PENGUIN CLASSICS

PENGUIN ENGLISH POETS

GENERAL EDITOR: CHRISTOPHER RICKS

THE PRELUDE

THE FOUR TEXTS (1798, 1799, 1805, 1850)

WILLIAM WORDSWORTH was born in the Lake District in April 1770, and died there eighty years later on 23 April 1850. He had three brothers and a sister, Dorothy, to whom throughout his life he was especially close. When she was six and he was nearly eight, their mother died. Dorothy was sent away to be brought up by relatives and a year later William was sent to Hawkshead Grammar School, scene of the great childhood episodes of *The Prelude*.

Wordsworth was cared for in lodgings and led a life of exceptional freedom, roving over the fells that surrounded the village. The death of his father, agent to the immensely powerful landowner Sir James Lowther, broke in on this happiness when he was thirteen, but did not halt the education through nature that complemented his Hawkshead studies and became the theme of his poetry.

As an undergraduate at Cambridge Wordsworth travelled (experiencing the French Revolution at first hand) and wrote poetry. His twenties were spent as a wanderer, in France, Wales, London, the Lakes, Dorset and Germany. In France he fathered a child whom he did not meet until she was nine because of the War. In 1795 he was reunited with Dorothy, and met Coleridge, with whom he published *Lyrical Ballads* in 1798, and to whom he addressed *The Prelude*, his epic study of human consciousness.

In the last days of the century Wordsworth and Dorothy found a settled home at Dove Cottage, Grasmere. Here Wordsworth wrote much of his best-loved poetry, and Dorothy her famous *Journals*. In 1802 Wordsworth married Dorothy's closest friend, Mary Hutchinson.

Gradually he established himself as the great poet of his age, a turning-point coming with the collected edition of 1815. From 1813 Wordsworth and his family lived at Rydal Mount in the neighbouring valley to Grasmere. In 1843 he became Poet Laureate.

JONATHAN WORDSWORTH, descended from the poet's younger brother Christopher, Master of Trinity, Cambridge, is Chairman of the Wordsworth Trust, Grasmere, University Lecturer in Romantic Studies at Oxford, and a Fellow of St Catherine's. He has edited much of Wordsworth's poetry, and more than one hundred titles in the Woodstock Facsimile series *Revolution and Romanticism*. He is author of *The Music of Humanity, The Borders of Vision, Ancestral Voices* and *Visionary Gleam.*

WILLIAM WORDSWORTH

The Prelude

THE FOUR TEXTS (1798, 1799, 1805, 1850)

Edited by JONATHAN WORDSWORTH

PENGUIN BOOKS

For A.S.W.

PENGUIN BOOKS

Published by the Penguin Group
Penguin Books Ltd, 80 Strand, London WC2R 0RL, England
Penguin Putnam Inc., 375 Hudson Street, New York, New York 10014, USA
Penguin Books Australia Ltd, 250 Camberwell Road, Camberwell, Victoria 3124, Australia
Penguin Books Canada Ltd, 10 Alcorn Avenue, Toronto, Ontario, Canada M4V 3B2
Penguin Books India (P) Ltd, 11 Community Centre, Panchsheel Park, New Delhi – 110 017, India
Penguin Books (NZ) Ltd, Cnr Rosedale and Airborne Roads, Albany, Auckland, New Zealand
Penguin Books (South Africa) (Pty) Ltd, 24 Sturdee Avenue, Rosebank 2196, South Africa

Penguin Books Ltd, Registered Offices: 80 Strand, London WC2R 0RL, England

www.penguin.com

This edition published 1995
6

Set in 10/11.5 pt Monophoto Ehrhardt
Typeset by Datix International Limited, Bungay, Suffolk
Printed in England by Clays Ltd, St Ives plc

CONTENTS

ACKNOWLEDGEMENTS

I am grateful to my fellow Trustees for permission to publish texts based on MSS at the Wordsworth Library, Grasmere. In making this new edition I have been conscious of a debt to the Cornell Editors, Stephen Parrish, James Butler, and above all Mark Reed; to the Penguin team, especially Christopher Ricks, Paul Keegan and Antony Wood; to past editors of *The Prelude*, Ernest de Selincourt, Helen Darbishire and James Maxwell; to Anne Semmes and Henry Wordsworth.

Jonathan Wordsworth

TABLE OF DATES

1770 *7 April* William Wordsworth born at Cockermouth, Cumberland, second son of John Wordsworth (1741–83), lawyer and agent to Sir James Lowther, later Earl of Lonsdale.

16 August Mary Hutchinson born at Penrith, Cumberland, home of Wordsworth's grandparents (marries poet 1802, dies 1859).

1771 *25 December* Birth of Dorothy Wordsworth, only sister of poet (d. 1855).

1772 *21 October* Birth of Samuel Taylor Coleridge (d. 1834).

4 December Birth of John Wordsworth, sailor brother of poet and Dorothy (drowned 5 February 1805).

1774 *9 June* Birth of Christopher, fifth and last child of John and Ann Wordsworth (later Master of Trinity, Cambridge; d. 1846).

1778 *c. 8 March* Ann Wordsworth, poet's mother, dies aged 30, probably of pneumonia (*1805* V 256–60).

June Dorothy sent to live with cousins in Halifax, on the grounds that she could not properly be brought up in all-male household.

1779 *c. 15 May* Wordsworth sent to Hawkshead Grammar School (*1799* I 258 ff.), where he lives (at one point with all three brothers) in lodgings with Ann Tyson (*1805* IV 16–28, 207–21).

1783 *30 December* Unexpected death of poet's father, John Wordsworth, aged 42 (*1799* I 349–60).

1785 First extant poem, *Bicentenary Verses*, on the foundation of Hawkshead Grammar School.

1786 *12 June* Death, aged 32, of the Revd William Taylor, Fellow of Emmanuel College, Cambridge, headmaster of Hawkshead Grammar School since 1781 (*1805* X 489–514).

1786–7 Composition of long, Gothic, partly autobiographical *Vale of Esthwaite* (surviving only in fragments).

1787 *March* Appearance in *European Magazine* of first published poem, *Sonnet, On Seeing Miss Helen Maria Williams Weep at a Tale of Distress.*
Early summer Reunion at Penrith of Wordsworth and Dorothy (living with relatives at Halifax for previous nine years) coincides with 'blessed time of early love' for Mary Hutchinson, Dorothy's close friend (*1805* VI 208–45, XI 315–25).
30 October Takes up residence at St John's College, Cambridge (*1805*, III, IV 39–55, VI 1–109, IX 226–36).

1788 Unsuccessful suit against Lord Lonsdale for repayment of £4,625 owed to John Wordsworth at his death (repaid to the family by Lonsdale's heir, 1803).
Summer Wordsworth spends nine weeks of Cambridge long vacation at Hawkshead (*1805* IV), giving rise to accounts of Dedication Scene (ll. 316–45) and Discharged Soldier (ll. 363–504).

1788–9 Composition of *An Evening Walk* (published 1793).

1789 *14 July* Fall of Bastille.

1790 *10 July–mid-October* Walking tour with Robert Jones (Cambridge student from mountainous North Wales) through France and the Alps, and back down the Rhine (*1805* VI 332–705); notable especially for Crossing of the Alps and Simplon Pass (ll. 494–572).

1791 *21 January* Wordsworth awarded BA without honours; moves to London.
May–August Stays with Jones in Wales; remarkable for climbing of Snowdon (*1805* XIII 1–73).

26 November Crosses to France, visiting the National Assembly in Paris, and probably the Jacobin Club (*1805* IX 40–80), before leaving for Orleans on 5 December.

1792 *Spring* Meets Annette Vallon; moves to Blois and is converted by French army officer and nobleman Michel Beaupuy to the cause of the people (*1805* IX 127–550).
Early summer Writes *Descriptive Sketches* (published 1793); Beaupuy's regiment leaves for service on Rhine, 27 July.
10 August Louis XVI deposed (*1805* X 39–54).
2–6 September Austrian invasion provokes massacre of royalist and other prisoners in Paris (*1805* X 62–82).
22 September Republic proclaimed, following unexpected victory over invaders at Valmy on 20th (*1805* X 24–31).
29 October Wordsworth in Paris en route for London (*1805* X 1–188), presumably intending to raise money and return to marry Annette; leaves France end of November.
15 December Anne Caroline Wordsworth baptized in Orleans Cathedral.

1793 *21 January* Execution of Louis XVI.
29 January Evening Walk and *Descriptive Sketches* published.
1 February France declares war on England; England follows suit on 11th, as it proves, dividing Wordsworth from Annette and Caroline till 1802 (Peace of Amiens).
16 February Publication of William Godwin's *Enquiry Concerning Political Justice* (*1805* X 805–29); approximate date of Wordsworth's unpublished Painite, rather than Godwinian, political tract *Letter to the Bishop of Llandaff*, attacking hereditary titles, defending execution of Louis.
Late July–early August Crosses Salisbury Plain on foot (*1805* XII 312–53), visiting Tintern Abbey for first time en route for North Wales; while staying with Jones, August–September, composes a version of *Salisbury Plain.*
7 October Execution of Gorsas, first of the Girondins (with whom Wordsworth was politically in sympathy) to be guillotined. Carlyle's story that Wordsworth returned to Paris at this time and saw Gorsas die is in the highest degree improbable. He was no Scarlet Pimpernel.

1794 *April–May* Wordsworth and Dorothy spend six weeks together at Windy Brow in Keswick; *Salisbury Plain* completed, *Evening Walk* and *Descriptive Sketches* heavily and interestingly revised.

10 June–26 July The Great Terror: Robespierre, presiding over the Committee of Public Safety, sends 1,376 people to the guillotine in Paris – as opposed to 1,251 in the previous fifteen months (*1805* X 329–45).

27 July Robespierre loses control in the National Convention, attempts suicide, and is guillotined next day; Wordsworth hears the news with 'glee', while crossing Levens Sands c. 20 August (*1805* X 529–52).

1795 *c. 9 January* Wordsworth receives legacy of £900 at the death from tuberculosis of Raisley Calvert (younger brother of a Hawkshead schoolfriend), designed to enable him to write instead of taking a job (*1805* XIII 349–67).

February–August Wordsworth in London; becomes a disciple of Godwin, whom he meets nine times, after being introduced to him on 27 February by William Frend (Unitarian mentor of Coleridge till sacked by Cambridge for his political views) at a gathering of radicals that included Holcroft (lately on trial for high treason).

Late August–September Wordsworth, on visit to Bristol, meets Southey and Coleridge.

26 September Wordsworth and Dorothy go to live at Racedown, a substantial house lent them by the Pinneys near Bridport in Dorset, taking with them the child Basil Montague (aged two-and-a-half) who has been entrusted to their care.

4 October Coleridge marries Sara Fricker.

October–November Wordsworth rewrites *Salisbury Plain* as *Adventures on Salisbury Plain* with new Godwinian slant. Letter gets through from Annette, mentioning half a dozen others sent but not received.

1796 *c. March* Wordsworth experiences some form of mental or moral crisis, probably brought on by reading the second edition of Godwin's *Political Justice* (*1805* X 878–920).

16 April Publication of Coleridge's *Poems on Various Sub-*

jects, including *Religious Musings*, read and admired by Wordsworth.

Autumn Wordsworth's only play, *The Borderers*, begun.

1797 *c. March Borderers* completed.

May–June First version of *Ruined Cottage* written.

c. 5 June Coleridge arrives on a visit to Racedown, taking the Wordsworths back with him to Nether Stowey on 4 July, where on the 7th they lease Alfoxden House.

c. 5 November Coleridge writes *Kubla Khan*; half-length version of *Ancient Mariner* complete by 20th.

c. 10 December Borderers turned down by Covent Garden, together with Coleridge's *Osorio.*

1798 *10 January* Coleridge receives annuity from Wedgwood brothers, enabling him to write rather than becoming Unitarian minister.

February Discharged Soldier (*1805* IX 363–504) written as independent poem; Coleridge's *Frost at Midnight* composed, and, embodying the same pantheist message, Wordsworth's *Pedlar* is written into *The Ruined Cottage*, which has now become part of *The Recluse*.

6 March Scheme for *The Recluse* announced in letter.

c. 13 March Goody Blake and Harry Gill, earliest of Wordsworth's lyrical ballads, completed (*The Thorn* and others following in quick succession).

10–13 July Having taken *Lyrical Ballads* MSS to the press, Wordsworth composes *Tintern Abbey* on tour of Wye.

16–19 September Coleridge and Wordsworths journey to Hamburg, he going on to Ratzeburg (30th), they to Goslar (6 October).

October First *Prelude* composition in *MS JJ: Was It For This* written, together with drafts of the boat-stealing episode (*1799* I 81–129), *Nutting*, and version of *There Was A Boy* (*1805* V 389–413) as first-person narrative.

November–December Composition (among other poetry) of first three Lucy poems and skating episode (*1799* I 150–85).

1799 *January–early February* 'Spots of time' sequence (*1799* I 258–374) composed; *1799* Part I complete before the Wordsworths leave Goslar on 23 February.

Late February–late April Wordsworths on walking tour that starts in Harz Forest (*1805* VII 347–90) and includes two visits to Coleridge, now at Göttingen.

13 May Wordsworths at Sockburn-on-Tees, home of the Hutchinson family, where they stay till the end of year.

Autumn 1799 Part II composed, and Part I revised; no working MSS survive.

25–6 October Coleridge, in England since mid-July, arrives at Sockburn; accompanies Wordsworth and his brother John (back from two-year voyage) on Lake District walking tour, ending c. 20 November.

18-19 November Wordsworth composes Glad Preamble (incorporated in *Prelude* as *1805* I–54, January 1804) on two-day walk from Ullswater to Grasmere to rent Dove Cottage. Coleridge returns to Sockburn, falls lastingly (and hopelessly) in love with Mary Hutchinson's younger sister Sara, and goes south to be a journalist in London.

Early December Transcription of 1799 *Prelude* in twin fair copy MSS, *MS V* copied by Dorothy and *MS U* copied by Mary Hutchinson.

20 December Having walked across the country from Sockburn via Wensleydale, Wordsworth and Dorothy take possession of Dove Cottage, their home till 1808.

1800 *January–early March* Composition of Prospectus to *The Recluse*, *Brothers*, *Hart-Leap Well* and bulk of *Home at Grasmere* (intended as first book of *The Recluse*).

6 April–4 May Coleridge's first visit to Dove Cottage; a second volume for *Lyrical Ballads* agreed upon.

29 June Coleridges (poet, wife and Hartley) arrive at Dove Cottage, stay till 23 July when they move into Greta Hall, 12 miles away at Keswick.

13 September Wordsworth at work on Preface to *Lyrical Ballads* (later described by Coleridge as 'half the child of my own brain').

4 October *Christabel* Part II completed, for inclusion in

Lyrical Ballads, second volume; two readings greeted with delight at Dove Cottage, but followed on 6th by decision that poem shall be published separately with Wordsworth's *Pedlar* (too long? too distinct from poetry of everyday life described in Preface?). Coleridge does not go on to write Part III of *Christabel*.

11 October Wordsworth at work on *Michael* as *Lyrical Ballads* replacement for *Christabel*.

18 December Last sheets of copy for *Lyrical Ballads* sent off.

1801 *7 January* John Wordsworth, aged 28, sworn in as captain of the *Earl of Abergavenny*, largest merchant ship in the East India Company's fleet.

c. 25 January Publication of *Lyrical Ballads* in two volumes, dated 1800, with Wordsworth's name on the title-page.

Spring 1799 *Prelude* revised for John to take on voyage.

Early December Wordsworth translating Chaucer.

21 December Wordsworth takes up *The Pedlar*, and on 28th is at work on a third part for *1799*, bringing story down to Cambridge; presumably composes *1805* III 1–167, in which *Pedlar* material is incorporated (ll. 330–56).

1802 *24 February* Coleridge notebook-entry reveals Wordsworth's intention to marry Mary Hutchinson.

Spring–early summer Wordsworth writing short poems and lyrics, including *Intimations* stanzas 1–4 and *Leech Gatherer*; *Pedlar* revisions, but no work on *Prelude*.

4 April Coleridge writes first version of *Dejection: An Ode*, addressed as despairing poetic love letter to Sara Hutchinson (*1805* XI 332–4).

27 March–16 May 1803 Peace of Amiens: only truce in war with France, 1793–1814.

9 July–6 October Wordsworth and Dorothy leave Grasmere on a journey that takes them via the Hutchinsons' new farm in Yorkshire to London, Dover and Calais, where they spend a month with Annette and Caroline; thence, with a week spent in London, back to Gallow Hill, where Wordsworth and Mary are married on 4 October, and finally, with Mary, to Grasmere. The journey produces

many of Wordsworth's greatest sonnets, including *Westminster Bridge* and *To Toussaint l'Ouverture.*
7 September Lamb shows the Wordsworths Bartholomew Fair (*1805* VII 648–94) and, on the same visit, Tipu's Tiger (IV 301–4).
7 November Wordsworth translating Tasso, *Orlando Furioso.*

1803 Threats of French invasion cause Wordsworth to enlist in Westmorland Volunteers, and call forth patriotic sonnets (among them *To the Men of Kent, October 1803*); otherwise little composition.
18 June Birth of poet's eldest son, John (d. 1875).
c. mid-July Hazlitt (expert portrait-painter as well as writer) visits Lake District and paints both Wordsworth and Coleridge; neither portrait seems to have survived.
15 August Wordsworth, Coleridge and Dorothy set out on Scottish tour, Coleridge on the 16th visiting in Carlisle gaol the forger Hatfield who had bigamously married Mary of Buttermere (*1805* VII 320–59). Tour includes visits to Burns' house and grave, and meeting with Walter Scott; provides material for poems of 1804–5, including *Yarrow Unvisited.*
October Wordsworth, said by Coleridge to be at work on *The Recluse*, reincorporates *The Pedlar* in *The Ruined Cottage* (*MS E*), strongly suggesting that he has in mind a plan for *The Excursion* (first mentioned in March 1804; published in 1814 as 'A Portion of *The Recluse*', with the full-length *Ruined Cottage* as Book I).
20 December Coleridge arrives at Dove Cottage, en route for London and the Mediterranean in search of health.

1804 *4 January* Wordsworth reads Coleridge 'the second part of his divine self-biography' (*1799* II) 'in the highest and outermost of Grasmere'.
14 January Coleridge leaves for south.
Late January–early March Wordsworth at work on new five-book version of *Prelude* for Coleridge to take abroad (comprising *1805* I–III, a single-book version of IV and V, plus the newly-written Climbing of Snowdon (finally

1805 XIII 1–65) and revised Spots of Time (finally XI 257–388). Also with Coleridge in mind, a collection of Wordsworth's unpublished verse (*MS M*) is prepared, *Intimations* is completed, and a number of other lyrics are composed, including *Ode to Duty* and *Daffodils*.

c. 10 March Though the five-book *Prelude* is complete, or very nearly so, Wordsworth decides to reorganize his material and work towards a longer version; by 18 March Coleridge has been sent *1805* I–V in almost their final shape.

9 April Coleridge sails for Malta on the *Speedwell*, Wordsworth at work on *1805* VI (recording his own foreign travels).

29 April Book VI complete, Wordsworth probably goes on to write XI and X (a) – carrying the poet's French experience and involvement in revolutionary politics up to the death of Robespierre, X 566 – before a summer break.

16 August Dora Wordsworth born (d. 1847).

7 October Wordsworth back at work on *Prelude*; writes Books VIII, VII (probably) and X (b) before Christmas.

Early November Probable date of *Kitten and the Falling Leaves* (echoed *1805* VII 294, 387, 470–3).

2 December Napoleon, with Pope in attendance, crowns himself Emperor (*1805* X 930–40).

1805 *5 February* John Wordsworth drowned as *Earl of Abergavenny* sinks off Portland; news reaches Dove Cottage on 11th, putting a stop to any composition.

c. 20 May Thirteen-book *Prelude* completed, Books XI–XIII (all short, and containing much old work) in previous three weeks.

3 June *Stepping Westward* composed on basis of 1803 Scottish tour, newly written up by Dorothy; *Solitary Reaper* follows on 5 November.

29 November Dorothy 'engaged in making a fair and final transcript' of *Prelude* (*MS A*).

26 December Two-thirds of *Prelude* transcribed; Wordsworth, 'very anxious to get forward with *The Recluse*', is 'reading for the nourishment of his mind preparatory to beginning'.

1806 *January–early March* Mary copying *Prelude MS B*; Wordsworth already making early corrections to *A*.
Early January Waggoner written.
Late March–mid-May Wordsworth spends three enjoyable weeks in London, visits Christopher (now Chaplain to the Archbishop at Lambeth) and the Beaumonts, sees Sir George's picture *Piel Castle in a Storm* (inspiration of *Elegiac Stanzas*, last and greatest of his elegies for John, composed on return to Grasmere).
15 June Thomas Wordsworth born (d. 1812).
Summer Wordsworth goes back to *Home at Grasmere*, adding a few lines and switching Prospectus to end, in effort to get started on central section of *Recluse.*
17 August Coleridge, abroad for two-and-a-half years, lands on south coast; reluctant to meet friends and family, lingers in London till late October.
Early September Constable, on painting tour of Lake District, meets Wordsworth; not impressed.
26 October Wordsworth family, now too large for Dove Cottage, sets out for Coleorton, Leicestershire, where Beaumont has lent them a farmhouse for the winter; joined by Sara Hutchinson in Kendal with news that Coleridge has at last come north. Uneasy meeting with Coleridge, who has put on weight and seems not himself.
24 November Coleridge's separation from his wife reported by Dorothy.
21 December Coleridge and Hartley come to stay with the Wordsworths at Coleorton.

1807 *Early January* Wordsworth reads *The Prelude* to Coleridge (to whom it has been addressed from the first); reading prompts Coleridge to write *To William Wordsworth*, last major poem.
Spring Blake poems, including *The Divine Image* and *Tiger*, copied by Wordsworth into his commonplace-book (from Benjamin Heath Malkin, who had access to a copy of *Innocence and Experience, Father's Memoirs of His Child*, 1806, xviii–xli).
Mid-April–early May Wordsworths in London.

8 May Appearance of *Poems in Two Volumes.*
10 June Wordsworths leave Coleorton, returning to Grasmere on 10 July, after period in Yorkshire.
4 November De Quincey, who has hero-worshipped Wordsworth since he was at school, and been in correspondence with him since May 1803, arrives at Dove Cottage (where, as tenant in succession to Wordsworth, he is to experience his most appalling opium-dreams).

1808 *16 January White Doe of Rylstone* completed (in emulation of Scott's popular *Lay of the Last Minstrel*).
Late February–early April Wordsworth in London, sees Coleridge, shilly-shallies about publishing *White Doe.*
Late May Wordsworths move half a mile across valley to Allan Bank, regarded by them as 'temple of abomination' when first built in 1805.
Summer Tuft of Primroses, including the sacking of the Grande Chartreuse (*1850* 421–89), written for *Recluse.*
30 August Signing of Convention of Cintra (British agreement to repatriate French army captured in Peninsular War); seen by Wordsworth and others as betrayal of freedom-fighters.
1 September Coleridge comes to visit Allan Bank; stays for two not always easy years.
6 September Birth of Catharine Wordsworth (d. 1812).
October Protest meetings over Convention of Cintra; Wordsworth's pamphlet (written with help from Coleridge) complete in original form by end of year.
Early November De Quincey too comes to live at Allan Bank; stays till February.
27 December First instalment of *Convention of Cintra* printed in *Courier*, others despatched to London.

1809 *January* Wordsworth decides to publish *Convention* in pamphlet form; De Quincey leaves for London c. 20 February to see it through press.
27 May Convention of Cintra finally published.
1 June First issue of Coleridge's *Friend* appears.
Mid-June–early November Wordsworth at work on Introduction for Joseph Wilkinson's *Select Views in Cumberland,*

Westmorland and Lancashire (first version of *Guide to Lakes*); copied by 17 November.
c. 20 October De Quincey moves into Dove Cottage.
26 October 1805 X 662–5, 689–727 ('Bliss was it in that dawn to be alive') published in *Friend* over Wordsworth's name.
December–May 1810 Probable date of *Excursion* Book II; Books III–V written by March 1812.
14 December Early part of Wordsworth's essay on education, *Reply to Mathetes*, published in *Friend*; concluded in issue of 4 January (over initials M.M.).
28 December 1805 I 428–89 ('Wisdom and spirit of the universe' up to skating episode) published in *Friend.*

1810 *22 February* First of Wordsworth's three *Essays upon Epitaphs* appears in *Friend* (other two written at this stage, but never published by Wordsworth).
15 March Last issue of *Friend.*
12 May Birth of William Wordsworth Jr (d. 1883).
4 July–early September Wordsworth makes trip to Coleorton and Hindwell (Thomas Hutchinson's farm in Wales), accompanied on first leg by Dorothy; period remarkable for passionate tenderness of poet's correspondence with Mary (brought to light in 1977).
Late October Basil Montagu passes on Wordsworth's remarks on the difficulty of living with Coleridge; Coleridge wounded and angry; friendship never fully recovers.

1811 *c. early June* Wordsworths move into Rectory, last and saddest of their homes at Grasmere (no longer standing).
Mid-October Wordsworth teaches briefly at Grasmere school (now the gingerbread shop) to observe workings of Dr Bell's Madras System of education.

1812 *Mid-April–mid-June* Wordsworth in London to make peace with Coleridge; reconciliation arranged through Lamb and Crabb Robinson, statements drawn up, meetings take place, Wordsworth attends Coleridge's lectures, some degree of harmony restored.
11 May Chance meetings with Byron and Moore; as well

as the Beaumonts, Lamb, De Quincey and Rogers (old friends), Wordsworth sees on this visit Uvedale Price, Constable, Humphry Davy, Joanna Baillie, Mrs Barbauld and many others.

4 June Death of Catharine Wordsworth (who has always been frail and subject to convulsions); news reaches London on 10th. *Surprised by Joy*, Wordsworth's sonnet for Catharine, belongs to 1813–14.

August–September Visit of Dr Bell to Grasmere.

1 December Thomas Wordsworth dies of measles, buried beside Catharine.

1813 *January 1813–late May 1814* Composition of *Excursion* VI–IX, together with the lament for death of the Solitary's children in Book III (1814 text, pp. 124–6).

26 April Through patronage of Lord Lonsdale, Wordsworth becomes Distributor of Stamps (civil servant with responsibility for stamp duties) for Westmorland and part of Cumberland.

12 May Household moves to Rydal Mount in neighbouring valley (with deaths of the children and proximity of their graves, the anyhow damp and inconvenient Rectory had become impossible to live in).

4 November Southey becomes Poet Laureate (Scott having turned the honour down).

1814 *Mid-July–early September* Tour of Scotland with Mary, and Sara Hutchinson; remarkable chiefly for meeting with James Hogg, the Ettrick shepherd, and composition of *Yarrow Visited.*

Early August Excursion published.

Late October Laodamia composed.

1815 *January* Writing Preface to *Poems* 1815.

Early April Publication of *Poems* 1815, first Collected Edition of Wordsworth.

2 June Publication of *White Doe of Rylstone.*

11 June Haydon makes life-mask of Wordsworth, as preparation for introducing him (with Keats, Newton and Voltaire) into his 12 × 15 foot painting *Christ's Entry into Jerusalem* – now in Cincinnati.

1816 *28 February* Marriage in Paris of Caroline Wordsworth and Jean-Baptiste-Martin Beaudouin; Dorothy arranges to go, but allows political situation to deter her.
May–June Coleridge's *Christabel, Kubla Khan and The Pains of Sleep* goes through three editions.
Late May Publication of Wordsworth's *Thanksgiving Ode* and *Letter to a Friend of Robert Burns.*

1817 *17 April Vernal Ode* composed.
Summer Evening of Extraordinary Splendour composed.
July Coleridge publishes *Biographia Literaria* and *Sibylline Leaves.*
28 December 'Immortal Dinner' takes place in Haydon's studio, with Wordsworth, Keats and a very tipsy Lamb.

1818 *c.13 April* Wordsworth, canvassing energetically for the tory Lowthers since previous December, publishes *Two Addresses to the Freeholders of Westmorland.* No significant poetry composed.

1819 Probable date of the first major *Prelude* revision, maybe prompted by John Carter's transcription of *MS C.*
Late April Peter Bell published.
June Waggoner published.
November Three-volume edition of Coleridge's *Friend.*

1820 *May Duddon Sonnets* published, *Vaudracour and Julia* (*1805* IX 556–935, telling obliquely of the poet's love for Annette Vallon) extracted from *Prelude* and published separately.
11 July–7 November Continental tour with Mary and Dorothy and Crabb Robinson, retracing in the Alps the poet's route of 1790; meeting in Paris with Annette and Caroline and Caroline's two daughters.
Late July Miscellaneous Poems (four-volume Collected Edition) published, plus second edition of *Excursion.*

1821 Dorothy and Mary writing accounts of the 1820 tour, Wordsworth composing his verse *Memorials* and sonnets for *Ecclesiastical Sketches* (both published in March 1822).
23 February Keats dies in Rome, aged 25.

1822 *c. late April* First separate publication of Wordsworth's *Guide, Description of the Scenery of the Lakes.*
8 July Shelley drowns in the Gulf of Spezia, aged 29.

1824 First American Collected Edition of Wordsworth (4 volumes, Boston).
19 April Death of Byron at Missolonghi, aged 36.
August–October Tour of North Wales.

1825 *c. February* Publication of Hazlitt's *Spirit of the Age.*
May Coleridge publishes *Aids to Reflection.*

1827 *7 February* Death of Sir George Beaumont (patron of Coleridge, Wordsworth and Constable, founder of the National Gallery).
May Poetical Works published in 5 volumes; some new work, old poems carefully revised (for the worse, as Wordsworth's friends make clear).
12 August Blake dies.

1828 *Early December Power of Sound* drafted (completed c. November 1829).
21 June–7 August Continental tour with Dora and Coleridge.
August Coleridge's *Poetical Works* in three volumes. Single-volume piracy of Wordsworth by Galignani, Paris.

1829 Galignani single-volume piracy of Coleridge–Shelley–Keats (for the last two, with status of unauthorized first Collected Works).

1830 *18 September* Death of Hazlitt.

1831 *19 September* Wordsworth and Dora visit the dying Sir Walter Scott at Abbotsford before his departure for Italy, then make tour of Highlands; *Yarrow Revisited* composed to celebrate friendship of almost 30 years.

1832 *Winter–spring* Second major *Prelude* revision, leading to transcription of *MS D.*
3 February Crabbe dies.

June New four-volume *Poetical Works.*
21 September Death of Scott (after return to Abbotsford).
Autumn MS D already being submitted to revision; Dorothy becomes chronic invalid.

1833 *July–August* Steamboat tour with Crabb Robinson to Isle of Man, Staffa and Iona; composition of *St Bees Head.*

1834 Deaths of Coleridge (25 July) and Lamb (27 December).

1835 *January* Publication of *Yarrow Revisited and Other Poems*, Wordsworth's most successful single volume, with important political Appendix.
16 May Death of Felicia Hemans.
23 June Death of Sara Hutchinson, for 30 years a member of the Wordsworth household.
21 November Death of James Hogg, following upon those of Scott, Coleridge, Lamb, Crabbe and Hemans, prompts Wordsworth to write *Extempore Effusion* (modelled on Dunbar's *Lament for the Makers*).

1836–7 Six-volume *Poetical Works* (reprinted six times before publication of the single-volume edition of 1845).

1837 *19 March–August* Wordsworth visits Rome and Venice with Crabb Robinson and Moxon (his publisher); poet 67, but highly productive. Last Continental tour.

1838 *June* Wordsworth's sonnets collected in single volume.
July–April 1839 Third major period of *Prelude* revision: *MS D* twice revised before transcription of *E* (printer's copy).

1841 *10 January* Annette Vallon dies; buried at Père Lachaise.
11 May Dora Wordsworth marries minor poet and man of letters, Edward Quillinan, at Bath.

1842 *April Poems Chiefly of Early and Late Years*, including first publication of *Adventures on Salisbury Plain* (1795, revised as *Guilt and Sorrow*) and *Borderers*, together with *Memorials of a Tour in Italy* (notably *Musings Near Aquapendente*) and the last of his major lyrics, *Airey-Force Valley.*

Winter 1842–3 'Fenwick Notes', on the circumstances of Wordsworth's individual poems, dictated to Isabella Fenwick, friend of his late years.

1843 *21 March* Death of Southey; succeeded as Poet Laureate by Wordsworth in April.

1845 *25 April* Borrows Samuel Rogers' court-dress, and Humphry Davy's sword, to attend Queen's Ball in London.
4 May Meets Tennyson (his successor as Poet Laureate).
November Single-volume *Poems*, with vignette of Rydal Mount on title-page; reissued 1847.

1847 *9 July* Dora Wordsworth dies of tuberculosis, aged 42.

1849 *6 January* Death of Hartley Coleridge, 'child of all the Vale'.

1849–50 Six-volume *Poetical Works*, with Wordsworth's final revisions.

1850 *23 April* Wordsworth dies, aged 80.
July Publication of *The Prelude* (title chosen by Mary).

1855 *25 January* Death of Dorothy Wordsworth (after more than 20 years an invalid).

1859 *17 January 1859* Death of Mary Wordsworth.

INTRODUCTION

The Prelude is a poem of many versions. Like Whitman, Wordsworth lived to be an old man, and kept bringing his work up to date. Unlike Whitman, who printed nine different texts of *Leaves of Grass* in the years 1855–91, Wordsworth left his poem in manuscript. His problem was that *The Prelude* (known in his lifetime as 'The Poem to Coleridge') was an autobiography. It was, Wordsworth told Sir George Beaumont on 1 May 1805, 'a thing unprecedented in literary history that a man should talk so much about himself'. Publication, he felt, could be justified only by completion of his grand scheme for *The Recluse*, of which *The Prelude* was a subordinate part. In 1814 he felt able to publish the less egocentric *Excursion* (with the words 'A Portion of *The Recluse*' on the title-page), but even when it became clear that the larger scheme would never be completed, he stuck to his view that *The Prelude* could not be printed on its own. As a result, Wordsworth's great epic of human consciousness was for almost half a century known only to members of his immediate circle.

The Prelude finally appeared in July 1850, three months after Wordsworth's death. Concerned as it was with the French Revolution, and finished originally in the year of Beethoven's *Fidelio* and Scott's *Lay of the Last Minstrel*, it seemed out of date next to the poem of the moment, Tennyson's *In Memoriam.* Many Victorians continued to prefer *The Excursion*, on which they had been brought up. It has been left to twentieth-century scholars to consolidate *The Prelude*'s position among the great English long poems by editing early versions preserved among manuscripts at the Wordsworth Library, Grasmere. Presented below are four texts spanning the years 1798–1850: (1) the first *Prelude* draft, *Was It For This*, a self-contained poem of 150 lines composed in Germany in October 1798; (2) the two-part *Prelude*, completed in 968 lines in December 1799, and first published in 1973; (3) *The Prelude* as completed in thirteen books in May 1805, revised over the course of the next year, and first published in 1926; (4) the first edition of *The Prelude*, made ready for the press by Wordsworth and published (with some unwarranted tinkerings) by his executors in 1850. The poems of 1805 and 1850 are offered as parallel texts.

Was It For This, here for the first time presented as a separate, annotated version of *The Prelude*, is of immense importance. Short as it is, it takes for its theme 'The Growth of a Poet's Mind', containing in embryo the discussion of education through nature central to all later versions. As he began to write Wordsworth did not know that he was embarked on a major poem. He and his sister Dorothy had recently come to the German town of Goslar in East Saxony, where they were to stay in cold and discomfort, and with very little money, until 23 February 1799. The poet was worrying about his failure to get on with writing the philosophical *Recluse*, planned with Coleridge in the spring and intended to be his life's work. As his draft opens he is asking himself reproachful questions in verse. His thoughts are in mid-flow, seemingly in mid-sentence:

> was it for this
> That one, the fairest of all rivers, loved
> To blend his murmurs with my nurse's song . . .
>
> For this didst thou,
> Oh Derwent, travelling over the green plains
> Near my sweet birthplace, didst thou, beauteous stream,
> Give ceaseless music to the night and day . . .
>
> Was it for this that I, a four years' child,
> Beneath thy scars and in thy silent pools
> Made one long bathing of a summer's day . . .

Wordsworth is writing fast, and his questioning has an urgency, yet the poetry forms itself naturally into a rhetorical pattern. Stylized reiteration of 'Was it for this' had been used by a number of eighteenth-century writers, Pope and Thomson among them, and is probably a development of hints in Virgil. English examples tend to derive from a passage in Milton's *Samson Agonistes*. Addressing his fallen son, now blinded and captive to the Philistines, Manoah asks:

> For this did the angel twice descend – for this
> Ordained thy nurture holy, as of a plant,
> Select and sacred? (ll. 361–3)

Wordsworth had not fatally abused his powers as a poet, but nevertheless saw himself in autumn 1798 as failing to put them to the purposes for which they had been ordained. As *Was It For This* develops, his sense of having been a 'chosen son' sends him back to examine his 'nurture' among the Cumbrian hills. There he finds, not the childhood of reassuring nostalgic memory, but moments of sublime intensity amid 'high objects' and 'eternal things' of nature. Pain and fear, exemplified in the bird's-nesting and woodcock-snaring episodes (*WIFT* 30–46, 76–97), are seen in these conditions to be 'sanctified' by the 'discipline' of nature's presence. In a magnificent phrase the poet claims, not just for himself, but for us all, the capacity to 'recognize|A grandeur in the beatings of the heart'. *The Prelude* has found its theme.

No one had ever written such poetry before. There had been painters – John Robert Cozens and Francis Towne among them – capable of embodying in landscape the Burkean sublime, but no poet had emerged of sufficient stature to body it forth in words. Extending *Was It For This*, Wordsworth takes a backward glance at *Paradise Lost*, the great precursor-poem that will be inspiration and challenge to each successive *Prelude* version (see *WIFT* 98–9n.). He then presents to us *The Prelude*'s earliest myth of origins. '. . . oh bounteous power', he writes, addressing a Platonic 'eternal spirit' who has 'His life in unimaginable things' and is 'apparent chiefly as the soul|Of our first sympathies':

> oh bounteous power,
> In childhood, in rememberable days,
> How often did thy love renew for me
> Those naked feelings which when thou wouldst form
> A living thing thou sendest like a breeze
> Into its infant being (*WIFT* 109–14)

For Wordsworth in October 1798 (three months after the pantheist affirmations of *Tintern Abbey*), it is the inspiring love of this 'Soul of things' that fits

> Our new existence to existing things,
> And in our dawn of being constitute[s]
> The bond of union betwixt life and joy. (*WIFT* 121–3)

In what is clearly a deliberate rounding off of his poem, Wordsworth concludes *Was It For This* by asserting the importance of 'primordial feelings' to the 'noblest ends' of later life. He then goes on, with the same inspired assurance, to compose the boat-stealing episode (*1799* I 82–129), seemingly for insertion within the structure of *Was It For This*, together with a version of *There Was a Boy* (*1805* V 389–413) in first-person narrative, and a number of lesser drafts. Effectively what is taking shape is a version of *1799* Part I. Despite Wordsworth's writing at this period three of the Lucy poems, *Ruth*, and much else, a short form of Part I seems to have been complete before Christmas 1798. *There Was A Boy* and *Nutting* could have been included, but probably weren't. The skating episode (*1799* I 150–85) too had been written, but was for some reason not incorporated until the following year. Among passages in the final text of *1799* Part I that had not yet been composed were the home-amusements section (ll. 206–33), added in late 1799, and the 'spots of time' sequence (ll. 258–374), inserted before the Wordsworths left Goslar in February.

For the composition of Part II in autumn 1799 there is little manuscript evidence. The Wordsworths were back in England, at Sockburn, County Durham, home of Mary Hutchinson, the poet's future wife. With a poem on childhood completed in draft, there was an obvious logic to writing a sequel on adolescence. In terms of Burke's famous definitions, the child's encounters with the sublime in Part I gave way in Part II to the boy's growing response to the beautiful. In moving on from *Was It For This*, however, Wordsworth had cut his lines on the Platonic 'soul of our first sympathies'; amid the discussion of boyhood in Part II we find, unexpectedly, a replacement. As before, Wordsworth is asking what have been the sources of the imaginative power so strikingly shown in his early memories. And as before, the question takes him back to infancy. He is thinking, though, in different terms. 'Subjected to the discipline of love', the Infant Babe at his mother's breast offers a new humanist myth with psychological implications a hundred years ahead of its time. Where in *Was It For This* it had been the 'eternal spirit' whose love, entering 'like a breeze', enlivened the 'infant being', now we are offered a child who 'gather[s] passion from his mother's eye'. 'Such feelings', Wordsworth adds,

> pass into his torpid life
> Like an awakening breeze, and hence his mind,
> Even in the first trial of its powers,
> Is prompt and watchful . . . (*1799* II 274–7)

It is now the mother – at once part of, and representative of, general nature – who 'fits|Our new existence to existing things'. Along the child's

> infant veins are interfused
> The gravitation and the filial bond
> Of nature that connect him with the world. (II 292–4)

No longer is Wordsworth thinking, as in *Tintern Abbey*, of a divine presence – 'the life of things' – 'interfused' through every aspect of the natural world. The bond with nature that establishes the child's humanity is one of blood.

The two-part *Prelude* was finished and transcribed early in December 1799, a matter of days before William and Dorothy Wordsworth moved into their first permanent home together, at Dove Cottage, Grasmere. Dorothy concluded *MS V*, her transcript of the 1799 *Prelude*, not with 'The End' or 'Finis', but with the words 'End of the Second Part', implying presumably that she thought the poem might be extended. In the event there was a period of revision in spring 1801, associated with preparing a manuscript for their sea-captain younger brother John to take on voyage. And in December Wordsworth began work on the opening of a third part, bringing the account of his education down to Cambridge, and probably completing a version of *1805* III 1–167.

There may have been unrecorded work on *The Prelude* at other times (summer 1803 is a possibility), but in January 1804 the poet made a wholly new start. Coleridge was ill and heading for the Mediterranean, as Keats would later do, in search of health. On the 4th he records in his *Notebook*, 'in the highest and outermost of Grasmere, Wordsworth read to me the second part of his divine self-biography'. Coleridge left Grasmere for London (and ultimately Malta) on the 14th; work probably began at once on a new version of the 'self-biography' for him to take with him when he sailed.

Rather than just extending the poem, Wordsworth at this point reorganized his material, extracting the 'spots of time' sequence from Part I for use at a later stage. Probably this means that he had already decided to incorporate the Glad Preamble (*1805* I 1–54) as an introduction, and either written, or decided to write, the necessary link-passage, ll. 55–271. The Preamble had, as John Finch showed in 1970, been composed as a free-standing effusion on 18–19 November 1799 (see *1805* I 1–54n.). Had Wordsworth intended it for *The Prelude*, it could have been included in the fair copy MSS of the two-part poem, transcribed the following month. It is hard to believe, given the abruptness of its opening, that he didn't regard *1799* as needing an introduction. The joyous Preamble, however, was not designed for the job – and could not be adapted for it without a transition leading into the self-reproachful questioning, 'Was it for this . . .'.

Mark Reed has suggested that the Preamble was incorporated in *The Prelude*, and the link-passage (sometimes known as the post-Preamble) composed, as early as 1801. It may be so. As always, his assessment of evidence is detailed and scrupulous. It hinges, however, on somewhat complex interpretation of phrasing in letters of 1801 and 1804, and I find myself not entirely convinced. I don't see why Wordsworth should add a long and grandiose introduction to his poem at a time when he was merely revising and extending the 1799 text. Certainly failure to get *The Recluse* under way in *Home at Grasmere* (spring 1800) could have led to the image of the poet as false steward at the end of the post-Preamble, but why the Miltonic posturing in ll. 157–219 over possible topics for an epic? At no stage is it likely that Wordsworth seriously considered writing an epic in the old-fashioned narrative mode. And there is no sign that he ever gave serious thought to the half-dozen topics that he mentions. He has taken his cue from Milton's early ambition to write a national epic, and is claiming (as Milton does in *Paradise Lost*) heroic status for the new and different poetry he is writing. The time when that claim is likely to have been made is January 1804, when (after yet another failure, in October 1803, to engage with *The Recluse*) Wordsworth came to see *The Prelude* in larger, more Miltonic, terms.

By early March 1804, Wordsworth was embarked on the fifth and final book of a new ambitious *Prelude*, with a structure that shows a loss and regaining of the paradise of imaginative vision. The first three books had reached the form taken in 1805; the fourth contained material later expanded to create *1805* IV and V; the fifth opened with the Climbing of Snowdon (written February 1804, and appearing finally in Book XIII) and concluded with a revised version of the two major Spots of Time (written January 1799, and used finally in Book XI). In structural terms, imagination, fostered by nature in childhood and adolescence, is 'impaired' (to use Wordsworth's later term) as the poet experiences 'an inner falling-off' at Cambridge. It is then 'restored' in the epiphany on Snowdon, the Spots of Time serving as an explanation as to how this has come about:

> So feeling comes in aid
> Of feeling, and diversity of strength
> Attends us if but once we have been strong. (*1805* XI 325–7)

Whether this impressive interim *Prelude* was completed when, c. 10 March, Wordsworth decided once again to reorganize his material, it is impossible to say. If not, it very nearly was. Drafts in *MS W*, where the poem was being assembled, show that the most that Wordsworth had still to write was a brief linking passage in the final book.

Once again Wordsworth's decision to keep going on *The Prelude* was connected with anxiety over *The Recluse.* Coleridge, on whom he relied with touching faith to provide material for a central philosophical section, was leaving the country, possibly dying. On 6 March Wordsworth wrote to him in London:

I finished five or six days ago another book of my poem, amounting to 650 lines. And now I am positively arrived at the subject I spoke of in my last. When this next book is done, which I shall begin in two or three days time, I shall consider the work as finished. Farewell.

I am very anxious to have your notes for *The Recluse.* I cannot say how much importance I attach to this. If it should please God that I survive you, I should reproach myself for ever in writing the work if I had neglected to procure this help.

On the 29th, having heard from Coleridge of an attack of diarrhoea (described to many different friends: Coleridge was not one to waste potential drama), Wordsworth wrote in still more desperate tones:

Your last letter but one, informing us of your late attack, was the severest shock to me, I think, I have ever received . . . I cannot help saying that I would gladly have given three fourths of my possessions for your letter on *The Recluse* at that time. I cannot say what a load it would be to me, should I survive you and you die without this memorial left behind. Do for Heaven's sake put this out of the reach of accident immediately.

To write *The Recluse* was for Wordsworth a duty to mankind, the purpose of his life. Unable to proceed with the central section, he went on with the prefatory poem that he did know how to write.

By 18 March 1804 Wordsworth was able to send Coleridge the first five books of *The Prelude* in almost their final shape. To achieve this he had in the previous week turned Book IV of the five-book poem into a near-final version of *1805* Books IV and V. Of the 400–500 lines that were added, no doubt some were old material, but Wordsworth was writing fast; the only major sequence he is likely to have had by him to incorporate at this stage was the Quixote Dream (*1805* V 51–168), written in February but probably not part of the five-book poem. The Spots of Time and Climbing of Snowdon were now laid aside for future use, and Wordsworth moved rapidly on into Book VI (Cambridge and The Alps), completed by 29 April. At this point he claimed in a letter to Richard Sharp to have written 'between two and three thousand lines, accurately near three thousand . . . namely four books, and a third of another'. To which he added:

I am at present in the seventh book of this work, which will turn out far longer than I ever dreamed of. It seems a frightful deal to say about oneself, and of course will never be published (during my lifetime I mean) till another work [*The Recluse*] has been written and published, of sufficient importance to justify me in giving my own history to the world.

When Wordsworth offers line-totals for his recent work, one can seldom be sure of what he is taking into account. In this case it is fairly certain that the four whole books he has completed are III, IV, V and VI; the problem is to identify the extra 'third'. Reed believes that the poet has gone straight on into Book VII (London), and completed 200 lines or so. I think myself that whether or not the book he has embarked on is VII, the post-Preamble (I 55–271) is quite as likely to be the extra 'third' that he has in mind. Wordsworth has in fact written a great deal more than he claims. In reaching our conclusions Reed and I both ignore the material composed in February–early March for the final book of the five-book *Prelude*, on the grounds that it has not yet found a place in the new poem. A future editor could argue that half of the final Book XI (almost the whole, if one includes the revised Spots of Time) *plus* a third of XIII (Climbing of Snowdon) should be taken into the equation. His case would be strengthened because, as Reed points out, work on Book XI materials in *MS W* seems to have continued after the five-book scheme was abandoned.

It is in fact far from clear in what order the books of *The Prelude* were composed. In an attempt to induce clarity I commented in the Norton Critical Edition (1979):

The probable order of composition of [Wordsworth's] last eight books is VI, IX, the first half of X, VIII, VII, the second half of X, XI, XII, XIII. Not that the individual books were normally of a single moment: most contain earlier work, and many the work of several earlier periods. There is nothing careless or piecemeal about the structure of *1805*, but it is the result of frequent rethinking, not of a single well-executed plan. (p. 516)

The last two sentences remain useful as a corrective, the first may well need some correction itself. Since his great Cornell edition came out, Reed has generously responded to my request for a brief statement of his position to print in this Introduction:

Book I 1–54 probably date from late 1799, and I 55–271 perhaps from spring 1801 or, and certainly by, early 1804. The order of basic organization of the several Books III–XIII may be broadly summarized as: III (late 1801–early 1804); IV–V (early 1804); VI, XI, VII, IX, first half of X (spring 1804; VII possibly late 1804); VIII, XII, second half of X, XIII (late 1804–spring 1805).

Some differences between the two accounts are more apparent than real. Reed places Book XI in spring 1804, when the materials were gathered in *MS W*, I place it a year later when the materials were adapted to form a book of the 1805 *Prelude.* The second half of Book X (which was drafted as a separate book, and printed as such in *1850*) is a case in which I have gone for the earlier dating, Reed for the later. There is no doubt that much of X (b) was complete before Wordsworth's letter to Beaumont of 30 November 1804; Reed places its composition after that of XII on the evidence of further drafting in *MS Z* c. April 1805. More contentious are the dating of the post-Preamble (where Reed continues to prefer spring 1801, and I think 1804 decidedly more probable) and of Book VII, Wordsworth's partly satirical treatment of the Underworld of London.

As with our views on the post-Preamble, Reed and I differ in our dating of Book VII partly because we are giving weight to different kinds of evidence. He has straightforwardness on his side: why should the 'seventh book' that Wordsworth was composing in late April 1804 not be Book VII? Perhaps it was. But supporting manuscript evidence is sparse, and there are different ways of assessing probabilities. Reed places London (Book VII) between the two French books (VI and IX in the final order). An alternative logic would have Wordsworth move straight on from his first unpolitical experience in France in 1790 (VI) to his commitment to the Revolution in the year-long visit of 1791–2 (IX), and the period leading up to Robespierre's death in July 1794 (X [a]). The fact that these are the only books of *The Prelude* for which no drafts survive very probably means that they were in a single manuscript, now lost, and strongly suggests that they belonged to a single period.

My own positioning of VII in autumn 1804 to some extent depends on the connection (notably at ll. 294, 387 and 470–3) with Wordsworth's *Kitten and the Falling Leaves.* It should be said at once that there is no firm dating for the poem. It is almost certain, however, that the baby watching the kitten is Dora (born August 1804) and highly likely that the leaves fell in that particular fall. Reed's suggestion of autumn 1805 as a date for the poem is plausible on other grounds, but raises the question as to why there should be connections with *The Prelude* at all. The nature of the links makes it clear that the poem came first, yet *The Prelude* was completed in May 1805. A single reminiscence might perhaps have been introduced in revision while Book VII was being copied (Dorothy records that two-thirds of *The Prelude* has been transcribed by 26 December 1805), but there are three such links – and widely spaced.

In all probability Wordsworth after breaking up the five-book *Prelude* in early March 1804, and sending Coleridge *1805* I–V to take with him to the Mediterranean, wrote the French books, VI, IX and X (a). This brought him up to the death of Robespierre, and to what is effectively the end of his direct political involvement in the Revolution. There he stopped for the summer. There were excellent reasons for doing so – he needed a rest, there were visitors to Dove Cottage, there was Dora's impending birth – but it is also doubtful whether he had decided what to write next. The drafts of *MS Y* show that in the event his thoughts went back to childhood, the material of Book I. Prompted, as Dorothy tells us, by reading Cowper (almost certainly the recently published *Yardley Oak*), Wordsworth in early October 1804 drafted Book VIII, 'Retrospect: Love of Nature Leading to Love of Mankind'. The first lines that he wrote (later transferred, to confuse scholars of the future, to the opening of VII) show him taking stock:

> Five years are vanished since I first poured out,
> Saluted by that animating breeze
> Which met me issuing from the city's walls,
> A glad preamble to this verse. I sang

Aloud in dithyrambic fervour, deep
But short-lived uproar, like a torrent sent
Out of the bowels of a bursting cloud
Down Scafell or Blencathra's rugged sides,
A waterspout from heaven. But 'twas not long
Ere the interrupted stream broke forth once more
And flowed awhile in strength, then stopped for years –
Not heard again until a little space
Before last primrose-time.

Retrospectively Wordsworth makes *The Prelude* a Grasmere poem. Composition is taken back five years to the date of the opening lines (the Glad Preamble, November 1799), rather than six (as in the correction of *1850*) to the poem's true origins at Goslar in October 1798. On the other hand he gives a clear account of *The Prelude*'s growth, from the initial 'waterspout' of inspired creativity (*1799* Part I), to the second 'breaking-forth' of the stream (Part II), the gap of years (with no substantial composition, 1800–3), and the new beginning in winter 1804. 'Beloved friend', Wordsworth continues, in surely needless self-reproach,

The assurances then given unto myself
Which did beguile me of some heavy thoughts
At thy departure to a foreign land
Have failed; for slowly doth the work advance.
Through the whole summer have I been at rest,
Partly from voluntary holiday
And part through outward hindrance. But I heard
After the hour of sunset yester-even,
Sitting within doors betwixt light and dark,
A voice that stirred me. 'Twas a little band,
A choir of redbreasts . . .
. . . sent in by Winter to bespeak
For the old man a welcome . . . (VII 13–27)

In his final text (VII 49–53) Wordsworth contrives at this point an elegant backward link to the 'mild creative breeze' of the Preamble (I 43) –

The last night's genial feeling overflowed
Upon this morning, and my favourite grove –
Now tossing its dark boughs in sun and wind –
Spreads through me a commotion like its own,
Something that fits me for the poet's task –

– in *MS Y* the linking had been of more immediate relevance:

The last night's genial feeling overflows
Upon this morning, efficacious more
By reason that my song must now return,
If she desert not her appointed path,
Back into nature's bosom.
Since that time
When with reluctance I withdrew from France
The story hath demanded less regard
To time and place; and where I lived, and how,
Hath been no longer scrupulously traced.

The first five lines take us on into Book VIII, the second (later used at XIII 334–7) refer us back to X 188–9 – 'In this frame of mind|Reluctantly to England I returned' – confirming that a narrative corresponding to Books IX and X (a) had been composed in the early summer.

It is difficult to think Book VIII entirely a success. Wordsworth returned to his Cumbrian childhood in an attempt to show the dawn, not of imagination (as in Part/Book I), but of human-heartedness, the love of humanity that had underlain his commitment to the Revolution ('my heart was all|Given to the people, and my love was theirs', IX 125–6). Drafts in *MS Y* (not surprisingly unused) show that at the time he was feeling an extraordinary ambivalence. Because of the contrast offered him by human littleness, the sensitive spirit 'cleaves|Exclusively to nature':

If upon mankind
He looks, and on the human maladies
Before his eyes, what finds he there to this
Framed answerably? – what but sordid men,

> And transient occupations, and desires
> Ignoble and depraved.

It is in this context that Wordsworth moves on from the pastoralism of VIII into his study of city life in VII.

Readers of *The Prelude* must often have wondered how it is that, having passed through a whole book on London they come, towards the end of Book VIII, on the poet's first entry into the city. Quite as surprising is the claim that 'more than elsewhere|Is possible', 'the unity of man' is set forth in London (VIII 826–7). 'Turn where'er we may', we are told at ll. 838–41, the town is

> Profusely sown with individual sights
> Of courage, and integrity, and truth
> And tenderness . . .

This after Londoners have been dismissed in the conclusion of Book VII as 'slaves unrespited of low pursuits', whose only unity is to live 'amid the same perpetual flow|Of trivial objects, melted and reduced|To one identity' (VII 700–3). Presumably what happened was that after trying in VIII to believe in a London full of tenderness and integrity – as he had tried to portray solitary Grasmere shepherds in terms of human-heartedness – Wordsworth decided to give the city a book to itself. He did so, it would seem, not entirely in a satirical spirit. Though threatened by what seemed to him an alien and anonymous way of life, he was also drawn to its hellish colour and bustle. Descending into its Underworld he could assess his own imaginative power and resilience.

It is clear that when he wrote what we know as Book VIII of *The Prelude* in October 1804 Wordsworth regarded it as following the French books (VI, IX and X [a]). Going on to compose VII at the end of the month, he probably thought of it as standing next in order. We don't know when the French books assumed their final positions, and, lacking the manuscript, we can't tell how much they had to be adapted. Important changes were made, however, in giving VII precedence over VIII. 'Five years are vanished . . .', which had been the opening of VIII, was switched to VII, creating the impression that VII was the first work of autumn 1804. A new opening was composed for VIII, setting up a contrast between the maniac energy of London's Bartholomew Fair (VII 648–94) and the peaceful idyll of the fair beneath Helvellyn (VIII 1–61). And (we must infer, though in this case there is no manuscript evidence) the address 'Preceptress stern . . . to thee I willingly return' (ll. 678 ff.) was inserted in VIII to gloss over the awkwardness of Wordsworth's retaining his original London material.

On 30 November Wordsworth tells Sharp that he has 'dispatched 1,600 or 1,700 lines' of 'the poem on [his] own earlier life' since the summer break. 'Dispatched' is not a very precise term, but it seems that the poet has both completed Book VII and cut down the *MS Y* drafts to form a coherent version of VIII. In their final shape the two books total 1,609 lines. On Christmas Day we have another helpful line-count, Wordsworth telling Beaumont that he has 'written upwards of 2,000 verses during the last ten weeks'. By a natural progression, Wordsworth has moved from London in VII, on to X (b), with its treatment of political alienation and personal crisis in the period following Robespierre's death. It seems that 400 or so lines have been completed of what is regarded at this stage as a separate book (and may, or may not, have been regarded as following X [a]). As Reed has emphasized, the material was to receive its final shape in *MS X* in April 1805, but line-counting evidence suggesting that the bulk had been written by Christmas has support in the text. At X 934–5 we come on Wordsworth's vehement biblical image of the French 'dog' returning to the 'vomit' of monarchy, as Napoleon crowns himself Emperor (2 December 1804) and the Republic comes to an end.

At Christmas 1804 it would seem that the first ten books of the thirteen-book 1805 *Prelude* were complete but for final reworkings. What order they stood in in the poet's mind we have no means of telling. Broadly he could be said to be working still on the paradise-lost-and-regained pattern established in the five-book poem. There had been no concerted attempt to show a fall from innocence into experience (primal imagination impaired), but in the poet's history of developing consciousness the 'inner falling-off' at Cambridge was now paralleled in the turning aside from nature represented by London and by political involvement. Ahead of Wordsworth as he wrote was the material he had set aside from his earlier conclusion, notably the Climbing of Snowdon and the Spots of Time. His rationalization in *MS W* of materials that were to form Book XI ('Imagination, How Impaired and Restored') suggests that very soon after breaking up the five-book poem in March 1804 he had decided on a new role for the Spots of Time, leading up to the epiphany of Snowdon, rather than following it by way of explanation. If this was the case, his main task in the first weeks of 1805 was probably reorganization, the writing in of link-passages and other revision designed to give the poem an overall coherence.

It seems that when news of the death at sea of the Wordsworths' brother John brought work to a stop on 11 February, what remained to be done was to put finishing touches to X (b) and XI and compose XII and XIII. Both these final books contain a great deal of old material, and both (like Book XI) turned out to be brief. Wordsworth, when he got back to work in early April, was in a hurry. Writing was distraction from his grief, and he could feel that he was doing it for John. On 1 May he tells Beaumont that, unable to write an elegy on his brother, he has gone back to *The Prelude*: 'you will be glad to hear that I have added 300 lines to it in the course of last week. Two books more will conclude it.' However much work he had done on XI in March 1804, it sounds as if he is now claiming credit for its composition. On 3 June he tells the same correspondent, 'I have the pleasure to say that I finished my poem about a fortnight ago.' XII and XIII, it seems, have also taken roughly a week apiece.

Pleasure in finishing *The Prelude* was muted. 'I had looked forward to the day', Wordsworth tells Beaumont,

> as a most happy one, and was indeed grateful to God for giving me life to complete the work, such as it is. But it was not a happy day for me; I was dejected on many accounts. When I looked back upon the performance it seemed to have a dead weight about it, the reality so far short of the expectation. It was the first long labour that I had finished, and the doubt whether I should ever live to write *The Recluse*, and the sense which I had of this poem being so far below what I had seemed capable of executing, depressed me much. Above all, many heavy thoughts of my poor departed brother hung upon me – the joy which I should have had

in showing him the manuscript, and a thousand other vain fancies and dreams.

'This work may be considered as a sort of portico to *The Recluse*', Wordsworth continues,

part of the same building, which I hope erelong to begin with in earnest; and if I am permitted to bring it to a conclusion, and to write, further, a narrative poem of the epic kind, I shall consider the *task* of my life as over.

Wordsworth would not be permitted to bring *The Recluse* to a conclusion. In summer 1806 he would rationalize *Home at Grasmere* (the attempt he had made on Book I in 1800), and he would return more than once to the manuscript in the hope of making a fresh start, but the only new work he was to produce for the daunting philosophical centrepiece of *The Recluse* was the sad fragment of 1808, *The Tuft of Primroses.* The narrative poem was less of a problem. Wordsworth's reference to epic has confused critics. The term was used loosely, and has after all no single definition. Wordsworth was writing to his patron, and wished to sound impressive. He is referring in fact to *The Excursion*, planned as early as the letter to De Quincey of 6 March 1804, and published in 1814, with 'A Portion of *The Recluse*' on the title-page. Publication of the autobiographical 'portico', meanwhile, could not in Wordsworth's view be warranted until the unwritable central portion was completed.

Dorothy put the situation very well to Lady Beaumont on 29 November 1805. *The Prelude* was in a sort of limbo, but that was not likely to mean it could be left alone:

I am now engaged in making a fair and final transcript of the poem on his own life – I mean *final* till it is prepared for the press, which will not be for many years. No doubt before that time he will, either from the suggestions of his friends, or his own, or both, have some alterations to make, but it appears to us at present to be finished.

'Us' in the final clause was Dorothy and Mary, Wordsworth's two chief amanuenses, each of whom had transcribed the two-part *Prelude* in 1799, and each of whom was now at work on an *1805* fair copy. Dorothy especially knew the poet too well to suppose that their work would be allowed to stand. Comparison of her text, *MS A*, with Mary's, *MS B*, shows that in addition to helping his helpers by reading difficult manuscripts and establishing the poem for them to copy, Wordsworth in fact revised early parts of the work in fair copy before later parts had been transcribed. When, in February 1806, the two copies were completed there is no evidence that he stopped revising.

How often Wordsworth revised *The Prelude* in the years 1805–50 we cannot know. An entry in the painter Joseph Farington's *Diary* shows that corrections were being made as early as November 1806 in preparation for meeting Coleridge (who had returned from Malta in August, but not felt up to seeing either his family or his closest friends). Others certainly followed the reading of the poem at Coleorton in January that prompted Coleridge to write his last major poem, the admiring *To William Wordsworth*:

An Orphic tale indeed,
A tale divine of high and passionate thoughts
To their own music chanted. Ah, great bard,
Ere yet that last swell, dying, awed the air,
With stedfast ken I viewed thee in the choir
Of ever-enduring men. (ll. 38–43)

The first of three wholesale *Prelude* revisions that we know to have taken place (each associated with a new fair copy manuscript) belongs to c. 1819. What prompted the new revision is less than clear. Wordsworth had completed *The Excursion*, and published it in 1814 as 'A Portion of *The Recluse*', then a year later gone on to print the first Collected Edition of his *Poems*. His Preface to *The Excursion*, setting out the scheme for *The Recluse* in needlessly ambitious terms, had put him under new pressure. For no obvious reason two philosophical sections were projected, when for sixteen years Wordsworth had been unable to write the single one implied in earlier (private) references. At some point he did return briefly to *Home at Grasmere* in hopes of making a new start, but the attempt was forlorn. The task of bringing *The Prelude* up to date was no doubt a welcome alternative.

The new fair copy, *MS C*, was transcribed by Wordsworth's 23-year-old clerk, John Carter, in a handsome volume, bound in quarter-calf and seemingly bought for the purpose. Perhaps it was designed by Wordsworth as a gift for patron or friend; possibly it was to be retained by Carter himself. Either way, it was never completed. And it seems to have provoked – rather than followed – the extensive reworkings from this period found in *MS A* (Dorothy's manuscript of *1805*). In publishing what he terms the '*C*-stage *Prelude*', Reed has speculated impressively on the status of Carter's volume, and particularly on why *C* never became the authoritative text. Revisions at the *C* Stage were heavy and largely unfortunate. Reed detects not merely a tendency to poetic elaboration and artificiality, but 'a strong infusion of body–spirit opposition and of stoic and Christian pessimism and piety'. There are occasional moments of inspiration – menacing new details, for instance, for the Simplon Pass,

> Huge fragments of primeval mountain spread
> In powerless ruin, blocks as huge aloft
> Impending, nor permitted yet to fall . . . (Reed II, p. 109)

– and occasional surprises: the vehemence with which the poet (canvassing at this period for the tory Lowthers) describes the royalist officers at Blois: 'Inflamed with passion, blind with prejudice|And stung with injury' (Reed II, p. 162). But there can be no doubt that most of the reworking is gratuitous.

The details of *1805* VI 339–42, for example, plain and visible to the mind's eye –

> A fellow student and myself (he too
> A mountaineer) together sallied forth
> And, staff in hand, on foot pursued our way
> Towards the distant Alps.

– are padded out to form a strained and disembodied dialogue:

> A fellow student, reared on Clywd's banks
> Mid Cambrian hills, accepted from my voice
> Bold invitation with no timid mind

And, sallying forth on foot, we took our way
Towards the distant Alps. (Reed II, p. 101)

The striking lines from *1805* Book XIII –

Thy love is human merely; this proceeds
More from the brooding soul, and is divine. (ll. 164–5)

– come to seem too daring in their claim for divinity in man, and are followed at the *C* Stage by a pious corrective:

Passion from all disturbing influence pure,
Foretaste of beatific sentiment
Bestowed in mercy on a world condemned
To mutability, pain and grief,
Terrestrial nature's sure inheritance. (Reed II, p. 225)

It is a strange fact that none of the three longer passages of *C*-stage elaboration cited above persists into the 1850 *Prelude.* Indeed none is found in the base text of *MS D*, c. January 1832. Reed allows us to see for the first time that *C* has proved an aberration. *MS A* still has authority as the base text of *D* is created; new readings in *C* are ignored, or accepted only in part. There is, however, no settled pattern of revision. Though *D* may reject concessions to Anglicanism found in *C*, it introduces 'Dust as we are, the immortal spirit grows' (*1850* I 340) and replaces *1805* 'I worshipped then among the depths of things|As my soul bade me', by 'Worshipping then among the depth of things|As piety ordained' (*1850* XII 184–5). On the credit side, *D* is responsible for the moving affirmation –

yet for me
Life's morning radiance hath not left the hills,
Her dew is on the flowers. (*1850* VI 50–2)

– but it produces too the sentimental diminishment of the Infant Babe, once 'powerful in all sentiments of grief|Of exultation, fear, and joy', now 'Frail creature . . . helpless as frail':

Is there a flower, to which he points with hand
Too weak to gather it, already love
Drawn from love's purest earthly fount for him
Hath beautified that flower . . . (*1850* II 245–8)

And *D* it is that introduces the obsequious address to Burke (*1850* VII 512–43), described by J. C. Maxwell in his edition of *The Prelude* (Penguin, 1971) as 'perhaps the most striking single example of insertion in later revision of sympathies alien to the earlier Wordsworth'.

Mary Wordsworth's transcription of *MS D* is marked by a charming letter from her daughter, Dora, to Maria Kinnaird, 18 February 1832:

Father is particularly well and busier than 1000 bees. Mother and he work like slaves from morning to night – an arduous work – correcting a long poem, written 30 years back . . . and not to be published during his life, The Growth of his own Mind – the ante-chapel, as he calls it, to *The Recluse*.

Eight months later, on 15 October, Dora tells the same correspondent that the poet 'is very busy, but not doing much good, I fear, as he is only correcting what was written some 30 years ago'. Probably in fact he was already revising *MS D*, transcribed in the spring. To do good, in this context, would have been to make progress with *The Recluse*. Manuscripts show that before starting the *Prelude* revisions that led to *MS D*, Wordsworth had gone back one last time to *Home at Grasmere* – the attempt on *The Recluse* which he had known as early as March 1800 wasn't going to work. As he took up *The Prelude* in 1832 he must have been close to admitting that the philosophical section(s) of his great work would never be written.

The admission came finally in May 1838, when Wordsworth told the Boston publisher, George Ticknor, that 'he had undertaken something beyond his powers to accomplish'. On 18 August, Isabella Fenwick, friend of the poet's later years, tells Henry Taylor that he has been working at *The Prelude* for the past month, so as to 'leave it in a state fit for publication'. And on 28 March she gives a wholly unthinking account of his progress:

> Every evening that the weather would permit of it he has been here and has told me of his day's work – of the difficulties he has had, and how he had overcome them, of the *beautiful* additions he had made, and all the why and wherefore of each alteration . . .

Wordsworth was putting into these last intensive *Prelude* revisions all the energies that should have gone into *The Recluse.* His posthumous fame was going to rest on what he had been telling himself for almost forty years was a relatively unimportant part of the scheme. The poem must be as good as he could make it. Fortunately there are not too many '*beautiful* additions'. We hear that man is 'born|Of dust, and kindred to the worm' (*1850* VIII 487–8), that imagination (which we have not regarded as moralized) 'trains|To meekness, and exalts by humble faith' (*1850* XIII 27–8). And we watch as the Climbing of Snowdon, great climax of *The Prelude*, is fudged into unmeaning by a Wordsworth frightened at the boldness of his own earlier self. His intuitions may not have changed very much, but times had – and attitudes, and the language of spiritual experience. There was no longer the freedom to speculate seen in the period before and just after the Revolution. Though he left many striking assertions untouched, Wordsworth did not feel able to confront Victorian readers with the 'image of a mighty mind', human, yet feeding upon the 'infinity' of its own inner greatness. He could not portray such a mind as 'exalted by an underpresence' that may be either 'The sense of God, or whatsoe'er is dim|Or vast in its own [finite] being'.

Among Wordsworth's latest revisions was his saddest. Final corrections to *MS D* led in 1839 to the transcription of the printer's copy, *E*; but *E* too seems to have been three times revised. On the second occasion the poet put the finishing touch to the new conclusion to the 'spots of time' sequence, which he had been fidgeting with in *D*. 'All these were spectacles and sounds', Wordsworth had written impressively in 1799,

> to which
> I often would repair, and thence would drink
> As at a fountain. And I do not doubt
> That in this later time, when storm and rain

Beat on my roof at midnight, or by day
When I am in the woods, unknown to me
The workings of my spirit thence are brought. (*1805* XI 382–8)

'And I do not doubt' – the poet's words had had the force of a creed, proclaiming a faith in the mind's strength and self-sufficiency that was central to *The Prelude.* By 1839 ten gratuitous lines have been added to the sequence, but the final shaping has especial pathos, telling us of an old man who has quite forgotten the power of his original experience, the force of his original claims for inspiration and imaginative strength:

All these were kindred spectacles and sounds
To which I oft repaired, and thence would drink,
As at a fountain; and on winter nights,
Down to this very time, when storm and rain
Beat on my roof, or, haply, at noon-day,
While in a grove I walk, whose lofty trees,
Laden with summer's thickest foliage, rock
In a strong wind, some workings of the spirit,
Some inward agitations thence are brought,
Whate'er their office, whether to beguile
Thoughts over busy in the course they took,
Or animate an hour of vacant ease. (*1850* XII 324–35)

The Spots of Time, which since January 1799 have supported each successive version of *The Prelude* with their theory of the imagination nourished and inspired by early experience, dwindle now to the memories of an old-age pensioner – ways to head off thoughts 'over busy', or while the time away.

PRELUDE MANUSCRIPTS

MS JJ	Notebook in use at Goslar in October–November 1798, containing the beginnings of *The Prelude*, including *Was It For This* and the original first-person draft of *There Was A Boy.*
MS 18A	Notebook used to assemble a near-complete version of *1799* Part I before the Wordsworths left Goslar on 23 February 1799; containing also *There Are Who Tell Us* (*There Was A Boy*, in third person, worked up into discussion of education for *The Recluse*).
MS RV	Fair copy of *1799* Part II, autumn 1799.
MS V	Fair copy of completed two-part *Prelude*, made by Dorothy Wordsworth, early December 1799, and base text for the poem as printed in this volume. Heavily revised January–February 1804.
MS U	Duplicate fair copy of two-part *Prelude*, made at the same period as *MS V* by Mary Hutchinson.
MS WW	Twenty-three leaves from tiny pocket-notebook used by Wordsworth during outdoor composition in February 1804, containing barely legible pencil-drafts of Climbing of Snowdon, and much else.
MS W	Notebook used to assemble short-lived five-book *Prelude* of February–early March 1804.
MS Y	Important notebook of October 1804, containing the Beaupuy section of *1805* Book IX (written in early summer), together with original drafts of VIII and material finally used in XI and XII.

MS X Notebook of October 1804 containing early version of *1805* VII.

MS Z Notebook of April–May 1805 with Books XI and XII of *1805* in original form.

MS A Fair copy of *Prelude* in thirteen books, made by Dorothy Wordsworth, November 1804–February 1805, and base copy for the text in this volume. Last revised in 1832.

MS B Duplicate fair copy of *1805*, made at the same period as *MS A* by Mary Wordsworth (née Hutchinson).

MS C Fair copy of revised thirteen-book *Prelude*, made by Wordsworth's clerk, John Carter, c. 1819. Lacks final book and last half of XII, and never regarded by the poet as an authoritative text.

MS D First MS of *The Prelude* in fourteen books, made by Mary Wordsworth early in 1832; heavily revised at the end of the year and again in 1838–9.

MS E Printer's copy for the posthumous first edition of *The Prelude* published in July 1850, inaccurately transcribed by the poet's daughter Dora and her cousin Elizabeth Cookson, March–May 1839, and several times revised.

TEXTS

Of the four texts presented below, the first two offer no great problems. *Was It For This* derives from *MS JJ* of October 1798, the two-part *Prelude* from *MS V* (Dorothy Wordsworth's fair copy of December 1799) and, where that is defective, from *MS U*, transcribed by Mary Hutchinson at the same moment. In both cases arriving at a text is helped by the Cornell *Prelude 1798–9* of Stephen Parrish (whose inspiration as General Editor of the Series goes unseen and unsung). The full-length *Preludes* are another matter. There can be no perfect text of *1805*. Such is the complexity of the manuscripts that no two editors (and no single editor on different occasions) will arrive at an identical version. The text of *1850*, where it is based (as has been normal) on the manuscripts, will be similarly variable.

De Selincourt in his great parallel-text edition of 1926, to which all subsequent editors must be indebted, made two important policy decisions. He selected *MS A* as his base text for *1805*, and he concluded that the posthumous first edition must be checked against the manuscripts to create a text of *1850* more nearly representing the poet's final intentions. The decision to base *1805* on *MS A* has been followed by all subsequent editors until the Cornell *Thirteen-book 'Prelude'* of 1991, in which Reed has attempted to present Wordsworth's final intentions at 'the *A/B* stage'. In a series concerned dominantly with the manuscripts and their implications, it is an interesting and valuable thing to do; but it is not I think more likely to provide a sound reading text. As De Selincourt noted, *MS A* (like *MS V* of *1799*), is treated by Wordsworth as the authoritative manuscript – being, for instance, used for revisions at the *C* and *D* Stages. *MS B* does at times have corrections that are independent of *A*, and perhaps to be regarded as substantive, but is essentially a second copy.

Ideally one would avoid all questions of priority by choosing as base text the original fair copy of *MS A.* But no such thing ever existed. The manuscript has been heavily revised, and corrections to early parts of the poem were made – often, like Blake's early corrections to *Vala*, made over erasure – while later books were being copied. There never was a fair copy that represented a single point in time – that is to say, a single version of *The Prelude.* In practice, transcription of *MS A* (whether as base text or as part of the composite *A/B*) has to be of the fair copy as it stood after initial corrections had been completed. Though hard to retrieve, this did exist. We can get near it. Not so, in my view, the final *A/B* stage. The principle behind Reed's choice is the same as De Selincourt's (or mine) – he attempts to single out the *Prelude* of a particular moment – but the text in his case rests on a state of affairs in the poet's head. We have to posit that where *MSS A* and *B* differ, Wordsworth knew which *B* readings he fancied, regarding them as part of an ideal text that existed in his mind, and not on paper. I should much prefer to have followed the Cornell text, or at least been able to conform to its line-numbering, but have with great reluctance stayed in the De Selincourt camp. Though deriving much from Reed's scholarship, the *1805* text printed below is based on *MS A* after what is deemed to be the initial stage of correction.

Editors of the fourteen-book *Prelude* are faced with a similarly difficult choice. In publishing the first edition in July 1850, the poet's executors – his son-in-law, Edward Quillinan (minor poet, husband of Dora), his clerk from the Stamp Office, John Carter (transcriber, thirty years earlier, of *MS C*, and thus with a stake in *The Prelude*), and his nephew, Christopher (writer in 1851 of the poet's official *Memoirs* and future Bishop of Lincoln) – made unwarranted alterations to the printer's copy, *MS E.* Logic would therefore suggest a reprinting of *E.* But *E* turns out to be a poor manuscript, transcribed from the final state of *D*, not by Dorothy, sadly now in her dotage, or by Mary, but by younger helpers who did not have the same experience or skill. To retrieve the *Prelude* that Wordsworth's executors should have printed, one has to go back a stage further, to corrected *MS D* (following *E* at points where it has been revised by the poet and therefore presumably represents an updating).

The process of correcting the printed first edition by reference to the manuscripts began with De Selincourt in 1926, and was taken a stage further by Maxwell in 1971. In 1979 the Norton Critical Edition offered a text of *1850* actually founded upon the manuscripts: Owen's thoroughgoing Cornell volume (1985) has a similar basis. Such logics are persuasive. The first edition of *The Prelude* is not an authorized text. We know it to be fallible. Manuscripts enable us to deduce the poet's intentions. But still, the first edition is a fact of literary history, the poem as it was first known to Wordsworth's public. It is the poem greeted memorably by the *Eclectic Review* as 'a large fossil relic, imperfect and magnificent . . . newly dug up, and with the fresh earth and the old dim subsoil meeting and mingling round it' – the poem slighted by Macaulay in his journal on 28 July 1850: 'It is to the last degree Jacobinical, indeed Socialist. I understand perfectly why Wordsworth did not choose to publish it in his lifetime.' In a situation in which texts of *1850* based on the manuscripts have been progressively refined, the time may now be right for a return to the version originally printed.

THIS EDITION

The Prelude is in many ways a very accessible poem; it is also nearly two hundred years old. The aim of this new Penguin edition has been to present the different versions in a way that is helpful and undistracting. Spelling in the three early texts is modernized, and punctuation editorial. Clearly this differentiates them from *1850*, where the text of the first edition has been reproduced exactly. It has seemed best, however, to aim at integrity within the individual texts rather than overall consistency (to provide in the early texts only such punctuation as exists in the manuscripts would be unhelpful, to repunctuate the first edition seems probably a mistake). Particular care has been taken in the notes to discuss instances where the poetry is confusing or unclear. References and scholarly paraphernalia have been kept to a workable minimum. It has been assumed that those who wish to follow the textual history of the poem in detail will turn to photographs and transcripts of the manuscripts in the Cornell editions of Parrish, Reed and Owen. No apparatus criticus is offered, but all major cases are noted in which the text of the first edition appears, on the basis of *MSS D* and *E*, to diverge from Wordsworth's intention. In general, textual variants are noted when they contribute significantly to our sense of the poet's creativity or of the poem's development.

Modernizing the spelling of Wordsworth's manuscript-poetry, like establishing the text, forces the editor into controversial decisions. The reader's convenience has to be weighed against claims for authenticity, scholarly rigour. Only *Was It For This*, however, survives in the poet's hand. To preserve original spelling in *1799* and *1805* is to preserve the choices and idiosyncrasies of his helpers. It can be argued that period spelling is a guide to pronunciation, but even where this is true it is doubtfully useful.

It could only be distracting if we as readers attempted to hear Wordsworth's version of Regency English, with its 'strong tincture of the northern *burr*, like the crust on wine' (Hazlitt, *My First Acquaintance With Poets*). Pronunciation has changed a great deal in two hundred years (usually leaving the spelling unaffected), and English is spoken far more widely. As a poet Wordsworth wished above all to reach out, and was above all sensitive to the tendency of language to create barriers. Though he regarded Chaucer's language as still intelligible, he spent much time in 1801–2 translating him, attempting to make him more available. He would have had no sympathy for preserving old spellings/forms when their unfamiliarity might be the cause of uncertainty, or give his poetry an antiquated air. His writing, he tells us in the Preface to *Lyrical Ballads*, is designed 'to interest mankind permanently'. He sought a permanent language to embody what seemed to him abiding human values.

Spellings that do not affect pronunciation ('eugh-trees', 'craggs', 'untill', 'chace', for instance, and the names 'Trompington', 'Gloster', 'Beaupuis') have been corrected without hesitation; others that do make a difference to the sound of the verse ('sate', 'spake', 'hath', 'doth') are modernized on the grounds of gain outweighing loss. Contractions ('slippry', 'givst') have been spelt out, on the assumption that few readers would in practice stress the extra syllable. Final 'ed's have been marked where they should be sounded ('fixèd face'), and monosyllabic forms (notably 'blest' as opposed to 'blessed') used where they exist and are appropriate. Capitalization – used with little discrimination in the manuscripts, and now incorrectly taken to be a form of emphasis – has been retained only for references to God (direct and indirect) and for personifications that assert themselves as such (Lady Sorrow).

Old spelling has been retained in certain cases where the poet seems to be highlighting an archaic form for poetic effect: the strong past participle of the verb 'to climb' ('having clomb|The Heights of Kendal', *1805* IV 1–2), or the word 'enough' in its rare plural form ('Enow there are . . . Enow to think . . .', V 153, 156). More significant is Wordsworth's use of verbal forms that cannot be modernized because of the metre: 'morning shines,|Nor heedeth man's perverseness' (XI 22–3), 'Here keepest thou thy individual state' (XIII 190). Frequently these are associated with the pronoun 'thou'; and as that cannot be altered, it has seemed logical to retain the few examples of 'ye' in the second person plural: 'ye knew him well, ye cliffs|And islands of Winander' (V 389–90).

Wordsworth's own comments on editing (quoted with effect by Maxwell) show a strong sense of priorities. 'A correct text is the first object of an editor', he tells Walter Scott on 7 November 1805,

> then such notes as explain difficult or unintelligible passages, or throw light upon them; and lastly, which is of much less importance, notes pointing out passages or authors to which the poet has been endebted – not in the piddling way of phrase here and phrase there (which is detestable as a general practice), but where the poet has really had essential obligations either as to matter or manner.

Scott was editing Dryden. Wordsworth was superintending the transcription of *The Prelude*, in effect editing himself. His text now needs a great deal more annotation than he envisaged – not least in the area of borrowings that causes him such irritation. He could take for granted, as a modern editor cannot, that readers would appreciate passing allusion: to the Bible, to Coleridge, to Shakespeare, to Cowper, above all to Milton. Describing *The Prelude*'s new theme of inner consciousness, Wordsworth asserts grandly at III 182–3, 'This is in truth heroic argument|And genuine prowess.' The poetry has little meaning unless we make the implied comparison with *Paradise Lost* IX 13–47, where Milton places himself in the epic tradition, asserting the superiority of his own Christian 'argument' over the war poetry of Homer and Virgil:

> sad task, yet argument
> Not less but more heroic than the wrath
> Of stern Achilles on his foe pursued
> Thrice fugitive about Troy wall, or rage
> Of Turnus for Lavinia disespoused . . .

'Essential obligation' does not always take the form of allusions that ask to be recognized. It may indeed break the surface 'phrase here and phrase there'. But almost always it contributes to a larger pattern. For the editor of Wordsworth there is little danger of descending to 'piddling' indebtedness. Notes offer readers the chance to trace underlying relationship, and to take the subtler points of allusion.

With his anxieties about 'the sad incompetence of human speech' and his demand that the reader be 'in a healthful state of association', Wordsworth might well have accepted that *The Prelude* would come to require 'such notes as explain difficult or unintelligible passages, or throw light upon them'. Many cases of difficulty have been sorted out in the present edition by repunctuation (that of *1805* throwing light upon parallel passages in *1850*), but no doubtful meaning in any version of the poem has gone unnoted. One or two have proved wholly baffling. Only the writer could tell us what he meant by capping his lucid and remarkable statement 'Points have we all of us within our souls|Where all stand single' with the words 'this I feel, and make|Breathings for incommunicable powers' (III 186–8).

ABBREVIATIONS

Prelude versions:	*WIFT*: *Was It For This* (original *Prelude* draft of October 1798) *1799*: Two-part *Prelude* of 1798–9 *1805*: Thirteen-book *Prelude* of 1805 *1850*: Fourteen-book *Prelude* of 1850
AM	Samuel Taylor Coleridge, *The Ancient Mariner* (1798 text)
Bicentenary Studies	*Bicentenary Wordsworth Studies*, ed. Jonathan Wordsworth (Ithaca, NY, 1970)
Butler	*'The Ruined Cottage' and 'The Pedlar'*, ed. James Butler, Cornell *Wordsworth* (Ithaca, NY, 1979)
BV	Jonathan Wordsworth, *William Wordsworth: The Borders of Vision* (Oxford and New York, 1982)
BNYPL	*Bulletin of the New York Public Library*
Chronology	Mark L. Reed, (i) *Wordsworth: Chronology of the Early Years, 1770–99*; (ii) *Wordsworth: Chronology of the Middle Years, 1800–15* (Cambridge, MA, 1967, 1975)
FM	Samuel Taylor Coleridge, *Frost at Midnight*, text of 1798 (Woodstock Facsimile, '*Fears in Solitude*', etc, Oxford and New York, 1989)

JEGP	*Journal of English and Germanic Philology*
Johnson	Samuel Johnson, *Dictionary of the English Language* (2 vols, 1786)
Lakes Tour	Revd William Gilpin, *Observations, Relative Chiefly to Picturesque Beauty, made in Cumberland and Westmorland* (2 vols, 1786)
Maxwell	William Wordsworth, *The Prelude: A Parallel Text*, ed. J. C. Maxwell, Penguin Classics (London and New York, 1971)
Memoirs	Christopher Wordsworth, *Memoirs of William Wordsworth* (2 vols, 1851)
Norton *Prelude*	*William Wordsworth: 'The Prelude', 1799, 1805, 1850*, ed. Jonathan Wordsworth, M. H. Abrams and Stephen Gill (New York, 1979)
Notebooks	*Notebooks of Samuel Taylor Coleridge*, ed. Kathleen Coburn (8 vols, New York, 1957–90)
NQ	*Notes and Queries*
Oxford	*Poetical Works of William Wordsworth*, ed. E. de Selincourt and Helen Darbishire (5 vols, Oxford and New York, 1940–9)
OED	*Oxford English Dictionary*
Oxford *Prelude*	*William Wordsworth, 'The Prelude'*, ed. E. de Selincourt (1926), 2nd ed. revised Helen Darbishire (Oxford and New York, 1959)
Owen	*The Fourteen-book 'Prelude'*, ed. W. J. B. Owen, Cornell *Wordsworth* (Ithaca, NY, 1985)

Parrish	*'The Prelude', 1798–9*, ed. Stephen Parrish, Cornell *Wordsworth* (Ithaca, NY, 1977)
PL	John Milton, *Paradise Lost*
PMLA	*Publications of the Modern Language Association of America*
Prose Works	*Prose Works of William Wordsworth*, ed. W. J. B. Owen and J. W. Smyser (3 vols, Oxford and New York, 1974)
Recollections	Thomas de Quincey, *Recollections of the Lakes and the Lake Poets*, ed. David Wright, Penguin Classics (London, 1970; New York, 1971)
Reed	*The Thirteen-book 'Prelude'*, ed. Mark L. Reed, Cornell *Wordsworth* (2 vols, Ithaca, NY, 1991)
RES	*Review of English Studies*
Rooke	Samuel Taylor Coleridge, *The Friend*, ed. Barbara Rooke, Bollingen *Coleridge* (2 vols, Princeton, NJ, 1969)
Sublime and Beautiful	Edmund Burke, *Enquiry into the Sublime and Beautiful*, ed. James T. Boulton (London, 1958)
TA	*Tintern Abbey*
Ward	Thomas de Quincey, *Confessions of an English Opium-Eater and Other Writings*, ed. Aileen Ward, Signet Classics (New York, 1966)
WC	*The Wordsworth Circle*
West, *Guide*	Thomas West, *A Guide to the Lakes*, 3rd ed., 1784, Woodstock Facsimile (Oxford and New York, 1989)

Wordsworth's Hawkshead	T. W. Thompson, *Wordsworth's Hawkshead*, ed. Robert Woof (Oxford, 1970)
Wye Tour	Revd William Gilpin, *Observations on the River Wye*, 1782, Woodstock Facsimile (Oxford and New York, 1991)

FURTHER READING

Editions of Wordsworth and Coleridge

Beer, John, *Poems of S. T. Coleridge*, selected and ed., Everyman, (revised ed. London, 1993)

Bollingen *Coleridge* (Princeton, NJ), especially:
(i) *Lectures 1795 on Politics and Religion*, ed. Lewis Patton and Peter Mann (1971)
(ii) *Essays on His Times*, ed. David Erdman (3 vols, 1978)
(iii) *The Friend*, ed. Barbara Rooke (2 vols, 1969)

Coburn, Kathleen, ed., *Notebooks of Samuel Taylor Coleridge* (8 vols, New York, 1957–90)

Cornell *Wordsworth* (Ithaca), especially:
(i) *'The Ruined Cottage' and 'The Pedlar'*, ed. James Butler (1979)
(ii) *'The Prelude' 1798–9*, ed. Stephen Parrish (1977)
(iii) *The Thirteen-book 'Prelude'*, ed. Mark L. Reed (1991)
(iv) *The Fourteen-book 'Prelude'*, ed. W. J. B. Owen (1985)

de Selincourt, E., and Helen Darbishire, eds, *Poetical Works of William Wordsworth* (5 vols, Oxford and New York, 1940–9)

de Selincourt, E., ed., *Letters of William and Dorothy Wordsworth* (Oxford and New York): *The Early Years, 1787–1805*, revised Chester L. Shaver (1967); *The Middle Years, 1806–11*, revised Mary Moorman (1969); *The Middle Years, 1812–20*, revised Mary Moorman and Alan G. Hill (1970); *The Later Years, 1821–53*, revised Alan G. Hill (4 vols, 1978–88); *A Supplement of New Letters*, ed. Alan G. Hill (1993)

de Selincourt, E., ed., William Wordsworth, *Guide to the Lakes*, Oxford Reprints (Oxford, 1970)

Gill, Stephen, *Poems of William Wordsworth*, selected and ed., New Oxford Standard Authors (Oxford and New York, 1984)

Griggs, Earl Leslie, ed., *Collected Letters of Samuel Taylor Coleridge* (6 vols, Oxford, 1956–71)

Owen, W. J. B. and Jane Worthington Smyser, *Prose Works of William Wordsworth* (3 vols, Oxford and New York, 1974)

Walford Davies, Damian, ed., *William Wordsworth, Selected Poems*, Everyman (London, 1994)

Woodstock Facsimile Series, *Revolution and Romanticism*, selected and introduced, Jonathan Wordsworth (Oxford and New York), especially:
- (i) Wordsworth, *The Excursion*, first ed., 1814 (1991)
- (ii) Wordsworth, *Poems*, 2 vols, 1815 (1989)
- (iii) Wordsworth, *The Prelude*, first ed., 1850 (1993)
- (iv) Coleridge, *Poems on Various Subjects*, 1796 (1990)
- (v) Coleridge, '*Fears in Solitude*', '*France, An Ode*' *and* '*Frost at Midnight*', first ed., 1798 (1989)
- (vi) Coleridge, *Sibylline Leaves*, 1817 (1990)

Woof, Pamela, ed., *Dorothy Wordsworth: The Grasmere Journals* (Oxford, 1990; New York, 1993)

Wordsworth, Jonathan, ed., '*The Pedlar*', '*Tintern Abbey*' *and the Two-part* '*Prelude*' (Cambridge and New York, 1985)

Wordsworth, Jonathan, M. H. Abrams and Stephen Gill, eds, '*The Prelude*', *1799, 1805 and 1850*, Norton Critical Edition (New York, 1979)

Background

Abrams, M. H., *The Mirror and the Lamp* (New York, 1953)

Burke, Edmund, *Enquiry into the Sublime and Beautiful*,

1757, ed. James T. Boulton (London, 1958); *Reflections on the Revolution in France*, 1790, ed. C. C. O'Brien (London, 1968)

George, M. Dorothy, *London Life in the Eighteenth Century*, 1925 (reissued London, 1965)

Gill, Stephen, *William Wordsworth: A Life* (Oxford and New York, 1989)

Gilpin, Revd William, *Observations, Relative Chiefly to Picturesque Beauty, made in Cumberland and Westmorland* (2 vols, 1786); *Observations on the River Wye* (1782)

Godwin, William, *Political Justice*, first ed., 2 vols, 1793, Woodstock Facsimile (Oxford and New York, 1992); *Caleb Williams*, 1794, ed. David McCracken, Oxford Novels (Oxford, 1970)

Goodwin, Albert, *Friends of Liberty: The English Democratic Movement in the Age of the French Revolution* (London, 1979)

Hartley, David, *Observations on Man*, 1749, with notes by Herman Pistorius (3 vols, 1791)

Hayden, Donald E., *Wordsworth's Walking-tour of 1790* (Tulsa, 1983)

Lefebvre, Georges, *The French Revolution*, trans. (i) E. M. Evanson (London, 1962), (ii) J. H. Stewart and J. Friguglietti (London, 1964)

Legouis, Emile, *William Wordsworth and Annette Vallon* (London, 1922; Reprint Services, Temecula, CA)

Locke, John, *The Educational Writings of John Locke*, ed. James L. Axtell (Cambridge, 1968)

Moorman, Mary, *William Wordsworth: A Biography: The Early Years: 1770–1803* (Oxford, 1957); *The Later Years: 1803–50* (Oxford, 1968)

Paine, Thomas, *Thomas Paine Reader*, ed. Michael Foot and Isaac Kramnick, Penguin Classics (London, 1987)

Price, Richard, *A Discourse of the Love of Our Country*, 1789, Woodstock Facsimile (Oxford and New York, 1992)

Robinson, Henry Crabb, *On Books and Their Writers*, ed. E. J. Morley (3 vols, London, 1938)

Roe, Nicholas, *Wordsworth and Coleridge: The Radical Years* (Oxford, 1988; New York, 1990)

Roland, Jeanne Marie de la Platière, *An Appeal to Impartial Posterity*, 1795, Woodstock Facsimile (Oxford and New York, 1990)

Schneider, Ben Ross Jr, *Wordsworth's Cambridge Education* (Cambridge, 1957)

Thompson, E. P., *The Making of the English Working Class* (London, 1963; reissued 1968)

Thompson, T. W., *Wordsworth's Hawkshead*, ed. Robert Woof (Oxford, 1970)

West, Thomas, *A Guide to the Lakes*, 3rd ed., 1784, Woodstock Facsimile (Oxford and New York, 1989)

Williams, Helen Maria, *Letters Written in France in the Summer of 1790*, Woodstock Facsimile (Oxford and New York, 1989)

Wollstonecraft, Mary, *A Wollstonecraft Anthology*, ed. Janet Todd (Bloomington, IN, 1977)

Wordsworth, Christopher, *Memoirs of William Wordsworth* (2 vols, 1851)

Wordsworth, Jonathan, 'The Infinite I AM: Coleridge and the Ascent of Being', *Coleridge's Imagination*, ed. Richard Gravil, Lucy Newlyn and Nicholas Roe (Cambridge and New York, 1985), 22–52; *Ancestral Voices: Fifty Books from the Romantic Period* (Oxford and New York, 1991); *Visionary Gleam: Forty Books from the Romantic Period* (Oxford and New York, 1993)

Critical works

Abrams, M. H., *Natural Supernaturalism: Tradition and Revolution in Romantic Literature* (Oxford and New York, 1971); 'The Correspondent Breeze: A Romantic Metaphor', *English Romantic Poets*, ed. M. H. Abrams (Oxford, 1960; revised, 1965), 37–54

Ellis, David, *Wordsworth, Freud and the Spots of Time* (Cambridge and New York, 1985)

Finch, John Alban, 'Wordsworth's Two-Handed Engine', *Bicentenary Wordsworth Studies*, ed. Jonathan Wordsworth (Ithaca, NY, 1970), 1–13

Gill, Stephen, *William Wordsworth: 'The Prelude'*, Landmarks of Literature (Cambridge and New York, 1991)

Hanley, Keith, 'Crossings Out: The Problem of Textual Passage in *The Prelude*', *Romantic Revisions*, ed. Robert Brinkley and Keith Hanley (Cambridge and New York, 1992), 103–36

Havens, Raymond Dexter, *The Mind of the Poet* (2 vols, Baltimore, MD, 1941)

Jacobus, Mary, *Romanticism, Writing and Sexual Difference: Essays on 'The Prelude'* (Oxford and New York, 1989)

Johnston, Kenneth R., *Wordsworth and 'The Recluse'* (New Haven, CT, 1984)

Landon, Carol, 'Some Sidelights on *The Prelude*', *Bicentenary Wordsworth Studies*, ed. Jonathan Wordsworth (Ithaca, NY, 1970), 359–76

Lindenberger, Herbert, *On Wordsworth's 'Prelude'* (Princeton, NJ, 1963); 'The Reception of *The Prelude*', *Bulletin of the New York Public Library*, lxiv (1960), 196–208

McFarland, Thomas, *Romanticism and the Forms of Ruin* (Princeton, NJ, 1981)

Rehder, Robert, 'Wordsworth's Imagination', forthcoming in *Wordsworth Circle*

Roe, Nicholas, 'Imagining Robespierre', *Coleridge's Imagination*, ed. Richard Gravil, Lucy Newlyn and Nicholas Roe (Cambridge and New York, 1985), 161–78; 'Revising the Revolution', *Romantic Revisions*, ed. Robert Brinkley and Keith Hanley (Cambridge and New York, 1992), 87–103

Wordsworth, Jonathan, 'The Five-Book *Prelude* of Early Spring 1804', *Journal of English and Germanic Philology*, lxxvi (January 1977), 1–25; 'That Wordsworth Epic', *Wordsworth Circle*, xi (winter 1980), 34–5; *William Wordsworth: The Borders of Vision* (Oxford and New York, 1983); 'Wordsworth's "Dim and Perilous Way"', *Revolution and English Romanticism*, ed. Keith Hanley and Raman Selden (Hassocks, Sussex, 1990), 205–23; 'Revision as Making: *The Prelude* and its Peers', *Romantic Revisions*, ed. Robert Brinkley and Keith Hanley (Cambridge and New York, 1992), 18–43

The Prelude

THE FOUR TEXTS

WAS IT FOR THIS

Was it for this
That one, the fairest of all rivers, loved
To blend his murmurs with my nurse's song,
And from his alder shades and rocky falls,
And from his fords and shallows, sent a voice
To intertwine my dreams? For this didst thou,
O Derwent, travelling over the green plains
Near my sweet birth-place, didst thou, beauteous stream,
Give ceaseless music to the night and day,
Which with its steady cadence tempering
Our human waywardness, composed by thoughts
To more than infant softness, giving me
Amid the fretful tenements of man
A knowledge, a dim earnest, of the calm
That nature breathes among her woodland haunts?
Was it for this (and now I speak of things
That have been, and that are, no gentle dreams
Complacent, fashioned fondly to adorn
The time of unrememberable being),
Was it for this that I, a four years' child,
Beneath thy scars and in thy silent pools
Made one long bathing of a summer's day,
Basked in the sun, or plunged into thy streams,
Alternate, all a summer's day, or coursed
Over thy sandy plains, and dashed the flowers
Of yellow groundsel – or, when the hill-tops,
The woods, and all the distant mountains,
Were bronzed with a deep radiance, stood alone
A naked savage in the thunder-shower?

For this in springtime, when on southern banks
The shining sun had from his knot of leaves
Decoyed the primrose flower, and when the vales
And woods were warm, was I a rover then
In the high places, on the lonely peaks,
Among the mountains and the winds? Though mean,
And though inglorious, were my views, the end
Was not ignoble. Oh, when I have hung
Above the raven's nest, have hung alone
By half-inch fissures in the slippery rock
But ill sustained, and almost (as it seemed)
Suspended by the wind which blew amain
Against the naked crag, ah, then,
While on the perilous edge I hung alone,
With what strange utterance did the loud dry wind
Blow through my ears! The sky seemed not a sky
Of earth – and with what motion moved the clouds!

Ah, not in vain ye beings of the hills,
And ye that walk the woods and open heaths
By moon or starlight, thus, from my first day
Of childhood, did ye love to interweave
The passions that build up our human soul
Not with the mean and vulgar works of man,
But with high objects, with eternal things,
With life and nature, purifying thus
The elements of feeling and of thought,
And sanctifying by such discipline
Both pain and fear, until we recognize
A grandeur in the beatings of the heart.
Ah, not in vain ye spirits of the springs,
And ye that have your voices in the clouds,
And ye that are familiars of the lakes
And standing pools, ah, not for trivial ends
Through snow and sunshine and the sparkling plains
Of moonlight frost, and through the stormy day,
Did ye with such assiduous love pursue
Your favourite and your joy. I may not think
A vulgar hope was yours when ye employed

Such ministry, when ye through many a year
Thus, by the agency of boyish sports,
Impressed upon the streams, the woods, the hills –
Impressed upon all forms – the characters
Of danger and desire, and thus did make
The surface of the universal earth
With meanings of delight, of hope and fear,
Work like a sea.

For this, when on the withered mountain-slope
The frost and breath of frosty wind had nipped
The last autumnal crocus, did I love
To range through half the night among the cliffs
And the smooth hollows where the woodcocks ran
Along the moonlight turf? In thought and wish
That time, my shoulder all with springes hung,
I was a fell destroyer. Gentle powers,
Who give us happiness and call it peace,
When scudding on from snare to snare I plied
My anxious visitation, hurrying on,
Still hurrying, hurrying onward, how my heart
Panted; among the lonely yew-trees and the crags
That looked upon me, how my bosom beat
With hope and fear! Sometimes strong desire
Resistless overcame me and the bird
That was the captive of another's toils
Became my prey, and when the deed was done
I heard among the solitary hills
Low breathings coming after me and sounds
Of undistinguishable motion, steps
Almost as silent as the turf they trod.

Nor while, though doubting yet not lost, I tread
The mazes of this argument, and paint
How nature by collateral interest
And by extrinsic passion peopled first
My mind with beauteous objects, may I well
Forget what might demand a loftier song,
How oft the eternal spirit – he that has

His life in unimaginable things,
And he who painting what he is in all
The visible imagery of all the worlds
Is yet apparent chiefly as the soul
Of our first sympathies – oh bounteous power,
In childhood, in rememberable days,
How often did thy love renew for me
Those naked feelings which when thou wouldst form
A living thing thou sendest like a breeze
Into its infant being. Soul of things,
How often did thy love renew for me
Those hallowed and pure motions of the sense
Which seem in their simplicity to own
An intellectual charm – that calm delight
Which (if I err not) surely must belong
To those first-born affinities which fit
Our new existence to existing things,
And in our dawn of being constitute
The bond of union betwixt life and joy.

Yes, I remember when the changeful earth
And twice five seasons on my mind had stamped
The faces of the changeful year, even then,
A child, I held unconscious intercourse
With the eternal beauty, drinking in
A pure organic pleasure from the lines
Of curling mist, or from the smooth expanse
Of waters coloured by the cloudless moon.
The sands of Westmorland, the creeks and bays
Of Cumbria's rocky limits, they can tell
How when the sea threw off his evening shade
And to the shepherd's hut beneath the crags
Did send sweet notice of the rising moon,
How I have stood, to images like this
A stranger, linking with the spectacle
No body of associated forms,
And bearing with me no peculiar sense
Of quietness or peace – yet I have stood
Even while my eye has moved o'er three long leagues

Of shining water, gathering, as it seemed,
New pleasure like a bee among the flowers.
Nor unsubservient even to noblest ends
Are these primordial feelings. How serene,
How calm these seem amid the swell
Of human passion – even yet I feel
Their tranquillizing power.

THE TWO-PART *PRELUDE* OF 1799

First Part

Was it for this
That one, the fairest of all rivers, loved
To blend his murmurs with my nurse's song,
And from his alder shades and rocky falls,
And from his fords and shallows, sent a voice
That flowed along my dreams? For this didst thou,
O Derwent, travelling over the green plains
Near my 'sweet birthplace', didst thou, beauteous stream,
Make ceaseless music through the night and day,
Which with its steady cadence tempering
Our human waywardness, composed my thoughts
To more than infant softness, giving me
Among the fretful dwellings of mankind
A knowledge, a dim earnest, of the calm
Which nature breathes among the fields and groves?
Beloved Derwent, fairest of all streams,
Was it for this that I, a four years' child,
A naked boy, among thy silent pools
Made one long bathing of a summer's day,
Basked in the sun, or plunged into thy streams,
Alternate, all a summer's day, or coursed
Over the sandy fields, and dashed the flowers
Of yellow groundsel – or, when crag and hill,
The woods, and distant Skiddaw's lofty height,
Were bronzed with a deep radiance, stood alone
A naked savage in the thunder-shower?

And afterwards ('twas in a later day,
Though early), when upon the mountain-slope
The frost and breath of frosty wind had snapped

The last autumnal crocus, 'twas my joy
To wander half the night among the cliffs
And the smooth hollows where the woodcocks ran
Along the moonlight turf. In thought and wish
That time, my shoulder all with springes hung,
I was a fell destroyer. Gentle powers,
Who give us happiness and call it peace,
When scudding on from snare to snare I plied
My anxious visitation, hurrying on,
Still hurrying, hurrying onward, how my heart
Panted; among the scattered yew-trees and the crags
That looked upon me, how my bosom beat
With expectation! Sometimes strong desire
Resistless overpowered me, and the bird
Which was the captive of another's toils
Became my prey, and when the deed was done
I heard among the solitary hills
Low breathings coming after me, and sounds
Of undistinguishable motion, steps
Almost as silent as the turf they trod.

Nor less in springtime, when on southern banks
The shining sun had from his knot of leaves
Decoyed the primrose flower, and when the vales
And woods were warm, was I a rover then
In the high places, on the lonesome peaks,
Among the mountains and the winds. Though mean,
And though inglorious, were my views, the end
Was not ignoble. Oh, when I have hung
Above the raven's nest, by knots of grass
Or half-inch fissures in the slippery rock
But ill sustained, and almost (as it seemed)
Suspended by the blast which blew amain
Shouldering the naked crag, oh, at that time,
While on the perilous ridge I hung alone,
With what strange utterance did the loud dry wind
Blow through my ears! The sky seemed not a sky
Of earth – and with what motion moved the clouds!

The mind of man is fashioned and built up
Even as a strain of music. I believe
That there are spirits which, when they would form
A favoured being, from his very dawn
Of infancy do open out the clouds
As at the touch of lightning, seeking him
With gentle visitation – quiet powers,
Retired, and seldom recognized, yet kind,
And to the very meanest not unknown –
With me, though, rarely in my early days
They communed. Others too there are, who use,
Yet haply aiming at the self-same end,
Severer interventions, ministry
More palpable – and of their school was I.

They guided me: one evening led by them
I went alone into a shepherd's boat,
A skiff that to a willow-tree was tied
Within a rocky cave, its usual home.
The moon was up, the lake was shining clear
Among the hoary mountains; from the shore
I pushed, and struck the oars, and struck again
In cadence, and my little boat moved on
Just like a man who walks with stately step
Though bent on speed. It was an act of stealth
And troubled pleasure. Not without the voice
Of mountain echoes did my boat move on,
Leaving behind her still on either side
Small circles glittering idly in the moon
Until they melted all into one track
Of sparkling light.

A rocky steep uprose
Above the cavern of the willow-tree,
And now, as suited one who proudly rowed
With his best skill, I fixed a steady view
Upon the top of that same craggy ridge,
The bound of the horizon – for behind
Was nothing but the stars and the grey sky.

She was an elfin pinnace; twenty times
I dipped my oars into the silent lake,
And as I rose upon the stroke my boat
Went heaving through the water like a swan –
When, from behind that rocky steep (till then
The bound of the horizon) a huge cliff,
As if with voluntary power instinct,
Upreared its head. I struck, and struck again,
And, growing still in stature, the huge cliff
Rose up between me and the stars, and still,
With measured motion, like a living thing
Strode after me. With trembling hands I turned
And through the silent water stole my way
Back to the cavern of the willow-tree.
There in her mooring-place I left my bark,
And through the meadows homeward went with grave
And serious thoughts; and after I had seen
That spectacle, for many days my brain
Worked with a dim and undetermined sense
Of unknown modes of being. In my thoughts
There was a darkness – call it solitude,
Or blank desertion. No familiar shapes
Of hourly objects, images of trees,
Of sea or sky, no colours of green fields,
But huge and mighty forms that do not live
Like living men moved slowly through my mind
By day, and were the trouble of my dreams.

Ah, not in vain ye beings of the hills,
And ye that walk the woods and open heaths
By moon or star-light, thus, from my first dawn
Of childhood, did ye love to intertwine
The passions that build up our human soul
Not with the mean and vulgar works of man,
But with high objects, with eternal things,
With life and nature, purifying thus
The elements of feeling and of thought,
And sanctifying by such discipline
Both pain and fear, until we recognize

A grandeur in the beatings of the heart.
Nor was this fellowship vouchsafed to me
With stinted kindness. In November days
When vapours rolling down the valleys made
A lonely scene more lonesome, among woods
At noon, and mid the calm of summer nights
When by the margin of the trembling lake
Beneath the gloomy hills I homeward went
In solitude, such intercourse was mine.

And in the frosty season, when the sun
Was set, and visible for many a mile
The cottage-windows through the twilight blazed,
I heeded not the summons. Clear and loud
The village clock tolled six; I wheeled about
Proud and exulting, like an untired horse
That cares not for its home. All shod with steel
We hissed along the polished ice in games
Confederate, imitative of the chase
And woodland pleasures – the resounding horn,
The pack loud bellowing, and the hunted hare.
So through the darkness and the cold we flew,
And not a voice was idle. With the din,
Meanwhile, the precipices rang aloud,
The leafless trees and every icy crag
Tinkled like iron; while the distant hills
Into the tumult sent an alien sound
Of melancholy, not unnoticed – while the stars
Eastward were sparkling clear, and in the west
The orange sky of evening died away.

Not seldom from the uproar I retired
Into a silent bay, or sportively
Glanced sideway, leaving the tumultuous throng,
To cut across the shadow of a star
That gleamed upon the ice. And oftentimes,
When we had given our bodies to the wind
And all the shadowy banks on either side
Came sweeping through the darkness, spinning still

The rapid line of motion, then at once
Have I, reclining back upon my heels,
Stopped short – yet still the solitary cliffs
Wheeled by me, even as if the earth had rolled
With visible motion her diurnal round!
Behind me did they stretch in solemn train,
Feebler and feebler, and I stood and watched
Till all was tranquil as a summer sea.

Ye powers of earth, ye genii of the springs,
And ye that have your voices in the clouds,
And ye that are familiars of the lakes
And of the standing pools, I may not think
A vulgar hope was yours when ye employed
Such ministry – when ye through many a year
Thus, by the agency of boyish sports,
On caves and trees, upon the woods and hills,
Impressed upon all forms the characters
Of danger or desire, and thus did make
The surface of the universal earth
With meanings of delight, of hope and fear,
Work like a sea.

Not uselessly employed,
I might pursue this theme through every change
Of exercise and sport to which the year
Did summon us in its delightful round.
We were a noisy crew; the sun in heaven
Beheld not vales more beautiful than ours,
Nor saw a race in happiness and joy
More worthy of the fields where they were sown.
I would record with no reluctant voice
Our home amusements by the warm peat-fire
At evening, when with pencil and with slate
(In square divisions parcelled out, and all
With crosses and with cyphers scribbled o'er)
We schemed and puzzled, head opposed to head,
In strife too humble to be named in verse;
Or round the naked table, snow-white deal,

Cherry or maple, sat in close array,
And to the combat – loo or whist – led on
A thick-ribbed army, not, as in the world,
Discarded and ungratefully thrown by
Even for the very service they had wrought,
But husbanded through many a long campaign.
Oh, with what echoes on the board they fell –
Ironic diamonds, hearts of sable hue,
Queens gleaming through their splendour's last decay,
Knaves wrapt in one assimilating gloom,
And kings indignant at the shame incurred
By royal visages. Meanwhile abroad
The heavy rain was falling, or the frost
Raged bitterly with keen and silent tooth,
And, interrupting the impassioned game,
Oft from the neighbouring lake the splitting ice,
While it sank down towards the water, sent
Among the meadows and the hills its long
And frequent yellings, imitative some
Of wolves that howl along the Bothnic main.

Nor with less willing heart would I rehearse
The woods of autumn, and their hidden bowers
With milk-white clusters hung; the rod and line
(True symbol of the foolishness of hope)
Which with its strong enchantment led me on
By rocks and pools, where never summer star
Impressed its shadow, to forlorn cascades
Among the windings of the mountain-brooks;
The kite in sultry calms from some high hill
Sent up, ascending thence till it was lost
Among the fleecy clouds – in gusty days
Launched from the lower grounds, and suddenly
Dashed headlong and rejected by the storm.
All these, and more, with rival claims demand
Grateful acknowledgement. It were a song
Venial, and such as (if I rightly judge)
I might protract unblamed, but I perceive
That much is overlooked, and we should ill

Attain our object if, from delicate fears
Of breaking in upon the unity
Of this my argument, I should omit
To speak of such effects as cannot here
Be regularly classed, yet tend no less
To the same point, the growth of mental power
And love of nature's works.

Ere I had seen
Eight summers – and 'twas in the very week
When I was first transplanted to thy vale,
Belovèd Hawkshead, when thy paths, thy shores
And brooks, were like a dream of novelty
To my half-infant mind – I chanced to cross
One of those open fields which, shaped like ears,
Make green peninsulas on Esthwaite's lake.
Twilight was coming on, yet through the gloom
I saw distinctly on the opposite shore,
Beneath a tree and close by the lake side,
A heap of garments, as if left by one
Who there was bathing. Half an hour I watched
And no one owned them; meanwhile the calm lake
Grew dark with all the shadows on its breast,
And now and then a leaping fish disturbed
The breathless stillness. The succeeding day
There came a company, and in their boat
Sounded with iron hooks and with long poles.
At length the dead man, mid that beauteous scene
Of trees and hills and water, bolt upright
Rose with his ghastly face. I might advert
To numerous accidents in flood or field,
Quarry or moor, or mid the winter snows,
Distresses and disasters, tragic facts
Of rural history that impressed my mind
With images to which in following years
Far other feelings were attached – with forms
That yet exist with independent life,
And, like their archetypes, know no decay.

There are in our existence spots of time
Which with distinct preeminence retain
A fructifying virtue, whence, depressed
By trivial occupations and the round
Of ordinary intercourse, our minds –
Especially the imaginative power –
Are nourished and invisibly repaired;
Such moments chiefly seem to have their date
In our first childhood.

I remember well
('Tis of an early season that I speak,
The twilight of rememberable life),
While I was yet an urchin, one who scarce
Could hold a bridle, with ambitious hopes
I mounted, and we rode towards the hills.
We were a pair of horsemen: honest James
Was with me, my encourager and guide.
We had not travelled long ere some mischance
Disjoined me from my comrade, and, through fear
Dismounting, down the rough and stony moor
I led my horse, and stumbling on, at length
Came to a bottom where in former times
A man, the murderer of his wife, was hung
In irons. Mouldered was the gibbet-mast;
The bones were gone, the iron and the wood;
Only a long green ridge of turf remained
Whose shape was like a grave. I left the spot,
And reascending the bare slope I saw
A naked pool that lay beneath the hills,
The beacon on the summit, and more near
A girl who bore a pitcher on her head
And seemed with difficult steps to force her way
Against the blowing wind. It was in truth
An ordinary sight, but I should need
Colours and words that are unknown to man
To paint the visionary dreariness
Which, while I looked all round for my lost guide,
Did at that time invest the naked pool,

The beacon on the lonely eminence,
The woman and her garments vexed and tossed
By the strong wind.

Nor less I recollect
(Long after, though my childhood had not ceased)
Another scene which left a kindred power
Implanted in my mind. One Christmas-time,
The day before the holidays began,
Feverish, and tired, and restless, I went forth
Into the fields, impatient for the sight
Of those three horses which should bear us home,
My brothers and myself. There was a crag,
An eminence, which from the meeting-point
Of two highways ascending overlooked
At least a long half-mile of those two roads,
By each of which the expected steeds might come –
The choice uncertain. Thither I repaired
Up to the highest summit. 'Twas a day
Stormy, and rough, and wild, and on the grass
I sat half sheltered by a naked wall.
Upon my right hand was a single sheep,
A whistling hawthorn on my left, and there,
Those two companions at my side, I watched
With eyes intensely straining, as the mist
Gave intermitting prospects of the wood
And plain beneath.

Ere I to school returned
That dreary time, ere I had been ten days
A dweller in my father's house, he died,
And I and my two brothers (orphans then)
Followed his body to the grave. The event,
With all the sorrow which it brought, appeared
A chastisement; and when I called to mind
That day so lately passed, when from the crag
I looked in such anxiety of hope,
With trite reflections of morality,
Yet with the deepest passion, I bowed low

To God who thus corrected my desires.
And afterwards the wind and sleety rain
And all the business of the elements,
The single sheep, and the one blasted tree,
And the bleak music of that old stone wall,
The noise of wood and water, and the mist
Which on the line of each of those two roads
Advanced in such indisputable shapes –
All these were spectacles and sounds to which
I often would repair, and thence would drink
As at a fountain. And I do not doubt
That in this later time, when storm and rain
Beat on my roof at midnight, or by day
When I am in the woods, unknown to me
The workings of my spirit thence are brought.

Nor, sedulous as I have been to trace
How nature by collateral interest,
And by extrinsic passion, peopled first
My mind with forms or beautiful or grand
And made me love them, may I well forget
How other pleasures have been mine, and joys
Of subtler origin – how I have felt
Not seldom, even in that tempestuous time,
Those hallowed and pure motions of the sense
Which seem in their simplicity to own
An intellectual charm, that calm delight
Which (if I err not) surely must belong
To those first-born affinities that fit
Our new existence to existing things,
And in our dawn of being constitute
The bond of union betwixt life and joy.

Yes, I remember when the changeful earth
And twice five seasons on my mind had stamped
The faces of the moving year, even then,
A child, I held unconscious intercourse
With the eternal beauty, drinking in
A pure organic pleasure from the lines

Of curling mist, or from the level plain
Of waters coloured by the steady clouds.
The sands of Westmorland, the creeks and bays
Of Cumbria's rocky limits, they can tell
How when the sea threw off his evening shade
And to the shepherd's hut beneath the crags
Did send sweet notice of the rising moon,
How I have stood, to images like these
A stranger, linking with the spectacle
No body of associated forms,
And bringing with me no peculiar sense
Of quietness or peace – yet I have stood
Even while my eye has moved o'er three long leagues
Of shining water, gathering, as it seemed,
Through the wide surface of that field of light
New pleasure, like a bee among the flowers.

Thus often in those fits of vulgar joy
Which through all seasons on a child's pursuits
Are prompt attendants, mid that giddy bliss
Which like a tempest works along the blood
And is forgotten, even then I felt
Gleams like the flashing of a shield. The earth
And common face of nature spoke to me
Rememberable things – sometimes, 'tis true,
By quaint associations, yet not vain
Nor profitless, if haply they impressed
Collateral objects and appearances,
Albeit lifeless then and doomed to sleep
Until maturer seasons called them forth
To impregnate and to elevate the mind.
And if the vulgar joy by its own weight
Wearied itself out of the memory,
The scenes which were a witness of that joy
Remained in their substantial lineaments
Depicted on the brain, and to the eye
Were visible, a daily sight. And thus
By the impressive agency of fear,
By pleasure and repeated happiness –

So frequently repeated – and by force
Of obscure feelings representative
Of joys that were forgotten, these same scenes,
So beauteous and majestic in themselves,
Though yet the day was distant, did at length
Become habitually dear, and all
Their hues and forms were by invisible links
Allied to the affections.

I began
My story early, feeling (as I fear)
The weakness of a human love for days
Disowned by memory – ere the birth of spring
Planting my snowdrops among winter snows.
Nor will it seem to thee, my friend, so prompt
In sympathy, that I have lengthened out
With fond and feeble tongue a tedious tale.
Meanwhile my hope has been that I might fetch
Reproaches from my former years, whose power
May spur me on, in manhood now mature,
To honourable toil. Yet should it be
That this is but an impotent desire –
That I by such inquiry am not taught
To understand myself, nor thou to know
With better knowledge how the heart was framed
Of him thou lovest – need I dread from thee
Harsh judgements if I am so loth to quit
Those recollected hours that have the charm
Of visionary things, and lovely forms
And sweet sensations, that throw back our life
And make our infancy a visible scene
On which the sun is shining?

Second Part

Thus far, my friend, have we retraced the way
Through which I travelled when I first began
To love the woods and fields. The passion yet
Was in its birth, sustained as might befall
By nourishment that came unsought; for still
From week to week, from month to month, we lived
A round of tumult. Duly were our games
Prolonged in summer till the daylight failed.
No chair remained before the doors, the bench
And threshold steps were empty; fast asleep
The labourer and the old man who had sat
A later lingerer – yet the revelry
Continued and the loud uproar! At last,
When all the ground was dark and the huge clouds
Were edged with twinkling stars, to bed we went
With weary joints and with a beating mind.
Ah, is there one who ever has been young
And needs a monitory voice to tame
The pride of virtue and of intellect?
And is there one, the wisest and the best
Of all mankind, who does not sometimes wish
For things which cannot be – who would not give,
If so he might, to duty and to truth
The eagerness of infantine desire?
A tranquillizing spirit presses now
On my corporeal frame, so wide appears
The vacancy between me and those days,
Which yet have such self-presence in my heart
That sometimes when I think of them I seem
Two consciousnesses – conscious of myself,

And of some other being.

A grey stone
Of native rock, left midway in the square
Of our small market-village, was the home
And centre of these joys; and when, returned
After long absence, thither I repaired,
I found that it was split, and gone to build
A smart assembly-room that perked and flared
With wash and rough-cast, elbowing the ground
Which had been ours. But let the fiddle scream,
And be ye happy! Yet I know, my friends,
That more than one of you will think with me
Of those soft starry nights, and that old dame
From whom the stone was named, who there had sat
And watched her table with its huckster's wares,
Assiduous for the length of sixty years.

We ran a boisterous race: the year spun round
With giddy motion: But the time approached
That brought with it a regular desire
For calmer pleasures – when the beauteous scenes
Of nature were collaterally attached
To every scheme of holiday delight,
And every boyish sport, less grateful else
And languidly pursued. When summer came
It was the pastime of our afternoons
To beat along the plain of Windermere
With rival oars, and the selected bourne
Was now an island musical with birds
That sang for ever, now a sister isle
Beneath the oak's umbrageous covert, sown,
With lilies-of-the-valley like a field,
And now a third small island where remained
An old stone table and one mouldered cave –
A hermit's history. In such a race,
So ended, disappointment could be none,
Uneasiness, or pain, or jealousy;
We rested in the shade, all pleased alike,

Conquered or conqueror. Thus our selfishness
Was mellowed down, and thus the pride of strength
And the vainglory of superior skill
Were interfused with objects which subdued
And tempered them, and gradually produced
A quiet independence of the heart.
And to my friend who knows me I may add
Unapprehensive of reproof that hence
Ensued a diffidence and modesty,
And I was taught to feel (perhaps too much)
The self-sufficing power of solitude.

No delicate viands sapped our bodily strength:
More than we wished we knew the blessing then
Of vigorous hunger, for our daily meals
Were frugal, Sabine fare – and then, exclude
A little weekly stipend, and we lived
Through three divisions of the quartered year
In penniless poverty. But now, to school
Returned from the half-yearly holidays
We came with purses more profusely filled,
Allowance which abundantly sufficed
To gratify the palate with repasts
More costly than the dame of whom I spoke,
That ancient woman, and her board, supplied.
Hence inroads into distant vales, and long
Excursions far away among the hills,
Hence rustic dinners on the cool green ground –
Or in the woods, or by a river-side
Or fountain – festive banquets, that provoked
The languid action of a natural scene
By pleasure of corporeal appetite.

Nor is my aim neglected if I tell
How twice in the long length of those half-years
We from our funds perhaps with bolder hand
Drew largely, anxious for one day at least
To feel the motion of the galloping steed.
And with the good old innkeeper, in truth

I needs must say, that sometimes we have used
Sly subterfuge, for the intended bound
Of the day's journey was too distant far
For any cautious man: a structure famed
Beyond its neighbourhood – the antique walls
Of a large abbey, with its fractured arch,
Belfry, and images, and living trees,
A holy scene! Along the smooth green turf
Our horses grazed. In more than inland peace
Left by the winds that overpass the vale,
In that sequestered ruin trees and towers –
Both silent and both motionless alike –
Hear all day long the murmuring sea that beats
Incessantly upon a craggy shore.

Our steeds remounted and the summons given,
With whip and spur we by the chantry flew
In uncouth race, and left the cross-legged knight
And the stone abbot, and that single wren
Which one day sang so sweetly in the nave
Of the old church that, though from recent showers
The earth was comfortless, and, touched by faint
Internal breezes, from the roofless walls
The shuddering ivy dripped large drops, yet still
So sweetly mid the gloom the invisible bird
Sang to itself that there I could have made
My dwelling-place, and lived for ever there
To hear such music. Through the walls we flew
And down the valley, and, a circuit made
In wantonness of heart, through rough and smooth
We scampered homeward. Oh, ye rocks and streams,
And that still spirit of the evening air,
Even in this joyous time I sometimes felt
Your presence, when with slackened step we breathed
Along the sides of the steep hills, or when,
Lightened by gleams of moonlight from the sea,
We beat with thundering hoofs the level sand.

There was a row of ancient trees, since fallen,

That on the margin of a jutting land
Stood near the Lake of Coniston, and made,
With its long boughs above the water stretched,
A gloom through which a boat might sail along
As in a cloister. An old hall was near,
Grotesque and beautiful, its gavel-end
And huge round chimneys to the top o'ergrown
With fields of ivy. Thither we repaired
('Twas even a custom with us) to the shore,
And to that cool piazza. They who dwelt
In the neglected mansion-house supplied
Fresh butter, tea-kettle and earthenware,
And chafing-dish with smoking coals; and so
Beneath the trees we sat in our small boat,
And in the covert ate our delicate meal
Upon the calm smooth lake. It was a joy
Worthy the heart of one who is full grown
To rest beneath those horizontal boughs
And mark the radiance of the setting sun,
Himself unseen, reposing on the top
Of the high eastern hills. And there I said,
That beauteous sight before me, there I said
(Then first beginning in my thoughts to mark
That sense of dim similitude which links
Our moral feelings with external forms)
That in whatever region I should close
My mortal life I would remember you,
Fair scenes – that dying I would think on you,
My soul would send a longing look to you,
Even as that setting sun, while all the vale
Could nowhere catch one faint memorial gleam,
Yet with the last remains of his last light
Still lingered, and a farewell lustre threw
On the dear mountain-tops where first he rose.
'Twas then my fourteenth summer, and these words
Were uttered in a casual access
Of sentiment, a momentary trance
That far outran the habit of my mind.

Upon the eastern shore of Windermere
Above the crescent of a pleasant bay
There was an inn – no homely-featured shed,
Brother of the surrounding cottages,
But 'twas a splendid place, the door beset
With chaises, grooms, and liveries, and within
Decanters, glasses and the blood-red wine.
In ancient times, or ere the Hall was built
On the large island, had the dwelling been
More worthy of a poet's love, a hut
Proud of its one bright fire and sycamore shade.
But though the rhymes were gone which once inscribed
The threshold, and large golden characters
On the blue-frosted signboard had usurped
The place of the old lion, in contempt
And mockery of the rustic painter's hand,
Yet to this hour the spot to me is dear
With all its foolish pomp. The garden lay
Upon a slope surmounted by the plain
Of a small bowling-green; beneath us stood
A grove, with gleams of water through the trees
And over the tree-tops – nor did we want
Refreshment, strawberries and mellow cream –
And there, through half an afternoon, we played
On the smooth platform, and the shouts we sent
Made all the mountains ring. But ere the fall
Of night, when in our pinnace we returned
Over the dusky lake, and to the beach
Of some small island steered our course, with one,
The minstrel of our troop, and left him there,
And rowed off gently while he blew his flute
Alone upon the rock, oh, then the calm
And dead still water lay upon my mind
Even with a weight of pleasure, and the sky,
Never before so beautiful, sank down
Into my heart and held me like a dream.

Thus day by day my sympathies increased,
And thus the common range of visible things

Grew dear to me. Already I began
To love the sun – a boy I loved the sun
Not as I since have loved him (as a pledge
And surety of my earthly life, a light
Which while I view I feel I am alive),
But for this cause, that I had seen him lay
His beauty on the morning hills, had seen
The western mountain touch his setting orb
In many a thoughtless hour, when from excess
Of happiness my blood appeared to flow
With its own pleasure, and I breathed with joy.
And from like feelings, humble though intense
(To patriotic and domestic love
Analogous) the moon to me was dear,
For I would dream away my purposes
Standing to look upon her while she hung
Midway between the hills, as if she knew
No other region, but belonged to thee –
Yea, appertained by a peculiar right
To thee and thy grey huts, my native vale!

Those incidental charms which first attached
My heart to rural objects day by day
Grew weaker, and I hasten on to tell
How nature – intervenient till this time,
And secondary – now at length was sought
For her own sake. But who shall parcel out
His intellect by geometric rules,
Split like a province into round and square?
Who knows the individual hour in which
His habits were first sown, even as a seed?
Who that shall point as with a wand, and say
'This portion of the river of my mind
Came from yon fountain'? Thou, my friend, art one
More deeply read in thy own thoughts, no slave
Of that false secondary power by which
In weakness we create distinctions, then
Believe our puny boundaries are things
Which we perceive, and not which we have made.

To thee, unblinded by these outward shows,
The unity of all has been revealed,
And thou wilt doubt with me, less aptly skilled
Than many are to class the cabinet
Of their sensations, and in voluble phrase
Run through the history and birth of each
As of a single independent thing.
Hard task to analyse a soul, in which
Not only general habits and desires,
But each most obvious and particular thought –
Not in a mystical and idle sense,
But in the words of reason deeply weighed –
Has no beginning.

Blest the infant babe
(For with my best conjectures I would trace
The progress of our being), blest the babe
Nursed in his mother's arms, the babe who sleeps
Upon his mother's breast, who when his soul
Claims manifest kindred with an earthly soul,
Does gather passion from his mother's eye.
Such feelings pass into his torpid life
Like an awakening breeze, and hence his mind,
Even in the first trial of its powers,
Is prompt and watchful, eager to combine
In one appearance all the elements
And parts of the same object, else detached
And loth to coalesce. Thus day by day
Subjected to the discipline of love,
His organs and recipient faculties
Are quickened, are more vigorous; his mind spreads,
Tenacious of the forms which it receives.
In one beloved presence – nay and more,
In that most apprehensive habitude
And those sensations which have been derived
From this belovèd presence – there exists
A virtue which irradiates and exalts
All objects through all intercourse of sense.
No outcast he, bewildered and depressed! –

Along his infant veins are interfused
The gravitation and the filial bond
Of nature that connect him with the world.
Emphatically such a being lives
An inmate of this *active* universe.
From nature largely he receives, nor so
Is satisfied, but largely gives again;
For feeling has to him imparted strength,
And – powerful in all sentiments of grief,
Of exultation, fear, and joy – his mind,
Even as an agent of the one great mind,
Creates, creator and receiver both,
Working but in alliance with the works
Which it beholds. Such, verily, is the first
Poetic spirit of our human life –
By uniform control of after years
In most abated and suppressed, in some
Through every change of growth or of decay
Preeminent till death.

From early days,
Beginning not long after that first time
In which, a babe, by intercourse of touch
I held mute dialogues with my mother's heart,
I have endeavoured to display the means
Whereby this infant sensibility,
Great birthright of our being, was in me
Augmented and sustained. Yet is a path
More difficult before me, and I fear
That in its broken windings we shall need
The chamois' sinews and the eagle's wing.
For now a trouble came into my mind
From obscure causes. I was left alone
Seeking this visible world, nor knowing why.
The props of my affections were removed,
And yet the building stood as if sustained
By its own spirit. All that I beheld
Was dear to me, and from this cause it came
That now to nature's finer influxes

My mind lay open – to that more exact
And intimate communion which our hearts
Maintain with the minuter properties
Of objects which already are beloved,
And of those only.

Many are the joys
Of youth, but oh, what happiness to live
When every hour brings palpable access
Of knowledge, when all knowledge is delight,
And sorrow is not there! The seasons came,
And every season brought a countless store
Of modes and temporary qualities
Which but for this most watchful power of love
Had been neglected, left a register
Of permanent relations else unknown.
Hence life, and change, and beauty, solitude
More active even than 'best society',
Society made sweet as solitude
By silent inobtrusive sympathies,
And gentle agitations of the mind
From manifold distinctions (difference
Perceived in things where to the common eye
No difference is), and hence, from the same source,
Sublimer joy. For I would walk alone
In storm and tempest, or in starlight nights
Beneath the quiet heavens, and at that time
Would feel whate'er there is of power in sound
To breathe an elevated mood, by form
Or image unprofaned. And I would stand
Beneath some rock, listening to sounds that are
The ghostly language of the ancient earth,
Or make their dim abode in distant winds.
Thence did I drink the visionary power.
I deem not profitless these fleeting moods
Of shadowy exaltation; not for this,
That they are kindred to our purer mind
And intellectual life, but that the soul –
Remembering how she felt, but what she felt

Remembering not – retains an obscure sense
Of possible sublimity, to which
With growing faculties she doth aspire,
With faculties still growing, feeling still
That whatsoever point they gain they still
Have something to pursue.

And not alone
In grandeur and in tumult, but no less
In tranquil scenes, that universal power
And fitness in the latent qualities
And essences of things, by which the mind
Is moved with feelings of delight, to me
Came strengthened with a superadded soul,
A virtue not its own. My morning walks
Were early: oft before the hours of school
I travelled round our little lake, five miles
Of pleasant wandering. Happy time! – more dear
For this, that one was by my side, a friend
Then passionately loved. With heart how full
Will he peruse these lines – this page, perhaps
A blank to other men – for many years
Have since flowed in between us, and (our minds
Both silent to each other) at this time
We live as if those hours had never been.
Nor seldom did I lift our cottage latch
Far earlier, and before the vernal thrush
Was audible, among the hills I sat
Alone upon some jutting eminence
At the first hour of morning, when the vale
Lay quiet in an utter solitude.
How shall I trace the history, where seek
The origin of what I then have felt?
Oft in those moments such a holy calm
Did overspread my soul that I forgot
The agency of sight, and what I saw
Appeared like something in myself, a dream,
A prospect in my mind.

'Twere long to tell
What spring and autumn, what the winter snows,
And what the summer shade, what day and night,
The evening and the morning, what my dreams
And what my waking thoughts, supplied to nurse
That spirit of religious love in which
I walked with nature. But let this at least
Be not forgotten, that I still retained
My first creative sensibility,
That by the regular action of the world
My soul was unsubdued. A plastic power
Abode with me, a forming hand, at times
Rebellious, acting in a devious mood,
A local spirit of its own, at war
With general tendency, but for the most
Subservient strictly to the external things
With which it communed. An auxiliar light
Came from my mind, which on the setting sun
Bestowed new splendour; the melodious birds,
The gentle breezes, fountains that ran on
Murmuring so sweetly in themselves, obeyed
A like dominion, and the midnight storm
Grew darker in the presence of my eye.
Hence my obeisance, my devotion hence,
And *hence* my transport!

Nor should this, perchance,
Pass unrecorded, that I still had loved
The exercise and produce of a toil
Than analytic industry to me
More pleasing, and whose character I deem
Is more poetic, as resembling more
Creative agency – I mean to speak
Of that interminable building reared
By observation of affinities
In objects where no brotherhood exists
To common minds. My seventeenth year was come,
And, whether from this habit rooted now
So deeply in my mind, or, from excess

Of the great social principle of life
Coercing all things into sympathy,
To unorganic natures I transferred
My own enjoyments, or, the power of truth
Coming in revelation, I conversed
With things that really are, I at this time
Saw blessings spread around me like a sea.
Thus did my days pass on, and now at length
From nature and her overflowing soul
I had received so much that all my thoughts
Were steeped in feeling.

I was only then
Contented when with bliss ineffable
I felt the sentiment of being, spread
O'er all that moves, and all that seemeth still;
O'er all that, lost beyond the reach of thought
And human knowledge, to the human eye
Invisible, yet liveth to the heart;
O'er all that leaps, and runs, and shouts, and sings,
Or beats the gladsome air; o'er all that glides
Beneath the wave, yea, in the wave itself
And mighty depth of waters. Wonder not
If such my transports were, for in all things
I saw one life, and felt that it was joy;
One song they sang, and it was audible –
Most audible then when the fleshly ear,
O'ercome by grosser prelude of that strain,
Forgot its functions and slept undisturbed.

If this be error, and another faith
Find easier access to the pious mind,
Yet were I grossly destitute of all
Those human sentiments which make this earth
So dear, if I should fail with grateful voice
To speak of you, ye mountains and ye lakes
And sounding cataracts, ye mists and winds
That dwell among the hills where I was born.
If in my youth I have been pure in heart,

If, mingling with the world, I am content
With my own modest pleasures, and have lived
With God and nature communing, removed
From little enmities and low desires,
The gift is yours – if in these times of fear,
This melancholy waste of hopes o'erthrown,
If, mid indifference and apathy
And wicked exultation, when good men
On every side fall off, we know not how,
To selfishness (disguised in gentle names
Of peace and quiet and domestic love,
Yet mingled, not unwillingly, with sneers
On visionary minds), if in this time
Of dereliction and dismay I yet
Despair not of our nature, but retain
A more than Roman confidence, a faith
That fails not, in all sorrow my support,
The blessing of my life, the gift is yours,
Ye mountains, thine o nature! Thou hast fed
My lofty speculations, and in thee
For this uneasy heart of ours I find
A never-failing principle of joy
And purest passion.

Thou, my friend, wast reared
In the great city, mid far other scenes,
But we by different roads at length have gained
The self-same bourne. And from this cause to thee
I speak unapprehensive of contempt,
The insinuated scoff of coward tongues,
And all that silent language which so oft
In conversation betwixt man and man
Blots from the human countenance all trace
Of beauty and of love. For thou hast sought
The truth in solitude, and thou art one
The most intense of nature's worshippers –
In many things my brother, chiefly here
In this my deep devotion. Fare thee well!
Health and the quiet of a healthful mind

Attend thee, seeking oft the haunts of men –
But yet more often living with thyself,
And for thyself – so haply shall thy days
Be many, and a blessing to mankind.

THE THIRTEEN-BOOK *PRELUDE* OF 1805

Book First

INTRODUCTION – CHILDHOOD AND SCHOOL-TIME

Oh there is blessing in this gentle breeze
That blows from the green fields and from the clouds
And from the sky; it beats against my cheek,
And seems half conscious of the joy it gives.
Oh welcome messenger! Oh welcome friend!
A captive greets thee, coming from a house
Of bondage, from yon city's walls set free,
A prison where he has been long immured.
Now I am free, enfranchised and at large,
May fix my habitation where I will.
What dwelling shall receive me? In what vale
Shall be my harbour? Underneath what grove
Shall I take up my home, and what sweet stream
Shall with its murmurs lull me to my rest?
The earth is all before me! With a heart
Joyous, nor scared at its own liberty,
I look about, and should the guide I choose
Be nothing better than a wandering cloud,
I cannot miss my way. I breathe again!
Trances of thought and mountings of the mind
Come fast upon me. It is shaken off –
As by miraculous gift 'tis shaken off –
That burden of my own unnatural self,
The heavy weight of many a weary day
Not mine, and such as were not made for me.
Long months of peace (if such bold word accord
With any promises of human life),
Long months of ease and undisturbed delight
Are mine in prospect. Whither shall I turn,

THE FOURTEEN-BOOK *PRELUDE* OF 1850

Book First

INTRODUCTION – CHILDHOOD AND SCHOOL-TIME

O there is blessing in this gentle breeze,
A visitant that while it fans my cheek
Doth seem half-conscious of the joy it brings
From the green fields, and from yon azure sky.
Whate'er its mission, the soft breeze can come
To none more grateful than to me; escaped
From the vast city, where I long had pined
A discontented sojourner: now free,
Free as a bird to settle where I will.
What dwelling shall receive me? in what vale
Shall be my harbour? underneath what grove
Shall I take up my home? and what clear stream
Shall with its murmur lull me into rest?
The earth is all before me. With a heart
Joyous, nor scared at its own liberty,
I look about; and should the chosen guide
Be nothing better than a wandering cloud,
I cannot miss my way. I breathe again!
Trances of thought and mountings of the mind
Come fast upon me: it is shaken off,
That burthen of my own unnatural self,
The heavy weight of many a weary day
Not mine, and such as were not made for me.
Long months of peace (if such bold word accord
With any promises of human life),
Long months of ease and undisturbed delight
Are mine in prospect; whither shall I turn,

By road or pathway, or through open field,
Or shall a twig, or any floating thing
Upon the river, point me out my course?

Enough that I am free, for months to come
May dedicate myself to chosen tasks –
May quit the tiresome sea and dwell on shore,
If not a settler on the soil, at least
To drink wild water, and to pluck green herbs,
And gather fruits fresh from their native tree.
Nay more – if I may trust myself, this hour
Hath brought a gift that consecrates my joy,
For I, methought, while the sweet breath of heaven
Was blowing on my body, felt within
A corresponding mild creative breeze,
A vital breeze which travelled gently on
O'er things which it had made, and is become
A tempest, a redundant energy
Vexing its own creation. 'Tis a power
That does not come unrecognized, a storm
Which, breaking up a long-continued frost,
Brings with it vernal promises, the hope
Of active days, of dignity and thought,
Of prowess in an honourable field,
Pure passions, virtue, knowledge, and delight,
The holy life of music and of verse.

Thus far, o friend, did I, not used to make
A present joy the matter of my song,
Pour out that day my soul in measured strains
Even in the very words which I have here
Recorded. To the open fields I told
A prophecy: poetic numbers came
Spontaneously, and clothed in priestly robe
My spirit, thus singled out, as it might seem,
For holy services. Great hopes were mine!
My own voice cheered me, and – far more – the mind's
Internal echo of the imperfect sound.
To both I listened, drawing from them both

By road or pathway, or through trackless field,
Up hill or down, or shall some floating thing
Upon the river point me out my course?

Dear Liberty! Yet what would it avail
But for a gift that consecrates the joy?
For I, methought, while the sweet breath of heaven
Was blowing on my body, felt within
A correspondent breeze, that gently moved
With quickening virtue, but is now become
A tempest, a redundant energy,
Vexing its own creation. Thanks to both,
And their congenial powers, that, while they join
In breaking up a long-continued frost,
Bring with them vernal promises, the hope
Of active days urged on by flying hours, –
Days of sweet leisure, taxed with patient thought
Abstruse, nor wanting punctual service high,
Matins and vespers of harmonious verse!

Thus far, O Friend! did I, not used to make
A present joy the matter of a song,
Pour forth that day my soul in measured strains
That would not be forgotten, and are here
Recorded: to the open fields I told
A prophecy: poetic numbers came
Spontaneously to clothe in priestly robe
A renovated spirit singled out,
Such hope was mine, for holy services.
My own voice cheered me, and, far more, the mind's
Internal echo of the imperfect sound;
To both I listened, drawing from them both

A cheerful confidence in things to come.

Whereat, being not unwilling now to give
A respite to this passion, I paced on
Gently, with careless steps, and came erelong
To a green shady place where down I sat
Beneath a tree, slackening my thoughts by choice
And settling into gentler happiness.
'Twas autumn, and a calm and placid day
With warmth as much as needed from a sun
Two hours declined towards the west, a day
With silver clouds and sunshine on the grass,
And, in the sheltered grove where I was couched,
A perfect stillness. On the ground I lay
Passing through many thoughts, yet mainly such
As to myself pertained. I made a choice
Of one sweet vale whither my steps should turn,
And saw, methought, the very house and fields
Present before my eyes. Nor did I fail
To add meanwhile assurance of some work
Of glory there forthwith to be begun –
Perhaps too there performed. Thus long I lay
Cheered by the genial pillow of the earth
Beneath my head, soothed by a sense of touch
From the warm ground, that balanced me (else lost
Entirely), seeing nought, nought hearing, save
When here and there, about the grove of oaks
Where was my bed, an acorn from the trees
Fell audibly and with a startling sound.

Thus occupied in mind, I lingered here
Contented, nor rose up until the sun
Had almost touched the horizon; bidding then
A farewell to the city left behind,
Even with the chance equipment of that hour
I journeyed towards the vale which I had chosen.
It was a splendid evening, and my soul
Did once again make trial of the strength
Restored to her afresh. Nor did she want

A cheerful confidence in things to come.

Content and not unwilling now to give
A respite to this passion, I paced on
With brisk and eager steps; and came, at length,
To a green shady place, where down I sate
Beneath a tree, slackening my thoughts by choice,
And settling into gentler happiness.
'Twas autumn, and a clear and placid day,
With warmth, as much as needed, from a sun
Two hours declined towards the west; a day
With silver clouds, and sunshine on the grass,
And in the sheltered and the sheltering grove
A perfect stillness. Many were the thoughts
Encouraged and dismissed, till choice was made
Of a known Vale, whither my feet should turn,
Nor rest till they had reached the very door
Of the one cottage which methought I saw.
No picture of mere memory ever looked
So fair; and while upon the fancied scene
I gazed with growing love, a higher power
Than Fancy gave assurance of some work
Of glory there forthwith to be begun,
Perhaps too there performed. Thus long I mused,
Nor e'er lost sight of what I mused upon,
Save when, amid the stately grove of oaks,
Now here, now there, an acorn, from its cup
Dislodged, through sere leaves rustled, or at once
To the bare earth dropped with a startling sound.
From that soft couch I rose not, till the sun
Had almost touched the horizon; casting then
A backward glance upon the curling cloud
Of city smoke, by distance ruralised;
Keen as a Truant or a Fugitive,
But as a Pilgrim resolute, I took,
Even with the chance equipment of that hour,
The road that pointed toward the chosen Vale.
It was a splendid evening, and my soul
Once more made trial of her strength, nor lacked

Eolian visitations, but the harp
Was soon defrauded, and the banded host
Of harmony dispersed in straggling sounds –
And lastly utter silence. 'Be it so!
It is an injury', said I, 'to this day
To think of any thing but present joy.'
So, like a peasant, I pursued my road
Beneath the evening sun, nor had one wish
Again to bend the sabbath of that time
To a servile yoke. What need of many words? –
A pleasant loitering journey, through two days
Continued, brought me to my hermitage.

I spare to speak, my friend, of what ensued:
The admiration and the love, the life
In common things – the endless store of things
Rare, or at least so seeming, every day
Found all about me in one neighbourhood –
The self-congratulation, the complete
Composure, and the happiness entire.
But speedily a longing in me rose
To brace myself to some determined aim,
Reading or thinking, either to lay up
New stores, or rescue from decay the old
By timely interference. I had hopes
Still higher, that with a frame of outward life
I might endue, might fix in a visible home,
Some portion of those phantoms of conceit
That had been floating loose about so long,
And to such beings temperately deal forth
The many feelings that oppressed my heart.
But I have been discouraged: gleams of light
Flash often from the east, then disappear
And mock me with a sky that ripens not
Into a steady morning. If my mind,
Remembering the sweet promise of the past,
Would gladly grapple with some noble theme,
Vain is her wish – where'er she turns she finds
Impediments from day to day renewed.

Æolian visitations; but the harp
Was soon defrauded, and the banded host
Of harmony dispersed in straggling sounds,
And lastly utter silence! 'Be it so;
Why think of any thing but present good?'
So, like a home-bound labourer I pursued
My way beneath the mellowing sun, that shed
Mild influence; nor left in me one wish
Again to bend the Sabbath of that time
To a servile yoke. What need of many words?
A pleasant loitering journey, through three days
Continued, brought me to my hermitage.
I spare to tell of what ensued, the life
In common things – the endless store of things,
Rare, or at least so seeming, every day
Found all about me in one neighbourhood –
The self-congratulation, and, from morn
To night, unbroken cheerfulness serene.
But speedily an earnest longing rose
To brace myself to some determined aim,
Reading or thinking; either to lay up
New stores, or rescue from decay the old
By timely interference: and therewith
Came hopes still higher, that with outward life
I might endue some airy phantasies
That had been floating loose about for years,
And to such beings temperately deal forth
The many feelings that oppressed my heart.
That hope hath been discouraged; welcome light
Dawns from the east, but dawns to disappear
And mock me with a sky that ripens not
Into a steady morning: if my mind,
Remembering the bold promise of the past,
Would gladly grapple with some noble theme,
Vain is her wish; where'er she turns she finds
Impediments from day to day renewed.

And now it would content me to yield up
Those lofty hopes awhile, for present gifts
Of humbler industry. But, o dear friend,
The poet, gentle creature as he is,
Has like the lover his unruly times –
His fits when he is neither sick nor well,
Though no distress be near him but his own
Unmanageable thoughts. The mind itself,
The meditative mind, best pleased perhaps
While she as duteous as the mother dove
Sits brooding, lives not always to that end,
But has less quiet instincts – goadings-on
That drive her as in trouble through the groves.
With me is now such passion, which I blame
No otherwise than as it lasts too long.

When, as becomes a man who would prepare
For such a glorious work, I through myself
Make rigorous inquisition, the report
Is often cheering; for I neither seem
To lack that first great gift, the vital soul,
Nor general truths, which are themselves a sort
Of elements and agents, under-powers,
Subordinate helpers of the living mind.
Nor am I naked in external things –
Forms, images – nor numerous other aids
Of less regard, though won perhaps with toil
And needful to build up a poet's praise.
Time, place, and manners, these I seek, and these
I find in plenteous store, but nowhere such
As may be singled out with steady choice –
No little band of yet remembered names
Whom I, in perfect confidence, might hope
To summon back from lonesome banishment
And make them inmates in the hearts of men
Now living, or to live in times to come.
Sometimes, mistaking vainly (as I fear)
Proud spring-tide swellings for a regular sea,
I settle on some British theme, some old

And now it would content me to yield up
Those lofty hopes awhile, for present gifts
Of humbler industry. But, oh, dear Friend!
The Poet, gentle creature as he is,
Hath, like the Lover, his unruly times;
His fits when he is neither sick nor well,
Though no distress be near him but his own
Unmanageable thoughts: his mind, best pleased
While she as duteous as the mother dove
Sits brooding, lives not always to that end,
But like the innocent bird, hath goadings on
That drive her as in trouble through the groves;
With me is now such passion, to be blamed
No otherwise than as it lasts too long.

When, as becomes a man who would prepare
For such an arduous work, I through myself
Make rigorous inquisition, the report
Is often cheering; for I neither seem
To lack that first great gift, the vital soul,
Nor general Truths, which are themselves a sort
Of Elements and Agents, Under-powers,
Subordinate helpers of the living mind:
Nor am I naked of external things,
Forms, images, nor numerous other aids
Of less regard, though won perhaps with toil
And needful to build up a Poet's praise.
Time, place, and manners do I seek, and these
Are found in plenteous store, but nowhere such
As may be singled out with steady choice;
No little band of yet remembered names
Whom I, in perfect confidence, might hope
To summon back from lonesome banishment,
And make them dwellers in the hearts of men
Now living, or to live in future years.
Sometimes the ambitious Power of choice, mistaking
Proud spring-tide swellings for a regular sea,
Will settle on some British theme, some old

Romantic tale by Milton left unsung;
More often, resting at some gentle place
Within the groves of chivalry, I pipe
Among the shepherds, with reposing knights
Sit by a fountain-side, and hear their tales.

Sometimes, more sternly moved, I would relate
How vanquished Mithridates northward passed,
And, hidden in the cloud of years, became
That Odin, father of a race by whom
Perished the Roman Empire; how the friends
And followers of Sertorius, out of Spain
Flying, found shelter in the Fortunate Isles
And left their usages, their arts and laws,
To disappear by a slow gradual death,
To dwindle and to perish one by one,
Starved in those narrow bounds – but not the soul
Of liberty, which fifteen hundred years
Survived, and, when the European came
With skill and power that could not be withstood,
Did, like a pestilence, maintain its hold
And wasted down by glorious death that race
Of natural heroes. Or I would record
How, in tyrannic times, some unknown man,
Unheard of in the chronicles of kings,
Suffered in silence for the love of truth;
How that one Frenchman, through continued force
Of meditation on the inhuman deeds

Romantic tale by Milton left unsung;
More often turning to some gentle place
Within the groves of Chivalry, I pipe
To shepherd swains, or seated harp in hand,
Amid reposing knights by a river side
Or fountain, listen to the grave reports
Of dire enchantments faced and overcome
By the strong mind, and tales of warlike feats,
Where spear encountered spear, and sword with sword
Fought, as if conscious of the blazonry
That the shield bore, so glorious was the strife;
Whence inspiration for a song that winds
Through ever changing scenes of votive quest
Wrongs to redress, harmonious tribute paid
To patient courage and unblemished truth,
To firm devotion, zeal unquenchable,
And Christian meekness hallowing faithful loves.
Sometimes, more sternly moved, I would relate
How vanquished Mithridates northward passed,
And, hidden in the cloud of years, became
Odin, the Father of a race by whom
Perished the Roman Empire: how the friends
And followers of Sertorius, out of Spain
Flying, found shelter in the Fortunate Isles,
And left their usages, their arts and laws,
To disappear by a slow gradual death,
To dwindle and to perish one by one,
Starved in those narrow bounds: but not the soul
Of Liberty, which fifteen hundred years
Survived, and, when the European came
With skill and power that might not be withstood,
Did, like a pestilence, maintain its hold
And wasted down by glorious death that race
Of natural heroes: or I would record
How, in tyrannic times, some high-souled man,
Unnamed among the chronicles of kings,
Suffered in silence for Truth's sake: or tell,
How that one Frenchman, through continued force
Of meditation on the inhuman deeds

Of the first conquerors of the Indian Isles,
Went single in his ministry across
The ocean (not to comfort the oppressed,
But, like a thirsty wind, to roam about
Withering the oppressor); how Gustavus found
Help at his need in Dalecarlia's mines;
How Wallace fought for Scotland, left the name
Of Wallace to be found like a wild flower
All over his dear country – left the deeds
Of Wallace, like a family of ghosts,
To people the steep rocks and river banks,
Her natural sanctuaries, with a local soul
Of independence and stern liberty.
Sometimes it suits me better to shape out
Some tale from my own heart, more near akin
To my own passions and habitual thoughts,
Some variegated story, in the main
Lofty, with interchange of gentler things.
But deadening admonitions will succeed
And the whole beauteous fabric seems to lack
Foundation, and withal appears throughout
Shadowy and unsubstantial.

                                        Then, last wish –
My last and favourite aspiration – then
I yearn towards some philosophic song
Of truth that cherishes our daily life,
With meditations passionate from deep
Recesses in man's heart, immortal verse
Thoughtfully fitted to the Orphean lyre;
But from this awful burden I full soon
Take refuge and beguile myself with trust
That mellower years will bring a riper mind
And clearer insight. Thus from day to day
I live a mockery of the brotherhood
Of vice and virtue, with no skill to part
Vague longing that is bred by want of power
From paramount impulse not to be withstood;
A timorous capacity from prudence;

Of those who conquered first the Indian Isles,
Went single in his ministry across
The Ocean; not to comfort the oppressed,
But, like a thirsty wind, to roam about
Withering the Oppressor: how Gustavus sought
Help at his need in Dalecarlia's mines:
How Wallace fought for Scotland; left the name
Of Wallace to be found, like a wild flower,
All over his dear Country; left the deeds
Of Wallace, like a family of Ghosts,
To people the steep rocks and river banks,
Her natural sanctuaries, with a local soul
Of independence and stern liberty.
Sometimes it suits me better to invent
A tale from my own heart, more near akin
To my own passions and habitual thoughts;
Some variegated story, in the main
Lofty, but the unsubstantial structure melts
Before the very sun that brightens it,
Mist into air dissolving! Then a wish,
My best and favourite aspiration, mounts
With yearning toward some philosophic song
Of Truth that cherishes our daily life;
With meditations passionate from deep
Recesses in man's heart, immortal verse
Thoughtfully fitted to the Orphean lyre;
But from this awful burthen I full soon
Take refuge and beguile myself with trust
That mellower years will bring a riper mind
And clearer insight. Thus my days are past
In contradiction; with no skill to part
Vague longing, haply bred by want of power,
From paramount impulse not to be withstood,
A timorous capacity from prudence,

From circumspection, infinite delay.
Humility and modest awe themselves
Betray me, serving often for a cloak
To a more subtle selfishness, that now
Does lock my functions up in blank reserve,
Now dupes me by an over-anxious eye
That with a false activity beats off
Simplicity and self-presented truth.
Ah, better far than this to stray about
Voluptuously through fields and rural walks
And ask no record of the hours given up
To vacant musing, unreproved neglect
Of all things, and deliberate holiday.
Far better never to have heard the name
Of zeal and just ambition, than to live
Thus baffled by a mind that every hour
Turns recreant to her task, takes heart again,
Then feels immediately some hollow thought
Hang like an interdict upon her hopes.
This is my lot; for either still I find
Some imperfection in the chosen theme,
Or see of absolute accomplishment
Much wanting – so much wanting in myself
That I recoil and droop, and seek repose
In indolence from vain perplexity,
Unprofitably travelling towards the grave
Like a false steward who has much received
And renders nothing back.

                                        Was it for this
That one, the fairest of all rivers, loved
To blend his murmurs with my nurse's song,
And from his alder shades and rocky falls,
And from his fords and shallows, sent a voice
That flowed along my dreams? For this, didst thou,
O Derwent, travelling over the green plains
Near my 'sweet birthplace', didst thou, beauteous stream,
Make ceaseless music through the night and day
Which with its steady cadence tempering

moral responsibility to do something w/ his gifts

INDOLENCE?

From circumspection, infinite delay.
Humility and modest awe themselves
Betray me, serving often for a cloak
To a more subtle selfishness; that now
Locks every function up in blank reserve,
Now dupes me, trusting to an anxious eye
That with intrusive restlessness beats off
Simplicity and self-presented truth.
Ah! better far than this, to stray about
Voluptuously through fields and rural walks,
And ask no record of the hours, resigned
To vacant musing, unreproved neglect
Of all things, and deliberate holiday.
Far better never to have heard the name
Of zeal and just ambition, than to live
Baffled and plagued by a mind that every hour
Turns recreant to her task; takes heart again,
Then feels immediately some hollow thought
Hang like an interdict upon her hopes.
This is my lot; for either still I find
Some imperfection in the chosen theme,
Or see of absolute accomplishment
Much wanting, so much wanting, in myself,
That I recoil and droop, and seek repose
In listlessness from vain perplexity,
Unprofitably travelling toward the grave,
Like a false steward who hath much received
And renders nothing back.

Was it for this
That one, the fairest of all rivers, loved
To blend his murmurs with my nurse's song,
And, from his alder shades and rocky falls,
And from his fords and shallows, sent a voice
That flowed along my dreams? For this, didst thou,
O Derwent! winding among grassy holms
Where I was looking on, a babe in arms,
Make ceaseless music that composed my thoughts
To more than infant softness, giving me

Our human waywardness, composed my thoughts
To more than infant softness, giving me
Among the fretful dwellings of mankind
A knowledge, a dim earnest, of the calm
Which nature breathes among the hills and groves?
When, having left his mountains, to the towers
Of Cockermouth that beauteous river came,
Behind my father's house he passed, close by,
Along the margin of our terrace-walk.
He was a playmate whom we dearly loved –
Oh, many a time have I, a five years' child,
A naked boy, in one delightful rill,
A little mill-race severed from his stream,
Made one long bathing of a summer's day,
Basked in the sun, and plunged and basked again
Alternate, all a summer's day, or coursed
Over the sandy fields, leaping through groves
Of yellow groundsel; or, when crag and hill,
The woods, and distant Skiddaw's lofty height,
Were bronzed with a deep radiance, stood alone
Beneath the sky as if I had been born
On Indian plains and from my mother's hut
Had run abroad in wantonness to sport,
A naked savage in the thunder-shower.

Fair seed-time had my soul, and I grew up
Fostered alike by beauty and by fear,
Much favoured in my birthplace, and no less
In that belovèd vale to which erelong
I was transplanted. Well I call to mind
('Twas at an early age, ere I had seen
Nine summers) when upon the mountain-slope
The frost, and breath of frosty wind, had snapped
The last autumnal crocus, 'twas my joy
To wander half the night among the cliffs
And the smooth hollows where the woodcocks ran
Along the open turf. In thought and wish
That time, my shoulder all with springes hung,
I was a fell destroyer. On the heights

Amid the fretful dwellings of mankind
A foretaste, a dim earnest, of the calm
That Nature breathes among the hills and groves.
When he had left the mountains and received
On his smooth breast the shadow of those towers
That yet survive, a shattered monument
Of feudal sway, the bright blue river passed
Along the margin of our terrace walk;
A tempting playmate whom we dearly loved.
Oh, many a time have I, a five years' child,
In a small mill-race severed from his stream,
Made one long bathing of a summer's day;
Basked in the sun, and plunged and basked again
Alternate, all a summer's day, or scoured
The sandy fields, leaping through flowery groves
Of yellow ragwort; or when rock and hill,
The woods, and distant Skiddaw's lofty height,
Were bronzed with deepest radiance, stood alone
Beneath the sky, as if I had been born
On Indian plains, and from my mother's hut
Had run abroad in wantonness, to sport
A naked savage, in the thunder shower.

Fair seed-time had my soul, and I grew up
Fostered alike by beauty and by fear:
Much favoured in my birth-place, and no less
In that beloved Vale to which erelong
We were transplanted – there were we let loose
For sports of wider range. Ere I had told
Ten birth-days, when among the mountain slopes
Frost, and the breath of frosty wind, had snapped
The last autumnal crocus, 'twas my joy
With store of springes o'er my shoulder hung
To range the open heights where woodcocks run
Along the smooth green turf. Through half the night,
Scudding away from snare to snare, I plied
That anxious visitation ; – moon and stars

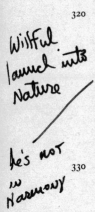

Scudding away from snare to snare, I plied
My anxious visitation, hurrying on,
Still hurrying, hurrying onward. Moon and stars
Were shining o'er my head; I was alone,
And seemed to be a trouble to the peace
That was among them. Sometimes it befell
In these night wanderings that a strong desire
O'erpowered my better reason, and the bird
Which was the captive of another's toils
Became my prey; and when the deed was done
I heard among the solitary hills
Low breathings coming after me, and sounds
Of undistinguishable motion, steps
Almost as silent as the turf they trod.

Nor less in springtime, when on southern banks
The shining sun had from his knot of leaves
Decoyed the primrose flower, and when the vales
And woods were warm, was I a plunderer then
In the high places, on the lonesome peaks
Where'er among the mountains and the winds
The mother-bird had built her lodge. Though mean
My object and inglorious, yet the end
Was not ignoble. Oh, when I have hung
Above the raven's nest, by knots of grass
And half-inch fissures in the slippery rock
But ill sustained, and almost (as it seemed)
Suspended by the blast which blew amain
Shouldering the naked crag, oh, at that time
While on the perilous ridge I hung alone,
With what strange utterance did the loud dry wind
Blow through my ears! The sky seemed not a sky
Of earth – and with what motion moved the clouds!

The mind of man is framed even like the breath
And harmony of music; there is a dark
Invisible workmanship that reconciles
Discordant elements, and makes them move
In one society. Ah me, that all

Were shining o'er my head. I was alone,
And seemed to be a trouble to the peace
That dwelt among them. Sometimes it befel
In these night wanderings, that a strong desire
O'erpowered my better reason, and the bird
Which was the captive of another's toil
Became my prey; and when the deed was done
I heard among the solitary hills
Low breathings coming after me, and sounds
Of undistinguishable motion, steps
Almost as silent as the turf they trod.

Nor less when spring had warmed the cultured Vale,
Moved we as plunderers where the mother-bird
Had in high places built her lodge; though mean
Our object and inglorious, yet the end
Was not ignoble. Oh! when I have hung
Above the raven's nest, by knots of grass
And half-inch fissures in the slippery rock
But ill sustained, and almost (so it seemed)
Suspended by the blast that blew amain,
Shouldering the naked crag, oh, at that time
While on the perilous ridge I hung alone,
With what strange utterance did the loud dry wind
Blow through my ear! the sky seemed not a sky
Of earth – and with what motion moved the clouds!

Dust as we are, the immortal spirit grows
Like harmony in music; there is a dark
Inscrutable workmanship that reconciles
Discordant elements, makes them cling together
In one society. How strange that all

The terrors, all the early miseries,
Regrets, vexations, lassitudes, that all
The thoughts and feelings which have been infused
Into my mind, should ever have made up
The calm existence that is mine when I
Am worthy of myself. Praise to the end –
Thanks likewise for the means! But I believe
That nature, oftentimes, when she would frame
A favoured being, from his earliest dawn
Of infancy doth open out the clouds
As at the touch of lightning, seeking him
With gentlest visitation; not the less,
Though haply aiming at the self-same end,
Does it delight her sometimes to employ
Severer interventions, ministry
More palpable – and so she dealt with me.

One evening (surely I was led by her)
I went alone into a shepherd's boat,
A skiff that to a willow-tree was tied
Within a rocky cave, its usual home.
'Twas by the shores of Patterdale, a vale
Wherein I was a stranger, thither come
A schoolboy-traveller at the holidays.
Forth rambled from the village inn alone
No sooner had I sight of this small skiff,
Discovered thus by unexpected chance,
Than I unloosed her tether and embarked.
The moon was up, the lake was shining clear
Among the hoary mountains; from the shore
I pushed, and struck the oars, and struck again
In cadence, and my little boat moved on
Even like a man who walks with stately step
Though bent on speed. It was an act of stealth
And troubled pleasure, nor without the voice
Of mountain-echoes did my boat move on,
Leaving behind her still on either side
Small circles glittering idly in the moon
Until they melted all into one track

The terrors, pains, and early miseries,
Regrets, vexations, lassitudes interfused
Within my mind, should e'er have borne a part,
And that a needful part, in making up
The calm existence that is mine when I
Am worthy of myself! Praise to the end!
Thanks to the means which Nature deigned to employ;
Whether her fearless visitings, or those
That came with soft alarm, like hurtless light
Opening the peaceful clouds; or she may use
Severer interventions, ministry
More palpable, as best might suit her aim.

One summer evening (led by her) I found
A little boat tied to a willow tree
Within a rocky cave, its usual home.
Straight I unloosed her chain, and stepping in
Pushed from the shore. It was an act of stealth
And troubled pleasure, nor without the voice
Of mountain-echoes did my boat move on;
Leaving behind her still, on either side,
Small circles glittering idly in the moon,
Until they melted all into one track

Of sparkling light.

A rocky steep uprose
Above the cavern of the willow-tree,
And now, as suited one who proudly rowed
With his best skill, I fixed a steady view
Upon the top of that same craggy ridge,
The bound of the horizon – for behind
Was nothing but the stars and the grey sky.
She was an elfin pinnace; lustily
I dipped my oars into the silent lake,
And as I rose upon the stroke my boat
Went heaving through the water like a swan –
When, from behind that craggy steep (till then
The bound of the horizon) a huge cliff,
As if with voluntary power instinct,
Upreared its head. I struck and struck again,
And, growing still in stature, the huge cliff
Rose up between me and the stars, and still,
With measured motion, like a living thing
Strode after me. With trembling hands I turned
And through the silent water stole my way
Back to the cavern of the willow-tree.
There in her mooring-place I left my bark,
And through the meadows homeward went with grave
And serious thoughts; and after I had seen
That spectacle, for many days my brain
Worked with a dim and undetermined sense
Of unknown modes of being. In my thoughts
There was a darkness – call it solitude
Or blank desertion. No familiar shapes
Of hourly objects, images of trees,
Of sea or sky, no colours of green fields,
But huge and mighty forms that do not live
Like living men moved slowly through my mind
By day, and were the trouble of my dreams.

Wisdom and spirit of the universe –
Thou soul that art the eternity of thought,

Of sparkling light. But now, like one who rows,
Proud of his skill, to reach a chosen point
With an unswerving line, I fixed my view
Upon the summit of a craggy ridge,
The horizon's utmost boundary; far above
Was nothing but the stars and the grey sky.
She was an elfin pinnace; lustily
I dipped my oars into the silent lake,
And, as I rose upon the stroke, my boat
Went heaving through the water like a swan;
When, from behind that craggy steep till then
The horizon's bound, a huge peak, black and huge,
As if with voluntary power instinct
Upreared its head. I struck and struck again,
And growing still in stature the grim shape
Towered up between me and the stars, and still,
For so it seemed, with purpose of its own
And measured motion like a living thing,
Strode after me. With trembling oars I turned,
And through the silent water stole my way
Back to the covert of the willow tree;
There in her mooring-place I left my bark, –
And through the meadows homeward went, in grave
And serious mood; but after I had seen
That spectacle, for many days, my brain
Worked with a dim and undetermined sense
Of unknown modes of being; o'er my thoughts
There hung a darkness, call it solitude
Or blank desertion. No familiar shapes
Remained, no pleasant images of trees,
Of sea or sky, no colours of green fields;
But huge and mighty forms, that do not live
Like living men, moved slowly through the mind
By day, and were a trouble to my dreams.

Wisdom and Spirit of the universe!
Thou Soul that art the eternity of thought,

That givest to forms and images a breath
And everlasting motion – not in vain
By day or star-light thus from my first dawn
Of childhood didst thou intertwine for me
The passions that build up our human soul,
Not with the mean and vulgar works of man,
But with high objects, with enduring things,
With life and nature, purifying thus
The elements of feeling and of thought,
And sanctifying by such discipline
Both pain and fear, until we recognize
A grandeur in the beatings of the heart.
Nor was this fellowship vouchsafed to me
With stinted kindness. In November days
When vapours rolling down the valleys made
A lonely scene more lonesome, among woods
At noon, and mid the calm of summer nights
When by the margin of the trembling lake
Beneath the gloomy hills I homeward went
In solitude, such intercourse was mine –
'Twas mine among the fields both day and night,
And by the waters all the summer long.

And in the frosty season, when the sun
Was set, and visible for many a mile
The cottage-windows through the twilight blazed,
I heeded not the summons. Happy time
It was indeed for all of us – to me
It was a time of rapture! Clear and loud
The village clock tolled six; I wheeled about
Proud and exulting like an untired horse
That cares not for its home. All shod with steel
We hissed along the polished ice in games
Confederate, imitative of the chase
And woodland pleasures – the resounding horn,
The pack loud bellowing, and the hunted hare.
So through the darkness and the cold we flew,
And not a voice was idle. With the din,
Meanwhile, the precipices rang aloud,

That givest to forms and images a breath
And everlasting motion, not in vain
By day or star-light thus from my first dawn
Of childhood didst thou intertwine for me
The passions that build up our human soul;
Not with the mean and vulgar works of man,
But with high objects, with enduring things –
With life and nature, purifying thus
The elements of feeling and of thought,
And sanctifying, by such discipline,
Both pain and fear, until we recognise
A grandeur in the beatings of the heart.
Nor was this fellowship vouchsafed to me
With stinted kindness. In November days,
When vapours rolling down the valley made
A lonely scene more lonesome, among woods,
At noon and 'mid the calm of summer nights,
When, by the margin of the trembling lake,
Beneath the gloomy hills homeward I went
In solitude, such intercourse was mine;
Mine was it in the fields both day and night,
And by the waters, all the summer long.

And in the frosty season, when the sun
Was set, and visible for many a mile
The cottage windows blazed through twilight gloom,
I heeded not their summons: happy time
It was indeed for all of us – for me
It was a time of rapture! Clear and loud
The village clock tolled six, – I wheeled about,
Proud and exulting like an untired horse
That cares not for his home. All shod with steel,
We hissed along the polished ice in games
Confederate, imitative of the chase
And woodland pleasures, – the resounding horn,
The pack loud chiming, and the hunted hare.
So through the darkness and the cold we flew,
And not a voice was idle; with the din
Smitten, the precipices rang aloud;

The leafless trees and every icy crag
Tinkled like iron; while the distant hills
Into the tumult sent an alien sound
Of melancholy, not unnoticed – while the stars
Eastward were sparkling clear, and in the west
The orange sky of evening died away.

Not seldom from the uproar I retired
Into a silent bay, or sportively
Glanced sideway, leaving the tumultuous throng,
To cut across the image of a star
That gleamed upon the ice. And oftentimes,
When we had given our bodies to the wind
And all the shadowy banks on either side
Came sweeping through the darkness, spinning still
The rapid line of motion, then at once
Have I, reclining back upon my heels,
Stopped short – yet still the solitary cliffs
Wheeled by me, even as if the earth had rolled
With visible motion her diurnal round!
Behind me did they stretch in solemn train,
Feebler and feebler, and I stood and watched
Till all was tranquil as a dreamless sleep.

Ye presences of nature, in the sky
Or on the earth, ye visions of the hills
And souls of lonely places, can I think
A vulgar hope was yours when ye employed
Such ministry – when ye through many a year
Haunting me thus among my boyish sports,
On caves and trees, upon the woods and hills,
Impressed upon all forms the characters
Of danger or desire, and thus did make
The surface of the universal earth
With triumph and delight, and hope and fear,
Work like a sea?

Not uselessly employed,
I might pursue this theme through every change

The leafless trees and every icy crag
Tinkled like iron; while far distant hills
Into the tumult sent an alien sound
Of melancholy not unnoticed, while the stars
Eastward were sparkling clear, and in the west
The orange sky of evening died away.
Not seldom from the uproar I retired
Into a silent bay, or sportively
Glanced sideway, leaving the tumultuous throng,
To cut across the reflex of a star
That fled, and, flying still before me, gleamed
Upon the glassy plain; and oftentimes,
When we had given our bodies to the wind,
And all the shadowy banks on either side
Came sweeping through the darkness, spinning still
The rapid line of motion, then at once
Have I, reclining back upon my heels,
Stopped short; yet still the solitary cliffs
Wheeled by me – even as if the earth had rolled
With visible motion her diurnal round!
Behind me did they stretch in solemn train,
Feebler and feebler, and I stood and watched
Till all was tranquil as a dreamless sleep.

Ye Presences of Nature in the sky
And on the earth! Ye Visions of the hills!
And Souls of lonely places! can I think
A vulgar hope was yours when ye employed
Such ministry, when ye through many a year
Haunting me thus among my boyish sports,
On caves and trees, upon the woods and hills,
Impressed upon all forms the characters
Of danger or desire; and thus did make
The surface of the universal earth
With triumph and delight, with hope and fear,
Work like a sea?

Not uselessly employed,
Might I pursue this theme through every change

Of exercise and play to which the year
Did summon us in its delightful round.
We were a noisy crew; the sun in heaven
Beheld not vales more beautiful than ours,
Nor saw a race in happiness and joy
More worthy of the fields where they were sown.
I would record with no reluctant voice
The woods of autumn, and their hazel-bowers
With milk-white clusters hung, the rod and line
(True symbol of the foolishness of hope)
Which with its strong enchantment led us on
By rocks and pools shut out from every star
All the green summer, to forlorn cascades
Among the windings of the mountain brooks.
Unfading recollections! – at this hour
The heart is almost mine with which I felt
From some hill-top on sunny afternoons
The kite high up among the fleecy clouds
Pull at its rein like an impatient courser,
Or, from the meadows sent on gusty days,
Beheld her breast the wind, then suddenly
Dashed headlong and rejected by the storm.

Ye lowly cottages in which we dwelt,
A ministration of your own was yours,
A sanctity, a safeguard, and a love!
Can I forget you, being as ye were
So beautiful among the pleasant fields
In which ye stood? Or can I here forget
The plain and seemly countenance with which
Ye dealt out your plain comforts? Yet had ye
Delights and exultations of your own:
Eager and never weary we pursued
Our home amusements by the warm peat-fire
At evening, when with pencil and with slate
(In square divisions parcelled out, and all
With crosses and with cyphers scribbled o'er)
We schemed and puzzled, head opposed to head,
In strife too humble to be named in verse;

Of exercise and play, to which the year
Did summon us in his delightful round.

We were a noisy crew; the sun in heaven
Beheld not vales more beautiful than ours;
Nor saw a band in happiness and joy
Richer, or worthier of the ground they trod.
I could record with no reluctant voice
The woods of autumn, and their hazel bowers
With milk-white clusters hung; the rod and line,
True symbol of hope's foolishness, whose strong
And unreproved enchantment led us on
By rocks and pools shut out from every star,
All the green summer, to forlorn cascades
Among the windings hid of mountain brooks.
– Unfading recollections! at this hour
The heart is almost mine with which I felt,
From some hill-top on sunny afternoons,
The paper kite high among fleecy clouds
Pull at her rein like an impetuous courser;
Or, from the meadows sent on gusty days,
Beheld her breast the wind, then suddenly
Dashed headlong, and rejected by the storm.

Ye lowly cottages wherein we dwelt,
A ministration of your own was yours;
Can I forget you, being as you were
So beautiful among the pleasant fields
In which ye stood? or can I here forget
The plain and seemly countenance with which
Ye dealt out your plain comforts? Yet had ye
Delights and exultations of your own.
Eager and never weary we pursued
Our home-amusements by the warm peat-fire
At evening, when with pencil, and smooth slate
In square divisions parcelled out and all
With crosses and with cyphers scribbled o'er,
We schemed and puzzled, head opposed to head
In strife too humble to be named in verse:

Or round the naked table, snow-white deal,
Cherry or maple, sat in close array,
And to the combat – loo or whist – led on
A thick-ribbed army, not, as in the world,
Neglected and ungratefully thrown by
Even for the very service they had wrought,
But husbanded through many a long campaign.
Uncouth assemblage was it, where no few
Had changed their functions – some, plebeian cards
Which fate, beyond the promise of their birth,
Had glorified, and called to represent
The persons of departed potentates.
Oh, with what echoes on the board they fell!
Ironic diamonds – clubs, hearts, diamonds, spades,
A congregation piteously akin!
Cheap matter did they give to boyish wit,
Those sooty knaves, precipitated down
With scoffs and taunts like Vulcan out of heaven;
The paramount ace, a moon in her eclipse;
Queens gleaming through their splendour's last decay,
And monarchs surly at the wrongs sustained
By royal visages. Meanwhile abroad
The heavy rain was falling, or the frost
Raged bitterly with keen and silent tooth,
And, interrupting the impassioned game,
From Esthwaite's neighbouring lake the splitting ice,
While it sank down towards the water, sent
Among the meadows and the hills its long
And dismal yellings, like the noise of wolves
When they are howling round the Bothnic Main.

Nor, sedulous as I have been to trace
How nature by extrinsic passion first
Peopled my mind with beauteous forms or grand
And made me love them, may I well forget
How other pleasures have been mine, and joys
Of subtler origin – how I have felt,
Not seldom even in that tempestuous time,
Those hallowed and pure motions of the sense

Or round the naked table, snow-white deal,
Cherry or maple, sate in close array,
And to the combat, Loo or Whist, led on
A thick-ribbed army; not, as in the world,
Neglected and ungratefully thrown by
Even for the very service they had wrought,
But husbanded through many a long campaign.
Uncouth assemblage was it, where no few
Had changed their functions; some, plebeian cards
Which Fate, beyond the promise of their birth,
Had dignified, and called to represent
The persons of departed potentates.
Oh, with what echoes on the board they fell!
Ironic diamonds, – clubs, hearts, diamonds, spades,
A congregation piteously akin!
Cheap matter offered they to boyish wit,
Those sooty knaves, precipitated down
With scoffs and taunts, like Vulcan out of heaven:
The paramount ace, a moon in her eclipse,
Queens gleaming through their splendour's last decay,
And monarchs surly at the wrongs sustained
By royal visages. Meanwhile abroad
Incessant rain was falling, or the frost
Raged bitterly, with keen and silent tooth;
And, interrupting oft that eager game,
From under Esthwaite's splitting fields of ice
The pent-up air, struggling to free itself,
Gave out to meadow grounds and hills a loud
Protracted yelling, like the noise of wolves
Howling in troops along the Bothnic Main.

Nor, sedulous as I have been to trace
How Nature by extrinsic passion first
Peopled the mind with forms sublime or fair,
And made me love them, may I here omit
How other pleasures have been mine, and joys
Of subtler origin; how I have felt,
Not seldom even in that tempestuous time,
Those hallowed and pure motions of the sense

Which seem in their simplicity to own
An intellectual charm – that calm delight
Which (if I err not) surely must belong
To those first-born affinities that fit
Our new existence to existing things,
And in our dawn of being constitute
The bond of union betwixt life and joy.

Yes, I remember when the changeful earth
And twice five seasons on my mind had stamped
The faces of the moving year – even then,
A child, I held unconscious intercourse
With the eternal beauty, drinking in
A pure organic pleasure from the lines
Of curling mist, or from the level plain
Of waters coloured by the steady clouds.

The sands of Westmorland, the creeks and bays
Of Cumbria's rocky limits, they can tell
How when the sea threw off his evening shade
And to the shepherd's hut beneath the crags
Did send sweet notice of the rising moon,
How I have stood, to fancies such as these
(Engrafted in the tenderness of thought)
A stranger, linking with the spectacle
No conscious memory of a kindred sight,
And bringing with me no peculiar sense
Of quietness or peace – yet I have stood
Even while mine eye has moved o'er three long leagues
Of shining water, gathering as it seemed
Through every hair-breadth of that field of light
New pleasure like a bee among the flowers.

Thus often in those fits of vulgar joy
Which through all seasons on a child's pursuits
Are prompt attendants, mid that giddy bliss
Which like a tempest works along the blood
And is forgotten, even then I felt
Gleams like the flashing of a shield. The earth

Which seem, in their simplicity, to own
An intellectual charm; that calm delight
Which, if I err not, surely must belong
To those first-born affinities that fit
Our new existence to existing things,
And, in our dawn of being, constitute
The bond of union between life and joy.

Yes, I remember when the changeful earth,
And twice five summers on my mind had stamped
The faces of the moving year, even then
I held unconscious intercourse with beauty
Old as creation, drinking in a pure
Organic pleasure from the silver wreaths
Of curling mist, or from the level plain
Of waters coloured by impending clouds.

The sands of Westmoreland, the creeks and bays
Of Cumbria's rocky limits, they can tell
How, when the Sea threw off his evening shade,
And to the shepherd's hut on distant hills
Sent welcome notice of the rising moon,
How I have stood, to fancies such as these
A stranger, linking with the spectacle
No conscious memory of a kindred sight,
And bringing with me no peculiar sense
Of quietness or peace; yet have I stood,
Even while mine eye hath moved o'er many a league
Of shining water, gathering as it seemed
Through every hair-breadth in that field of light
New pleasure like a bee among the flowers.

Thus oft amid those fits of vulgar joy
Which, through all seasons, on a child's pursuits
Are prompt attendants, 'mid that giddy bliss
Which, like a tempest, works along the blood
And is forgotten; even then I felt
Gleams like the flashing of a shield; – the earth

And common face of nature spoke to me
Rememberable things – sometimes, 'tis true,
By chance collisions and quaint accidents
(Like those ill-sorted unions, work supposed
Of evil-minded fairies), yet not vain
Nor profitless if haply they impressed
Collateral objects and appearances,
Albeit lifeless then and doomed to sleep
Until maturer seasons called them forth
To impregnate and to elevate the mind.
And if the vulgar joy by its own weight
Wearied itself out of the memory,
The scenes which were a witness of that joy
Remained in their substantial lineaments
Depicted on the brain, and to the eye
Were visible, a daily sight. And thus,
By the impressive discipline of fear,
By pleasure and repeated happiness –
So frequently repeated – and by force
Of obscure feelings representative
Of joys that were forgotten, these same scenes,
So beauteous and majestic in themselves,
Though yet the day was distant, did at length
Become habitually dear, and all
Their hues and forms were by invisible links
Allied to the affections.

I began
My story early, feeling (as I fear)
The weakness of a human love for days
Disowned by memory – ere the birth of spring
Planting my snowdrops among winter snows.
Nor will it seem to thee, my friend, so prompt
In sympathy, that I have lengthened out
With fond and feeble tongue a tedious tale.
Meanwhile, my hope has been that I might fetch
Invigorating thoughts from former years,
Might fix the wavering balance of my mind,
And haply meet reproaches too whose power

And common face of Nature spake to me
Rememberable things; sometimes, 'tis true,
By chance collisions and quaint accidents
(Like those ill-sorted unions, work supposed
Of evil-minded fairies), yet not vain
Nor profitless, if haply they impressed
Collateral objects and appearances,
Albeit lifeless then, and doomed to sleep
Until maturer seasons called them forth
To impregnate and to elevate the mind.
– And if the vulgar joy by its own weight
Wearied itself out of the memory,
The scenes which were a witness of that joy
Remained in their substantial lineaments
Depicted on the brain, and to the eye
Were visible, a daily sight; and thus
By the impressive discipline of fear,
By pleasure and repeated happiness,
So frequently repeated, and by force
Of obscure feelings representative
Of things forgotten, these same scenes so bright,
So beautiful, so majestic in themselves,
Though yet the day was distant, did become
Habitually dear, and all their forms
And changeful colours by invisible links
Were fastened to the affections.

I began
My story early – not misled, I trust,
By an infirmity of love for days
Disowned by memory – ere the breath of spring
Planting my snowdrops among winter snows:
Nor will it seem to thee, O Friend! so prompt
In sympathy, that I have lengthened out
With fond and feeble tongue a tedious tale.
Meanwhile, my hope has been, that I might fetch
Invigorating thoughts from former years;
Might fix the wavering balance of my mind,
And haply meet reproaches too, whose power

May spur me on, in manhood now mature,
To honourable toil. Yet should these hopes
Be vain, and thus should neither I be taught
To understand myself, nor thou to know
With better knowledge how the heart was framed
Of him thou lovest, need I dread from thee
Harsh judgements if I am so loth to quit
Those recollected hours that have the charm
Of visionary things, and lovely forms
And sweet sensations, that throw back our life
And almost make our infancy itself
A visible scene on which the sun is shining?
   One end hereby at least has been attained –
My mind has been revived – and if this mood
Desert me not, I will forthwith bring down
Through later years the story of my life.
The road lies plain before me; 'tis a theme
Single and of determined bounds, and hence
I choose it rather at this time than work
Of ampler or more varied argument.

May spur me on, in manhood now mature,
To honourable toil. Yet should these hopes
Prove vain, and thus should neither I be taught
To understand myself, nor thou to know
With better knowledge how the heart was framed
Of him thou lovest; need I dread from thee
Harsh judgments, if the song be loth to quit
Those recollected hours that have the charm
Of visionary things, those lovely forms
And sweet sensations that throw back our life,
And almost make remotest infancy
A visible scene, on which the sun is shining?

One end at least hath been attained; my mind
Hath been revived, and if this genial mood
Desert me not, forthwith shall be brought down
Through later years the story of my life.
The road lies plain before me; – 'tis a theme
Single and of determined bounds; and hence
I choose it rather at this time, than work
Of ampler or more varied argument,
Where I might be discomfited and lost:
And certain hopes are with me, that to thee
This labour will be welcome, honoured Friend!

Book Second

SCHOOL-TIME (CONTINUED)

Thus far, o friend, have we, though leaving much
Unvisited, endeavoured to retrace
My life through its first years, and measured back
The way I travelled when I first began
To love the woods and fields. The passion yet
Was in its birth, sustained as might befall
By nourishment that came unsought; for still
From week to week, from month to month, we lived
A round of tumult. Duly were our games
Prolonged in summer till the daylight failed;
No chair remained before the doors, the bench
And threshold steps were empty; fast asleep
The labourer, and the old man who had sat
A later lingerer – yet the revelry
Continued and the loud uproar. At last,
When all the ground was dark, and the huge clouds
Were edged with twinkling stars, to bed we went
With weary joints and with a beating mind.

Ah, is there one who ever has been young
And needs a monitory voice to tame
The pride of virtue and of intellect?
And is there one, the wisest and the best
Of all mankind, who does not sometimes wish
For things which cannot be – who would not give,
If so he might, to duty and to truth
The eagerness of infantine desire?
A tranquillizing spirit presses now
On my corporeal frame, so wide appears
The vacancy between me and those days

Book Second

SCHOOL-TIME (CONTINUED)

Thus far, O Friend! have we, though leaving much
Unvisited, endeavoured to retrace
The simple ways in which my childhood walked;
Those chiefly that first led me to the love
Of rivers, woods, and fields. The passion yet
Was in its birth, sustained as might befal
By nourishment that came unsought; for still
From week to week, from month to month, we lived
A round of tumult. Duly were our games
Prolonged in summer till the day-light failed:
No chair remained before the doors; the bench
And threshold steps were empty; fast asleep
The labourer, and the old man who had sate
A later lingerer; yet the revelry
Continued and the loud uproar: at last,
When all the ground was dark, and twinkling stars
Edged the black clouds, home and to bed we went,
Feverish with weary joints and beating minds.
Ah! is there one who ever has been young,
Nor needs a warning voice to tame the pride
Of intellect and virtue's self-esteem?
One is there, though the wisest and the best
Of all mankind, who covets not at times
Union that cannot be; – who would not give,
If so he might, to duty and to truth
The eagerness of infantine desire?
A tranquillising spirit presses now
On my corporeal frame, so wide appears
The vacancy between me and those days

Which yet have such self-presence in my mind
That sometimes when I think of them I seem
Two consciousnesses – conscious of myself
And of some other being. A grey stone
Of native rock, left midway in the square
Of our small market-village, was the home
And centre of these joys; and when, returned
After long absence, thither I repaired,
I found that it was split, and gone to build
A smart assembly-room that perked and flared
With wash and rough-cast, elbowing the ground
Which had been ours. But let the fiddle scream,
And be ye happy! Yet, my friends, I know
That more than one of you will think with me
Of those soft starry nights, and that old dame
From whom the stone was named, who there had sat
And watched her table with its huckster's wares
Assiduous through the length of sixty years.

We ran a boisterous race: the year spun round
With giddy motion. But the time approached
That brought with it a regular desire
For calmer pleasures – when the beauteous forms
Of nature were collaterally attached
To every scheme of holiday delight,
And every boyish sport, less grateful else
And languidly pursued. When summer came
It was the pastime of our afternoons
To beat along the plain of Windermere
With rival oars, and the selected bourne
Was now an island musical with birds
That sang for ever, now a sister isle
Beneath the oak's umbrageous covert, sown
With lilies-of-the-valley like a field,
And now a third small island where remained
An old stone table and a mouldered cave –
A hermit's history. In such a race,

Which yet have such self-presence in my mind,
That, musing on them, often do I seem
Two consciousnesses, conscious of myself
And of some other Being. A rude mass
Of native rock, left midway in the square
Of our small market village, was the goal
Or centre of these sports; and when, returned
After long absence, thither I repaired,
Gone was the old grey stone, and in its place
A smart Assembly-room usurped the ground
That had been ours. There let the fiddle scream,
And be ye happy! Yet, my Friends! I know
That more than one of you will think with me
Of those soft starry nights, and that old Dame
From whom the stone was named, who there had sate,
And watched her table with its huckster's wares
Assiduous, through the length of sixty years.

We ran a boisterous course; the year span round
With giddy motion. But the time approached
That brought with it a regular desire
For calmer pleasures, when the winning forms
Of Nature were collaterally attached
To every scheme of holiday delight
And every boyish sport, less grateful else
And languidly pursued.

When summer came,
Our pastime was, on bright half-holidays,
To sweep along the plain of Windermere
With rival oars; and the selected bourne
Was now an Island musical with birds
That sang and ceased not; now a Sister Isle
Beneath the oaks' umbrageous covert, sown
With lilies of the valley like a field;
And now a third small Island, where survived
In solitude the ruins of a shrine
Once to Our Lady dedicated, and served
Daily with chaunted rites. In such a race

So ended, disappointment could be none,
Uneasiness, or pain, or jealousy;
We rested in the shade, all pleased alike,
Conquered and conqueror. Thus the pride of strength
And the vainglory of superior skill
Were interfused with objects which subdued
And tempered them, and gradually produced
A quiet independence of the heart.
And to my friend who knows me I may add
Unapprehensive of reproof that hence
Ensued a diffidence and modesty,
And I was taught to feel (perhaps too much)
The self-sufficing power of solitude.

No delicate viands sapped our bodily strength:
More than we wished we knew the blessing then
Of vigorous hunger, for our daily meals
Were frugal, Sabine fare – and then, exclude
A little weekly stipend, and we lived
Through three divisions of the quartered year
In penniless poverty. But now to school
Returned from the half-yearly holidays
We came with purses more profusely filled,
Allowance which abundantly sufficed
To gratify the palate with repasts
More costly than the dame of whom I spoke,
That ancient woman, and her board, supplied.
Hence inroads into distant vales, and long
Excursions far away among the hills,
Hence rustic dinners on the cool green ground –
Or in the woods, or near a river-side,
Or by some shady fountain – while soft airs
Among the leaves were stirring, and the sun
Unfelt shone sweetly round us in our joy.

Nor is my aim neglected if I tell
How twice in the long length of those half-years
We from our funds perhaps with bolder hand
Drew largely, anxious for one day at least

So ended, disappointment could be none,
Uneasiness, or pain, or jealousy:
We rested in the shade, all pleased alike,
Conquered and conqueror. Thus the pride of strength,
And the vain-glory of superior skill,
Were tempered; thus was gradually produced
A quiet independence of the heart;
And to my Friend who knows me I may add,
Fearless of blame, that hence for future days
Ensued a diffidence and modesty,
And I was taught to feel, perhaps too much,
The self-sufficing power of Solitude.

Our daily meals were frugal, Sabine fare!
More than we wished we knew the blessing then
Of vigorous hunger – hence corporeal strength
Unsapped by delicate viands; for, exclude
A little weekly stipend, and we lived
Through three divisions of the quartered year
In penniless poverty. But now to school
From the half-yearly holidays returned,
We came with weightier purses, that sufficed
To furnish treats more costly than the Dame
Of the old grey stone, from her scant board, supplied.
Hence rustic dinners on the cool green ground,
Or in the woods, or by a river side
Or shady fountains, while among the leaves
Soft airs were stirring, and the mid-day sun
Unfelt shone brightly round us in our joy.
Nor is my aim neglected if I tell
How sometimes, in the length of those half-years,
We from our funds drew largely; – proud to curb,

To feel the motion of the galloping steed.
And with the good old innkeeper, in truth,
On such occasion sometimes we employed
Sly subterfuge; for the intended bound
Of the day's journey was too distant far
For any cautious man: a structure famed
Beyond its neighbourhood – the antique walls
Of that large abbey which within the Vale
Of Nightshade, to St Mary's honour built,
Stands yet a mouldering pile with fractured arch,
Belfry, and images, and living trees,
A holy scene! Along the smooth green turf
Our horses grazed. To more than inland peace
Left by the sea wind passing overhead
(Though wind of roughest temper) trees and towers
May in that valley oftentimes be seen
Both silent and both motionless alike,
Such is the shelter that is there, and such
The safeguard for repose and quietness.

Our steeds remounted and the summons given,
With whip and spur we by the chantry flew
In uncouth race, and left the cross-legged knight,
And the stone-abbot, and that single wren
Which one day sang so sweetly in the nave
Of the old church that, though from recent showers
The earth was comfortless, and, touched by faint
Internal breezes – sobbings of the place
And respirations – from the roofless walls
The shuddering ivy dripped large drops, yet still
So sweetly mid the gloom the invisible bird
Sang to itself that there I could have made
My dwelling-place, and lived for ever there
To hear such music. Through the walls we flew
And down the valley, and, a circuit made
In wantonness of heart, through rough and smooth
We scampered homeward. Oh, ye rocks and streams,
And that still spirit of the evening air,
Even in this joyous time I sometimes felt

And eager to spur on, the galloping steed;
And with the courteous inn-keeper, whose stud
Supplied our want, we haply might employ
Sly subterfuge, if the adventure's bound
Were distant: some famed temple where of yore
The Druids worshipped, or the antique walls
Of that large abbey, where within the Vale
Of Nightshade, to St. Mary's honour built,
Stands yet a mouldering pile with fractured arch,
Belfry, and images, and living trees,
A holy scene! Along the smooth green turf
Our horses grazed. To more than inland peace
Left by the west wind sweeping overhead
From a tumultuous ocean, trees and towers
In that sequestered valley may be seen,
Both silent and both motionless alike;
Such the deep shelter that is there, and such
The safeguard for repose and quietness.

Our steeds remounted and the summons given,
With whip and spur we through the chauntry flew
In uncouth race, and left the cross-legged knight,
And the stone-abbot, and that single wren
Which one day sang so sweetly in the nave
Of the old church, that – though from recent showers
The earth was comfortless, and touched by faint
Internal breezes, sobbings of the place
And respirations, from the roofless walls
The shuddering ivy dripped large drops – yet still
So sweetly 'mid the gloom the invisible bird
Sang to herself, that there I could have made
My dwelling-place, and lived for ever there
To hear such music. Through the walls we flew
And down the valley, and, a circuit made
In wantonness of heart, through rough and smooth
We scampered homewards. Oh, ye rocks and streams,
And that still spirit shed from evening air!
Even in this joyous time I sometimes felt

Your presence, when with slackened step we breathed
Along the sides of the steep hills, or when,
Lighted by gleams of moonlight from the sea,
We beat with thundering hoofs the level sand.

Upon the eastern shore of Windermere
Above the crescent of a pleasant bay,
There was an inn – no homely-featured shed,
Brother of the surrounding cottages,
But 'twas a splendid place, the door beset
With chaises, grooms, and liveries, and within
Decanters, glasses, and the blood-red wine.
In ancient times, or ere the Hall was built
On the large island, had this dwelling been
More worthy of a poet's love, a hut
Proud of its one bright fire and sycamore shade.
But though the rhymes were gone which once inscribed
The threshold, and large golden characters
On the blue-frosted signboard had usurped
The place of the old lion, in contempt
And mockery of the rustic painter's hand,
Yet to this hour the spot to me is dear
With all its foolish pomp. The garden lay
Upon a slope surmounted by the plain
Of a small bowling-green; beneath us stood
A grove, with gleams of water through the trees
And over the tree-tops – nor did we want
Refreshment, strawberries and mellow cream –
And there, through half an afternoon, we played
On the smooth platform, and the shouts we sent
Made all the mountains ring. But ere the fall
Of night, when in our pinnace we returned
Over the dusky lake, and to the beach
Of some small island steered our course, with one,
The minstrel of our troop, and left him there,
And rowed off gently while he blew his flute
Alone upon the rock, oh then the calm
And dead still water lay upon my mind

Your presence, when with slackened step we breathed
Along the sides of the steep hills, or when
Lighted by gleams of moonlight from the sea
We beat with thundering hoofs the level sand.

Midway on long Winander's eastern shore,
Within the crescent of a pleasant bay,
A tavern stood; no homely-featured house,
Primeval like its neighbouring cottages,
But 'twas a splendid place, the door beset
With chaises, grooms, and liveries, and within
Decanters, glasses, and the blood-red wine.
In ancient times, and ere the Hall was built
On the large island, had this dwelling been
More worthy of a poet's love, a hut,
Proud of its own bright fire and sycamore shade.
But – though the rhymes were gone that once inscribed
The threshold, and large golden characters,
Spread o'er the spangled sign-board, had dislodged
The old Lion and usurped his place, in slight
And mockery of the rustic painter's hand –
Yet, to this hour, the spot to me is dear
With all its foolish pomp. The garden lay
Upon a slope surmounted by a plain
Of a small bowling-green; beneath us stood
A grove, with gleams of water through the trees
And over the tree-tops; nor did we want
Refreshment, strawberries and mellow cream.
There, while through half an afternoon we played
On the smooth platform, whether skill prevailed
Or happy blunder triumphed, bursts of glee
Made all the mountains ring. But, ere night-fall,
When in our pinnace we returned at leisure
Over the shadowy lake, and to the beach
Of some small island steered our course with one,
The Minstrel of the Troop, and left him there,
And rowed off gently, while he blew his flute
Alone upon the rock – oh, then, the calm
And dead still water lay upon my mind

Even with a weight of pleasure, and the sky,
Never before so beautiful, sank down
Into my heart and held me like a dream.

Thus daily were my sympathies enlarged,
And thus the common range of visible things
Grew dear to me. Already I began
To love the sun – a boy I loved the sun
Not as I since have loved him (as a pledge
And surety of our earthly life, a light
Which while we view we feel we are alive),
But for this cause, that I had seen him lay
His beauty on the morning hills, had seen
The western mountain touch his setting orb
In many a thoughtless hour, when from excess
Of happiness my blood appeared to flow
With its own pleasure, and I breathed with joy.
And from like feelings, humble though intense
(To patriotic and domestic love
Analogous) the moon to me was dear,
For I would dream away my purposes
Standing to look upon her while she hung
Midway between the hills, as if she knew
No other region, but belonged to thee –
Yea, appertained by a peculiar right
To thee and thy grey huts, my darling vale!

Those incidental charms which first attached
My heart to rural objects day by day
Grew weaker, and I hasten on to tell
How nature – intervenient till this time,
And secondary – now at length was sought
For her own sake. But who shall parcel out
His intellect by geometric rules,
Split like a province into round and square?
Who knows the individual hour in which
His habits were first sown, even as a seed?
Who that shall point as with a wand, and say
'This portion of the river of my mind

Even with a weight of pleasure, and the sky,
Never before so beautiful, sank down
Into my heart, and held me like a dream!
Thus were my sympathies enlarged, and thus
Daily the common range of visible things
Grew dear to me: already I began
To love the sun; a boy I loved the sun,
Not as I since have loved him, as a pledge
And surety of our earthly life, a light
Which we behold and feel we are alive;
Nor for his bounty to so many worlds –
But for this cause, that I had seen him lay
His beauty on the morning hills, had seen
The western mountain touch his setting orb,
In many a thoughtless hour, when, from excess
Of happiness, my blood appeared to flow
For its own pleasure, and I breathed with joy.
And, from like feelings, humble though intense,
To patriotic and domestic love
Analogous, the moon to me was dear;
For I could dream away my purposes,
Standing to gaze upon her while she hung
Midway between the hills, as if she knew
No other region, but belonged to thee,
Yea, appertained by a peculiar right
To thee and thy grey huts, thou one dear Vale!

Those incidental charms which first attached
My heart to rural objects, day by day
Grew weaker, and I hasten on to tell
How Nature, intervenient till this time
And secondary, now at length was sought
For her own sake. But who shall parcel out
His intellect by geometric rules,
Split like a province into round and square?
Who knows the individual hour in which
His habits were first sown, even as a seed?
Who that shall point as with a wand and say
'This portion of the river of my mind

Came from yon fountain'? Thou, my friend, art one
More deeply read in thy own thoughts; to thee
Science appears but what in truth she is,
Not as our glory and our absolute boast,
But as a succedaneum and a prop
To our infirmity. Thou art no slave
Of that false secondary power by which
In weakness we create distinctions, then
Deem that our puny boundaries are things
Which we perceive, and not which we have made.
To thee, unblinded by these outward shows,
The unity of all has been revealed,
And thou wilt doubt with me, less aptly skilled
Than many are to class the cabinet
Of their sensations, and in voluble phrase
Run through the history and birth of each
As of a single independent thing.
Hard task to analyse a soul, in which
Not only general habits and desires,
But each most obvious and particular thought –
Not in a mystical and idle sense
But in the words of reason deeply weighed –
Has no beginning.

Blest the infant babe
(For with my best conjectures I would trace
The progress of our being), blest the babe
Nursed in his mother's arms, the babe who sleeps
Upon his mother's breast, who when his soul
Claims manifest kindred with an earthly soul,
Does gather passion from his mother's eye!
Such feelings pass into his torpid life
Like an awakening breeze, and hence his mind,
Even in the first trial of its powers,
Is prompt and watchful, eager to combine
In one appearance all the elements
And parts of the same object, else detached
And loth to coalesce. Thus day by day
Subjected to the discipline of love,

Came from yon fountain?' Thou, my Friend! art one
More deeply read in thy own thoughts; to thee
Science appears but what in truth she is,
Not as our glory and our absolute boast,
But as a succedaneum, and a prop
To our infirmity. No officious slave
Art thou of that false secondary power
By which we multiply distinctions, then
Deem that our puny boundaries are things
That we perceive, and not that we have made.
To thee, unblinded by these formal arts,
The unity of all hath been revealed,
And thou wilt doubt, with me less aptly skilled
Than many are to range the faculties
In scale and order, class the cabinet
Of their sensations, and in voluble phrase
Run through the history and birth of each
As of a single independent thing.
Hard task, vain hope, to analyse the mind,
If each most obvious and particular thought,
Not in a mystical and idle sense,
But in the words of Reason deeply weighed,
Hath no beginning.

Blest the infant Babe,
(For with my best conjecture I would trace
Our Being's earthly progress,) blest the Babe,
Nursed in his Mother's arms, who sinks to sleep
Rocked on his Mother's breast; who with his soul
Drinks in the feelings of his Mother's eye!
For him, in one dear Presence, there exists
A virtue which irradiates and exalts
Objects through widest intercourse of sense.
No outcast he, bewildered and depressed:
Along his infant veins are interfused
The gravitation and the filial bond
Of nature that connect him with the world.
Is there a flower, to which he points with hand
Too weak to gather it, already love

His organs and recipient faculties
Are quickened, are more vigorous; his mind spreads
Tenacious of the forms which it receives.
In one belovèd presence – nay and more,
In that most apprehensive habitude
And those sensations which have been derived
From this beloved presence – there exists
A virtue which irradiates and exalts
All objects through all intercourse of sense.
No outcast he, bewildered and depressed! –
Along his infant veins are interfused
The gravitation and the filial bond
Of nature that connect him with the world.
Emphatically such a being lives
An inmate of this *active* universe.
From nature largely he receives, nor so
Is satisfied, but largely gives again;
For feeling has to him imparted strength,
And – powerful in all sentiments of grief,
Of exultation, fear, and joy – his mind,
Even as an agent of the one great mind,
Creates, creator and receiver both,
Working but in alliance with the works
Which it beholds. Such, verily, is the first
Poetic spirit of our human life –
By uniform control of after years
In most abated and suppressed, in some
Through every change of growth or of decay
Pre-eminent till death.

From early days,
Beginning not long after that first time
In which, a babe, by intercourse of touch
I held mute dialogues with my mother's heart,
I have endeavoured to display the means
Whereby the infant sensibility,
Great birthright of our being, was in me
Augmented and sustained. Yet is a path
More difficult before me, and I fear

Drawn from love's purest earthly fount for him
Hath beautified that flower; already shades
Of pity cast from inward tenderness
Do fall around him upon aught that bears
Unsightly marks of violence or harm.
Emphatically such a Being lives,
Frail creature as he is, helpless as frail,
An inmate of this active universe.
For feeling has to him imparted power
That through the growing faculties of sense
Doth like an agent of the one great Mind
Create, creator and receiver both,
Working but in alliance with the works
Which it beholds. – Such, verily, is the first
Poetic spirit of our human life,
By uniform control of after years,
In most, abated or suppressed; in some,
Through every change of growth and of decay,
Pre-eminent till death.

From early days,
Beginning not long after that first time
In which, a Babe, by intercourse of touch
I held mute dialogues with my Mother's heart,
I have endeavoured to display the means
Whereby this infant sensibility,
Great birthright of our being, was in me
Augmented and sustained. Yet is a path
More difficult before me; and I fear

That in its broken windings we shall need
The chamois' sinews and the eagle's wing.
For now a trouble came into my mind
From unknown causes: I was left alone
Seeking the visible world, nor knowing why.
The props of my affections were removed,
And yet the building stood as if sustained
By its own spirit! All that I beheld
Was dear to me, and from this cause it came
That now to nature's finer influxes
My mind lay open – to that more exact
And intimate communion which our hearts
Maintain with the minuter properties
Of objects which already are beloved,
And of those only.

Many are the joys
Of youth, but oh, what happiness to live
When every hour brings palpable access
Of knowledge, when all knowledge is delight,
And sorrow is not there! The seasons came,
And every season to my notice brought
A store of transitory qualities
Which but for this most watchful power of love
Had been neglected, left a register
Of permanent relations, else unknown.
Hence life, and change, and beauty, solitude
More active even than 'best society',
Society made sweet as solitude
By silent inobtrusive sympathies,
And gentle agitations of the mind
From manifold distinctions (difference
Perceived in things where to the common eye
No difference is), and hence, from the same source,
Sublimer joy. For I would walk alone
In storm and tempest, or in starlight nights
Beneath the quiet heavens, and at that time
Have felt whate'er there is of power in sound
To breathe an elevated mood, by form

That in its broken windings we shall need
The chamois' sinews, and the eagle's wing:
For now a trouble came into my mind
From unknown causes. I was left alone
Seeking the visible world, nor knowing why.
The props of my affections were removed,
And yet the building stood, as if sustained
By its own spirit! All that I beheld
Was dear, and hence to finer influxes
The mind lay open to a more exact
And close communion. Many are our joys
In youth, but oh! what happiness to live
When every hour brings palpable access
Of knowledge, when all knowledge is delight,
And sorrow is not there! The seasons came,
And every season wheresoe'er I moved
Unfolded transitory qualities,
Which, but for this most watchful power of love,
Had been neglected; left a register
Of permanent relations, else unknown.
Hence life, and change, and beauty, solitude
More active even than 'best society' –
Society made sweet as solitude
By silent inobtrusive sympathies,
And gentle agitations of the mind
From manifold distinctions, difference
Perceived in things, where, to the unwatchful eye,
No difference is, and hence, from the same source,
Sublimer joy; for I would walk alone,
Under the quiet stars, and at that time
Have felt whate'er there is of power in sound
To breathe an elevated mood, by form

Or image unprofaned. And I would stand
Beneath some rock, listening to sounds that are
The ghostly language of the ancient earth,
Or make their dim abode in distant winds.
Thence did I drink the visionary power.
I deem not profitless those fleeting moods
Of shadowy exultation; not for this,
That they are kindred to our purer mind
And intellectual life, but that the soul –
Remembering how she felt, but what she felt
Remembering not – retains an obscure sense
Of possible sublimity, to which
With growing faculties she doth aspire,
With faculties still growing, feeling still
That whatsoever point they gain they still
Have something to pursue.

And not alone
In grandeur and in tumult, but no less
In tranquil scenes, that universal power
And fitness in the latent qualities
And essences of things, by which the mind
Is moved by feelings of delight, to me
Came strengthened with a superadded soul,
A virtue not its own. My morning walks
Were early: oft before the hours of school
I travelled round our little lake, five miles
Of pleasant wandering. Happy time! – more dear
For this, that one was by my side, a friend
Then passionately loved. With heart how full
Will he peruse these lines – this page, perhaps
A blank to other men – for many years
Have since flowed in between us, and (our minds
Both silent to each other) at this time
We live as if those hours had never been.
Nor seldom did I lift our cottage latch
Far earlier, and before the vernal thrush
Was audible, among the hills I sat

Or image unprofaned; and I would stand,
If the night blackened with a coming storm,
Beneath some rock, listening to notes that are
The ghostly language of the ancient earth,
Or make their dim abode in distant winds.
Thence did I drink the visionary power;
And deem not profitless those fleeting moods
Of shadowy exultation: not for this,
That they are kindred to our purer mind
And intellectual life; but that the soul,
Remembering how she felt, but what she felt
Remembering not, retains an obscure sense
Of possible sublimity, whereto
With growing faculties she doth aspire,
With faculties still growing, feeling still
That whatsoever point they gain, they yet
Have something to pursue.

And not alone,
'Mid gloom and tumult, but no less 'mid fair
And tranquil scenes, that universal power
And fitness in the latent qualities
And essences of things, by which the mind
Is moved with feelings of delight, to me
Came, strengthened with a superadded soul,
A virtue not its own. My morning walks
Were early; – oft before the hours of school
I travelled round our little lake, five miles
Of pleasant wandering. Happy time! more dear
For this, that one was by my side, a Friend,
Then passionately loved; with heart how full
Would he peruse these lines! For many years
Have since flowed in between us, and, our minds
Both silent to each other, at this time
We live as if those hours had never been.
Nor seldom did I lift our cottage latch
Far earlier, ere one smoke-wreath had risen
From human dwelling, or the vernal thrush
Was audible; and sate among the woods

Alone upon some jutting eminence
At the first hour of morning, when the vale
Lay quiet in an utter solitude.
How shall I trace the history, where seek
The origin of what I then have felt?
Oft in those moments such a holy calm
Did overspread my soul that I forgot
That I had bodily eyes, and what I saw
Appeared like something in myself, a dream,
A prospect in my mind.

'Twere long to tell
What spring and autumn, what the winter snows,
And what the summer shade, what day and night,
The evening and the morning, what my dreams
And what my waking thoughts, supplied to nurse
That spirit of religious love in which
I walked with nature. But let this at least
Be not forgotten, that I still retained
My first creative sensibility,
That by the regular action of the world
My soul was unsubdued. A plastic power
Abode with me, a forming hand, at times
Rebellious, acting in a devious mood,
A local spirit of its own, at war
With general tendency, but for the most
Subservient strictly to the external things
With which it communed. An auxiliar light
Came from my mind, which on the setting sun
Bestowed new splendour; the melodious birds,
The gentle breezes, fountains that ran on
Murmuring so sweetly in themselves, obeyed
A like dominion, and the midnight storm
Grew darker in the presence of my eye.
Hence my obeisance, my devotion hence,
And hence my transport!

Nor should this perchance
Pass unrecorded, that I still had loved

Alone upon some jutting eminence,
At the first gleam of dawn-light, when the Vale,
Yet slumbering, lay in utter solitude.
How shall I seek the origin? where find
Faith in the marvellous things which then I felt?
Oft in these moments such a holy calm
Would overspread my soul, that bodily eyes
Were utterly forgotten, and what I saw
Appeared like something in myself, a dream,
A prospect in the mind.

'Twere long to tell
What spring and autumn, what the winter snows,
And what the summer shade, what day and night,
Evening and morning, sleep and waking, thought
From sources inexhaustible, poured forth
To feed the spirit of religious love
In which I walked with Nature. But let this
Be not forgotten, that I still retained
My first creative sensibility;
That by the regular action of the world
My soul was unsubdued. A plastic power
Abode with me; a forming hand, at times
Rebellious, acting in a devious mood;
A local spirit of his own, at war
With general tendency, but, for the most,
Subservient strictly to external things
With which it communed. An auxiliar light
Came from my mind, which on the setting sun
Bestowed new splendour; the melodious birds,
The fluttering breezes, fountains that run on
Murmuring so sweetly in themselves, obeyed
A like dominion, and the midnight storm
Grew darker in the presence of my eye:
Hence my obeisance, my devotion hence,
And hence my transport.

Nor should this, perchance,
Pass unrecorded, that I still had loved

The exercise and produce of a toil
Than analytic industry to me
More pleasing, and whose character I deem
Is more poetic, as resembling more
Creative agency – I mean to speak
Of that interminable building reared
By observation of affinities
In objects where no brotherhood exists
To common minds. My seventeenth year was come,
And, whether from this habit rooted now
So deeply in my mind, or, from excess
Of the great social principle of life
Coercing all things into sympathy,
To unorganic natures I transferred
My own enjoyments, or, the power of truth
Coming in revelation, I conversed
With things that really are, I at this time
Saw blessings spread around me like a sea.
Thus did my days pass on, and now at length
From nature and her overflowing soul
I had received so much that all my thoughts
Were steeped in feeling.

I was only then
Contented when with bliss ineffable
I felt the sentiment of being, spread
O'er all that moves, and all that seemeth still;
O'er all that, lost beyond the reach of thought
And human knowledge, to the human eye
Invisible, yet liveth to the heart;
O'er all that leaps and runs, and shouts and sings,
Or beats the gladsome air; o'er all that glides
Beneath the wave, yea, in the wave itself
And mighty depth of waters. Wonder not
If such my transports were, for in all things
I saw one life, and felt that it was joy.
One song they sang, and it was audible
Most audible then when the fleshly ear,

The exercise and produce of a toil,
Than analytic industry to me
More pleasing, and whose character I deem
Is more poetic as resembling more
Creative agency. The song would speak
Of that interminable building reared
By observation of affinities
In objects where no brotherhood exists
To passive minds. My seventeenth year was come;
And, whether from this habit rooted now
So deeply in my mind, or from excess
In the great social principle of life
Coercing all things into sympathy,
To unorganic natures were transferred
My own enjoyments; or the power of truth
Coming in revelation, did converse
With things that really are; I, at this time,
Saw blessings spread around me like a sea.
Thus while the days flew by, and years passed on,
From Nature and her overflowing soul,
I had received so much, that all my thoughts
Were steeped in feeling; I was only then
Contented, when with bliss ineffable
I felt the sentiment of Being spread
O'er all that moves and all that seemeth still;
O'er all that, lost beyond the reach of thought
And human knowledge, to the human eye
Invisible, yet liveth to the heart;
O'er all that leaps and runs, and shouts and sings,
Or beats the gladsome air; o'er all that glides
Beneath the wave, yea, in the wave itself,
And mighty depth of waters. Wonder not
If high the transport, great the joy I felt,
Communing in this sort through earth and heaven
With every form of creature, as it looked
Towards the Uncreated with a countenance
Of adoration, with an eye of love.
One song they sang, and it was audible,
Most audible, then, when the fleshly ear,

O'ercome by grosser prelude of that strain,
Forgot its functions and slept undisturbed.

If this be error, and another faith
Find easier access to the pious mind,
Yet were I grossly destitute of all
Those human sentiments which make this earth
So dear, if I should fail with grateful voice
To speak of you, ye mountains and ye lakes
And sounding cataracts, ye mists and winds
That dwell among the hills where I was born.
If in my youth I have been pure in heart,
If, mingling with the world, I am content
With my own modest pleasures, and have lived
With God and nature communing, removed
From little enmities and low desires,
The gift is yours – if in these times of fear,
This melancholy waste of hopes o'erthrown,
If, mid indifference and apathy
And wicked exultation, when good men
On every side fall off, we know not how,
To selfishness (disguised in gentle names
Of peace and quiet and domestic love,
Yet mingled not unwillingly with sneers
On visionary minds), if in this time
Of dereliction and dismay I yet
Despair not of our nature, but retain
A more than Roman confidence, a faith
That fails not, in all sorrow my support,
The blessing of my life, the gift is yours,
Ye mountains, thine, o nature! Thou hast fed
My lofty speculations, and in thee
For this uneasy heart of ours I find
A never-failing principle of joy
And purest passion.

Thou, my friend, wert reared
In the great city, mid far other scenes,

O'ercome by humblest prelude of that strain,
Forgot her functions, and slept undisturbed.

If this be error, and another faith
Find easier access to the pious mind,
Yet were I grossly destitute of all
Those human sentiments that make this earth
So dear, if I should fail with grateful voice
To speak of you, ye mountains, and ye lakes
And sounding cataracts, ye mists and winds
That dwell among the hills where I was born.
If in my youth I have been pure in heart,
If, mingling with the world, I am content
With my own modest pleasures, and have lived
With God and Nature communing, removed
From little enmities and low desires,
The gift is yours; if in these times of fear,
This melancholy waste of hopes o'erthrown,
If, 'mid indifference and apathy,
And wicked exultation when good men
On every side fall off, we know not how,
To selfishness, disguised in gentle names
Of peace and quiet and domestic love,
Yet mingled not unwillingly with sneers
On visionary minds; if, in this time
Of dereliction and dismay, I yet
Despair not of our nature, but retain
A more than Roman confidence, a faith
That fails not, in all sorrow my support,
The blessing of my life; the gift is yours,
Ye winds and sounding cataracts! 'tis yours,
Ye mountains! thine, O Nature! Thou hast fed
My lofty speculations; and in thee,
For this uneasy heart of ours, I find
A never-failing principle of joy
And purest passion.

Thou, my Friend! wert reared
In the great city, 'mid far other scenes;

But we by different roads at length have gained
The self-same bourne. And for this cause to thee
I speak unapprehensive of contempt,
The insinuated scoff of coward tongues,
And all that silent language which so oft
In conversation betwixt man and man
Blots from the human countenance all trace
Of beauty and of love. For thou hast sought
The truth in solitude, and thou art one,
The most intense of nature's worshippers –
In many things my brother, chiefly here
In this my deep devotion. Fare thee well!
Health and the quiet of a healthful mind
Attend thee – seeking oft the haunts of men,
And yet more often living with thyself,
And for thyself – so haply shall thy days
Be many, and a blessing to mankind.

But we, by different roads, at length have gained
The self-same bourne. And for this cause to thee
I speak, unapprehensive of contempt,
The insinuated scoff of coward tongues,
And all that silent language which so oft
In conversation between man and man
Blots from the human countenance all trace
Of beauty and of love. For thou hast sought
The truth in solitude, and, since the days
That gave thee liberty, full long desired
To serve in Nature's temple, thou hast been
The most assiduous of her ministers;
In many things my brother, chiefly here
In this our deep devotion.

Fare thee well!
Health and the quiet of a healthful mind
Attend thee! seeking oft the haunts of men,
And yet more often living with thyself,
And for thyself, so haply shall thy days
Be many, and a blessing to mankind.

Book Third

RESIDENCE AT CAMBRIDGE

It was a dreary morning when the chaise
Rolled over the flat plains of Huntingdon
And through the open windows first I saw
The long-backed chapel of King's College rear
His pinnacles above the dusky groves.
Soon afterwards, we espied upon the road
A student clothed in gown and tasselled cap;
He passed – nor was I master of my eyes
Till he was left a hundred yards behind.
The place, as we approached, seemed more and more
To have an eddy's force, and sucked us in
More eagerly at every step we took.
Onward we drove beneath the castle; down
By Magdalene Bridge we went and crossed the Cam,
And at the *Hoop* we landed, famous inn.

My spirit was up, my thoughts were full of hope;
Some friends I had – acquaintances who there
Seemed friends – poor simple schoolboys, now hung round
With honour and importance. In a world
Of welcome faces up and down I roved;
Questions, directions, counsel and advice,
Flowed in upon me from all sides. Fresh day
Of pride and pleasure! – To myself I seemed
A man of business and expense, and went
From shop to shop about my own affairs,
To tutors or to tailors as befell,

Book Third

RESIDENCE AT CAMBRIDGE

It was a dreary morning when the wheels
Rolled over a wide plain o'erhung with clouds,
And nothing cheered our way till first we saw
The long-roofed chapel of King's College lift
Turrets and pinnacles in answering files,
Extended high above a dusky grove.

Advancing, we espied upon the road
A student clothed in gown and tasselled cap,
Striding along as if o'ertasked by Time,
Or covetous of exercise and air;
He passed – nor was I master of my eyes
Till he was left an arrow's flight behind.
As near and nearer to the spot we drew,
It seemed to suck us in with an eddy's force.
Onward we drove beneath the Castle; caught,
While crossing Magdalene Bridge, a glimpse of Cam;
And at the *Hoop* alighted, famous Inn.

My spirit was up, my thoughts were full of hope;
Some friends I had, acquaintances who there
Seemed friends, poor simple school-boys, now hung round
With honour and importance: in a world
Of welcome faces up and down I roved;
Questions, directions, warnings and advice,
Flowed in upon me, from all sides; fresh day
Of pride and pleasure! to myself I seemed
A man of business and expense, and went
From shop to shop about my own affairs,
To Tutor or to Tailor, as befel,

From street to street with loose and careless heart.
I was the dreamer, they the dream! I roamed
Delighted through the motley spectacle:
Gowns, grave or gaudy, doctors, students, streets,
Lamps, gateways, flocks of churches, courts and towers –
Strange transformation for a mountain youth,
A northern villager. As if by word
Of magic or some fairy's power, at once
Behold me rich in moneys and attired
In splendid clothes, with hose of silk, and hair
Glittering like rimy trees when frost is keen –
My lordly dressing-gown, I pass it by,
With other signs of manhood which supplied
The lack of beard! The weeks went roundly on,
With invitations, suppers, wine and fruit,
Smooth housekeeping within, and all without
Liberal and suiting gentleman's array.

The Evangelist St John my patron was:
Three gloomy courts are his, and in the first
Was my abiding-place, a nook obscure.
Right underneath, the College kitchens made
A humming sound, less tuneable than bees
But hardly less industrious, with shrill notes
Of sharp command and scolding intermixed.
Near me was Trinity's loquacious clock
Who never let the quarters, night or day,
Slip by him unproclaimed, and told the hours
Twice over with a male and female voice.
Her pealing organ was my neighbour too,
And from my bedroom I in moonlight nights
Could see right opposite, a few yards off,
The antechapel where the statue stood
Of Newton with his prism and silent face.

From street to street with loose and careless mind.

I was the Dreamer, they the Dream; I roamed
Delighted through the motley spectacle;
Gowns grave, or gaudy, doctors, students, streets,
Courts, cloisters, flocks of churches, gateways, towers:
Migration strange for a stripling of the hills,
A northern villager.

As if the change
Had waited on some Fairy's wand, at once
Behold me rich in monies, and attired
In splendid garb, with hose of silk, and hair
Powdered like rimy trees, when frost is keen.
My lordly dressing-gown, I pass it by,
With other signs of manhood that supplied
The lack of beard. – The weeks went roundly on,
With invitations, suppers, wine and fruit,
Smooth housekeeping within, and all without
Liberal, and suiting gentleman's array.

The Evangelist St. John my patron was:
Three Gothic courts are his, and in the first
Was my abiding-place, a nook obscure;
Right underneath, the College kitchens made
A humming sound, less tuneable than bees,
But hardly less industrious; with shrill notes
Of sharp command and scolding intermixed.
Near me hung Trinity's loquacious clock,
Who never let the quarters, night or day,
Slip by him unproclaimed, and told the hours
Twice over with a male and female voice.
Her pealing organ was my neighbour too;
And from my pillow, looking forth by light
Of noon or favouring stars, I could behold
The antechapel where the statue stood
Of Newton with his prism and silent face,
The marble index of a mind for ever
Voyaging through strange seas of Thought, alone.

Of College labours, of the lecturer's room
(All studded round, as thick as chairs could stand,
With loyal students faithful to their books,
Half-and-half idlers, hardy recusants,
And honest dunces), of important days –
Examinations, when the man was weighed
As in the balance! – of excessive hopes,
Tremblings withal and commendable fears,
Small jealousies and triumphs good or bad,
I make short mention. Things they were which then
I did not love, nor do I love them now:
Such glory was but little sought by me,
And little won. But it is right to say
That even so early, from the first crude days
Of settling-time in this my new abode,
Not seldom I had melancholy thoughts
From personal and family regards
(Wishing to hope without a hope), some fears
About my future worldly maintenance,
And, more than all, a strangeness in my mind,
A feeling that I was not for that hour,
Nor for that place. But wherefore be cast down?
Why should I grieve? I was a chosen son.
For hither I had come with holy powers
And faculties (whether to work or feel)
To apprehend all passions and all moods
Which time and place and season do impress
Upon the visible universe, and work
Like changes there by force of my own mind.
I was a freeman – in the purest sense
Was free – and to majestic ends was strong.
I do not speak of learning, moral truth
Or understanding, 'twas enough for me
To know that I was otherwise endowed.

When the first glitter of the show was passed,
And the first dazzle of the taper-light,
As if with a rebound my mind returned
Into its former self. Oft did I leave

Of College labours, of the Lecturer's room
All studded round, as thick as chairs could stand,
With loyal students faithful to their books,
Half-and-half idlers, hardy recusants,
And honest dunces – of important days,
Examinations, when the man was weighed
As in a balance! of excessive hopes,
Tremblings withal and commendable fears,
Small jealousies, and triumphs good or bad,
Let others that know more speak as they know.
Such glory was but little sought by me,
And little won. Yet from the first crude days
Of settling time in this untried abode,
I was disturbed at times by prudent thoughts,
Wishing to hope without a hope, some fears
About my future worldly maintenance,
And, more than all, a strangeness in the mind,
A feeling that I was not for that hour,
Nor for that place. But wherefore be cast down?
For (not to speak of Reason and her pure
Reflective acts to fix the moral law
Deep in the conscience, nor of Christian Hope,
Bowing her head before her sister Faith
As one far mightier), hither I had come,
Bear witness Truth, endowed with holy powers
And faculties, whether to work or feel.
Oft when the dazzling show no longer new
Had ceased to dazzle, ofttimes did I quit

My comrades, and the crowd, buildings and groves,
And walked along the fields, the level fields,
With heaven's blue concave reared above my head.
And now it was that, through such change entire
And this first absence from those shapes sublime
Wherewith I had been conversant, my mind
Seemed busier in itself than heretofore –
At least I more directly recognized
My powers and habits. Let me dare to speak
A higher language, say that now I felt
The strength and consolation which were mine.
As if awakened, summoned, roused, constrained,
I looked for universal things, perused
The common countenance of earth and heaven,
And turning the mind in upon itself
Pored, watched, expected, listened, spread my thoughts
And spread them with a wider creeping; felt
Incumbencies more awful, visitings
Of the upholder of the tranquil soul,
Which underneath all passion lives secure
A steadfast life. But peace, it is enough
To notice that I was ascending now
To such community with highest truth.

A track pursuing not untrod before,
From deep analogies by thought supplied
Or consciousnesses not to be subdued,
To every natural form, rock, fruit or flower,

My comrades, leave the crowd, buildings and groves,
And as I paced alone the level fields
Far from those lovely sights and sounds sublime
With which I had been conversant, the mind
Drooped not; but there into herself returning,
With prompt rebound seemed fresh as heretofore.
At least I more distinctly recognised
Her native instincts: let me dare to speak
A higher language, say that now I felt
What independent solaces were mine,
To mitigate the injurious sway of place
Or circumstance, how far soever changed
In youth, or *to* be changed in manhood's prime;
Or for the few who shall be called to look
On the long shadows in our evening years,
Ordained precursors to the night of death.
As if awakened, summoned, roused, constrained,
I looked for universal things; perused
The common countenance of earth and sky:
Earth, nowhere unembellished by some trace
Of that first Paradise whence man was driven;
And sky, whose beauty and bounty are expressed
By the proud name she bears – the name of Heaven.
I called on both to teach me what they might;
Or turning the mind in upon herself
Pored, watched, expected, listened, spread my thoughts
And spread them with a wider creeping; felt
Incumbencies more awful, visitings
Of the Upholder of the tranquil soul,
That tolerates the indignities of Time,
And, from the centre of Eternity
All finite motions overruling, lives
In glory immutable. But peace! enough
Here to record that I was mounting now
To such community with highest truth –
A track pursuing, not untrod before,
From strict analogies by thought supplied
Or consciousnesses not to be subdued.
To every natural form, rock, fruit or flower,

Even the loose stones that cover the highway,
I gave a moral life – I saw them feel,
Or linked them to some feeling. The great mass
Lay bedded in a quickening soul, and all
That I beheld respired with inward meaning.
Thus much for the one presence, and the life
Of the great whole; suffice it here to add
That whatsoe'er of terror or of love
Or beauty, nature's daily face put on
From transitory passion, unto this
I was as wakeful even as waters are
To the sky's motion, in a kindred sense
Of passion was obedient as a lute
That waits upon the touches of the wind.
So was it with me in my solitude:
So, often among multitudes of men.
Unknown, unthought of, yet I was most rich,
I had a world about me – 'twas my own,
I made it; for it only lived to me
And to the God who looked into my mind.

Such sympathies would sometimes show themselves
By outward gestures and by visible looks –
Some called it madness – such indeed it was,
If childlike fruitfulness in passing joy,
If steady moods of thoughtfulness matured
To inspiration, sort with such a name;
If prophecy be madness; if things viewed
By poets of old time, and higher up
By the first men, earth's first inhabitants,
May in these tutored days no more be seen
With undisordered sight. But leaving this,
It was no madness; for I had an eye
Which in my strongest workings evermore
Was looking for the shades of difference
As they lie hid in all exterior forms,
Near or remote, minute or vast – an eye
Which from a stone, a tree, a withered leaf,
To the broad ocean and the azure heavens

Even the loose stones that cover the high-way,
I gave a moral life: I saw them feel,
Or linked them to some feeling: the great mass
Lay bedded in a quickening soul, and all
That I beheld respired with inward meaning.
Add that whate'er of Terror or of Love
Or Beauty, Nature's daily face put on
From transitory passion, unto this
I was as sensitive as waters are
To the sky's influence in a kindred mood
Of passion; was obedient as a lute
That waits upon the touches of the wind.
Unknown, unthought of, yet I was most rich –
I had a world about me – 'twas my own;
I made it, for it only lived to me,
And to the God who sees into the heart.
Such sympathies, though rarely, were betrayed
By outward gestures and by visible looks:
Some called it madness – so indeed it was,
If child-like fruitfulness in passing joy,
If steady moods of thoughtfulness matured
To inspiration, sort with such a name;
If prophecy be madness; if things viewed
By poets in old time, and higher up
By the first men, earth's first inhabitants,
May in these tutored days no more be seen
With undisordered sight. But leaving this,
It was no madness, for the bodily eye
Amid my strongest workings evermore
Was searching out the lines of difference
As they lie hid in all external forms,
Near or remote, minute or vast, an eye
Which from a tree, a stone, a withered leaf,
To the broad ocean and the azure heavens

Spangled with kindred multitudes of stars,
Could find no surface where its power might sleep,
Which spake perpetual logic to my soul,
And by an unrelenting agency
Did bind my feelings even as in a chain.

And here, o friend, have I retraced my life
Up to an eminence, and told a tale
Of matters which not falsely I may call
The glory of my youth. Of genius, power,
Creation and divinity itself
I have been speaking, for my theme has been
What passed within me! Not of outward things
Done visibly for other minds – words, signs,
Symbols or actions – but of my own heart
Have I been speaking, and my youthful mind.
O heavens, how awful is the might of souls,
And what they do within themselves while yet
The yoke of earth is new to them, the world
Nothing but a wild field where they were sown!
This is in truth heroic argument
And genuine prowess, which I wished to touch
With hand however weak, but in the main
It lies far hidden from the reach of words.
Points have we all of us within our souls
Where all stand single; this I feel, and make
Breathings for incommunicable powers.
Yet each man is a memory to himself,
And therefore, now that I must quit this theme,
I am not heartless, for there's not a man
That lives who hath not had his godlike hours,
And knows not what majestic sway we have
As natural beings in the strength of nature.

Enough, for now into a populous plain
We must descend. A traveller I am,
And all my tale is of myself – even so –
So be it, if the pure in heart delight
To follow me, and thou, o honoured friend,

Spangled with kindred multitudes of stars,
Could find no surface where its power might sleep;
Which spake perpetual logic to my soul,
And by an unrelenting agency
Did bind my feelings even as in a chain.

And here, O Friend! have I retraced my life
Up to an eminence, and told a tale
Of matters which not falsely may be called
The glory of my youth. Of genius, power,
Creation and divinity itself
I have been speaking, for my theme has been
What passed within me. Not of outward things
Done visibly for other minds, words, signs,
Symbols or actions, but of my own heart
Have I been speaking, and my youthful mind.
O Heavens! how awful is the might of souls,
And what they do within themselves while yet
The yoke of earth is new to them, the world
Nothing but a wild field where they were sown.
This is, in truth, heroic argument,
This genuine prowess, which I wished to touch
With hand however weak, but in the main
It lies far hidden from the reach of words.
Points have we all of us within our souls
Where all stand single; this I feel, and make
Breathings for incommunicable powers;
But is not each a memory to himself,
And, therefore, now that we must quit this theme,
I am not heartless, for there's not a man
That lives who hath not known his god-like hours,
And feels not what an empire we inherit
As natural beings in the strength of Nature.

No more: for now into a populous plain
We must descend. A Traveller I am,
Whose tale is only of himself; even so,
So be it, if the pure of heart be prompt
To follow, and if thou, my honoured Friend!

Who in my thoughts art ever at my side,
Uphold as heretofore my fainting steps.

It has been told already how my sight
Was dazzled by the novel show, and how
Erelong I did into myself return.
So did it seem, and so in truth it was –
Yet this was but short lived. Thereafter came
Observance less devout: I had made a change
In climate, and my nature's outward coat
Changed also, slowly and insensibly.
To the deep quiet and majestic thoughts
Of loneliness succeeded empty noise
And superficial pastimes, now and then
Forced labour, and more frequently forced hopes,
And (worse than all) a treasonable growth
Of indecisive judgements that impaired
And shook the mind's simplicity. And yet
This was a gladsome time. Could I behold –
Who, less insensible than sodden clay
On a sea-river's bed at ebb of tide,
Could have beheld – with undelighted heart
So many happy youths (so wide and fair
A congregation in its budding-time
Of health, and hope, and beauty), all at once
So many divers samples of the growth
Of life's sweet season – could have seen unmoved
That miscellaneous garland of wild flowers
Upon the matron temples of a place
So famous through the world? To me at least
It was a goodly prospect; for, through youth,
Though I had been trained up to stand unpropped,
And independent musings pleased me so
That spells seemed on me when I was alone,
Yet could I only cleave to solitude
In lonesome places. If a throng was near,
That way I leaned by nature, for my heart
Was social and loved idleness and joy.

Who in these thoughts art ever at my side,
Support, as heretofore, my fainting steps.

It hath been told, that when the first delight
That flashed upon me from this novel show
Had failed, the mind returned into herself;
Yet true it is, that I had made a change
In climate, and my nature's outward coat
Changed also slowly and insensibly.
Full oft the quiet and exalted thoughts
Of loneliness gave way to empty noise
And superficial pastimes; now and then
Forced labour, and more frequently forced hopes;
And, worst of all, a treasonable growth
Of indecisive judgments, that impaired
And shook the mind's simplicity. – And yet
This was a gladsome time. Could I behold –
Who, less insensible than sodden clay
In a sea-river's bed at ebb of tide,
Could have beheld, – with undelighted heart,
So many happy youths, so wide and fair
A congregation in its budding-time
Of health, and hope, and beauty, all at once
So many divers samples from the growth
Of life's sweet season – could have seen unmoved
That miscellaneous garland of wild flowers
Decking the matron temples of a place
So famous through the world? To me, at least,
It was a goodly prospect: for, in sooth,
Though I had learnt betimes to stand unpropped,
And independent musings pleased me so
That spells seemed on me when I was alone,
Yet could I only cleave to solitude
In lonely places; if a throng was near
That way I leaned by nature; for my heart
Was social, and loved idleness and joy.

Not seeking those who might participate
My deeper pleasures (nay, I had not once,
Though not unused to mutter lonesome songs,
Even with myself divided such delight,
Or looked that way for aught that might be clothed
In human language), easily I passed
From the remembrances of better things,
And slipped into the weekday works of youth,
Unburdened, unalarmed, and unprofaned.
Caverns there were within my mind which sun
Could never penetrate, yet did there not
Want store of leafy arbours where the light
Might enter in at will. Companionships,
Friendships, acquaintances, were welcome all;
We sauntered, played, we rioted, we talked
Unprofitable talk at morning hours,
Drifted about along the streets and walks,
Read lazily in lazy books, went forth
To gallop through the country in blind zeal
Of senseless horsemanship, or on the breast
Of Cam sailed boisterously, and let the stars
Come out, perhaps, without one quiet thought.

Such was the tenor of the opening act
In this new life. Imagination slept,
And yet not utterly. I could not print
Ground where the grass had yielded to the steps
Of generations of illustrious men,
Unmoved. I could not always lightly pass
Through the same gateways, sleep where they had slept,
Wake where they waked, range that enclosure old,
That garden of great intellects, undisturbed.
Place also by the side of this dark sense
Of nobler feeling, that those spiritual men,
Even the great Newton's own ethereal self,
Seemed humbled in these precincts, thence to be
The more belovèd – invested here with tasks
Of life's plain business, as a daily garb

Not seeking those who might participate
My deeper pleasures (nay, I had not once,
Though not unused to mutter lonesome songs,
Even with myself divided such delight,
Or looked that way for aught that might be clothed
In human language), easily I passed
From the remembrances of better things,
And slipped into the ordinary works
Of careless youth, unburthened, unalarmed.
Caverns there were within my mind which sun
Could never penetrate, yet did there not
Want store of leafy *arbours* where the light
Might enter in at will. Companionships,
Friendships, acquaintances, were welcome all.
We sauntered, played, or rioted; we talked
Unprofitable talk at morning hours;
Drifted about along the streets and walks,
Read lazily in trivial books, went forth
To gallop through the country in blind zeal
Of senseless horsemanship, or on the breast
Of Cam sailed boisterously, and let the stars
Come forth, perhaps without one quiet thought.

Such was the tenor of the second act
In this new life. Imagination slept,
And yet not utterly. I could not print
Ground where the grass had yielded to the steps
Of generations of illustrious men,
Unmoved. I could not always lightly pass
Through the same gateways, sleep where they had slept,
Wake where they waked, range that inclosure old,
That garden of great intellects, undisturbed.
Place also by the side of this dark sense
Of noble feeling, that those spiritual men,
Even the great Newton's own ethereal self,
Seemed humbled in these precincts thence to be
The more endeared. Their several memories here
(Even like their persons in their portraits clothed
With the accustomed garb of daily life)

(Dictators at the plough), a change that left
All genuine admiration unimpaired.

Beside the pleasant mills of Trumpington
I laughed with Chaucer; in the hawthorn-shade
Heard him, while birds were warbling, tell his tales
Of amorous passion. And that gentle bard,
Chosen by the muses for their page of state –
Sweet Spenser, moving through his clouded heaven
With the moon's beauty and the moon's soft pace –
I called him brother, Englishman, and friend!
Yea, our blind poet, who in his later day
Stood almost single, uttering odious truth
(Darkness before, and danger's voice behind),
Soul awful, if the earth has ever lodged
An awful soul, I seemed to see him here
Familiarly, and in his scholar's dress
Bounding before me, yet a stripling youth –
A boy, no better, with his rosy cheeks
Angelical, keen eye, courageous look,
And conscious step of purity and pride.

Among the band of my compeers was one,
My class-fellow at school, whose chance it was
To lodge in the apartments which had been,
Time out of mind, honoured by Milton's name –
The very shell reputed of the abode
Which he had tenanted. O temperate bard!
One afternoon, the first time I set foot
In this thy innocent nest and oratory,
Seated with others in a festive ring
Of commonplace convention, I to thee
Poured out libations, to thy memory drank
Within my private thoughts, till my brain reeled,
Never so clouded by the fumes of wine
Before that hour, or since. Thence forth I ran
From that assembly, through a length of streets
Ran ostrich-like, to reach our chapel-door

Put on a lowly and a touching grace
Of more distinct humanity, that left
All genuine admiration unimpaired.

Beside the pleasant Mill of Trompington
I laughed with Chaucer in the hawthorn shade;
Heard him, while birds were warbling, tell his tales
Of amorous passion. And that gentle Bard,
Chosen by the Muses for their Page of State –
Sweet Spenser, moving through his clouded heaven
With the moon's beauty and the moon's soft pace,
I called him Brother, Englishman, and Friend!
Yea, our blind Poet, who, in his later day,
Stood almost single; uttering odious truth –
Darkness before, and danger's voice behind,
Soul awful – if the earth has ever lodged
An awful soul – I seemed to see him here
Familiarly, and in his scholar's dress
Bounding before me, yet a stripling youth –
A boy, no better, with his rosy cheeks
Angelical, keen eye, courageous look,
And conscious step of purity and pride.
Among the band of my compeers was one
Whom chance had stationed in the very room
Honoured by Milton's name. O temperate Bard!
Be it confest that, for the first time, seated
Within thy innocent lodge and oratory,
One of a festive circle, I poured out
Libations, to thy memory drank, till pride
And gratitude grew dizzy in a brain
Never excited by the fumes of wine
Before that hour, or since. Then, forth I ran
From the assembly; through a length of streets,
Ran, ostrich-like, to reach our chapel door

In not a desperate or opprobrious time,
Albeit long after the importunate bell
Had stopped, with wearisome Cassandra-voice
No longer haunting the dark winter night.
(Call back, o friend, a moment to thy mind,
The place itself and fashion of the rites.)
Upshouldering in a dislocated lump
With shallow ostentatious carelessness
My surplice, gloried in and yet despised,
I clove in pride through the inferior throng
Of the plain burghers, who in audience stood
On the last skirts of their permitted ground,
Beneath the pealing organ. Empty thoughts! –
I am ashamed of them; and that great bard,
And thou, o friend, who in thy ample mind
Has stationed me for reverence and love,
Ye will forgive the weakness of that hour,
In some of its unworthy vanities
Brother of many more.

In this mixed sort
The months passed on, remissly, not given up
To wilful alienation from the right,
Or walks of open scandal, but in vague
And loose indifference, easy likings, aims
Of a low pitch – duty and zeal dismissed,
Yet nature, or a happy course of things,
Not doing in their stead the needful work.
The memory languidly revolved, the heart
Reposed in noontide rest, the inner pulse
Of contemplation almost failed to beat.
Rotted as by a charm, my life became
A floating island, an amphibious thing,
Unsound, of spongy texture, yet withal
Not wanting a fair face of water weeds
And pleasant flowers. The thirst of living praise,
A reverence for the glorious dead, the sight
Of those long vistas, catacombs in which
Perennial minds lie visibly entombed,

In not a desperate or opprobrious time,
Albeit long after the importunate bell
Had stopped, with wearisome Cassandra voice
No longer haunting the dark winter night.
Call back, O Friend! a moment to thy mind
The place itself and fashion of the rites.
With careless ostentation shouldering up
My surplice, through the inferior throng I clove
Of the plain Burghers, who in audience stood
On the last skirts of their permitted ground,
Under the pealing organ. Empty thoughts!
I am ashamed of them: and that great Bard,
And thou, O Friend! who in thy ample mind
Hast placed me high above my best deserts,
Ye will forgive the weakness of that hour,
In some of its unworthy vanities,
Brother to many more.

In this mixed sort
The months passed on, remissly, not given up
To wilful alienation from the right,
Or walks of open scandal, but in vague
And loose indifference, easy likings, aims
Of a low pitch – duty and zeal dismissed,
Yet Nature, or a happy course of things
Not doing in their stead the needful work.
The memory languidly revolved, the heart
Reposed in noontide rest, the inner pulse
Of contemplation almost failed to beat.
Such life might not inaptly be compared
To a floating island, an amphibious spot
Unsound, of spongy texture, yet withal
Not wanting a fair face of water weeds
And pleasant flowers. The thirst of living praise,
Fit reverence for the glorious Dead, the sight
Of those long vistas, sacred catacombs,
Where mighty *minds* lie visibly entombed,

Have often stirred the heart of youth, and bred
A fervent love of rigorous discipline.
Alas, such high commotion touched not me!
No look was in these walls to put to shame
My easy spirits and discountenance
Their light composure, far less to instil
A calm resolve of mind, firmly addressed
To puissant efforts. Nor was this the blame
Of others but my own; I should in truth
As far as doth concern my single self,
Misdeem most widely, lodging it elsewhere.
For I, bred up in nature's lap, was even
As a spoiled child, and (rambling like the wind
As I had done in daily intercourse
With those delicious rivers, solemn heights
And mountains, ranging like a fowl of the air)
I was ill-tutored for captivity –
To quit my pleasure, and from month to month
Take up a station calmly on the perch
Of sedentary peace. Those lovely forms
Had also left less space within my mind,
Which, wrought upon instinctively, had found
A freshness in those objects of its love,
A winning power beyond all other power.
Not that I slighted books – that were to lack
All sense – but other passions had been mine,
More fervent, making me less prompt perhaps
To indoor study than was wise or well,
Or suited to my years.

Yet I could shape
The image of a place which – soothed and lulled
As I had been, trained up in paradise
Among sweet garlands and delightful sounds,
Accustomed in my loneliness to walk
With nature magisterially – yet I
Methinks could shape the image of a place
Which with its aspect should have bent me down
To instantaneous service, should at once

Have often stirred the heart of youth, and bred
A fervent love of rigorous discipline. –
Alas! such high emotion touched not me.
Look was there none within these walls to shame
My easy spirits, and discountenance
Their light composure, far less to instil
A calm resolve of mind, firmly addressed
To puissant efforts. Nor was this the blame
Of others but my own; I should, in truth,
As far as doth concern my single self,
Misdeem most widely, lodging it elsewhere:
For I, bred up 'mid Nature's luxuries,
Was a spoiled child, and rambling like the wind,
As I had done in daily intercourse
With those crystalline rivers, solemn heights,
And mountains, ranging like a fowl of the air,
I was ill-tutored for captivity;
To quit my pleasure, and, from month to month,
Take up a station calmly on the perch
Of sedentary peace. Those lovely forms
Had also left less space within my mind,
Which, wrought upon instinctively, had found
A freshness in those objects of her love,
A winning power, beyond all other power.
Not that I slighted books, – that were to lack
All sense, – but other passions in me ruled,
Passions more fervent, making me less prompt
To in-door study than was wise or well,
Or suited to those years. Yet I, though used
In magisterial liberty to rove,
Culling such flowers of learning as might tempt
A random choice, could shadow forth a place
(If now I yield not to a flattering dream)
Whose studious aspect should have bent me down
To instantaneous service; should at once

Have made me pay to science and to arts
And written lore – acknowledged my liege lord –
A homage frankly offered up, like that
Which I had paid to nature. Toil and pains
In this recess which I have bodied forth
Should spread from heart to heart, and stately groves,
Majestic edifices, should not want
A corresponding dignity within.
The congregating temper which pervades
Our unripe years, not wasted, should be made
To minister to works of high attempt,
Which the enthusiast would perform with love.
Youth should be awed, possessed, as with a sense
Religious, of what holy joy there is
In knowledge, if it be sincerely sought
For its own sake – in glory, and in praise,
If but by labour won, and to endure.
The passing day should learn to put aside
Her trappings here, should strip them off abashed
Before antiquity and steadfast truth
And strong book-mindedness; and over all
Should be a healthy sound simplicity,
A seemly plainness – name it as you will,
Republican, or pious.

If these thoughts
Be a gratuitous emblazonry
That does but mock this recreant age, at least
Let folly and false-seeming (we might say)
Be free to affect whatever formal gait
Of moral or scholastic discipline
Shall raise them highest in their own esteem –
Let them parade among the schools at will,
But spare the house of God. Was ever known
The witless shepherd who would drive his flock
With serious repetition to a pool
Of which 'tis plain to sight they never taste?
A weight must surely hang on days begun
And ended with worst mockery. Be wise,

Have made me pay to science and to arts
And written lore, acknowledged my liege lord,
A homage frankly offered up, like that
Which I had paid to Nature. Toil and pains
In this recess, by thoughtful Fancy built,
Should spread from heart to heart; and stately groves,
Majestic edifices, should not want
A corresponding dignity within.
The congregating temper that pervades
Our unripe years, not wasted, should be taught
To minister to works of high attempt –
Works which the enthusiast would perform with love.
Youth should be awed, religiously possessed
With a conviction of the power that waits
On knowledge, when sincerely sought and prized
For its own sake, on glory and on praise
If but by labour won, and fit to endure
The passing day; should learn to put aside
Her trappings here, should strip them off abashed
Before antiquity and stedfast truth
And strong book-mindedness; and over all
A healthy sound simplicity should reign,
A seemly plainness, name it what you will,
Republican or pious.

If these thoughts
Are a gratuitous emblazonry
That mocks the recreant age *we* live in, then
Be Folly and False-seeming free to affect
Whatever formal gait of discipline
Shall raise them highest in their own esteem –
Let them parade among the Schools at will,
But spare the House of God. Was ever known
The witless shepherd who persists to drive
A flock that thirsts not to a pool disliked?
A weight must surely hang on days begun
And ended with such mockery. Be wise,

Ye presidents and deans, and to your bells
Give seasonable rest, for 'tis a sound
Hollow as ever vexed the tranquil air,
And your officious doings bring disgrace
On the plain steeples of our English Church
Whose worship mid remotest village trees
Suffers for this. Even science too, at hand
In daily sight of such irreverence,
Is smitten thence with an unnatural taint,
Loses her just authority, falls beneath
Collateral suspicion, else unknown.
This obvious truth did not escape me then,
Unthinking as I was, and I confess
That, having in my native hills given loose
To a schoolboy's dreaming, I had raised a pile
Upon the basis of the coming time,
Which now before me melted fast away –
Which could not live, scarcely had life enough
To mock the builder

Oh, what joy it were
To see a sanctuary for our country's youth
With such a spirit in it as might be
Protection for itself, a virgin grove
Primeval in its purity and depth,
Where, though the shades were filled with cheerfulness,
Nor indigent of songs warbled from crowds
In under-coverts, yet the countenance
Of the whole place should wear a stamp of awe –
A habitation sober and demure
For ruminating creatures, a domain
For quiet things to wander in, a haunt
In which the heron might delight to feed
By the shy rivers, and the pelican
Upon the cypress-spire in lonely thought
Might sit and sun himself. Alas, alas,
In vain for such solemnity we look!
Our eyes are crossed by butterflies, our ears
Hear chattering popinjays – the inner heart

Ye Presidents and Deans, and, till the spirit
Of ancient times revive, and youth be trained
At home in pious service, to your bells
Give seasonable rest, for 'tis a sound
Hollow as ever vexed the tranquil air;
And your officious doings bring disgrace
On the plain steeples of our English Church,
Whose worship, 'mid remotest village trees,
Suffers for this. Even Science, too, at hand
In daily sight of this irreverence,
Is smitten thence with an unnatural taint,
Loses her just authority, falls beneath
Collateral suspicion, else unknown.
This truth escaped me not, and I confess,
That having 'mid my native hills given loose
To a schoolboy's vision, I had raised a pile
Upon the basis of the coming time,
That fell in ruins round me. Oh, what joy
To see a sanctuary for our country's youth
Informed with such a spirit as might be
Its own protection; a primeval grove,
Where, though the shades with cheerfulness were filled,
Nor indigent of songs warbled from crowds
In under-coverts, yet the countenance
Of the whole place should bear a stamp of awe;
A habitation sober and demure
For ruminating creatures; a domain
For quiet things to wander in; a haunt
In which the heron should delight to feed
By the shy rivers, and the pelican
Upon the cypress spire in lonely thought
Might sit and sun himself. – Alas! Alas!
In vain for such solemnity I looked;
Mine eyes were crossed by butterflies, ears vexed
By chattering popinjays; the inner heart

Is trivial, and the impresses without
Are of a gaudy region.

Different sight
Those venerable doctors saw of old,
When all who dwelt within these famous walls
Led in abstemiousness a studious life,
When, in forlorn and naked chambers cooped
And crowded, o'er their ponderous books they sat
Like caterpillars eating out their way
In silence, or with keen devouring noise
Not to be tracked or fathered. Princes then
At matins froze, and couched at curfew-time,
Trained up through piety and zeal to prize
Spare diet, patient labour, and plain weeds.
O seat of arts, renowned throughout the world,
Far different service in those homely days
The nurslings of the muses underwent
From their first childhood – in that glorious time
When learning, like a stranger come from far,
Sounding through Christian lands her trumpet, roused
The peasant and the king; when boys and youths,
The growth of ragged villages and huts,
Forsook their homes, and (errant in the quest
Of patron, famous school or friendly nook
Where, pensioned, they in shelter might sit down)
From town to town and through wide scattered realms
Journeyed with their huge folios in their hands,
And often, starting from some covert place,
Saluted the chance comer on the road
Crying, 'An obolus, a penny give
To a poor scholar'; when illustrious men,
Lovers of truth by penury constrained –
Bucer, Erasmus, or Melanchthon – read
Before the doors and windows of their cells
By moonshine, through mere lack of taper-light.

But peace to vain regrets! We see but darkly
Even when we look behind us, and best things

Seemed trivial, and the impresses without
Of a too gaudy region.

Different sight
Those venerable Doctors saw of old,
When all who dwelt within these famous walls
Led in abstemiousness a studious life;
When, in forlorn and naked chambers cooped
And crowded, o'er the ponderous books they hung
Like caterpillars eating out their way
In silence, or with keen devouring noise
Not to be tracked or fathered. Princes then
At matins froze, and couched at curfew-time,
Trained up through piety and zeal to prize
Spare diet, patient labour, and plain weeds.
O seat of Arts! renowned throughout the world!
Far different service in those homely days
The Muses' modest nurslings underwent
From their first childhood: in that glorious time
When Learning, like a stranger come from far,
Sounding through Christian lands her trumpet, roused
Peasant and king; when boys and youths, the growth
Of ragged villages and crazy huts,
Forsook their homes, and, errant in the quest
Of Patron, famous school or friendly nook,
Where, pensioned, they in shelter might sit down.
From town to town and through wide scattered realms
Journeyed with ponderous folios in their hands;
And often, starting from some covert place,
Saluted the chance comer on the road,
Crying, 'An obolus, a penny give
To a poor scholar!' – when illustrious men,
Lovers of truth, by penury constrained,
Bucer, Erasmus, or Melancthon, read
Before the doors or windows of their cells
By moonshine through mere lack of taper light.

But peace to vain regrets! We see but darkly
Even when we look behind us, and best things

Are not so pure by nature that they needs
Must keep to all (as fondly all believe)
Their highest promise. If the mariner,
When at reluctant distance he has passed
Some fair enticing island, did but know
What fate might have been his, could he have brought
His bark to land upon the wished-for spot,
Good cause full often would he have to bless
The belt of churlish surf that scared him thence,
Or haste of the inexorable wind.
For me, I grieve not; happy is the man
Who only misses what I missed, who falls
No lower than I fell.

I did not love
(As hath been noticed heretofore) the guise
Of our scholastic studies, could have wished
The river to have had an ampler range
And freer pace. But this I tax not; far,
Far more I grieved to see among the band
Of those who in the field of contest stood
As combatants, passions that did to me
Seem low and mean – from ignorance of mine,
In part, and want of just forbearance, yet
My wiser mind grieves now for what I saw.
Willingly did I part from these, and turn
Out of their track to travel with the shoal
Of more unthinking natures: easy minds
And pillowy, and not wanting love that makes
The day pass lightly on when foresight sleeps,
And wisdom and the pledges interchanged
With our own inner being are forgot.

To books, our daily fare prescribed, I turned
With sickly appetite, and when I went
At other times in quest of my own food
I chased not steadily the manly deer,
But laid me down to any casual feast
Of wild wood-honey, or, with truant eyes

Are not so pure by nature that they needs
Must keep to all, as fondly all believe,
Their highest promise. If the mariner,
When at reluctant distance he hath passed
Some tempting island, could but know the ills
That must have fallen upon him had he brought
His bark to land upon the wished-for shore,
Good cause would oft be his to thank the surf
Whose white belt scared him thence, or wind that blew
Inexorably adverse: for myself
I grieve not; happy is the gownèd youth,
Who only misses what I missed, who falls
No lower than I fell.

I did not love,
Judging not ill perhaps, the timid course
Of our scholastic studies; could have wished
To see the river flow with ampler range
And freer pace; but more, far more, I grieved
To see displayed among an eager few,
Who in the field of contest persevered,
Passions unworthy of youth's generous heart
And mounting spirit, pitiably repaid,
When so disturbed, whatever palms are won.
From these I turned to travel with the shoal
Of more unthinking natures, easy minds
And pillowy; yet not wanting love that makes
The day pass lightly on, when foresight sleeps,
And wisdom and the pledges interchanged
With our own inner being are forgot.

Unruly, peeped about for vagrant fruit.
And as for what pertains to human life,
The deeper passions working round me here
(Whether of envy, jealousy, pride, shame,
Ambition, emulation, fear, or hope,
Or those of dissolute pleasure) were by me
Unshared, and only now and then observed –
So little was their hold upon my being,
As outward things that might administer
To knowledge or instruction. Hushed, meanwhile,
Was the under-soul, locked up in such a calm
That not a leaf of the great nature stirred.

Yet was this deep vacation not given up
To utter waste. Hitherto I had stood
In my own mind remote from human life –
At least from what we commonly so name –
Even as a shepherd on a promontory
Who lacking occupation looks far forth
Into the endless sea, and rather makes
Than finds what he beholds. And sure it is
That this first transit from the smooth delights
And wild outlandish walks of simple youth
To something that resembled an approach
Towards mortal business (to a privileged world
Within a world, a midway residence
With all its intervenient imagery)
Did better suit my visionary mind,
Far better, than to have been bolted forth,
Thrust out abruptly into fortune's way
Among the conflicts of substantial life –
By a more just gradation did lead on
To higher things, more naturally matured
For permanent possession, better fruits,
Whether of truth or virtue, to ensue.

In playful zest of fancy did we note
(How could we less?) the manners and the ways
Of those who in the livery were arrayed

Yet was this deep vacation not given up
To utter waste. Hitherto I had stood
In my own mind remote from social life,
(At least from what we commonly so name,)
Like a lone shepherd on a promontory
Who lacking occupation looks far forth
Into the boundless sea, and rather makes
Than finds what he beholds. And sure it is,
That this first transit from the smooth delights
And wild outlandish walks of simple youth
To something that resembles an approach
Towards human business, to a privileged world
Within a world, a midway residence
With all its intervenient imagery,
Did better suit my visionary mind,
Far better, than to have been bolted forth,
Thrust out abruptly into Fortune's way
Among the conflicts of substantial life;
By a more just gradation did lead on
To higher things; more naturally matured,
For permanent possession, better fruits,
Whether of truth or virtue, to ensue.
In serious mood, but oftener, I confess,
With playful zest of fancy did we note
(How could we less?) the manners and the ways
Of those who lived distinguished by the badge

Of good or evil fame – of those with whom
By frame of academic discipline
Perforce we were connected, men whose sway
And whose authority of office served
To set our minds on edge, and did no more.
Nor wanted we rich pastime of this kind,
Found everywhere but chiefly in the ring
Of the grave elders, men unscoured, grotesque
In character, tricked out like aged trees
Which through the lapse of their infirmity
Give ready place to any random seed
That chooses to be reared upon their trunks.
Here on my view, confronting as it were
Those shepherd swains whom I had lately left,
Did flash a different image of old age
(How different!) yet both withal alike
A book of rudiments for the unpractised sight –
Objects embossed, and which with sedulous care
Nature holds up before the eye of youth
In her great school, with further view perhaps
To enter early on her tender scheme
Of teaching comprehension with delight
And mingling playful with pathetic thoughts.

The surfaces of artificial life
And manners finely spun, the delicate race
Of colours, lurking, gleaming up and down
Through that state arras woven with silk and gold –
This wily interchange of snaky hues,
Willingly and unwillingly revealed –
I had not learned to watch; and at this time,
Perhaps, had such been in my daily sight
I might have been indifferent thereto
As hermits are to tales of distant things.
Hence for these rarities elaborate
Having no relish yet, I was content
With the more homely produce rudely piled

Of good or ill report; or those with whom
By frame of Academic discipline
We were perforce connected, men whose sway
And known authority of office served
To set our minds on edge, and did no more.
Nor wanted we rich pastime of this kind,
Found everywhere, but chiefly in the ring
Of the grave Elders, men unscoured, grotesque
In character, tricked out like aged trees
Which through the lapse of their infirmity
Give ready place to any random seed
That chooses to be reared upon their trunks.

Here on my view, confronting vividly
Those shepherd swains whom I had lately left,
Appeared a different aspect of old age;
How different! yet both distinctly marked,
Objects embossed to catch the general eye,
Or portraitures for special use designed,
As some might seem, so aptly do they serve
To illustrate Nature's book of rudiments –
That book upheld as with maternal care
When she would enter on her tender scheme
Of teaching comprehension with delight,
And mingling playful with pathetic thoughts.

The surfaces of artificial life
And manners finely wrought, the delicate race
Of colours, lurking, gleaming up and down
Through that state arras woven with silk and gold;
This wily interchange of snaky hues,
Willingly or unwillingly revealed,
I neither knew nor cared for; and as such
Were wanting here, I took what might be found

In this our coarser warehouse. At this day
I smile in many a mountain-solitude
At passages and fragments that remain
Of that inferior exhibition, played
By wooden images, a theatre
For wake or fair. And oftentimes do flit
Remembrances before me of old men,
Old humourists, who have been long in their graves,
And having almost in my mind put off
Their human names, have into phantoms passed
Of texture midway betwixt life and books.

I play the loiterer, 'tis enough to note
That here in dwarf proportions were expressed
The limbs of the great world – its goings-on
Collaterally portrayed as in mock fight,
A tournament of blows, some hardly dealt
Though short of mortal combat – and whate'er
Might of this pageant be supposed to hit
A simple rustic's notice, this way less,
More that way, was not wasted upon me.
And yet this spectacle may well demand
A more substantial name: no mimic show,
Itself a living part of a live whole,
A creek of the vast sea. For all degrees
And shapes of spurious fame and short-lived praise
Here sat in state, and, fed with daily alms,
Retainers won away from solid good.
And here was labour, his own bond-slave; hope,
That never set the pains against the prize;
Idleness halting with his weary clog,
And poor misguided shame, and witless fear,
And simple pleasure, foraging for death;
Honour misplaced, and dignity astray;
Feuds, factions, flatteries, enmity, and guile;
Murmuring submission, and bald government
(The idol weak as the idolator),
And decency and custom starving truth,

Of less elaborate fabric. At this day
I smile, in many a mountain solitude
Conjuring up scenes as obsolete in freaks
Of character, in points of wit as broad,
As aught by wooden images performed
For entertainment of the gaping crowd
At wake or fair. And oftentimes do flit
Remembrances before me of old men –
Old humourists, who have been long in their graves,
And having almost in my mind put off
Their human names, have into phantoms passed
Of texture midway between life and books.

I play the loiterer: 'tis enough to note
That here in dwarf proportions were expressed
The limbs of the great world; its eager strifes
Collaterally pourtrayed, as in mock fight,
A tournament of blows, some hardly dealt
Though short of mortal combat; and whate'er
Might in this pageant be supposed to hit
An artless rustic's notice, this way less,
More that way, was not wasted upon me –
And yet the spectacle may well demand
A more substantial name, no mimic show,
Itself a living part of a live whole,
A creek in the vast sea; for, all degrees
And shapes of spurious fame and short-lived praise
Here sate in state, and fed with daily alms
Retainers won away from solid good;
And here was Labour, his own bond-slave; Hope,
That never set the pains against the prize;
Idleness halting with his weary clog,
And poor misguided Shame, and witless Fear,
And simple Pleasure foraging for Death;
Honour misplaced, and Dignity astray;
Feuds, factions, flatteries, enmity, and guile
Murmuring submission, and bald government,
(The idol weak as the idolator,)
And Decency and Custom starving Truth,

And blind authority beating with his staff
The child that might have led him; emptiness
Followed as of good omen, and meek worth
Left to itself unheard of and unknown.

Of these and other kindred notices
I cannot say what portion is in truth
The naked recollection of that time,
And what may rather have been called to life
By after-meditation. But delight
That, in an easy temper lulled asleep,
Is still with innocence its own reward,
This surely was not wanting. Carelessly
I gazed, roving as through a cabinet
Or wide museum (thronged with fishes, gems,
Birds, crocodiles, shells) where little can be seen
Well understood, or naturally endeared,
Yet still does every step bring something forth
That quickens, pleases, stings – and here and there
A casual rarity is singled out
And has its brief perusal, then gives way
To others, all supplanted in their turn.
Meanwhile amid this gaudy congress, framed
Of things by nature most unneighbourly,
The head turns round and cannot right itself,
And though an aching and a barren sense
Of gay confusion still be uppermost,
With few wise longings and but little love,
Yet something to the memory sticks at last
Whence profit may be drawn in times to come.

Thus in submissive idleness, my friend,
The labouring time of autumn, winter, spring –
Nine months – rolled pleasingly away; the tenth
Returned me to my native hills again.

And blind Authority beating with his staff
The child that might have led him; Emptiness
Followed as of good omen, and meek Worth
Left to herself unheard of and unknown.

Of these and other kindred notices
I cannot say what portion is in truth
The naked recollection of that time,
And what may rather have been called to life
By after-meditation. But delight
That, in an easy temper lulled asleep,
Is still with Innocence its own reward,
This was not wanting. Carelessly I roamed
As through a wide museum from whose stores
A casual rarity is singled out
And has its brief perusal, then gives way
To others, all supplanted in their turn;
Till 'mid this crowded neighbourhood of things
That are by nature most unneighbourly,
The head turns round and cannot right itself;
And though an aching and a barren sense
Of gay confusion still be uppermost,
With few wise longings and but little love,
Yet to the memory something cleaves at last,
Whence profit may be drawn in times to come.

Thus in submissive idleness, my Friend!
The labouring time of autumn, winter, spring,
Eight months! rolled pleasingly away; the ninth
Came and returned me to my native hills.

Book Fourth

SUMMER VACATION

A pleasant sight it was when, having clomb
The Heights of Kendal, and that dreary moor
Was crossed, at length as from a rampart's edge
I overlooked the bed of Windermere.
I bounded down the hill, shouting amain
A lusty summons to the farther shore
For the old ferryman, and when he came
I did not step into the well-known boat
Without a cordial welcome. Thence right forth
I took my way, now drawing towards home,
To that sweet valley where I had been reared;
'Twas but a short hour's walk ere, veering round,
I saw the snow-white church upon its hill
Sit like a thronèd lady, sending out
A gracious look all over its domain.
Glad greetings had I, and some tears perhaps,
From my old dame, so motherly and good,
While she perused me with a parent's pride.
The thoughts of gratitude shall fall like dew

Book Fourth

SUMMER VACATION

Bright was the summer's noon when quickening steps
Followed each other till a dreary moor
Was crossed, a bare ridge clomb, upon whose top
Standing alone, as from a rampart's edge,
I overlooked the bed of Windermere,
Like a vast river, stretching in the sun.
With exultation, at my feet I saw
Lake, islands, promontories, gleaming bays,
A universe of Nature's fairest forms
Proudly revealed with instantaneous burst,
Magnificent, and beautiful, and gay.
I bounded down the hill shouting amain
For the old Ferryman; to the shout the rocks
Replied, and when the Charon of the flood
Had staid his oars, and touched the jutting pier,
I did not step into the well-known boat
Without a cordial greeting. Thence with speed
Up the familiar hill I took my way
Towards that sweet Valley where I had been reared;
'Twas but a short hour's walk, ere veering round
I saw the snow-white church upon her hill
Sit like a thronèd Lady, sending out
A gracious look all over her domain.
Yon azure smoke betrays the lurking town;
With eager footsteps I advance and reach
The cottage threshold where my journey closed.
Glad welcome had I, with some tears, perhaps,
From my old Dame, so kind and motherly,
While she perused me with a parent's pride.
The thoughts of gratitude shall fall like dew

Upon thy grave, good creature! While my heart
Can beat I never will forget thy name.
Heaven's blessing be upon thee where thou liest
After thy innocent and busy stir
In narrow cares, thy little daily growth
Of calm enjoyments – after eighty years,
And more than eighty, of untroubled life –
Childless, yet by the strangers to thy blood
Honoured with little less than filial love.
Great joy was mine to see thee once again,
Thee and thy dwelling, and a throng of things
About its narrow precincts, all beloved
And many of them seeming yet my own!

Why should I speak of what a thousand hearts
Have felt, and every man alive can guess?
The rooms, the court, the garden were not left
Long unsaluted, and the spreading pine
And broad stone table underneath its boughs –
Our summer seat in many a festive hour –
And that unruly child of mountain birth,
The froward brook, which, soon as he was boxed
Within our garden, found himself at once
As if by trick insidious and unkind,
Stripped of his voice and left to dimple down
Without an effort and without a will
A channel pavèd by the hand of man.
I looked at him and smiled, and smiled again,
And in the press of twenty thousand thoughts,
'Ha', quoth I, 'pretty prisoner, are you there!'
And now (reviewing soberly that hour)
I marvel that a fancy did not flash
Upon me, and a strong desire, straightway –
At sight of such an emblem that showed forth
So aptly my late course of even days
And all their smooth enthralment – to pen down
A satire on myself. My aged dame
Was with me, at my side; she guided me,
I willing – nay, nay, wishing – to be led.

Upon thy grave, good creature! While my heart
Can beat never will I forget thy name.
Heaven's blessing be upon thee where thou liest
After thy innocent and busy stir
In narrow cares, thy little daily growth
Of calm enjoyments, after eighty years,
And more than eighty, of untroubled life,
Childless, yet by the strangers to thy blood
Honoured with little less than filial love.
What joy was mine to see thee once again,
Thee and thy dwelling, and a crowd of things
About its narrow precincts all beloved,
And many of them seeming yet my own!
Why should I speak of what a thousand hearts
Have felt, and every man alive can guess?
The rooms, the court, the garden were not left
Long unsaluted, nor the sunny seat
Round the stone table under the dark pine,
Friendly to studious or to festive hours;
Nor that unruly child of mountain birth,
The famous brook, who, soon as he was boxed
Within our garden, found himself at once,
As if by trick insidious and unkind,
Stripped of his voice and left to dimple down
(Without an effort and without a will)
A channel paved by man's officious care.
I looked at him and smiled, and smiled again,
And in the press of twenty thousand thoughts,
'Ha,' quoth I, 'pretty prisoner, are you there!'
Well might sarcastic Fancy then have whispered,
'An emblem here behold of thy own life;
In its late course of even days with all
Their smooth enthralment;' but the heart was full,
Too full for that reproach. My aged Dame
Walked proudly at my side : she guided me;
I willing, nay – nay, wishing to be led.

The face of every neighbour whom I met
Was as a volume to me; some I hailed
Far off, upon the road or at their work,
Unceremonious greetings interchanged
With half the length of a long field between.
Among my schoolfellows I scattered round
A salutation that was more constrained,
Though earnest – doubtless with a little pride,
But with more shame, for my habiliments,
The transformation and the gay attire.

Delighted did I take my place again
At our domestic table, and, dear friend,
Relating simply as my wish has been
A poet's history, can I leave untold
The joy with which I laid me down at night
In my accustomed bed, more welcome now
Perhaps than if it had been more desired
Or been more often thought of with regret? –
That bed whence I had heard the roaring wind
And clamorous rain – that bed where I so oft
Had lain awake on breezy nights to watch
The moon in splendour couched among the leaves
Of a tall ash that near our cottage stood,
Had watched her with fixed eyes while to and fro
In the dark summit of the moving tree
She rocked with every impulse of the wind.

Among the faces which it pleased me well
To see again was one by ancient right
Our inmate, a rough terrier of the hills,
By birth and call of nature preordained
To hunt the badger and unearth the fox
Among the impervious crags, but having been
From youth our own adopted, he had passed
Into a gentler service. And when first
The boyish spirit flagged, and day by day
Along my veins I kindled with the stir,
The fermentation, and the vernal heat

– The face of every neighbour whom I met
Was like a volume to me; some were hailed
Upon the road, some busy at their work,
Unceremonious greetings interchanged
With half the length of a long field between.
Among my schoolfellows I scattered round
Like recognitions, but with some constraint
Attended, doubtless, with a little pride,
But with more shame, for my habiliments,
The transformation wrought by gay attire.
Not less delighted did I take my place
At our domestic table: and, dear Friend!
In this endeavour simply to relate
A Poet's history, may I leave untold
The thankfulness with which I laid me down
In my accustomed bed, more welcome now
Perhaps than if it had been more desired
Or been more often thought of with regret;
That lowly bed whence I had heard the wind
Roar and the rain beat hard, where I so oft
Had lain awake on summer nights to watch
The moon in splendour couched among the leaves
Of a tall ash, that near our cottage stood;
Had watched her with fixed eyes while to and fro
In the dark summit of the waving tree
She rocked with every impulse of the breeze.

Among the favourites whom it pleased me well
To see again, was one by ancient right
Our inmate, a rough terrier of the hills;
By birth and call of nature pre-ordained
To hunt the badger and unearth the fox
Among the impervious crags, but having been
From youth our own adopted, he had passed
Into a gentler service. And when first
The boyish spirit flagged, and day by day
Along my veins I kindled with the stir,
The fermentation, and the vernal heat

Of poesy, affecting private shades
Like a sick lover, then this dog was used
To watch me, an attendant and a friend,
Obsequious to my steps early and late –
Though often of such dilatory walk
Tired, and uneasy at the halts I made.
A hundred times, when in these wanderings
I have been busy with the toil of verse
(Great pains and little progress) and at once
Some fair enchanting image in my mind
Rose up full-formed like Venus from the sea,
Have I sprung forth towards him and let loose
My hand upon his back with stormy joy,
Caressing him again and yet again.
And when in the public roads at eventide
I sauntered, like a river murmuring
And talking to itself, at such a season
It was his custom to jog on before;
But duly, whensoever he had met
A passenger approaching, would he turn
To give me timely notice, and straightway,
Punctual to such admonishment, I hushed
My voice, composed my gait, and shaped myself
To give and take a greeting that might save
My name from piteous rumours such as wait
On men suspected to be crazed in brain.

Those walks well worthy to be prized and loved –
Regretted, that word too was on my tongue,
But they were richly laden with all good
And cannot be remembered but with thanks
And gratitude and perfect joy of heart –
Those walks did now like a returning spring
Come back on me again. When first I made
Once more the circuit of our little lake,
If ever happiness hath lodged with man
That day consummate happiness was mine,
Wide-spreading, steady, calm, contemplative.

Of poesy, affecting private shades
Like a sick Lover, then this dog was used
To watch me, an attendant and a friend,
Obsequious to my steps early and late,
Though often of such dilatory walk
Tired, and uneasy at the halts I made.
A hundred times when, roving high and low,
I have been harassed with the toil of verse,
Much pains and little progress, and at once
Some lovely Image in the song rose up
Full-formed, like Venus rising from the sea;
Then have I darted forwards to let loose
My hand upon his back with stormy joy,
Caressing him again and yet again.
And when at evening on the public way
I sauntered, like a river murmuring
And talking to itself when all things else
Are still, the creature trotted on before;
Such was his custom; but whene'er he met
A passenger approaching, he would turn
To give me timely notice, and straightway,
Grateful for that admonishment, I hushed
My voice, composed my gait, and, with the air
And mien of one whose thoughts are free, advanced
To give and take a greeting that might save
My name from piteous rumours, such as wait
On men suspected to be crazed in brain.

Those walks well worthy to be prized and loved –
Regretted! – that word, too, was on my tongue,
But they were richly laden with all good,
And cannot be remembered but with thanks
And gratitude, and perfect joy of heart –
Those walks in all their freshness now came back
Like a returning Spring. When first I made
Once more the circuit of our little lake,
If ever happiness hath lodged with man,
That day consummate happiness was mine,
Wide-spreading, steady, calm, contemplative.

The sun was set, or setting, when I left
Our cottage-door, and evening soon brought on
A sober hour – not winning or serene,
For cold and raw the air was, and untuned –
But as a face we love is sweetest then
When sorrow damps it, or, whatever look
It chance to wear is sweetest if the heart
Have fulness in itself, even so with me
It fared that evening. Gently did my soul
Put off her veil, and self-transmuted stood
Naked as in the presence of her God.
As on I walked, a comfort seemed to touch
A heart that had not been disconsolate;
Strength came where weakness was not known to be,
At least not felt; and restoration came
Like an intruder knocking at the door
Of unacknowledged weariness.

I took
The balance in my hand and weighed myself.
I saw but little, and thereat was pleased! –
Little did I remember, and even this
Still pleased me more. But I had hopes and peace
And swellings of the spirits, was rapt and soothed,
Conversed with promises, had glimmering views
How life pervades the undecaying mind –
How the immortal soul with godlike power
Informs, creates, and thaws the deepest sleep
That time can lay upon her – how, on earth,
Man, if he do but live within the light
Of high endeavours, daily spreads abroad
His being with a strength that cannot fail.
Nor was there want of milder thoughts: of love,
Of innocence and holiday repose,
And more than pastoral quiet in the heart
Of amplest projects, and a peaceful end
At last, or glorious, by endurance won.
Thus musing, in a wood I sat me down
Alone, continuing there to muse; meanwhile

The sun was set, or setting, when I left
Our cottage door, and evening soon brought on
A sober hour, not winning or serene,
For cold and raw the air was, and untuned;
But as a face we love is sweetest then
When sorrow damps it, or, whatever look
It chance to wear, is sweetest if the heart
Have fulness in herself; even so with me
It fared that evening. Gently did my soul
Put off her veil, and, self-transmuted, stood
Naked, as in the presence of her God.
While on I walked, a comfort seemed to touch
A heart that had not been disconsolate:
Strength came where weakness was not known to be,
At least not felt; and restoration came
Like an intruder knocking at the door
Of unacknowledged weariness. I took
The balance, and with firm hand weighed myself.
– Of that external scene which round me lay,
Little, in this abstraction, did I see;
Remembered less; but I had inward hopes
And swellings of the spirit, was rapt and soothed,
Conversed with promises, had glimmering views
How life pervades the undecaying mind;
How the immortal soul with God-like power
Informs, creates, and thaws the deepest sleep
That time can lay upon her; how on earth,
Man, if he do but live within the light
Of high endeavours, daily spreads abroad
His being armed with strength that cannot fail.
Nor was there want of milder thoughts, of love
Of innocence, and holiday repose;
And more than pastoral quiet, 'mid the stir
Of boldest projects, and a peaceful end
At last, or glorious, by endurance won.
Thus musing, in a wood I sate me down
Alone, continuing there to muse: the slopes

The mountain-heights were slowly overspread
With darkness, and before a rippling breeze
The long lake lengthened out its hoary line.
And in the sheltered coppice where I sat,
Around me from among the hazel leaves
(Now here, now there, stirred by the straggling wind)
Came intermittingly a breath-like sound,
A respiration short and quick, which oft –
Yea, might I say, again and yet again –
Mistaking for the panting of my dog,
The off-and-on companion of my walk,
I turned my head to look if he were there.

A freshness also found I at this time
In human life – the life I mean of those
Whose occupations really I loved –
The prospect often touched me with surprise,
Crowded and full and changed, as seemed to me,
Even as a garden in the heat of spring
After an eight-days' absence. For – to omit
The things which were the same and yet appeared
So different – amid this solitude,
The little vale where was my chief abode,
'Twas not indifferent to a youthful mind
To note perhaps some sheltered seat in which
An old man had been used to sun himself,
Now empty; pale-faced babes whom I had left
In arms, known children of the neighbourhood,
Now rosy prattlers tottering up and down;
And growing girls whose beauty, filched away
With all its pleasant promises, was gone
To deck some slighted playmate's homely cheek.

Yes, I had something of another eye,
And often looking round was moved to smiles
Such as a delicate work of humour breeds.
I read, without design, the opinions, thoughts
Of those plain-living people, in a sense
Of love and knowledge; with another eye

And heights meanwhile were slowly overspread
With darkness, and before a rippling breeze
The long lake lengthened out its hoary line,
And in the sheltered coppice where I sate,
Around me from among the hazel leaves,
Now here, now there, moved by the straggling wind,
Came ever and anon a breath-like sound,
Quick as the pantings of the faithful dog,
The off and on companion of my walk;
And such, at times, believing them to be,
I turned my head to look if he were there;
Then into solemn thought I passed once more.

A freshness also found I at this time
In human Life, the daily life of those
Whose occupations really I loved;
The peaceful scene oft filled me with surprise
Changed like a garden in the heat of spring
After an eight-days' absence. For (to omit
The things which were the same and yet appeared
Far otherwise) amid this rural solitude,
A narrow Vale where each was known to all,
'Twas not indifferent to a youthful mind
To mark some sheltering bower or sunny nook,
Where an old man had used to sit alone,
Now vacant; pale-faced babes whom I had left
In arms, now rosy prattlers at the feet
Of a pleased grandame tottering up and down;
And growing girls whose beauty, filched away
With all its pleasant promises, was gone
To deck some slighted playmate's homely cheek.

Yes, I had something of a subtler sense,
And often looking round was moved to smiles
Such as a delicate work of humour breeds;
I read, without design, the opinions, thoughts,
Of those plain-living people now observed
With clearer knowledge; with another eye

I saw the quiet woodman in the woods,
The shepherd on the hills. With new delight
(This chiefly) did I view my grey-haired dame,
Saw her go forth to church or other work
Of state, equipped in monumental trim:
Short velvet cloak, her bonnet of the like,
A mantle such as Spanish cavaliers
Wore in old time. Her smooth domestic life –
Affectionate without uneasiness –
Her talk, her business, pleased me; and no less
Her clear though shallow stream of piety
That ran on sabbath days a fresher course.
With thoughts unfelt till now I saw her read
Her bible on the Sunday afternoons,
And loved the book when she had dropped asleep
And made of it a pillow for her head.

Nor less do I remember to have felt
Distinctly manifested at this time
A dawning, even as of another sense:
A human-heartedness about my love
For objects hitherto the gladsome air
Of my own private being and no more –
Which I had loved even as a blessèd spirit
Or angel if he were to dwell on earth
Might love, in individual happiness.
But now there opened on me other thoughts
Of change, congratulation and regret,
A new-born feeling! It spread far and wide:
The trees, the mountains, shared it, and the brooks,
The stars of heaven – now seen in their old haunts –
White Sirius glittering o'er the southern crags,
Orion with his belt, and those fair Seven
(Acquaintances of every little child)
And Jupiter, my own belovèd star!
Whatever shadings of mortality
Had fallen upon these objects heretofore
Were different in kind – not tender (strong,
Deep, gloomy were they and severe, the scatterings

I saw the quiet woodman in the woods,
The shepherd roam the hills. With new delight,
This chiefly, did I note my grey-haired Dame;
Saw her go forth to church or other work
Of state, equipped in monumental trim;
Short velvet cloak, (her bonnet of the like),
A mantle such as Spanish Cavaliers
Wore in old time. Her smooth domestic life,
Affectionate without disquietude,
Her talk, her business, pleased me; and no less
Her clear though shallow stream of piety
That ran on Sabbath days a fresher course;
With thoughts unfelt till now I saw her read
Her Bible on hot Sunday afternoons,
And loved the book, when she had dropped asleep
And made of it a pillow for her head.

Nor less do I remember to have felt,
Distinctly manifested at this time,
A human-heartedness about my love
For objects hitherto the absolute wealth
Of my own private being and no more:
Which I had loved, even as a blessed spirit
Or Angel, if he were to dwell on earth,
Might love in individual happiness.
But now there opened on me other thoughts
Of change, congratulation or regret,
A pensive feeling! It spread far and wide;
The trees, the mountains shared it, and the brooks,
The stars of Heaven, now seen in their old haunts –
White Sirius glittering o'er the southern crags,
Orion with his belt, and those fair Seven,
Acquaintances of every little child,
And Jupiter, my own beloved star!
Whatever shadings of mortality,
Whatever imports from the world of death
Had come among these objects heretofore,
Were, in the main, of mood less tender: strong,
Deep, gloomy were they, and severe; the scatterings

Of childhood) – and moreover had given way
In later youth to beauty, and to love
Enthusiastic, to delight and joy.

As one who hangs down-bending from the side
Of a slow-moving boat upon the breast
Of a still water, solacing himself
With such discoveries as his eye can make
Beneath him in the bottom of the deeps,
Sees many beauteous sights (weeds, fishes, flowers,
Grots, pebbles, roots of trees) and fancies more,
Yet often is perplexed and cannot part
The shadow from the substance – rocks and sky,
Mountains and clouds, from that which is indeed
The region, and the things which there abide
In their true dwelling – now is crossed by gleam
Of his own image, by a sunbeam now,
And motions that are sent he knows not whence,
Impediments that make his task more sweet;
Such pleasant office have we long pursued
Incumbent o'er the surface of past time
With like success. Nor have we often looked
On more alluring shows (to me, at least),
More soft, or less ambiguously descried,
Than those which now we have been passing by,
And where we still are lingering.

Yet in spite
Of all these new employments of the mind,
There was an inner falling off. I loved,
Loved deeply, all that I had loved before –
More deeply even than ever – but a swarm
Of heady thoughts jostling each other, gauds
And feast and dance and public revelry
And sports and games (less pleasing in themselves,
Than as they were a badge glossy and fresh
Of manliness and freedom), these did now
Seduce me from the firm habitual quest
Of feeding pleasures, from that eager zeal,

Of awe or tremulous dread, that had given way
In later youth to yearnings of a love
Enthusiastic, to delight and hope.

As one who hangs down-bending from the side
Of a slow-moving boat, upon the breast
Of a still water, solacing himself
With such discoveries as his eye can make
Beneath him in the bottom of the deep,
Sees many beauteous sights – weeds, fishes, flowers,
Grots, pebbles, roots of trees, and fancies more,
Yet often is perplexed and cannot part
The shadow from the substance, rocks and sky,
Mountains and clouds, reflected in the depth
Of the clear flood, from things which there abide
In their true dwelling; now is crossed by gleam
Of his own image, by a sun-beam now,
And wavering motions sent he knows not whence,
Impediments that make his task more sweet;
Such pleasant office have we long pursued
Incumbent o'er the surface of past time
With like success, nor often have appeared
Shapes fairer or less doubtfully discerned
Than these to which the Tale, indulgent Friend!
Would now direct thy notice. Yet in spite
Of pleasure won, and knowledge not withheld,
There was an inner falling off – I loved,
Loved deeply all that had been loved before,
More deeply even than ever: but a swarm
Of heady schemes jostling each other, gawds,
And feast and dance, and public revelry,
And sports and games (too grateful in themselves,
Yet in themselves less grateful, I believe,
Than as they were a badge glossy and fresh
Of manliness and freedom) all conspired
To lure my mind from firm habitual quest
Of feeding pleasures, to depress the zeal

Those yearnings, which had every day been mine –
A wild, unworldly-minded youth, given up
To nature and to books, or, at the most,
From time to time, by inclination shipped
One among many in societies
That were, or seemed, as simple as myself.
But now was come a change. It would demand
Some skill, and longer time than may be spared,
To paint even to myself these vanities,
And how they wrought. But sure it is that now
Contagious air did oft environ me,
Unknown among these haunts in former days.
The very garments that I wore appeared
To prey upon my strength, and stopped the course
And quiet stream of self-forgetfulness.
Something there was about me that perplexed
The authentic sight of reason, pressed too closely
On that religious dignity of mind
That is the very faculty of truth –
Which wanting (either from the very first
A function never lighted up, or else
Extinguished), man, a creature great and good,
Seems but a pageant plaything with vile claws,
And this great frame of breathing elements,
A senseless idol.

This vague heartless chase
Of trivial pleasures was a poor exchange
For books and nature at that early age.
'Tis true some casual knowledge might be gained
Of character or life; but at that time,
Of manners put to school I took small note,
And all my deeper passions lay elsewhere.
Far better had it been to exalt the mind
By solitary study, to uphold
Intense desire by thought and quietness –
And yet, in chastisement of these regrets,
The memory of one particular hour

And damp those yearnings which had once been mine –
A wild, unworldly-minded youth, given up
To his own eager thoughts. It would demand
Some skill, and longer time than may be spared,
To paint these vanities, and how they wrought
In haunts where they, till now, had been unknown.
It seemed the very garments that I wore
Preyed on my strength, and stopped the quiet stream
Of self-forgetfulness.

Yes, that heartless chase
Of trivial pleasures was a poor exchange
For books and nature at that early age.
'Tis true, some casual knowledge might be gained
Of character or life; but at that time,
Of manners put to school I took small note,
And all my deeper passions lay elsewhere.
Far better had it been to exalt the mind
By solitary study, to uphold
Intense desire through meditative peace;
And yet, for chastisement of these regrets,
The memory of one particular hour

Does here rise up against me!

In a throng,
A festal company of maids and youths,
Old men and matrons staid – promiscuous rout,
A medley of all tempers – I had passed
The night in dancing, gaiety, and mirth,
With din of instruments and shuffling feet
And glancing forms and tapers glittering
And unaimed prattle flying up and down,
Spirits upon the stretch, and here and there
Slight shocks of young love-liking interspersed
That mounted up like joy into the head
And tingled through the veins. Ere we retired
The cock had crowed, the sky was bright with day;
Two miles I had to walk along the fields
Before I reached my home. Magnificent
The morning was, a memorable pomp,
More glorious than I ever had beheld.
The sea was laughing at a distance; all
The solid mountains were as bright as clouds,
Grain-tinctured, drenched in empyrean light;
And in the meadows and the lower grounds
Was all the sweetness of a common dawn –
Dews, vapours, and the melody of birds,
And labourers going forth into the fields.
Ah, need I say, dear friend, that to the brim
My heart was full? I made no vows, but vows
Were then made for me: bond unknown to me
Was given that I should be, else sinning greatly,
A dedicated spirit. On I walked
In blessedness, which even yet remains.

Strange rendezvous my mind was at that time,
A parti-coloured show of grave and gay,
Solid and light, short-sighted and profound –
Of inconsiderate habits and sedate
Consorting in one mansion unreproved.
I knew the worth of that which I possessed,

Doth here rise up against me. 'Mid a throng
Of maids and youths, old men, and matrons staid,
A medley of all tempers, I had passed
The night in dancing, gaiety, and mirth,
With din of instruments and shuffling feet,
And glancing forms, and tapers glittering,
And unaimed prattle flying up and down;
Spirits upon the stretch, and here and there
Slight shocks of young love-liking interspersed,
Whose transient pleasure mounted to the head,
And tingled through the veins. Ere we retired,
The cock had crowed, and now the eastern sky
Was kindling, not unseen, from humble copse
And open field, through which the pathway wound,
And homeward led my steps. Magnificent
The morning rose, in memorable pomp,
Glorious as e'er I had beheld – in front,
The sea lay laughing at a distance; near,
The solid mountains shone, bright as the clouds,
Grain-tinctured, drenched in empyrean light;
And in the meadows and the lower grounds
Was all the sweetness of a common dawn –
Dews, vapours, and the melody of birds,
And labourers going forth to till the fields.

Ah! need I say, dear Friend! that to the brim
My heart was full; I made no vows, but vows
Were then made for me; bond unknown to me
Was given, that I should be, else sinning greatly,
A dedicated Spirit. On I walked
In thankful blessedness, which yet survives.

Strange rendezvous! My mind was at that time
A parti-coloured show of grave and gay,
Solid and light, short-sighted and profound;
Of inconsiderate habits and sedate,
Consorting in one mansion unreproved.
The worth I knew of powers that I possessed,

Though slighted and misused. Besides in truth
That summer, swarming as it did with thoughts
Transient and loose, yet wanted not a store
Of primitive hours, when – by these hindrances
Unthwarted – I experienced in myself
Conformity as just as that of old
To the end and written spirit of God's works,
Whether held forth in nature or in man.

From many wanderings that have left behind
Remembrances not lifeless, I will here
Single out one, then pass to other themes.
A favourite pleasure hath it been with me
From time of earliest youth to walk alone
Along the public way, when, for the night
Deserted, in its silence it assumes
A character of deeper quietness
Than pathless solitudes. At such an hour
Once, ere these summer months were passed away,
I slowly mounted up a steep ascent
Where the road's watery surface, to the ridge

Though slighted and too oft misused. Besides,
That summer, swarming as it did with thoughts
Transient and idle, lacked not intervals
When Folly from the frown of fleeting Time
Shrunk, and the mind experienced in herself
Conformity as just as that of old
To the end and written spirit of God's works,
Whether held forth in Nature or in Man,
Through pregnant vision, separate or conjoined.

When from our better selves we have too long
Been parted by the hurrying world, and droop,
Sick of its business, of its pleasures tired,
How gracious, how benign, is Solitude;
How potent a mere image of her sway;
Most potent when impressed upon the mind
With an appropriate human centre – hermit,
Deep in the bosom of the wilderness;
Votary (in vast cathedral, where no foot
Is treading, where no other face is seen)
Kneeling at prayers; or watchman on the top
Of lighthouse, beaten by Atlantic waves;
Or as the soul of that great Power is met
Sometimes embodied on a public road,
When, for the night deserted, it assumes
A character of quiet more profound
Than pathless wastes.

Once, when those summer months
Were flown, and autumn brought its annual show
Of oars with oars contending, sails with sails,
Upon Winander's spacious breast, it chanced
That – after I had left a flower-decked room
(Whose in-door pastime, lighted up, survived
To a late hour), and spirits overwrought
Were making night do penance for a day
Spent in a round of strenuous idleness –
My homeward course led up a long ascent,
Where the road's watery surface, to the top

Of that sharp rising, glittered in the moon
And seemed before my eyes another stream
Creeping with silent lapse to join the brook
That murmured in the valley.

On I went
Tranquil, receiving in my own despite
Amusement, as I slowly passed along,
From such near objects as from time to time
Perforce intruded on the listless sense
Quiescent and disposed to sympathy,
With an exhausted mind worn out by toil
And all unworthy of the deeper joy
Which waits on distant prospect – cliff or sea,
The dark blue vault and universe of stars.
Thus did I steal along that silent road,
My body from the stillness drinking in
A restoration like the calm of sleep,
But sweeter far. Above, before, behind,
Around me, all was peace and solitude:
I looked not round, nor did the solitude
Speak to my eye, but it was heard and felt.
Oh happy state – what beauteous pictures now
Rose in harmonious imagery! They rose
As from some distant region of my soul
And came along like dreams; yet such as left
Obscurely mingled with their passing forms
A consciousness of animal delight,
A self-possession felt in every pause
And every gentle movement of my frame.

While thus I wandered, step by step led on,
It chanced a sudden turning of the road
Presented to my view an uncouth shape,
So near that, slipping back into the shade
Of a thick hawthorn, I could mark him well,
Myself unseen. He was of stature tall,
A foot above man's common measure tall,

Of that sharp rising, glittered to the moon
And bore the semblance of another stream
Stealing with silent lapse to join the brook
That murmured in the vale. All else was still;
No living thing appeared in earth or air,
And, save the flowing water's peaceful voice,
Sound there was none – but, lo! an uncouth shape,
Shown by a sudden turning of the road,
So near that, slipping back into the shade
Of a thick hawthorn, I could mark him well,
Myself unseen. He was of stature tall,
A span above man's common measure, tall,

Stiff in his form, and upright, lank and lean –
A man more meagre, as it seemed to me,
Was never seen abroad by night or day.
His arms were long, and bare his hands; his mouth
Showed ghastly in the moonlight; from behind,
A milestone propped him, and his figure seemed
Half sitting, and half standing. I could mark
That he was clad in military garb,
Though faded yet entire. He was alone,
Had no attendant, neither dog, nor staff,
Nor knapsack; in his very dress appeared
A desolation, a simplicity,
That seemed akin to solitude. Long time
Did I peruse him with a mingled sense
Of fear and sorrow. From his lips meanwhile
There issued murmuring sounds, as if of pain
Or of uneasy thought; yet still his form
Kept the same steadiness, and at his feet
His shadow lay, and moved not. In a glen
Hard by, a village stood, whose roofs and doors
Were visible among the scattered trees,
Scarce distant from the spot an arrow's flight.
I wished to see him move, but he remained
Fixed to his place, and still from time to time
Sent forth a murmuring voice of dead complaint,
Groans scarcely audible.

Without self-blame
I had not thus prolonged my watch; and now,
Subduing my heart's specious cowardice,
I left the shady nook where I had stood
And hailed him. Slowly from his resting-place
He rose, and with a lean and wasted arm
In measured gesture lifted to his head
Returned my salutation, then resumed
His station as before. And when erelong
I asked his history, he in reply
Was neither slow nor eager, but unmoved
And with a quiet uncomplaining voice,

Stiff, lank, and upright; a more meagre man
Was never seen before by night or day.
Long were his arms, pallid his hands; his mouth
Looked ghastly in the moonlight: from behind,
A mile-stone propped him; I could also ken
That he was clothed in military garb,
Though faded, yet entire. Companionless,
No dog attending, by no staff sustained,
He stood, and in his very dress appeared
A desolation, a simplicity,
To which the trappings of a gaudy world
Make a strange back-ground. From his lips, ere long,
Issued low muttered sounds, as if of pain
Or some uneasy thought; yet still his form
Kept the same awful steadiness – at his feet
His shadow lay, and moved not. From self-blame
Not wholly free, I watched him thus; at length
Subduing my heart's specious cowardice,
I left the shady nook where I had stood
And hailed him. Slowly from his resting-place
He rose, and with a lean and wasted arm
In measured gesture lifted to his head
Returned my salutation; then resumed
His station as before; and when I asked
His history, the veteran, in reply,
Was neither slow nor eager; but, unmoved,
And with a quiet uncomplaining voice,

A stately air of mild indifference,
He told in simple words a soldier's tale –
That in the tropic islands he had served,
Whence he had landed scarcely ten days past;
That on his landing he had been dismissed,
And now was travelling to his native home.
At this, I turned and looked towards the village
But all were gone to rest, the fires all out,
And every silent window to the moon
Shone with a yellow glitter. 'No one there',
Said I, 'is waking; we must measure back
The way which we have come. Behind yon wood
A labourer dwells, and (take it on my word)
He will not murmur should we break his rest,
And with a ready heart will give you food
And lodging for the night.' At this he stooped
And from the ground took up an oaken staff
By me yet unobserved – a traveller's staff
Which I suppose from his slack hand had dropped,
And lain till now neglected in the grass.

Towards the cottage without more delay
We shaped our course. As it appeared to me
He travelled without pain, and I beheld
With ill-suppressed astonishment his tall
And ghastly figure moving at my side;
Nor, while we journeyed thus, could I forbear
To question him of what he had endured
From hardship, battle, or the pestilence.
He all the while was in demeanour calm,
Concise in answer. Solemn and sublime
He might have seemed, but that in all he said
There was a strange half-absence, and a tone
Of weakness and indifference, as of one
Remembering the importance of his theme
But feeling it no longer. We advanced
Slowly, and ere we to the wood were come
Discourse had ceased. Together on we passed
In silence through the shades gloomy and dark;

A stately air of mild indifference,
He told in few plain words a soldier's tale –
That in the Tropic Islands he had served,
Whence he had landed scarcely three weeks past;
That on his landing he had been dismissed,
And now was travelling towards his native home.
This heard, I said, in pity, 'Come with me.'
He stooped, and straightway from the ground took up
An oaken staff by me yet unobserved –
A staff which must have dropt from his slack hand
And lay till now neglected in the grass.
Though weak his step and cautious, he appeared
To travel without pain, and I beheld,
With an astonishment but ill suppressed,
His ghostly figure moving at my side;
Nor could I, while we journeyed thus, forbear
To turn from present hardships to the past,
And speak of war, battle, and pestilence,
Sprinkling this talk with questions, better spared,
On what he might himself have seen or felt.
He all the while was in demeanour calm,
Concise in answer; solemn and sublime
He might have seemed, but that in all he said
There was a strange half-absence, as of one
Knowing too well the importance of his theme,
But feeling it no longer. Our discourse
Soon ended, and together on we passed
In silence through a wood gloomy and still.

Then, turning up along an open field,
We gained the cottage. At the door I knocked,
Calling aloud 'My friend, here is a man
By sickness overcome. Beneath your roof
This night let him find rest, and give him food,
If food he need, for he is faint and tired.'
Assured that now my comrade would repose
In comfort, I entreated that henceforth
He would not linger in the public ways
But ask for timely furtherance, and help
Such as his state required. At this reproof,
With the same ghastly mildness in his look
He said 'My trust is in the God of Heaven,
And in the eye of him that passes me!'

The cottage door was speedily unlocked;
And now the soldier touched his hat again
With his lean hand, and in a voice that seemed
To speak with a reviving interest
Till then unfelt, he thanked me. I returned
The blessing of the poor unhappy man,
And so we parted. Back I cast a look,
And lingered near the door a little space,
Then sought with quiet heart my distant home.

Up-turning, then, along an open field,
We reached a cottage. At the door I knocked,
And earnestly to charitable care
Commended him as a poor friendless man,
Belated and by sickness overcome.
Assured that now the traveller would repose
In comfort, I entreated that henceforth
He would not linger in the public ways,
But ask for timely furtherance and help
Such as his state required. At this reproof,
With the same ghastly mildness in his look,
He said, 'My trust is in the God of Heaven,
And in the eye of him who passes me!'

The cottage door was speedily unbarred,
And now the soldier touched his hat once more
With his lean hand, and in a faltering voice,
Whose tone bespake reviving interests
Till then unfelt, he thanked me; I returned
The farewell blessing of the patient man,
And so we parted. Back I cast a look,
And lingered near the door a little space,
Then sought with quiet heart my distant home.

Book Fifth
BOOKS

Even in the steadiest mood of reason, when
All sorrow for thy transitory pains
Goes out, it grieves me for thy state, o man,
Thou paramount creature, and thy race, while ye
Shall sojourn on this planet – not for woes
Which thou endurest (that weight, albeit huge,
I charm away), but for those palms achieved
Through length of time, by study and hard thought,
The honours of thy high endowments. There
My sadness finds its fuel.

Hitherto
In progress through this verse my mind hath looked
Upon the speaking face of earth and heaven
As her prime teacher, intercourse with man
Established by the sovereign intellect,
Who through that bodily image has diffused
A soul divine which we participate,
A deathless spirit. Thou also, man, hast wrought,
For commerce of thy nature with itself,
Things worthy of unconquerable life;
And yet we feel – we cannot choose but feel –
That these must perish. Tremblings of the heart
It gives to think that the immortal being
No more shall need such garments. And yet man,
As long as he shall be the child of earth,
Might almost 'weep to have' what he may lose,
Nor be himself extinguished, but survive
Abject, depressed, forlorn, disconsolate.
A thought is with me sometimes, and I say

Book Fifth
BOOKS

When Contemplation, like the night-calm felt
Through earth and sky, spreads widely, and sends deep
Into the soul its tranquillising power,
Even then I sometimes grieve for thee, O Man,
Earth's paramount Creature! not so much for woes
That thou endurest; heavy though that weight be,
Cloud-like it mounts, or touched with light divine
Doth melt away; but for those palms achieved,
Through length of time, by patient exercise
Of study and hard thought; there, there, it is
That sadness finds its fuel. Hitherto,
In progress through this Verse, my mind hath looked
Upon the speaking face of earth and heaven
As her prime teacher, intercourse with man
Established by the sovereign Intellect,
Who through that bodily image hath diffused,
As might appear to the eye of fleeting time,
A deathless spirit. Thou also, man! hast wrought,
For commerce of thy nature with herself,
Things that aspire to unconquerable life;
And yet we feel – we cannot choose but feel –
That they must perish. Tremblings of the heart
It gives, to think that our immortal being
No more shall need such garments; and yet man,
As long as he shall be the child of earth,
Might almost 'weep to have' what he may lose,
Nor be himself extinguished, but survive,
Abject, depressed, forlorn, disconsolate.
A thought is with me sometimes, and I say, –

'Should earth by inward throes be wrenched throughout,
Or fire be sent from far to wither all
Her pleasant habitations, and dry up
Old ocean in his bed, left singed and bare,
Yet would the living presence still subsist
Victorious, and composure would ensue,
And kindlings like the morning – presage sure,
Though slow perhaps, of a returning day.
But all the meditations of mankind,
Yea, all the adamantine holds of truth
By reason built, or passion (which itself
Is highest reason in a soul sublime),
The consecrated works of bard and sage,
Sensuous or intellectual, wrought by men,
Twin labourers and heirs of the same hopes –
Where would they be? Oh, why has not the mind
Some element to stamp her image on
In nature somewhat nearer to her own?
Why, gifted with such powers to send abroad
Her spirit, must it lodge in shrines so frail?'

One day, when in the hearing of a friend
I had given utterance to thoughts like these,
He answered with a smile that in plain truth
'Twas going far to seek disquietude;
But on the front of his reproof confessed
That he at sundry seasons had himself
Yielded to kindred hauntings – and forthwith
Added that once upon a summer's noon
While he was sitting in a rocky cave
By the sea-side (perusing, as it chanced,
The famous history of the errant knight
Recorded by Cervantes) these same thoughts
Came to him, and to height unusual rose
While listlessly he sat, and having closed
The book, had turned his eyes towards the sea.
On poetry and geometric truth
(The knowledge that endures), upon these two
And their high privilege of lasting life

Should the whole frame of earth by inward throes
Be wrenched, or fire come down from far to scorch
Her pleasant habitations, and dry up
Old Ocean, in his bed left singed and bare,
Yet would the living Presence still subsist
Victorious, and composure would ensue,
And kindlings like the morning – presage sure
Of day returning and of life revived.
But all the meditations of mankind,
Yea, all the adamantine holds of truth
By reason built, or passion, which itself
Is highest reason in a soul sublime;
The consecrated works of Bard and Sage,
Sensuous or intellectual, wrought by men,
Twin labourers and heirs of the same hopes;
Where would they be? Oh! why hath not the Mind
Some element to stamp her image on
In nature somewhat nearer to her own?
Why, gifted with such powers to send abroad
Her spirit, must it lodge in shrines so frail?

One day, when from my lips a like complaint
Had fallen in presence of a studious friend,
He with a smile made answer, that in truth
'Twas going far to seek disquietude;
But on the front of his reproof confessed
That he himself had oftentimes given way
To kindred hauntings. Whereupon I told,
That once in the stillness of a summer's noon,
While I was seated in a rocky cave
By the sea-side, perusing, so it chanced,
The famous history of the errant knight
Recorded by Cervantes, these same thoughts
Beset me, and to height unusual rose,
While listlessly I sate, and, having closed
The book, had turned my eyes toward the wide sea.
On poetry and geometric truth,
And their high privilege of lasting life,

Exempt from all internal injury,
He mused – upon these chiefly – and at length,
His senses yielding to the sultry air,
Sleep seized him and he passed into a dream.

He saw before him an arabian waste,
A desert, and he fancied that himself
Was sitting there in the wide wilderness
Alone upon the sands. Distress of mind
Was growing in him when, behold, at once
To his great joy a man was at his side,
Upon a dromedary mounted high!
He seemed an arab of the Bedouin tribes;
A lance he bore, and underneath one arm
A stone, and in the opposite hand a shell
Of a surpassing brightness. Much rejoiced
The dreaming man that he should have a guide
To lead him through the desert, and he thought –
While questioning himself what this strange freight
Which the newcomer carried through the waste
Could mean – the arab told him that the stone
(To give it in the language of the dream)
Was Euclid's *Elements*. 'And this', said he,
'This other', pointing to the shell, 'this book
Is something of more worth.' And at the word
The stranger, said my friend continuing,
Stretched forth the shell towards me, with command
That I should hold it to my ear. I did so
And heard that instant in an unknown tongue,
Which yet I understood, articulate sounds,
A loud prophetic blast of harmony,
An ode in passion uttered, which foretold
Destruction to the children of the earth
By deluge now at hand.

No sooner ceased
The song, but with calm look the arab said
That all was true, that it was even so
As had been spoken, and that he himself

From all internal injury exempt,
I mused, upon these chiefly: and at length,
My senses yielding to the sultry air,
Sleep seized me, and I passed into a dream.
I saw before me stretched a boundless plain
Of sandy wilderness, all black and void,
And as I looked around, distress and fear
Came creeping over me, when at my side,
Close at my side, an uncouth shape appeared
Upon a dromedary, mounted high.
He seemed an Arab of the Bedouin tribes:
A lance he bore, and underneath one arm
A stone, and in the opposite hand a shell
Of a surpassing brightness. At the sight
Much I rejoiced, not doubting but a guide
Was present, one who with unerring skill
Would through the desert lead me; and while yet
I looked and looked, self-questioned what this freight
Which the new-comer carried through the waste
Could mean, the Arab told me that the stone
(To give it in the language of the dream)
Was 'Euclid's Elements;' and 'This,' said he,
'Is something of more worth;' and at the word
Stretched forth the shell, so beautiful in shape,
In colour so resplendent, with command
That I should hold it to my ear. I did so,
And heard that instant in an unknown tongue,
Which yet I understood, articulate sounds,
A loud prophetic blast of harmony;
An Ode, in passion uttered, which foretold
Destruction to the children of the earth
By deluge, now at hand. No sooner ceased
The song, than the Arab with calm look declared
That all would come to pass of which the voice
Had given forewarning, and that he himself

Was going then to bury those two books –
The one that held acquaintance with the stars
And wedded man to man by purest bond
Of nature, undisturbed by space or time;
The other that was a god, yea many gods,
Had voices more than all the winds, and was
A joy, a consolation, and a hope.
My friend continued, strange as it may seem
I wondered not, although I plainly saw
The one to be a stone, the other a shell,
Nor doubted once but that they both were books,
Having a perfect faith in all that passed.

A wish was now engendered in my fear
To cleave unto this man, and I begged leave
To share his errand with him. On he passed
Not heeding me; I followed, and took note
That he looked often backward with wild look,
Grasping his twofold treasure to his side.
Upon a dromedary, lance in rest
He rode, I keeping pace with him; and now
I fancied that he was the very knight
Whose tale Cervantes tells, yet not the knight,
But was an arab of the desert too –
Of these was neither, and was both at once.
His countenance meanwhile grew more disturbed,
And, looking backwards when he looked, I saw
A glittering light, and asked him whence it came.
'It is', said he, 'the waters of the deep
Gathering upon us.' Quickening then his pace,
He left me. I called after him aloud;
He heeded not, but with his twofold charge
Beneath his arm, before me, full in view,
I saw him riding o'er the desert sands
With the fleet waters of the drowning world
In chase of him. Whereat I waked in terror,
And saw the sea before me, and the book
In which I had been reading at my side.

Was going then to bury those two books:
The one that held acquaintance with the stars,
And wedded soul to soul in purest bond
Of reason, undisturbed by space or time;
The other that was a god, yea many gods,
Had voices more than all the winds, with power
To exhilarate the spirit, and to soothe,
Through every clime, the heart of human kind.
While this was uttering, strange as it may seem,
I wondered not, although I plainly saw
The one to be a stone, the other a shell;
Nor doubted once but that they both were books,
Having a perfect faith in all that passed.
Far stronger, now, grew the desire I felt
To cleave unto this man; but when I prayed
To share his enterprise, he hurried on
Reckless of me: I followed, not unseen,
For oftentimes he cast a backward look,
Grasping his twofold treasure. – Lance in rest,
He rode, I keeping pace with him; and now
He, to my fancy, had become the knight
Whose tale Cervantes tells; yet not the knight,
But was an Arab of the desert too;
Of these was neither, and was both at once.
His countenance, meanwhile, grew more disturbed;
And, looking backwards when he looked, mine eyes
Saw, over half the wilderness diffused,
A bed of glittering light: I asked the cause:
'It is,' said he, 'the waters of the deep
Gathering upon us;' quickening then the pace
Of the unwieldly creature he bestrode,
He left me: I called after him aloud;
He heeded not; but, with his twofold charge
Still in his grasp, before me, full in view,
Went hurrying o'er the illimitable waste,
With the fleet waters of a drowning world
In chase of him; whereat I waked in terror,
And saw the sea before me, and the book,
In which I had been reading, at my side.

Full often, taking from the world of sleep
This arab phantom which my friend beheld,
This semi-Quixote, I to him have given
A substance, fancied him a living man –
A gentle dweller in the desert, crazed
By love and feeling and internal thought
Protracted among endless solitudes –
Have shaped him, in the oppression of his brain,
Wandering upon this quest, and thus equipped.
And I have scarcely pitied him, have felt
A reverence for a being thus employed,
And thought that in the blind and awful lair
Of such a madness reason did lie couched.
Enow there are on earth to take in charge
Their wives, their children, and their virgin loves,
Or whatsoever else the heart holds dear –
Enow to think of these – yea, will I say,
In sober contemplation of the approach
Of such great overthrow, made manifest
By certain evidence, that I methinks
Could share that maniac's anxiousness, could go
Upon like errand. Oftentimes at least
Me hath such deep entrancement half possessed
When I have held a volume in my hand
(Poor earthly casket of immortal verse),
Shakespeare, or Milton, labourers divine!

Mighty, indeed supreme, must be the power
Of living nature, which could thus so long
Detain me from the best of other thoughts.
Even in the lisping time of infancy
And (later down) in prattling childhood – even
While I was travelling back among those days –
How could I ever play an ingrate's part?
Once more should I have made those bowers resound,
And intermingled strains of thankfulness
With their own thoughtless melodies. At least
It might have well beseemed me to repeat

Full often, taking from the world of sleep
This Arab phantom, which I thus beheld,
This semi-Quixote, I to him have given
A substance, fancied him a living man,
A gentle dweller in the desert, crazed
By love and feeling, and internal thought
Protracted among endless solitudes;
Have shaped him wandering upon this quest!
Nor have I pitied him; but rather felt
Reverence was due to a being thus employed;
And thought that, in the blind and awful lair
Of such a madness, reason did lie couched.
Enow there are on earth to take in charge
Their wives, their children, and their virgin loves,
Or whatsoever else the heart holds dear;
Enow to stir for these; yea, will I say,
Contemplating in soberness the approach
Of an event so dire, by signs in earth
Or heaven made manifest, that I could share
That maniac's fond anxiety, and go
Upon like errand. Oftentimes at least
Me hath such strong entrancement overcome,
When I have held a volume in my hand,
Poor earthly casket of immortal verse,
Shakespeare, or Milton, labourers divine!

Great and benign, indeed, must be the power
Of living nature, which could thus so long
Detain me from the best of other guides
And dearest helpers, left unthanked, unpraised,
Even in the time of lisping infancy;
And later down, in prattling childhood even,
While I was travelling back among those days,
How could I ever play an ingrate's part?
Once more should I have made those bowers resound,
By intermingling strains of thankfulness
With their own thoughtless melodies; at least
It might have well beseemed me to repeat

Some simply fashioned tale, to tell again
In slender accents of sweet verse some tale
That did bewitch me then and soothes me now.
O friend, o poet, brother of my soul,
Think not that I could ever pass along
Untouched by these remembrances – no, no,
But I was hurried forward by a stream
And could not stop. Yet wherefore should I speak?
Why call upon a few weak words to say
What is already written in the hearts
Of all that breathe – what in the path of all
Drops daily from the tongue of every child,
Wherever man is found? The trickling tear
Upon the cheek of listening infancy
Tells it, and the insuperable look
That drinks as if it never could be full.

That portion of my story I shall leave
There registered. Whatever else there be
Of power or pleasure, sown or fostered thus,
Peculiar to myself, let that remain
Where it lies hidden in its endless home
Among the depths of time. And yet it seems
That here, in memory of all books which lay
Their sure foundations in the heart of man
(Whether by native prose, or numerous verse)
That in the name of all inspirèd souls,
From Homer the great thunderer, from the voice
Which roars along the bed of Jewish song,
And that, more varied and elaborate,
Those trumpet-tones of harmony that shake
Our shores in England – from those loftiest notes
Down to the low and wren-like warblings made
For cottagers and spinners at the wheel
And weary travellers when they rest themselves
By the highways and hedges, ballad tunes,
Food for the hungry ears of little ones
And of old men who have survived their joy –
It seemeth, in behalf of these, the works,

Some simply fashioned tale, to tell again,
In slender accents of sweet verse, some tale
That did bewitch me then, and soothes me now.
O Friend! O Poet! brother of my soul,
Think not that I could pass along untouched
By these remembrances. Yet wherefore speak?
Why call upon a few weak words to say
What is already written in the hearts
Of all that breathe? – what in the path of all
Drops daily from the tongue of every child,
Wherever man is found? The trickling tear
Upon the cheek of listening Infancy
Proclaims it, and the insuperable look
That drinks as if it never could be full.

That portion of my story I shall leave
There registered: whatever else of power
Or pleasure sown, or fostered thus, may be
Peculiar to myself, let that remain
Where still it works, though hidden from all search
Among the depths of time. Yet is it just
That here, in memory of all books which lay
Their sure foundations in the heart of man,
Whether by native prose, or numerous verse,
That in the name of all inspirèd souls,
From Homer the great Thunderer, from the voice
That roars along the bed of Jewish song,
And that more varied and elaborate,
Those trumpet-tones of harmony that shake
Our shores in England, – from those loftiest notes
Down to the low and wren-like warblings, made
For cottagers and spinners at the wheel,
And sun-burnt travellers resting their tired limbs,
Stretched under wayside hedge-rows, ballad tunes,
Food for the hungry ears of little ones,
And of old men who have survived their joys:
'Tis just that in behalf of these, the works,

And of the men who framed them (whether known,
Or sleeping nameless in their scattered graves),
That I should here assert their rights, attest
Their honours, and should once for all pronounce
Their benediction, speak of them as powers
For ever to be hallowed – only less,
For what we may become and what we need,
Than nature's self, which is the breath of God.

Rarely and with reluctance would I stoop
To transitory themes, yet I rejoice –
And, by these thoughts admonished, must speak out
Thanksgivings from my heart – that I was reared
Safe from an evil which these days have laid
Upon the children of the land, a pest
That might have dried me up body and soul.
This verse is dedicate to nature's self,
And things that teach as nature teaches; then
Oh where had been the man, the poet where –
Where had we been, we two, belovèd friend –
If we, in lieu of wandering as we did
Through heights and hollows and bye-spots of tales
Rich with indigenous produce (open ground
Of fancy, happy pastures ranged at will)
Had been attended, followed, watched, and noosed,
Each in his several melancholy walk
Stringed like a poor man's heifer at its feed,
Led through the lanes in forlorn servitude –
Or rather, like a stallèd ox shut out
From touch of growing grass, that may not taste
A flower till it have yielded up its sweets
A prelibation to the mower's scythe.

Behold the parent hen amid her brood –
Though fledged and feathered, and well pleased to part
And straggle from her presence, still a brood,
And she herself from the maternal bond
Still undischarged. Yet does she little more

And of the men that framed them, whether known,
Or sleeping nameless in their scattered graves,
That I should here assert their rights, attest
Their honours, and should, once for all, pronounce
Their benediction; speak of them as Powers
For ever to be hallowed; only less,
For what we are and what we may become,
Than Nature's self, which is the breath of God,
Or His pure Word by miracle revealed.

Rarely and with reluctance would I stoop
To transitory themes; yet I rejoice,
And, by these thoughts admonished, will pour out
Thanks with uplifted heart, that I was reared
Safe from an evil which these days have laid
Upon the children of the land, a pest
That might have dried me up, body and soul.
This verse is dedicate to Nature's self,
And things that teach as Nature teaches: then,
Oh! where had been the Man, the Poet where,
Where had we been, we two, beloved Friend!
If in the season of unperilous choice,
In lieu of wandering, as we did, through vales
Rich with indigenous produce, open ground
Of Fancy, happy pastures ranged at will,
We had been followed, hourly watched, and noosed,
Each in his several melancholy walk
Stringed like a poor man's heifer at its feed,
Led through the lanes in forlorn servitude;
Or rather like a stallèd ox debarred
From touch of growing grass, that may not taste
A flower till it have yielded up its sweets
A prelibation to the mower's scythe.

Behold the parent hen amid her brood,
Though fledged and feathered, and well pleased to part
And straggle from her presence, still a brood,
And she herself from the maternal bond
Still undischarged; yet doth she little more

Than move with them in tenderness and love,
A centre of the circle which they make;
And now and then – alike from need of theirs
And call of her own natural appetites –
She scratches, ransacks up the earth for food,
Which they partake at pleasure. Early died
My honoured mother, she who was the heart
And hinge of all our learnings and our loves;
She left us destitute and, as we might,
Trooping together.

Little suits it me
To break upon the sabbath of her rest
With any thought that looks at others' blame,
Nor would I praise her but in perfect love.
Hence am I checked, but I will boldly say
In gratitude, and for the sake of truth,
Unheard by her, that she (not falsely taught,
Fetching her goodness rather from times past
Than shaping novelties from those to come)
Had no presumption, no such jealousy,
Nor did by habit of her thoughts mistrust
Our nature, but had virtual faith that he
Who fills the mother's breasts with innocent milk
Does also for our nobler part provide,
Under his great correction and control,
As innocent instincts, and as innocent food.
This was her creed, and therefore she was pure
From feverish dread of error and mishap
And evil (overweeningly so called)
Was not puffed up by false unnatural hopes,
Nor selfish with unnecessary cares,
Nor with impatience from the season asked
More than its timely produce – rather loved
The hours for what they are, than from regards
Glanced on their promises in restless pride.
Such was she; not from faculties more strong
Than others have, but from the times perhaps

Than move with them in tenderness and love,
A centre to the circle which they make;
And now and then, alike from need of theirs
And call of her own natural appetites,
She scratches, ransacks up the earth for food,
Which they partake at pleasure. Early died
My honoured Mother, she who was the heart
And hinge of all our learnings and our loves:
She left us destitute, and, as we might,
Trooping together. Little suits it me
To break upon the sabbath of her rest
With any thought that looks at others' blame;
Nor would I praise her but in perfect love.
Hence am I checked: but let me boldly say,
In gratitude, and for the sake of truth,
Unheard by her, that she, not falsely taught,
Fetching her goodness rather from times past,
Than shaping novelties for times to come,
Had no presumption, no such jealousy,
Nor did by habit of her thoughts mistrust
Our nature, but had virtual faith that He
Who fills the mother's breast with innocent milk,
Doth also for our nobler part provide,
Under His great correction and control,
As innocent instincts, and as innocent food;
Or draws for minds that are left free to trust
In the simplicities of opening life
Sweet honey out of spurned or dreaded weeds.
This was her creed, and therefore she was pure
From anxious fear of error or mishap,
And evil, overweeningly so called;
Was not puffed up by false unnatural hopes,
Nor selfish with unnecessary cares,
Nor with impatience from the season asked
More than its timely produce, rather loved
The hours for what they are, than from regard
Glanced on their promises in restless pride.
Such was she – not from faculties more strong
Than others have, but from the times, perhaps,

And spot in which she lived, and through a grace
Of modest meekness, simple-mindedness,
A heart that found benignity and hope,
Being itself benign.

My drift has scarcely
I fear been obvious, for I have recoiled
From showing as it is the monster birth
Engendered by these too industrious times.
Let few words paint it! 'Tis a child – no child,
But a dwarf man! – in knowledge, virtue, skill,
In what he is not and in what he is,
The noontide shadow of a man complete.
A worshipper of worldly seemliness,
Not quarrelsome (for that were far beneath
His dignity), with gifts he bubbles o'er
As generous as a fountain. Selfishness
May not come near him, gluttony or pride;
The wandering beggars propagate his name,
Dumb creatures find him tender as a nun.
Yet deem him not for this a naked dish
Of goodness merely, he is garnished out.
Arch are his notices, and nice his sense
Of the ridiculous; deceit and guile,
Meanness and falsehood, he detects, can treat
With apt and graceful laughter; nor is blind
To the broad follies of the licensed world;
Though shrewd, yet innocent himself withal,
And can read lectures upon innocence!

He is fenced round (nay armed, for aught we know,
In panoply complete) and fear itself,
Natural or supernatural alike,
Unless it leap upon him in a dream,
Touches him not. Briefly, the moral part
Is perfect, and in learning and in books
He is a prodigy. His discourse moves slow,
Massy and ponderous as a prison door,
Tremendously embossed with terms of art;

And spot in which she lived, and through a grace
Of modest meekness, simple-mindedness,
A heart that found benignity and hope,
Being itself benign.

My drift I fear
Is scarcely obvious; but, that common sense
May try this modern system by its fruits,
Leave let me take to place before her sight
A specimen pourtrayed with faithful hand.
Full early trained to worship seemliness,
This model of a child is never known
To mix in quarrels; that were far beneath
Its dignity; with gifts he bubbles o'er
As generous as a fountain; selfishness
May not come near him, nor the little throng
Of flitting pleasures tempt him from his path;
The wandering beggars propagate his name,
Dumb creatures find him tender as a nun,
And natural or supernatural fear,
Unless it leap upon him in a dream,
Touches him not. To enhance the wonder, see
How arch his notices, how nice his sense
Of the ridiculous; not blind is he
To the broad follies of the licensed world,
Yet innocent himself withal, though shrewd,
And can read lectures upon innocence;

Rank growth of propositions overruns
The stripling's brain; the path in which he treads
Is choked with grammars; cushion of divine
Was never such a type of thought profound
As is the pillow where he rests his head.
The ensigns of the empire which he holds,
The globe and sceptre of his royalties,
Are telescopes and crucibles and maps.
Ships he can guide across the pathless sea,
And tell you all their cunning; he can read
The inside of the earth, and spell the stars;
He knows the policies of foreign lands,
Can string you names of districts, cities, towns,
The whole world over, tight as beads of dew
Upon a gossamer thread! He sifts, he weighs,
Takes nothing upon trust: his teachers stare,
The country people pray for God's good grace
And tremble at his deep experiments.
All things are put to question. He must live
Knowing that he grows wiser every day
Or else not live at all – and seeing too
Each little drop of wisdom as it falls
Into the dimpling cistern of his heart.
Meanwhile old grandame earth is grieved to find
The playthings which her love designed for him
Unthought of: in their woodland beds the flowers
Weep, and the riversides are all forlorn.

Now this is hollow – 'tis a life of lies
From the beginning, and in lies must end.
Forth bring him to the air of common sense
And, fresh and showy as it is, the corpse
Slips from us into powder. Vanity,
That is his soul. There lives he, and there moves –
It is the soul of every thing he seeks –
That gone, nothing is left which he can love.
Nay, if a thought of purer birth should rise
To carry him towards a better clime,
Some busy helper still is on the watch

A miracle of scientific lore,
Ships he can guide across the pathless sea,
And tell you all their cunning; he can read
The inside of the earth, and spell the stars;
He knows the policies of foreign lands;
Can string you names of districts, cities, towns,
The whole world over, tight as beads of dew
Upon a gossamer thread; he sifts, he weighs;
All things are put to question; he must live
Knowing that he grows wiser every day
Or else not live at all, and seeing too
Each little drop of wisdom as it falls
Into the dimpling cistern of his heart:
For this unnatural growth the trainer blame,
Pity the tree. – Poor human vanity,
Wert thou extinguished, little would be left
Which he could truly love; but how escape?
For, ever as a thought of purer birth
Rises to lead him toward a better clime,
Some intermeddler still is on the watch
To drive him back, and pound him, like a stray,
Within the pinfold of his own conceit.
Meanwhile old grandame earth is grieved to find
The playthings, which her love designed for him,
Unthought of: in their woodland beds the flowers
Weep, and the river sides are all forlorn.

To drive him back, and pound him like a stray
Within the pinfold of his own conceit,
Which is his home, his natural dwelling place.
Oh, give us once again the wishing-cap
Of Fortunatus and the invisible coat
Of Jack the Giant-killer, Robin Hood
And Sabra in the forest with St George!
The child whose love is here, at least does reap
One precious gain – that he forgets himself.

These mighty workmen of our later age
Who with a broad highway have overbridged
The froward chaos of futurity,
Tamed to their bidding; they who have the art
To manage books, and things, and make them work
Gently on infant minds as does the sun
Upon a flower – the tutors of our youth,
The guides, the wardens of our faculties
And stewards of our labour, watchful men
And skilful in the usury of time,
Sages who in their prescience would control
All accidents, and to the very road
Which they have fashioned would confine us down
Like engines – when will they be taught
That in the unreasoning progress of the world
A wiser spirit is at work for us,
A better eye than theirs, most prodigal
Of blessings and most studious of our good,
Even in what seem our most unfruitful hours?

There was a boy – ye knew him well, ye cliffs
And islands of Winander! – many a time
At evening, when the stars had just begun
To move along the edges of the hills,
Rising or setting, would he stand alone
Beneath the trees or by the glimmering lake,
And there, with fingers interwoven, both hands
Pressed closely palm to palm and to his mouth
Uplifted, he as through an instrument

Oh! give us once again the wishing cap
Of Fortunatus, and the invisible coat
Of Jack the Giant-killer, Robin Hood,
And Sabra in the forest with St. George!
The child, whose love is here, at least, doth reap
One precious gain, that he forgets himself.

These mighty workmen of our later age,
Who, with a broad highway, have overbridged
The froward chaos of futurity,
Tamed to their bidding; they who have the skill
To manage books, and things, and make them act
On infant minds as surely as the sun
Deals with a flower; the keepers of our time,
The guides and wardens of our faculties,
Sages who in their prescience would control
All accidents, and to the very road
Which they have fashioned would confine us down,
Like engines; when will their presumption learn,
That in the unreasoning progress of the world
A wiser spirit is at work for us,
A better eye than theirs, most prodigal
Of blessings, and most studious of our good,
Even in what seem our most unfruitful hours?

There was a Boy: ye knew him well, ye cliffs
And islands of Winander! – many a time
At evening, when the earliest stars began
To move along the edges of the hills,
Rising or setting, would he stand alone
Beneath the trees or by the glimmering lake,
And there, with fingers interwoven, both hands
Pressed closely palm to palm, and to his mouth
Uplifted, he, as through an instrument,

Blew mimic hootings to the silent owls
That they might answer him. And they would shout
Across the watery vale, and shout again
Responsive to his call, with quivering peals
And long halloos and screams, and echoes loud
Redoubled and redoubled – concourse wild
Of mirth and jocund din. And when it chanced
That pauses of deep silence mocked his skill,
Then sometimes in that silence while he hung
Listening, a gentle shock of mild surprise
Has carried far into his heart the voice
Of mountain torrents; or the visible scene
Would enter unawares into his mind
With all its solemn imagery, its rocks,
Its woods, and that uncertain heaven, received
Into the bosom of the steady lake.

This boy was taken from his mates, and died
In childhood ere he was full ten years old.
Fair are the woods, and beauteous is the spot,
The vale where he was born. The churchyard hangs
Upon a slope above the village-school,
And there, along that bank, when I have passed
At evening, I believe that oftentimes
A full half-hour together I have stood
Mute, looking at the grave in which he lies.
Even now, methinks, I have before my sight
That self-same village church; I see her sit
(The thronèd lady spoken of erewhile)
On her green hill, forgetful of this boy
Who slumbers at her feet – forgetful too
Of all her silent neighbourhood of graves,
And listening only to the gladsome sounds
That, from the rural school ascending, play
Beneath her and about her. May she long
Behold a race of young ones like to those
With whom I herded! – easily indeed
We might have fed upon a fatter soil
Of arts and letters, but be that forgiven –

Blew mimic hootings to the silent owls,
That they might answer him; and they would shout
Across the watery vale, and shout again,
Responsive to his call, with quivering peals,
And long halloos and screams, and echoes loud,
Redoubled and redoubled, concourse wild
Of jocund din; and, when a lengthened pause
Of silence came and baffled his best skill,
Then sometimes, in that silence while he hung
Listening, a gentle shock of mild surprise
Has carried far into his heart the voice
Of mountain torrents; or the visible scene
Would enter unawares into his mind,
With all its solemn imagery, its rocks,
Its woods, and that uncertain heaven, received
Into the bosom of the steady lake.

This Boy was taken from his mates, and died
In childhood, ere he was full twelve years old.
Fair is the spot, most beautiful the vale
Where he was born; the grassy churchyard hangs
Upon a slope above the village school,
And through that churchyard when my way has led
On summer evenings, I believe that there
A long half hour together I have stood
Mute, looking at the grave in which he lies!
Even now appears before the mind's clear eye
That self-same village church; I see her sit
(The thronèd Lady whom erewhile we hailed)
On her green hill, forgetful of this Boy
Who slumbers at her feet, – forgetful, too,
Of all her silent neighbourhood of graves,
And listening only to the gladsome sounds
That, from the rural school ascending, play
Beneath her and about her. May she long
Behold a race of young ones like to those
With whom I herded! – (easily, indeed,
We might have fed upon a fatter soil
Of arts and letters – but be that forgiven) –

A race of real children, not too wise,
Too learnèd, or too good, but wanton, fresh,
And bandied up and down by love and hate;
Fierce, moody, patient, venturous, modest, shy,
Mad at their sports like withered leaves in winds;
Though doing wrong and suffering, and full oft
Bending beneath our life's mysterious weight
Of pain and fear, yet still in happiness
Not yielding to the happiest upon earth.
Simplicity in habit, truth in speech,
Be these the daily strengtheners of their minds;
May books and nature be their early joy,
And knowledge rightly honoured with that name –
Knowledge not purchased with the loss of power!

Well do I call to mind the very week
When I was first entrusted to the care
Of that sweet valley – when its paths, its shores
And brooks, were like a dream of novelty
To my half-infant thoughts – that very week,
While I was roving up and down alone
Seeking I knew not what, I chanced to cross
One of those open fields which, shaped like ears,
Make green peninsulas on Esthwaite's Lake.
Twilight was coming on, yet through the gloom
I saw distinctly on the opposite shore
A heap of garments, left, as I supposed,
By one who there was bathing. Long I watched,
But no one owned them; meanwhile the calm lake
Grew dark with all the shadows on its breast,
And now and then a fish up-leaping snapped
The breathless stillness. The succeeding day
(Those unclaimed garments telling a plain tale)
Went there a company, and in their boat
Sounded with grappling irons and long poles.
At length, the dead man, mid that beauteous scene

A race of real children; not too wise,
Too learned, or too good; but wanton, fresh,
And bandied up and down by love and hate;
Not unresentful where self-justified;
Fierce, moody, patient, venturous, modest, shy;
Mad at their sports like withered leaves in winds;
Though doing wrong and suffering, and full oft
Bending beneath our life's mysterious weight
Of pain, and doubt, and fear, yet yielding not
In happiness to the happiest upon earth.
Simplicity in habit, truth in speech,
Be these the daily strengtheners of their minds;
May books and Nature be their early joy!
And knowledge, rightly honoured with that name –
Knowledge not purchased by the loss of power!

Well do I call to mind the very week
When I was first intrusted to the care
Of that sweet Valley; when its paths, its shores,
And brooks were like a dream of novelty
To my half-infant thoughts; that very week,
While I was roving up and down alone,
Seeking I knew not what, I chanced to cross
One of those open fields, which, shaped like ears,
Make green peninsulas on Esthwaite's Lake:
Twilight was coming on, yet through the gloom
Appeared distinctly on the opposite shore
A heap of garments, as if left by one
Who might have there been bathing. Long I watched,
But no one owned them; meanwhile the calm lake
Grew dark with all the shadows on its breast,
And, now and then, a fish up-leaping snapped
The breathless stillness. The succeeding day,
Those unclaimed garments telling a plain tale
Drew to the spot an anxious crowd; some looked
In passive expectation from the shore,
While from a boat others hung o'er the deep,
Sounding with grappling irons and long poles.
At last, the dead man, 'mid that beauteous scene

Of trees and hills and water, bolt upright
Rose with his ghastly face – a spectre shape,
Of terror even. And yet no vulgar fear,
Young as I was (a child not nine years old),
Possessed me, for my inner eye had seen
Such sights before among the shining streams
Of fairyland, the forests of romance.
Thence came a spirit hallowing what I saw
With decoration and ideal grace,
A dignity, a smoothness, like the works
Of Grecian art and purest poesy.

I had a precious treasure at that time,
A little yellow canvas-covered book,
A slender abstract of the *Arabian Tales*;
And when I learned, as now I first did learn
From my companions in this new abode,
That this dear prize of mine was but a block
Hewn from a mighty quarry – in a word,
That there were four large volumes, laden all
With kindred matter – 'twas in truth to me
A promise scarcely earthly. Instantly
I made a league, a covenant with a friend
Of my own age, that we should lay aside
The moneys we possessed, and hoard up more,
Till our joint savings had amassed enough
To make this book our own. Through several months
Religiously did we preserve that vow,
And spite of all temptation hoarded up
And hoarded up; but firmness failed at length,
Nor were we ever masters of our wish.

And afterwards, when to my father's house
Returning at the holidays I found
That golden store of books which I had left
Open to my enjoyment once again,
What heart was mine! Full often through the course
Of those glad respites in the summer-time
When armed with rod and line we went abroad

Of trees and hills and water, bolt upright
Rose, with his ghastly face, a spectre shape
Of terror; yet no soul-debasing fear,
Young as I was, a child not nine years old,
Possessed me, for my inner eye had seen
Such sights before, among the shining streams
Of faëry land, the forest of romance.
Their spirit hallowed the sad spectacle
With decoration of ideal grace;
A dignity, a smoothness, like the works
Of Grecian art, and purest poesy.

A precious treasure had I long possessed,
A little yellow, canvas-covered book,
A slender abstract of the Arabian tales;
And, from companions in a new abode,
When first I learnt, that this dear prize of mine
Was but a block hewn from a mighty quarry –
That there were four large volumes, laden all
With kindred matter, 'twas to me, in truth,
A promise scarcely earthly. Instantly,
With one not richer than myself, I made
A covenant that each should lay aside
The moneys he possessed, and hoard up more,
Till our joint savings had amassed enough
To make this book our own. Through several months,
In spite of all temptation, we preserved
Religiously that vow; but firmness failed,
Nor were we ever masters of our wish.

And when thereafter to my father's house
The holidays returned me, there to find
That golden store of books which I had left,
What joy was mine! How often in the course
Of those glad respites, though a soft west wind
Ruffled the waters to the angler's wish

For a whole day together, I have lain
Down by thy side, o Derwent, murmuring stream,
On the hot stones and in the glaring sun,
And there have read, devouring as I read,
Defrauding the day's glory – desperate –
Till with a sudden bound of smart reproach
Such as an idler deals with in his shame
I to my sport betook myself again.

A gracious spirit o'er this earth presides,
And o'er the heart of man: invisibly
It comes, directing those to works of love
Who care not, know not, think not what they do.
The tales that charm away the wakeful night
In Araby, romances, legends penned
For solace by the light of monkish lamps;
Fictions for ladies, of their love, devised
By youthful squires; adventures endless, spun
By the dismantled warrior in old age
Out of the bowels of those very thoughts
In which his youth did first extravagate –
These spread like day, and something in the shape
Of these will live till man shall be no more.
Dumb yearnings, hidden appetites, are ours,
And they must have their food. Our childhood sits,
Our simple childhood sits, upon a throne
That has more power than all the elements.
I guess not what this tells of being past,
Nor what it augurs of the life to come,
But so it is. And in that dubious hour,
That twilight when we first begin to see
This dawning earth, to recognize, expect,
And, in the long probation that ensues
(The time of trial, ere we learn to live
In reconcilement with our stinted powers),
To endure this state of meagre vassalage,
Unwilling to forego, confess, submit,
Uneasy and unsettled – yoke-fellows

For a whole day together, have I lain
Down by thy side, O Derwent! murmuring stream,
On the hot stones, and in the glaring sun,
And there have read, devouring as I read,
Defrauding the day's glory, desperate!
Till with a sudden bound of smart reproach,
Such as an idler deals with in his shame,
I to the sport betook myself again.

A gracious spirit o'er this earth presides,
And o'er the heart of man: invisibly
It comes, to works of unreproved delight,
And tendency benign, directing those
Who care not, know not, think not what they do.
The tales that charm away the wakeful night
In Araby, romances; legends penned
For solace by dim light of monkish lamps;
Fictions, for ladies of their love, devised
By youthful squires; adventures endless, spun
By the dismantled warrior in old age,
Out of the bowels of those very schemes
In which his youth did first extravagate;
These spread like day, and something in the shape
Of these will live till man shall be no more.
Dumb yearnings, hidden appetites, are ours,
And *they must* have their food. Our childhood sits,
Our simple childhood, sits upon a throne
That hath more power than all the elements.
I guess not what this tells of Being past,
Nor what it augurs of the life to come;
But so it is, and, in that dubious hour,
That twilight when we first begin to see
This dawning earth, to recognise, expect,
And in the long probation that ensues,
The time of trial, ere we learn to live
In reconcilement with our stinted powers;
To endure this state of meagre vassalage,
Unwilling to forego, confess, submit,
Uneasy and unsettled, yoke-fellows

To custom, mettlesome, and not yet tamed
And humbled down – oh, then we feel, we feel,
We know, when we have friends! Ye dreamers, then –
Forgers of lawless tales! – we bless you then
(Impostors, drivellers, dotards, as the ape
Philosophy will call you), then we feel
With what, and how great might ye are in league,
Who make our wish, our power, our thought a deed,
An empire, a possession; ye whom time
And seasons serve – all faculties – to whom
Earth crouches, the elements are potter's clay,
Space like a heaven filled up with northern lights,
Here, nowhere, there, and everywhere at once.

It might demand a more impassioned strain
To tell of later pleasures, linked to these,
A tract of the same isthmus which we cross
In progress from our native continent
To earth and human life – I mean to speak
Of that delightful time of growing youth
When cravings for the marvellous relent,
And we begin to love what we have seen;
And sober truth, experience, sympathy,
Take stronger hold of us, and words themselves
Move us with conscious pleasure. I am sad
At thought of raptures now for ever flown;
Even unto tears I sometimes could be sad
To think of, to read over, many a page –
Poems withal of name – which at the time
Did never fail to entrance me, and are now
Dead in my eyes as is a theatre
Fresh emptied of spectators. Thirteen years,
Or haply less, I might have seen when first
My ears began to open to the charm
Of words in tuneful order, found them sweet
For *their own sakes* – a passion and a power –

To custom, mettlesome, and not yet tamed
And humbled down; oh! then we feel, we feel,
We know where we have friends. Ye dreamers, then,
Forgers of daring tales! we bless you then,
Impostors, drivellers, dotards, as the ape
Philosophy will call you: *then* we feel
With what, and how great might ye are in league,
Who make our wish, our power, our thought a deed,
An empire, a possession, – ye whom time
And seasons serve; all Faculties to whom
Earth crouches, the elements are potter's clay,
Space like a heaven filled up with northern lights,
Here, nowhere, there, and everywhere at once.

Relinquishing this lofty eminence
For ground, though humbler, not the less a tract
Of the same isthmus, which our spirits cross
In progress from their native continent
To earth and human life, the Song might dwell
On that delightful time of growing youth,
When craving for the marvellous gives way
To strengthening love for things that we have seen;
When sober truth and steady sympathies,
Offered to notice by less daring pens,
Take firmer hold of us, and words themselves
Move us with conscious pleasure.

I am sad
At thought of raptures now for ever flown;
Almost to tears I sometimes could be sad
To think of, to read over, many a page,
Poems withal of name, which at that time
Did never fail to entrance me, and are now
Dead in my eyes, dead as a theatre
Fresh emptied of spectators. Twice five years
Or less I might have seen, when first my mind
With conscious pleasure opened to the charm
Of words in tuneful order, found them sweet
For their own *sakes*, a passion, and a power;

And phrases pleased me chosen for delight,
For pomp, or love.

Oft in the public roads,
Yet unfrequented, while the morning light
Was yellowing the hill-tops, with that dear friend
(The same whom I have mentioned heretofore)
I went abroad, and for the better part
Of two delightful hours we strolled along
By the still borders of the misty lake
Repeating favourite verses with one voice,
Or conning more, as happy as the birds
That round us chanted. Well might we be glad,
Lifted above the ground by airy fancies
More bright than madness or the dreams of wine.
And though full oft the objects of our love
Were false, and in their splendour overwrought,
Yet surely at such time no vulgar power
Was working in us – nothing less in truth
Than that most noble attribute of man
(Though yet untutored and inordinate),
That wish for something loftier, more adorned,
Than is the common aspect, daily garb,
Of human life. What wonder then if sounds
Of exultation echoed through the groves!
For images, and sentiments, and words,
And everything with which we had to do
In that delicious world of poesy,
Kept holiday, a never-ending show
With music, incense, festival, and flowers!

Here must I pause: this only will I add,
From heart-experience and in humblest sense
Of modesty, that he who in his youth
A wanderer among the woods and fields
With living nature hath been intimate,
Not only in that raw unpractised time
Is stirred to ecstasy (as others are)
By glittering verse, but he does furthermore,

And phrases pleased me chosen for delight,
For pomp, or love. Oft, in the public roads
Yet unfrequented, while the morning light
Was yellowing the hill tops, I went abroad
With a dear friend, and for the better part
Of two delightful hours we strolled along
By the still borders of the misty lake,
Repeating favourite verses with one voice,
Or conning more, as happy as the birds
That round us chaunted. Well might we be glad,
Lifted above the ground by airy fancies,
More bright than madness or the dreams of wine;
And, though full oft the objects of our love
Were false, and in their splendour overwrought,
Yet was there surely then no vulgar power
Working within us, – nothing less, in truth,
Than that most noble attribute of man,
Though yet untutored and inordinate,
That wish for something loftier, more adorned,
Than is the common aspect, daily garb,
Of human life. What wonder, then, if sounds
Of exultation echoed through the groves!
For, images, and sentiments, and words,
And everything encountered or pursued
In that delicious world of poesy,
Kept holiday, a never-ending show,
With music, incense, festival, and flowers!

Here must we pause: this only let me add,
From heart-experience, and in humblest sense
Of modesty, that he, who in his youth
A daily wanderer among woods and fields
With living Nature hath been intimate,
Not only in that raw unpractised time
Is stirred to extasy, as others are,
By glittering verse; but further, doth receive,

In measure only dealt out to himself,
Receive enduring touches of deep joy
From the great nature that exists in works
Of mighty poets. Visionary power
Attends upon the motions of the winds
Embodied in the mystery of words;
There darkness makes abode, and all the host
Of shadowy things do work their changes there,
As in a mansion like their proper home.
Even forms and substances are circumfused
By that transparent veil with light divine,
And through the turnings intricate of verse
Present themselves as objects recognized
In flashes, and with a glory scarce their own.

Thus far a scanty record is deduced
Of what I owed to books in early life;
Their later influence yet remains untold,
But as this work was taking in my thoughts
Proportions that seemed larger than had first
Been meditated, I was indisposed
To any further progress at a time
When these acknowledgements were left unpaid.

In measure only dealt out to himself,
Knowledge and increase of enduring joy
From the great Nature that exists in works
Of mighty Poets. Visionary power
Attends the motions of the viewless winds,
Embodied in the mystery of words:
There, darkness makes abode, and all the host
Of shadowy things work endless changes, – there,
As in a mansion like their proper home,
Even forms and substances are circumfused
By that transparent veil with light divine,
And, through the turnings intricate of verse,
Present themselves as objects recognised,
In flashes, and with glory not their own.

Book Sixth

CAMBRIDGE AND THE ALPS

The leaves were yellow when to Furness Fells,
The haunt of shepherds, and to cottage life
I bade adieu, and, one among the flock
Who by that season are convened, like birds
Trooping together at the fowler's lure,
Went back to Granta's cloisters – not so fond
Or eager, though as gay and undepressed
In spirit, as when I thence had taken flight
A few short months before. I turned my face
Without repining from the mountain pomp
Of autumn, and its beauty (entered in
With calmer lakes and louder streams); and you,
Frank-hearted maids of rocky Cumberland,
You and your not unwelcome days of mirth,
I quitted, and your nights of revelry,
And in my own unlovely cell sat down
In lightsome mood. Such privilege has youth,
That cannot take long leave of pleasant thoughts!

We need not linger o'er the ensuing time,
But let me add at once that now, the bonds
Of indolent and vague society
Relaxing in their hold, I lived henceforth
More to myself, read more, reflected more,
Felt more, and settled daily into habits
More promising. Two winters may be passed
Without a separate notice; many books
Were read in process of this time – devoured,
Tasted or skimmed, or studiously perused –
Yet with no settled plan. I was detached

CROSSING SIMPLON PASS

Book Sixth

CAMBRIDGE AND THE ALPS

The leaves were fading when to Esthwaite's banks
And the simplicities of cottage life
I bade farewell; and, one among the youth
Who, summoned by that season, reunite
As scattered birds troop to the fowler's lure,
Went back to Granta's cloisters, not so prompt
Or eager, though as gay and undepressed
In mind, as when I thence had taken flight
A few short months before. I turned my face
Without repining from the coves and heights
Clothed in the sunshine of the withering fern;
Quitted, not loth, the mild magnificence
Of calmer lakes and louder streams; and you,
Frank-hearted maids of rocky Cumberland,
You and your not unwelcome days of mirth,
Relinquished, and your nights of revelry,
And in my own unlovely cell sate down
In lightsome mood – such privilege has youth
That cannot take long leave of pleasant thoughts.

The bonds of indolent society
Relaxing in their hold, henceforth I lived
More to myself. Two winters may be passed
Without a separate notice: many books
Were skimmed, devoured, or studiously perused,
But with no settled plan. I was detached

Internally from academic cares,
From every hope of prowess and reward,
And wished to be a lodger in that house
Of letters, and no more – and should have been
Even such, but for some personal concerns
That hung about me in my own despite
Perpetually, no heavy weight, but still
A baffling and a hindrance, a control
Which made the thought of planning for myself
A course of independent study seem
An act of disobedience towards them
Who loved me, proud rebellion and unkind.
This bastard virtue – rather let it have
A name it more deserves, this cowardice –
Gave treacherous sanction to that over-love
Of freedom planted in me from the first,
And indolence, by force of which I turned
From regulations even of my own
As from restraints and bonds. And who can tell,
Who knows what thus may have been gained, both then
And at a later season, or preserved –
What love of nature, what original strength
Of contemplation, what intuitive truths
The deepest and the best, and what research
Unbiassed, unbewildered, and unawed?

The poet's soul was with me at that time,
Sweet meditations, the still overflow
Of happiness and truth. A thousand hopes
Were mine, a thousand tender dreams, of which
No few have since been realized, and some
Do yet remain, hopes for my future life.
Four years and thirty, told this very week,
Have I been now a sojourner on earth,
And yet the morning gladness is not gone
Which then was in my mind. Those were the days
Which also first encouraged me to trust
With firmness (hitherto but lightly touched

Internally from academic cares;
Yet independent study seemed a course
Of hardy disobedience toward friends
And kindred, proud rebellion and unkind.
This spurious virtue, rather let it bear
A name it now deserves, this cowardice,
Gave treacherous sanction to that over-love
Of freedom which encouraged me to turn
From regulations even of my own
As from restraints and bonds. Yet who can tell –
Who knows what thus may have been gained, both then
And at a later season, or preserved;
What love of nature, what original strength
Of contemplation, what intuitive truths,
The deepest and the best, what keen research,
Unbiassed, unbewildered, and unawed?

The Poet's soul was with me at that time;
Sweet meditations, the still overflow
Of present happiness, while future years
Lacked not anticipations, tender dreams,
No few of which have since been realised;
And some remain, hopes for my future life.
Four years and thirty, told this very week,
Have I been now a sojourner on earth,
By sorrow not unsmitten; yet for me
Life's morning radiance hath not left the hills,
Her dew is on the flowers. Those were the days
Which also first emboldened me to trust
With firmness, hitherto but lightly touched

With such a daring thought) that I might leave
Some monument behind me which pure hearts
Should reverence. The instinctive humbleness,
Upheld even by the very name and thought
Of printed books and authorship, began
To melt away; and further, the dread awe
Of mighty names was softened down and seemed
Approachable, admitting fellowship
Of modest sympathy. Such aspect now,
Though not familiarly, my mind put on:
I loved, and I enjoyed – that was my chief
And ruling business – happy in the strength
And loveliness of imagery and thought.

All winter long, whenever free to take
My choice, did I at nights frequent our groves
And tributary walks – the last, and oft
The only one, who had been lingering there
Through hours of silence till the porter's bell,
A punctual follower on the stroke of nine,
Rang with its blunt unceremonious voice,
Inexorable summons! Lofty elms,
Inviting shades of opportune recess,
Did give composure to a neighbourhood
Unpeaceful in itself. A single tree
There was (no doubt yet standing there), an ash
With sinuous trunk, boughs exquisitely wreathed.
Up from the ground and almost to the top
The trunk and master branches everywhere
Were green with ivy, and the lightsome twigs
And outer spray profusely tipped with seeds
That hung in yellow tassels and festoons,
Moving or still – a favourite trimmed out
By winter for himself, as if in pride,
And with outlandish grace. Oft have I stood
Foot-bound uplooking at this lovely tree
Beneath a frosty moon. The hemisphere
Of magic fiction, verse of mine perhaps
May never tread, but scarcely Spenser's self

By such a daring thought, that I might leave
Some monument behind me which pure hearts
Should reverence. The instinctive humbleness,
Maintained even by the very name and thought
Of printed books and authorship, began
To melt away; and further, the dread awe
Of mighty names was softened down and seemed
Approachable, admitting fellowship
Of modest sympathy. Such aspect now,
Though not familiarly, my mind put on,
Content to observe, to achieve, and to enjoy.

All winter long, whenever free to choose,
Did I by night frequent the College groves
And tributary walks; the last, and oft
The only one, who had been lingering there
Through hours of silence, till the porter's bell,
A punctual follower on the stroke of nine,
Rang with its blunt unceremonious voice,
Inexorable summons! Lofty elms,
Inviting shades of opportune recess,
Bestowed composure on a neighbourhood
Unpeaceful in itself. A single tree
With sinuous trunk, boughs exquisitely wreathed,
Grew there; an ash which Winter for himself
Decked as in pride, and with outlandish grace:
Up from the ground, and almost to the top,
The trunk and every master branch were green
With clustering ivy, and the lightsome twigs
And outer spray profusely tipped with seeds
That hung in yellow tassels, while the air
Stirred them, not voiceless. Often have I stood
Foot-bound uplooking at this lovely tree
Beneath a frosty moon. The hemisphere
Of magic fiction, verse of mine perchance
May never tread; but scarcely Spenser's self

Could have more tranquil visions in his youth –
More bright appearances could scarcely see
Of human forms and superhuman powers –
Than I beheld standing on winter nights
Alone beneath this fairy-work of earth.

'Twould be a waste of labour to detail
The rambling studies of a truant youth –
Which further may be easily divined,
What, and what kind they were. My inner knowledge
(This barely will I note) was oft in depth
And delicacy like another mind
Sequestered from my outward taste in books.
And yet the books which then I loved the most
Are dearest to me now; for, being versed
In living nature, I had there a guide
Which opened frequently my eyes, else shut,
A standard which was usefully applied,
Even when unconsciously, to other things
Which less I understood. In general terms
I was a better judge of thoughts than words,
Misled as to these latter, not alone
By common inexperience of youth
But by the trade in classic niceties
(Delusion to young scholars incident,
And old ones also) by that overprized
And dangerous craft of picking phrases out
From languages that want the living voice
To make of them a nature to the heart –
To tell us what is passion, what is truth,
What reason, what simplicity and sense.

Yet must I not entirely overlook
The pleasure gathered from the elements
Of geometric science. I had stepped
In these enquiries but a little way,
No farther than the threshold (with regret
Sincere I mention this), but there I found
Enough to exalt, to cheer me, and compose.

Could have more tranquil visions in his youth,
Or could more bright appearances create
Of human forms with superhuman powers,
Than I beheld loitering on calm clear nights
Alone, beneath this fairy work of earth.

On the vague reading of a truant youth
'Twere idle to descant. My inner judgment
Not seldom differed from my taste in books,
As if it appertained to another mind,
And yet the books which then I valued most
Are dearest to me *now*; for, having scanned,
Not heedlessly, the laws, and watched the forms
Of Nature, in that knowledge I possessed
A standard, often usefully applied,
Even when unconsciously, to things removed
From a familiar sympathy. – In fine,
I was a better judge of thoughts than words,
Misled in estimating words, not only
By common inexperience of youth,
But by the trade in classic niceties,
The dangerous craft of culling term and phrase
From languages that want the living voice
To carry meaning to the natural heart;
To tell us what is passion, what is truth,
What reason, what simplicity and sense.

Yet may we not entirely overlook
The pleasure gathered from the rudiments
Of geometric science. Though advanced
In these inquiries, with regret I speak,
No farther than the threshold, there I found
Both elevation and composed delight:

With Indian awe and wonder, ignorance
Which even was cherished, did I meditate
Upon the alliance of those simple, pure
Proportions and relations with the frame
And laws of nature – how they could become
Herein a leader to the human mind –
And made endeavours frequent to detect
The process by dark guesses of my own.
Yet from this source more frequently I drew
A pleasure calm and deeper, a still sense
Of permanent and universal sway
And paramount endowment in the mind,
An image not unworthy of the one
Surpassing life which – out of space and time,
Nor touched by welterings of passion – is,
And has the name of, God. Transcendent peace
And silence did await upon these thoughts
That were a frequent comfort to my youth.

And as I have read of one by shipwreck thrown
With fellow-sufferers whom the waves had spared
Upon a region uninhabited,
An island of the deep, who, having brought
To land a single volume and no more –
A treatise of geometry – was used,
Although of food and clothing destitute
And beyond common wretchedness depressed,
To part from company and take this book
(Then first a self-taught pupil in those truths)
To spots remote and corners of the isle
By the sea-side, and draw his diagrams
With a long stick upon the sand, and thus
Did oft beguile his sorrow and almost
Forget his feeling – even so (if things
Producing like effect, from outward cause

With Indian awe and wonder, ignorance pleased
With its own struggles, did I meditate
On the relation those abstractions bear
To Nature's laws, and by what process led,
Those immaterial agents bowed their heads
Duly to serve the mind of earth-born man;
From star to star, from kindred sphere to sphere,
From system on to system without end.

More frequently from the same source I drew
A pleasure quiet and profound, a sense
Of permanent and universal sway,
And paramount belief; there, recognised
A type, for finite natures, of the one
Supreme Existence, the surpassing life
Which – to the boundaries of space and time,
Of melancholy space and doleful time,
Superior, and incapable of change,
Nor touched by welterings of passion – is,
And hath the name of, God. Transcendent peace
And silence did await upon these thoughts
That were a frequent comfort to my youth.

'Tis told by one whom stormy waters threw,
With fellow-sufferers by the shipwreck spared,
Upon a desert coast, that having brought
To land a single volume, saved by chance,
A treatise of Geometry, he wont,
Although of food and clothing destitute,
And beyond common wretchedness depressed,
To part from company and take this book
(Then first a self-taught pupil in its truths)
To spots remote, and draw his diagrams
With a long staff upon the sand, and thus
Did oft beguile his sorrow, and almost
Forget his feeling: so (if like effect
From the same cause produced, 'mid outward things

So different, may rightly be compared),
So was it with me then, and so will be
With poets ever. Mighty is the charm
Of those abstractions to a mind beset
With images and haunted by itself,
And specially delightful unto me
Was that clear synthesis built up aloft
So gracefully, even then when it appeared
No more than as a plaything, or a toy
Embodied to the sense – not what it is
In verity, an independent world
Created out of pure intelligence.

Such dispositions then were mine, almost
Through grace of heaven and inborn tenderness.
And not to leave the picture of that time
Imperfect, with these habits I must rank
A melancholy (from humours of the blood
In part, and partly taken up) that loved
A pensive sky, sad days, and piping winds,
The twilight more than dawn, autumn than spring –
A treasured and luxurious gloom, of choice
And inclination mainly, and the mere
Redundancy of youth's contentedness.
Add unto this a multitude of hours
Pilfered away by what the bard who sang
Of the enchanter Indolence has called
'Good-natured lounging', and behold a map
Of my collegiate life – far less intense
Than duty called for, or, without regard
To duty, might have sprung up of itself
By change of accidents, or even (to speak
Without unkindness) in another place.

So different, may rightly be compared),
So was it then with me, and so will be
With Poets ever. Mighty is the charm
Of those abstractions to a mind beset
With images, and haunted by herself,
And specially delightful unto me
Was that clear synthesis built up aloft
So gracefully; even then when it appeared
Not more than a mere plaything, or a toy
To sense embodied: not the thing it is
In verity, an independent world,
Created out of pure intelligence.

Such dispositions then were mine unearned
By aught, I fear, of genuine desert –
Mine, through heaven's grace and inborn aptitudes.
And not to leave the story of that time
Imperfect, with these habits must be joined,
Moods melancholy, fits of spleen, that loved
A pensive sky, sad days, and piping winds,
The twilight more than dawn, autumn than spring;
A treasured and luxurious gloom of choice
And inclination mainly, and the mere
Redundancy of youth's contentedness.
– To time thus spent, add multitudes of hours
Pilfered away, by what the Bard who sang
Of the Enchanter Indolence hath called
'Good-natured lounging,' and behold a map
Of my collegiate life – far less intense
Than duty called for, or, without regard
To duty, *might* have sprung up of itself
By change of accidents, or even, to speak
Without unkindness, in another place.
Yet why take refuge in that plea? – the fault,
This I repeat, was mine; mine be the blame.

In summer among distant nooks I roved
(Dovedale, or Yorkshire dales, or through bye-tracts
Of my own native region) and was blest
Between those sundry wanderings with a joy
Above all joys, that seemed another morn
Risen on mid noon: the presence, friend, I mean
Of that sole sister, she who has been long
Thy treasure also, thy true friend and mine,
Now after separation desolate
Restored to me – such absence that she seemed
A gift then first bestowed. The gentle banks
Of Emont, hitherto unnamed in song,
And that monastic castle, on a flat
Low-standing by the margin of the stream,
A mansion not unvisited of old
By Sidney, where, in sight of our Helvellyn,
Some snatches he might pen, for aught we know,
Of his *Arcadia*, by fraternal love
Inspired – that river and that mouldering dome
Have seen us sit in many a summer hour,
My sister and myself, when, having climbed
In danger through some window's open space,
We looked abroad, or on the turret's head
Lay listening to the wild flowers and the grass
As they gave out their whispers to the wind.

Another maid there was, who also breathed
A gladness o'er that season, then to me
By her exulting outside look of youth
And placid under-countenance first endeared –

In summer, making quest for works of art,
Or scenes renowned for beauty, I explored
That streamlet whose blue current works its way
Between romantic Dovedale's spiry rocks;
Pried into Yorkshire dales, or hidden tracts
Of my own native region, and was blest
Between these sundry wanderings with a joy
Above all joys, that seemed another morn
Risen on mid noon; blest with the presence, Friend!
Of that sole Sister, her who hath been long
Dear to thee also, thy true friend and mine,
Now, after separation desolate,
Restored to me – such absence that she seemed
A gift then first bestowed. The varied banks
Of Emont, hitherto unnamed in song,
And that monastic castle, 'mid tall trees,
Low-standing by the margin of the stream,
A mansion visited (as fame reports)
By Sidney, where, in sight of our Helvellyn,
Or stormy Cross-fell, snatches he might pen
Of his Arcadia, by fraternal love
Inspired; – that river and those mouldering towers
Have seen us side by side, when, having clomb
The darksome windings of a broken stair,
And crept along a ridge of fractured wall,
Not without trembling, we in safety looked
Forth, through some Gothic window's open space,
And gathered with one mind a rich reward
From the far-stretching landscape, by the light
Of morning beautified, or purple eve;
Or, not less pleased, lay on some turret's head,
Catching from tufts of grass and hare-bell flowers
Their faintest whisper to the passing breeze,
Given out while mid-day heat oppressed the plains.

Another maid there was, who also shed
A gladness o'er that season, then to me,
By her exulting outside look of youth
And placid under-countenance, first endeared;

That other spirit, Coleridge, who is now
So near to us, that meek confiding heart
So reverenced by us both. O'er paths and fields
In all that neighbourhood, through narrow lanes
Of eglantine and through the shady woods,
And o'er the Border Beacon and the waste
Of naked pools and common crags that lay
Exposed on the bare fell, was scattered love,
A spirit of pleasure and youth's golden gleam.
O friend, we had not seen thee at that time,
And yet a power is on me and a strong
Confusion, and I seem to plant thee there!
Far art thou wandered now in search of health
And milder breezes – melancholy lot –
But thou art with us, with us in the past,
The present, with us in the times to come.
There is no grief, no sorrow, no despair,
No languor, no dejection, no dismay,
No absence scarcely can there be, for those
Who love as we do. Speed thee well! Divide
Thy pleasure with us; thy returning strength,
Receive it daily as a joy of ours;
Share with us thy fresh spirits, whether gift
Of gales Etesian or of loving thoughts.

I too have been a wanderer – but alas,
How different is the fate of different men
Though twins almost in genius and in mind!
Unknown unto each other (yea, and breathing
As if in different elements) we were framed
To bend at last to the same discipline,
Predestined if two beings ever were
To seek the same delights, and have one health,
One happiness. Throughout this narrative,
Else sooner ended, I have known full well
For whom I thus record the birth and growth
Of gentleness, simplicity, and truth,
And joyous loves that hallow innocent days
Of peace and self-command. Of rivers, fields,

That other spirit, Coleridge! who is now
So near to us, that meek confiding heart,
So reverenced by us both. O'er paths and fields
In all that neighbourhood, through narrow lanes
Of eglantine, and through the shady woods,
And o'er the Border Beacon, and the waste
Of naked pools, and common crags that lay
Exposed on the bare fell, were scattered love,
The spirit of pleasure, and youth's golden gleam.
O Friend! we had not seen thee at that time,
And yet a power is on me, and a strong
Confusion, and I seem to plant thee there.
Far art thou wandered now in search of health
And milder breezes, – melancholy lot!
But thou art with us, with us in the past,
The present, with us in the times to come.
There is no grief, no sorrow, no despair,
No languor, no dejection, no dismay,
No absence scarcely can there be, for those
Who love as we do. Speed thee well! divide
With us thy pleasure; thy returning strength,
Receive it daily as a joy of ours;
Share with us thy fresh spirits, whether gift
Of gales Etesian or of tender thoughts.

I, too, have been a wanderer; but, alas!
How different the fate of different men.
Though mutually unknown, yea nursed and reared
As if in several elements, we were framed
To bend at last to the same discipline,
Predestined, if two beings ever were,
To seek the same delights, and have one health,
One happiness. Throughout this narrative,
Else sooner ended, I have borne in mind
For whom it registers the birth, and marks the growth,
Of gentleness, simplicity, and truth,
And joyous loves, that hallow innocent days
Of peace and self-command. Of rivers, fields,

And groves I speak to thee, my friend – to thee
Who, yet a liveried schoolboy in the depths
Of the huge city, on the leaded roof
Of that wide edifice, thy home and school,
Wast used to lie and gaze upon the clouds
Moving in heaven, or haply, tired of this,
To shut thine eyes and by internal light
See trees, and meadows, and thy native stream,
Far distant, thus beheld from year to year
Of thy long exile. Nor could I forget
In this late portion of my argument
That scarcely had I finally resigned
My rights among those academic bowers
When thou wert thither guided. From the heart
Of London, and from cloisters there, thou camest,
And didst sit down in temperance and peace,
A rigorous student. What a stormy course
Then followed! Oh, it is a pang that calls
For utterance to think how small a change
Of circumstances might to thee have spared
A world of pain, ripened ten thousand hopes
For ever withered.

Through this retrospect
Of my own college life I still have had
Thy after-sojourn in the self-same place
Present before my eyes, have played with times
(I speak of private business of the thought)
And accidents as children do with cards,
Or as a man who when his house is built,
A frame locked up in wood and stone, doth still
In impotence of mind by his fireside
Rebuild it to his liking. I have thought
Of thee, thy learning, gorgeous eloquence,
And all the strength and plumage of thy youth,
Thy subtle speculations, toils abstruse
Among the schoolmen, and Platonic forms
Of wild ideal pageantry, shaped out
From things well-matched or ill, and words for things –

And groves I speak to thee, my Friend! to thee,
Who, yet a liveried schoolboy, in the depths
Of the huge city, on the leaded roof
Of that wide edifice, thy school and home,
Wert used to lie and gaze upon the clouds
Moving in heaven; or, of that pleasure tired,
To shut thine eyes, and by internal light
See trees, and meadows, and thy native stream,
Far distant, thus beheld from year to year
Of a long exile. Nor could I forget,
In this late portion of my argument,
That scarcely, as my term of pupilage
Ceased, had I left those academic bowers
When thou wert thither guided. From the heart
Of London, and from cloisters there, thou camest,
And didst sit down in temperance and peace,
A rigorous student. What a stormy course
Then followed. Oh! it is a pang that calls
For utterance, to think what easy change
Of circumstances might to thee have spared
A world of pain, ripened a thousand hopes,
For ever withered. Through this retrospect
Of my collegiate life I still have had
Thy after-sojourn in the self-same place
Present before my eyes, have played with times
And accidents as children do with cards,
Or as a man, who, when his house is built,
A frame locked up in wood and stone, doth still,
As impotent fancy prompts, by his fireside,
Rebuild it to his liking. I have thought
Of thee, thy learning, gorgeous eloquence,
And all the strength and plumage of thy youth,
Thy subtle speculations, toils abstruse
Among the schoolmen, and Platonic forms
Of wild ideal pageantry, shaped out
From things well-matched or ill, and words for things,

The self-created sustenance of a mind
Debarred from nature's living images,
Compelled to be a life unto itself,
And unrelentingly possessed by thirst
Of greatness, love, and beauty. Not alone,
Ah, surely not in singleness of heart,
Should I have seen the light of evening fade
Upon the silent Cam, if we had met
Even at that early time. I needs must hope,
Must feel, must trust, that my maturer age
And temperature less willing to be moved,
My calmer habits and more steady voice,
Would with an influence benign have soothed
Or chased away the airy wretchedness
That battened on thy youth. But thou hast trod,
In watchful meditation thou hast trod
A march of glory, which does put to shame
These vain regrets; health suffers in thee, else
Such grief for thee would be the weakest thought
That ever harboured in the breast of man.

A passing word erewhile did lightly touch
On wanderings of my own, and now to these
My poem leads me with an easier mind.
The employments of three winters when I wore
A student's gown have been already told,
Or shadowed forth as far as there is need;
When the third summer brought its liberty,
A fellow student and myself (he too
A mountaineer) together sallied forth
And, staff in hand, on foot pursued our way
Towards the distant Alps. An open slight
Of college cares and study was the scheme,
Nor entertained without concern for those
To whom my worldly interests were dear.
But nature then was sovereign in my heart,
And mighty forms, seizing a youthful fancy,
Had given a charter to irregular hopes.

The self-created sustenance of a mind
Debarred from Nature's living images,
Compelled to be a life unto herself,
And unrelentingly possessed by thirst
Of greatness, love, and beauty. Not alone,
Ah! surely not in singleness of heart
Should I have seen the light of evening fade
From smooth Cam's silent waters: had we met,
Even at that early time, needs must I trust
In the belief, that my maturer age,
My calmer habits, and more steady voice,
Would with an influence benign have soothed,
Or chased away, the airy wretchedness
That battened on thy youth. But thou hast trod
A march of glory, which doth put to shame
These vain regrets; health suffers in thee, else
Such grief for thee would be the weakest thought
That ever harboured in the breast of man.

A passing word erewhile did lightly touch
On wanderings of my own, that now embraced
With livelier hope a region wider far.

When the third summer freed us from restraint,
A youthful friend, he too a mountaineer,
Not slow to share my wishes, took his staff,
And sallying forth, we journeyed side by side,
Bound to the distant Alps. A hardy slight
Did this unprecedented course imply
Of college studies and their set rewards;
Nor had, in truth, the scheme been formed by me
Without uneasy forethought of the pain,
The censures, and ill-omening of those
To whom my worldly interests were dear.
But Nature then was sovereign in my mind,
And mighty forms, seizing a youthful fancy,
Had given a charter to irregular hopes.

In any age, without an impulse sent
From work of nations and their goings-on,
I should have been possessed by like desire,
But 'twas a time when Europe was rejoiced,
France standing on the top of golden hours,
And human nature seeming born again.

Bound, as I said, to the Alps, it was our lot
To land at Calais on the very eve
Of that great federal day; and there we saw,
In a mean city and among a few,
How bright a face is worn when joy of one
Is joy of tens of millions. Southward thence
We took our way, direct through hamlets, towns,
Gaudy with relics of that festival,
Flowers left to wither on triumphal arcs,
And window-garlands. On the public roads –
And once, three days successively, through paths
By which our toilsome journey was abridged –
Among sequestered villages we walked
And found benevolence and blessedness
Spread like a fragrance everywhere, like spring
That leaves no corner of the land untouched.
Where elms for many and many a league in files
With their thin umbrage, on the stately roads
Of that great kingdom, rustled o'er our heads
For ever near us as we paced along,
'Twas sweet at such a time (with such delights
On every side, in prime of youthful strength)
To feed a poet's tender melancholy
And fond conceit of sadness, to the noise
And gentle undulation which they made.
Unhoused beneath the evening star we saw
Dances of liberty, and in late hours

In any age of uneventful calm
Among the nations, surely would my heart
Have been possessed by similar desire;
But Europe at that time was thrilled with joy,
France standing on the top of golden hours,
And human nature seeming born again.

Lightly equipped, and but a few brief looks
Cast on the white cliffs of our native shore
From the receding vessel's deck, we chanced
To land at Calais on the very eve
Of that great federal day; and there we saw,
In a mean city, and among a few,
How bright a face is worn when joy of one
Is joy for tens of millions. Southward thence
We held our way, direct through hamlets, towns,
Gaudy with reliques of that festival,
Flowers left to wither on triumphal arcs,
And window-garlands. On the public roads,
And, once, three days successively, through paths
By which our toilsome journey was abridged,
Among sequestered villages we walked
And found benevolence and blessedness
Spread like a fragrance everywhere, when spring
Hath left no corner of the land untouched:
Where elms for many and many a league in files
With their thin umbrage, on the stately roads
Of that great kingdom, rustled o'er our heads,
For ever near us as we paced along:
How sweet at such a time, with such delight
On every side, in prime of youthful strength,
To feed a Poet's tender melancholy
And fond conceit of sadness, with the sound
Of undulations varying as might please
The wind that swayed them; once, and more than once
Unhoused beneath the evening star we saw
Dances of liberty, and, in late hours

Of darkness, dances in the open air.

Among the vine-clad hills of Burgundy,
Upon the bosom of the gentle Soane
We glided forward with the flowing stream.
Swift Rhone, thou wert the wings on which we cut
Between thy lofty rocks! Enchanting show
Those woods and farms and orchards did present,
And single cottages and lurking towns –
Reach after reach, procession without end
Of deep and stately vales. A lonely pair
Of Englishmen we were, and sailed along
Clustered together with a merry crowd
Of those emancipated, with a host
Of travellers, chiefly delegates returning
From the great spousals newly solemnized
At their chief city, in the sight of Heaven.
Like bees they swarmed, gaudy and gay as bees;
Some vapoured in the unruliness of joy,
And flourished with their swords as if to fight
The saucy air. In this blithe company
We landed, took with them our evening meal,
Guests welcome almost as the angels were
To Abraham of old. The supper done,
With flowing cups elate and happy thoughts
We rose at signal given, and formed a ring
And hand in hand danced round and round the board.
All hearts were open, every tongue was loud
With amity and glee. We bore a name
Honoured in France, the name of Englishmen,
And hospitably did they give us hail
As their forerunners in a glorious course –
And round and round the board they danced again!

With this same throng our voyage we pursued
At early dawn. The monastery bells

Of darkness, dances in the open air
Deftly prolonged, though grey-haired lookers on
Might waste their breath in chiding.

Under hills –
The vine-clad hills and slopes of Burgundy,
Upon the bosom of the gentle Saone
We glided forward with the flowing stream.
Swift Rhone! thou wert the *wings* on which we cut
A winding passage with majestic ease
Between thy lofty rocks. Enchanting show
Those woods and farms and orchards did present,
And single cottages and lurking towns,
Reach after reach, succession without end
Of deep and stately vales! A lonely pair
Of strangers, till day closed, we sailed along,
Clustered together with a merry crowd
Of those emancipated, a blithe host
Of travellers, chiefly delegates returning
From the great spousals newly solemnised
At their chief city, in the sight of Heaven.
Like bees they swarmed, gaudy and gay as bees;
Some vapoured in the unruliness of joy,
And with their swords flourished as if to fight
The saucy air. In this proud company
We landed – took with them our evening meal,
Guests welcome almost as the angels were
To Abraham of old. The supper done,
With flowing cups elate and happy thoughts
We rose at signal given, and formed a ring
And, hand in hand, danced round and round the board;
All hearts were open, every tongue was loud
With amity and glee; we bore a name
Honoured in France, the name of Englishmen,
And hospitably did they give us hail,
As their forerunners in a glorious course;
And round and round the board we danced again.
With these blithe friends our voyage we renewed
At early dawn. The monastery bells

Made a sweet jingling in our youthful ears;
The rapid river, flowing without noise,
And every spire we saw among the rocks,
Spoke with a sense of peace – at intervals
Touching the heart amid the boisterous crew
With which we were environed. Having parted
From this glad rout, the Convent of Chartreuse
Received us two days afterwards, and there
We rested in an awful solitude –
Thence onward to the country of the Swiss.

Made a sweet jingling in our youthful ears;
The rapid river flowing without noise,
And each uprising or receding spire
Spake with a sense of peace, at intervals
Touching the heart amid the boisterous crew
By whom we were encompassed. Taking leave
Of this glad throng, foot-travellers side by side,
Measuring our steps in quiet, we pursued
Our journey, and ere twice the sun had set
Beheld the Convent of Chartreuse, and there
Rested within an awful *solitude*:
Yes, for even then no other than a place
Of soul-affecting *solitude* appeared
That far-famed region, though our eyes had seen,
As toward the sacred mansion we advanced,
Arms flashing, and a military glare
Of riotous men commissioned to expel
The blameless inmates, and belike subvert
That frame of social being, which so long
Had bodied forth the ghostliness of things
In silence visible and perpetual calm.
– 'Stay, stay your sacrilegious hands!' – The voice
Was Nature's, uttered from her Alpine throne;
I heard it then and seem to hear it now –
'Your impious work forbear, perish what may,
Let this one temple last, be this one spot
Of earth devoted to eternity!'
She ceased to speak, but while St. Bruno's pines
Waved their dark tops, not silent as they waved,
And while below, along their several beds,
Murmured the sister streams of Life and Death,
Thus by conflicting passions pressed, my heart
Responded; 'Honour to the patriot's zeal!
Glory and hope to new-born Liberty!
Hail to the mighty projects of the time!
Discerning sword that Justice wields, do thou
Go forth and prosper; and, ye purging fires,
Up to the loftiest towers of Pride ascend,
Fanned by the breath of angry Providence.

But oh! if Past and Future be the wings
On whose support harmoniously conjoined
Moves the great spirit of human knowledge, spare
These courts of mystery, where a step advanced
Between the portals of the shadowy rocks
Leaves far behind life's treacherous vanities,
For penitential tears and trembling hopes
Exchanged – to equalise in God's pure sight
Monarch and peasant: be the house redeemed
With its unworldly votaries, for the sake
Of conquest over sense, hourly achieved
Through faith and meditative reason, resting
Upon the word of heaven-imparted truth,
Calmly triumphant; and for humbler claim
Of that imaginative impulse sent
From these majestic floods, yon shining cliffs,
The untransmuted shapes of many worlds,
Cerulean ether's pure inhabitants,
These forests unapproachable by death,
That shall endure as long as man endures,
To think, to hope, to worship, and to feel,
To struggle, to be lost within himself
In trepidation, from the blank abyss
To look with bodily eyes, and be consoled.'
Not seldom since that moment have I wished
That thou, O Friend! the trouble or the calm
Hadst shared, when, from profane regards apart,
In sympathetic reverence we trod
The floors of those dim cloisters, till that hour,
From their foundation, strangers to the presence
Of unrestricted and unthinking man.
Abroad, how cheeringly the sunshine lay
Upon the open lawns! Vallombre's groves
Entering, we fed the soul with darkness; thence
Issued, and with uplifted eyes beheld,
In different quarters of the bending sky,
The cross of Jesus stand erect, as if
Hands of angelic powers had fixed it there,
Memorial reverenced by a thousand storms;

'Tis not my present purpose to retrace
That variegated journey step by step;
A march it was of military speed,
And earth did change her images and forms
Before us fast as clouds are changed in heaven.
Day after day, up early and down late,
From vale to vale, from hill to hill we went,
From province on to province did we pass,
Keen hunters in a chase of fourteen weeks,
Eager as birds of prey, or as a ship
Upon the stretch when winds are blowing fair.
Sweet coverts did we cross of pastoral life,
Enticing valleys – greeted them and left
Too soon, while yet the very flash and gleam
Of salutation were not passed away.
Oh, sorrow for the youth who could have seen
Unchastened, unsubdued, unawed, unraised
To patriarchal dignity of mind
And pure simplicity of wish and will,
Those sanctified abodes of peaceful man!
My heart leaped up when first I did look down
On that which was first seen of those deep haunts,
A green recess, an aboriginal vale,
Quiet, and lorded over and possessed
By naked huts, wood-built, and sown like tents
Or Indian cabins over the fresh lawns
And by the river-side.

Yet then, from the undiscriminating sweep
And rage of one State-whirlwind, insecure.

'Tis not my present purpose to retrace
That variegated journey step by step.
A march it was of military speed,
And Earth did change her images and forms
Before us, fast as clouds are changed in heaven.
Day after day, up early and down late,
From hill to vale we dropped, from vale to hill
Mounted – from province on to province swept,
Keen hunters in a chase of fourteen weeks,
Eager as birds of prey, or as a ship
Upon the stretch, when winds are blowing fair:
Sweet coverts did we cross of pastoral life,
Enticing valleys, greeted them and left
Too soon, while yet the very flash and gleam
Of salutation were not passed away.
Oh! sorrow for the youth who could have seen
Unchastened, unsubdued, unawed, unraised
To patriarchal dignity of mind,
And pure simplicity of wish and will,
Those sanctified abodes of peaceful man,
Pleased (though to hardship born, and compassed round
With danger, varying as the seasons change),
Pleased with his daily task, or, if not pleased,
Contented, from the moment that the dawn
(Ah! surely not without attendant gleams
Of soul-illumination) calls him forth
To industry, by glistenings flung on rocks,
Whose evening shadows lead him to repose.

Well might a stranger look with bounding heart
Down on a green recess, the first I saw
Of those deep haunts, an aboriginal vale,
Quiet and lorded over and possessed
By naked huts, wood-built, and sown like tents
Or Indian cabins over the fresh lawns
And by the river side.

That day we first
Beheld the summit of Mont Blanc, and grieved
To have a soulless image on the eye
Which had usurped upon a living thought
That never more could be. The wondrous Vale
Of Chamouny did on the following dawn,
With its dumb cataracts and streams of ice,
A motionless array of mighty waves,
Five rivers broad and vast, make rich amends,
And reconciled us to realities.
There small birds warble from the leafy trees,
The eagle soareth in the element;
There does the reaper bind the yellow sheaf,
The maiden spread the haycock in the sun,
While winter like a tamèd lion walks,
Descending from the mountain to make sport
Among the cottages by beds of flowers.

Whate'er in this wide circuit we beheld
Or heard was fitted to our unripe state
Of intellect and heart. By simple strains
Of feeling, the pure breath of real life,
We were not left untouched. With such a book
Before our eyes we could not choose but read
A frequent lesson of sound tenderness,
The universal reason of mankind,
The truth of young and old. Nor, side by side
Pacing, two brother pilgrims, or alone
Each with his humour, could we fail to abound
(Craft this which has been hinted at before)
In dreams and fictions pensively composed –
Dejection taken up for pleasure's sake,
And gilded sympathies. The willow wreath,
Even among those solitudes sublime,
And sober posies of funereal flowers
Culled from the gardens of the Lady Sorrow,
Did sweeten many a meditative hour.

That very day,
From a bare ridge we also first beheld
Unveiled the summit of Mont Blanc, and grieved
To have a soulless image on the eye
That had usurped upon a living thought
That never more could be. The wondrous Vale
Of Chamouny stretched far below, and soon
With its dumb cataracts and streams of ice,
A motionless array of mighty waves,
Five rivers broad and vast, made rich amends,
And reconciled us to realities;
There small birds warble from the leafy trees,
The eagle soars high in the element,
There doth the reaper bind the yellow sheaf,
The maiden spread the haycock in the sun,
While Winter like a well-tamed lion walks,
Descending from the mountain to make sport
Among the cottages by beds of flowers.

Whate'er in this wide circuit we beheld,
Or heard, was fitted to our unripe state
Of intellect and heart. With such a book
Before our eyes, we could not choose but read
Lessons of genuine brotherhood, the plain
And universal reason of mankind,
The truths of young and old. Nor, side by side
Pacing, two social pilgrims, or alone
Each with his humour, could we fail to abound
In dreams and fictions, pensively composed:
Dejection taken up for pleasure's sake,
And gilded sympathies, the willow wreath,
And sober posies of funereal flowers,
Gathered among those solitudes sublime
From formal gardens of the lady Sorrow,
Did sweeten many a meditative hour.

Yet still in me, mingling with these delights,
Was something of stern mood, an under-thirst
Of vigour never utterly asleep.
Far different dejection once was mine –
A deep and genuine sadness then I felt –
The circumstances I will here relate
Even as they were. Upturning with a band
Of travellers, from the Valais we had clomb
Along the road that leads to Italy;
A length of hours, making of these our guides
Did we advance, and having reached an inn
Among the mountains, we together ate
Our noon's repast, from which the travellers rose
Leaving us at the board. Erelong we followed,
Descending by the beaten road that led
Right to a rivulet's edge, and there broke off.
The only track now visible was one
Upon the further side, right opposite,
And up a lofty mountain. This we took
After a little scruple, and short pause,
And climbed with eagerness, though not at length
Without surprise and some anxiety
On finding that we did not overtake
Our comrades gone before. By fortunate chance,
While every moment now increased our doubts,
A peasant met us, and from him we learned
That to the place which had perplexed us first
We must descend, and there should find the road,
Which in the stony channel of the stream
Lay a few steps, and then along its banks –
And further, that thenceforward all our course
Was downwards with the current of that stream.
Hard of belief, we questioned him again,
And all the answers which the man returned
To our inquiries – in their sense and substance,
Translated by the feelings which we had –
Ended in this, that we had crossed the Alps.

Yet still in me with those soft luxuries
Mixed something of stern mood, an under-thirst
Of vigour seldom utterly allayed.
And from that source how different a sadness
Would issue, let one incident make known.
When from the Vallais we had turned, and clomb
Along the Simplon's steep and rugged road,
Following a band of muleteers, we reached
A halting-place, where all together took
Their noon-tide meal. Hastily rose our guide,
Leaving us at the board; awhile we lingered,
Then paced the beaten downward way that led
Right to a rough stream's edge, and there broke off;
The only track now visible was one
That from the torrent's further brink held forth
Conspicuous invitation to ascend
A lofty mountain. After brief delay
Crossing the unbridged stream, that road we took,
And clomb with eagerness, till anxious fears
Intruded, for we failed to overtake
Our comrades gone before. By fortunate chance,
While every moment added doubt to doubt,
A peasant met us, from whose mouth we learned
That to the spot which had perplexed us first
We must descend, and there should find the road,
Which in the stony channel of the stream
Lay a few steps, and then along its banks;
And, that our future course, all plain to sight,
Was downwards, with the current of that stream.
Loth to believe what we so grieved to hear,
For still we had hopes that pointed to the clouds,
We questioned him again, and yet again;
But every word that from the peasant's lips
Came in reply, translated by our feelings,
Ended in this, – *that we had crossed the Alps.*

Imagination – lifting up itself
Before the eye and progress of my song
Like an unfathered vapour, here that power,
In all the might of its endowments, came
Athwart me! I was lost as in a cloud,
Halted without a struggle to break through;
And now, recovering, to my soul I say
'I recognize thy glory.' In such strength
Of usurpation, in such visitings
Of awful promise, when the light of sense
Goes out in flashes that have shown to us
The invisible world, does greatness make abode,
There harbours whether we be young or old.
Our destiny, our nature, and our home,
Is with infinitude, and only there –
With hope it is, hope that can never die,
Effort, and expectation, and desire,
And something evermore about to be.
The mind beneath such banners militant
Thinks not of spoils or trophies, nor of aught
That may attest its prowess, blest in thoughts
That are their own perfection and reward –
Strong in itself, and in the access of joy
Which hides it like the overflowing Nile.

The dull and heavy slackening which ensued
Upon those tidings by the peasant given
Was soon dislodged. Downwards we hurried fast,
And entered with the road which we had missed
Into a narrow chasm. The brook and road
Were fellow-travellers in this gloomy pass,
And with them did we journey several hours
At a slow step. The immeasurable height
Of woods decaying, never to be decayed,
The stationary blasts of waterfalls,
And everywhere along the hollow rent
Winds thwarting winds, bewildered and forlorn,
The torrents shooting from the clear blue sky,

Imagination – here the Power so called
Through sad incompetence of human speech,
That awful Power rose from the mind's abyss
Like an unfathered vapour that enwraps,
At once, some lonely traveller. I was lost;
Halted without an effort to break through;
But to my conscious soul I now can say –
'I recognise thy glory:' in such strength
Of usurpation, when the light of sense
Goes out, but with a flash that has revealed
The invisible world, doth greatness make abode,
There harbours; whether we be young or old,
Our destiny, our being's heart and home,
Is with infinitude, and only there;
With hope it is, hope that can never die,
Effort, and expectation, and desire,
And something evermore about to be.
Under such banners militant, the soul
Seeks for no trophies, struggles for no spoils
That may attest her prowess, blest in thoughts
That are their own perfection and reward,
Strong in herself and in beatitude
That hides her, like the mighty flood of Nile
Poured from his fount of Abyssinian clouds
To fertilise the whole Egyptian plain.

The melancholy slackening that ensued
Upon those tidings by the peasant given
Was soon dislodged. Downwards we hurried fast,
And, with the half-shaped road which we had missed,
Entered a narrow chasm. The brook and road
Were fellow-travellers in this gloomy strait,
And with them did we journey several hours
At a slow pace. The immeasurable height
Of woods decaying, never to be decayed,
The stationary blasts of waterfalls,
And in the narrow rent at every turn
Winds thwarting winds, bewildered and forlorn,
The torrents shooting from the clear blue sky,

The rocks that muttered close upon our ears,
Black drizzling crags that spoke by the wayside
As if a voice were in them, the sick sight
And giddy prospect of the raving stream,
The unfettered clouds and region of the heavens,
Tumult and peace, the darkness and the light –
Were all like workings of one mind, the features
Of the same face, blossoms upon one tree,
Characters of the great apocalypse,
The types and symbols of eternity,
Of first, and last, and midst, and without end.

That night our lodging was an Alpine house,
An inn, or hospital (as they are named),
Standing in that same valley by itself
And close upon the confluence of two streams –
A dreary mansion, large beyond all need,
With high and spacious rooms, deafened and stunned
By noise of waters, making innocent sleep
Lie melancholy among weary bones.

Uprisen betimes, our journey we renewed
Led by the stream, ere noonday magnified
Into a lordly river, broad and deep,
Dimpling along in silent majesty
With mountains for its neighbours, and in view
Of distant mountains and their snowy tops –
And thus proceeding to Locarno's Lake,
Fit resting-place for such a visitant.
Locarno, spreading out in width like heaven,
And Como – thou, a treasure by the earth
Kept to itself, a darling bosomed up
In Abyssinian privacy – I spoke
Of thee, thy chestnut woods, and garden-plots
Of Indian corn tended by dark-eyed maids,
Thy lofty steeps, and pathways roofed with vines
Winding from house to house, from town to town

The rocks that muttered close upon our ears,
Black drizzling crags that spake by the way-side
As if a voice were in them, the sick sight
And giddy prospect of the raving stream,
The unfettered clouds and region of the Heavens,
Tumult and peace, the darkness and the light –
Were all like workings of one mind, the features
Of the same face, blossoms upon one tree;
Characters of the great Apocalypse,
The types and symbols of Eternity,
Of first, and last, and midst, and without end.

That night our lodging was a house that stood
Alone within the valley, at a point
Where, tumbling from aloft, a torrent swelled
The rapid stream whose margin we had trod;
A dreary mansion, large beyond all need,
With high and spacious rooms, deafened and stunned
By noise of waters, making innocent sleep
Lie melancholy among weary bones.

Uprisen betimes, our journey we renewed,
Led by the stream, ere noon-day magnified
Into a lordly river, broad and deep,
Dimpling along in silent majesty,
With mountains for its neighbours, and in view
Of distant mountains and their snowy tops,
And thus proceeding to Locarno's Lake,
Fit resting-place for such a visitant.
Locarno! spreading out in width like Heaven,
How dost thou cleave to the poetic heart,
Bask in the sunshine of the memory;
And Como! thou, a treasure whom the earth
Keeps to herself, confined as in a depth
Of Abyssinian privacy. I spake
Of thee, thy chestnut woods, and garden plots
Of Indian corn tended by dark-eyed maids;
Thy lofty steeps, and pathways roofed with vines,
Winding from house to house, from town to town,

(Sole link that binds them to each other), walks,
League after league, and cloistral avenues
Where silence is if music be not there:
While yet a youth undisciplined in verse,
Through fond ambition of my heart I told
Your praises, nor can I approach you now
Ungreeted by a more melodious song,
Where tones of learnèd art and nature mixed
May frame enduring language. Like a breeze
Or sunbeam over your domain I passed
In motion without pause; but ye have left
Your beauty with me, an impassioned sight
Of colours and of forms, whose power is sweet
And gracious, almost (might I dare to say?)
As virtue is, or goodness – sweet as love,
Or the remembrance of a noble deed,
Or gentlest visitations of pure thought
When God, the giver of all joy, is thanked
Religiously in silent blessedness –
Sweet as this last itself, for such it is.

Through those delightful pathways we advanced
Two days, and still in presence of the lake,
Which winding up among the Alps now changed
Slowly its lovely countenance and put on
A sterner character. The second night,
In eagerness, and by report misled
Of those Italian clocks that speak the time
In fashion different from ours, we rose
By moonshine, doubting not that day was near
And that meanwhile, coasting the water's edge
As hitherto, and with as plain a track
To be our guide, we might behold the scene
In its most deep repose. We left the town
Of Gravedona with this hope, but soon
Were lost, bewildered among woods immense,
Where, having wandered for a while, we stopped
And on a rock sat down to wait for day.

Sole link that binds them to each other; walks,
League after league, and cloistral avenues,
Where silence dwells if music be not there:
While yet a youth undisciplined in verse,
Through fond ambition of that hour, I strove
To chant your praise; nor can approach you now
Ungreeted by a more melodious Song,
Where tones of Nature smoothed by learned Art
May flow in lasting current. Like a breeze
Or sunbeam over your domain I passed
In motion without pause; but ye have left
Your beauty with me, a serene accord
Of forms and colours, passive, yet endowed
In their submissiveness with power as sweet
And gracious, almost might I dare to say,
As virtue is, or goodness; sweet as love,
Or the remembrance of a generous deed,
Or mildest visitations of pure thought,
When God, the giver of all joy, is thanked
Religiously, in silent blessedness;
Sweet as this last herself, for such it is.

With those delightful pathways we advanced,
For two days' space, in presence of the Lake,
That, stretching far among the Alps, assumed
A character more stern. The second night,
From sleep awakened, and misled by sound
Of the church clock telling the hours with strokes
Whose import then we had not learned, we rose
By moonlight, doubting not that day was nigh,
And that meanwhile, by no uncertain path,
Along the winding margin of the lake,
Led, as before, we should behold the scene
Hushed in profound repose. We left the town
Of Gravedona with this hope; but soon
Were lost, bewildered among woods immense,
And on a rock sate down, to wait for day.

An open place it was and overlooked
From high the sullen water underneath
On which a dull red image of the moon
Lay bedded, changing oftentimes its form
Like an uneasy snake. Long time we sat,
For scarcely more than one hour of the night
(Such was our error) had been gone when we
Renewed our journey. On the rock we lay
And wished to sleep but could not for the stings
Of insects which with noise like that of noon
Filled all the woods. The cry of unknown birds,
The mountains – more by darkness visible
And their own size, than any outward light –
The breathless wilderness of clouds, the clock
That told with unintelligible voice
The widely parted hours, the noise of streams
And sometimes rustling motions nigh at hand
Which did not leave us free from personal fear,
And lastly the withdrawing moon, that set
Before us while she yet was high in heaven –
These were our food, and such a summer night
Did to that pair of golden days succeed,
With now and then a doze and snatch of sleep
On Como's banks, the same delicious lake.

But here I must break off, and quit at once
(Though loth) the record of these wanderings,
A theme which may seduce me else beyond
All reasonable bounds. Let this alone
Be mentioned as a parting word, that not
In hollow exultation, dealing forth
Hyperboles of praise comparative,
Not rich one moment to be poor for ever,
Not prostrate, overborne, as if the mind
Itself were nothing, a mean pensioner
On outward forms – did we in presence stand
Of that magnificent region. On the front
Of this whole song is written that my heart

An open place it was, and overlooked,
From high, the sullen water far beneath,
On which a dull red image of the moon
Lay bedded, changing oftentimes its form
Like an uneasy snake. From hour to hour
We sate and sate, wondering, as if the night
Had been ensnared by witchcraft. On the rock
At last we stretched our weary limbs for sleep,
But *could not* sleep, tormented by the stings
Of insects, which, with noise like that of noon,
Filled all the woods; the cry of unknown birds;
The mountains more by blackness visible
And their own size, than any outward light;
The breathless wilderness of clouds; the clock
That told, with unintelligible voice,
The widely parted hours; the noise of streams,
And sometimes rustling motions nigh at hand,
That did not leave us free from personal fear;
And, lastly, the withdrawing moon, that set
Before us, while she still was high in heaven; –
These were our food; and such a summer's night
Followed that pair of golden days that shed
On Como's Lake, and all that round it lay,
Their fairest, softest, happiest influence.

But here I must break off, and bid farewell
To days, each offering some new sight, or fraught
With some untried adventure, in a course
Prolonged till sprinklings of autumnal snow
Checked our unwearied steps. Let this alone
Be mentioned as a parting word, that not
In hollow exultation, dealing out
Hyperboles of praise comparative;
Not rich one moment to be poor for ever;
Not prostrate, overborne, as if the mind
Herself were nothing, a mere pensioner
On outward forms – did we in presence stand
Of that magnificent region. On the front
Of this whole Song is written that my heart

Must in such temple needs have offered up
A different worship. Finally whate'er
I saw, or heard, or felt, was but a stream
That flowed into a kindred stream, a gale
That helped me forwards, did administer
To grandeur and to tenderness – to the one
Directly, but to tender thoughts by means
Less often instantaneous in effect –
Conducted me to these along a path
Which in the main was more circuitous.

Oh, most belovèd friend, a glorious time,
A happy time that was! Triumphant looks
Were then the common language of all eyes:
As if awaked from sleep, the nations hailed
Their great expectancy; the fife of war
Was then a spirit-stirring sound indeed,
A blackbird's whistle in a vernal grove.
We left the Swiss exulting in the fate
Of their near neighbours, and, when shortening fast
Our pilgrimage – nor distant far from home –
We crossed the Brabant armies on the fret
For battle in the cause of liberty.
A stripling, scarcely of the household then
Of social life, I looked upon these things
As from a distance (heard, and saw, and felt,
Was touched, but with no intimate concern),
I seemed to move among them as a bird
Moves through the air, or as a fish pursues
Its business in its proper element.
I needed not that joy, I did not need
Such help: the ever-living universe
And independent spirit of pure youth
Were with me at that season, and delight
Was in all places spread around my steps
As constant as the grass upon the fields.

Must, in such Temple, needs have offered up
A different worship. Finally, whate'er
I saw, or heard, or felt, was but a stream
That flowed into a kindred stream; a gale,
Confederate with the current of the soul,
To speed my voyage; every sound or sight,
In its degree of power, administered
To grandeur or to tenderness, – to the one
Directly, but to tender thoughts by means
Less often instantaneous in effect;
Led me to these by paths that, in the main,
Were more circuitous, but not less sure
Duly to reach the point marked out by Heaven.

Oh, most belovèd Friend! a glorious time,
A happy time that was; triumphant looks
Were then the common language of all eyes;
As if awaked from sleep, the Nations hailed
Their great expectancy: the fife of war
Was then a spirit-stirring sound indeed,
A black-bird's whistle in a budding grove.
We left the Swiss exulting in the fate
Of their near neighbours; and, when shortening fast
Our pilgrimage, nor distant far from home,
We crossed the Brabant armies on the fret
For battle in the cause of Liberty.
A stripling, scarcely of the household then
Of social life, I looked upon these things
As from a distance; heard, and saw, and felt,
Was touched, but with no intimate concern;
I seemed to move along them, as a bird
Moves through the air, or as a fish pursues
Its sport, or feeds in its proper element;
I wanted not that joy, I did not need
Such help; the ever-living universe,
Turn where I might, was opening out its glories,
And the independent spirit of pure youth
Called forth, at every season, new delights
Spread round my steps like sunshine o'er green fields.

Book Seventh
RESIDENCE IN LONDON

Five years are vanished since I first poured out,
Saluted by that animating breeze
Which met me issuing from the city's walls
A glad preamble to this verse. I sang
Aloud in dithyrambic fervour, deep
But short-lived uproar, like a torrent sent
Out of the bowels of a bursting cloud
Down Scafell or Blencathra's rugged sides,
A waterspout from heaven. But 'twas not long
Ere the interrupted stream broke forth once more
And flowed awhile in strength, then stopped for years –
Not heard again until a little space
Before last primrose-time. Belovèd friend,
The assurances then given unto myself
Which did beguile me of some heavy thoughts
At thy departure to a foreign land
Have failed; for slowly does this work advance.
Through the whole summer have I been at rest,
Partly from voluntary holiday
And part through outward hindrance. But I heard
After the hour of sunset yester-even,
Sitting within doors betwixt light and dark,
A voice that stirred me. 'Twas a little band,
A choir of redbreasts gathered somewhere near
My threshold – minstrels from the distant woods
And dells, sent in by Winter to bespeak
For the old man a welcome, to announce
With preparation artful and benign
(Yea the most gentle music of the year)
That their rough lord had left the surly north

Book Seventh

RESIDENCE IN LONDON

Six changeful years have vanished since I first
Poured out (saluted by that quickening breeze
Which met me issuing from the City's walls)
A glad preamble to this Verse: I sang
Aloud, with fervour irresistible
Of short-lived transport, like a torrent bursting,
From a black thunder-cloud, down Scafell's side
To rush and disappear. But soon broke forth
(So willed the Muse) a less impetuous stream,
That flowed awhile with unabating strength,
Then stopped for years; not audible again
Before last primrose-time. Belovèd Friend!
The assurance which then cheered some heavy thoughts
On thy departure to a foreign land
Has failed; too slowly moves the promised work.
Through the whole summer have I been at rest,
Partly from voluntary holiday,
And part through outward hindrance. But I heard,
After the hour of sunset yester-even,
Sitting within doors between light and dark,
A choir of redbreasts gathered somewhere near
My threshold, – minstrels from the distant woods
Sent in on Winter's service, to announce,
With preparation artful and benign,
That the rough lord had left the surly North

And has begun his journey.

A delight
At this unthought-of greeting unawares
Smote me, a sweetness of the coming time,
And, listening, I half whispered 'We will be,
Ye heartsome choristers, ye and I will be
Brethren, and in the hearing of bleak winds
Will chant together.' And thereafter, walking
By later twilight on the hills, I saw
A glow-worm from beneath a dusky shade
Or canopy of yet unwithered fern
Clear-shining, like a hermit's taper seen
Through a thick forest. Silence touched me here
No less than sound had done before: the child
Of summer, lingering, shining by itself,
The voiceless worm on the unfrequented hills,
Seemed sent on the same errand with the choir
Of winter that had warbled at my door,
And the whole year seemed tenderness and love.
The last night's genial feeling overflowed
Upon this morning, and my favourite grove –
Now tossing its dark boughs in sun and wind –
Spreads through me a commotion like its own,
Something that fits me for the poet's task,
Which we will now resume with cheerful hope,
Nor checked by aught of tamer argument
That lies before us, needful to be told.

Returned from that excursion, soon I bade
Farewell for ever to the private bowers
Of gownèd students – quitted these, no more
To enter them – and pitched my vagrant tent
A casual dweller and at large among
The unfenced regions of society.
Yet undetermined to what plan of life
I should adhere, and seeming thence to have
A little space of intermediate time
Loose and at full command, to London first

On his accustomed journey. The delight,
Due to this timely notice, unawares
Smote me, and, listening, I in whispers said,
'Ye heartsome Choristers, ye and I will be
Associates, and, unscared by blustering winds,
Will chant together.' Thereafter, as the shades
Of twilight deepened, going forth, I spied
A glow-worm underneath a dusky plume
Or canopy of yet unwithered fern,
Clear-shining, like a hermit's taper seen
Through a thick forest. Silence touched me here
No less than sound had done before; the child
Of Summer, lingering, shining, by herself,
The voiceless worm on the unfrequented hills,
Seemed sent on the same errand with the choir
Of Winter that had warbled at my door,
And the whole year breathed tenderness and love.

The last night's genial feeling overflowed
Upon this morning, and my favourite grove,
Tossing in sunshine its dark boughs aloft,
As if to make the strong wind visible,
Wakes in me agitations like its own,
A spirit friendly to the Poet's task,
Which we will now resume with lively hope,
Nor checked by aught of tamer argument
That lies before us, needful to be told.

Returned from that excursion, soon I bade
Farewell for ever to the sheltered seats
Of gowned students, quitted hall and bower,
And every comfort of that privileged ground,
Well pleased to pitch a vagrant tent among
The unfenced regions of society.

Yet, undetermined to what course of life
I should adhere, and seeming to possess
A little space of intermediate time
At full command, to London first I turned,

I turned, if not in calmness, nevertheless
In no disturbance of excessive hope –
At ease from all ambition personal,
Frugal as there was need, and though self-willed,
Yet temperate and reserved, and wholly free
From dangerous passions. 'Twas at least two years
Before this season when I first beheld
That mighty place, a transient visitant,
And now it pleased me my abode to fix
Single in the wide waste. To have a house
It was enough (what matter for a home?)
That owned me, living cheerfully abroad
With fancy on the stir from day to day
And all my young affections out of doors.

There was a time when whatsoe'er is feigned
Of airy palaces and gardens built
By genii of romance, or has in grave
Authentic history been set forth of Rome,
Alcairo, Babylon or Persepolis,
Or given upon report by pilgrim friars
Of golden cities ten months' journey deep
Among Tartarian wilds, fell short, far short,
Of that which I in simpleness believed
And thought of London – held me by a chain
Less strong of wonder and obscure delight.
I know not that herein I shot beyond
The common mark of childhood, but I well
Remember that among our flock of boys
Was one, a cripple from the birth, whom chance
Summoned from school to London – fortunate
And envied traveller! And when he returned
After short absence, and I first set eyes
Upon his person, verily (though strange
The thing may seem) I was not wholly free
From disappointment to behold the same
Appearance, the same body, not to find
Some change, some beams of glory brought away

In no disturbance of excessive hope,
By personal ambition unenslaved,
Frugal as there was need, and, though self-willed,
From dangerous passions free. Three years had flown
Since I had felt in heart and soul the shock
Of the huge town's first presence, and had paced
Her endless streets, a transient visitant:
Now fixed amid that concourse of mankind
Where Pleasure whirls about incessantly,
And life and labour seem but one, I filled
An idler's place; an idler well content
To have a house (what matter for a home?)
That owned him; living cheerfully abroad
With unchecked fancy ever on the stir,
And all my young affections out of doors.

There was a time when whatsoe'er is feigned
Of airy palaces, and gardens built
By Genii of romance; or hath in grave
Authentic history been set forth of Rome,
Alcairo, Babylon, or Persepolis;
Or given upon report by pilgrim friars,
Of golden cities ten months' journey deep
Among Tartarian wilds – fell short, far short,
Of what my fond simplicity believed
And thought of London – held me by a chain
Less strong of wonder and obscure delight.
Whether the bolt of childhood's Fancy shot
For me beyond its ordinary mark,
'Twere vain to ask; but in our flock of boys
Was One, a cripple from his birth, whom chance
Summoned from school to London; fortunate
And envied traveller! When the Boy returned,
After short absence, curiously I scanned
His mien and person, nor was free, in sooth,
From disappointment, not to find some change
In look and air, from that new region brought,

From that new region. Much I questioned him,
And every word he uttered on my ears
Fell flatter than a cagèd parrot's note
That answers unexpectedly awry
And mocks the prompter's listening. Marvellous things
My fancy had shaped forth, of sights and shows,
Processions, equipages, lords and dukes,
The King, and the King's palace, and not last
Or least (Heaven bless him!) the renowned Lord Mayor –
Dreams hardly less intense than those which wrought
A change of purpose in young Whittington
When he in friendlessness, a drooping boy,
Sat on a stone and heard the bells speak out
Articulate music. Above all, one thought
Baffled my understanding: how men lived
Even next-door neighbours (as we say) yet still
Strangers, and knowing not each other's names.

Oh, wondrous power of words! How sweet they are
According to the meaning which they bring!
Vauxhall and Ranelagh – I then had heard
Of your green groves and wilderness of lamps,
Your gorgeous ladies, fairy cataracts
And pageant fireworks! Nor must we forget
Those other wonders, different in kind
Though scarcely less illustrious in degree:
The river proudly bridged, the giddy top
And Whispering Gallery of St Paul's, the tombs
Of Westminster, the Giants of Guildhall,
Bedlam and the two figures at its gates,
Streets without end and churches numberless,
Statues with flowery gardens in vast squares,

As if from Fairy-land. Much I questioned him;
And every word he uttered, on my ears
Fell flatter than a cagèd parrot's note,
That answers unexpectedly awry,
And mocks the prompter's listening. Marvellous things
Had vanity (quick Spirit that appears
Almost as deeply seated and as strong
In a Child's heart as fear itself) conceived
For my enjoyment. Would that I could now
Recal what then I pictured to myself,
Of mitred Prelates, Lords in ermine clad,
The King, and the King's Palace, and, not last,
Nor least, Heaven bless him! the renowned Lord Mayor:
Dreams not unlike to those which once begat
A change of purpose in young Whittington,
When he, a friendless and a drooping boy,
Sate on a stone, and heard the bells speak out
Articulate music. Above all, one thought
Baffled my understanding: how men lived
Even next-door neighbours, as we say, yet still
Strangers, not knowing each the other's name.

O, wond'rous power of words, by simple faith
Licensed to take the meaning that we love!
Vauxhall and Ranelagh! I then had heard
Of your green groves, and wilderness of lamps
Dimming the stars, and fireworks magical,
And gorgeous ladies, under splendid domes,
Floating in dance, or warbling high in air
The songs of spirits! Nor had Fancy fed
With less delight upon that other class
Of marvels, broad-day wonders permanent:
The River proudly bridged; the dizzy top
And Whispering Gallery of St Paul's; the tombs
Of Westminster; the Giants of Guildhall;
Bedlam, and those carved maniacs at the gates,
Perpetually recumbent; Statues – man,
And the horse under him – in gilded pomp
Adorning flowery gardens, 'mid vast squares;

The Monument and armoury of the Tower.
These fond imaginations of themselves
Had long before given way in season due,
Leaving a throng of others in their stead;
And now I looked upon the real scene,
Familiarly perused it day by day,
With keen and lively pleasure even there
Where disappointment was the strongest, pleased
Through courteous self-submission, as a tax
Paid to the object by prescriptive right –
A thing that ought to be.

Shall I give way,
Copying the impression of the memory,
(Though things remembered idly do half seem
The work of fancy) shall I, as the mood
Inclines me, here describe for pastime's sake
Some portion of that motley imagery,
A vivid pleasure of my youth, and now,
Among the lonely places that I love,
A frequent daydream for my riper mind?
And first the look and aspect of the place,
The broad highway appearance as it strikes
On strangers of all ages; the quick dance
Of colours, lights, and forms; the Babel din;
The endless stream of men, and moving things;
From hour to hour the illimitable walk
Still among streets with clouds and sky above;
The wealth, the bustle and the eagerness,
The glittering chariots with their pampered steeds,
Stalls, barrows, porters; midway in the street
The scavenger, who begs with hat in hand;
The labouring hackney-coaches, the rash speed
Of coaches travelling far whirled on with horn
Loud blowing, and the sturdy drayman's team
Ascending from some alley of the Thames
And striking right across the crowded Strand
Till the fore-horse veer round with punctual skill;
Here, there and everywhere a weary throng,

The Monument, and that Chamber of the Tower
Where England's sovereigns sit in long array,
Their steeds bestriding, – every mimic shape
Cased in the gleaming mail the monarch wore,
Whether for gorgeous tournament addressed,
Or life or death upon the battle-field.
Those bold imaginations in due time
Had vanished, leaving others in their stead:
And now I looked upon the living scene;
Familiarly perused it; oftentimes,
In spite of strongest disappointment, pleased
Through courteous self-submission, as a tax
Paid to the object by prescriptive right.

Rise up, thou monstrous ant-hill on the plain
Of a too busy world! Before me flow,
Thou endless stream of men and moving things!
Thy every-day appearance, as it strikes –
With wonder heightened, or sublimed by awe –
On strangers, of all ages; the quick dance
Of colours, lights, and forms; the deafening din;

The comers and the goers face to face,
Face after face; the string of dazzling wares,
Shop after shop, with symbols, blazoned names,
And all the tradesman's honours overhead –
Here, fronts of houses, like a title-page,
With letters huge inscribed from top to toe;
Stationed above the door, like guardian saints,
There, allegoric shapes, female or male,
Or physiognomies of real men,
Land-warriors, kings, or admirals of the sea,
Boyle, Shakespeare, Newton, or the attractive head
Of some Scotch doctor, famous in his day.

Meanwhile the roar continues, till at length,
Escaped as from an enemy, we turn
Abruptly into some sequestered nook
Still as a sheltered place when winds blow loud.
At leisure, thence, through tracts of thin resort
And sights and sounds that come at intervals,
We take our way. A raree-show is here
With children gathered round; another street
Presents a company of dancing dogs,
Or dromedary with an antic pair
Of monkeys on his back, a minstrel band
Of Savoyards, or, single and alone,
An English ballad-singer. Private courts
Gloomy as coffins, and unsightly lanes
Thrilled by some female vendor's scream (belike
The very shrillest of all London cries),
May then entangle us awhile,
Conducted through those labyrinths unawares
To privileged regions and inviolate
Where from their airy lodges studious lawyers
Look out on waters, walks, and gardens green.

Thence back into the throng, until we reach,
Following the tide that slackens by degrees,
Some half-frequented scene where wider streets
Bring straggling breezes of suburban air.

The comers and the goers face to face,
Face after face; the string of dazzling wares,
Shop after shop, with symbols, blazoned names,
And all the tradesman's honours overhead:
Here, fronts of houses, like a title-page,
With letters huge inscribed from top to toe,
Stationed above the door, like guardian saints;
There, allegoric shapes, female or male,
Or physiognomies of real men,
Land-warriors, kings, or admirals of the sea,
Boyle, Shakspeare, Newton, or the attractive head
Of some quack-doctor, famous in his day.

Meanwhile the roar continues, till at length,
Escaped as from an enemy, we turn
Abruptly into some sequestered nook,
Still as a sheltered place when winds blow loud!
At leisure, thence, through tracts of thin resort,
And sights and sounds that come at intervals,
We take our way. A raree-show is here,
With children gathered round; another street
Presents a company of dancing dogs,
Or dromedary, with an antic pair
Of monkeys on his back; a minstrel band
Of Savoyards; or, single and alone,
An English ballad-singer. Private courts,
Gloomy as coffins, and unsightly lanes
Thrilled by some female vendor's scream, belike
The very shrillest of all London cries,
May then entangle our impatient steps;
Conducted through those labyrinths, unawares,
To privileged regions and inviolate,
Where from their airy lodges studious lawyers
Look out on waters, walks, and gardens green.

Thence back into the throng, until we reach,
Following the tide that slackens by degrees,
Some half-frequented scene, where wider streets
Bring straggling breezes of suburban air.

Here files of ballads dangle from dead walls,
Advertisements of giant-size from high
Press forward in all colours on the sight:
These, bold in conscious merit, lower down,
That – fronted with a most imposing word –
Is peradventure one in masquerade.
As on the broadening causeway we advance
Behold a face turned up towards us, strong
In lineaments, and red with over-toil.
'Tis one perhaps already met elsewhere,
A travelling cripple, by the trunk cut short
And stumping with his arms. In sailor's garb
Another lies at length beside a range
Of written characters with chalk inscribed
Upon the smooth flat stones. The nurse is here,
The bachelor that loves to sun himself,
The military idler, and the dame
That field-ward takes her walk in decency.

Now homeward through the thickening hubbub, where
See – among less distinguishable shapes –
The Italian, with his frame of images
Upon his head, with basket at his waist
The Jew, the stately and slow-moving Turk
With freight of slippers piled beneath his arm.
Briefly, we find (if tired of random sights,
And haply to that search our thoughts should turn)
Among the crowd, conspicuous less or more
As we proceed, all specimens of man
Through all the colours which the sun bestows,
And every character of form and face:
The Swede, the Russian; from the genial south,
The Frenchman and the Spaniard; from remote
America, the hunter Indian; Moors,
Malays, Lascars, the Tartar and Chinese,
And negro ladies in white muslin gowns.

Here files of ballads dangle from dead walls;
Advertisements, of giant-size, from high
Press forward, in all colours, on the sight;
These, bold in conscious merit, lower down;
That, fronted with a most imposing word,
Is, peradventure, one in masquerade.
As on the broadening causeway we advance,
Behold, turned upwards, a face hard and strong
In lineaments, and red with over-toil.
'Tis one encountered here and everywhere;
A travelling cripple, by the trunk cut short,
And stumping on his arms. In sailor's garb
Another lies at length, beside a range
Of well-formed characters, with chalk inscribed
Upon the smooth flat stones: the Nurse is here,
The Bachelor, that loves to sun himself,
The military Idler, and the Dame,
That field-ward takes her walk with decent steps.

Now homeward through the thickening hubbub, where
See, among less distinguishable shapes,
The begging scavenger, with hat in hand;
The Italian, as he thrids his way with care,
Steadying, far-seen, a frame of images
Upon his head; with basket at his breast
The Jew; the stately and slow-moving Turk,
With freight of slippers piled beneath his arm!

Enough; – the mighty concourse I surveyed
With no unthinking mind, well pleased to note
Among the crowd all specimens of man,
Through all the colours which the sun bestows,
And every character of form and face:
The Swede, the Russian; from the genial south,
The Frenchman and the Spaniard; from remote
America, the Hunter-Indian; Moors,
Malays, Lascars, the Tartar, the Chinese,
And Negro Ladies in white muslin gowns.

At leisure let us view from day to day,
As they present themselves, the spectacles
Within doors: troops of wild beasts, birds and beasts
Of every nature, from all climes convened,
And, next to these, those mimic sights that ape
The absolute presence of reality,
Expressing as in mirror sea and land,
And what earth is, and what she has to show.
I do not here allude to subtlest craft
By means refined attaining purest ends,
But imitations fondly made in plain
Confession of man's weakness and his loves.
Whether the painter – fashioning a work
To nature's circumambient scenery,
And with his greedy pencil taking in
A whole horizon on all sides – with power
Like that of angels or commissioned spirits
Plant us upon some lofty pinnacle,
Or in a ship on waters (with a world
Of life, and life-like mockery, to east,
To west, beneath, behind us, and before),
Or more mechanic artist represent
By scale exact, in model, wood or clay,
From shading colours also borrowing help,
Some miniature of famous spots and things,
Domestic or the boast of foreign realms:
The Firth of Forth, and Edinborough throned
On crags, fit empress of that mountain land;
St Peter's Church, or (more aspiring aim)
In microscopic vision, Rome itself;
Or else perhaps some rural haunt, the Falls
Of Tivoli; and high upon that steep
The Temple of the Sibyl – every tree
Through all the landscape, tuft, stone, scratch minute,
And every cottage lurking in the rocks –
All that the traveller sees when he is there.

Add to these exhibitions mute and still
Others of wider scope, where living men,

At leisure, then, I viewed, from day to day,
The spectacles within doors, – birds and beasts
Of every nature, and strange plants convened
From every clime; and, next, those sights that ape
The absolute presence of reality,
Expressing, as in mirror, sea and land,
And what earth is, and what she has to shew.
I do not here allude to subtlest craft,
By means refined attaining purest ends,
But imitations, fondly made in plain
Confession of man's weakness and his loves.
Whether the Painter, whose ambitious skill
Submits to nothing less than taking in
A whole horizon's circuit, do with power,
Like that of angels or commissioned spirits,
Fix us upon some lofty pinnacle,
Or in a ship on waters, with a world
Of life, and life-like mockery beneath,
Above, behind, far stretching and before;
Or more mechanic artist represent
By scale exact, in model, wood or clay,
From blended colours also borrowing help,
Some miniature of famous spots or things, –
St. Peter's Church; or, more aspiring aim,
In microscopic vision, Rome herself;
Or, haply, some choice rural haunt, – the Falls
Of Tivoli; and, high upon that steep,
The Sibyl's mouldering Temple! every tree,
Villa, or cottage, lurking among rocks
Throughout the landscape; tuft, stone scratch minute –
All that the traveller sees when he is there.

And to these exhibitions, mute and still,
Others of wider scope, where living men,

Music, and shifting pantomimic scenes,
Together joined their multifarious aid
To heighten the allurement. Need I fear
To mention by its name (as in degree
Lowest of these and humblest in attempt,
Though richly graced with honours of its own)
Half-rural Sadler's Wells? Though at that time
Intolerant, as is the way of youth
Unless itself be pleased, I more than once
Here took my seat, and mauger frequent fits
Of irksomeness, with ample recompense
Saw singers, rope-dancers, giants and dwarfs,
Clowns, conjurors, posture-masters, harlequins,
Amid the uproar of the rabblement
Perform their feats. Nor was it mean delight
To watch crude nature work in untaught minds,
To note the laws and progress of belief –
Though obstinate on this way, yet on that
How willingly we travel, and how far! –
To have, for instance, brought upon the scene
The champion, Jack the Giant-killer: lo!
He dons his coat of darkness, on the stage
Walks, and achieves his wonders, from the eye
Of living mortal safe as is the moon
'Hid in her vacant interlunar cave'.
Delusion bold! – and faith must needs be coy –
How is it wrought? His garb is black, the word
'*Invisible*' flames forth upon his chest.

Nor was it unamusing here to view
Those samples as of ancient comedy
And Thespian times, dramas of living men,
And recent things yet warm with life: a sea-fight,
Shipwreck, or some domestic incident
The fame of which is scattered through the land;
Such as of late this daring brotherhood
Set forth (too holy theme for such a place,
And doubtless treated with irreverence
Albeit with their very best of skill),

Music, and shifting pantomimic scenes,
Diversified the allurement. Need I fear
To mention by its name, as in degree,
Lowest of these and humblest in attempt,
Yet richly graced with honours of her own,
Half-rural Sadler's Wells? Though at that time
Intolerant, as is the way of youth
Unless itself be pleased, here more than once
Taking my seat, I saw (nor blush to add,
With ample recompense) giants and dwarfs,
Clowns, conjurors, posture-masters, harlequins,
Amid the uproar of the rabblement,
Perform their feats. Nor was it mean delight
To watch crude Nature work in untaught minds;
To note the laws and progress of belief;
Though obstinate on this way, yet on that
How willingly we travel, and how far!
To have, for instance, brought upon the scene
The champion, Jack the Giant-killer: Lo!
He dons his coat of darkness; on the stage
Walks, and achieves his wonders, from the eye
Of living Mortal covert, 'as the moon
Hid in her vacant interlunar cave.'
Delusion bold! and how can it be wrought?
The garb he wears is black as death, the word
'*Invisible*' flames forth upon his chest.

Here, too, were 'forms and pressures of the time,'
Rough, bold, as Grecian comedy displayed
When Art was young; dramas of living men,
And recent things yet warm with life; a sea-fight,
Shipwreck, or some domestic incident
Divulged by Truth and magnified by Fame,
Such as the daring brotherhood of late
Set forth, too serious theme for that light place –

I mean, o distant friend, a story drawn
From our own ground, *The Maid of Buttermere*,
And how the spoiler came 'a bold bad man'
To God unfaithful, children, wife, and home,
And wooed the artless daughter of the hills,
And wedded her, in cruel mockery
Of love and marriage bonds. O friend, I speak
With tender recollection of that time
When first we saw the maiden, then a name
By us unheard of – in her cottage-inn
Were welcomed and attended on by her,
Both stricken with one feeling of delight,
An admiration of her modest mien
And carriage, marked by unexampled grace.
Not unfamiliarly we since that time
Have seen her, her discretion have observed,
Her just opinions, female modesty,
Her patience, and retirèdness of mind
Unsoiled by commendation and the excess
Of public notice. This memorial verse
Comes from the poet's heart, and is her due –
For we were nursed (as almost might be said)
On the same mountains; children at one time,
Must haply often on the self-same day
Have from our several dwellings gone abroad
To gather daffodils on Coker's stream.

These last words uttered, to my argument
I was returning, when – with sundry forms
Mingled, that in the way which I must tread
Before me stand – thy image rose again,
Mary of Buttermere! She lives in peace
Upon the ground where she was born and reared;
Without contamination does she live
In quietness, without anxiety.
Beside the mountain-chapel sleeps in earth
Her newborn infant, fearless as a lamb
That thither comes from some unsheltered place
To rest beneath the little rock-like pile

I mean, O distant Friend! a story drawn
From our own ground, – the Maid of Buttermere, –
And how, unfaithful to a virtuous wife
Deserted and deceived, the spoiler came
And wooed the artless daughter of the hills,
And wedded her, in cruel mockery
Of love and marriage bonds. These words to thee
Must needs bring back the moment when we first,
Ere the broad world rang with the maiden's name,
Beheld her serving at the cottage inn,
Both stricken, as she entered or withdrew,
With admiration of her modest mien
And carriage, marked by unexampled grace.
We since that time not unfamiliarly
Have seen her, – her discretion have observed,
Her just opinions, delicate reserve,
Her patience, and humility of mind
Unspoiled by commendation and the excess
Of public notice – an offensive light
To a meek spirit suffering inwardly.

From this memorial tribute to my theme
I was returning, when, with sundry forms
Commingled – shapes which met me in the way
That we must tread – thy image rose again,
Maiden of Buttermere! She lives in peace
Upon the spot where she was born and reared;
Without contamination doth she live
In quietness, without anxiety:
Beside the mountain chapel, sleeps in earth
Her new-born infant, fearless as a lamb
That, thither driven from some unsheltered place,
Rests underneath the little rock-like pile

When storms are blowing. Happy are they both,
Mother and child! These feelings – in themselves
Trite – do yet scarcely seem so when I think
Of those ingenuous moments of our youth
Ere yet by use we have learnt to slight the crimes
And sorrows of the world. Those days are now
My theme, and, mid the numerous scenes which they
Have left behind them, foremost I am crossed
Here by remembrance of two figures, one
A rosy babe, who for a twelvemonth's space
Perhaps had been of age to deal about
Articulate prattle, child as beautiful
As ever sat upon a mother's knee;
The other was the parent of that babe –
But on the mother's cheek the tints were false,
A painted bloom.

'Twas at a theatre
That I beheld this pair; the boy had been
The pride and pleasure of all lookers-on
In whatsoever place, but seemed in this
A sort of alien scattered from the clouds.
Of lusty vigour, more than infantine,
He was in limbs, in face a cottage rose
Just three parts blown – a cottage-child, but ne'er
Saw I, by cottage or elsewhere, a babe
By nature's gifts so honoured. Upon a board
Whence an attendant of the theatre
Served out refreshments, had this child been placed,
And there he sat, environed with a ring
Of chance spectators, chiefly dissolute men
And shameless women – treated and caressed –
Ate, drank, and with the fruit and glasses played,
While oaths, indecent speech, and ribaldry
Were rife about him as are songs of birds
In springtime after showers. The mother too
Was present, but of her I know no more
Than hath been said, and scarcely at this time
Do I remember her. But I behold

When storms are raging. Happy are they both –
Mother and child! – These feelings, in themselves
Trite, do yet scarcely seem so when I think
On those ingenuous moments of our youth
Ere we have learnt by use to slight the crimes
And sorrows of the world. Those simple days
Are now my theme; and, foremost of the scenes,
Which yet survive in memory, appears
One, at whose centre sate a lovely Boy,
A sportive infant, who, for six months' space,
Not more, had been of age to deal about
Articulate prattle – Child as beautiful
As ever clung around a mother's neck,
Or father fondly gazed upon with pride.
There, too, conspicuous for stature tall
And large dark eyes, beside her infant stood
The mother; but, upon her cheeks diffused,
False tints too well accorded with the glare
From play-house lustres thrown without reserve
On every object near. The Boy had been
The pride and pleasure of all lookers-on
In whatsoever place, but seemed in this
A sort of alien scattered from the clouds.
Of lusty vigour, more than infantine
He was in limb, in cheek a summer rose
Just three parts blown – a cottage-child – if e'er,
By cottage-door on breezy mountain side,
Or in some sheltering vale, was seen a babe
By Nature's gifts so favoured. Upon a board
Decked with refreshments had this child been placed,
His little stage in the vast theatre,
And there he sate surrounded with a throng
Of chance spectators, chiefly dissolute men
And shameless women, treated and caressed;
Ate, drank, and with the fruit and glasses played,
While oaths and laughter and indecent speech
Were rife about him as the songs of birds
Contending after showers. The mother now
Is fading out of memory, but I see

The lovely boy as I beheld him then
Among the wretched and the falsely gay,
Like one of those who walked with hair unsinged
Amid the fiery furnace. He has since
Appeared to me ofttimes as if embalmed
By nature, through some special privilege
Stopped at the growth he had – destined to live,
To be, to have been, come and go, a child
And nothing more, no partner in the years
That bear us forward to distress and guilt,
Pain and abasement – beauty in such excess
Adorned him in that miserable place.
So have I thought of him a thousand times,
And seldom otherwise. But he perhaps,
Mary, may now have lived till he could look
With envy on thy nameless babe that sleeps
Beside the mountain-chapel undisturbed.

It was but little more than three short years
Before the season which I speak of now
When first, a traveller from our pastoral hills,
Southward two hundred miles I had advanced
And for the first time in my life did hear
The voice of woman utter blasphemy –
Saw woman as she is to open shame
Abandoned, and the pride of public vice.
Full surely from the bottom of my heart
I shuddered, but the pain was almost lost,
Absorbed and buried in the immensity
Of the effect: a barrier seemed at once
Thrown in, that from humanity divorced
The human form, splitting the race of man
In twain, yet leaving the same outward shape.
Distress of mind ensued upon this sight
And ardent meditation. Afterwards
A milder sadness on such spectacles
Attended – thought, commiseration, grief
For the individual and the overthrow
Of her soul's beauty – farther at that time

The lovely Boy as I beheld him then
Among the wretched and the falsely gay,
Like one of those who walked with hair unsinged
Amid the fiery furnace. Charms and spells
Muttered on black and spiteful instigation
Have stopped, as some believe, the kindliest growths.
Ah, with how different spirit might a prayer
Have been preferred, that this fair creature, checked
By special privilege of Nature's love,
Should in his childhood be detained for ever!
But with its universal freight the tide
Hath rolled along, and this bright innocent,
Mary! may now have lived till he could look
With envy on thy nameless babe that sleeps,
Beside the mountain chapel, undisturbed.

Four rapid years had scarcely then been told
Since, travelling southward from our pastoral hills,
I heard, and for the first time in my life,
The voice of woman utter blasphemy –
Saw woman as she is, to open shame
Abandoned, and the pride of public vice;
I shuddered, for a barrier seemed at once
Thrown in, that from humanity divorced
Humanity, splitting the race of man
In twain, yet leaving the same outward form.
Distress of mind ensued upon the sight
And ardent meditation. Later years
Brought to such spectacle a milder sadness,
Feelings of pure commiseration, grief
For the individual and the overthrow
Of her soul's beauty; farther I was then

Than this I was but seldom led. In truth
The sorrow of the passion stopped me here.

I quit this painful theme; enough is said
To show what thoughts must often have been mine
At theatres, which then were my delight –
A yearning made more strong by obstacles
Which slender funds imposed. Life then was new,
The senses easily pleased. The lustres, lights,
The carving and the gilding, paint and glare,
And all the mean upholstery of the place,
Wanted not animation in my sight,
Far less the living figures on the stage,
Solemn or gay – whether some beauteous dame
Advanced in radiance through a deep recess
Of thick entangled forest, like the moon
Opening the clouds; or sovereign king, announced
With flourishing trumpets, came in full-blown state
Of the world's greatness, winding round with train
Of courtiers, banners, and a length of guards,
Or captive led in abject weeds and jingling
His slender manacles; or romping girl
Bounced, leapt, and pawed the air; or mumbling sire,
A scare-crow pattern of old age patched up
Of all the tatters of infirmity
All loosely put together, hobbled in,
Stumping upon a cane with which he smites,
From time to time, the solid boards, and makes them
Prate somewhat loudly of the whereabout
Of one so overloaded with his years.
But what of this? The laugh, the grin, grimace,
And all the antics and buffoonery,
The least of them not lost, were all received
With charitable pleasure. Through the night,
Between the show and many-headed mass
Of the spectators, and each little nook

But seldom led, or wished to go; in truth
The sorrow of the passion stopped me there.

But let me now, less moved, in order take
Our argument. Enough is said to show
How casual incidents of real life,
Observed where pastime only had been sought,
Outweighed, or put to flight, the set events
And measured passions of the stage, albeit
By Siddons trod in the fulness of her power.
Yet was the theatre my dear delight;
The very gilding, lamps and painted scrolls,
And all the mean upholstery of the place,
Wanted not animation, when the tide
Of pleasure ebbed but to return as fast
With the ever-shifting figures of the scene,
Solemn or gay: whether some beauteous dame
Advanced in radiance through a deep recess
Of thick entangled forest, like the moon
Opening the clouds; or sovereign king, announced
With flourishing trumpet, came in full-blown state
Of the world's greatness, winding round with train
Of courtiers, banners, and a length of guards;
Or captive led in abject weeds, and jingling
His slender manacles; or romping girl
Bounced, leapt, and pawed the air; or mumbling sire,
A scare-crow pattern of old age dressed up
In all the tatters of infirmity
All loosely put together, hobbled in,
Stumping upon a cane with which he smites,
From time to time, the solid boards, and makes them
Prate somewhat loudly of the whereabout
Of one so overloaded with his years.
But what of this! the laugh, the grin, grimace,
The antics striving to outstrip each other,
Were all received, the least of them not lost,
With an unmeasured welcome. Through the night,
Between the show, and many-headed mass
Of the spectators, and each several nook

That had its fray or brawl, how eagerly
And with what flashes (as it were) the mind
Turned this way, that way – sportive and alert
And watchful as a kitten when at play,
While winds are blowing round her, among grass
And rustling leaves. Enchanting age and sweet –
Romantic almost, looked at through a space,
How small, of intervening years! For then,
Though surely no mean progress had been made
In meditations holy and sublime,
Yet something of a girlish childlike gloss
Of novelty survived for scenes like these –
Pleasure that had been handed down from times
When at a country-playhouse, having caught
In summer through the fractured wall, a glimpse
Of daylight, at the thought of where I was
I gladdened more than if I had beheld
Before me some bright cavern of romance,
Or than we do when on our beds we lie
At night, in warmth, when rains are beating hard.

The matter which detains me now will seem
To many neither dignified enough
Nor arduous, and is doubtless in itself
Humble and low – yet not to be despised
By those who have observed the curious props
By which the perishable hours of life
Rest on each other, and the world of thought
Exists and is sustained. More lofty themes,
Such as at least do wear a prouder face,
Might here be spoken of, but when I think
Of these I feel the imaginative power
Languish within me. Even then it slept
When wrought upon by tragic sufferings,
The heart was full; amid my sobs and tears
It slept even in the season of my youth.
For though I was most passionately moved

Filled with its fray or brawl, how eagerly
And with what flashes, as it were, the mind
Turned this way – that way! sportive and alert
And watchful, as a kitten when at play,
While winds are eddying round her, among straws
And rustling leaves. Enchanting age and sweet!
Romantic almost, looked at through a space,
How small, of intervening years! For then,
Though surely no mean progress had been made
In meditations holy and sublime,
Yet something of a girlish child-like gloss
Of novelty survived for scenes like these;
Enjoyment haply handed down from times
When at a country-playhouse, some rude barn
Tricked out for that proud use, if I perchance
Caught, on a summer evening through a chink
In the old wall, an unexpected glimpse
Of daylight, the bare thought of where I was
Gladdened me more than if I had been led
Into a dazzling cavern of romance,
Crowded with Genii busy among works
Not to be looked at by the common sun.

The matter that detains us now may seem,
To many, neither dignified enough
Nor arduous, yet will not be scorned by them,
Who, looking inward, have observed the ties
That bind the perishable hours of life
Each to the other, and the curious props
By which the world of memory and thought
Exists and is sustained. More lofty themes,
Such as at least do wear a prouder face,
Solicit our regard; but when I think
Of these, I feel the imaginative power
Languish within me; even then it slept,
When, pressed by tragic sufferings, the heart
Was more than full; amid my sobs and tears
It slept, even in the pregnant season of youth.
For though I was most passionately moved

And yielded to the changes of the scene
With most obsequious feeling, yet all this
Passed not beyond the suburbs of the mind.
If aught there were of real grandeur here
'Twas only then when gross realities,
The incarnation of the spirits that moved
Amid the poet's beauteous world – called forth
With that distinctness which a contrast gives,
Or opposition – made me recognize
As by a glimpse, the things which I had shaped
And yet not shaped, had seen and scarcely seen,
Had felt, and thought of in my solitude.

Pass we from entertainments that are such
Professedly, to others titled higher,
Yet (in the estimate of youth at least)
More near akin to these than names imply,
I mean the brawls of lawyers in their courts
Before the ermined judge, or that great stage
Where senators – tongue-favoured men – perform,
Admired and envied. Oh, the beating heart
When one among the prime of these rose up,
One of whose name from childhood we had heard
Familiarly, a household term like those,
The Bedfords, Gloucesters, Salisburys, of old
Which the fifth Harry talks of. Silence! hush!
This is no trifler, no short-flighted wit,
Nor stammerer of a minute, painfully
Delivered. No, the orator hath yoked
The hours, like young Aurora, to his car –
Oh, presence of delight, can patience e'er
Grow weary of attending on a track
That kindles with such glory? Marvellous –
The enchantment spreads and rises – all are rapt,
Astonished! Like a hero in romance
He winds away his never-ending horn!
Words follow words, sense seems to follow sense –
What memory and what logic! – till the strain,

And yielded to all changes of the scene
With an obsequious promptness, yet the storm
Passed not beyond the suburbs of the mind;
Save when realities of act and mien,
The incarnation of the spirits that move
In harmony amid the Poet's world,
Rose to ideal grandeur, or, called forth
By power of contrast, made me recognise,
As at a glance, the things which I had shaped,
And yet not shaped, had seen and scarcely seen,
When, having closed the mighty Shakspeare's page,
I mused, and thought, and felt, in solitude.

Pass we from entertainments, that are such
Professedly, to others titled higher,
Yet, in the estimate of youth at least,
More near akin to those than names imply, –
I mean the brawls of lawyers in their courts
Before the ermined judge, or that great stage
Where senators, tongue-favoured men, perform,
Admired and envied. Oh! the beating heart,
When one among the prime of these rose up, –
One, of whose name from childhood we had heard
Familiarly, a household term, like those,
The Bedfords, Glosters, Salsburys, of old
Whom the fifth Harry talks of. Silence! hush!
This is no trifler, no short-flighted wit,
No stammerer of a minute, painfully
Delivered. No! the Orator hath yoked
The Hours, like young Aurora, to his car:
Thrice welcome Presence! how can patience e'er
Grow weary of attending on a track
That kindles with such glory! All are charmed,
Astonished; like a hero in romance,
He winds away his never-ending horn;
Words follow words, sense seems to follow sense:
What memory and what logic! till the strain

Transcendent, superhuman as it is,
Grows tedious even in a young man's ear.

Transcendent, superhuman as it seemed,
Grows tedious even in a young man's ear.

Genius of Burke! forgive the pen seduced
By specious wonders, and too slow to tell
Of what the ingenuous, what bewildered men,
Beginning to mistrust their boastful guides,
And wise men, willing to grow wiser, caught,
Rapt auditors! from thy most eloquent tongue –
Now mute, for ever mute in the cold grave.
I see him, – old, but vigorous in age, –
Stand like an oak whose stag-horn branches start
Out of its leafy brow, the more to awe
The younger brethren of the grove. But some –
While he forewarns, denounces, launches forth,
Against all systems built on abstract rights,
Keen ridicule; the majesty proclaims
Of Institutes and Laws, hallowed by time;
Declares the vital power of social ties
Endeared by Custom; and with high disdain,
Exploding upstart Theory, insists
Upon the allegiance to which men are born –
Some – say at once a froward multitude –
Murmur (for truth is hated, where not loved)
As the winds fret within the Æolian cave,
Galled by their monarch's chain. The times were big
With ominous change, which, night by night, provoked
Keen struggles, and black clouds of passion raised;
But memorable moments intervened,
When Wisdom, like the Goddess from Jove's brain,
Broke forth in armour of resplendent words,
Startling the Synod. Could a youth, and one
In ancient story versed, whose breast had heaved
Under the weight of classic eloquence,
Sit, see, and hear, unthankful, uninspired?

Nor did the Pulpit's oratory fail
To achieve its higher triumph. Not unfelt
Were its admonishments, nor lightly heard

These are grave follies; other public shows
The capital city teems with, of a kind
More light – and where but in the holy church?
There have I seen a comely bachelor,
Fresh from a toilette of two hours, ascend
The pulpit, with seraphic glance look up,
And, in a tone elaborately low
Beginning, lead his voice through many a maze
A minuet course, and, winding up his mouth
From time to time into an orifice
Most delicate, a lurking eyelet, small
And only not invisible, again
Open it out, diffusing thence a smile
Of rapt irradiation, exquisite.
Meanwhile the Evangelists, Isaiah, Job,
Moses, and he who penned, the other day,
The Death of Abel, Shakespeare, Doctor Young,
And Ossian (doubt not, 'tis the naked truth)
Summoned from streamy Morven – each and all
Must in their turn lend ornament and flowers
To entwine the crook of eloquence with which
This pretty shepherd, pride of all the plains,
Leads up and down his captivated flock.

I glance but at a few conspicuous marks,
Leaving ten thousand others that do each –
In hall or court, conventicle or shop,
In public room or private, park or street –
With fondness reared on his own pedestal,
Look out for admiration. Folly, vice,
Extravagance in gesture, mien, and dress,
And all the strife of singularity
(Lies to the ear, and lies to every sense),
Of these, and of the living shapes they wear,
There is no end. Such candidates for regard,
Although well pleased to be where they were found,

The awful truths delivered thence by tongues
Endowed with various power to search the soul;
Yet ostentation, domineering, oft
Poured forth harangues, how sadly out of place! –
There have I seen a comely bachelor,
Fresh from a toilette of two hours, ascend
His rostrum, with seraphic glance look up,
And, in a tone elaborately low
Beginning, lead his voice through many a maze
A minuet course; and, winding up his mouth,
From time to time, into an orifice
Most delicate, a lurking eyelet, small,
And only not invisible, again
Open it out, diffusing thence a smile
Of rapt irradiation, exquisite.
Meanwhile the Evangelists, Isaiah, Job,
Moses, and he who penned, the other day,
The Death of Abel, Shakspeare, and the Bard
Whose genius spangled o'er a gloomy theme
With fancies thick as his inspiring stars,
And Ossian (doubt not, 'tis the naked truth)
Summoned from streamy Morven – each and all
Would, in their turns, lend ornaments and flowers
To entwine the crook of eloquence that helped
This pretty Shepherd, pride of all the plains,
To rule and guide his captivated flock.

I glance but at a few conspicuous marks,
Leaving a thousand others, that, in hall,
Court, theatre, conventicle, or shop,
In public room or private, park or street,
Each fondly reared on his own pedestal,
Looked out for admiration. Folly, vice,
Extravagance in gesture, mien, and dress,
And all the strife of singularity,
Lies to the ear, and lies to every sense –
Of these, and of the living shapes they wear,
There is no end. Such candidates for regard,
Although well pleased to be where they were found,

I did not hunt after or greatly prize,
Nor made unto myself a secret boast
Of reading them with quick and curious eye,
But as a common produce – things that are
Today, tomorrow will be – took of them
Such willing note as, on some errand bound
Of pleasure or of love, some traveller might
(Among a thousand other images)
Of sea-shells that bestud the sandy beach,
Or daisies swarming through the fields in June.

But foolishness and madness in parade,
Though most at home in this their dear domain,
Are scattered everywhere, no rarities
Even to the rudest novice of the schools.
O friend, one feeling was there which belonged
To this great city by exclusive right –

I did not hunt after, nor greatly prize,
Nor made unto myself a secret boast
Of reading them with quick and curious eye;
But, as a common produce, things that are
To-day, to-morrow will be, took of them
Such willing note, as, on some errand bound
That asks not speed, a Traveller might bestow
On sea-shells that bestrew the sandy beach,
Or daisies swarming through the fields of June.

But foolishness and madness in parade,
Though most at home in this their dear domain,
Are scattered everywhere, no rarities,
Even to the rudest novice of the Schools.
Me, rather, it employed, to note, and keep
In memory, those individual sights
Of courage, or integrity, or truth,
Or tenderness, which there, set off by foil,
Appeared more touching. One will I select;
A Father – for he bore that sacred name –
Him saw I, sitting in an open square,
Upon a corner-stone of that low wall,
Wherein were fixed the iron pales that fenced
A spacious grass-plot; there, in silence, sate
This One Man, with a sickly babe outstretched
Upon his knee, whom he had thither brought
For sunshine, and to breathe the fresher air.
Of those who passed, and me who looked at him,
He took no heed; but in his brawny arms
(The Artificer was to the elbow bare,
And from his work this moment had been stolen)
He held the child, and, bending over it,
As if he were afraid both of the sun
And of the air, which he had come to seek,
Eyed the poor babe with love unutterable.

As the black storm upon the mountain top
Sets off the sunbeam in the valley, so

How often in the overflowing streets
Have I gone forwards with the crowd, and said
Unto myself 'The face of everyone
That passes by me is a mystery!'
Thus have I looked, nor ceased to look, oppressed
By thoughts of what and whither, when and how,
Until the shapes before my eyes became
A second-sight procession such as glides
Over still mountains, or appears in dreams,
And all the ballast of familiar life –
The present and the past, hope, fear, all stays,
All laws, of acting, thinking, speaking man –
Went from me, neither knowing me, nor known.
And once, far travelled in such mood, beyond
The reach of common indications, lost
Amid the moving pageant, 'twas my chance
Abruptly to be smitten with the view
Of a blind beggar, who, with upright face,
Stood propped against a wall, upon his chest
Wearing a written paper to explain
The story of the man and who he was.
My mind did at this spectacle turn round
As with the might of waters, and it seemed
To me that in this label was a type
Or emblem of the utmost that we know
Both of ourselves and of the universe;
And, on the shape of this unmoving man,
His fixèd face and sightless eyes, I looked
As if admonished from another world.

Though reared upon the base of outward things,
These chiefly are such structures as the mind
Builds for itself. Scenes different there are,
Full-formed, which take, with small internal help,
Possession of the faculties: the peace
Of night, for instance, the solemnity
Of nature's intermediate hours of rest
When the great tide of human life stands still,

That huge fermenting mass of human-kind
Serves as a solemn back-ground, or relief,
To single forms and objects, whence they draw,
For feeling and contemplative regard,
More than inherent liveliness and power.
How oft, amid those overflowing streets,
Have I gone forward with the crowd, and said
Unto myself, 'The face of every one
That passes by me is a mystery!'
Thus have I looked, nor ceased to look, oppressed
By thoughts of what and whither, when and how,
Until the shapes before my eyes became
A second-sight procession, such as glides
Over still mountains, or appears in dreams;
And once, far-travelled in such mood, beyond
The reach of common indication, lost
Amid the moving pageant, I was smitten
Abruptly, with the view (a sight not rare)
Of a blind Beggar, who, with upright face,
Stood, propped against a wall, upon his chest
Wearing a written paper, to explain
His story, whence he came, and who he was.
Caught by the spectacle my mind turned round
As with the might of waters; an apt type
This label seemed of the utmost we can know,
Both of ourselves and of the universe;
And, on the shape of that unmoving man,
His steadfast face and sightless eyes, I gazed,
As if admonished from another world.

Though reared upon the base of outward things,
Structures like these the excited spirit mainly
Builds for herself; scenes different there are,
Full-formed, that take, with small internal help,
Possession of the faculties, – the peace
That comes with night; the deep solemnity
Of nature's intermediate hours of rest,
When the great tide of human life stands still;

The business of the day to come unborn,
Of that gone by locked up as in the grave;
The calmness, beauty, of the spectacle,
Sky, stillness, moonshine, empty streets, and sounds
Unfrequent as in deserts; at late hours
Of winter evenings, when unwholesome rains
Are falling hard, with people yet astir,
The feeble salutation from the voice
Of some unhappy woman now and then
Heard as we pass, when no one looks about,
Nothing is listened to. But these I fear
Are falsely catalogued – things that are, are not,
Even as we give them welcome, or assist,
Are prompt or are remiss. What say you then
To times when half the city shall break out
Full of one passion (vengeance, rage, or fear)
To executions, to a street on fire,
Mobs, riots, or rejoicings? From those sights
Take one, an annual festival, the fair
Holden where martyrs suffered in past time,
And named of St Bartholomew. There see
A work that's finished to our hands, that lays –
If any spectacle on earth can do –
The whole creative powers of man asleep!
For once the muse's help will we implore
And she shall lodge us, wafted on her wings,
Above the press and danger of the crowd,
Upon some showman's platform.

What a hell
For eyes and ears, what anarchy and din
Barbarian and infernal – 'tis a dream
Monstrous in colour, motion, shape, sight, sound!
Below, the open space, through every nook
Of the wide area, twinkles, is alive
With heads; the midway region and above
Is thronged with staring pictures and huge scrolls,
Dumb proclamations of the prodigies,

The business of the day to come, unborn,
Of that gone by, locked up, as in the grave;
The blended calmness of the heavens and earth,
Moonlight and stars, and empty streets, and sounds
Unfrequent as in deserts; at late hours
Of winter evenings, when unwholesome rains
Are falling hard, with people yet astir,
The feeble salutation from the voice
Of some unhappy woman, now and then
Heard as we pass, when no one looks about,
Nothing is listened to. But these, I fear,
Are falsely catalogued; things that are, are not,
As the mind answers to them, or the heart
Is prompt, or slow, to feel. What say you, then,
To times, when half the city shall break out
Full of one passion, vengeance, rage, or fear?
To executions, to a street on fire,
Mobs, riots, or rejoicings? From these sights
Take one, – that ancient festival, the Fair,
Holden where martyrs suffered in past time,
And named of St. Bartholomew; there, see
A work completed to our hands, that lays,
If any spectacle on earth can do,
The whole creative powers of man asleep! –
For once, the Muse's help will we implore,
And she shall lodge us, wafted on her wings,
Above the press and danger of the crowd,
Upon some showman's platform. What a shock
For eyes and ears! what anarchy and din,
Barbarian and infernal, – a phantasma,
Monstrous in colour, motion, shape, sight, sound!
Below, the open space, through every nook
Of the wide area, twinkles, is alive
With heads; the midway region, and above,
Is thronged with staring pictures and huge scrolls,
Dumb proclamations of the Prodigies;

And chattering monkeys dangling from their poles,
And children whirling in their roundabouts;
With those that stretch the neck and strain the eyes,
And crack the voice in rivalship (the crowd
Inviting), with buffoons against buffoons
Grimacing, writhing, screaming – him who grinds
The hurdy-gurdy, at the fiddle weaves,
Rattles the salt-box, thumps the kettle-drum,
And him who at the trumpet puffs his cheeks,
The silver-collared negro with his timbrel,
Equestrians, tumblers, women, girls, and boys,
Blue-breeched, pink-vested, and with towering plumes.
All moveables of wonder, from all parts,
Are here: albinos, painted Indians, dwarfs,
The horse of knowledge and the learned pig,
The stone-eater, the man that swallows fire,
Giants, ventriloquists, the invisible girl,
The bust that speaks and moves its goggling eyes,
The wax-work, clock-work, all the marvellous craft
Of modern Merlins, wild beasts, puppet-shows,
All out-o'-the-way, far-fetched, perverted things,
All freaks of nature, all Promethean thoughts
Of man – his dulness, madness, and their feats –
All jumbled up together to make up
This parliament of monsters. Tents and booths
Meanwhile, as if the whole were one vast mill,
Are vomiting, receiving, on all sides,
Men, women, three-years' children, babes in arms.

Oh, blank confusion, and a type not false
Of what the mighty city is itself
To all except a straggler here and there –
To the whole swarm of its inhabitants –
An undistinguishable world to men,
The slaves unrespited of low pursuits
Living amid the same perpetual flow
Of trivial objects, melted and reduced
To one identity by differences

With chattering monkeys dangling from their poles,
And children whirling in their roundabouts;
With those that stretch the neck and strain the eyes,
And crack the voice in rivalship, the crowd
Inviting; with buffoons against buffoons
Grimacing, writhing, screaming, – him who grinds
The hurdy-gurdy, at the fiddle weaves,
Rattles the salt-box, thumps the kettle-drum,
And him who at the trumpet puffs his cheeks,
The silver-collared Negro with his timbrel,
Equestrians, tumblers, women, girls, and boys,
Blue-breeched, pink-vested, with high-towering plumes. –
All moveables of wonder, from all parts,
Are here – Albinos, painted Indians, Dwarfs,
The Horse of knowledge, and the learned Pig,
The Stone-eater, the man that swallows fire,
Giants, Ventriloquists, the Invisible Girl,
The Bust that speaks and moves its goggling eyes,
The Wax-work, Clock-work, all the marvellous craft
Of modern Merlins, Wild Beasts, Puppet-shows,
All out-o'-the-way, far-fetched, perverted things,
All freaks of nature, all Promethean thoughts
Of man, his dullness, madness, and their feats
All jumbled up together, to compose
A Parliament of Monsters. Tents and Booths
Meanwhile, as if the whole were one vast mill,
Are vomiting, receiving on all sides,
Men, Women, three-years' Children, Babes in arms.

Oh, blank confusion! true epitome
Of what the mighty City is herself,
To thousands upon thousands of her sons,
Living amid the same perpetual whirl
Of trivial objects, melted and reduced
To one identity, by differences

That have no law, no meaning, and no end –
Oppression under which even highest minds
Must labour, whence the strongest are not free.
But though the picture weary out the eye,
By nature an unmanageable sight,
It is not wholly so to him who looks
In steadiness, who hath among least things
An under-sense of greatest – sees the parts
As parts, but with a feeling of the whole.
This (of all acquisitions first) awaits
On sundry and most widely different modes
Of education; nor with least delight
On that through which I passed. Attention comes,
And comprehensiveness and memory,
From early converse with the works of God
Among all regions, chiefly where appear
Most obviously simplicity and power.
By influence habitual to the mind
The mountain's outline and its steady form
Gives a pure grandeur, and its presence shapes
The measure and the prospect of the soul
To majesty. Such virtue have the forms
Perennial of the ancient hills; nor less
The changeful language of their countenances
Gives movement to the thoughts, and multitude,
With order and relation. This (if still
As hitherto with freedom I may speak
And the same perfect openness of mind,
Not violating any just restraint,
As I would hope, of real modesty),
This did I feel in that vast receptacle.
The spirit of nature was upon me here;

That have no law, no meaning, and no end –
Oppression, under which even highest minds
Must labour, whence the strongest are not free.
But though the picture weary out the eye,
By nature an unmanageable sight,
It is not wholly so to him who looks
In steadiness, who hath among least things
An under-sense of greatest; sees the parts
As parts, but with a feeling of the whole.
This, of all acquisitions, first awaits
On sundry and most widely different modes
Of education, nor with least delight
On that through which I passed. Attention springs,
And comprehensiveness and memory flow,
From early converse with the works of God
Among all regions; chiefly where appear
Most obviously simplicity and power.
Think, how the everlasting streams and woods,
Stretched and still stretching far and wide, exalt
The roving Indian, on his desert sands:
What grandeur not unfelt, what pregnant show
Of beauty, meets the sun-burnt Arab's eye:
And, as the sea propels, from zone to zone,
Its currents; magnifies its shoals of life
Beyond all compass; spreads, and sends aloft
Armies of clouds, – even so, its powers and aspects
Shape for mankind, by principles as fixed,
The views and aspirations of the soul
To majesty. Like virtue have the forms
Perennial of the ancient hills; nor less
The changeful language of their countenances
Quickens the slumbering mind, and aids the thoughts,
However multitudinous, to move
With order and relation. This, if still,
As hitherto, in freedom I may speak,
Not violating any just restraint,
As may be hoped, of real modesty, –
This did I feel, in London's vast domain.
The Spirit of Nature was upon me there;

The soul of beauty and enduring life
Was present as a habit, and diffused –
Through meagre lines and colours, and the press
Of self-destroying, transitory things –
Composure and ennobling harmony.

The soul of Beauty and enduring Life
Vouchsafed her inspiration, and diffused,
Through meagre lines and colours, and the press
Of self-destroying, transitory things,
Composure, and ennobling Harmony.

Book Eighth

RETROSPECT – LOVE OF NATURE LEADING TO LOVE OF MANKIND

What sounds are those, Helvellyn, which are heard
Up to thy summit, through the depth of air
Ascending as if distance had the power
To make the sounds more audible? What crowd
Is yon, assembled in the gay green field?
Crowd seems it, solitary hill, to thee,
Though but a little family of men
(Twice twenty), with their children and their wives,
And here and there a stranger interspersed.
It is a summer festival, a fair,
Such as – on this side now, and now on that,
Repeated through his tributary vales –
Helvellyn in the silence of his rest
Sees annually, if storms be not abroad
And mists have left him an unshrouded head.
Delightful day it is for all who dwell
In this secluded glen, and eagerly
They give it welcome.

Long ere heat of noon
Behold the cattle are driven down; the sheep
That have for traffic been culled out are penned
In cotes that stand together on the plain
Ranged side by side; the chaffering is begun.
The heifer lows, uneasy at the voice
Of a new master; bleat the flocks aloud.
Booths are there none: a stall or two is here,
A lame man or a blind (the one to beg,
The other to make music), hither too
From far, with basket slung upon her arm

Book Eighth

RETROSPECT – LOVE OF NATURE LEADING TO LOVE OF MAN

What sounds are those, Helvellyn, that are heard
Up to thy summit, through the depth of air
Ascending, as if distance had the power
To make the sounds more audible? What crowd
Covers, or sprinkles o'er, yon village green?
Crowd seems it, solitary hill! to thee,
Though but a little family of men,
Shepherds and tillers of the ground – betimes
Assembled with their children and their wives,
And here and there a stranger interspersed.
They hold a rustic fair – a festival,
Such as, on this side now, and now on that,
Repeated through his tributary vales,
Helvellyn, in the silence of his rest,
Sees annually, if clouds towards either ocean
Blown from their favourite resting-place, or mists
Dissolved, have left him an unshrouded head.
Delightful day it is for all who dwell
In this secluded glen, and eagerly
They give it welcome. Long ere heat of noon,
From byre or field the kine were brought; the sheep
Are penned in cotes; the chaffering is begun.
The heifer lows, uneasy at the voice
Of a new master; bleat the flocks aloud.
Booths are there none; a stall or two is here;
A lame man or a blind, the one to beg,
The other to make music; hither, too,
From far, with basket, slung upon her arm,

Of hawker's wares – books, pictures, combs, and pins –
Some aged woman finds her way again,
Year after year a punctual visitant;
The showman with his freight upon his back,
And once perchance in lapse of many years
Prouder itinerant, mountebank, or he
Whose wonders in a covered wain lie hid.
But one is here, the loveliest of them all,
Some sweet lass of the valley, looking out
For gains – and who that sees her would not buy?
Fruits of her father's orchard, apples, pears
(On that day only to such office stooping),
She carries in her basket, and walks round
Among the crowd, half pleased with, half ashamed
Of her new calling, blushing restlessly.
The children now are rich, the old man now
Is generous, so gaiety prevails
Which all partake of, young and old.

Immense
Is the recess, the circumambient world
Magnificent, by which they are embraced.
They move about upon the soft green field;
How little they (they and their doings) seem,
Their herds and flocks about them, they themselves,
And all which they can further or obstruct –
Through utter weakness pitiably dear
As tender infants are – and yet how great!
For all things serve them: them the morning light
Loves as it glistens on the silent rocks;
And them the silent rocks, which now from high
Look down upon them; the reposing clouds,

Of hawker's wares – books, pictures, combs, and pins –
Some aged woman finds her way again,
Year after year, a punctual visitant!
There also stands a speech-maker by rote,
Pulling the strings of his boxed raree-show;
And in the lapse of many years may come
Prouder itinerant, mountebank, or he
Whose wonders in a covered wain lie hid.
But one there is, the loveliest of them all,
Some sweet lass of the valley, looking out
For gains, and who that sees her would not buy?
Fruits of her father's orchard, are her wares,
And with the ruddy produce, she walks round
Among the crowd, half pleased with half ashamed
Of her new office, blushing restlessly.
The children now are rich, for the old to-day
Are generous as the young; and, if content
With looking on, some ancient wedded pair
Sit in the shade together, while they gaze,
'A cheerful smile unbends the wrinkled brow,
The days departed start again to life,
And all the scenes of childhood reappear,
Faint, but more tranquil, like the changing sun
To him who slept at noon and wakes at eve.'
Thus gaiety and cheerfulness prevail,
Spreading from young to old, from old to young,
And no one seems to want his share. – Immense
Is the recess, the circumambient world
Magnificent, by which they are embraced:
They move about upon the soft green turf:
How little they, they and their doings, seem,
And all that they can further or obstruct!
Through utter weakness pitiably dear,
As tender infants are: and yet how great!
For all things serve them: them the morning light
Loves, as it glistens on the silent rocks;
And them the silent rocks, which now from high
Look down upon them; the reposing clouds;

The lurking brooks from their invisible haunts;
And old Helvellyn, conscious of the stir.
And the blue sky that roofs their calm abode.

With deep devotion, nature, did I feel
In that great city what I owed to thee:
High thoughts of God and man, and love of man,
Triumphant over all those loathsome sights
Of wretchedness and vice, a watchful eye,
Which, with the outside of our human life
Not satisfied, must read the inner mind.
For I already had been taught to love
My fellow-beings, to such habits trained
Among the woods and mountains, where I found
In thee a gracious guide to lead me forth
Beyond the bosom of my family,
My friends and youthful playmates. 'Twas thy power
That raised the first complacency in me
And noticeable kindliness of heart,
Love human to the creature in himself
As he appeared, a stranger in my path,
Before my eyes a brother of this world –
Thou first didst with those motions of delight
Inspire me.

I remember, far from home
Once having strayed while yet a very child,
I saw a sight – and with what joy and love!
It was a day of exhalations spread
Upon the mountains, mists and steam-like fogs
Redounding everywhere, not vehement
But calm and mild, gentle and beautiful,
With gleams of sunshine on the eyelet-spots
And loopholes of the hills – wherever seen,
Hidden by quiet process, and as soon
Unfolded, to be huddled up again.
Along a narrow valley and profound
I journeyed, when, aloft above my head,
Emerging from the silvery vapours, lo,

The wild brooks prattling from invisible haunts;
And old Helvellyn, conscious of the stir
Which animates this day their calm abode.
With deep devotion, Nature, did I feel,
In that enormous City's turbulent world
Of men and things, what benefit I owed
To thee, and those domains of rural peace,

A shepherd and his dog, in open day!
Girt round with mists they stood and looked about
From that enclosure small, inhabitants
Of an aërial island floating on,
As seemed, with that abode in which they were,
A little pendant area of grey rocks
By the soft wind breathed forward. With delight
As bland almost, one evening I beheld,
And at as early age (the spectacle
Is common, but by me was then first seen)
A shepherd in the bottom of a vale,
Towards the centre standing, who with voice,
And hand waved to and fro as need required,
Gave signal to his dog, thus teaching him
To chase along the mazes of steep crags
The flock he could not see. And so the brute
(Dear creature!) with a man's intelligence
Advancing, or retreating on his steps,
Through every pervious strait to right or left
Thridded a way unbaffled; while the flock
Fled upwards from the terror of his bark
Through rocks and seams of turf with liquid gold
Irradiate – that deep farewell-light by which
The setting sun proclaims the love he bears
To mountain regions.

Beauteous the domain
Where to the sense of beauty first my heart
Was opened, tract more exquisitely fair
Than is that paradise of ten thousand trees,
Or Gehol's famous gardens, in a clime
Chosen from widest empire, for delight
Of the Tartarian dynasty composed
Beyond that mighty wall, not fabulous
(China's stupendous mound), by patient skill
Of myriads and boon nature's lavish help:
Scene linked to scene, and evergrowing change,
Soft, grand, or gay, with palaces and domes
Of pleasure spangled over, shady dells

Where to the sense of beauty first my heart
Was opened; tract more exquisitely fair
Than that famed paradise of ten thousand trees,
Or Gehol's matchless gardens, for delight
Of the Tartarian dynasty composed
(Beyond that mighty wall, not fabulous,
China's stupendous mound) by patient toil
Of myriads and boon nature's lavish help;
There, in a clime from widest empire chosen,
Fulfilling (could enchantment have done more?)
A sumptuous dream of flowery lawns, with domes
Of pleasure sprinkled over, shady dells

For eastern monasteries, sunny mounds
With temples crested, bridges, gondolas,
Rocks, dens, and groves of foliage taught to melt
Into each other their obsequious hues –
Going and gone again, in subtle chase
Too fine to be pursued – or standing forth
In no discordant opposition, strong
And gorgeous as the colours side by side
Bedded among the plumes of tropic birds;
And mountains over all, embracing all,
And all the landscape endlessly enriched
With waters running, falling, or asleep.

But lovelier far than this, the paradise
Where I was reared; in nature's primitive gifts
Favoured no less, and more to every sense
Delicious, seeing that the sun and sky,
The elements, and seasons in their change,
Do find their dearest fellow-labourer there
The heart of man – a district on all sides
The fragrance breathing of humanity:
Man free, man working for himself, with choice
Of time, and place, and object; by his wants,
His comforts, native occupations, cares,
Conducted on to individual ends
Or social, and still followed by a train
Unwooed, unthought-of even – simplicity,
And beauty, and inevitable grace.
Yea, doubtless, at an age when but a glimpse
Of those resplendent gardens, with their frame
Imperial and elaborate ornaments,
Would to a child be transport over-great,
When but a half-hour's roam through such a place
Would leave behind a dance of images
That shall break in upon his sleep for weeks,
Even then the common haunts of the green earth,
With the ordinary human interests
Which they embosom (all without regard
As both may seem) are fastening on the heart

For eastern monasteries, sunny mounts
With temples crested, bridges, gondolas,
Rocks, dens, and groves of foliage taught to melt
Into each other their obsequious hues,
Vanished and vanishing in subtle chase,
Too fine to be pursued; or standing forth
In no discordant opposition, strong
And gorgeous as the colours side by side
Bedded among rich plumes of tropic birds;
And mountains over all, embracing all;
And all the landscape, endlessly enriched
With waters running, falling, or asleep.

But lovelier far than this, the paradise
Where I was reared; in Nature's primitive gifts
Favoured no less, and more to every sense
Delicious, seeing that the sun and sky,
The elements, and seasons as they change,
Do find a worthy fellow-labourer there –
Man free, man working for himself, with choice
Of time, and place, and object; by his wants,
His comforts, native occupations, cares,
Cheerfully led to individual ends
Or social, and still followed by a train
Unwooed, unthought-of even – simplicity,
And beauty, and inevitable grace.

Yea, when a glimpse of those imperial bowers
Would to a child be transport over-great,
When but a half-hour's roam through such a place
Would leave behind a dance of images,
That shall break in upon his sleep for weeks;
Even then the common haunts of the green earth,
And ordinary interests of man,
Which they embosom, all without regard
As both may seem, are fastening on the heart

Insensibly, each with the other's help,
So that we love, not knowing that we love,
And feel, not knowing whence our feeling comes.

Such league have these two principles of joy
In our affections. I have singled out
Some moments, the earliest that I could, in which
Their several currents, blended into one –
Weak yet, and gathering imperceptibly –
Flowed in by gushes. My first human love,
As has been mentioned, did incline to those
Whose occupations and concerns were most
Illustrated by nature and adorned,
And shepherds were the men who pleased me first:
Not such as in Arcadian fastnesses
Sequestered handed down among themselves
(So ancient poets sing) the golden age;
Nor such – a second race, allied to these –
As Shakespeare in the wood of Arden placed
Where Phoebe sighed for the false Ganymede,
Or there where Florizel and Perdita
Together danced, queen of the feast and king;
Nor such as Spenser fabled. True it is
That I had heard (what he perhaps had seen)
Of maids at sunrise bringing in from far
Their maybush, and along the streets in flocks
Parading with a song of taunting rhymes
Aimed at the laggards slumbering within doors –
Had also heard, from those who yet remembered,
Tales of the maypole dance, and flowers that decked
The posts and the kirk-pillars, and of youths,
That each one with his maid at break of day
By annual custom issued forth in troops
To drink the waters of some favourite well,
And hang it round with garlands.

This, alas,
Was but a dream: the times had scattered all

Insensibly, each with the other's help.
For me, when my affections first were led
From kindred, friends, and playmates, to partake
Love for the human creature's absolute self,
That noticeable kindliness of heart
Sprang out of fountains, there abounding most
Where sovereign Nature dictated the tasks
And occupations which her beauty adorned,
And Shepherds were the men that pleased me first;
Not such as Saturn ruled 'mid Latian wilds,
With arts and laws so tempered, that their lives
Left, even to us toiling in this late day,
A bright tradition of the golden age;
Not such as, 'mid Arcadian fastnesses
Sequestered, handed down among themselves
Felicity, in Grecian song renowned;
Nor such as, when an adverse fate had driven,
From house and home, the courtly band whose fortunes
Entered, with Shakspeare's genius, the wild woods
Of Arden, amid sunshine or in shade,
Culled the best fruits of Time's uncounted hours,
Ere Phœbe sighed for the false Ganymede;
Or there where Perdita and Florizel
Together danced, Queen of the feast, and King;
Nor such as Spenser fabled. True it is,
That I had heard (what he perhaps had seen)
Of maids at sunrise bringing in from far
Their May-bush, and along the street in flocks
Parading with a song of taunting rhymes,
Aimed at the laggards slumbering within doors;
Had also heard, from those who yet remembered,
Tales of the May-pole dance, and wreaths that decked
Porch, door-way, or kirk-pillar; and of youths,
Each with his maid, before the sun was up,
By annual custom, issuing forth in troops,
To drink the waters of some sainted well,
And hang it round with garlands. Love survives;
But, for such purpose, flowers no longer grow:
The times, too sage, perhaps too proud, have dropped

These lighter graces, and the rural ways
And manners which it was my chance to see
In childhood were severe and unadorned,
The unluxuriant produce of a life
Intent on little but substantial needs –
Yet beautiful – and beauty that was felt.
But images of danger and distress
And suffering, these took deepest hold of me:
Man suffering among awful powers and forms.
Of this I heard and saw enough to make
The imagination restless, nor was free
Myself from frequent perils. Nor were tales
Wanting – the tragedies of former times,
Or hazards and escapes, which in my walks
I carried with me among crags and woods
And mountains – and of these may here be told
One, as recorded by my household dame.

At the first falling of autumnal snow
A shepherd and his son one day went forth
(Thus did the matron's tale begin) to seek
A straggler of their flock. They both had ranged
Upon this service the preceding day
All over their own pastures and beyond,
And now at sunrise sallying out again
Renewed their search, begun where from Dove Crag –
Ill home for bird so gentle – they looked down
On Deepdale Head and Brothers Water, named
From those two brothers that were drowned therein.
Thence northward, having passed by Arthur's Seat
To Fairfield's highest summit, on the right
Leaving St Sunday's Pike, to Grisedale Tarn
They shot, and over that cloud-loving hill
Seat Sandal (a fond lover of the clouds),
Thence up Helvellyn, a superior mount
With prospect underneath of Striding Edge
And Grisedale's houseless vale, along the brink
Of Russet Cove and those two other coves
Huge skeletons of crags, which from the trunk

These lighter graces; and the rural ways
And manners which my childhood looked upon
Were the unluxuriant produce of a life
Intent on little but substantial needs,
Yet rich in beauty, beauty that was felt.
But images of danger and distress,
Man suffering among awful Powers and Forms;
Of this I heard, and saw enough to make
Imagination restless; nor was free
Myself from frequent perils; nor were tales
Wanting, – the tragedies of former times,
Hazards and strange escapes, of which the rocks
Immutable and everflowing streams,
Where'er I roamed, were speaking monuments.

Of old Helvellyn spread their arms abroad
And make a stormy harbour for the winds.
Far went those shepherds in their devious quest,
From mountain ridges peeping as they passed
Down into every glen; at length the boy
Said 'Father, with your leave, I will go back
And range the ground which we have searched before.'
So speaking, southward down the hill the lad
Sprang like a gust of wind, crying aloud
'I know where I shall find him.'

'For take note',
Said here my grey-haired dame, 'that though the storm
Drive one of these poor creatures miles and miles,
If he can crawl he will return again
To his own hills, the spots where when a lamb
He learnt to pasture at his mother's side.'
After so long a labour, suddenly
Bethinking him of this, the boy
Pursued his way towards a brook whose course
Was through that unfenced tract of mountain-ground
Which to his father's little farm belonged,
The home and ancient birthright of their flock.
Down the deep channel of the stream he went,
Prying through every nook; meanwhile the rain
Began to fall upon the mountain-tops –
Thick storm and heavy which for three hours' space
Abated not – and all that time the boy
Was busy in his search, until at length
He spied the sheep upon a plot of grass,
An island in the brook. It was a place
Remote and deep, piled round with rocks where foot
Of man or beast was seldom used to tread;
But now, when everywhere the summer grass
Had failed, this one adventurer, hunger-pressed,
Had left his fellows and made his way alone
To the green plot of pasture in the brook.
Before the boy knew well what he had seen
He leapt upon the island with proud heart

And with a prophet's joy. Immediately
The sheep sprang forward to the further shore
And was borne headlong by the roaring flood.
At this the boy looked round him, and his heart
Fainted with fear. Thrice did he turn his face
To either brink, nor could he summon up
The courage that was needful to leap back
Cross the tempestuous torrent. So he stood,
A prisoner on the island, not without
More than one thought of death and his last hour.

Meanwhile the father had returned alone
To his own house; and now at the approach
Of evening he went forth to meet his son,
Conjecturing vainly for what cause the boy
Had stayed so long. The shepherd took his way
Up his own mountain-grounds, where as he walked
Along the steep that overhung the brook
He seemed to hear a voice, which was again
Repeated, like the whistling of a kite.
At this, not knowing why (as oftentimes
Long afterwards he has been heard to say)
Down to the brook he went, and tracked its course
Upwards among the o'erhanging rocks; nor thus
Had he gone far ere he espied the boy
Where on that little plot of ground he stood
Right in the middle of the roaring stream,
Now stronger every moment and more fierce.
The sight was such as no one could have seen
Without distress and fear. The shepherd heard
The outcry of his son, he stretched his staff
Towards him, bade him leap – which word scarce said,
The boy was safe within his father's arms.

Smooth life had flock and shepherd in old time,
Long springs and tepid winters on the banks
Of delicate Galesus – and no less
Those scattered along Adria's myrtle shores –
Smooth life the herdsman, and his snow-white herd

Smooth life had flock and shepherd in old time,
Long springs and tepid winters, on the banks
Of delicate Galesus; and no less
Those scattered along Adria's myrtle shores:
Smooth life had herdsman, and his snow-white herd

To triumphs and to sacrificial rites
Devoted, on the inviolable stream
Of rich Clitumnus; and the goatherd lived
As sweetly underneath the pleasant brows
Of cool Lucretilis, where the pipe was heard
Of Pan, the invisible god, thrilling the rocks
With tutelary music, from all harm
The fold protecting. I myself (mature
In manhood then) have seen a pastoral tract
Like one of these, where fancy might run wild,
Though under skies less generous and serene;
Yet there, as for herself, had nature framed
A pleasure-ground, diffused a fair expanse
Of level pasture, islanded with groves
And banked with woody risings – but the plain
Endless, here opening widely out, and there
Shut up in lesser lakes or beds of lawn
And intricate recesses, creek or bay
Sheltered within a shelter, where at large
The shepherd strays, a rolling hut his home.
Thither he comes with springtime, there abides
All summer, and at sunrise ye may hear
His flute or flageolet resounding far.
There's not a nook or hold of that vast space,
Nor strait where passage is, but it shall have
In turn its visitant, telling there his hours
In unlaborious pleasure, with no task
More toilsome than to carve a beechen bowl
For spring or fountain, which the traveller finds
When through the region he pursues at will
His devious course.

A glimpse of such sweet life
I saw when from the melancholy walls
Of Goslar, once imperial, I renewed
My daily walk along that cheerful plain
Which, reaching to her gates, spreads east and west
And northwards from beneath the mountainous verge
Of the Hercynian forest. Yet, hail to you,

To triumphs and to sacrificial rites
Devoted, on the inviolable stream
Of rich Clitumnus; and the goat-herd lived
As calmly, underneath the pleasant brows
Of cool Lucretilis, where the pipe was heard
Of Pan, Invisible God, thrilling the rocks
With tutelary music, from all harm
The fold protecting. I myself, mature
In manhood then, have seen a pastoral tract
Like one of these, where Fancy might run wild,
Though under skies less generous, less serene:
There, for her own delight had Nature framed
A pleasure-ground, diffused a fair expanse
Of level pasture, islanded with groves
And banked with woody risings; but the Plain
Endless, here opening widely out, and there
Shut up in lesser lakes or beds of lawn
And intricate recesses, creek or bay
Sheltered within a shelter, where at large
The shepherd strays, a rolling hut his home.
Thither he comes with spring-time, there abides
All summer, and at sunrise ye may hear
His flageolet to liquid notes of love
Attuned, or sprightly fife resounding far.
Nook is there none, nor tract of that vast space
Where passage opens, but the same shall have
In turn its visitant, telling there his hours
In unlaborious pleasure, with no task
More toilsome than to carve a beechen bowl
For spring or fountain, which the traveller finds,
When through the region he pursues at will
His devious course. A glimpse of such sweet life
I saw when, from the melancholy walls
Of Goslar, once imperial, I renewed
My daily walk along that wide champaign,
That, reaching to her gates, spreads east and west,
And northwards, from beneath the mountainous verge
Of the Hercynian forest. Yet, hail to you

Your rocks and precipices – ye that seize
The heart with firmer grasp – your snows and streams
Ungovernable, and your terrifying winds
That howled so dismally when I have been
Companionless among your solitudes!
There 'tis the shepherd's task the winter long
To wait upon the storms: of their approach
Sagacious, from the height he drives his flock
Down into sheltering coves, and feeds them there
Through the hard time, long as the storm is locked
(So do they phrase it), bearing from the stalls
A toilsome burden up the craggy ways
To strew it on the snow. And when the spring
Looks out, and all the mountains dance with lambs,
He through the enclosures won from the steep waste,
And through the lower heights, hath gone his rounds;
And when the flock with warmer weather climbs
Higher and higher, him his office leads
To range among them, through the hills dispersed,
And watch their goings – whatsoever track
Each wanderer chooses for itself – a work
That lasts the summer through. He quits his home
At day-spring, and no sooner does the sun
Begin to strike him with a fire-like heat
Than he lies down upon some shining place,
And breakfasts with his dog. When he has stayed
(As for the most he does) beyond his time,
He springs up with a bound, and then away! –
Ascending fast with his long pole in hand,
Or winding in and out among the crags.

What need to follow him through what he does
Or sees in his day's march? He feels himself,
In those vast regions where his service is,
A freeman, wedded to his life of hope
And hazard, and hard labour interchanged

Moors, mountains, headlands, and ye hollow vales,
Ye long deep channels for the Atlantic's voice,
Powers of my native region! Ye that seize
The heart with firmer grasp! Your snows and streams
Ungovernable, and your terrifying winds,
That howl so dismally for him who treads
Companionless your awful solitudes!
There, 'tis the shepherd's task the winter long
To wait upon the storms: of their approach
Sagacious, into sheltering coves he drives
His flock, and thither from the homestead bears
A toilsome burden up the craggy ways,
And deals it out, their regular nourishment
Strewn on the frozen snow. And when the spring
Looks out, and all the pastures dance with lambs,
And when the flock, with warmer weather, climbs
Higher and higher, him his office leads
To watch their goings, whatsoever track
The wanderers choose. For this he quits his home
At day-spring, and no sooner doth the sun
Begin to strike him with a fire-like heat,
Than he lies down upon some shining rock,
And breakfasts with his dog. When they have stolen,
As is their wont, a pittance from strict time,
For rest not needed or exchange of love,
Then from his couch he starts; and now his feet
Crush out a livelier fragrance from the flowers
Of lowly thyme, by Nature's skill enwrought
In the wild turf: the lingering dews of morn
Smoke round him, as from hill to hill he hies,
His staff protending like a hunter's spear,
Or by its aid leaping from crag to crag,
And o'er the brawling beds of unbridged streams.
Philosophy, methinks, at Fancy's call,
Might deign to follow him through what he does
Or sees in his day's march; himself he feels,
In those vast regions where his service lies,
A freeman, wedded to his life of hope
And hazard, and hard labour interchanged

With that majestic indolence so dear
To native man. A rambling schoolboy, thus
Have I beheld him, without knowing why
Have felt his presence in his own domain
As of a lord and master, or a power,
Or genius – under nature, under God,
Presiding – and severest solitude
Seemed more commanding oft when he was there.
Seeking the raven's nest and suddenly
Surprised with vapours, or on rainy days
When I have angled up the lonely brooks,
Mine eyes have glanced upon him few steps off,
In size a giant, stalking through the fog,
His sheep like Greenland bears. At other times,
When round some shady promontory turning,
His form hath flashed upon me glorified
By the deep radiance of the setting sun;
Or him have I descried in distant sky
A solitary object and sublime
Above all height, like an aërial cross
As it is stationed on some spiry rock
Of the Chartreuse for worship.

Thus was man
Ennobled outwardly before mine eyes,
And thus my heart at first was introduced
To an unconscious love and reverence
Of human nature; hence the human form
To me was like an index of delight,
Of grace and honour, power and worthiness.
Meanwhile this creature (spiritual almost
As those of books, but more exalted far,
Far more of an imaginative form)
Was not a Corin of the groves, who lives
For his own fancies, or to dance by the hour
In coronal, with Phyllis in the midst,
But, for the purposes of kind, a man
With the most common – husband, father – learnt,
Could teach, admonish, suffered with the rest

With that majestic indolence so dear
To native man. A rambling school-boy, thus
I felt his presence in his own domain,
As of a lord and master, or a power,
Or genius, under Nature, under God,
Presiding; and severest solitude
Had more commanding looks when he was there.
When up the lonely brooks on rainy days
Angling I went, or trod the trackless hills
By mists bewildered, suddenly mine eyes
Have glanced upon him distant a few steps,
In size a giant, stalking through thick fog,
His sheep like Greenland bears; or, as he stepped
Beyond the boundary line of some hill-shadow,
His form hath flashed upon me, glorified
By the deep radiance of the setting sun:
Or him have I descried in distant sky,
A solitary object and sublime,
Above all height! like an aerial cross
Stationed alone upon a spiry rock
Of the Chartreuse, for worship. Thus was man
Ennobled outwardly before my sight,
And thus my heart was early introduced
To an unconscious love and reverence
Of human nature; hence the human form
To me became an index of delight,
Of grace and honour, power and worthiness.
Meanwhile this creature – spiritual almost
As those of books, but more exalted far;
Far more of an imaginative form
Than the gay Corin of the groves, who lives
For his own fancies, or to dance by the hour,
In coronal, with Phyllis in the midst –
Was, for the purposes of kind, a man
With the most common; husband, father; learned,
Could teach, admonish; suffered with the rest

From vice and folly, wretchedness and fear.
Of this I little saw, cared less for it,
But something must have felt.

Call ye these appearances
Which I beheld of shepherds in my youth,
This sanctity of nature given to man,
A shadow, a delusion – ye who are fed
By the dead letter, not the spirit of things,
Whose truth is not a motion or a shape
Instinct with vital functions, but a block
Or waxen image which yourselves have made
And ye adore! But blessèd be the God
Of nature and of man that this was so,
That men did at the first present themselves
Before my untaught eyes thus purified,
Removed, and at a distance that was fit.
And so we all of us in some degree
Are led to knowledge – whencesoever led,
And howsoever – were it otherwise,
And we found evil fast as we find good
In our first years (or think that it is found),
How could the innocent heart bear up and live?
But doubly fortunate my lot: not here
Alone, that something of a better life
Perhaps was round me than it is the privilege
Of most to move in, but that first I looked
At man through objects that were great and fair,
First communed with him by their help. And thus
Was founded a sure safeguard and defence
Against the weight of meanness, selfish cares,
Coarse manners, vulgar passions, that beat in
On all sides from the ordinary world
In which we traffic. Starting from this point
I had my face towards the truth, began
With an advantage, furnished with that kind
Of prepossession without which the soul
Receives no knowledge that can bring forth good –
No genuine insight ever comes to her –

From vice and folly, wretchedness and fear;
Of this I little saw, cared less for it,
But something must have felt.

Call ye these appearances –
Which I beheld of shepherds in my youth,
This sanctity of Nature given to man –
A shadow, a delusion, ye who pore
On the dead letter, miss the spirit of things;
Whose truth is not a motion or a shape
Instinct with vital functions, but a block
Or waxen image which yourselves have made,
And ye adore! But blessed be the God
Of Nature and of Man that this was so;
That men before my inexperienced eyes
Did first present themselves thus purified,
Removed, and to a distance that was fit:
And so we all of us in some degree
Are led to knowledge, wheresoever led,
And howsoever; were it otherwise,
And we found evil fast as we find good
In our first years, or think that it is found,
How could the innocent heart bear up and live!
But doubly fortunate my lot; not here
Alone, that something of a better life
Perhaps was round me than it is the privilege
Of most to move in, but that first I looked
At Man through objects that were great or fair;
First communed with him by their help. And thus
Was founded a sure safeguard and defence
Against the weight of meanness, selfish cares,
Coarse manners, vulgar passions, that beat in
On all sides from the ordinary world
In which we traffic. Starting from this point
I had my face turned toward the truth, began
With an advantage furnished by that kind
Of prepossession, without which the soul
Receives no knowledge that can bring forth good,
No genuine insight ever comes to her.

Happy in this, that I with nature walked,
Not having a too early intercourse
With the deformities of crowded life,
And those ensuing laughters and contempts
Self-pleasing, which if we would wish to think
With admiration and respect of man
Will not permit us, but pursue the mind
That to devotion willingly would be raised,
Into the temple and the temple's heart.

Yet do not deem, my friend, though thus I speak
Of man as having taken in my mind
A place thus early which might almost seem
Pre-eminent, that this was really so.
Nature herself was at this unripe time
But secondary to my own pursuits
And animal activities, and all
Their trivial pleasures; and long afterwards
When those had died away, and nature did
For her own sake become my joy, even then
(And upwards through late youth, until not less
Than three-and-twenty summers had been told)
Was man in my affections and regards
Subordinate to her, her awful forms
And viewless agencies – a passion she,
A rapture often, and immediate joy
Ever at hand; he distant, but a grace
Occasional, an accidental thought,
His hour being not yet come. Far less had then
The inferior creatures, beast or bird, attuned
My spirit to that gentleness of love,
Won from me those minute obeisances
Of tenderness which I may number now
With my first blessings. Nevertheless on these
The light of beauty did not fall in vain,
Or grandeur circumfuse them to no end.

From the restraint of over-watchful eyes
Preserved, I moved about, year after year,
Happy, and now most thankful that my walk
Was guarded from too early intercourse
With the deformities of crowded life,
And those ensuing laughters and contempts,
Self-pleasing, which, if we would wish to think
With a due reverence on earth's rightful lord,
Here placed to be the inheritor of heaven,
Will not permit us; but pursue the mind,
That to devotion willingly would rise,
Into the temple and the temple's heart.

Yet deem not, Friend! that human kind with me
Thus early took a place pre-eminent;
Nature herself was, at this unripe time,
But secondary to my own pursuits
And animal activities, and all
Their trivial pleasures; and when these had drooped
And gradually expired, and Nature, prized
For her own sake, became my joy, even then –
And upwards through late youth, until not less
Than two-and-twenty summers had been told –
Was Man in my affections and regards
Subordinate to her, her visible forms
And viewless agencies: a passion, she,
A rapture often, and immediate love
Ever at hand; he, only a delight
Occasional, an accidental grace,
His hour being not yet come. Far less had then
The inferior creatures, beast or bird, attuned
My spirit to that gentleness of love
(Though they had long been carefully observed),
Won from me those minute obeisances
Of tenderness, which I may number now
With my first blessings. Nevertheless, on these
The light of beauty did not fall in vain,
Or grandeur circumfuse them to no end.

Why should I speak of tillers of the soil? –
The ploughman and his team; or men and boys
In festive summer busy with the rake,
Old men and ruddy maids and little ones
All out together, and in sun and shade
Dispersed among the hay-grounds alder-fringed;
The quarryman, far heard, that blasts the rocks;
The fishermen in pairs, the one to row
And one to drop the net, plying their trade
'Mid tossing lakes and tumbling boats' and winds
Whistling; the miner (melancholy man!)
That works by taper-light while all the hills
Are shining with the glory of the day.

But when that first poetic faculty
Of plain imagination and severe –
No longer a mute influence of the soul,
An element of the nature's inner self –
Began to have some promptings to put on
A visible shape, and to the works of art,
The notions and the images of books,
Did knowingly conform itself (by these
Inflamed, and proud of that her new delight),
There came among these shapes of human life
A wilfulness of fancy and conceit
Which gave them new importance to the mind –
And nature and her objects beautified
These fictions as (in some sort) in their turn
They burnished her. From touch of this new power
Nothing was safe: the elder-tree that grew
Beside the well-known charnelhouse had then
A dismal look, the yew-tree had its ghost
That took its station there for ornament.
Then common death was none, common mishap,
But matter for this humour everywhere –
The tragic, super-tragic, else left short.
Then, if a widow, staggering with the blow
Of her distress, was known to have made her way
To the cold grave in which her husband slept,

But when that first poetic faculty
Of plain Imagination and severe,
No longer a mute influence of the soul,
Ventured, at some rash Muse's earnest call,
To try her strength among harmonious words;
And to book-notions and the rules of art
Did knowingly conform itself; there came
Among the simple shapes of human life
A wilfulness of fancy and conceit;
And Nature and her objects beautified
These fictions, as in some sort, in their turn,
They burnished her. From touch of this new power
Nothing was safe: the elder-tree that grew
Beside the well-known charnel-house had then
A dismal look: the yew-tree had its ghost,
That took his station there for ornament:
The dignities of plain occurrence then
Were tasteless, and truth's golden mean, a point
Where no sufficient pleasure could be found.
Then, if a widow, staggering with the blow
Of her distress, was known to have turned her steps
To the cold grave in which her husband slept,

One night – or haply more than one – through pain
Or half-insensate impotence of mind,
The fact was caught at greedily, and there
She was a visitant the whole year through
Wetting the turf with never-ending tears,
And all the storms of heaven must beat on her!

Through wild obliquities could I pursue
Among all objects of the fields and groves
These cravings: when the foxglove, one by one,
Upwards through every stage of its tall stem
Had shed its bells, and stood by the wayside
Dismantled, with a single one perhaps
Left at the ladder's top, with which the plant
Appeared to stoop – as slender blades of grass
Tipped with a bead of rain or dew – behold
If such a sight were seen, would fancy bring
Some vagrant thither with her babes and seat her
Upon the turf beneath the stately flower
Drooping in sympathy, and making so
A melancholy crest above the head
Of the lorn creature while her little ones,
(All unconcerned with her unhappy plight)
Were sporting with the purple cups that lay
Scattered upon the ground.

There was a copse,
An upright bank of wood and woody rock
That opposite our rural dwelling stood,
In which a sparkling patch of diamond light
Was in bright weather duly to be seen
On summer afternoons, within the wood
At the same place. 'Twas doubtless nothing more
Than a black rock, which, wet with constant springs,
Glistered far seen from out its lurking-place
As soon as ever the declining sun
Had smitten it. Beside our cottage hearth
Sitting with open door, a hundred times
Upon this lustre have I gazed, that seemed

One night, or haply more than one, through pain
Or half-insensate impotence of mind,
The fact was caught at greedily, and there
She must be visitant the whole year through,
Wetting the turf with never-ending tears.

Through quaint obliquities I might pursue
These cravings; when the fox-glove, one by one,
Upwards through every stage of the tall stem,
Had shed beside the public way its bells,
And stood of all dismantled, save the last
Left at the tapering ladder's top, that seemed
To bend as doth a slender blade of grass
Tipped with a rain-drop, Fancy loved to seat,
Beneath the plant despoiled, but crested still
With this last relic, soon itself to fall,
Some vagrant mother, whose arch little ones,
All unconcerned by her dejected plight,
Laughed as with rival eagerness their hands
Gathered the purple cups that round them lay,
Strewing the turf's green slope.

A diamond light
(Whene'er the summer sun, declining, smote
A smooth rock wet with constant springs) was seen
Sparkling from out a copse-clad bank that rose
Fronting our cottage. Oft beside the hearth
Seated, with open door, often and long
Upon this restless lustre have I gazed,

To have some meaning which I could not find –
And now it was a burnished shield, I fancied,
Suspended over a knight's tomb who lay
Inglorious, buried in the dusky wood;
An entrance now into some magic cave
Or palace for a fairy of the rock.
Nor would I, though not certain whence the cause
Of the effulgence, thither have repaired
Without a precious bribe, and day by day
And month by month I saw the spectacle,
Nor ever once have visited the spot
Unto this hour.

Thus sometimes were the shapes
Of wilful fancy grafted upon feelings
Of the imagination, and they rose
In worth accordingly. My present theme
Is to retrace the way that led me on
Through nature to the love of human-kind;
Nor could I with such object overlook
The influence of this power which turned itself
Instinctively to human passions, things
Least understood – of this adulterate power –
For so it may be called, and without wrong,
When with that first compared. Yet in the midst
Of these vagaries, with an eye so rich
As mine, through the chance (on me not wasted)
Of having been brought up in such a grand
And lovely region, I had forms distinct
To steady me. These thoughts did oft revolve
About some centre palpable, which at once
Incited them to motion, and controlled;
And whatsoever shape the fit might take,
And whencesoever it might come, I still
At all times had a real solid world
Of images about me – did not pine
As one in cities bred might do (as thou,
Belovèd friend, hast told me that thou didst,
Great spirit as thou art) in endless dreams

That made my fancy restless as itself.
'Twas now for me a burnished silver shield
Suspended over a knight's tomb, who lay
Inglorious, buried in the dusky wood:
An entrance now into some magic cave
Or palace built by fairies of the rock;
Nor could I have been bribed to disenchant
The spectacle, by visiting the spot.
Thus wilful Fancy, in no hurtful mood,
Engrafted far-fetched shapes on feelings bred
By pure Imagination: busy Power
She was, and with her ready pupil turned
Instinctively to human passions, then
Least understood. Yet, 'mid the fervent swarm
Of these vagaries, with an eye so rich
As mine was through the bounty of a grand
And lovely region, I had forms distinct
To steady me: each airy thought revolved
Round a substantial centre, which at once
Incited it to motion, and controlled.
I did not pine like one in cities bred,
As was thy melancholy lot, dear Friend!
Great Spirit as thou art, in endless dreams

Of sickliness, disjoining, joining, things
Without the light of knowledge. Where the harm
If, when the woodman languished with disease
From sleeping night by night among the woods
Within his sod-built cabin, Indian-wise,
I called the pangs of disappointed love
And all the long etcetera of such thought
To help him to his grave? Meanwhile the man,
If not already from the woods retired
To die at home, was haply (as I knew)
Pining alone among the gentle airs,
Birds, running streams, and hills so beautiful
On golden evenings, while the charcoal-pile
Breathed up its smoke, an image of his ghost
Or spirit that was soon to take its flight.

Of sickliness, disjoining, joining, things
Without the light of knowledge. Where the harm,
If, when the woodman languished with disease
Induced by sleeping nightly on the ground
Within his sod-built cabin, Indian-wise,
I called the pangs of disappointed love,
And all the sad etcetera of the wrong,
To help him to his grave. Meanwhile the man,
If not already from the woods retired
To die at home, was haply as I knew,
Withering by slow degrees, 'mid gentle airs,
Birds, running streams, and hills so beautiful
On golden evenings, while the charcoal pile
Breathed up its smoke, an image of his ghost
Or spirit that full soon must take her flight.
Nor shall we not be tending towards that point
Of sound humanity to which our Tale
Leads, though by sinuous ways, if here I shew
How Fancy, in a season when she wove
Those slender cords, to guide the unconscious Boy
For the Man's sake, could feed at Nature's call
Some pensive musings which might well beseem
Maturer years.

A grove there is whose boughs
Stretch from the western marge of Thurston-mere,
With length of shade so thick, that whoso glides
Along the line of low-roofed water, moves
As in a cloister. Once – while, in that shade
Loitering, I watched the golden beams of light
Flung from the setting sun, as they reposed
In silent beauty on the naked ridge
Of a high eastern hill – thus flowed my thoughts
In a pure stream of words fresh from the heart:
Dear native Regions, wheresoe'er shall close
My mortal course, there will I think on you;
Dying, will cast on you a backward look;
Even as this setting sun (albeit the Vale
Is no where touched by one memorial gleam)

There came a time of greater dignity
Which had been gradually prepared and now
Rushed in as if on wings – the time in which
The pulse of being everywhere was felt –
When all the several frames of things, like stars
Through every magnitude distinguishable,
Were half confounded in each other's blaze,
One galaxy of life and joy. Then rose
Man, inwardly contemplated, and present
In my own being, to a loftier height,
As of all visible natures crown, and first
In capability of feeling what
Was to be felt – in being rapt away
By the divine effect of power and love –
As, more than anything we know, instinct
With godhead, and by reason and by will
Acknowledging dependency sublime.

Erelong, transported hence as in a dream,
I found myself begirt with temporal shapes
Of vice and folly thrust upon my view,
Objects of sport, and ridicule, and scorn,
Manners and characters discriminate,
And little busy passions that eclipsed,
As well they might, the impersonated thought,
The idea, or abstraction of the kind.
An idler among academic bowers,
Such was my new condition (as at large
Has been set forth) yet here the vulgar light
Of present, actual, superficial life,
Gleaming through colouring of other times,
Old usages and local privilege,

Doth with the fond remains of his last power
Still linger, and a farewell lustre sheds
On the dear mountain-tops where first he rose.

Enough of humble arguments; recal,
My Song! those high emotions which thy voice
Has heretofore made known; that bursting forth
Of sympathy, inspiring and inspired,
When everywhere a vital pulse was felt,
And all the several frames of things, like stars,
Through every magnitude distinguishable,
Shone mutually indebted, or half lost
Each in the other's blaze, a galaxy
Of life and glory. In the midst stood Man,
Outwardly, inwardly contemplated,
As, of all visible natures, crown, though born
Of dust, and kindred to the worm; a Being,
Both in perception and discernment, first
In every capability of rapture,
Through the divine effect of power and love;
As, more than anything we know, instinct
With godhead, and, by reason and by will,
Acknowledging dependency sublime.

Ere long, the lonely mountains left, I moved,
Begirt, from day to day, with temporal shapes
Of vice and folly thrust upon my view,
Objects of sport, and ridicule, and scorn,
Manners and characters discriminate,
And little bustling passions that eclipse,
As well they might, the impersonated thought,
The idea, or abstraction of the kind.

An idler among academic bowers,
Such was my new condition, as at large
Has been set forth; yet here the vulgar light
Of present, actual, superficial life,
Gleaming through colouring of other times,
Old usages and local privilege,

Thereby was softened, almost solemnized,
And rendered apt and pleasing to the view.
This notwithstanding, being brought more near
As I was now to guilt and wretchedness,
I trembled, thought of human life at times
With an indefinite terror and dismay –
Such as the storms and angry elements
Had bred in me, but gloomier far, a dim
Analogy to uproar and misrule,
Disquiet, danger, and obscurity.

It might be told – but wherefore speak of things
Common to all? – that, seeing, I essayed
To give relief, began to deem myself
A moral agent (judging between good
And evil, not as for the mind's delight
But for her safety) one who was to *act*,
As sometimes to the best of my weak means
I did, by human sympathy impelled –
And through dislike and most offensive pain
Was to the truth conducted; of this faith
Never forsaken, that by acting well,
And understanding, I should learn to love
The end of life and everything we know.

Preceptress stern that didst instruct me next,
London, to thee I willingly return!
Erewhile my verse played only with the flowers
Enwrought upon thy mantle, satisfied
With this amusement, and a simple look
Of childlike inquisition now and then
Cast upwards on thine eye to puzzle out
Some inner meanings which might harbour there.
Yet did I not give way to this light mood
Wholly beguiled, as one incapable
Of higher things, and ignorant that high things
Were round me. Never shall I forget the hour,
The moment rather say, when, having thridded
The labyrinth of suburban villages,

Was welcome, softened, if not solemnised.
This notwithstanding, being brought more near
To vice and guilt, forerunning wretchedness,
I trembled, – thought, at times, of human life
With an indefinite terror and dismay,
Such as the storms and angry elements
Had bred in me; but gloomier far, a dim
Analogy to uproar and misrule,
Disquiet, danger, and obscurity.

It might be told (but wherefore speak of things
Common to all?) that, seeing, I was led
Gravely to ponder – judging between good
And evil, not as for the mind's delight
But for her guidance – one who was to *act*,
As sometimes to the best of feeble means
I did, by human sympathy impelled:
And, through dislike and most offensive pain,
Was to the truth conducted; of this faith
Never forsaken, that, by acting well,
And understanding, I should learn to love
The end of life, and every thing we know.

Grave Teacher, stern Preceptress! for at times
Thou canst put on an aspect most severe;
London, to thee I willingly return.
Erewhile my verse played idly with the flowers
Enwrought upon thy mantle; satisfied
With that amusement, and a simple look
Of child-like inquisition now and then
Cast upwards on thy countenance, to detect
Some inner meanings which might harbour there.
But how could I in mood so light indulge,
Keeping such fresh remembrance of the day,
When, having thridded the long labyrinth
Of the suburban villages, I first

At length I did unto myself first seem
To enter the great city. On the roof
Of an itinerant vehicle I sat,
With vulgar men about me, vulgar forms
Of houses, pavements, streets, of men and things –
Mean shapes on every side – but at the time
When to myself it fairly might be said
(The very moment that I seemed to know)
'The threshold now is overpast', great God
That aught *external* to the living mind
Should have such mighty sway, yet so it was!
A weight of ages did at once descend
Upon my heart – no thought embodied, no
Distinct remembrances, but weight and power,
Power growing with the weight! Alas, I feel
That I am trifling; 'twas a moment's pause,
All that took place within me came and went
As in a moment, and I only now
Remember that it was a thing divine.

As when a traveller has from open day
With torches passed into some vault of earth,
The grotto of Antiparos or the den
Of Yordas among Craven's mountain tracts;
He looks and sees the cavern spread and grow
Widening itself on all sides, sees, or thinks
He sees, erelong the roof above his head,
Which instantly unsettles and recedes –
Substance and shadow, light and darkness, all
Commingled, making up a canopy
Of shapes and forms and tendencies to shape
That shift and vanish, change and interchange
Like spectres – ferment quiet and sublime
Which after a short space works less and less,
Till, every effort, every motion gone,
The scene before him lies in perfect view
Exposed and lifeless as a written book!
But let him pause awhile and look again
And a new quickening shall succeed, at first

Entered thy vast dominion? On the roof
Of an itinerant vehicle I sate,
With vulgar men about me, trivial forms
Of houses, pavement, streets, of men and things, –
Mean shapes on every side: but, at the instant,
When to myself it fairly might be said,
The threshold now is overpast, (how strange
That aught external to the living mind
Should have such mighty sway! yet so it was),
A weight of ages did at once descend
Upon my heart; no thought embodied, no
Distinct remembrances, but weight and power, –
Power growing under weight: alas! I feel
That I am trifling: 'twas a moment's pause, –
All that took place within me came and went
As in a moment; yet with Time it dwells,
And grateful memory, as a thing divine.

The curious traveller, who, from open day,
Hath passed with torches into some huge cave,
The Grotto of Antiparos, or the Den
In old time haunted by that Danish Witch,
Yordas; he looks around and sees the vault
Widening on all sides; sees, or thinks he sees,
Erelong, the massy roof above his head,
That instantly unsettles and recedes, –
Substance and shadow, light and darkness, all
Commingled, making up a canopy
Of shapes and forms and tendencies to shape
That shift and vanish, change and interchange
Like spectres, – ferment silent and sublime!
That after a short space works less and less,
Till, every effort, every motion gone,
The scene before him stands in perfect view
Exposed, and lifeless as a written book! –
But let him pause awhile, and look again,
And a new quickening shall succeed, at first

Beginning timidly, then creeping fast
Through all which he beholds. The senseless mass,
In its projections, wrinkles, cavities,
Through all its surface, with all colours streaming
Like a magician's airy pageant, parts,
Unites, embodying everywhere some pressure
Or image, recognized or new, some type
Or picture of the world: forests and lakes,
Ships, rivers, towers, the warrior clad in mail,
The prancing steed, the pilgrim with his staff,
The mitred bishop and the thronèd king –
A spectacle to which there is no end.

No otherwise had I at first been moved
With such a swell of feeling, followed soon
By a blank sense of greatness passed away –
And afterwards continued to be moved –
In presence of that vast metropolis,
The fountain of my country's destiny
And of the destiny of earth itself;
That great emporium, chronicle at once
And burial-place of passions, and their home
Imperial and chief living residence.

With strong sensations teeming as it did
Of past and present, such a place must needs
Have pleased me in those times. I sought not then
Knowledge, but craved for power – and power I found
In all things. Nothing had a circumscribed
And narrow influence, but all objects, being
Themselves capacious, also found in me
Capaciousness and amplitude of mind.
Such is the strength and glory of our youth!
The human nature unto which I felt
That I belonged, and which I loved and reverenced,
Was not a punctual presence, but a spirit

Beginning timidly, then creeping fast,
Till the whole cave, so late a senseless mass,
Busies the eye with images and forms
Boldly assembled, – here is shadowed forth
From the projections, wrinkles, cavities,
A variegated landscape, – there the shape
Of some gigantic warrior clad in mail,
The ghostly semblance of a hooded monk,
Veiled nun, or pilgrim resting on his staff:
Strange congregation! yet not slow to meet
Eyes that perceive through minds that can inspire.

Even in such sort had I at first been moved,
Nor otherwise continued to be moved,
As I explored the vast metropolis,
Fount of my country's destiny and the world's;
That great emporium, chronicle at once
And burial-place of passions, and their home
Imperial, their chief living residence.

With strong sensations teeming as it did
Of past and present, such a place must needs
Have pleased me, seeking knowledge at that time
Far less than craving power; yet knowledge came,
Sought or unsought, and influxes of power
Came, of themselves, or at her call derived
In fits of kindliest apprehensiveness,
From all sides, when whate'er was in itself
Capacious found, or seemed to find, in me
A correspondent amplitude of mind;
Such is the strength and glory of our youth!
The human nature unto which I felt
That I belonged, and reverenced with love,
Was not a punctual presence, but a spirit

Living in time and space, and far diffused –
In this my joy, in this my dignity
Consisted. The external universe,
By striking upon what is found within,
Had given me this conception, with the help
Of books and what they picture and record.

'Tis true, the history of my native land,
With those of Greece compared and popular Rome
(Events not lovely nor magnanimous,
But harsh and unaffecting in themselves
And in our high-wrought modern narratives
Stripped of their humanizing soul, the life
Of manners and familiar incidents)
Had never much delighted me. And less
Than other minds I had been used to owe
The pleasure which I found in place or thing
To extrinsic transitory accidents,
To records or traditions; but a sense
Of what had been here done, and suffered here
Through ages – and was doing, suffering, still –
Weighed with me, could support the test of thought,
Was like the enduring majesty and power
Of independent nature. And not seldom
Even individual remembrances,
By working on the shapes before my eyes,
Became like vital functions of the soul;
And out of what had been, what was, the place
Was thronged with impregnations, like those wilds
In which my early feelings had been nursed,
And naked valleys full of caverns, rocks
And audible seclusions, dashing lakes,
Echoes and waterfalls, and pointed crags
That into music touch the passing wind.

Thus here imagination also found
An element that pleased her, tried her strength
Among new objects – simplified, arranged,
Impregnated my knowledge, made it live –

Diffused through time and space, with aid derived
Of evidence from monuments, erect,
Prostrate, or leaning towards their common rest
In earth, the widely scattered wreck sublime
Of vanished nations, or more clearly drawn
From books and what they picture and record.

'Tis true, the history of our native land,
With those of Greece compared and popular Rome,
And in our high-wrought modern narratives
Stript of their harmonising soul, the life
Of manners and familiar incidents,
Had never much delighted me. And less
Than other intellects had mine been used
To lean upon extrinsic circumstance
Of record or tradition; but a sense
Of what in the Great City had been done
And suffered, and was doing, suffering, still,
Weighed with me, could support the test of thought;
And, in despite of all that had gone by,
Or was departing never to return,
There I conversed with majesty and power
Like independent natures. Hence the place
Was thronged with impregnations like the Wilds
In which my early feelings had been nursed –
Bare hills and valleys, full of caverns, rocks,
And audible seclusions, dashing lakes,
Echoes and waterfalls, and pointed crags
That into music touch the passing wind.
Here then my young imagination found
No uncongenial element; could here
Among new objects serve or give command,
Even as the heart's occasions might require,
To forward reason's else too scrupulous march.

And the result was elevating thoughts
Of human nature. Neither guilt nor vice,
Debasement of the body or the mind,
Nor all the misery forced upon my sight
(Which was not lightly passed, but often scanned
Most feelingly) could overthrow my trust
In what we may become, induce belief
That I was ignorant, had been falsely taught,
A solitary, who with vain conceits
Had been inspired, and walked about in dreams.
When from that rueful prospect overcast
And in eclipse my meditations turned,
Lo, everything that was indeed divine
Retained its purity inviolate
And unencroached upon, nay, seemed brighter far
For this deep shade in counterview, this gloom
Of opposition, such as showed itself
To the eyes of Adam (yet in Paradise
Though fallen from bliss) when 'in the east he saw
Darkness ere day's mid course, and morning light
More orient in the western cloud, that drew
O'er the blue firmament a radiant white,
Descending slow with something heavenly fraught'.

Add also that among the multitudes
Of that great city oftentimes was seen
Affectingly set forth – more than elsewhere
Is possible – the unity of man,
One spirit over ignorance and vice
Predominant; in good and evil hearts
One sense for moral judgements, as one eye
For the sun's light. When strongly breathed upon
By this sensation (whencesoe'er it comes,
Of union or communion) does the soul
Rejoice as in her highest joy; for there,
There chiefly, has she feeling whence she is,
And passing through all natures rests with God.

The effect was, still more elevated views
Of human nature. Neither vice nor guilt,
Debasement undergone by body or mind,
Nor all the misery forced upon my sight,
Misery not lightly passed, but sometimes scanned
Most feelingly, could overthrow my trust
In what we *may* become; induce belief
That I was ignorant, had been falsely taught,
A solitary, who with vain conceits
Had been inspired, and walked about in dreams.
From those sad scenes when meditation turned,
Lo! every thing that was indeed divine
Retained its purity inviolate,
Nay brighter shone, by this portentous gloom
Set off; such opposition as aroused
The mind of Adam, yet in Paradise
Though fallen from bliss, when in the East he saw
Darkness ere day's mid course, and morning light
More orient in the western cloud, that drew
O'er the blue firmament a radiant white,
Descending slow with something heavenly fraught.

Add also, that among the multitudes
Of that huge city, oftentimes was seen
Affectingly set forth, more than elsewhere
Is possible, the unity of man,
One spirit over ignorance and vice
Predominant, in good and evil hearts;
One sense for moral judgments, as one eye
For the sun's light. The soul when smitten thus
By a sublime *idea*, whencesoe'er
Vouchsafed for union or communion, feeds
On the pure bliss, and takes her rest with God.

And is not, too, that vast abiding-place
Of human creatures, turn where'er we may,
Profusely sown with individual sights
Of courage, and integrity, and truth
And tenderness, which, here set off by foil,
Appears more touching? In the tender scenes
Chiefly was my delight, and one of these
Never will be forgotten. 'Twas a man
Whom I saw sitting in an open square
Close to the iron paling that fenced in
The spacious grass-plot; on the corner-stone
Of the low wall in which the pales were fixed
Sat this one man, and with a sickly babe
Upon his knee, whom he had thither brought
For sunshine, and to breathe the fresher air.
Of those who passed, and me who looked at him,
He took no note; but in his brawny arms
(The artificer was to the elbow bare,
And from his work this moment had been stolen)
He held the child, and, bending over it
As if he were afraid both of the sun
And of the air which he had come to seek,
He eyed it with unutterable love.

Thus were my thoughts attracted more and more
By slow gradations towards human-kind,
And to the good and ill of human life.
Nature had led me on, and now I seemed
To travel independent of her help
As if I had forgotten her – but no,
My fellow beings still were unto me
Far less than she was. Though the scale of love
Were filling fast, 'twas light as yet compared
With that in which her mighty objects lay.

Thus from a very early age, O Friend!
My thoughts by slow gradations had been drawn
To human-kind, and to the good and ill
Of human life: Nature had led me on;
And oft amid the 'busy hum' I seemed
To travel independent of her help,
As if I had forgotten her; but no,
The world of human-kind outweighed not hers
In my habitual thoughts; the scale of love,
Though filling daily, still was light, compared
With that in which *her* mighty objects lay.

Book Ninth

RESIDENCE IN FRANCE

As oftentimes a river (it might seem)
Yielding in part to old remembrances,
Part swayed by fear to tread an onward road
That leads direct to the devouring sea,
Turns and will measure back his course – far back,
Towards the very regions which he crossed
In his first outset – so have we long time
Made motions retrograde, in like pursuit
Detained. But now we start afresh: I feel
An impulse to precipitate my verse.
Fair greetings to this shapeless eagerness,
Whene'er it comes, needful in work so long,
Thrice needful to the argument which now
Awaits us – oh, how much unlike the past! –
One which, though bright the promise, will be found
Ere far we shall advance, ungenial, hard
To treat of, and forbidding in itself.

Free as a colt at pasture on the hills
I ranged at large through the metropolis,
Month after month. Obscurely did I live,
Not courting the society of men
By literature, or elegance, or rank,

Book Ninth

RESIDENCE IN FRANCE

Even as a river, – partly (it might seem)
Yielding to old remembrances, and swayed
In part by fear to shape a way direct,
That would engulph him soon in the ravenous sea –
Turns, and will measure back his course, far back,
Seeking the very regions which he crossed
In his first outset; so have we, my Friend!
Turned and returned with intricate delay.
Or as a traveller, who has gained the brow
Of some aerial Down, while there he halts
For breathing-time, is tempted to review
The region left behind him; and, if aught
Deserving notice have escaped regard,
Or been regarded with too careless eye,
Strives, from that height, with one and yet one more
Last look, to make the best amends he may:
So have we lingered. Now we start afresh
With courage, and new hope risen on our toil.
Fair greetings to this shapeless eagerness,
Whene'er it comes! needful in work so long,
Thrice needful to the argument which now
Awaits us! Oh, how much unlike the past!

Free as a colt at pasture on the hill,
I ranged at large, through London's wide domain,
Month after month. Obscurely did I live,
Not seeking frequent intercourse with men,
By literature, or elegance, or rank,

Distinguished – in the midst of things, it seemed,
Looking as from a distance on the world
That moved about me. Yet insensibly
False preconceptions were corrected thus
And errors of the fancy rectified
(Alike with reference to men and things),
And sometimes from each quarter were poured in
Novel imaginations and profound.
A year thus spent, this field (with small regret
Save only for the bookstalls in the streets,
Wild produce, hedgerow fruit, on all sides hung
To lure the sauntering traveller from his track)
I quitted, and betook myself to France,
Led thither chiefly by a personal wish
To speak the language more familiarly,
With which intent I chose for my abode
A city on the borders of the Loire.

Through Paris lay my readiest path, and there
I sojourned a few days and visited
In haste each spot of old and recent fame –
The latter chiefly – from the Field of Mars
Down to the suburbs of St Antony,
And from Mont Martyr southward to the Dome
Of Geneviève. In both her clamorous halls
(The National Synod and the Jacobins)
I saw the revolutionary power
Toss like a ship at anchor, rocked by storms;
The Arcades I traversed in the Palace huge
Of Orleans, coasted round and round the line
Of tavern, brothel, gaming-house and shop,
Great rendezvous of worst and best, the walk
Of all who had a purpose, or had not.
I stared, and listened with a stranger's ears
To hawkers and haranguers (hubbub wild!)
And hissing factionists with ardent eyes,
In knots, or pairs, or single – ant-like swarms
Of builders and subverters, every face

Distinguished. Scarcely was a year thus spent
Ere I forsook the crowded solitude,
With less regret for its luxurious pomp,
And all the nicely-guarded shows of art,
Than for the humble book-stalls in the streets,
Exposed to eye and hand where'er I turned.

France lured me forth; the realm that I had crossed
So lately, journeying toward the snow-clad Alps.
But now, relinquishing the scrip and staff,
And all enjoyment which the summer sun
Sheds round the steps of those who meet the day
With motion constant as his own, I went
Prepared to sojourn in a pleasant town,
Washed by the current of the stately Loire.

Through Paris lay my readiest course, and there
Sojourning a few days, I visited,
In haste, each spot of old or recent fame,
The latter chiefly; from the field of Mars
Down to the suburbs of St. Antony,
And from Mont Martyr southward to the Dome
Of Geneviève. In both her clamorous Halls,
The National Synod and the Jacobins,
I saw the Revolutionary Power
Toss like a ship at anchor, rocked by storms;
The Arcades I traversed, in the Palace huge
Of Orleans; coasted round and round the line
Of Tavern, Brothel, Gaming-house, and Shop,
Great rendezvous of worst and best, the walk
Of all who had a purpose, or had not;
I stared and listened, with a stranger's ears,
To Hawkers and Haranguers, hubbub wild!
And hissing Factionists with ardent eyes,
In knots, or pairs, or single. Not a look
Hope takes, or Doubt or Fear is forced to wear,
But seemed there present; and I scanned them all,

That hope or apprehension could put on –
Joy, anger and vexation, in the midst
Of gaiety and dissolute idleness.

Where silent zephyrs sported with the dust
Of the Bastille I sat in the open sun,
And from the rubbish gathered up a stone
And pocketed the relic in the guise
Of an enthusiast; yet, in honest truth,
Though not without some strong incumbences,
And glad – could living man be otherwise? –
I looked for something which I could not find,
Affecting more emotion than I felt.
For 'tis most certain, that the utmost force
Of all these various objects which may show
The temper of my mind as then it was
Seemed less to recompense the traveller's pains –
Less moved me, gave me less delight – than did
A single picture merely, hunted out
Among other sights: the *Magdalen* of Le Brun,
A beauty exquisitely wrought, fair face
And rueful, with its ever-flowing tears.

But hence to my more permanent residence
I hasten. There, by novelties in speech,
Domestic manners, customs, gestures, looks,
And all the attire of ordinary life,
Attention was at first engrossed, and thus
Amused and satisfied I scarcely felt
The shock of these concussions, unconcerned,
Tranquil almost, and careless as a flower
Glassed in a greenhouse – or a parlour-shrub
When every bush and tree, the country through,
Is shaking to the roots – indifference this
Which may seem strange; but I was unprepared
With needful knowledge, had abruptly passed
Into a theatre of which the stage
Was busy with an action far advanced.

Watched every gesture uncontrollable,
Of anger, and vexation, and despite,
All side by side, and struggling face to face,
With gaiety and dissolute idleness.

Where silent zephyrs sported with the dust
Of the Bastille, I sate in the open sun,
And from the rubbish gathered up a stone,
And pocketed the relic, in the guise
Of an enthusiast; yet, in honest truth,
I looked for something that I could not find,
Affecting more emotion than I felt;
For 'tis most certain, that these various sights,
However potent their first shock, with me
Appeared to recompense the traveller's pains
Less than the painted Magdalene of Le Brun,
A beauty exquisitely wrought, with hair
Dishevelled, gleaming eyes, and rueful cheek
Pale and bedropped with everflowing tears.

But hence to my more permanent abode
I hasten; there, by novelties in speech,
Domestic manners, customs, gestures, looks,
And all the attire of ordinary life,
Attention was engrossed; and, thus amused,
I stood, 'mid those concussions, unconcerned,
Tranquil almost, and careless as a flower
Glassed in a green-house, or a parlour shrub
That spreads its leaves in unmolested peace,
While every bush and tree, the country through,
Is shaking to the roots: indifference this
Which may seem strange: but I was unprepared
With needful knowledge, had abruptly passed
Into a theatre, whose stage was filled
And busy with an action far advanced.

Like others I had read, and eagerly
Sometimes, the master pamphlets of the day,
Nor wanted such half-insight as grew wild
Upon that meagre soil, helped out by talk
And public news; but having never chanced
To see a regular chronicle which might show
(If any such indeed existed then)
Whence the main organs of the public power
Had sprung – their transmigrations, when and how
Accomplished – giving thus unto events
A form and body, all things were to me
Loose and disjointed, and the affections left
Without a vital interest. At that time,
Moreover, the first storm was overblown,
And the strong hand of outward violence
Locked up in quiet. For myself (I fear
Now in connection with so great a theme
To speak, as I must be compelled to do,
Of one so unimportant), a short time
I loitered, and frequented night by night
Routs, card-tables, the formal haunts of men
Whom in the city privilege of birth
Sequestered from the rest, societies
Where, through punctilios of elegance
And deeper causes, all discourse – alike
Of good and evil – of the time was shunned
With studious care. But 'twas not long ere this
Proved tedious, and I gradually withdrew
Into a noisier world, and thus did soon
Become a patriot – and my heart was all
Given to the people, and my love was theirs.

A knot of military officers
That to a regiment appertained which then
Was stationed in the city were the chief
Of my associates; some of these wore swords
Which had been seasoned in the wars, and all
Were men well-born – at least laid claim to such
Distinction, as the chivalry of France.

Like others, I had skimmed, and sometimes read
With care, the master pamphlets of the day;
Nor wanted such half-insight as grew wild
Upon that meagre soil, helped out by talk
And public news; but having never seen
A chronicle that might suffice to show
Whence the main organs of the public power
Had sprung, their transmigrations, when and how
Accomplished, giving thus unto events
A form and body; all things were to me
Loose and disjointed, and the affections left
Without a vital interest. At that time,
Moreover, the first storm was overblown,
And the strong hand of outward violence
Locked up in quiet. For myself, I fear
Now in connection with so great a theme
To speak (as I must be compelled to do)
Of one so unimportant; night by night
Did I frequent the formal haunts of men,
Whom, in the city, privilege of birth
Sequestered from the rest, societies
Polished in arts, and in punctilio versed;
Whence, and from deeper causes, all discourse
Of good and evil of the time was shunned
With scrupulous care; but these restrictions soon
Proved tedious, and I gradually withdrew
Into a noisier world, and thus ere long
Became a patriot; and my heart was all
Given to the people, and my love was theirs.

A band of military Officers,
Then stationed in the city, were the chief
Of my associates: some of these wore swords
That had been seasoned in the wars, and all
Were men well-born; the chivalry of France.

In age and temper differing, they had yet
One spirit ruling in them all, alike
(Save only one, hereafter to be named)
Were bent upon undoing what was done.
This was their rest, and only hope; therewith
No fear had they of bad becoming worse,
For worst to them was come – nor would have stirred,
Or deemed it worth a moment's while to stir,
In anything, save only as the act
Looked thitherward. One, reckoning by years,
Was in the prime of manhood, and erewhile
He had sat lord in many tender hearts,
Though heedless of such honours now, and changed:
His temper was quite mastered by the times,
And they had blighted him, had eat away
The beauty of his person, doing wrong
Alike to body and to mind. His port,
Which once had been erect and open, now
Was stooping and contracted, and a face,
By nature lovely in itself, expressed
As much as any that was ever seen
A ravage out of season, made by thoughts
Unhealthy and vexatious. At the hour,
The most important of each day, in which
The public news was read, the fever came
A punctual visitant to shake this man,
Disarmed his voice and fanned his yellow cheek
Into a thousand colours. While he read,
Or mused, his sword was haunted by his touch
Continually, like an uneasy place
In his own body.

'Twas in truth an hour
Of universal ferment. Mildest men
Were agitated, and commotions, strife
Of passion and opinion, filled the walls
Of peaceful houses with unquiet sounds.
The soil of common life was at that time
Too hot to tread upon! Oft said I then,

In age and temper differing, they had yet
One spirit ruling in each heart; alike
(Save only one, hereafter to be named)
Were bent upon undoing what was done:
This was their rest and only hope; therewith
No fear had they of bad becoming worse,
For worst to them was come; nor would have stirred,
Or deemed it worth a moment's thought to stir,
In any thing, save only as the act
Looked thitherward. One, reckoning by years,
Was in the prime of manhood, and erewhile
He had sate lord in many tender hearts;
Though heedless of such honours now, and changed:
His temper was quite mastered by the times,
And they had blighted him, had eaten away
The beauty of his person, doing wrong
Alike to body and to mind: his port,
Which once had been erect and open, now
Was stooping and contracted, and a face,
Endowed by Nature with her fairest gifts
Of symmetry and light and bloom, expressed,
As much as any that was ever seen,
A ravage out of season, made by thoughts
Unhealthy and vexatious. With the hour,
That from the press of Paris duly brought
Its freight of public news, the fever came,
A punctual visitant, to shake this man,
Disarmed his voice and fanned his yellow cheek
Into a thousand colours; while he read,
Or mused, his sword was haunted by his touch
Continually, like an uneasy place
In his own body. 'Twas in truth an hour
Of universal ferment; mildest men
Were agitated; and commotions, strife
Of passion and opinion, filled the walls
Of peaceful houses with unquiet sounds.
The soil of common life, was, at that time,
Too hot to tread upon. Oft said I then,

And not then only, 'What a mockery this
Of history, the past and that to come!
Now do I feel how I have been deceived
Reading of nations and their works in faith –
Faith given to vanity and emptiness –
Oh, laughter for the page that would reflect
To future times the face of what now is!'
The land all swarmed with passion, like a plain
Devoured by locusts – Carra, Gorsas – add
A hundred other names forgotten now,
Nor to be heard of more. Yet were they powers
Like earthquakes, shocks repeated day by day,
And felt through every nook of town and field.
The men already spoken of as chief
Of my associates were prepared for flight
To augment the band of emigrants in arms
Upon the borders of the Rhine, and leagued
With foreign foes mustered for instant war.
This was their undisguised intent, and they
Were waiting with the whole of their desires
The moment to depart.

An Englishman,
Born in a land the name of which appeared
To license some unruliness of mind –
A stranger, with youth's further privilege,
And that indulgence which a half-learnt speech
Wins from the courteous – I, who had been else
Shunned and not tolerated, freely lived
With these defenders of the Crown, and talked,
And heard their notions; nor did they disdain
The wish to bring me over to their cause.
But though untaught by thinking or by books
To reason well of polity or law,
And nice distinctions – then on every tongue –
Of natural rights and civil, and to acts
Of nations and their passing interests

And not then only, 'What a mockery this
Of history, the past and that to come!
Now do I feel how all men are deceived,
Reading of nations and their works, in faith,
Faith given to vanity and emptiness;
Oh! laughter for the page that would reflect
To future times the face of what now is!'
The land all swarmed with passion, like a plain
Devoured by locusts, – Carra, Gorcas, – add
A hundred other names, forgotten now,
Nor to be heard of more; yet, they were powers,
Like earthquakes, shocks repeated day by day,
And felt through every nook of town and field.

Such was the state of things. Meanwhile the chief
Of my associates stood prepared for flight
To augment the band of emigrants in arms
Upon the borders of the Rhine, and leagued
With foreign foes mustered for instant war.
This was their undisguised intent, and they
Were waiting with the whole of their desires
The moment to depart.

An Englishman,
Born in a land whose very name appeared
To license some unruliness of mind;
A stranger, with youth's further privilege,
And the indulgence that a half-learnt speech
Wins from the courteous; I, who had been else
Shunned and not tolerated, freely lived
With these defenders of the Crown, and talked,
And heard their notions; nor did they disdain
The wish to bring me over to their cause.

But though untaught by thinking or by books
To reason well of polity or law,
And nice distinctions, then on every tongue,
Of natural rights and civil; and to acts
Of nations and their passing interests,

(I speak comparing these with other things)
Almost indifferent – even the historian's tale
Prizing but little otherwise than I prized
Tales of the poets: as it made my heart
Beat high and filled my fancy with fair forms,
Old heroes and their sufferings and their deeds –
Yet in the regal sceptre, and the pomp
Of orders and degrees, I nothing found
Then, or had ever even in crudest youth,
That dazzled me; but rather what my soul
Mourned for, or loathed, beholding that the best
Ruled not, and feeling that they ought to rule.

For, born in a poor district (and which yet
Retaineth more of ancient homeliness,
Manners erect, and frank simplicity,
Than any other nook of English land),
It was my fortune scarcely to have seen
Through the whole tenor of my school-day time
The face of one, who, whether boy or man,
Was vested with attention or respect
Through claims of wealth or blood. Nor was it least
Of many debts which afterwards I owed
To Cambridge and an academic life
That something there was holden up to view
Of a republic, where all stood thus far
Upon equal ground, that they were brothers all
In honour, as of one community –
Scholars and gentlemen – where, furthermore,
Distinction lay open to all that came,
And wealth and titles were in less esteem
Than talents and successful industry.
Add unto this, subservience from the first
To God and nature's single sovereignty
(Familiar presences of awful power),
And fellowship with venerable books
To sanction the proud workings of the soul
And mountain liberty. It could not be
But that one tutored thus, who had been formed

(If with unworldly ends and aims compared)
Almost indifferent, even the historian's tale
Prizing but little otherwise than I prized
Tales of the poets, as it made the heart
Beat high, and filled the fancy with fair forms,
Old heroes and their sufferings and their deeds;
Yet in the regal sceptre, and the pomp
Of orders and degrees, I nothing found
Then, or had ever, even in crudest youth,
That dazzled me, but rather what I mourned
And ill could brook, beholding that the best
Ruled not, and feeling that they ought to rule.

For, born in a poor district, and which yet
Retaineth more of ancient homeliness,
Than any other nook of English ground,
It was my fortune scarcely to have seen,
Through the whole tenor of my school-day time,
The face of one, who, whether boy or man,
Was vested with attention or respect
Through claims of wealth or blood; nor was it least
Of many benefits, in later years
Derived from academic institutes
And rules, that they held something up to view
Of a Republic, where all stood thus far
Upon equal ground; that we were brothers all
In honour, as in one community,
Scholars and gentlemen; where, furthermore,
Distinction open lay to all that came,
And wealth and titles were in less esteem
Than talents, worth, and prosperous industry.
Add unto this, subservience from the first
To presences of God's mysterious power
Made manifest in Nature's sovereignty,
And fellowship with venerable books,
To sanction the proud workings of the soul,
And mountain liberty. It could not be
But that one tutored thus should look with awe

To thought and moral feeling in the way
This story hath described, should look with awe
Upon the faculties of man, receive
Gladly the highest promises, and hail
As best the government of equal rights
And individual worth. And hence, o friend,
If at the first great outbreak I rejoiced
Less than might well befit my youth, the cause
In part lay here, that unto me the events
Seemed nothing out of nature's certain course,
A gift that rather was come late than soon.
No wonder then if advocates like these
Whom I have mentioned, at this riper day
Were impotent to make my hopes put on
The shape of theirs, my understanding bend
In honour to their honour. Zeal, which yet
Had slumbered, now in opposition burst
Forth like a polar summer: every word
They uttered was a dart by counter-winds
Blown back upon themselves. Their reason seemed
Confusion-stricken by a higher power
Than human understanding, their discourse
Maimed, spiritless – and, in their weakness strong,
I triumphed.

Meantime day by day the roads,
While I consorted with these royalists,
Were crowded with the bravest youth of France,
And all the promptest of her spirits, linked
In gallant soldiership, and posting on
To meet the war upon her frontier bounds.
Yet at this very moment do tears start
Into mine eyes (I do not say I weep –
I wept not then – but tears have dimmed my sight)
In memory of the farewells of that time,
Domestic severings, female fortitude
At dearest separation, patriot love
And self-devotion, and terrestrial hope
Encouraged with a martyr's confidence.

Upon the faculties of man, receive
Gladly the highest promises, and hail,
As best, the government of equal rights
And individual worth. And hence, O Friend!
If at the first great outbreak I rejoiced
Less than might well befit my youth, the cause
In part lay here, that unto me the events
Seemed nothing out of nature's certain course,
A gift that was come rather late than soon.
No wonder, then, if advocates like these,
Inflamed by passion, blind with prejudice,
And stung with injury, at this riper day,
Were impotent to make my hopes put on
The shape of theirs, my understanding bend
In honour to their honour: zeal, which yet
Had slumbered, now in opposition burst
Forth like a Polar summer: every word
They uttered was a dart, by counter-winds
Blown back upon themselves; their reason seemed
Confusion-stricken by a higher power
Than human understanding, their discourse
Maimed, spiritless; and, in their weakness strong,
I triumphed.

Meantime, day by day, the roads
Were crowded with the bravest youth of France,
And all the promptest of her spirits, linked
In gallant soldiership, and posting on
To meet the war upon her frontier bounds.
Yet at this very moment do tears start
Into mine eyes: I do not say I weep –
I wept not then, – but tears have dimmed my sight,
In memory of the farewells of that time,
Domestic severings, female fortitude
At dearest separation, patriot love
And self-devotion, and terrestrial hope,
Encouraged with a martyr's confidence;

Even files of strangers merely, seen but once
And for a moment, men from far with sound
Of music, martial tunes, and banners spread,
Entering the city – here and there a face
Or person singled out among the rest,
Yet still a stranger and beloved as such –
Even by these passing spectacles my heart
Was oftentimes uplifted, and they seemed
Like arguments from Heaven that 'twas a cause
Good, and which no one could stand up against
Who was not lost, abandoned, selfish, proud,
Mean, miserable, wilfully depraved,
Hater perverse of equity and truth.

Among that band of officers was one,
Already hinted at, of other mould –
A patriot, thence rejected by the rest,
And with an oriental loathing spurned
As of a different caste. A meeker man
Than this lived never, or a more benign –
Meek, though enthusiastic to the height
Of highest expectation. Injuries
Made *him* more gracious, and his nature then
Did breathe its sweetness out most sensibly,
As aromatic flowers on alpine turf
When foot has crushed them. He through the events
Of that great change wandered in perfect faith
As through a book, an old romance, or tale
Of fairy, or some dream of actions wrought
Behind the summer clouds. By birth he ranked
With the most noble, but unto the poor
Among mankind he was in service bound
As by some tie invisible, oaths professed
To a religious order. Man he loved
As man, and to the mean and the obscure,
And all the homely in their homely works,
Transferred a courtesy which had no air
Of condescension, but did rather seem
A passion and a gallantry, like that

Even files of strangers merely seen but once,
And for a moment, men from far with sound
Of music, martial tunes, and banners spread,
Entering the city, here and there a face,
Or person singled out among the rest,
Yet still a stranger and beloved as such;
Even by these passing spectacles my heart
Was oftentimes uplifted, and they seemed
Arguments sent from Heaven to prove the cause
Good, pure, which no one could stand up against,
Who was not lost, abandoned, selfish, proud,
Mean, miserable, wilfully depraved,
Hater perverse of equity and truth.

Among that band of Officers was one,
Already hinted at, of other mould –
A patriot, thence rejected by the rest,
And with an oriental loathing spurned,
As of a different caste. A meeker man
Than this lived never, nor a more benign,
Meek though enthusiastic. Injuries
Made *him* more gracious, and his nature then
Did breathe its sweetness out most sensibly,
As aromatic flowers on Alpine turf,
When foot hath crushed them. He through the events
Of that great change wandered in perfect faith,
As through a book, an old romance, or tale
Of Fairy, or some dream of actions wrought
Behind the summer clouds. By birth he ranked
With the most noble, but unto the poor
Among mankind he was in service bound,
As by some tie invisible, oaths professed
To a religious order. Man he loved
As man; and, to the mean and the obscure,
And all the homely in their homely works,
Transferred a courtesy which had no air
Of condescension; but did rather seem
A passion and a gallantry, like that

Which he, a soldier, in his idler day
Had paid to woman. Somewhat vain he was,
Or seemed so; yet it was not vanity
But fondness, and a kind of radiant joy
That covered him about when he was bent
On works of love or freedom, or revolved
Complacently the progress of a cause
Whereof he was a part – yet this was meek
And placid, and took nothing from the man
That was delightful. Oft in solitude
With him did I discourse about the end
Of civil government, and its wisest forms,
Of ancient prejudice and chartered rights,
Allegiance, faith, and laws by time matured,
Custom and habit, novelty and change –
Of self-respect and virtue in the few
For patrimonial honour set apart,
And ignorance in the labouring multitude.
For he, an upright man and tolerant,
Balanced these contemplations in his mind,
And I, who at that time was scarcely dipped
Into the turmoil, had a sounder judgement
Than afterwards, carried about me yet
With less alloy to its integrity
The experience of past ages, as (through help
Of books and common life) it finds its way
To youthful minds, by objects over-near
Not pressed upon, nor dazzled or misled
By struggling with the crowd for present ends.

But though not deaf and obstinate to find
Error without apology on the side
Of those who were against us, more delight
We took (and let this freely be confessed)
In painting to ourselves the miseries
Of royal courts, and that voluptuous life
Unfeeling where the man who is of soul
The meanest thrives the most, where dignity,
True personal dignity, abideth not –

Which he, a soldier, in his idler day
Had paid to woman: somewhat vain he was,
Or seemed so, yet it was not vanity,
But fondness, and a kind of radiant joy
Diffused around him, while he was intent
On works of love or freedom, or revolved
Complacently the progress of a cause,
Whereof he was a part: yet this was meek
And placid, and took nothing from the man
That was delightful. Oft in solitude
With him did I discourse about the end
Of civil government, and its wisest forms;
Of ancient loyalty, and chartered rights,
Custom and habit, novelty and change;
Of self-respect, and virtue in the few
For patrimonial honour set apart,
And ignorance in the labouring multitude.
For he, to all intolerance indisposed,
Balanced these contemplations in his mind;
And I, who at that time was scarcely dipped
Into the turmoil, bore a sounder judgment
Than later days allowed; carried about me,
With less alloy to its integrity,
The experience of past ages, as, through help
Of books and common life, it makes sure way
To youthful minds, by objects over near
Not pressed upon, nor dazzled or misled
By struggling with the crowd for present ends.

But though not deaf, nor obstinate to find
Error without excuse upon the side
Of them who strove against us, more delight
We took, and let this freely be confessed,
In painting to ourselves the miseries
Of royal courts, and that voluptuous life
Unfeeling, where the man who is of soul
The meanest thrives the most; where dignity,
True personal dignity, abideth not;

A light and cruel world, cut off from all
The natural inlets of just sentiment,
From lowly sympathy and chastening truth –
Where good and evil never have that name,
That which they ought to have, but wrong prevails,
And vice at home. We added dearest themes:
Man and his noble nature (as it is
The gift of God and lies in his own power),
His blind desires and steady faculties
Capable of clear truth – the one to break
Bondage, the other to build liberty
On firm foundations, making social life
(Through knowledge spreading and imperishable)
As just in regulation and as pure,
As individual in the wise and good.

We summoned up the honourable deeds
Of ancient story, thought of each bright spot
That could be found in all recorded time
Of truth preserved and error passed away;
Of single spirits that catch the flame from Heaven,
And how the multitude of men will feed
And fan each other – thought of sects, how keen
They are to put the appropriate nature on,
Triumphant over every obstacle
Of custom, language, country, love and hate,
And what they do and suffer for their creed,
How far they travel, and how long endure;
How quickly mighty nations have been formed
From least beginnings; how, together locked
By new opinions, scattered tribes have made
One body, spreading wide as clouds in heaven.
To aspirations then of our own minds
Did we appeal, and, finally, beheld
A living confirmation of the whole
Before us in a people risen up
Fresh as the morning star. Elate we looked
Upon their virtues, saw in rudest men

A light, a cruel, and vain world cut off
From the natural inlets of just sentiment,
From lowly sympathy and chastening truth;
Where good and evil interchange their names,
And thirst for bloody spoils abroad is paired
With vice at home. We added dearest themes –
Man and his noble nature, as it is
The gift which God has placed within his power,
His blind desires and steady faculties
Capable of clear truth, the one to break
Bondage, the other to build liberty
On firm foundations, making social life,
Through knowledge spreading and imperishable,
As just in regulation, and as pure
As individual in the wise and good.

We summoned up the honourable deeds
Of ancient Story, thought of each bright spot,
That would be found in all recorded time,
Of truth preserved and error passed away;
Of single spirits that catch the flame from Heaven,
And how the multitudes of men will feed
And fan each other; thought of sects, how keen
They are to put the appropriate nature on,
Triumphant over every obstacle
Of custom, language, country, love, or hate,
And what they do and suffer for their creed;
How far they travel, and how long endure;
How quickly mighty Nations have been formed,
From least beginnings; how, together locked
By new opinions, scattered tribes have made
One body, spreading wide as clouds in heaven.
To aspirations then of our own minds
Did we appeal; and, finally, beheld
A living confirmation of the whole
Before us, in a people from the depth
Of shameful imbecility uprisen,
Fresh as the morning star. Elate we looked
Upon their virtues; saw, in rudest men,

Self-sacrifice the firmest, generous love
And continence of mind, and sense of right
Uppermost in the midst of fiercest strife.

Oh sweet it is in academic groves –
Or such retirement, friend, as we have known
Among the mountains, by our Rotha's stream,
Greta, or Derwent, or some nameless rill –
To ruminate, with interchange of talk,
On rational liberty and hope in man,
Justice and peace. But far more sweet such toil
(Toil, say I, for it leads to thoughts abstruse)
If nature then be standing on the brink
Of some great trial, and we hear the voice
Of one devoted, one whom circumstance
Hath called upon to embody his deep sense
In action, give it outwardly a shape,
And that of benediction to the world.
Then doubt is not, and truth is more than truth –
A hope it is and a desire, a creed
Of zeal (by an authority divine
Sanctioned) of danger, difficulty, or death.
Such conversation, under Attic shades,
Did Dion hold with Plato, ripened thus
For a deliverer's glorious task, and such
He (on that ministry already bound)
Held with Eudemus and Timonides
Surrounded by adventurers in arms,
When those two vessels, with their daring freight
For the Sicilian tyrant's overthrow,
Sailed from Zacynthus – philosophic war,
Led by philosophers. With harder fate,
Though like ambition, such was he, o friend,
Of whom I speak. So Beaupuy – let the name
Stand near the worthiest of antiquity –
Fashioned his life; and many a long discourse,
With like persuasion honoured, we maintained,
He on his part accoutred for the worst.
He perished fighting (in supreme command,

Self-sacrifice the firmest; generous love,
And continence of mind, and sense of right,
Uppermost in the midst of fiercest strife.

Oh, sweet it is, in academic groves,
Or such retirement, Friend! as we have known
In the green dales beside our Rotha's stream,
Greta, or Derwent, or some nameless rill,
To ruminate, with interchange of talk,
On rational liberty, and hope in man,
Justice and peace. But far more sweet such toil –
Toil, say I, for it leads to thoughts abstruse –
If nature then be standing on the brink
Of some great trial, and we hear the voice
Of one devoted, – one whom circumstance
Hath called upon to embody his deep sense
In action, give it outwardly a shape,
And that of benediction, to the world.
Then doubt is not, and truth is more than truth, –
A hope it is, and a desire; a creed
Of zeal, by an authority Divine
Sanctioned, of danger, difficulty, or death.
Such conversation, under Attic shades,
Did Dion hold with Plato; ripened thus
For a Deliverer's glorious task, – and such
He, on that ministry already bound,
Held with Eudemus and Timonides,
Surrounded by adventurers in arms,
When those two vessels with their daring freight,
For the Sicilian Tyrant's overthrow,
Sailed from Zacynthus, – philosophic war,
Led by Philosophers. With harder fate,
Though like ambition, such was he, O Friend!
Of whom I speak. So Beaupuis (let the name
Stand near the worthiest of Antiquity)
Fashioned his life; and many a long discourse,
With like persuasion honoured, we maintained:
He, on his part, accoutred for the worst.
He perished fighting, in supreme command,

Upon the borders of the unhappy Loire)
For liberty against deluded men,
His fellow countrymen, and yet most blessed
In this, that he the fate of later times
Lived not to see, nor what we now behold
Who have as ardent hearts as he had then.

Along that very Loire, with festivals
Resounding at all hours, and innocent yet
Of civil slaughter, was our frequent walk;
Or in wide forests of the neighbourhood,
High woods and over-arched, with open space
On every side, and footing many a mile,
Inwoven roots and moss smooth as the sea,
A solemn region. Often in such place
From earnest dialogues I slipped in thought
And let remembrance steal to other times,
When hermits (from their sheds and caves forth-strayed)
Walked by themselves, so met in shades like these,
And if a devious traveller was heard
Approaching from a distance, as might chance,
With speed and echoes loud of trampling hoofs
From the hard floor reverberated, then
It was Angelica thundering through the woods
Upon her palfrey, or that gentler maid
Erminia, fugitive as fair as she.
Sometimes I saw, methought, a pair of knights
Joust underneath the trees, that as in storm
Did rock above their heads; anon the din
Of boisterous merriment and music's roar,
With sudden proclamation burst from haunt
Of satyrs in some viewless glade, with dance
Rejoicing o'er a female in the midst,
A mortal beauty, their unhappy thrall.
The width of those huge forests, unto me

Upon the borders of the unhappy Loire,
For liberty, against deluded men,
His fellow country-men; and yet most blessed
In this, that he the fate of later times
Lived not to see, nor what we now behold,
Who have as ardent hearts as he had then.

Along that very Loire, with festal mirth
Resounding at all hours, and innocent yet
Of civil slaughter, was our frequent walk;
Or in wide forests of continuous shade,
Lofty and over-arched, with open space
Beneath the trees, clear footing many a mile –
A solemn region. Oft amid those haunts,
From earnest dialogues I slipped in thought,
And let remembrance steal to other times,
When, o'er those interwoven roots, moss-clad,
And smooth as marble or a waveless sea,
Some Hermit, from his cell forth-strayed, might pace
In sylvan meditation undisturbed;
As on the pavement of a Gothic church
Walks a lone Monk, when service hath expired,
In peace and silence. But if e'er was heard, –
Heard, though unseen, – a devious traveller,
Retiring or approaching from afar
With speed and echoes loud of trampling hoofs
From the hard floor reverberated, then
It was Angelica thundering through the woods
Upon her palfrey, or that gentle maid
Erminia, fugitive as fair as she.
Sometimes methought I saw a pair of knights
Joust underneath the trees, that as in storm
Rocked high above their heads; anon, the din
Of boisterous merriment, and music's roar,
In sudden proclamation, burst from haunt
Of Satyrs in some viewless glade, with dance
Rejoicing o'er a female in the midst,
A mortal beauty, their unhappy thrall.
The width of those huge forests, unto me

A novel scene, did often in this way
Master my fancy while I wandered on
With that revered companion. And sometimes,
When to a convent in a meadow green
By a brookside we came – a roofless pile,
And not by reverential touch of time
Dismantled, but by violence abrupt –
In spite of those heart-bracing colloquies,
In spite of real fervour, and of that
Less genuine and wrought up within myself,
I could not but bewail a wrong so harsh,
And for the matin-bell (to sound no more)
Grieved, and the evening taper, and the cross
High on the topmost pinnacle, a sign
Admonitory, by the traveller
First seen above the woods.

And when my friend
Pointed upon occasion to the site
Of Romorantin, home of ancient kings;
To the imperial edifice of Blois;
Or to that rural castle, name now slipped
From my remembrance (where a lady lodged,
By the first Francis wooed, and, bound to him
In chains of mutual passion, from the tower,
As a tradition of the country tells,
Practised to commune with her royal knight
By cressets and love-beacons, intercourse
'Twixt her high-seated residence and his
Far off at Chambord on the plain beneath) –
Even here, though less than with the peaceful house
Religious, mid these frequent monuments
Of kings, their vices or their better deeds,
Imagination, potent to inflame
At times with virtuous wrath and noble scorn,
Did also often mitigate the force
Of civic prejudice, the bigotry
(So call it) of a youthful patriot's mind;
And on these spots with many gleams I looked

A novel scene, did often in this way
Master my fancy while I wandered on
With that revered companion. And sometimes –
When to a convent in a meadow green,
By a brook-side, we came, a roofless pile,
And not by reverential touch of Time
Dismantled, but by violence abrupt –
In spite of those heart-bracing colloquies,
In spite of real fervour, and of that
Less genuine and wrought up within myself –
I could not but bewail a wrong so harsh,
And for the Matin-bell to sound no more
Grieved, and the twilight taper, and the cross
High on the topmost pinnacle, a sign
(How welcome to the weary traveller's eyes!)
Of hospitality and peaceful rest.
And when the partner of those varied walks
Pointed upon occasion to the site
Of Romorentin, home of ancient kings,
To the imperial edifice of Blois,
Or to that rural castle, name now slipped
From my remembrance, where a lady lodged,
By the first Francis wooed, and bound to him
In chains of mutual passion, from the tower,
As a tradition of the country tells,
Practised to commune with her royal knight
By cressets and love-beacons, intercourse
'Twixt her high-seated residence and his
Far off at Chambord on the plain beneath;
Even here, though less than with the peaceful house
Religious, 'mid those frequent monuments
Of Kings, their vices and their better deeds,
Imagination, potent to inflame
At times with virtuous wrath and noble scorn,
Did also often mitigate the force
Of civic prejudice, the bigotry,
So call it, of a youthful patriot's mind;
And on these spots with many gleams I looked

Of chivalrous delight. Yet not the less,
Hatred of absolute rule, where will of one
Is law for all, and of that barren pride
In those who, by immunities unjust,
Betwixt the sovereign and the people stand
(His helpers and not theirs) laid stronger hold
Daily upon me – mixed with pity too
And love, for where hope is, there love will be
For the abject multitude.

And when we chanced
One day to meet a hunger-bitten girl,
Who crept along fitting her languid self
Unto a heifer's motion – by a cord
Tied to her arm, and picking thus from the lane
Its sustenance, while the girl with her two hands
Was busy knitting in a heartless mood
Of solitude – and at the sight my friend
In agitation said ''Tis against *that*
Which we are fighting!' I with him believed
Devoutly that a spirit was abroad
Which could not be withstood; that poverty,
At least like this, would in a little time
Be found no more; that we should see the earth
Unthwarted in her wish to recompense
The industrious and the lowly child of toil
(All institutes for ever blotted out
That legalized exclusion, empty pomp
Abolished, sensual state and cruel power,
Whether by edict of the one or few);
And finally, as sum and crown of all,
Should see the people having a strong hand
In making their own laws – whence better days
To all mankind.

But, these things set apart,
Was not the single confidence enough
To animate the mind that ever turned
A thought to human welfare: that henceforth

Of chivalrous delight. Yet not the less,
Hatred of absolute rule, where will of one
Is law for all, and of that barren pride
In them who, by immunities unjust,
Between the sovereign and the people stand,
His helper and not theirs, laid stronger hold
Daily upon me, mixed with pity too
And love; for where hope is, there love will be
For the abject multitude. And when we chanced
One day to meet a hunger-bitten girl,
Who crept along fitting her languid gait
Unto a heifer's motion, by a cord
Tied to her arm, and picking thus from the lane
Its sustenance, while the girl with pallid hands
Was busy knitting in a heartless mood
Of solitude, and at the sight my friend
In agitation said, ''Tis against *that*
That we are fighting,' I with him believed
That a benignant spirit was abroad
Which might not be withstood, that poverty
Abject as this would in a little time
Be found no more, that we should see the earth
Unthwarted in her wish to recompense
The meek, the lowly, patient child of toil,
All institutes for ever blotted out
That legalised exclusion, empty pomp
Abolished, sensual state and cruel power,
Whether by edict of the one or few;
And finally, as sum and crown of all,
Should see the people having a strong hand
In framing their own laws; whence better days
To all mankind. But, these things set apart,
Was not this single confidence enough
To animate the mind that ever turned
A thought to human welfare? That henceforth

Captivity by mandate without law
Should cease, and open accusation lead
To sentence in the hearing of the world,
And open punishment – if not the air
Be free to breathe in, and the heart of man
Dread nothing. Having touched this argument
I shall not (as my purpose was) take note
Of other matters which detained us oft
In thought or conversation – public acts,
And public persons, and the emotions wrought
Within our minds by the ever-varying wind
Of record and report which day by day
Swept over us – but I will here instead
Draw from obscurity a tragic tale,
Not in its spirit singular indeed
But haply worth memorial, as I heard
The events related by my patriot friend
And others who had borne a part therein.

Oh happy time of youthful lovers – thus
My story may begin – oh balmy time
In which a love-knot on a lady's brow
Is fairer than the fairest star in heaven!
To such inheritance of blessedness
Young Vaudracour was brought by years that had
A little overstepped his stripling prime.
A town of small repute in the heart of France
Was the youth's birthplace; there he vowed his love
To Julia, a bright maid, from parents sprung
Not mean in their condition, but with rights
Unhonoured of nobility – and hence
The father of the young man, who had place
Among that order, spurned the very thought
Of such alliance. From their cradles up,
With but a step between their several homes,
The pair had thriven together year by year,
Friend, playmates, twins in pleasure – after strife
And petty quarrels had grown fond again –
Each other's advocate, each other's help,

Captivity by mandate without law
Should cease; and open accusation lead
To sentence in the hearing of the world,
And open punishment, if not the air
Be free to breathe in, and the heart of man
Dread nothing. From this height I shall not stoop
To humbler matter that detained us oft
In thought or conversation, public acts,
And public persons, and emotions wrought
Within the breast, as ever-varying winds
Of record or report swept over us;
But I might here, instead, repeat a tale,
Told by my Patriot friend, of sad events,
That prove to what low depth had struck the roots,
How widely spread the boughs, of that old tree
Which, as a deadly mischief, and a foul
And black dishonour, France was weary of.

Oh, happy time of youthful lovers, (thus
The story might begin). Oh, balmy time,
In which a love-knot, on a lady's brow,
Is fairer than the fairest star in Heaven!
So might – and with that prelude *did* begin
The record; and, in faithful verse, was given
The doleful sequel.

But our little bark
On a strong river boldly hath been launched;
And from the driving current should we turn
To loiter wilfully within a creek,
Howe'er attractive, Fellow voyager!
Would'st thou not chide? Yet deem not my pains lost:
For Vaudracour and Julia (so were named
The ill-fated pair) in that plain tale will draw
Tears from the hearts of others, when their own
Shall beat no more. Thou, also, there mayst read,
At leisure, how the enamoured youth was driven,
By public power abased, to fatal crime,
Nature's rebellion against monstrous law;

Nor ever happy if they were apart.
A basis this for deep and solid love,
And endless constancy, and placid truth;
But – whatsoever of such treasures might,
Beneath the outside of their youth, have lain
Reserved for mellower years – his present mind
Was under fascination: he beheld
A vision, and he loved the thing he saw.

Arabian fiction never filled the world
With half the wonders that were wrought for him.
Earth lived in one great presence of the spring,
Life turned the meanest of her implements
Before his eyes to price above all gold,
The house she dwelt in was a sainted shrine,
Her chamber-window did surpass in glory
The portals of the east! All paradise
Could by the simple opening of a door
Let itself in upon him! Pathways, walks,
Swarmed with enchantment, till his spirit sank
Beneath the burden, overblessed for life.
This state was theirs, till – whether through effect
Of some delirious hour, or that the youth,
Seeing so many bars betwixt himself
And the dear haven where he wished to be
In honourable wedlock with his love,
Without a certain knowledge of his own
Was inwardly prepared to turn aside
From law and custom, and entrust himself
To nature for a happy end of all
(And thus abated of that pure reserve
Congenial to his loyal heart, with which
It would have pleased him to attend the steps
Of maiden so divinely beautiful),
I know not – but reluctantly must add
That Julia, yet without the name of wife,
Carried about her for a secret grief
The promise of a mother.

How, between heart and heart, oppression thrust
Her mandates, severing whom true love had joined,
Harassing both; until he sank and pressed
The couch his fate had made for him; supine,
Save when the stings of viperous remorse,
Trying their strength, enforced him to start up,
Aghast and prayerless. Into a deep wood
He fled, to shun the haunts of human kind;
There dwelt, weakened in spirit more and more;
Nor could the voice of Freedom, which through France
Full speedily resounded, public hope,
Or personal memory of his own worst wrongs,
Rouse him; but, hidden in those gloomy shades,
His days he wasted, – an imbecile mind.

To conceal
The threatened shame the parents of the maid
Found means to hurry her away by night
And unforewarned, that in a distant town
She might remain shrouded in privacy
Until the babe was born. When morning came
The lover, thus bereft, stung with his loss
And all uncertain whither he should turn,
Chafed like a wild beast in the toils. At length,
Following as his suspicions led, he found –
Oh joy! – sure traces of the fugitives,
Pursued them to the town where they had stopped,
And lastly to the very house itself
Which had been chosen for the maid's retreat.
The sequel may be easily divined:
Walks backwards, forwards, morning, noon and night
(When decency and caution would allow),
And Julia, who, whenever to herself
She happened to be left a moment's space,
Was busy at her casement, as a swallow
About its nest, erelong did thus espy
Her lover – thence a stolen interview
By night accomplished, with a ladder's help.

I pass the raptures of the pair; such theme
Hath by a hundred poets been set forth
In more delightful verse than skill of mine
Could fashion – chiefly by that darling bard
Who told of Juliet and her Romeo,
And of the lark's note heard before its time,
And of the streaks that laced the severing clouds
In the unrelenting east. 'Tis mine to tread
The humbler province of plain history,
And, without choice of circumstance, submissively
Relate what I have heard. The lovers came
To this resolve (with which they parted, pleased
And confident) that Vaudracour should hie
Back to his father's house, and there employ
Means aptest to obtain a sum of gold –

A final portion even, if that might be –
Which done, together they could then take flight
To some remote and solitary place
Where they might live with no one to behold
Their happiness, or to disturb their love.
Immediately, and with this mission charged,
Home to his father's house did he return
And there remained a time without hint given
Of his design; but if a word were dropped
Touching the matter of his passion, still,
In hearing of his father, Vaudracour
Persisted openly that nothing less
Than death should make him yield up hope to be
A blessèd husband of the maid he loved.

Incensed at such obduracy and slight
Of exhortations and remonstrances
The father threw out threats that by a mandate
Bearing the private signet of the state
He should be baffled of his mad intent –
And that should cure him. From this time the youth
Conceived a terror, and by night or day
Stirred nowhere without arms. Soon afterwards
His parents to their country seat withdrew
Upon some feigned occasion, and the son
Was left with one attendant in the house.
Retiring to his chamber for the night,
While he was entering at the door, attempts
Were made to seize him by three armèd men,
The instruments of ruffian power. The youth,
In the first impulse of his rage, laid one
Dead at his feet, and to the second gave
A perilous wound – which done, at sight
Of the dead man, he peacefully resigned
His person to the law, was lodged in prison,
And wore the fetters of a criminal.

Through three weeks' space (by means which love devised)

The maid in her seclusion had received
Tidings of Vaudracour, and how he sped
Upon his enterprise. Thereafter came
A silence; half a circle did the moon
Complete, and then a whole, and still the same
Silence. A thousand thousand fears and hopes
Stirred in mind – thoughts waking, thoughts of sleep,
Entangled in each other – and at last
Self-slaughter seemed her only resting-place.
So did she fare in her uncertainty.

At length, by interference of a friend
(One who had sway at court) the youth regained
His liberty, on promise to sit down
Quietly in his father's house, nor take
One step to reunite himself with her
Of whom his parents disapproved – hard law,
To which he gave consent only because
His freedom else could nowise be procured.
Back to his father's house he went, remained
Eight days, and then his resolution failed.
He fled to Julia, and the words with which
He greeted her were these: 'All right is gone –
Gone from me! Thou no longer now art mine,
I thine! A murderer, Julia, cannot love
An innocent woman – I behold thy face,
I see thee, and my misery is complete!'
She could not give him answer; afterwards
She coupled with his father's name some words
Of vehement indignation; but the youth
Checked her, nor would he hear of this; for thought
Unfilial, or unkind, had never once
Found harbour in his breast. The lovers, thus
United once again, together lived
For a few days, which were to Vaudracour
Days of dejection, sorrow and remorse
For that ill deed of violence which his hand
Had hastily committed; for the youth
Was of a loyal spirit, a conscience nice,

And over tender for the trial which
His fate had called him to. The father's mind,
Meanwhile, remained unchanged, and Vaudracour
Learned that a mandate had been newly issued
To arrest him on the spot. Oh pain it was
To part! He could not – and he lingered still
To the last moment of his time, and then
(At dead of night with snow upon the ground)
He left the city, and in villages
The most sequestered of the neighbourhood
Lay hidden for the space of several days,
Until, the horseman bringing back report
That he was nowhere to be found, the search
Was ended. Back returned the ill-fated youth,
And from the house where Julia lodged (to which
He now found open ingress, having gained
The affection of the family, who loved him
Both for his own, and for the maiden's sake)
One night retiring, he was seized.

But here
A portion of the tale may well be left
In silence, though my memory could add
Much how the youth (and in short space of time)
Was traversed from without; much, too, of thoughts
By which he was employed in solitude
Under privation and restraint, and what
Through dark and shapeless fear of things to come,
And what through strong compunction for the past,
He suffered, breaking down in heart and mind.
Such grace (if grace it were) had been vouchsafed –
Or such effect had through the father's want
Of power, or through his negligence, ensued –
That Vaudracour was suffered to remain,
Though under guard and without liberty,
In the same city with the unhappy maid
From whom he was divided. So they fared,
Objects of general concern, till, moved
With pity for their wrongs, the magistrate

(The same who had placed the youth in custody)
By application to the minister
Obtained his liberty upon condition
That to his father's house he should return.

He left his prison almost on the eve
Of Julia's travail. She had likewise been
(As from the time indeed, when she had first
Been brought for secrecy to this abode),
Though treated with consoling tenderness,
Herself a prisoner – a dejected one,
Filled with a lover's and a woman's fears –
And whensoe'er the mistress of the house
Entered the room for the last time at night
And Julia with a low and plaintive voice
Said 'You are coming then to lock me up!'
The housewife when these words (always the same)
Were by her captive languidly pronounced
Could never hear them uttered without tears.

A day or two before her childbed time
Was Vaudracour restored to her, and soon
As he might be permitted to return
Into her chamber after the child's birth,
The master of the family begged that all
The household might be summoned, doubting not
But that they might receive impressions then
Friendly to human kindness. Vaudracour
(This heard I from one present at the time)
Held up the newborn infant in his arms
And kissed, and blessed, and covered it with tears,
Uttering a prayer that he might never be
As wretched as his father. Then he gave
The child to her who bore it, and she too
Repeated the same prayer – took it again
And, muttering something faintly afterwards,
He gave the infant to the standers-by,
And wept in silence upon Julia's neck.

Two months did he continue in the house,
And often yielded up himself to plans
Of future happiness. 'You shall return,
Julia', said he, 'and to your father's house
Go with your child. You have been wretched, yet
It is a town where both of us were born –
None will reproach you, for our loves are known.
With ornaments the prettiest you shall dress
Your boy, as soon as he can run about,
And when he thus is at his play my father
Will see him from the window, and the child
Will by his beauty move his grandsire's heart,
So that it will be softened, and our loves
End happily, as they began.' These gleams
Appeared but seldom; oftener he was seen
Propping a pale and melancholy face
Upon the mother's bosom, resting thus
His head upon one breast, while from the other
The babe was drawing in its quiet food.
At other times, when he in silence long
And fixedly had looked upon her face,
He would exclaim, 'Julia, how much thine eyes
Have cost me!' During daytime when the child
Lay in its cradle, by its side he sat,
Not quitting it an instant. The whole town
In his unmerited misfortunes now
Took part, and if he either at the door
Or window for a moment with his child
Appeared, immediately the street was thronged;
While others, frequently without reserve,
Passed and repassed before the house to steal
A look at him.

Oft at this time he wrote
Requesting, since he knew that the consent
Of Julia's parents never could be gained
To a clandestine marriage, that his father
Would from the birthright of an eldest son
Exclude him, giving but (when this was done)

A sanction to his nuptials. Vain request,
To which no answer was returned! And now
From her own home the mother of his love
Arrived to apprise the daughter of her fixed
And last resolve, that, since all hope to move
The old man's heart proved vain, she must retire
Into a convent, and be there immured.
Julia was thunderstricken by these words,
And she insisted on a mother's rights
To take her child along with her – a grant
Impossible, as she at last perceived.
The persons of the house no sooner heard
Of this decision upon Julia's fate
Than everyone was overwhelmed with grief,
Nor could they frame a manner soft enough
To impart the tidings to the youth. But great
Was their astonishment when they beheld him
Receive the news in calm despondency,
Composed and silent, without outward sign
Of even the least emotion. Seeing this,
When Julia scattered some upbraiding words
Upon his slackness, he thereto returned
No answer, only took the mother's hand
(Who loved him scarcely less than her own child)
And kissed it, without seeming to be pressed
By any pain that 'twas the hand of one
Whose errand was to part him from his love
For ever.

In the city he remained
A season after Julia had retired
And in the convent taken up her home,
To the end that he might place his infant babe
With a fit nurse; which done, beneath the roof
Where now his little one was lodged, he passed
The day entire, and scarcely could at length
Tear himself from the cradle to return
Home to his father's house – in which he dwelt
Awhile, and then came back that he might see

Whether the babe had gained sufficient strength
To bear removal. He quitted this same town
For the last time, attendant by the side
Of a close-chair – a litter or sedan –
In which the child was carried. To a hill
Which rose at a league's distance from the town
The family of the house where he had lodged
Attended him, and parted from him there,
Watching below until he disappeared
On the hilltop. His eyes he scarcely took,
Through all that journey, from the chair in which
The babe was carried; and at every inn
Or place at which they halted or reposed
Laid him upon his knees, nor would permit
The hands of any but himself to dress
The infant or undress. By one of those
Who bore the chair these facts, at his return,
Were told, and in relating them he wept.

This was the manner in which Vaudracour
Departed with his infant, and thus reached
His father's house, where to the innocent child
Admittance was denied. The young man spoke
No word of indignation or reproof,
But of his father begged (a last request)
That a retreat might be assigned to him,
A house where in the country he might dwell
With such allowance as his wants required –
And the more lonely that the mansion was
'Twould be more welcome. To a lodge that stood
Deep in a forest, with leave given, at the age
Of four-and-twenty summers he retired;
And thither took with him his infant babe,
And one domestic for their common needs,
An aged woman. It consoled him here
To attend upon the orphan and perform
The office of a nurse to his young child,
Which, after a short time, by some mistake
Or indiscretion of the father, died.

The tale I follow to its last recess
Of suffering or of peace, I know not which –
Theirs be the blame who caused the woe, not mine.

From that time forth he never uttered word
To any living. An inhabitant
Of that same town in which the pair had left
So lively a remembrance of their griefs
By chance of business coming within reach
Of his retirement, to the spot repaired
With the intent to visit him; he reached
The house and only found the matron there,
Who told him that his pains were thrown away,
For that her master never uttered word
To living soul – not even to her. Behold
While they were speaking, Vaudracour approached,
But, seeing someone there, just as his hand
Was stretched towards the garden-gate, he shrunk,
And like a shadow glided out of view.
Shocked at his savage outside, from the place
The visitor retired.

Thus lived the youth,
Cut off from all intelligence with man,
And shunning even the light of common day.
Nor could the voice of freedom, which through France
Soon afterwards resounded, public hope,
Or personal memory of his own deep wrongs,
Rouse him; but in those solitary shades
His days he wasted – an imbecile mind.

Book Tenth

RESIDENCE IN FRANCE AND FRENCH REVOLUTION

It was a beautiful and silent day
That overspread the countenance of earth
(Then fading) with unusual quietness,
When from the Loire I parted, and through scenes
Of vineyard, orchard, meadow-ground and tilth,
Calm waters, gleams of sun, and breathless trees,
Towards the fierce metropolis turned my steps
Their homeward way to England. From his throne
The King had fallen; the congregated host –
Dire cloud, upon the front of which was written
The tender mercies of the dismal wind
That bore it – on the plains of liberty
Had burst innocuously. Say more, the swarm
That came elate and jocund, like a band
Of eastern hunters, to enfold in ring
Narrowing itself by moments, and reduce
To the last punctual spot of their despair
A race of victims (so they deemed), *themselves*
Had shrunk from sight of their own task, and fled
In terror. Desolation and dismay
Remained for them whose fancies had grown rank
With evil expectations: confidence
And perfect triumph to the better cause.

Book Tenth

RESIDENCE IN FRANCE – (CONTINUED)

It was a beautiful and silent day
That overspread the countenance of earth,
Then fading with unusual quietness, –
A day as beautiful as e'er was given
To soothe regret, though deepening what it soothed,
When by the gliding Loire I paused, and cast
Upon his rich domains, vineyard and tilth,
Green meadow-ground, and many-coloured woods,
Again, and yet again, a farewell look;
Then from the quiet of that scene passed on,
Bound to the fierce Metropolis. From his throne
The King had fallen, and that invading host –
Presumptuous cloud, on whose black front was written
The tender mercies of the dismal wind
That bore it – on the plains of Liberty
Had burst innocuous. Say in bolder words,
They – who had come elate as eastern hunters
Banded beneath the Great Mogul, when he
Erewhile went forth from Agra or Lahore,
Rajahs and Omrahs in his train, intent
To drive their prey enclosed within a ring
Wide as a province, but, the signal given,
Before the point of the life-threatening spear
Narrowing itself by moments – they, rash men,
Had seen the anticipated quarry turned
Into avengers, from whose wrath they fled
In terror. Disappointment and dismay
Remained for all whose fancies had run wild
With evil expectations; confidence
And perfect triumph for the better cause.

The state, as if to stamp the final seal
On her security, and to the world
Show what she was, a high and fearless soul –
Or rather in a spirit of thanks to those
Who had stirred up her slackening faculties
To a new transition – had assumed with joy
The body and the venerable name
Of a republic. Lamentable crimes,
'Tis true, had gone before this hour, the work
Of massacre, in which the senseless sword
Was prayed to as a judge; but these were past,
Earth free from them for ever, as was thought –
Ephemeral monsters, to be seen but once,
Things that could only show themselves and die!

This was the time in which, inflamed with hope,
To Paris I returned. Again I ranged,
More eagerly than I had done before,
Through the wide city, and in progress passed
The prison where the unhappy monarch lay,
Associate with his children and his wife
In bondage, and the palace, lately stormed
With roar of cannon and a numerous host.
I crossed (a black and empty area then)
The Square of the Carrousel, few weeks back
Heaped up with dead and dying – upon these
And other sights looking as doth a man
Upon a volume whose contents he knows
Are memorable but from him locked up,
Being written in a tongue he cannot read,
So that he questions the mute leaves with pain
And half upbraids their silence. But that night
When on my bed I lay, I was most moved
And felt most deeply in what world I was.
My room was high and lonely, near the roof
Of a large mansion or hotel, a spot

The State, as if to stamp the final seal
On her security, and to the world
Show what she was, a high and fearless soul,
Exulting in defiance, or heart-stung
By sharp resentment, or belike to taunt
With spiteful gratitude the baffled League,
That had stirred up her slackening faculties
To a new transition, when the King was crushed,
Spared not the empty throne, and in proud haste
Assumed the body and venerable name
Of a Republic. Lamentable crimes,
'Tis true, had gone before this hour, dire work
Of massacre, in which the senseless sword
Was prayed to as a judge; but these were past,
Earth free from them for ever, as was thought, –
Ephemeral monsters, to be seen but once!
Things that could only show themselves and die.

Cheered with this hope, to Paris I returned,
And ranged, with ardour heretofore unfelt,
The spacious city, and in progress passed
The prison where the unhappy Monarch lay,
Associate with his children and his wife
In bondage; and the palace, lately stormed
With roar of cannon by a furious host.
I crossed the square (an empty area then!)
Of the Carrousel, where so late had lain
The dead, upon the dying heaped, and gazed
On this and other spots, as doth a man
Upon a volume whose contents he knows
Are memorable, but from him locked up,
Being written in a tongue he cannot read,
So that he questions the mute leaves with pain,
And half upbraids their silence. But that night
I felt most deeply in what world I was,
What ground I trod on, and what air I breathed.
High was my room and lonely, near the roof
Of a large mansion or hotel, a lodge

That would have pleased me in more quiet times –
Nor was it wholly without pleasure then.
With unextinguished taper I kept watch,
Reading at intervals. The fear gone by
Pressed on me almost like a fear to come.
I thought of those September massacres,
Divided from me by a little month,
And felt and touched them, a substantial dread
(The rest was conjured up from tragic fictions
And mournful calendars of true history,
Remembrances and dim admonishments):
'The horse is taught his manage, and the wind
Of heaven wheels round and treads in his own steps;
Year follows year, the tide returns again,
Day follows day, all things have second birth;
The earthquake is not satisfied at once!'
And in such way I wrought upon myself
Until I seemed to hear a voice that cried
To the whole city 'Sleep no more!' To this
Add comments of a calmer mind, from which
I could not gather full security,
But at the best it seemed a place of fear
Unfit for the repose of night,
Defenceless as a wood where tigers roam.

Betimes next morning to the Palace Walk
Of Orleans I repaired, and entering there
Was greeted (among divers other notes)
By voices of the hawkers in the crowd
Bawling 'Denunciation of the crimes
Of Maximilian Robespierre'. The speech
Which in their hands they carried was the same
Which had been recently pronounced, the day
When Robespierre (well knowing for what mark
Some words of indirect reproof had been

That would have pleased me in more quiet times;
Nor was it wholly without pleasure then.
With unextinguished taper I kept watch,
Reading at intervals; the fear gone by
Pressed on me almost like a fear to come.
I thought of those September massacres,
Divided from me by one little month,
Saw them and touched: the rest was conjured up
From tragic fictions or true history,
Remembrances and dim admonishments.
The horse is taught his manage, and no star
Of wildest course but treads back his own steps;
For the spent hurricane the air provides
As fierce a successor; the tide retreats
But to return out of its hiding-place
In the great deep; all things have second birth;
The earthquake is not satisfied at once;
And in this way I wrought upon myself,
Until I seemed to hear a voice that cried,
To the whole city, 'Sleep no more.' The trance
Fled with the voice to which it had given birth;
But vainly comments of a calmer mind
Promised soft peace and sweet forgetfulness.
The place, all hushed and silent as it was,
Appeared unfit for the repose of night,
Defenceless as a wood where tigers roam.

With early morning towards the Palace-walk
Of Orleans eagerly I turned; as yet
The streets were still; not so those long Arcades;
There, 'mid a peal of ill-matched sounds and cries,
That greeted me on entering, I could hear
Shrill voices from the hawkers in the throng,
Bawling, 'Denunciation of the Crimes
Of Maximilian Robespierre'; the hand,
Prompt as the voice, held forth a printed speech,
The same that had been recently pronounced,
When Robespierre, not ignorant for what mark
Some words of indirect reproof had been

Intended) rose in hardihood, and dared
The man who had an ill surmise of him
To bring his charge in openness. Whereat,
When a dead pause ensued and no one stirred,
In silence of all present, from his seat
Louvet walked singly through the avenue
And took his station in the tribune, saying
'I, Robespierre, accuse thee!' 'Tis well known
What was the issue of that charge, and how
Louvet was left alone without support
Of his irresolute friends. But these are things
Of which I speak only as they were storm
Or sunshine to my individual mind,
No further.

Let me then relate that now,
In some sort seeing with my proper eyes
That liberty, and life, and death would soon
To the remotest corners of the land
Lie in the arbitrement of those who ruled
The capital city (what was struggled for,
And by what combatants victory must be won;
The indecision on their part whose aim
Seemed best, and the straightforward path of those
Who in attack or in defence alike
Were strong through their impiety), greatly I
Was agitated. Yea, I could almost
Have prayed that throughout earth upon all souls
Worthy of liberty – upon every soul
Matured to live in plainness and in truth –
The gift of tongues might fall, and men arrive
From the four quarters of the winds to do
For France what without help she could not do,
A work of honour. Think not that to this

Intended, rose in hardihood, and dared
The man who had an ill surmise of him
To bring his charge in openness; whereat,
When a dead pause ensued, and no one stirred,
In silence of all present, from his seat
Louvet walked single through the avenue,
And took his station in the Tribune, saying,
'I, Robespierre, accuse thee!' Well is known
The inglorious issue of that charge, and how
He, who had launched the startling thunderbolt,
The one bold man, whose voice the attack had sounded,
Was left without a follower to discharge
His perilous duty, and retire lamenting
That Heaven's best aid is wasted upon men
Who to themselves are false.

But these are things
Of which I speak, only as they were storm
Or sunshine to my individual mind,
No further. Let me then relate that now –
In some sort seeing with my proper eyes
That Liberty, and Life, and Death would soon
To the remotest corners of the land
Lie in the arbitrement of those who ruled
The capital City; what was struggled for,
And by what combatants victory must be won;
The indecision on their part whose aim
Seemed best, and the straightforward path of those
Who in attack or in defence were strong
Through their impiety – my inmost soul
Was agitated; yea, I could almost
Have prayed that throughout earth upon all men,
By patient exercise of reason made
Worthy of liberty, all spirits filled
With zeal expanding in Truth's holy light,
The gift of tongues might fall, and power arrive
From the four quarters of the winds to do
For France, what without help she could not do,
A work of honour; think not that to this

I added, work of safety: from such thought,
And the least fear about the end of things,
I was as far as angels are from guilt.

Yet did I grieve – nor only grieved – but thought
Of opposition and of remedies.
An insignificant stranger and obscure,
Mean as I was, and little graced with powers
Of eloquence even in my native speech,
And all unfit for tumult and intrigue,
Yet would I willingly have taken up
A service at this time for cause so great,
However dangerous. Inly I revolved
How much the destiny of man had still
Hung upon single persons – that there was,
Transcendent to all local patrimony,
One nature as there is one sun in heaven;
That objects, even as they are great, thereby
Do come within the reach of humblest eyes;
That man was only weak through his mistrust
And want of hope, where evidence divine
Proclaimed to him that hope should be most sure;
That, with desires heroic and firm sense,
A spirit thoroughly faithful to itself,
Unquenchable, unsleeping, undismayed,
Was as an instinct among men, a stream
That gathered up each petty straggling rill
And vein of water, glad to be rolled on
In safe obedience; that a mind whose rest
Was where it ought to be, in self-restraint,
In circumspection and simplicity,
Fell rarely in entire discomforture
Below its aim, or met with from without
A treachery that defeated it or foiled.

I added, work of safety: from all doubt
Or trepidation for the end of things
Far was I, far as angels are from guilt.

Yet did I grieve, nor only grieved, but thought
Of opposition and of remedies:
An insignificant stranger and obscure,
And one, moreover, little graced with power
Of eloquence even in my native speech,
And all unfit for tumult or intrigue,
Yet would I at this time with willing heart
Have undertaken for a cause so great
Service however dangerous. I revolved,
How much the destiny of Man had still
Hung upon single persons; that there was,
Transcendent to all local patrimony,
One nature, as there is one sun in heaven;
That objects, even as they are great, thereby
Do come within the reach of humblest eyes;
That Man is only weak through his mistrust
And want of hope where evidence divine
Proclaims to him that hope should be most sure;
Nor did the inexperience of my youth
Preclude conviction, that a spirit strong
In hope, and trained to noble aspirations,
A spirit throughly faithful to itself,
Is for Society's unreasoning herd
A domineering instinct, serves at once
For way and guide, a fluent receptacle
That gathers up each petty straggling rill
And vein of water, glad to be rolled on
In safe obedience; that a mind, whose rest
Is where it ought to be, in self-restraint,
In circumspection and simplicity,
Falls rarely in entire discomfiture
Below its aim, or meets with, from without,
A treachery that foils it or defeats;
And, lastly, if the means on human will,
Frail human will, dependent should betray

On the other side, I called to mind those truths
Which are the commonplaces of the schools,
A theme for boys, too trite even to be felt,
Yet, with a revelation's liveliness
In all their comprehensive bearings known
And visible to philosophers of old,
Men who (to business of the world untrained)
Lived in the shade – and to Harmodious known
And his compeer Aristogiton; known
To Brutus – that tyrannic power is weak,
Hath neither gratitude, nor faith, nor love,
Nor the support of good or evil men
To trust in; that the godhead which is ours
Can never utterly be charmed or stilled;
That nothing has a natural right to last
But equity and reason; that all else
Meets foes irreconcilable, and at best
Does live but by variety of disease.

Well might my wishes be intense, my thoughts
Strong and perturbed, not doubting at that time –
Creed which ten shameful years have not annulled –
But that the virtue of one paramount mind
Would have abashed those impious crests, have quelled
Outrage and bloody power, and, in despite
Of what the people were through ignorance
And immaturity (and in the teeth
Of desperate opposition from without),

Him who too boldly trusted them, I felt
That 'mid the loud distractions of the world
A sovereign voice subsists within the soul,
Arbiter undisturbed of right and wrong,
Of life and death, in majesty severe
Enjoining, as may best promote the aims
Of truth and justice, either sacrifice,
From whatsoever region of our cares
Or our infirm affections Nature pleads,
Earnest and blind, against the stern decree.

On the other side, I called to mind those truths
That are the common-places of the schools –
(A theme for boys, too hackneyed for their sires,)
Yet, with a revelation's liveliness,
In all their comprehensive bearings known
And visible to philosophers of old,
Men who, to business of the world untrained,
Lived in the shade; and to Harmodius known
And his compeer Aristogiton, known
To Brutus – that tyrannic power is weak
Hath neither gratitude, nor faith, nor love,
Nor the support of good or evil men
To trust in; that the godhead which is ours
Can never utterly be charmed or stilled;
That nothing hath a natural right to last
But equity and reason; that all else
Meets foes irreconcilable, and at best
Lives only by variety of disease.

Well might my wishes be intense, my thoughts
Strong and perturbed, not doubting at that time
But that the virtue of one paramount mind
Would have abashed those impious crests – have quelled
Outrage and bloody power, and, in despite
Of what the People long had been and were
Through ignorance and false teaching, sadder proof
Of immaturity, and in the teeth
Of desperate opposition from without –

Have cleared a passage for just government
And left a solid birthright to the state,
Redeemed according to example given
By ancient lawgivers. In this frame of mind
Reluctantly to England I returned,
Compelled by nothing less than absolute want
Of funds for my support; else (well assured
That I both was and must be of small worth,
No better than an alien in the land),
I doubtless should have made a common cause
With some who perished, haply perished too –
A poor mistaken and bewildered offering
Should to the breast of nature have gone back
With all my resolutions, all my hopes,
A poet only to myself, to men
Useless, and even, belovèd friend, a soul
To thee unknown!

When to my native land
(After a whole year's absence) I returned
I found the air yet busy with the stir
Of a contention which had been raised up
Against the traffickers in negro blood,
An effort which though baffled nevertheless
Had called back old forgotten principles
Dismissed from service, had diffused some truths

Have cleared a passage for just government,
And left a solid birthright to the State,
Redeemed, according to example given
By ancient lawgivers.

In this frame of mind,
Dragged by a chain of harsh necessity,
So seemed it, – now I thankfully acknowledge,
Forced by the gracious providence of Heaven, –
To England I returned, else (though assured
That I both was and must be of small weight,
No better than a landsman on the deck
Of a ship struggling with a hideous storm)
Doubtless, I should have then made common cause
With some who perished; haply perished too,
A poor mistaken and bewildered offering, –
Should to the breast of Nature have gone back,
With all my resolutions, all my hopes,
A Poet only to myself, to men
Useless, and even, beloved Friend! a soul
To thee unknown!

Twice had the trees let fall
Their leaves, as often Winter had put on
His hoary crown, since I had seen the surge
Beat against Albion's shore, since ear of mine
Had caught the accents of my native speech
Upon our native country's sacred ground.
A patriot of the world, how could I glide
Into communion with her sylvan shades,
Erewhile my tuneful haunt? It pleased me more
To abide in the great City, where I found
The general air still busy with the stir
Of that first memorable onset made
By a strong levy of humanity
Upon the traffickers in Negro blood;
Effort which, though defeated, had recalled
To notice old forgotten principles,
And through the nation spread a novel heat

And more of virtuous feeling through the heart
Of the English people. And no few of those
So numerous (little less in verity
Than a whole nation crying with one voice)
Who had been crossed in this their just intent
And righteous hope, thereby were well prepared
To let that journey sleep awhile, and join
Whatever other caravan appeared
To travel forward towards liberty
With more success. For me that strife had ne'er
Fastened on my affections, nor did now
Its unsuccessful issue much excite
My sorrow, having laid this faith to heart,
That if France prospered good men would not long
Pay fruitless worship to humanity,
And this most rotten branch of human shame
(Object, as seemed, of a superfluous pains)
Would fall together with its parent tree.

Such was my then belief – that there was one,
And only one, solicitude for all.
And now the strength of Britain was put forth
In league with the confederated host;
Not in my single self alone I found,
But in the minds of all ingenuous youth,
Change and subversion from this hour. No shock
Given to my moral nature had I known
Down to that very moment – neither lapse
Nor turn of sentiment that might be named
A revolution, save at this one time.
All else was progress on the self-same path
On which, with a diversity of pace,
I had been travelling: this a stride at once
Into another region. True it is,
'Twas not concealed with what ungracious eyes
Our native rulers from the very first
Had looked upon regenerated France,
Nor had I doubted that this day would come;
But in such contemplation I had thought

Of virtuous feeling. For myself, I own
That this particular strife had wanted power
To rivet my affections; nor did now
Its unsuccessful issue much excite
My sorrow; for I brought with me the faith
That, if France prospered, good men would not long
Pay fruitless worship to humanity,
And this most rotten branch of human shame,
Object, so seemed it, of superfluous pains,
Would fall together with its parent tree.
What, then, were my emotions, when in arms
Britain put forth her free-born strength in league,
Oh, pity and shame! with those confederate Powers!
Not in my single self alone I found,
But in the minds of all ingenuous youth,
Change and subversion from that hour. No shock
Given to my moral nature had I known
Down to that very moment; neither lapse
Nor turn of sentiment that might be named
A revolution, save at this one time;
All else was progress on the self-same path
On which, with a diversity of pace,
I had been travelling: this a stride at once
Into another region. As a light

Of general interests only, beyond this
Had never once foretasted the event.
Now had I other business, for I felt
The ravage of this most unnatural strife
In my own heart; there lay it like a weight
At enmity with all the tenderest springs
Of my enjoyments. I who with the breeze
Had played, a green leaf on the blessèd tree
Of my belovèd country – nor had wished
For happier fortune than to wither there –
Now from my pleasant station was cut off
And tossed about in whirlwinds. I rejoiced,
Yes, afterwards (truth painful to record)
Exulted in the triumph of my soul
When Englishmen by thousands were o'erthrown,
Left without glory on the field, or driven,
Brave hearts, to shameful flight. It was a grief –
Grief call it not, 'twas anything but that –
A conflict of sensations without name,
Of which he only who may love the sight
Of a village-steeple as I do can judge,
When in the congregation bending all
To their great Father, prayers were offered up
Or praises for our country's victories,
And, mid the simple worshippers perchance
I only, like an uninvited guest
Whom no one owned, sat silent – shall I add,
Fed on the day of vengeance yet to come!

Oh, much have they to account for who could tear
By violence, at one decisive rent,
From the best youth in England their dear pride,
Their joy in England. This, too, at a time
In which worst losses easily might wear
The best of names, when patriotic love
Did of itself in modesty give way
Like the precursor when the Deity
Is come whose harbinger he is – a time
In which apostasy from ancient faith

And pliant harebell, swinging in the breeze
On some grey rock – its birth-place – so had I
Wantoned, fast rooted on the ancient tower
Of my beloved country, wishing not
A happier fortune than to wither there:
Now was I from that pleasant station torn
And tossed about in whirlwind. I rejoiced,
Yea, afterwards – truth most painful to record! –
Exulted, in the triumph of my soul,
When Englishmen by thousands were o'erthrown,
Left without glory on the field, or driven,
Brave hearts! to shameful flight. It was a grief, –
Grief call it not, 'twas anything but that, –
A conflict of sensations without name,
Of which *he* only, who may love the sight
Of a village steeple, as I do, can judge,
When, in the congregation bending all
To their great Father, prayers were offered up,
Or praises for our country's victories;
And, 'mid the simple worshippers, perchance
I only, like an uninvited guest
Whom no one owned, sate silent, shall I add,
Fed on the day of vengeance yet to come.

Oh! much have they to account for, who could tear,
By violence, at one decisive rent,
From the best youth in England their dear pride,
Their joy, in England; this, too, at a time
In which worst losses easily might wean
The best of names, when patriotic love
Did of itself in modesty give way,
Like the Precursor when the Deity
Is come Whose harbinger he was; a time
In which apostasy from ancient faith

Seemed but conversion to a higher creed –
Withal a season dangerous and wild,
A time in which Experience would have plucked
Flowers out of any hedge to make thereof
A chaplet in contempt of his grey locks.

Ere yet the fleet of Britain had gone forth
On this unworthy service whereunto
The unhappy counsel of a few weak men
Had doomed it, I beheld the vessels lie,
A brood of gallant creatures – on the deep
I saw them in their rest – a sojourner
Through a whole month of calm and glassy days
In that delightful island which protects
Their place of convocation. There I heard
Each evening, walking by the still seashore,
A monitory sound which never failed –
The sunset cannon. When the orb went down
In the tranquillity of nature, came
That voice (ill requiem!), seldom heard by me
Without a spirit overcast, a deep
Imagination, thought of woes to come,
And sorrow for mankind, and pain of heart.

In France the men who for their desperate ends
Had plucked up mercy by the roots were glad
Of this new enemy. Tyrants, strong before
In devilish pleas, were ten times stronger now;
And thus, beset with foes on every side,
The goaded land waxed mad! The crimes of few
Spread into madness of the many; blasts
From hell came sanctified like airs from heaven.
The sternness of the just, the faith of those
Who doubted not that Providence had times
Of anger and of vengeance, theirs who throned
The human understanding paramount
And made of that their god, the hopes of those
Who were content to barter short-lived pangs
For a paradise of ages, the blind rage

Seemed but conversion to a higher creed;
Withal a season dangerous and wild,
A time when sage Experience would have snatched
Flowers out of any hedge-row to compose
A chaplet in contempt of his grey locks.

When the proud fleet that bears the red-cross flag
In that unworthy service was prepared
To mingle, I beheld the vessels lie,
A brood of gallant creatures, on the deep;
I saw them in their rest, a sojourner
Through a whole month of calm and glassy days
In that delightful island which protects
Their place of convocation – there I heard,
Each evening, pacing by the still sea-shore,
A monitory sound that never failed, –
The sunset cannon. While the orb went down
In the tranquillity of nature, came
That voice, ill requiem! seldom heard by me
Without a spirit overcast by dark
Imaginations, sense of woes to come,
Sorrow for human kind, and pain of heart.

In France, the men, who, for their desperate ends,
Had plucked up mercy by the roots, were glad
Of this new enemy. Tyrants, strong before
In wicked pleas, were strong as demons now;
And thus, on every side beset with foes,
The goaded land waxed mad; the crimes of few
Spread into madness of the many; blasts
From hell came sanctified like airs from heaven.
The sternness of the just, the faith of those
Who doubted not that Providence had times
Of vengeful retribution, theirs who throned
The human Understanding paramount
And made of that their God, the hopes of men
Who were content to barter short-lived pangs
For a paradise of ages, the blind rage

Of insolent tempers, the light vanity
Of intermeddlers, steady purposes
Of the suspicious, slips of the indiscreet,
And all the accidents of life, were pressed
Into one service, busy with one work.
The Senate was heart-stricken, not a voice
Uplifted, none to oppose or mitigate.

Domestic carnage now filled all the year
With feastdays: the old man from the chimney-nook,
The maiden from the bosom of her love,
The mother from the cradle of her babe,
The warrior from the field – all perished, all –
Friends, enemies, of all parties, ages, ranks,
Head after head, and never heads enough
For those who bade them fall. They found their joy,
They made it, ever thirsty, as a child
(If light desires of innocent little ones
May with such heinous appetites be matched)
Having a toy, a windmill, though the air
Do of itself blow fresh and makes the vane
Spin in his eyesight, he is not content,
But with the plaything at arm's length he sets
His front against the blast, and runs amain
To make it whirl the faster.

In the depth
Of these enormities even thinking minds
Forgot at seasons whence they had their being –
Forgot that such a sound was ever heard
As liberty upon earth; yet all beneath
Her innocent authority was wrought
Nor could have been, without her blessèd name.
The illustrious wife of Roland, in the hour

Of insolent tempers, the light vanity
Of intermeddlers, steady purposes
Of the suspicious, slips of the indiscreet,
And all the accidents of life were pressed
Into one service, busy with one work.
The Senate stood aghast, her prudence quenched,
Her wisdom stifled, and her justice scared,
Her frenzy only active to extol
Past outrages, and shape the way for new,
Which no one dared to oppose or mitigate.

Domestic carnage now filled the whole year
With feast-days; old men from the chimney-nook,
The maiden from the bosom of her love,
The mother from the cradle of her babe,
The warrior from the field – all perished, all –
Friends, enemies, of all parties, ages, ranks,
Head after head, and never heads enough
For those that bade them fall. They found their joy,
They made it proudly, eager as a child,
(If like desires of innocent little ones
May with such heinous appetites be compared),
Pleased in some open field to exercise
A toy that mimics with revolving wings
The motion of a wind-mill; though the air
Do of itself blow fresh, and make the vanes
Spin in his eyesight, *that* contents him not,
But, with the plaything at arm's length, he sets
His front against the blast, and runs amain,
That it may whirl the faster.

Amid the depth
Of those enormities, even thinking minds
Forgot, at seasons, whence they had their being;
Forgot that such a sound was ever heard
As Liberty upon earth: yet all beneath
Her innocent authority was wrought,
Nor could have been, without her blessed name.
The illustrious wife of Roland, in the hour

Of her composure, felt that agony
And gave it vent in her last words. O friend,
It was a lamentable time for man,
Whether a hope had e'er been his or not –
A woeful time for them whose hopes did still
Outlast the shock; most woeful for those few
(They had the deepest feeling of the grief)
Who still were flattered, and had trust in man.
Meanwhile, the invaders fared as they deserved!
The Herculean commonwealth had put forth her arms
And throttled with an infant godhead's might
The snakes about her cradle – that was well,
And as it should be, yet no cure for those
Whose souls were sick with pain of what would be
Hereafter brought in charge against mankind.

Most melancholy at the time, o friend,
Were my day-thoughts, my dreams were miserable.
Through months, through years, long after the last beat
Of those atrocities (I speak bare truth,
As if to thee alone in private talk)
I scarcely had one night of quiet sleep,
Such ghastly visions had I of despair,
And tyranny, and implements of death,
And long orations which in dreams I pleaded
Before unjust tribunals, with a voice
Labouring, a brain confounded, and a sense
Of treachery and desertion in the place
The holiest that I knew of – my own soul.

When I began at first in early youth
To yield myself to nature, when that strong
And holy passion overcame me first,
Neither the day nor night, evening or morn,

Of her composure, felt that agony,
And gave it vent in her last words. O Friend!
It was a lamentable time for man,
Whether a hope had e'er been his or not;
A woful time for them whose hopes survived
The shock; most woful for those few who still
Were flattered, and had trust in human kind:
They had the deepest feeling of the grief.
Meanwhile the Invaders fared as they deserved:
The Herculean Commonwealth had put forth her arms,
And throttled with an infant godhead's might
The snakes about her cradle; that was well,
And as it should be; yet no cure for them
Whose souls were sick with pain of what would be
Hereafter brought in charge against mankind.
Most melancholy at that time, O Friend!
Were my day-thoughts, – my nights were miserable;
Through months, through years, long after the last beat
Of those atrocities, the hour of sleep
To me came rarely charged with natural gifts,
Such ghastly visions had I of despair
And tyranny, and implements of death;
And innocent victims sinking under fear,
And momentary hope, and worn-out prayer,
Each in his separate cell, or penned in crowds
For sacrifice, and struggling with fond mirth
And levity in dungeons, where the dust
Was laid with tears. Then suddenly the scene
Changed, and the unbroken dream entangled me
In long orations, which I strove to plead
Before unjust tribunals, – with a voice
Labouring, a brain confounded, and a sense,
Death-like, of treacherous desertion, felt
In the last place of refuge – my own soul.

When I began in youth's delightful prime
To yield myself to Nature, when that strong
And holy passion overcame me first,
Nor day nor night, evening or morn, was free

Were free from the oppression. But, great God,
Who sendest thyself into this breathing world
Through nature and through every kind of life,
And makest man what he is – creature divine,
In single or in social eminence,
Above all these raised infinite ascents
When reason which enables him to be
Is not sequestered – what a change is here!
How different ritual for this after-worship,
What countenance to promote this second love!
That first was service but to things which lie
At rest within the bosom of thy will;
Therefore to serve was high beatitude,
The tumult was a gladness, and the fear
Ennobling, venerable – sleep secure,
And waking thoughts more rich than happiest dreams.

But as the ancient prophets were inflamed,
Nor wanted consolations of their own
And majesty of mind when they denounced
On towns and cities, wallowing in the abyss
Of their offences, punishment to come;
Or saw like other men, with bodily eyes,
Before them in some desolated place
The consummation of the wrath of Heaven;
So did some portions of that spirit fall
On me, to uphold me through those evil times,
And in their rage and dog-day heat I found
Something to glory in, as just and fit
And in the order of sublimest laws.
And even if that were not, amid the awe
Of unintelligible chastisement
I felt a kind of sympathy with power –

From its oppression. But, O Power Supreme!
Without Whose call this world would cease to breathe,
Who from the fountain of Thy grace dost fill
The veins that branch through every frame of life,
Making man what he is, creature divine,
In single or in social eminence,
Above the rest raised infinite ascents
When reason that enables him to be
Is not sequestered – what a change is here!
How different ritual for this after-worship,
What countenance to promote this second love!
The first was service paid to things which lie
Guarded within the bosom of Thy will.
Therefore to serve was high beatitude;
Tumult was therefore gladness, and the fear
Ennobling, venerable; sleep secure,
And waking thoughts more rich than happiest dreams.

But as the ancient Prophets, borne aloft
In vision, yet constrained by natural laws
With them to take a troubled human heart,
Wanted not consolations, nor a creed
Of reconcilement, then when they denounced,
On towns and cities, wallowing in the abyss
Of their offences, punishment to come;
Or saw, like other men, with bodily eyes,
Before them, in some desolated place,
The wrath consummate and the threat fulfilled;
So, with devout humility be it said,
So, did a portion of that spirit fall
On me uplifted from the vantage-ground
Of pity and sorrow to a state of being
That through the time's exceeding fierceness saw
Glimpses of retribution, terrible,
And in the order of sublime behests:
But, even if that were not, amid the awe
Of unintelligible chastisement,
Not only acquiescences of faith
Survived, but daring sympathies with power,

Motions raised up within me nevertheless
Which had relationship to highest things.
Wild blasts of music thus did find their way
Into the midst of terrible events,
So that worst tempests might be listened to.
Then was the truth received into my heart
That under heaviest sorrow earth can bring,
Griefs bitterest of ourselves or of our kind,
If from the affliction somewhere do not grow
Honour which could not else have been – a faith,
An elevation and a sanctity –
If new strength be not given or old restored,
The blame is ours, not nature's. When a taunt
Was taken up by scoffers in their pride,
Saying 'Behold the harvest which we reap
From popular government and equality!'
I saw that it was neither these nor aught
Of wild belief engrafted on their names
By false philosophy that caused the woe,
But that it was a reservoir of guilt
And ignorance filled up from age to age
That could no longer hold its loathsome charge,
But burst and spread in deluge through the land.

And as the desert has green spots, the sea
Small islands in the midst of stormy waves,
So that disastrous period did not want
Such sprinklings of all human excellence
As were a joy to hear of. Yet (nor less
For those bright spots, those fair examples given
Of fortitude and energy and love,
And human nature faithful to itself
Under worst trials) was I impelled to think
Of the glad time when first I traversed France
A youthful pilgrim – above all remembered
That day when through an arch that spanned the street,
A rainbow made of garish ornaments

Motions not treacherous or profane, else why
Within the folds of no ungentle breast
Their dread vibration to this hour prolonged?
Wild blasts of music thus could find their way
Into the midst of turbulent events;
So that worst tempests might be listened to.
Then was the truth received into my heart,
That, under heaviest sorrow earth can bring,
If from the affliction somewhere do not grow
Honour which could not else have been, a faith,
An elevation and a sanctity,
If new strength be not given nor old restored,
The blame is ours, not Nature's. When a taunt
Was taken up by scoffers in their pride,
Saying, 'Behold the harvest that we reap
From popular government and equality,'
I clearly saw that neither these nor aught
Of wild belief engrafted on their names
By false philosophy had caused the woe,
But a terrific reservoir of guilt
And ignorance filled up from age to age,
That could no longer hold its loathsome charge,
But burst and spread in deluge through the land.

And as the desert hath green spots, the sea
Small islands scattered amid stormy waves,
So *that* disastrous period did not want
Bright sprinklings of all human excellence,
To which the silver wands of saints in Heaven
Might point with rapturous joy. Yet not the less,
For those examples in no age surpassed
Of fortitude and energy and love,
And human nature faithful to herself
Under worst trials, was I driven to think
Of the glad times when first I traversed France
A youthful pilgrim; above all reviewed
That eventide, when under windows bright
With happy faces and with garlands hung,
And through a rainbow-arch that spanned the street,

(Triumphal pomp for liberty confirmed),
We walked, a pair of weary travellers,
Along the town of Arras, place from which
Issued that Robespierre who afterwards
Wielded the sceptre of the atheist crew.
When the calamity spread far and wide,
And this same city, which had even appeared
To outrun the rest in exultation, groaned
Under the vengeance of her cruel son,
As Lear reproached the winds I could almost
Have quarrelled with that blameless spectacle
For being yet an image in my mind
To mock me under such a strange reverse.

O friend, few happier moments have been mine
Through my whole life than that when first I heard
That this foul tribe of Moloch was o'erthrown
And their chief regent levelled with the dust.
The day was one which haply may deserve
A separate chronicle. Having gone abroad
From a small village where I tarried then,
To the same far-secluded privacy
I was returning. Over the smooth sands
Of Leven's ample estuary lay
My journey, and beneath a genial sun,
With distant prospect among gleams of sky
And clouds, and intermingled mountain-tops,
In one inseparable glory clad –
Creatures of one ethereal substance met
In consistory, like a diadem
Or crown of burning seraphs as they sit
In the empyrean. Underneath this show
Lay, as I knew, the nest of pastoral vales
Among whose happy fields I had grown up
From childhood. On the fulgent spectacle,
Which neither changed nor stirred nor passed away,
I gazed, and with a fancy more alive

Triumphal pomp for liberty confirmed,
I paced, a dear companion at my side,
The town of Arras, whence with promise high
Issued, on delegation to sustain
Humanity and right, *that* Robespierre,
He who thereafter, and in how short time!
Wielded the sceptre of the Atheist crew.
When the calamity spread far and wide –
And this same city, that did then appear
To outrun the rest in exultation, groaned
Under the vengeance of her cruel son,
As Lear reproached the winds – I could almost
Have quarrelled with that blameless spectacle
For lingering yet an image in my mind
To mock me under such a strange reverse.

O Friend! few happier moments have been mine
Than that which told the downfall of this Tribe
So dreaded, so abhorred. The day deserves
A separate record. Over the smooth sands
Of Leven's ample estuary lay
My journey, and beneath a genial sun,
With distant prospect among gleams of sky
And clouds, and intermingling mountain tops,
In one inseparable glory clad,
Creatures of one ethereal substance met
In consistory, like a diadem
Or crown of burning seraphs as they sit
In the empyrean. Underneath that pomp
Celestial, lay unseen the pastoral vales
Among whose happy fields I had grown up
From childhood. On the fulgent spectacle,
That neither passed away nor changed, I gazed

On this account – that I had chanced to find
That morning, ranging through the churchyard graves
Of Cartmel's rural town, the place in which
An honoured teacher of my youth was laid.
While we were schoolboys he had died among us,
And was borne hither, as I knew, to rest
With his own family. A plain stone, inscribed
With name, date, office, pointed out the spot,
To which a slip of verses was subjoined
(By his desire, as afterwards I learnt),
A fragment from the *Elegy* of Gray.
A week, or little less, before his death
He said to me 'My head will soon lie low!'
And when I saw the turf that covered him
After the lapse of full eight years, those words,
With sound of voice and countenance of the man,
Came back upon me, so that some few tears
Fell from me in my own despite. And now,
Thus travelling smoothly o'er the level sands,
I thought with pleasure of the verses graven
Upon his tombstone, saying to myself
'He loved the poets, and if now alive
Would have loved me, as one not destitute
Of promise, nor belying the kind hope
Which he had formed when I at his command
Began to spin, at first, my toilsome songs.'

Without me and within, as I advanced
All that I saw, or felt, or communed with,
Was gentleness and peace. Upon a small
And rocky island near, a fragment stood
(Itself like a sea-rock) of what had been
A Romish chapel, where in ancient times
Masses were said at the hour which suited those
Who crossed the sands with ebb of morning tide.
Not far from this still ruin all the plain
Was spotted with a variegated crowd
Of coaches, wains, and travellers, horse and foot,

Enrapt; but brightest things are wont to draw
Sad opposites out of the inner heart,
As even their pensive influence drew from mine.
How could it otherwise? for not in vain
That very morning had I turned aside
To seek the ground where, 'mid a throng of graves,
An honoured teacher of my youth was laid,
And on the stone were graven by his desire
Lines from the churchyard elegy of Gray.
This faithful guide, speaking from his death-bed,
Added no farewell to his parting counsel,
But said to me, 'My head will soon lie low;'
And when I saw the turf that covered him,
After the lapse of full eight years, those words,
With sound of voice and countenance of the Man,
Came back upon me, so that some few tears
Fell from me in my own despite. But now
I thought, still traversing that widespread plain,
With tender pleasure of the verses graven
Upon his tombstone, whispering to myself:
He loved the Poets, and, if now alive,
Would have loved me, as one not destitute
Of promise, nor belying the kind hope
That he had formed, when I at his command,
Began to spin, with toil, my earliest songs.

As I advanced, all that I saw or felt
Was gentleness and peace. Upon a small
And rocky island near, a fragment stood
(Itself like a sea rock) the low remains
(With shells encrusted, dark with briny weeds)
Of a dilapidated structure, once
A Romish chapel, where the vested priest
Said matins at the hour that suited those
Who crossed the sands with ebb of morning tide.
Not far from that still ruin all the plain
Lay spotted with a variegated crowd
Of vehicles and travellers, horse and foot,

Wading beneath the conduct of their guide
In loose procession through the shallow stream
Of inland water; the great sea meanwhile
Was at safe distance, far retired. I paused,
Unwilling to proceed, the scene appeared
So gay and cheerful, when – a traveller
Chancing to pass – I carelessly inquired
If any news were stirring. He replied
In the familiar language of the day
That *Robespierre was dead*. Nor was a doubt,
On further question, left within my mind
But that the tidings were substantial truth –
That he and his supporters all were fallen.

Great was my glee of spirit, great my joy
In vengeance, and eternal justice, thus
Made manifest. 'Come now, ye golden times',
Said I, forth-breathing on those open sands
A hymn of triumph, 'as the morning comes
Out of the bosom of the night, come ye!
Thus far our trust is verified: behold,
They who with clumsy desperation brought
Rivers of blood, and preached that nothing else
Could cleanse the Augean stable, by the might
Of their own helper have been swept away!
Their madness is declared and visible –
Elsewhere will safety now be sought, and earth
March firmly towards righteousness and peace.'
Then schemes I framed more calmly when and how
The madding factions might be tranquillized,
And – though through hardships manifold and long –
The mighty renovation would proceed.
Thus, interrupted by uneasy bursts
Of exultation, I pursued my way
Along that very shore which I had skimmed
In former times, when (spurring from the Vale
Of Nightshade, and St Mary's mouldering fane
And the stone abbot) after circuit made
In wantonness of heart, a joyous crew

Wading beneath the conduct of their guide
In loose procession through the shallow stream
Of inland waters; the great sea meanwhile
Heaved at safe distance, far retired. I paused,
Longing for skill to paint a scene so bright
And cheerful, but the foremost of the band
As he approached, no salutation given
In the familiar language of the day,
Cried, 'Robespierre is dead!' – nor was a doubt,
After strict question, left within my mind
That he and his supporters all were fallen.

Great was my transport, deep my gratitude
To everlasting Justice, by this fiat
Made manifest. 'Come now, ye golden times,'
Said I forth-pouring on those open sands
A hymn of triumph: 'as the morning comes
From out the bosom of the night, come ye:
Thus far our trust is verified; behold!
They who with clumsy desperation brought
A river of Blood, and preached that nothing else
Could cleanse the Augean stable, by the might
Of their own helper have been swept away;
Their madness stands declared and visible;
Elsewhere will safety now be sought, and earth
March firmly towards righteousness and peace.' –
Then schemes I framed more calmly, when and how
The madding factions might be tranquillised,
And how through hardships manifold and long
The glorious renovation would proceed.
Thus interrupted by uneasy bursts
Of exultation, I pursued my way
Along that very shore which I had skimmed
In former days, when – spurring from the Vale
Of Nightshade, and St. Mary's mouldering fane,
And the stone abbot, after circuit made
In wantonness of heart, a joyous band

Of schoolboys hastening to their distant home
Along the margin of the moonlight sea,
We beat with thundering hoofs the level sand.

Of school-boys hastening to their distant home
Along the margin of the moonlight sea –
We beat with thundering hoofs the level sand.

From this time forth in France, as is well known,
Authority put on a milder face,
Yet everything was wanting that might give
Courage to those who looked for good by light
Of rational experience – good I mean
At hand, and in the spirit of past aims.
The same belief I, nevertheless, retained:
The language of the Senate, and the acts
And public measures of the Government,
Though both of heartless omen, had not power
To daunt me. In the people was my trust
And in the virtues which mine eyes had seen,
And to the ultimate repose of things
I looked with unabated confidence.
I knew that wound external could not take
Life from the young Republic – that new foes
Would only follow in the path of shame
Their brethren, and her triumphs be in the end
Great, universal, irresistible.
This faith (which was an object in my mind
Of passionate intuition) had effect
Not small in dazzling me; for thus, through zeal,
Such victory I confounded in my thoughts
With one far higher and more difficult –
Triumphs of unambitious peace at home
And noiseless fortitude. Beholding still
Resistance strong as heretofore, I thought
That what was in degree the same was likewise
The same in quality, that as the worse
Of the two spirits then at strife remained

Book Eleventh

FRANCE – (CONCLUDED)

From that time forth, Authority in France
Put on a milder face; Terror had ceased,
Yet every thing was wanting that might give
Courage to them who looked for good by light
Of rational Experience, for the shoots
And hopeful blossoms of a second spring:
Yet, in me, confidence was unimpaired;
The Senate's language, and the public acts
And measures of the Government, though both
Weak, and of heartless omen, had not power
To daunt me; in the People was my trust:
And, in the virtues which mine eyes had seen,
I knew that wound external could not take
Life from the young Republic; that new foes
Would only follow, in the path of shame,
Their brethren, and her triumphs be in the end
Great, universal, irresistible.
This intuition led me to confound
One victory with another, higher far, –
Triumphs of unambitious peace at home,
And noiseless fortitude. Beholding still
Resistance strong as heretofore, I thought
That what was in degree the same was likewise
The same in quality, – that, as the worse
Of the two spirits then at strife remained

Untired, the better surely would preserve
The heart that first had roused him – never dreamt
That transmigration could be undergone,
A fall of being suffered, and of hope,
By creature that appeared to have received
Entire conviction what a great ascent
Had been accomplished, what high faculties
It had been called to.

Youth maintains, I knew,
In all conditions of society
Communion more direct and intimate
With nature and the inner strength she has,
And hence (ofttimes) no less with reason too,
Than age or manhood even. To nature then
Power had reverted: habit, custom, law,
Had left an interregnum's open space
For her to stir about in uncontrolled.
The warmest judgements and the most untaught
Found in events which every day brought forth
Enough to sanction them, and far, far more
To shake the authority of canons drawn
From ordinary practice. I could see
How Babel-like the employment was of those
Who, by the recent deluge stupefied,
With their whole souls went culling from the day
Its petty promises, to build a tower
For their own safety – laughed at gravest heads
Who, watching in their hate of France for signs
Of her disasters, if the stream of rumour
Brought with it one green branch, conceited thence
That not a single tree was left alive
In all her forests. How could I believe
That wisdom could, in any shape, come near
Men clinging to delusions so insane?
And thus, experience proving that no few
Of my opinions had been just, I took
Like credit to myself where less was due,
And thought that other notions were as sound –

Untired, the better, surely, would preserve
The heart that first had roused him. Youth maintains,
In all conditions of society,
Communion more direct and intimate
With Nature, – hence, ofttimes, with reason too –
Than age or manhood, even. To Nature, then,
Power had reverted: habit, custom, law,
Had left an interregnum's open space
For *her* to move about in, uncontrolled.
Hence could I see how Babel-like their task,
Who, by the recent deluge stupified,
With their whole souls went culling from the day
Its petty promises, to build a tower
For their own safety; laughed with my compeers
At gravest heads, by enmity to France
Distempered, till they found, in every blast
Forced from the street-disturbing newsman's horn,
For her great cause record or prophecy
Of utter ruin. How might we believe
That wisdom could, in any shape, come near
Men clinging to delusions so insane?
And thus, experience proving that no few
Of our opinions had been just, we took
Like credit to ourselves where less was due,
And thought that other notions were as sound,

Yea, could not but be right – because I saw
That foolish men opposed them.

To a strain
More animated I might here give way
And tell (since juvenile errors are my theme)
What in those days through Britain was performed
To turn *all* judgements out of their right course;
But this is passion over-near ourselves,
Reality too close and too intense,
And mingled up with something, in my mind,
Of scorn and condemnation personal
That would profane the sanctity of verse.
Our shepherds – this say merely – at that time
Thirsted to make the guardian-crook of law
A tool of murder. They who ruled the state
(Though with such awful proof before their eyes
That he who would sow death, reaps death, or worse,
And can reap nothing better) child-like longed
To imitate – not wise enough to avoid.
Giants in their impiety alone,
But in their weapons and their warfare base
As vermin working out of reach, they leagued
Their strength perfidiously to undermine
Justice and make an end of liberty.

But from these bitter truths I must return
To my own history. It hath been told
That I was led to take an eager part
In arguments of civil polity
Abruptly, and indeed before my time.
I had approached, like other youth, the shield
Of human nature from the golden side,
And would have fought even to the death to attest
The quality of the metal which I saw.
What there is best in individual man,
Of wise in passion and sublime in power,
What there is strong and pure in household love,
Benevolent in small societies

Yea, could not but be right, because we saw
That foolish men opposed them.

To a strain
More animated I might here give way,
And tell, since juvenile errors are my theme,
What in those days, through Britain, was performed
To turn *all* judgments out of their right course;
But this is passion over-near ourselves,
Reality too close and too intense,
And intermixed with something, in my mind,
Of scorn and condemnation personal,
That would profane the sanctity of verse.
Our Shepherds, this say merely, at that time
Acted, or seemed at least to act, like men
Thirsting to make the guardian crook of law
A tool of murder; they who ruled the State,
Though with such awful proof before their eyes
That he, who would sow death, reaps death, or worse,
And can reap nothing better, child-like longed
To imitate, not wise enough to avoid;
Or left (by mere timidity betrayed)
The plain straight road, for one no better chosen
Than if their wish had been to undermine
Justice, and make an end of Liberty.

But from these bitter truths I must return
To my own history. It hath been told
That I was led to take an eager part
In arguments of civil polity,
Abruptly, and indeed before my time:
I had approached, like other youths, the shield
Of human nature from the golden side,
And would have fought, even to the death, to attest
The quality of the metal which I saw.
What there is best in individual man,
Of wise in passion, and sublime in power,
Benevolent in small societies,

And great in large ones also when called forth
By great occasions – these were things of which
I something knew, yet even these (themselves
Felt deeply) were not thoroughly understood
By reason. Nay, far from it! They were yet,
As cause was given me afterwards to learn,
Not proof against the injuries of the day –
Lodged only at the sanctuary's door,
Not safe within its bosom. Thus prepared,
And with such general insight into evil,
And of the bounds which sever it from good,
As books and common intercourse with life
Must needs have given (to the noviciate mind,
When the world travels in a beaten road,
Guide faithful as is needed), I began
To think with fervour upon management
Of nations, what it is and ought to be,
And how their worth depended on their laws
And on the constitution of the state.

Oh pleasant exercise of hope and joy –
For great were the auxiliars which then stood
Upon our side, we who were strong in love!
Bliss was it in that dawn to be alive,
But to be young was very heaven! Oh times,
In which the meagre, stale, forbidding ways
Of custom, law, and statute, took at once
The attraction of a country in romance –
When reason seemed the most to assert her rights
When most intent on making of herself
A prime enchanter to assist the work
Which then was going forwards in her name!
Not favoured spots alone, but the whole earth,
The beauty wore of promise, that which sets
(To take an image which was felt, no doubt,
Among the bowers of Paradise itself)
The budding rose above the rose full-blown.
What temper at the prospect did not wake
To happiness unthought of? The inert

And great in large ones, I had oft revolved,
Felt deeply, but not thoroughly understood
By reason: nay, far from it; they were yet,
As cause was given me afterwards to learn,
Not proof against the injuries of the day;
Lodged only at the sanctuary's door,
Not safe within its bosom. Thus prepared,
And with such general insight into evil,
And of the bounds which sever it from good,
As books and common intercourse with life
Must needs have given – to the inexperienced mind,
When the world travels in a beaten road,
Guide faithful as is needed – I began
To meditate with ardour on the rule
And management of nations; what it is
And ought to be; and strove to learn how far
Their power or weakness, wealth or poverty,
Their happiness or misery, depends
Upon their laws, and fashion of the State.

O pleasant exercise of hope and joy!
For mighty were the auxiliars which then stood
Upon our side, us who were strong in love!
Bliss was it in that dawn to be alive,
But to be young was very Heaven! O times,
In which the meagre, stale, forbidding ways
Of custom, law, and statute, took at once
The attraction of a country in romance!
When Reason seemed the most to assert her rights
When most intent on making of herself
A prime enchantress – to assist the work,
Which then was going forward in her name!
Not favoured spots alone, but the whole Earth,
The beauty wore of promise – that which sets
(As at some moments might not be unfelt
Among the bowers of Paradise itself)
The budding rose above the rose full blown.
What temper at the prospect did not wake
To happiness unthought of? The inert

Were roused, and lively natures rapt away!
They who had fed their childhood upon dreams –
The playfellows of fancy, who had made
All powers of swiftness, subtlety, and strength
Their ministers, used to stir in lordly wise
Among the grandest objects of the sense
And deal with whatsoever they found there
As if they had within some lurking right
To wield it – they too, who, of gentle mood,
Had watched all gentle motions, and to these
Had fitted their own thoughts (schemers more mild,
And in the region of their peaceful selves),
Did now find helpers to their hearts' desire
And stuff at hand plastic as they could wish,
Were called upon to exercise their skill,
Not in Utopia – subterraneous fields,
Or some secreted island, heaven knows where! –
But in the very world which is the world
Of all of us, the place in which in the end
We find our happiness, or not at all.

Why should I not confess that earth was then
To me what an inheritance new-fallen
Seems, when the first time visited, to one
Who thither comes to find in it his home?
He walks about and looks upon the place
With cordial transport, moulds it and remoulds,
And is half pleased with things that are amiss,
'Twill be such joy to see them disappear.
An active partisan, I thus convoked
From every object pleasant circumstance
To suit my ends. I moved among mankind
With genial feelings still predominant,
When erring, erring on the better part
And in the kinder spirit; placable,
Indulgent ofttimes to the worst desires
(As, on one side, not uninformed that men
See as it has been taught them, and that time

Were roused, and lively natures rapt away!
They who had fed their childhood upon dreams,
The play-fellows of fancy, who had made
All powers of swiftness, subtilty, and strength
Their ministers, – who in lordly wise had stirred
Among the grandest objects of the sense,
And dealt with whatsoever they found there
As if they had within some lurking right
To wield it; – they, too, who of gentle mood
Had watched all gentle motions, and to these
Had fitted their own thoughts, schemers more mild,
And in the region of their peaceful selves; –
Now was it that *both* found, the meek and lofty
Did both find helpers to their hearts' desire,
And stuff at hand, plastic as they could wish, –
Were called upon to exercise their skill,
Not in Utopia, – subterranean fields, –
Or some secreted island, Heaven knows where!
But in the very world, which is the world
Of all of us, – the place where, in the end,
We find our happiness, or not at all!

Why should I not confess that Earth was then
To me, what an inheritance, new-fallen,
Seems, when the first time visited, to one
Who thither comes to find in it his home?
He walks about and looks upon the spot
With cordial transport, moulds it and remoulds,
And is half pleased with things that are amiss,
'Twill be such joy to see them disappear.

An active partisan, I thus convoked
From every object pleasant circumstance
To suit my ends; I moved among mankind
With genial feelings still predominant;
When erring, erring on the better part,
And in the kinder spirit; placable,
Indulgent, as not uninformed that men
See as they have been taught – Antiquity

Gives rights to error, on the other hand,
That throwing off oppression must be work
As well of licence as of liberty);
And above all – for this was more than all –
Not caring if the wind did now and then
Blow keen upon an eminence that gave
Prospect so large into futurity; happy,
In brief a child of nature as at first,
Diffusing only those affections wider
That from the cradle had grown up with me,
And losing, in no other way than light
Is lost in light, the weak in the more strong.

In the main outline such it might be said
Was my condition, till with open war
Britain opposed the liberties of France.
This threw me first out of the pale of love,
Soured and corrupted upwards to the source
My sentiments (was not, as hitherto,
A swallowing up of lesser things in great,
But change of them into their opposites),
And thus a way was opened for mistakes
And false conclusions of the intellect,
As gross in their degree, and in their kind
Far, far more dangerous. What had been a pride,
Was now a shame. My likings and my loves
Ran in new channels, leaving old ones dry,
And thus a blow, which in maturer age
Would but have touched the judgement, struck more deep
Into sensations near the heart. Meantime
As from the first wild theories were afloat,
Unto the subtleties of which at least
I had but lent a careless ear, assured
Of this, that time would soon set all things right –
Prove that the multitude had been oppressed,
And would be so no more.

But when events
Brought less encouragement, and unto these

Gives rights to error; and aware, no less,
That throwing off oppression must be work
As well of License as of Liberty;
And above all – for this was more than all –
Not caring if the wind did now and then
Blow keen upon an eminence that gave
Prospect so large into futurity;
In brief, a child of Nature, as at first,
Diffusing only those affections wider
That from the cradle had grown up with me,
And losing, in no other way than light
Is lost in light, the weak in the more strong.

In the main outline, such it might be said
Was my condition, till with open war
Britain opposed the liberties of France.
This threw me first out of the pale of love;
Soured and corrupted, upwards to the source,
My sentiments; was not, as hitherto,
A swallowing up of lesser things in great,
But change of them into their contraries;
And thus a way was opened for mistakes
And false conclusions, in degree as gross,
In kind more dangerous. What had been a pride,
Was now a shame; my likings and my loves
Ran in new channels, leaving old ones dry;
And hence a blow that, in maturer age,
Would but have touched the judgment, struck more deep
Into sensations near the heart: meantime,
As from the first, wild theories were afloat,
To whose pretensions, sedulously urged,
I had but lent a careless ear, assured
That time was ready to set all things right,
And that the multitude, so long oppressed,
Would be oppressed no more.

But when events
Brought less encouragement, and unto these

The immediate proof of principles no more
Could be entrusted (while the events themselves,
Worn out in greatness and in novelty,
Less occupied the mind, and sentiments
Could through my understanding's natural growth
No longer justify themselves through faith
Of inward consciousness, and hope that laid
Its hand upon its object), evidence
Safer, of universal application, such
As could not be impeached, was sought elsewhere.

And now, become oppressors in their turn,
Frenchmen had changed a war of self-defence
For one of conquest, losing sight of all
Which they had struggled for – and mounted up,
Openly in the view of earth and heaven,
The scale of liberty. I read her doom,
Vexed inly somewhat, it is true, and sore,
But not dismayed, nor taking to the shame
Of a false prophet; but, roused up, I stuck
More firmly to old tenets, and to prove
Their temper strained them more. And thus in heat
Of contest did opinions every day
Grow into consequence, till round my mind
They clung as if they were the life of it.

This was the time when all things tended fast
To depravation; the philosophy
That promised to abstract the hopes of man
Out of his feelings, to be fixed thenceforth
For ever in a purer element,
Found ready welcome. Tempting region that
For zeal to enter and refresh herself,
Where passions had the privilege to work,
And never hear the sound of their own names!
But (speaking more in charity) the dream

The immediate proof of principles no more
Could be entrusted, while the events themselves,
Worn out in greatness, stripped of novelty,
Less occupied the mind, and sentiments
Could through my understanding's natural growth
No longer keep their ground, by faith maintained
Of inward consciousness, and hope that laid
Her hand upon her object – evidence
Safer, of universal application, such
As could not be impeached, was sought elsewhere.

But now, become oppressors in their turn,
Frenchmen had changed a war of self-defence
For one of conquest, losing sight of all
Which they had struggled for: now mounted up,
Openly in the eye of earth and heaven,
The scale of liberty. I read her doom,
With anger vexed, with disappointment sore,
But not dismayed, nor taking to the shame
Of a false prophet. While resentment rose
Striving to hide, what nought could heal, the wounds
Of mortified presumption, I adhered
More firmly to old tenets, and, to prove
Their temper, strained them more; and thus, in heat
Of contest, did opinions every day
Grow into consequence, till round my mind
They clung, as if they were its life, nay more,
The very being of the immortal soul.

This was the time, when, all things tending fast
To depravation, speculative schemes –
That promised to abstract the hopes of Man
Out of his feelings, to be fixed thenceforth
For ever in a purer element –
Found ready welcome. Tempting region *that*
For Zeal to enter and refresh herself,
Where passions had the privilege to work,
And never hear the sound of their own names.
But, speaking more in charity, the dream

Was flattering to the young ingenuous mind,
Pleased with extremes, and not the least with that
Which makes the human reason's naked self
The object of its fervour. What delight! –
How glorious! – in self-knowledge and self-rule
To look through all the frailties of the world
And, with a resolute mastery shaking off
The accidents of nature, time and place,
That make up the weak being of the past,
Build social freedom on its only basis,
The freedom of the individual mind,
Which (to the blind restraint of general laws
Superior) magisterially adopts
One guide, the light of circumstances, flashed
Upon an independent intellect.

For, howsoe'er unsettled, never once
Had I thought ill of human-kind, or been
Indifferent to its welfare; but, inflamed
With thirst of a secure intelligence,
And sick of other passion, I pursued
A higher nature – wished that man should start
Out of the worm-like state in which he is,
And spread abroad the wings of liberty,
Lord of himself in undisturbed delight.
A noble aspiration! – yet I feel
The aspiration – but with other thoughts
And happier. For I was perplexed, and sought
To accomplish the transition by such means
As did not lie in nature – sacrificed
The exactness of a comprehensive mind
To scrupulous and microscopic views
That furnished out materials for a work
Of false imagination, placed beyond
The limits of experience and of truth.

Enough, no doubt, the advocates themselves
Of ancient institutions had performed
To bring disgrace upon their very names –

Flattered the young, pleased with extremes, nor least
With that which makes our Reason's naked self
The object of its fervour. What delight!
How glorious! in self-knowledge and self-rule,
To look through all the frailties of the world,
And, with a resolute mastery shaking off
Infirmities of nature, time, and place,
Build social upon personal Liberty,
Which, to the blind restraints of general laws
Superior, magisterially adopts
One guide, the light of circumstances, flashed
Upon an independent intellect.
Thus expectation rose again; thus hope,
From her first ground expelled, grew proud once more.
Oft, as my thoughts were turned to human kind,
I scorned indifference; but, inflamed with thirst
Of a secure intelligence, and sick
Of other longing, I pursued what seemed
A more exalted nature; wished that Man
Should start out of his earthy, worm-like state,
And spread abroad the wings of Liberty,
Lord of himself, in undisturbed delight –
A noble aspiration! *yet* I feel
(Sustained by worthier as by wiser thoughts)
The aspiration, nor shall ever cease
To feel it; – but return we to our course.

Enough, 'tis true – could such a plea excuse
Those aberrations – had the clamorous friends
Of ancient Institutions said and done
To bring disgrace upon their very names;

Disgrace, of which custom, and written law,
And sundry moral sentiments, as props
And emanations of these institutes,
Too justly bore a part. A veil had been
Uplifted. Why deceive ourselves? – 'twas so,
'Twas even so – and sorrow for the man
Who either had not eyes wherewith to see,
Or, seeing, hath forgotten! Let this pass,
Suffice it that a shock had then been given
To old opinions, and the minds of all men
Had felt it – that my mind was both let loose,
Let loose and goaded. After what has been
Already said of patriotic love,
And hinted at in other sentiments,
We need not linger long upon this theme.
This only may be said, that from the first
Having two natures in me (joy the one,
The other melancholy), and withal
A happy man, and therefore bold to look
On painful things – slow, somewhat, too, and stern
In temperament – I took the knife in hand
And, stopping not at parts less sensitive,
Endeavoured with my best of skill to probe
The living body of society
Even to the heart. I pushed without remorse
My speculations forward, yea, set foot
On nature's holiest places.

Time may come
When some dramatic story may afford
Shapes livelier to convey to thee, my friend,
What then I learned, or think I learned, of truth,
And the errors into which I was betrayed
By present objects, and by reasonings false
From the beginning, inasmuch as drawn
Out of a heart which had been turned aside
From nature by external accidents,
And which was thus confounded more and more,
Misguiding and misguided. Thus I fared,

Disgrace, of which, custom and written law,
And sundry moral sentiments as props
Or emanations of those institutes,
Too justly bore a part. A veil had been
Uplifted; why deceive ourselves? in sooth,
'Twas even so; and sorrow for the man
Who either had not eyes wherewith to see,
Or, seeing, had forgotten! A strong shock
Was given to old opinions; all men's minds
Had felt its power, and mine was both let loose,
Let loose and goaded. After what hath been
Already said of patriotic love,
Suffice it here to add, that, somewhat stern
In temperament, withal a happy man,
And therefore bold to look on painful things,
Free likewise of the world, and thence more bold,
I summoned my best skill, and toiled, intent
To anatomise the frame of social life,
Yea, the whole body of society
Searched to its heart. Share with me, Friend! the wish
That some dramatic tale, endued with shapes
Livelier, and flinging out less guarded words
Than suit the work we fashion, might set forth
What then I learned, or think I learned, of truth,
And the errors into which I fell, betrayed
By present objects, and by reasonings false
From their beginnings, inasmuch as drawn
Out of a heart that had been turned aside
From Nature's way by outward accidents,
And which was thus confounded, more and more
Misguided, and misguiding. So I fared,

Dragging all passions, notions, shapes of faith,
Like culprits to the bar; suspiciously
Calling the mind to establish in plain day
Her titles and her honours; now believing,
Now disbelieving; endlessly perplexed
With impulse, motive, right and wrong, the ground
Of moral obligation – what the rule
And what the sanction – till, demanding proof,
And seeking it in everything, I lost
All feeling of conviction, and (in fine)
Sick, wearied out with contrarieties,
Yielded up moral questions in despair
And for my future studies, as the sole
Employment of the enquiring faculty,
Turned towards mathematics, and their clear
And solid evidence.

Dragging all precepts, judgments, maxims, creeds,
Like culprits to the bar; calling the mind,
Suspiciously, to establish in plain day
Her titles and her honours; now believing,
Now disbelieving; endlessly perplexed
With impulse, motive, right and wrong, the ground
Of obligation, what the rule and whence
The sanction; till, demanding formal *proof*,
And seeking it in every thing, I lost
All feeling of conviction, and, in fine,
Sick, wearied out with contrarieties,
Yielded up moral questions in despair.

This was the crisis of that strong disease,
This the soul's last and lowest ebb; I drooped,
Deeming our blessed reason of least use
Where wanted most: 'The lordly attributes
Of will and choice,' I bitterly exclaimed,
'What are they but a mockery of a Being
Who hath in no concerns of his a test
Of good and evil; knows not what to fear
Or hope for, what to covet or to shun;
And who, if those could be discerned, would yet
Be little profited, would see, and ask
Where is the obligation to enforce?
And, to acknowledged law rebellious, still,
As selfish passion urged, would act amiss;
The dupe of folly, or the slave of crime.'

Depressed, bewildered thus, I did not walk
With scoffers, seeking light and gay revenge
From indiscriminate laughter, nor sate down
In reconcilement with an utter waste
Of intellect; such sloth I could not brook,
(Too well I loved, in that my spring of life,
Pains-taking thoughts, and truth, their dear reward)
But turned to abstract science, and there sought
Work for the reasoning faculty enthroned
Where the disturbances of space and time –

Ah, then it was
That thou, most precious friend – about this time
First known to me – didst lend a living help
To regulate my soul. And then it was
That the belovèd woman in whose sight
Those days were passed (now speaking in a voice
Of sudden admonition, like a brook
That does but cross a lonely road; and now
Seen, heard and felt, and caught at every turn,
Companion never lost through many a league)
Maintained for me a saving intercourse
With my true self. For, though impaired and changed
Much, as it seemed, I was no further changed
Than as a clouded, not a waning moon.
She, in the midst of all, preserved me still
A poet, made me seek beneath that name
My office upon earth, and nowhere else.
And lastly, nature's self, by human love
Assisted, through the weary labyrinth
Conducted me again to open day,
Revived the feelings of my earlier life,
Gave me that strength and knowledge full of peace,
Enlarged and never more to be disturbed,
Which through the steps of our degeneracy,
All degradation of this age, hath still
Upheld me, and upholds me at this day
In the catastrophe (for so they dream,
And nothing less) when, finally to close
And rivet up the gains of France, a Pope
Is summoned in to crown an Emperor –
This last opprobrium, when we see the dog
Returning to his vomit; when the sun
That rose in splendour, was alive, and moved
In exultation among living clouds,
Hath put his function and his glory off,
And, turned into a gewgaw, a machine,

Whether in matters various, properties
Inherent, or from human will and power
Derived – find no admission. Then it was –
Thanks to the bounteous Giver of all good! –
That the beloved Sister in whose sight
Those days were passed, now speaking in a voice
Of sudden admonition – like a brook
That did but *cross* a lonely road, and now
Is seen, heard, felt, and caught at every turn,
Companion never lost through many a league –
Maintained for me a saving intercourse
With my true self; for, though bedimmed and changed
Much, as it seemed, I was no further changed
Than as a clouded and a waning moon:
She whispered still that brightness would return,
She, in the midst of all, preserved me still
A Poet, made me seek beneath that name,
And that alone, my office upon earth;
And, lastly, as hereafter will be shown,
If willing audience fail not, Nature's self,
By all varieties of human love
Assisted, led me back through opening day
To those sweet counsels between head and heart
Whence grew that genuine knowledge, fraught with peace,
Which, through the later sinkings of this cause,
Hath still upheld me, and upholds me now
In the catastrophe (for so they dream,
And nothing less), when, finally to close
And seal up all the gains of France, a Pope
Is summoned in, to crown an Emperor –
This last opprobrium, when we see a people,
That once looked up in faith, as if to Heaven
For manna, take a lesson from the dog
Returning to his vomit; when the sun
That rose in splendour, was alive, and moved
In exultation with a living pomp
Of clouds – his glory's natural retinue –
Hath dropped all functions by the gods bestowed,
And, turned into a gewgaw, a machine,

Sets like an opera phantom.

Thus, o friend,
Through times of honour and through times of shame
Have I descended, tracing faithfully
The workings of a youthful mind beneath
The breath of great events – its hopes no less
Than universal, and its boundless love –
A story destined for thy ear, who now
Among the basest and the lowest fallen
Of all the race of men dost make abode,
Where Etna looketh down on Syracuse,
The city of Timoleon. Living God,
How are the mighty prostrated! They first,
They first of all that breathe, should have awaked
When the great voice was heard out of the tombs
Of ancient heroes. If for France I have grieved,
Who in the judgement of no few hath been
A trifler only in her proudest day –
Have been distressed to think of what she once
Promised, now is – a far more sober cause
Thine eyes must see of sorrow in a land
Strewed with the wreck of loftiest years, a land
Glorious indeed, substantially renowned
Of simple virtue once and manly praise,
Now without one memorial hope; not even
A hope to be deferred, for that would serve
To cheer the heart in such entire decay.

But indignation works where hope is not,
And thou, o friend, wilt be refreshed. There is
One great society alone on earth,
The noble living and the noble dead.
Thy consolation shall be there, and time
And nature shall before thee spread in store
Imperishable thoughts, the place itself
Be conscious of thy presence, and the dull
Sirocco air of its degeneracy
Turn as thou movest into a healthful breeze

Sets like an Opera phantom.

Thus, O Friend!
Through times of honour and through times of shame
Descending, have I faithfully retraced
The perturbations of a youthful mind
Under a long-lived storm of great events –
A story destined for thy ear, who now,
Among the fallen of nations, dost abide
Where Etna, over hill and valley, casts
His shadow stretching towards Syracuse,
The city of Timoleon! Righteous Heaven!
How are the mighty prostrated! They first,
They first of all that breathe should have awaked
When the great voice was heard from out the tombs
Of ancient heroes. If I suffered grief
For ill-requited France, by many deemed
A trifler only in her proudest day;
Have been distressed to think of what she once
Promised, now is; a far more sober cause
Thine eyes must see of sorrow in a land,
To the reanimating influence lost
Of memory, to virtue lost and hope,
Though with the wreck of loftier years bestrewn.

But indignation works where hope is not,
And thou, O Friend! wilt be refreshed. There is
One great society alone on earth:
The noble Living and the noble Dead.

To cherish and invigorate thy frame.

Thine be those motions strong and sanative,
A ladder for thy spirit to reascend
To health and joy and pure contentedness;
To me the grief confined, that thou art gone
From this last spot of earth where freedom now
Stands single in her only sanctuary –
A lonely wanderer art gone, by pain
Compelled and sickness, at this latter day,
This heavy time of change for all mankind.
I feel for thee, must utter what I feel:
The sympathies erewhile in part discharged
Gather afresh, and will have vent again.
My own delights do scarcely seem to me
My own delights! The lordly Alps themselves
(Those rosy peaks, from which the morning looks
Abroad on many nations) are not now
Since thy migration and departure, friend,
The gladsome image in my memory
Which they were used to be. To kindred scenes,
On errand (at a time, how different!)
Thou takest thy way, carrying a heart more ripe
For all divine enjoyment, with the soul
Which nature gives to poets, now by thought
Matured and in the summer of its strength.
Oh, wrap him in your shades, ye giant woods
On Etna's side; and thou, o flowery vale
Of Enna, is there not some nook of thine
From the first playtime of the infant earth
Kept sacred to restorative delight?

Child of the mountains, among shepherds reared,
Even from my earliest schoolday time I loved
To dream of Sicily, and now a strong
And vital promise wafted from that land

Thine be such converse strong and sanative,
A ladder for thy spirit to reascend
To health and joy and pure contentedness;
To me the grief confined, that thou art gone
From this last spot of earth, where Freedom now
Stands single in her only sanctuary;
A lonely wanderer art gone, by pain
Compelled and sickness, at this latter day,
This sorrowful reverse for all mankind.
I feel for thee, must utter what I feel:
The sympathies erewhile in part discharged,
Gather afresh, and will have vent again:
My own delights do scarcely seem to me
My own delights; the lordly Alps themselves,
Those rosy peaks, from which the Morning looks
Abroad on many nations, are no more
For me that image of pure gladsomeness
Which they were wont to be. Through kindred scenes,
For purpose, at a time, how different!
Thou tak'st thy way, carrying the heart and soul
That Nature gives to Poets, now by thought
Matured, and in the summer of their strength.
Oh! wrap him in your shades, ye giant woods,
On Etna's side; and thou, O flowery field
Of Enna! is there not some nook of thine,
From the first play-time of the infant world
Kept sacred to restorative delight,
When from afar invoked by anxious love?

Child of the mountains, among shepherds reared,
Ere yet familiar with the classic page,
I learnt to dream of Sicily; and lo,
The gloom, that, but a moment past, was deepened
At thy command, at her command gives way;
A pleasant promise, wafted from her shores,

Comes o'er my heart! There's not a single name
Of note belonging to that honoured isle –
Philosopher or bard, Empedocles,
Or Archimedes, deep and tranquil soul –
That is not like a comfort to my grief.
And, o Theocritus, so far have some
Prevailed among the powers of heaven and earth
By force of graces which were theirs, that they
Have had (as thou reportest) miracles
Wrought for them in old time. Yea, not unmoved,
When thinking of my own belovèd friend,
I hear thee tell how bees with honey fed
Divine Comates, by his tyrant lord
Within a chest imprisoned impiously –
How with their honey from the fields they came
And fed him there, alive, from month to month,
Because the goatherd, blessèd man, had lips
Wet with the muse's nectar.

Thus I soothe
The pensive moments by this calm fireside,
And find a thousand fancied images
That cheer the thoughts of those I love, and mine.
Our prayers have been accepted: thou wilt stand,
Not as an exile but a visitant
On Etna's top; by pastoral Arethuse
(Or if that fountain be indeed no more,

Comes o'er my heart: in fancy I behold
Her seas yet smiling, her once happy vales;
Nor can my tongue give utterance to a name
Of note belonging to that honoured isle,
Philosopher or Bard, Empedocles,
Or Archimedes, pure abstracted soul!
That doth not yield a solace to my grief:
And, O Theocritus, so far have some
Prevailed among the powers of heaven and earth,
By their endowments, good or great, that they
Have had, as thou reportest, miracles
Wrought for them in old time: yea, not unmoved,
When thinking on my own beloved friend,
I hear thee tell how bees with honey fed
Divine Comates, by his impious lord
Within a chest imprisoned; how they came
Laden from blooming grove or flowery field,
And fed him there, alive, month after month,
Because the goatherd, blessed man! had lips
Wet with the Muses' nectar.

Thus I soothe
The pensive moments by this calm fire-side,
And find a thousand bounteous images
To cheer the thoughts of those I love, and mine.
Our prayers have been accepted; thou wilt stand
On Etna's summit, above earth and sea,
Triumphant, winning from the invaded heavens
Thoughts without bound, magnificent designs,
Worthy of poets who attuned their harps
In wood or echoing cave, for discipline
Of heroes; or, in reverence to the gods,
'Mid temples, served by sapient priests, and choirs
Of virgins crowned with roses. Not in vain
Those temples, where they in their ruins yet
Survive for inspiration, shall attract
Thy solitary steps: and on the brink
Thou wilt recline of pastoral Arethuse;
Or, if that fountain be in truth no more,

Then near some other spring, which by the name
Thou gratulatest, willingly deceived)
Shalt linger as a gladsome votary,
And not a captive pining for his home.

Then, near some other spring, which, by the name
Thou gratulatest, willingly deceived,
I see thee linger a glad votary,
And not a captive pining for his home.

Book Eleventh

IMAGINATION, HOW IMPAIRED AND RESTORED

Long time has man's unhappiness and guilt
Detained us: with what dismal sights beset
For the outward view, and inwardly oppressed
With sorrow, disappointment, vexing thoughts,
Confusion of opinion, zeal decayed –
And lastly, utter loss of hope itself
And things to hope for! Not with these began
Our song, and not with these our song must end.
Ye motions of delight that through the fields
Stir gently, breezes and soft airs that breathe
The breath of paradise and find your way
To the recesses of the soul; ye brooks
Muttering along the stones, a busy noise
By day, a quiet one in silent night;
And you, ye groves, whose ministry it is
To interpose the covert of your shades,
Even as a sleep, betwixt the heart of man
And the uneasy world – 'twixt man himself
Not seldom, and his own unquiet heart –
Oh, that I had a music and a voice
Harmonious as your own, that I might tell

Book Twelfth

IMAGINATION AND TASTE, HOW IMPAIRED AND RESTORED

Long time have human ignorance and guilt
Detained us, on what spectacles of woe
Compelled to look, and inwardly oppressed
With sorrow, disappointment, vexing thoughts,
Confusion of the judgment, zeal decayed,
And, lastly, utter loss of hope itself
And things to hope for! Not with these began
Our song, and not with these our song must end. –
Ye motions of delight, that haunt the sides
Of the green hills; ye breezes and soft airs,
Whose subtle intercourse with breathing flowers,
Feelingly watched, might teach Man's haughty race
How without injury to take, to give
Without offence; ye who, as if to show
The wondrous influence of power gently used,
Bend the complying heads of lordly pines,
And, with a touch, shift the stupendous clouds
Through the whole compass of the sky; ye brooks,
Muttering along the stones, a busy noise
By day, a quiet sound in silent night;
Ye waves, that out of the great deep steal forth
In a calm hour to kiss the pebbly shore,
Not mute, and then retire, fearing no storm;
And you, ye groves, whose ministry it is
To interpose the covert of your shades,
Even as a sleep, between the heart of man
And outward troubles, between man himself,
Not seldom, and his own uneasy heart:
Oh! that I had a music and a voice
Harmonious as your own, that I might tell

What ye have done for me. The morning shines,
Nor heedeth man's perverseness; spring returns –
I saw the spring return when I was dead
To deeper hope, yet had I joy for her
And welcomed her benevolence, rejoiced
In common with the children of her love,
Plants, insects, beast in field, and bird in bower.
So neither were complacency, nor peace,
Nor tender yearnings, wanting for my good
Through those distracted times: in nature still
Glorying, I found a counterpoise in her
Which, when the spirit of evil was at height,
Maintained for me a secret happiness.
Her I resorted to, and loved so much
I seemed to love as much as heretofore –
And yet this passion, fervent as it was,
Had suffered change, how could there fail to be
Some change, if merely hence, that years of life
Were going on, and with them loss or gain
Inevitable, sure alternative?

This history, my friend, has chiefly told
Of intellectual power from stage to stage
Advancing hand in hand with love and joy,
And of imagination teaching truth,
Until that natural graciousness of mind
Gave way to overpressure of the times
And their disastrous issues. What availed,
When spells forbade the voyager to land,
The fragrance which did ever and anon
Give notice of the shore, from arbours breathed
Of blessèd sentiment and fearless love?
What did such sweet remembrances avail –
Perfidious then, as seemed – what served they then?
My business was upon the barren seas,
My errand was to sail to other coasts.
Shall I avow that I had hope to see –
I mean that future times would surely see –
The man to come parted as by a gulf

What ye have done for me. The morning shines,
Nor heedeth Man's perverseness; Spring returns, –
I saw the Spring return, and could rejoice,
In common with the children of her love,
Piping on boughs, or sporting on fresh fields,
Or boldly seeking pleasure nearer heaven
On wings that navigate cerulean skies.
So neither were complacency, nor peace,
Nor tender yearnings, wanting for my good
Through these distracted times; in Nature still
Glorying, I found a counterpoise in her,
Which, when the spirit of evil reached its height,
Maintained for me a secret happiness.

This narrative, my Friend! hath chiefly told
Of intellectual power, fostering love,
Dispensing truth, and, over men and things,
Where reason yet might hesitate, diffusing
Prophetic sympathies of genial faith:
So was I favoured – such my happy lot –
Until that natural graciousness of mind
Gave way to overpressure from the times
And their disastrous issues. What availed,
When spells forbade the voyager to land,
That fragrant notice of a pleasant shore
Wafted, at intervals, from many a bower
Of blissful gratitude and fearless love?
Dare I avow that wish was mine to see,
And hope that future times *would* surely see,
The man to come, parted, as by a gulph,

From him who had been; that I could no more
Trust the elevation which had made me one
With the great family that here and there
Is scattered through the abyss of ages past
(Sage, patriot, lover, hero), for it seemed
That their best virtues were not free from taint
Of something false and weak, which could not stand
The open eye of reason. Then I said
'Go to the poets; they will speak to thee
More perfectly of purer creatures! Yet
If reason be nobility in man
Can aught be more ignoble than the man
Whom they describe – would fasten if they may
Upon our love by sympathies of truth?'

Thus strangely did I war against myself –
A bigot to a new idolatry,
Did like a monk who has forsworn the world
Zealously labour to cut off my heart
From all the sources of her former strength,
And, as by simple waving of a wand
The wizard instantaneously dissolves
Palace or grove, even so did I unsoul
As readily by syllogistic words
(Some charm of logic, ever within reach)
Those mysteries of passion which have made,
And shall continue evermore to make –
In spite of all that reason has performed
And shall perform to exalt and to refine –
One brotherhood of all the human race
Through all the habitations of past years
And those to come. And hence an emptiness
Fell on the historian's page, and even on that
Of poets, pregnant with more absolute truth:
The works of both withered in my esteem,
Their sentence was, I thought, pronounced – their rights
Seemed mortal, and their empire passed away.

From him who had been; that I could no more
Trust the elevation which had made me one
With the great family that still survives
To illuminate the abyss of ages past,
Sage, warrior, patriot, hero; for it seemed
That their best virtues were not free from taint
Of something false and weak, that could not stand
The open eye of Reason. Then I said,
'Go to the Poets, they will speak to thee
More perfectly of purer creatures; – yet
If reason be nobility in man,
Can aught be more ignoble than the man
Whom they delight in, blinded as he is
By prejudice, the miserable slave
Of low ambition or distempered love?'

In such strange passion, if I may once more
Review the past, I warred against myself –
A bigot to a new idolatry –
Like a cowled monk who hath forsworn the world,
Zealously laboured to cut off my heart
From all the sources of her former strength;
And as, by simple waving of a wand,
The wizard instantaneously dissolves
Palace or grove, even so could I unsoul
As readily by syllogistic words
Those mysteries of being which have made,
And shall continue evermore to make,
Of the whole human race one brotherhood.

What then remained in such eclipse, what light
To guide or cheer? The laws of things which lie
Beyond the reach of human will or power,
The life of nature, by the God of love
Inspired – celestial presence ever pure –
These left, the soul of youth must needs be rich,
Whatever else be lost; and these were mine,
Not a deaf echo merely of the thought
(Bewildered recollections, solitary),
But living sounds. Yet in despite of this –
This feeling, which howe'er impaired or damped,
Yet having been once born can never die –
'Tis true that earth with all her appanage
Of elements and organs, storm and sunshine,
With its pure forms and colours, pomp of clouds,
Rivers and mountains, objects among which
It might be thought that no dislike or blame,
No sense of weakness or infirmity
Or aught amiss, could possibly have come,
Yea, even the visible universe was scanned
With something of a kindred spirit, fell
Beneath the domination of a taste
Less elevated, which did in my mind
With its more noble influence interfere,
Its animation and its deeper sway.

There comes (if need be now to speak of this
After such long detail of our mistakes),
There comes a time when reason – not the grand
And simple reason, but that humbler power
Which carries on its not inglorious work
By logic and minute analysis –
Is of all idols that which pleases most
The growing mind. A trifler would he be
Who on the obvious benefits should dwell
That rise out of this process; but to speak
Of all the narrow estimates of things
Which hence originate were a worthy theme
For philosophic verse. Suffice it here

What wonder, then, if, to a mind so far
Perverted, even the visible Universe
Fell under the dominion of a taste
Less spiritual, with microscopic view
Was scanned, as I had scanned the moral world?

To hint that danger cannot but attend
Upon a function rather proud to be
The enemy of falsehood, than the friend
Of truth – to sit in judgement, than to feel.

O soul of nature, excellent and fair,
That didst rejoice with me, with whom I too
Rejoiced through early youth, before the winds
And powerful waters, and in lights and shades
That marched and countermarched about the hills
In glorious apparition – now all eye
And now all ear, but ever with the heart
Employed and the majestic intellect –
O soul of nature that dost overflow
With passion and with life, what feeble men
Walk on this earth, how feeble have I been
When thou wert in thy strength! Nor this through stroke
Of human suffering such as justifies
Remissness and inaptitude of mind,
But through presumption; even in pleasure pleased
Unworthily, disliking here, and there
Liking, by rules of mimic art transferred
To things above all art. But more – for this,
Although a strong infection of the age,
Was never much my habit – giving way
To a comparison of scene with scene,
Bent overmuch on superficial things,
Pampering myself with meagre novelties
Of colour and proportion, to the moods
Of nature and the spirit of the place
Less sensible. Nor only did the love
Of sitting thus in judgement interrupt
My deeper feelings, but another cause,
More subtle and less easily explained,
That almost seems inherent in the creature –
Sensuous and intellectual as he is,
A twofold frame of body and of mind.

O Soul of Nature! excellent and fair!
That didst rejoice with me, with whom I, too,
Rejoiced through early youth, before the winds
And roaring waters, and in lights and shades
That marched and countermarched about the hills
In glorious apparition, Powers on whom
I daily waited, now all eye and now
All ear; but never long without the heart
Employed, and man's unfolding intellect:
O Soul of Nature! that, by laws divine
Sustained and governed, still dost overflow
With an impassioned life, what feeble ones
Walk on this earth! how feeble have I been
When thou wert in thy strength! Nor this through stroke
Of human suffering, such as justifies
Remissness and inaptitude of mind,
But through presumption; even in pleasure pleased
Unworthily, disliking here, and there
Liking; by rules of mimic art transferred
To things above all art; but more, – for this,
Although a strong infection of the age,
Was never much my habit – giving way
To a comparison of scene with scene,
Bent overmuch on superficial things,
Pampering myself with meagre novelties
Of colour and proportion; to the moods
Of time and season, to the moral power,
The affections and the spirit of the place,
Insensible. Nor only did the love
Of sitting thus in judgment interrupt
My deeper feelings, but another cause,
More subtle and less easily explained,
That almost seems inherent in the creature,
A twofold frame of body and of mind.

The state to which I now allude was one
In which the eye was master of the heart,
When that which is in every stage of life
The most despotic of our senses gained
Such strength in me as often held my mind
In absolute dominion

Gladly here,
Entering upon abstruser argument,
Would I endeavour to unfold the means
Which nature studiously employs to thwart
This tyranny, summons all the senses each
To counteract the other (and themselves)
And makes them all, and the objects with which all
Are conversant, subservient in their turn
To the great ends of liberty and power.
But this is matter for another song;
Here only let me add that my delights,
Such as they were, were sought insatiably,
Though 'twas a transport of the outward sense
Not of the mind – vivid but not profound –
Yet was I often greedy in the chase,
And roamed from hill to hill, from rock to rock,
Still craving combinations of new forms,
New pleasure, wider empire for the sight,
Proud of its own endowments, and rejoiced
To lay the inner faculties asleep.

Amid the turns and counterturns, the strife
And various trials of our complex being
As we grow up, such thraldom of that sense
Seems hard to shun. And yet I knew a maid
Who, young as I was then, conversed with things
In higher style. From appetites like these
She, gentle visitant, as well she might,
Was wholly free. Far less did critic rules
Or barren intermeddling subtleties
Perplex her mind, but (wise as women are
When genial circumstance hath favoured them)

I speak in recollection of a time
When the bodily eye, in every stage of life
The most despotic of our senses, gained
Such strength in *me* as often held my mind
In absolute dominion. Gladly here,
Entering upon abstruser argument,
Could I endeavour to unfold the means
Which Nature studiously employs to thwart
This tyranny, summons all the senses each
To counteract the other, and themselves,
And makes them all, and the objects with which all
Are conversant, subservient in their turn
To the great ends of Liberty and Power.
But leave we this: enough that my delights
(Such as they were) were sought insatiably.
Vivid the transport, vivid though not profound;
I roamed from hill to hill, from rock to rock,
Still craving combinations of new forms,
New pleasure, wider empire for the sight,
Proud of her own endowments, and rejoiced
To lay the inner faculties asleep.
Amid the turns and counterturns, the strife
And various trials of our complex being,
As we grow up, such thraldom of that sense
Seems hard to shun. And yet I knew a maid,
A young enthusiast, who escaped these bonds;
Her eye was not the mistress of her heart;
Far less did rules prescribed by passive taste,
Or barren intermeddling subtleties,
Perplex her mind; but, wise as women are
When genial circumstance hath favoured them,

She welcomed what was given, and craved no more.
Whatever scene was present to her eyes,
That was the best, to that she was attuned
Through her humility and lowliness,
And through a perfect happiness of soul,
Whose variegated feelings were in this
Sisters, that they were each some new delight.
For she was nature's inmate: her the birds
And every flower she met with, could they but
Have known her, would have loved. Methought such charm
Of sweetness did her presence breathe around
That all the trees, and all the silent hills,
And everything she looked on, should have had
An intimation how she bore herself
Towards them and to all creatures. God delights
In such a being; for her common thoughts
Are piety, her life is blessedness.

Even like this maid, before I was called forth
From the retirement of my native hills
I loved whate'er I saw – nor lightly loved,
But fervently – did never dream of aught
More grand, more fair, more exquisitely framed,
Than those few nooks to which my happy feet
Were limited. I had not at that time
Lived long enough, nor in the least survived
The first diviner influence of this world
As it appears to unaccustomed eyes.
I worshipped then among the depths of things
As my soul bade me; could I then take part
In aught but admiration, or be pleased
With anything but humbleness and love?
I felt, and nothing else; I did not judge –
I never thought of judging – with the gift
Of all this glory filled and satisfied.
And afterwards, when through the gorgeous Alps
Roaming, I carried with me the same heart.
In truth, this degradation – howsoe'er

She welcomed what was given, and craved no more;
Whate'er the scene presented to her view,
That was the best, to that she was attuned
By her benign simplicity of life,
And through a perfect happiness of soul,
Whose variegated feelings were in this
Sisters, that they were each some new delight.
Birds in the bower, and lambs in the green field,
Could they have known her, would have loved; methought
Her very presence such a sweetness breathed,
That flowers, and trees, and even the silent hills,
And every thing she looked on, should have had
An intimation how she bore herself
Towards them and to all creatures. God delights
In such a being; for her common thoughts
Are piety, her life is gratitude.

Even like this maid, before I was called forth
From the retirement of my native hills,
I loved whate'er I saw: nor lightly loved,
But most intensely; never dreamt of aught
More grand, more fair, more exquisitely framed
Than those few nooks to which my happy feet
Were limited. I had not at that time
Lived long enough, nor in the least survived
The first diviner influence of this world,
As it appears to unaccustomed eyes.
Worshipping then among the depth of things,
As piety ordained; could I submit
To measured admiration, or to aught
That should preclude humility and love?
I felt, observed, and pondered; did not judge,
Yea, never thought of judging; with the gift
Of all this glory filled and satisfied.
And afterwards, when through the gorgeous Alps
Roaming, I carried with me the same heart:
In truth, the degradation – howsoe'er

Induced, effect, in whatsoe'er degree,
Of custom that prepares such wantonness
As makes the greatest things give way to least,
Or any other cause which has been named,
Or, lastly, aggravated by the times
Which with their passionate sounds might often make
The milder minstrelsies of rural scenes
Inaudible – was transient. I had felt
Too forcibly, too early in my life,
Visitings of imaginative power
For this to last: I shook the habit off
Entirely and for ever, and again
In nature's presence stood, as I stand now,
A sensitive, and a *creative* soul.

There are in our existence spots of time
Which with distinct pre-eminence retain
A vivifying virtue, whence, depressed
By false opinion and contentious thought,
Or aught of heavier or more deadly weight
In trivial occupations and the round
Of ordinary intercourse, our minds
Are nourished and invisibly repaired –
A virtue by which pleasure is enhanced,
That penetrates, enables us to mount
When high, more high, and lifts us up when fallen.
This efficacious spirit chiefly lurks
Among those passages of life in which
We have had deepest feeling that the mind
Is lord and master, and that outward sense
Is but the obedient servant of her will.
Such moments, worthy of all gratitude,
Are scattered everywhere, taking their date
From our first childhood – in our childhood even
Perhaps are most conspicuous. Life with me,
As far as memory can look back, is full
Of this beneficent influence.

Induced, effect, in whatsoe'er degree,
Of custom that prepares a partial scale
In which the little oft outweighs the great;
Or any other cause that hath been named;
Or lastly, aggravated by the times
And their impassioned sounds, which well might make
The milder minstrelsies of rural scenes
Inaudible – was transient; I had known
Too forcibly, too early in my life,
Visitings of imaginative power
For this to last: I shook the habit off
Entirely and for ever, and again
In Nature's presence stood, as now I stand,
A sensitive being, a *creative* soul.

There are in our existence spots of time,
That with distinct pre-eminence retain
A renovating virtue, whence, depressed
By false opinion and contentious thought,
Or aught of heavier or more deadly weight,
In trivial occupations, and the round
Of ordinary intercourse, our minds
Are nourished and invisibly repaired;
A virtue, by which pleasure is enhanced,
That penetrates, enables us to mount,
When high, more high, and lifts us up when fallen.
This efficacious spirit chiefly lurks
Among those passages of life that give
Profoundest knowledge to what point, and how,
The mind is lord and master – outward sense
The obedient servant of her will. Such moments
Are scattered everywhere, taking their date
From our first childhood. I remember well,

At a time
When scarcely (I was then not six years old)
My hand could hold a bridle, with proud hopes
I mounted, and we rode towards the hills.
We were a pair of horsemen: honest James
Was with me, my encourager and guide.
We had not travelled long ere some mischance
Disjoined me from my comrade, and, through fear
Dismounting, down the rough and stony moor
I led my horse, and stumbling on, at length
Came to a bottom where in former times
A murderer had been hung in iron chains.
The gibbet-mast was mouldered down, the bones
And iron case were gone; but on the turf
Hard by, soon after that fell deed was wrought,
Some unknown hand had carved the murderer's name.
The monumental writing was engraven
In times long past, and still from year to year
By superstition of the neighbourhood
The grass is cleared away, and to this hour
The letters are all fresh and visible.
Faltering, and ignorant where I was, at length
I chanced to espy those characters inscribed
On the green sod. Forthwith I left the spot
And reascending the bare common saw
A naked pool that lay beneath the hills,
The beacon on the summit, and more near,
A girl who bore a pitcher on her head
And seemed with difficult steps to force her way
Against the blowing wind. It was in truth
An ordinary sight, but I should need
Colours and words that are unknown to man
To paint the visionary dreariness
Which, while I looked all round for my lost guide,
Did at that time invest the naked pool,
The beacon on the lonely eminence,
The woman and her garments vexed and tossed
By the strong wind.

That once, while yet my inexperienced hand
Could scarcely hold a bridle, with proud hopes
I mounted, and we journeyed towards the hills:
An ancient servant of my father's house
Was with me, my encourager and guide:
We had not travelled long, ere some mischance
Disjoined me from my comrade; and, through fear
Dismounting, down the rough and stony moor
I led my horse, and, stumbling on, at length
Came to a bottom, where in former times
A murderer had been hung in iron chains.
The gibbet-mast had mouldered down, the bones
And iron case were gone; but on the turf,
Hard by, soon after that fell deed was wrought,
Some unknown hand had carved the murderer's name.
The monumental letters were inscribed
In times long past; but still, from year to year,
By superstition of the neighbourhood,
The grass is cleared away, and to this hour
The characters are fresh and visible:
A casual glance had shown them, and I fled,
Faltering and faint, and ignorant of the road:
Then, reascending the bare common, saw
A naked pool that lay beneath the hills,
The beacon on the summit, and, more near,
A girl, who bore a pitcher on her head,
And seemed with difficult steps to force her way
Against the blowing wind. It was, in truth,
An ordinary sight; but I should need
Colours and words that are unknown to man,
To paint the visionary dreariness
Which, while I looked all round for my lost guide,
Invested moorland waste, and naked pool,
The beacon crowning the lone eminence,
The female and her garments vexed and tossed
By the strong wind. When, in the blessed hours

When, in a blessèd season
With those two dear ones – to my heart so dear –
When in the blessèd time of early love,
Long afterwards I roamed about
In daily presence of this very scene,
Upon the naked pool and dreary crags,
And on the melancholy beacon, fell
The spirit of pleasure and youth's golden gleam –
And think ye not with radiance more divine
From these remembrances, and from the power
They left behind? So feeling comes in aid
Of feeling, and diversity of strength
Attends us if but once we have been strong.
Oh, mystery of man, from what a depth
Proceed thy honours! I am lost, but see
In simple childhood something of the base
On which thy greatness stands – but this I feel,
That from thyself it is that thou must give,
Else never canst receive. The days gone by
Come back upon me from the dawn almost
Of life; the hiding-places of my power
Seem open, I approach, and then they close;
I see by glimpses now, when age comes on
May scarcely see at all; and I would give
While yet we may (as far as words can give)
A substance and a life to what I feel –
I would enshrine the spirit of the past
For future restoration. Yet another
Of these to me affecting incidents,
With which we will conclude.

One Christmas-time,
The day before the holidays began,
Feverish, and tired, and restless, I went forth
Into the fields, impatient for the sight
Of those two horses which should bear us home,
My brothers and myself. There was a crag,
An eminence, which from the meeting-point
Of two highways ascending, overlooked

Of early love, the loved one at my side,
I roamed, in daily presence of this scene,
Upon the naked pool and dreary crags,
And on the melancholy beacon, fell
A spirit of pleasure and youth's golden gleam;
And think ye not with radiance more sublime
For these remembrances, and for the power
They had left behind? So feeling comes in aid
Of feeling, and diversity of strength
Attends us, if but once we have been strong.
Oh! mystery of man, from what a depth
Proceed thy honours. I am lost, but see
In simple childhood something of the base
On which thy greatness stands; but this I feel,
That from thyself it comes, that thou must give,
Else never canst receive. The days gone by
Return upon me almost from the dawn
Of life: the hiding-places of man's power
Open; I would approach them, but they close.
I see by glimpses now; when age comes on,
May scarcely see at all; and I would give,
While yet we may, as far as words can give,
Substance and life to what I feel, enshrining,
Such is my hope, the spirit of the Past
For future restoration. – Yet another
Of these memorials: –

One Christmas-time,
On the glad eve of its dear holidays,
Feverish, and tired, and restless, I went forth
Into the fields, impatient for the sight
Of those led palfreys that should bear us home;
My brothers and myself. There rose a crag,
That, from the meeting-point of two highways
Ascending, overlooked them both, far stretched;

At least a long half-mile of those two roads,
By each of which the expected steeds might come –
The choice uncertain. Thither I repaired
Up to the highest summit. 'Twas a day
Stormy, and rough, and wild, and on the grass
I sat half sheltered by a naked wall.
Upon my right hand was a single sheep,
A whistling hawthorn on my left, and there,
With those companions at my side, I watched,
Straining my eyes intensely, as the mist
Gave intermitting prospect of the wood
And plain beneath. Ere I to school returned
That dreary time, ere I had been ten days
A dweller in my father's house, he died,
And I and my two brothers (orphans then)
Followed his body to the grave. The event,
With all the sorrow which it brought, appeared
A chastisement; and when I called to mind
That day so lately past, when from the crag
I looked in such anxiety of hope,
With trite reflections of morality,
Yet in the deepest passion, I bowed low
To God who thus corrected my desires.
And afterwards the wind and sleety rain
And all the business of the elements,
The single sheep, and the one blasted tree,
And the bleak music of that old stone wall,
The noise of wood and water, and the mist
Which on the line of each of those two roads
Advanced in such indisputable shapes –
All these were spectacles and sounds to which
I often would repair, and thence would drink
As at a fountain. And I do not doubt
That in this later time, when storm and rain
Beat on my roof at midnight, or by day
When I am in the woods, unknown to me
The workings of my spirit thence are brought.

Thither, uncertain on which road to fix
My expectation, thither I repaired,
Scout-like, and gained the summit; 'twas a day
Tempestuous, dark, and wild, and on the grass
I sate half-sheltered by a naked wall;
Upon my right hand couched a single sheep,
Upon my left a blasted hawthorn stood;
With those companions at my side, I watched,
Straining my eyes intensely, as the mist
Gave intermitting prospect of the copse
And plain beneath. Ere we to school returned, –
That dreary time, – ere we had been ten days
Sojourners in my father's house, he died,
And I and my three brothers, orphans then,
Followed his body to the grave. The event,
With all the sorrow that it brought, appeared
A chastisement; and when I called to mind
That day so lately past, when from the crag
I looked in such anxiety of hope;
With trite reflections of morality,
Yet in the deepest passion, I bowed low
To God, Who thus corrected my desires;
And, afterwards, the wind and sleety rain,
And all the business of the elements,
The single sheep, and the one blasted tree,
And the bleak music from that old stone wall,
The noise of wood and water, and the mist
That on the line of each of those two roads
Advanced in such indisputable shapes;
All these were kindred spectacles and sounds
To which I oft repaired, and thence would drink,
As at a fountain; and on winter nights,
Down to this very time, when storm and rain
Beat on my roof, or, haply, at noon-day,
While in a grove I walk, whose lofty trees,
Laden with summer's thickest foliage, rock
In a strong wind, some working of the spirit,
Some inward agitations thence are brought,

Thou wilt not languish here, o friend, for whom
I travel in these dim uncertain ways;
Thou wilt assist me as a pilgrim gone
In quest of highest truth. Behold me then
Once more in nature's presence, thus restored
Or otherwise, and strengthened once again
(With memory left of what had been escaped)
To habits of devoutest sympathy.

Whate'er their office, whether to beguile
Thoughts over busy in the course they took,
Or animate an hour of vacant ease.

Book Twelfth

SAME SUBJECT (CONTINUED)

From nature does emotion come, and moods
Of calmness equally are nature's gift –
This is her glory. These two attributes
Are sister horns that constitute her strength;
This twofold influence is the sun and shower
Of all her bounties, both in origin
And end alike benignant. Hence it is
That genius, which exists by interchange
Of peace and excitation, finds in her
His best and purest friend – from her receives
That energy by which he seeks the truth
(Is roused, aspires, grasps, struggles, wishes, craves),
From her, that happy stillness of the mind
Which fits him to receive it when unsought.

Such benefit may souls of humblest frame
Partake of, each in their degree; 'tis mine
To speak of what myself have known and felt.
Sweet task! – for words find easy way, inspired
By gratitude and confidence in truth.
Long time in search of knowledge desperate
I was benighted heart and mind, but now
On all sides day began to reappear,
And it was proved indeed that not in vain
I had been taught to reverence a power
That is the very quality and shape
And image of right reason – that matures
Her processes by steadfast laws; gives birth
To no impatient or fallacious hopes,
No heat of passion or excessive zeal,

Book Thirteenth

IMAGINATION AND TASTE, HOW IMPAIRED AND RESTORED – (CONCLUDED)

From Nature doth emotion come, and moods
Of calmness equally are Nature's gift:
This is her glory; these two attributes
Are sister horns that constitute her strength.
Hence Genius, born to thrive by interchange
Of peace and excitation, finds in her
His best and purest friend; from her receives
That energy by which he seeks the truth,
From her that happy stillness of the mind
Which fits him to receive it when unsought.

Such benefit the humblest intellects
Partake of, each in their degree; 'tis mine
To speak, what I myself have known and felt;
Smooth task! for words find easy way, inspired
By gratitude, and confidence in truth.
Long time in search of knowledge did I range
The field of human life, in heart and mind
Benighted; but, the dawn beginning now
To re-appear, 'twas proved that not in vain
I had been taught to reverence a Power
That is the visible quality and shape
And image of right reason; that matures
Her processes by steadfast laws; gives birth
To no impatient or fallacious hopes,
No heat of passion or excessive zeal,

No vain conceits; provokes to no quick turns
Of self-applauding intellect, but lifts
The being into magnanimity;
Holds up before the mind intoxicate
With present objects, and the busy dance
Of things that pass away, a temperate show
Of objects that endure, and by this course
Disposes her, when over fondly set
On leaving her incumbrances behind,
To seek in man (and in the frame of life,
Social and individual) what there is
Desirable, affecting, good or fair,
Of kindred permanence – the gifts divine
And universal, the pervading grace
That has been, is, and shall be. Above all
Did nature bring again that wiser mood,
More deeply re-established in my soul,
Which – seeing little worthy or sublime
In what we blazon with the pompous names
Of power and action – early tutored me
To look with feelings of fraternal love
Upon those unassuming things that hold
A silent station in this beauteous world.

Thus moderated, thus composed, I found
Once more in man an object of delight,
Of pure imagination, and of love;
And, as the horizon of my mind enlarged,
Again I took the intellectual eye
For my instructor, studious more to see
Great truths, than touch and handle little ones.
Knowledge was given accordingly: my trust
Was firmer in the feelings which had stood
The test of such a trial, clearer far
My sense of what was excellent and right;
The promise of the present time retired
Into its true proportion; sanguine schemes,
Ambitious virtues, pleased me less – I sought
For good in the familiar face of life,

No vain conceits; provokes to no quick turns
Of self-applauding intellect; but trains
To meekness, and exalts by humble faith;
Holds up before the mind intoxicate
With present objects, and the busy dance
Of things that pass away, a temperate show
Of objects that endure; and by this course
Disposes her, when over-fondly set
On throwing off incumbrances, to seek
In man, and in the frame of social life,
Whate'er there is desirable and good
Of kindred permanence, unchanged in form
And function, or, through strict vicissitude
Of life and death, revolving. Above all
Were re-established now those watchful thoughts
Which, seeing little worthy or sublime
In what the Historian's pen so much delights
To blazon – power and energy detached
From moral purpose – early tutored me
To look with feelings of fraternal love
Upon the unassuming things that hold
A silent station in this beauteous world.

Thus moderated, thus composed, I found
Once more in Man an object of delight,
Of pure imagination, and of love;
And, as the horizon of my mind enlarged,
Again I took the intellectual eye
For my instructor, studious more to see
Great truths, than touch and handle little ones.
Knowledge was given accordingly; my trust
Became more firm in feelings that had stood
The test of such a trial; clearer far
My sense of excellence – of right and wrong:
The promise of the present time retired
Into its true proportion; sanguine schemes,
Ambitious projects, pleased me less; I sought
For present good in life's familiar face,

And built thereon my hopes of good to come.

With settling judgements now of what would last
And what would disappear; prepared to find
Ambition, folly, madness, in the men
Who thrust themselves upon this passive world
As rulers of the world (to see in these,
Even when the public welfare is their aim,
Plans without thought, or bottomed on false thought
And false philosophy); having brought to test
Of solid life and true result the books
Of modern statists, and thereby perceived
The utter hollowness of what we name
The wealth of nations, where alone that wealth
Is lodged, and how increased; and having gained
A more judicious knowledge of what makes
The dignity of individual man –
Of man, no composition of the thought,
Abstraction, shadow, image, but the man
Of whom we read, the man whom we behold
With our own eyes – I could not but enquire,
Not with less interest than heretofore
But greater, though in spirit more subdued,
Why is this glorious creature to be found
One only in ten thousand? What one is,
Why may not many be? What bars are thrown
By nature in the way of such a hope?
Our animal wants and the necessities
Which they impose, are these the obstacles? –
If not, then others vanish into air.

Such meditations bred an anxious wish
To ascertain how much of real worth,
And genuine knowledge, and true power of mind,
Did at this day exist in those who lived
By bodily labour – labour far exceeding
Their due proportion – under all the weight
Of that injustice which upon ourselves
By composition of society

And built thereon my hopes of good to come.

With settling judgments now of what would last
And what would disappear; prepared to find
Presumption, folly, madness, in the men
Who thrust themselves upon the passive world
As Rulers of the world; to see in these,
Even when the public welfare is their aim,
Plans without thought, or built on theories
Vague and unsound; and having brought the books
Of modern statists to their proper test,
Life, human life, with all its sacred claims
Of sex and age, and heaven-descended rights,
Mortal, or those beyond the reach of death;
And having thus discerned how dire a thing
Is worshipped in that idol proudly named
'The Wealth of Nations,' *where* alone that wealth
Is lodged, and how increased; and having gained
A more judicious knowledge of the worth
And dignity of individual man,
No composition of the brain, but man
Of whom we read, the man whom we behold
With our own eyes – I could not but inquire –
Not with less interest than heretofore,
But greater, though in spirit more subdued –
Why is this glorious creature to be found
One only in ten thousand? What one is,
Why may not millions be? What bars are thrown
By Nature in the way of such a hope?
Our animal appetites and daily wants,
Are these obstructions insurmountable?
If not, then others vanish into air.
'Inspect the basis of the social pile:
Inquire,' said I, 'how much of mental power
And genuine virtue they possess who live
By bodily toil, labour exceeding far
Their due proportion, under all the weight
Of that injustice which upon ourselves

Ourselves entail. To frame such estimate
I chiefly looked (what need to look beyond?)
Among the natural abodes of men –
Fields with their rural works – recalled to mind
My earliest notices, with these compared
The observations of my later youth
Continued downwards to that very day.
For time had never been in which the throes
And mighty hopes of nations, and the stir
And tumult of the world, to me could yield
(How far soe'er transported and possessed)
Full measure of content, but still I craved
An intermixture of distinct regards
And truths of individual sympathy
Nearer ourselves. Such often might be gleaned
From that great city, else it must have been
A heart-depressing wilderness indeed –
Full soon to me a wearisome abode –
But much was wanting; therefore did I turn
To you, ye pathways and ye lonely roads,
Sought you, enriched with everything I prized,
With human kindness and with nature's joy.

Oh, next to one dear state of bliss, vouchsafed,
Alas, to few in this untoward world –
The bliss of walking daily in life's prime
Through field or forest with the maid we love
While yet our hearts are young, while yet we breathe
Nothing but happiness, living in some place
(Deep vale, or anywhere, the home of both)
From which it would be misery to stir –
Oh, next to such enjoyment of our youth,
In my esteem, next to such dear delight,
Was that of wandering on from day to day
Where I could meditate in peace, and find
The knowledge which I love, and teach the sound
Of poet's music to strange fields and groves;

Ourselves entail.' Such estimate to frame
I chiefly looked (what need to look beyond?)
Among the natural abodes of men,
Fields with their rural works; recalled to mind
My earliest notices; with these compared
The observations made in later youth,
And to that day continued. – For, the time
Had never been when throes of mighty Nations
And the world's tumult unto me could yield,
How far soe'er transported and possessed,
Full measure of content; but still I craved
An intermingling of distinct regards
And truths of individual sympathy
Nearer ourselves. Such often might be gleaned
From the great City, else it must have proved
To me a heart-depressing wilderness;
But much was wanting: therefore did I turn
To you, ye pathways, and ye lonely roads;
Sought you enriched with everything I prized,
With human kindnesses and simple joys.

Oh! next to one dear state of bliss, vouchsafed
Alas! to few in this untoward world,
The bliss of walking daily in life's prime
Through field or forest with the maid we love,
While yet our hearts are young, while yet we breathe
Nothing but happiness, in some lone nook,
Deep vale, or any where, the home of both,
From which it would be misery to stir:
Oh! next to such enjoyment of our youth,
In my esteem, next to such dear delight,
Was that of wandering on from day to day
Where I could meditate in peace, and cull
Knowledge that step by step might lead me on
To wisdom; or, as lightsome as a bird
Wafted upon the wind from distant lands,
Sing notes of greeting to strange fields or groves,

Converse with men, where if we meet a face
We almost meet a friend, on naked moors
With long long ways before, by cottage bench,
Or well-spring where the weary traveller rests.

I love a public road: few sights there are
That please me more – such object has had power
O'er my imagination since the dawn
Of childhood, when its disappearing line
Seen daily afar off, on one bare steep
Beyond the limits which my feet had trod,
Was like a guide into eternity,
At least to things unknown and without bound.
Even something of the grandeur which invests
The mariner who sails the roaring sea
Through storm and darkness, early in my mind
Surrounded too the wanderers of the earth –
Grandeur as much, and loveliness far more.
Awed have I been by strolling bedlamites;
From many other uncouth vagrants (passed
In fear) have walked with quicker step – but why
Take note of this? When I began to enquire,
To watch and question those I met, and held
Familiar talk with them, the lonely roads
Were schools to me in which I daily read
With most delight the passions of mankind,
There saw into the depth of human souls –
Souls that appear to have no depth at all
To vulgar eyes. And now, convinced at heart
How little that to which alone we give
The name of education has to do
With real feeling and just sense, how vain
A correspondence with the talking world

Which lacked not voice to welcome me in turn:
And, when that pleasant toil had ceased to please,
Converse with men, where if we meet a face
We almost meet a friend, on naked heaths
With long long ways before, by cottage bench,
Or well-spring where the weary traveller rests.

Who doth not love to follow with his eye
The windings of a public way? the sight,
Familiar object as it is, hath wrought
On my imagination since the morn
Of childhood, when a disappearing line,
One daily present to my eyes, that crossed
The naked summit of a far-off hill
Beyond the limits that my feet had trod,
Was like an invitation into space
Boundless, or guide into eternity.
Yes, something of the grandeur which invests
The mariner who sails the roaring sea
Through storm and darkness, early in my mind
Surrounded, too, the wanderers of the earth;
Grandeur as much, and loveliness far more.
Awed have I been by strolling Bedlamites;
From many other uncouth vagrants (passed
In fear) have walked with quicker step; but why
Take note of this? When I began to enquire,
To watch and question those I met, and speak
Without reserve to them, the lonely roads
Were open schools in which I daily read
With most delight the passions of mankind,
Whether by words, looks, sighs, or tears, revealed;
There saw into the depth of human souls,
Souls that appear to have no depth at all
To careless eyes. And – now convinced at heart
How little those formalities, to which
With overweening trust alone we give
The name of Education, have to do
With real feeling and just sense; how vain
A correspondence with the talking world

Proves to the most – and called to make good search
If man's estate, by doom of nature yoked
With toil, is therefore yoked with ignorance,
If virtue be indeed so hard to rear,
And intellectual strength so rare a boon –
I prized such walks still more. For there I found
Hope to my hope, and to my pleasure peace
And steadiness, and healing and repose
To every angry passion. There I heard,
From mouths of lowly men and of obscure,
A tale of honour – sounds in unison
With loftiest promises of good and fair.

There are who think that strong affections, love
Known by whatever name, is falsely deemed
A gift (to use a term which they would use)
Of vulgar nature – that its growth requires
Retirement, leisure, language purified
By manners thoughtful and elaborate –
That whoso feels such passion in excess
Must live within the very light and air
Of elegances that are made by man.
True is it, where oppression worse than death
Salutes the being at his birth, where grace
Of culture hath been utterly unknown,
And labour in excess and poverty
From day to day pre-occupy the ground
Of the affections, and to nature's self
Oppose a deeper nature – there indeed
Love cannot be. Nor does it easily thrive
In cities, where the human heart is sick,
And the eye feeds it not, and cannot feed.
Thus far – no further – is that inference good.

Yes, in those wanderings deeply did I feel
How we mislead each other, above all
How books mislead us – looking for their fame
To judgements of the wealthy few, who see
By artificial lights – how they debase

Proves to the most; and called to make good search
If man's estate, by doom of Nature yoked
With toil, be therefore yoked with ignorance;
If virtue be indeed so hard to rear,
And intellectual strength so rare a boon –
I prized such walks still more, for there I found
Hope to my hope, and to my pleasure peace
And steadiness, and healing and repose
To every angry passion. There I heard,
From mouths of men obscure and lowly, truths
Replete with honour; sounds in unison
With loftiest promises of good and fair.

There are who think that strong affection, love
Known by whatever name, is falsely deemed
A gift, to use a term which they would use,
Of vulgar nature; that its growth requires
Retirement, leisure, language purified
By manners studied and elaborate;
That whoso feels such passion in its strength
Must live within the very light and air
Of courteous usages refined by art.
True is it, where oppression worse than death
Salutes the being at his birth, where grace
Of culture hath been utterly unknown,
And poverty and labour in excess
From day to day pre-occupy the ground
Of the affections, and to Nature's self
Oppose a deeper nature; there, indeed,
Love cannot be; nor does it thrive with ease
Among the close and overcrowded haunts
Of cities, where the human heart is sick,
And the eye feeds it not, and cannot feed.
– Yes, in those wanderings deeply did I feel
How we mislead each other; above all,
How books mislead us, seeking their reward
From judgments of the wealthy Few, who see
By artificial lights; how they debase

The many for the pleasure of those few,
Effeminately level down the truth
To certain general notions for the sake
Of being understood at once (or else
Through want of better knowledge in the men
Who frame them), flattering thus our self-conceit
With pictures that ambitiously set forth
The differences, the outside marks by which
Society has parted man from man,
Neglectful of the universal heart.

Here, calling up to mind what then I saw,
A youthful traveller, and see daily now
Before me in my rural neighbourhood,
Here might I pause, and bend in reverence
To nature and the power of human minds,
To men as they are men within themselves.
How oft high service is performed within
When all the external man is rude in show –
Not like a temple rich with pomp and gold,
But a mere mountain chapel such as shields
Its simple worshippers from sun and shower.
'Of these', said I, 'shall be my song. Of these,
If future years mature me for the task,
Will I record the praises, making verse
Deal boldly with substantial things – in truth
And sanctity of passion speak of these,
That justice may be done, obeisance paid
Where it is due. Thus haply shall I teach,
Inspire – through unadulterated ears
Pour rapture, tenderness and hope – my theme
No other than the very heart of man
As found among the best of those who live
Not unexalted by religious hope,
Nor uninformed by books (good books, though few)
In nature's presence. Thence may I select
Sorrow that is not sorrow but delight,
And miserable love that is not pain
To hear of, for the glory that redounds

The Many for the pleasure of those Few;
Effeminately level down the truth
To certain general notions, for the sake
Of being understood at once, or else
Through want of better knowledge in the heads
That framed them; flattering self-conceit with words,
That, while they most ambitiously set forth
Extrinsic differences, the outward marks
Whereby society has parted man
From man, neglect the universal heart.

Here, calling up to mind what then I saw,
A youthful traveller, and see daily now
In the familiar circuit of my home,
Here might I pause, and bend in reverence
To Nature, and the power of human minds,
To men as they are men within themselves.
How oft high service is performed within,
When all the external man is rude in show, –
Not like a temple rich with pomp and gold,
But a mere mountain chapel, that protects
Its simple worshippers from sun and shower.
Of these, said I, shall be my song; of these,
If future years mature me for the task,
Will I record the praises, making verse
Deal boldly with substantial things; in truth
And sanctity of passion, speak of these,
That justice may be done, obeisance paid
Where it is due: thus haply shall I teach,
Inspire, through unadulterated ears
Pour rapture, tenderness, and hope, – my theme
No other than the very heart of man,
As found among the best of those who live,
Not unexalted by religious faith,
Nor uninformed by books, good books, though few,
In Nature's presence: thence may I select
Sorrow, that is not sorrow, but delight;
And miserable love, that is not pain
To hear of, for the glory that redounds

Therefrom to human-kind and what we are.'

Be mine to follow with no timid step
Where knowledge leads me: it shall be my pride
That I have dared to tread this holy ground
Speaking no dream, but things oracular,
Matter not lightly to be heard by those
Who to the letter of the outward promise
Do read the invisible soul – by men adroit
In speech, and for communion with the world
Accomplished – minds whose faculties are then
Most active when they are most eloquent,
And elevated most when most admired.
Men may be found of other mould than these
Who are their own upholders, to themselves
Encouragement, and energy, and will,
Expressing liveliest thoughts in lively words
As native passion dictates. Others too
There are among the walks of homely life
Still higher, men for contemplation framed,
Shy, and unpractised in the strife of phrase,
Meek men, whose very souls perhaps would sink
Beneath them, summoned to such intercourse.
Theirs is the language of the heavens, the power,
The thought, the image, and the silent joy.
Words are but under-agents in their souls;
When they are grasping with their greatest strength,
They do not breathe among them. This I speak
In gratitude to God, who feeds our hearts
For his own service – knoweth, loveth us,
When we are unregarded by the world.

Also about this time did I receive
Convictions still more strong than heretofore
Not only that the inner frame is good,
And graciously composed, but that, no less,
Nature through all conditions hath a power
To consecrate – if we have eyes to see –
The outside of her creatures, and to breathe

Therefrom to human kind, and what we are.
Be mine to follow with no timid step
Where knowledge leads me: it shall be my pride
That I have dared to tread this holy ground,
Speaking no dream, but things oracular;
Matter not lightly to be heard by those
Who to the letter of the outward promise
Do read the invisible soul; by men adroit
In speech, and for communion with the world
Accomplished; minds whose faculties are then
Most active when they are most eloquent,
And elevated most when most admired.
Men may be found of other mould than these,
Who are their own upholders, to themselves
Encouragement, and energy, and will,
Expressing liveliest thoughts in lively words
As native passion dictates. Others, too,
There are among the walks of homely life
Still higher, men for contemplation framed,
Shy, and unpractised in the strife of phrase;
Meek men, whose very souls perhaps would sink
Beneath them, summoned to such intercourse:
Theirs is the language of the heavens, the power,
The thought, the image, and the silent joy:
Words are but under-agents in their souls;
When they are grasping with their greatest strength,
They do not breathe among them: this I speak
In gratitude to God, Who feeds our hearts
For His own service; knoweth, loveth us,
When we are unregarded by the world.

Also, about this time did I receive
Convictions still more strong than heretofore,
Not only that the inner frame is good,
And graciously composed, but that, no less,
Nature for all conditions wants not power
To consecrate, if we have eyes to see,
The outside of her creatures, and to breathe

Grandeur upon the very humblest face
Of human life. I felt that the array
Of outward circumstance and visible form
Is to the pleasure of the human mind
What passion makes it; that, meanwhile, the forms
Of nature have a passion in themselves
That intermingles with those works of man
To which she summons him (although the works
Be mean, have nothing lofty of their own),
And that the genius of the poet hence
May boldly take his way among mankind
Wherever nature leads – that he has stood
By nature's side among the men of old,
And so shall stand for ever. Dearest friend,
Forgive me if I say that I (who long
Had harboured reverentially a thought
That poets, even as prophets, each with each
Connected in a mighty scheme of truth,
Have each for his peculiar dower a sense
By which he is enabled to perceive
Something unseen before), forgive me, friend,
If I, the meanest of this band, had hope
That unto me had also been vouchsafed
An influx – that in some sort I possessed
A privilege, and that a work of mine,
Proceeding from the depth of untaught things,
Enduring and creative, might become
A power like one of nature's.

To such mood
Once above all (a traveller at that time
Upon the Plain of Sarum) was I raised:
There on the pastoral downs without a track
To guide me, or along the bare white roads
Lengthening in solitude their dreary line,
While through those vestiges of ancient times
I ranged, and by the solitude o'ercome,
I had a reverie and saw the past,
Saw multitudes of men, and here and there

Grandeur upon the very humblest face
Of human life. I felt that the array
Of act and circumstance, and visible form,
Is mainly to the pleasure of the mind
What passion makes them; that meanwhile the forms
Of Nature have a passion in themselves,
That intermingles with those works of man
To which she summons him; although the works
Be mean, have nothing lofty of their own;
And that the Genius of the Poet hence
May boldly take his way among mankind
Wherever Nature leads; that he hath stood
By Nature's side among the men of old,
And so shall stand for ever. Dearest Friend!
If thou partake the animating faith
That Poets, even as Prophets, each with each
Connected in a mighty scheme of truth,
Have each his own peculiar faculty,
Heaven's gift, a sense that fits him to perceive
Objects unseen before, thou wilt not blame
The humblest of this band who dares to hope
That unto him hath also been vouchsafed
An insight that in some sort he possesses,
A privilege whereby a work of his,
Proceeding from a source of untaught things,
Creative and enduring, may become
A power like one of Nature's. To a hope
Not less ambitious once among the wilds
Of Sarum's Plain, my youthful spirit was raised;
There, as I ranged at will the pastoral downs
Trackless and smooth, or paced the bare white roads
Lengthening in solitude their dreary line,
Time with his retinue of ages fled
Backwards, nor checked his flight until I saw
Our dim ancestral Past in vision clear;
Saw multitudes of men, and, here and there,

A single Briton in his wolf-skin vest,
With shield and stone-axe, stride across the wold;
The voice of spears was heard, the rattling spear
Shaken by arms of mighty bone, in strength
Long mouldered, of barbaric majesty.
I called upon the darkness, and it took –
A midnight darkness seemed to come and take –
All objects from my sight; and lo, again
The desert visible by dismal flames!
It is the sacrificial altar, fed
With living men – how deep the groans! – the voice
Of those in the gigantic wicker thrills
Throughout the region far and near, pervades
The monumental hillocks, and the pomp
Is for both worlds, the living and the dead.

At other moments (for through that wide waste
Three summer days I roamed) when 'twas my chance
To have before me on the downy plain
Lines, circles, mounts, a mystery of shapes
Such as in many quarters yet survive,
With intricate profusion figuring o'er
The untilled ground – the work, as some divine,
Of infant science, imitative forms
By which the Druids covertly expressed
Their knowledge of the heavens, and imaged forth
The constellations – I was gently charmed,
Albeit with an antiquarian's dream,
And saw the bearded teachers, with white wands
Uplifted, pointing to the starry sky,
Alternately, and plain below, while breath
Of music seemed to guide them, and the waste
Was cheered with stillness and a pleasant sound.

This for the past, and things that may be viewed
Or fancied in the obscurities of time!
Nor is it, friend, unknown to thee: at least,
Thyself delighted, thou for my delight
Hast said (perusing some imperfect verse

A single Briton clothed in wolf-skin vest,
With shield and stone-axe, stride across the wold;
The voice of spears was heard, the rattling spear
Shaken by arms of mighty bone, in strength,
Long mouldered, of barbaric majesty.
I called on Darkness – but before the word
Was uttered, midnight darkness seemed to take
All objects from my sight; and lo! again
The Desert visible by dismal flames;
It is the sacrificial altar, fed
With living men – how deep the groans! the voice
Of those that crowd the giant wicker thrills
The monumental hillocks, and the pomp
Is for both worlds, the living and the dead.
At other moments (for through that wide waste
Three summer days I roamed) where'er the Plain
Was figured o'er with circles, lines, or mounds,
That yet survive, a work, as some divine,
Shaped by the Druids, so to represent
Their knowledge of the heavens, and image forth
The constellations; gently was I charmed
Into a waking dream, a reverie
That, with believing eyes, where'er I turned,
Beheld long-bearded teachers, with white wands
Uplifted, pointing to the starry sky,
Alternately, and plain below, while breath
Of music swayed their motions, and the waste
Rejoiced with them and me in those sweet sounds.

This for the past, and things that may be viewed
Or fancied in the obscurity of years
From monumental hints: and thou, O Friend!
Pleased with some unpremeditated strains

Which in that lonesome journey was composed)
That also I must then have exercised
Upon the vulgar forms of present things
And actual world of our familiar days,
A higher power – have caught from them a tone,
An image, and a character, by books
Not hitherto reflected. Call we this
But a persuasion taken up by thee
In friendship? Yet the mind is to herself
Witness and judge, and I remember well
That in life's everyday appearances
I seemed about this period to have sight
Of a new world – a world, too, that was fit
To be transmitted, and made visible
To other eyes, as having for its base
That whence our dignity originates,
That which both gives it being, and maintains
A balance, an ennobling interchange
Of action from within and from without:
The excellence, pure spirit, and best power,
Both of the object seen, and eye that sees.

That served those wanderings to beguile, hast said
That then and there my mind had exercised
Upon the vulgar forms of present things,
The actual world of our familiar days,
Yet higher power; had caught from them a tone,
An image, and a character, by books
Not hitherto reflected. Call we this
A partial judgment – and yet why? for *then*
We were as strangers; and I may not speak
Thus wrongfully of verse, however rude,
Which on thy young imagination, trained
In the great City, broke like light from far.
Moreover, each man's Mind is to herself
Witness and judge; and I remember well
That in life's every-day appearances
I seemed about this time to gain clear sight
Of a new world – a world, too, that was fit
To be transmitted, and to other eyes
Made visible; as ruled by those fixed laws
Whence spiritual dignity originates,
Which do both give it being and maintain
A balance, an ennobling interchange
Of action from without and from within;
The excellence, pure function, and best power
Both of the object seen, and eye that sees.

Book Thirteenth
CONCLUSION

In one of these excursions, travelling then
Through Wales on foot and with a youthful friend,
I left Bethgelert's huts at couching-time
And westward took my way to see the sun
Rise from the top of Snowdon. Having reached
The cottage at the mountain's foot, we there
Roused up the shepherd who by ancient right
Of office is the stranger's usual guide,
And after short refreshment sallied forth.

It was a summer's night, a close warm night,
Wan, dull and glaring, with a dripping mist
Low-hung and thick that covered all the sky
Half threatening storm and rain; but on we went
Unchecked, being full of heart and having faith
In our tried pilot. Little could we see
Hemmed round on every side with fog and damp,
And, after ordinary travellers' chat
With our conductor, silently we sank
Each into commerce with his private thoughts.
Thus did we breast the ascent, and by myself
Was nothing either seen or heard the while
Which took me from my musings, save that once
The shepherd's cur did to his own great joy
Unearth a hedgehog in the mountain crags
Round which he made a barking turbulent.
This small adventure (for even such it seemed
In that wild place and at the dead of night)
Being over and forgotten, on we wound

Book Fourteenth

CONCLUSION

In one of those excursions (may they ne'er
Fade from remembrance!) through the Northern tracts
Of Cambria ranging with a youthful friend,
I left Bethgelert's huts at couching-time,
And westward took my way, to see the sun
Rise from the top of Snowdon. To the door
Of a rude cottage at the mountain's base
We came, and roused the shepherd who attends
The adventurous stranger's steps, a trusty guide;
Then, cheered by short refreshment, sallied forth.

It was a close, warm, breezeless summer night,
Wan, dull, and glaring, with a dripping fog
Low-hung and thick that covered all the sky;
But, undiscouraged, we began to climb
The mountain-side. The mist soon girt us round,
And, after ordinary travellers' talk
With our conductor, pensively we sank
Each into commerce with his private thoughts:
Thus did we breast the ascent, and by myself
Was nothing either seen or heard that checked
Those musings or diverted, save that once
The shepherd's lurcher, who, among the crags,
Had to his joy unearthed a hedgehog, teased
His coiled-up prey with barkings turbulent.
This small adventure, for even such it seemed
In that wild place and at the dead of night,
Being over and forgotten, on we wound

In silence as before.

With forehead bent
Earthward, as if in opposition set
Against an enemy, I panted up
With eager pace, and no less eager thoughts.
Thus might we wear perhaps an hour away,
Ascending at loose distance each from each,
And I, as chanced, the foremost of the band –
When at my feet the ground appeared to brighten,
And with a step or two seemed brighter still;
Nor had I time to ask the cause of this,
For instantly a light upon the turf
Fell like a flash! I looked about, and lo,
The moon stood naked in the heavens at height
Immense above my head, and on the shore
I found myself of a huge sea of mist,
Which meek and silent rested at my feet.
A hundred hills their dusky backs upheaved
All over this still ocean; and beyond,
Far, far beyond, the vapours shot themselves
In headlands, tongues, and promontory shapes,
Into the sea – the real sea, that seemed
To dwindle and give up its majesty,
Usurped upon as far as sight could reach.
Meanwhile, the moon looked down upon this show
In single glory, and we stood, the mist
Touching our very feet. And from the shore
At distance not the third part of a mile
Was a blue chasm, a fracture in the vapour,
A deep and gloomy breathing-place through which
Mounted the roar of waters, torrents, streams
Innumerable, roaring with one voice!
The universal spectacle throughout
Was shaped for admiration and delight,
Grand in itself alone, but in that breach
Through which the homeless voice of waters rose,
That dark deep thoroughfare, had nature lodged
The soul, the imagination of the whole.

In silence as before. With forehead bent
Earthward, as if in opposition set
Against an enemy, I panted up
With eager pace, and no less eager thoughts.
Thus might we wear a midnight hour away,
Ascending at loose distance each from each,
And I, as chanced, the foremost of the band;
When at my feet the ground appeared to brighten,
And with a step or two seemed brighter still;
Nor was time given to ask or learn the cause,
For instantly a light upon the turf
Fell like a flash, and lo! as I looked up,
The Moon hung naked in a firmament
Of azure without cloud, and at my feet
Rested a silent sea of hoary mist.
A hundred hills their dusky backs upheaved
All over this still ocean; and beyond,
Far, far beyond, the solid vapours stretched,
In headlands, tongues, and promontory shapes,
Into the main Atlantic, that appeared
To dwindle, and give up his majesty,
Usurped upon far as the sight could reach.
Not so the ethereal vault; encroachment none
Was there, nor loss; only the inferior stars
Had disappeared, or shed a fainter light
In the clear presence of the full-orbed Moon,
Who, from her sovereign elevation, gazed
Upon the billowy ocean, as it lay
All meek and silent, save that through a rift –
Not distant from the shore whereon we stood,
A fixed, abysmal, gloomy, breathing-place –
Mounted the roar of waters, torrents, streams
Innumerable, roaring with one voice!
Heard over earth and sea, and, in that hour,
For so it seemed, felt by the starry heavens.

A meditation rose in me that night
Upon the lonely mountain when the scene
Had passed away, and it appeared to me
The perfect image of a mighty mind,
Of one that feeds upon infinity,
That is exalted by an underpresence,
The sense of God, or whatsoe'er is dim
Or vast in its own being. Above all,
One function of such mind had nature there
Exhibited by putting forth, and that
With circumstance most awful and sublime:
That domination which she oftentimes
Exerts upon the outward face of things,
So moulds them, and endues, abstracts, combines,
Or by abrupt and unhabitual influence
Does make one object so impress itself
Upon all others, and pervade them so,
That even the grossest minds must see and hear
And cannot choose but feel.

The power which these
Acknowledge when thus moved, which nature thus
Thrusts forth upon the senses, is the express
Resemblance, in the fullness of its strength
Made visible – a genuine counterpart
And brother – of the glorious faculty
Which higher minds bear with them as their own.
This is the very spirit in which they deal
With all the objects of the universe:
They from their native selves can send abroad
Like transformation, for themselves create
A like existence, and, whene'er it is
Created for them, catch it by an instinct.
Them the enduring and the transient both
Serve to exalt. They build up greatest things

When into air had partially dissolved
That vision, given to spirits of the night
And three chance human wanderers, in calm thought
Reflected, it appeared to me the type
Of a majestic intellect, its acts
And its possessions, what it has and craves,
What in itself it is, and would become.
There I beheld the emblem of a mind
That feeds upon infinity, that broods
Over the dark abyss, intent to hear
Its voices issuing forth to silent light
In one continuous stream; a mind sustained
By recognitions of transcendent power,
In sense conducting to ideal form,
In soul of more than mortal privilege.
One function, above all, of such a mind
Had Nature shadowed there, by putting forth,
'Mid circumstances awful and sublime,
That mutual domination which she loves
To exert upon the face of outward things,
So moulded, joined, abstracted, so endowed
With interchangeable supremacy,
That men, least sensitive, see, hear, perceive,
And cannot choose but feel. The power, which all
Acknowledge when thus moved, which Nature thus
To bodily sense exhibits, is the express
Resemblance of that glorious faculty
That higher minds bear with them as their own.
This is the very spirit in which they deal
With the whole compass of the universe:
They from their native selves can send abroad
Kindred mutations; for themselves create
A like existence; and, whene'er it dawns
Created for them, catch it, or are caught
By its inevitable mastery,
Like angels stopped upon the wing by sound
Of harmony from Heaven's remotest spheres.
Them the enduring and the transient both
Serve to exalt; they build up greatest things

From least suggestions, ever on the watch,
Willing to work and to be wrought upon.
They need not extraordinary calls
To rouse them: in a world of life they live,
By sensible impressions not enthralled,
But quickened, roused, and made thereby more fit
To hold communion with the invisible world.
Such minds are truly from the Deity,
For they are powers; and hence the highest bliss
That can be known is theirs – the consciousness
Of whom they are, habitually infused
Through every image and through every thought,
And all impressions. Hence religion, faith,
And endless occupation for the soul,
Whether discursive or intuitive;
Hence sovereignty within and peace at will,
Emotion which best foresight need not fear,
Most worthy then of trust when most intense;
Hence cheerfulness in every act of life;
Hence truth in moral judgements and delight
That fails not in the external universe.

Oh, who is he that has his whole life long
Preserved, enlarged, this freedom in himself? –
For this alone is genuine liberty.

From least suggestions; ever on the watch,
Willing to work and to be wrought upon,
They need not extraordinary calls
To rouse them; in a world of life they live,
By sensible impressions not enthralled,
But by their quickening impulse made more prompt
To hold fit converse with the spiritual world,
And with the generations of mankind
Spread over time, past, present, and to come,
Age after age, till Time shall be no more.
Such minds are truly from the Deity,
For they are Powers; and hence the highest bliss
That flesh can know is theirs – the consciousness
Of Whom they are, habitually infused
Through every image and through every thought,
And all affections by communion raised
From earth to heaven, from human to divine;
Hence endless occupation for the Soul,
Whether discursive or intuitive;
Hence cheerfulness for acts of daily life,
Emotions which best foresight need not fear,
Most worthy then of trust when most intense.
Hence, amid ills that vex and wrongs that crush
Our hearts – if here the words of Holy Writ
May with fit reverence be applied – that peace
Which passeth understanding, that repose
In moral judgments which from this pure source
Must come, or will by man be sought in vain.

Oh! who is he that hath his whole life long
Preserved, enlarged, this freedom in himself?
For this alone is genuine liberty:
Where is the favoured being who hath held
That course unchecked, unerring, and untired,
In one perpetual progress smooth and bright? –
A humbler destiny have we retraced,
And told of lapse and hesitating choice,
And backward wanderings along thorny ways:
Yet – compassed round by mountain solitudes,

Witness, ye solitudes where I received
My earliest visitations, careless then
Of what was given me, and where now I roam
A meditative, oft a suffering, man
And yet I trust with undiminished powers –
Witness, whatever falls my better mind
Revolving with the accidents of life
May have sustained, that howsoe'er misled
I never, in the quest of right and wrong,
Did tamper with myself from private aims;
Nor was in any of my hopes the dupe
Of selfish passions; nor did wilfully
Yield ever to mean cares and low pursuits;
But rather did with jealousy shrink back
From every combination that might aid
The tendency, too potent in itself,
Of habit to enslave the mind – I mean
Oppress it by the laws of vulgar sense
And substitute a universe of death,
The falsest of all worlds, in place of that
Which is divine and true

To fear and love
(To love as first and chief, for there fear ends)
Be this ascribed, to early intercourse
In presence of sublime and lovely forms
With the adverse principles of pain and joy –
Evil as one is rashly named by those
Who know not what they say. From love (for here
Do we begin and end) all grandeur comes,
All truth and beauty – from pervading love –
That gone, we are as dust.

Behold the fields
In balmy springtime full of rising flowers
And happy creatures! See that pair, the lamb
And the lamb's mother, and their tender ways
Shall touch thee to the heart! In some green bower
Rest, and be not alone, but have thou there

Within whose solemn temple I received
My earliest visitations, careless then
Of what was given me; and which now I range,
A meditative, oft a suffering man –
Do I declare – in accents which, from truth
Deriving cheerful confidence, shall blend
Their modulation with these vocal streams –
That, whatsoever falls my better mind,
Revolving with the accidents of life,
May have sustained, that, howsoe'er misled,
Never did I, in quest of right and wrong,
Tamper with conscience from a private aim;
Nor was in any public hope the dupe
Of selfish passions; nor did ever yield
Wilfully to mean cares or low pursuits,
But shrunk with apprehensive jealousy
From every combination which might aid
The tendency, too potent in itself,
Of use and custom to bow down the soul
Under a growing weight of vulgar sense,
And substitute a universe of death
For that which moves with light and life informed,
Actual, divine, and true. To fear and love,
To love as prime and chief, for there fear ends,
Be this ascribed; to early intercourse,
In presence of sublime or beautiful forms,
With the adverse principles of pain and joy –
Evil as one is rashly named by men
Who know not what they speak. By love subsists
All lasting grandeur, by pervading love;
That gone, we are as dust. – Behold the fields
In balmy spring-time full of rising flowers
And joyous creatures; see that pair, the lamb
And the lamb's mother, and their tender ways
Shall touch thee to the heart; thou callest this love,
And not inaptly so, for love it is,
Far as it carries thee. In some green bower
Rest, and be not alone, but have thou there

The one who is thy choice of all the world –
There linger, lulled and lost, and rapt away –
Be happy to thy fill! Thou callest this love
And so it is, but there is higher love
Than this, a love that comes into the heart
With awe and a diffusive sentiment –
Thy love is human merely; this proceeds
More from the brooding soul, and is divine.

This love more intellectual cannot be
Without imagination, which in truth
Is but another name for absolute strength
And clearest insight, amplitude of mind
And reason in her most exalted mood.
This faculty has been the moving soul
Of our long labour: we have traced the stream
From darkness and the very place of birth
In its blind cavern, whence is faintly heard
The sound of waters; followed it to light
And open day, accompanied its course
Among the ways of nature, afterwards
Lost sight of it bewildered and engulfed,
Then given it greeting as it rose once more
With strength, reflecting in its solemn breast
The works of man and face of human life;
And lastly, from its progress have we drawn
The feeling of life endless, the great thought
By which we live, infinity and God.

Imagination having been our theme,
So also has that intellectual love,
For they are each in each, and cannot stand
Dividually. Here must thou be, o man,
Strength to thyself – no helper hast thou here –
Here keepest thou thy individual state.
No other can divide with thee this work,
No secondary hand can intervene

The One who is thy choice of all the world:
There linger, listening, gazing, with delight
Impassioned, but delight how pitiable!
Unless this love by a still higher love
Be hallowed, love that breathes not without awe;
Love that adores, but on the knees of prayer,
By heaven inspired; that frees from chains the soul,
Lifted, in union with the purest, best,
Of earth-born passions, on the wings of praise
Bearing a tribute to the Almighty's Throne.

This spiritual Love acts not nor can exist
Without Imagination, which, in truth,
Is but another name for absolute power
And clearest insight, amplitude of mind,
And Reason in her most exalted mood.
This faculty hath been the feeding source
Of our long labour: we have traced the stream
From the blind cavern whence is faintly heard
Its natal murmur; followed it to light
And open day; accompanied its course
Among the ways of Nature, for a time
Lost sight of it bewildered and engulphed:
Then given it greeting as it rose once more
In strength, reflecting from its placid breast
The works of man and face of human life;
And lastly, from its progress have we drawn
Faith in life endless, the sustaining thought
Of human Being, Eternity, and God.

Imagination having been our theme,
So also hath that intellectual Love,
For they are each in each, and cannot stand
Dividually. – Here must thou be, O Man!
Power to thyself; no Helper hast thou here;
Here keepest thou in singleness thy state:
No other can divide with thee this work:
No secondary hand can intervene

To fashion this ability. 'Tis thine,
The prime and vital principle is thine
In the recesses of thy nature, far
From any reach of outward fellowship,
Else 'tis not thine at all. But joy to him,
Oh, joy to him who here has sown – has laid
Here the foundations of his future years –
For all that friendship, all that love can do,
All that a darling countenance can look
Or dear voice utter, to complete the man,
Perfect him (made imperfect in himself),
All shall be his. And he whose soul has risen
Up to the height of feeling intellect
Shall want no humbler tenderness, his heart
Be tender as a nursing mother's heart;
Of female softness shall his life be full,
Of little loves and delicate desires,
Mild interests and gentlest sympathies.

Child of my parents, sister of my soul,
Elsewhere have strains of gratitude been breathed
To thee for all the early tenderness
Which I from thee imbibed. And true it is
That later seasons owed to thee no less;
For, spite of thy sweet influence and the touch
Of other kindred hands that opened out
The springs of tender thought in infancy,
And spite of all which singly I had watched
Of elegance, and each minuter charm
In nature and in life, still to the last –
Even to the very going-out of youth,
The period which our story now has reached –
I too exclusively esteemed that love,
And sought that beauty, which (as Milton sings)
Has terror in it. Thou didst soften down
This over-sternness; but for thee, sweet friend,
My soul, too reckless of mild grace, had been
Far longer what by nature it was framed –
Longer retained its countenance severe –

To fashion this ability; 'tis thine,
The prime and vital principle is thine
In the recesses of thy nature, far
From any reach of outward fellowship,
Else is not thine at all. But joy to him,
Oh, joy to him who here hath sown, hath laid
Here, the foundation of his future years!
For all that friendship, all that love can do,
All that a darling countenance can look
Or dear voice utter, to complete the man,
Perfect him, made imperfect in himself,
All shall be his: and he whose soul hath risen
Up to the height of feeling intellect
Shall want no humbler tenderness; his heart
Be tender as a nursing mother's heart;
Of female softness shall his life be full,
Of humble cares and delicate desires,
Mild interests and gentlest sympathies.

Child of my parents! Sister of my soul!
Thanks in sincerest verse have been elsewhere
Poured out for all the early tenderness
Which I from thee imbibed: and 'tis most true
That later seasons owed to thee no less;
For, spite of thy sweet influence and the touch
Of kindred hands that opened out the springs
Of genial thought in childhood, and in spite
Of all that unassisted I had marked
In life or nature of those charms minute
That win their way into the heart by stealth
(Still to the very going-out of youth),
I too exclusively esteemed *that* love,
And sought *that* beauty, which, as Milton sings,
Hath terror in it. Thou didst soften down
This over-sternness; but for thee, dear Friend!
My soul, too reckless of mild grace, had stood
In her original self too confident,
Retained too long a countenance severe;

A rock with torrents roaring, with the clouds
Familiar, and a favourite of the stars;
But thou didst plant its crevices with flowers,
Hang it with shrubs that twinkle in the breeze,
And teach the little birds to build their nests
And warble in its chambers. At a time
When nature, destined to remain so long
Foremost in my affections, had fallen back
Into a second place, well pleased to be
A handmaid to a nobler than herself –
When every day brought with it some new sense
Of exquisite regard for common things,
And all the earth was budding with these gifts
Of more refined humanity – thy breath,
Dear sister, was a kind of gentler spring
That went before my steps.

With such a theme,
Coleridge, with this my argument, of thee
Shall I be silent? O most loving soul,
Placed on this earth to love and understand
And from thy presence shed the light of love,
Shall I be mute, ere thou be spoken of?
Thy gentle spirit to my heart of hearts
Did also find its way; and thus the life
Of all things and the mighty unity
In all which we behold, and feel, and are,

A rock with torrents roaring, with the clouds
Familiar, and a favourite of the stars:
But thou didst plant its crevices with flowers,
Hang it with shrubs that twinkle in the breeze,
And teach the little birds to build their nests
And warble in its chambers. At a time
When Nature, destined to remain so long
Foremost in my affections, had fallen back
Into a second place, pleased to become
A handmaid to a nobler than herself,
When every day brought with it some new sense
Of exquisite regard for common things,
And all the earth was budding with these gifts
Of more refined humanity, thy breath,
Dear Sister! was a kind of gentler spring
That went before my steps. Thereafter came
One whom with thee friendship had early paired;
She came, no more a phantom to adorn
A moment, but an inmate of the heart,
And yet a spirit, there for me enshrined
To penetrate the lofty and the low;
Even as one essence of pervading light
Shines, in the brightest of ten thousand stars,
And, the meek worm that feeds her lonely lamp
Couched in the dewy grass.

With such a theme,
Coleridge! with this my argument, of thee
Shall I be silent? O capacious Soul!
Placed on this earth to love and understand,
And from thy presence shed the light of love,
Shall I be mute, ere thou be spoken of?
Thy kindred influence to my heart of hearts
Did also find its way. Thus fear relaxed
Her overweening grasp; thus thoughts and things
In the self-haunting spirit learned to take
More rational proportions; mystery,
The incumbent mystery of sense and soul,
Of life and death, time and eternity,

Admitted more habitually a mild
Interposition, closelier gathering thoughts
Of man and his concerns, such as become
A human creature, be he who he may,
Poet, or destined to an humbler name.
And so the deep enthusiastic joy,
The rapture of the hallelujah sent
From all that breathes and is, was chastened, stemmed
And balanced by a reason which indeed
Is reason, duty and pathetic truth –
And God and man divided, as they ought,
Between them the great system of the world
Where man is sphered, and which God animates.

And now, o friend, this history is brought
To its appointed close. The discipline
And consummation of the poet's mind,
In everything that stood most prominent,
Have faithfully been pictured. We have reached
The time, which was our object from the first,
When we may (not presumptuously, I hope)
Suppose my powers so far confirmed, and such
My knowledge, as to make me capable
Of building up a work that should endure.
Yet much has been omitted, as need was –
Of books how much! – and even of the other wealth
Which is collected among woods and fields,
Far more. For nature's secondary grace,
That outward illustration which is hers,
Has hitherto been barely touched upon:
The charm more superficial, and yet sweet,
Which from her works finds way, contemplated
As they hold forth a genuine counterpart
And softening mirror of the moral world.

Yes, having tracked the main essential power –
Imagination – up her way sublime,
In turn might fancy also be pursued

Admitted more habitually a mild
Interposition – a serene delight
In closelier gathering cares, such as become
A human creature, howsoe'er endowed,
Poet, or destined for a humbler name;
And so the deep enthusiastic joy,
The rapture of the hallelujah sent
From all that breathes and is, was chastened, stemmed
And balanced by pathetic truth, by trust
In hopeful reason, leaning on the stay
Of Providence; and in reverence for duty,
Here, if need be, struggling with storms, and there
Strewing in peace life's humblest ground with herbs,
At every season green, sweet at all hours.

And now, O Friend! this history is brought
To its appointed close: the discipline
And consummation of a Poet's mind,
In everything that stood most prominent,
Have faithfully been pictured; we have reached
The time (our guiding object from the first)
When we may, not presumptuously, I hope,
Suppose my powers so far confirmed, and such
My knowledge as to make me capable
Of building up a Work that shall endure.
Yet much hath been omitted, as need was;
Of books how much! and even of the other wealth
That is collected among woods and fields,
Far more: for Nature's secondary grace
Hath hitherto been barely touched upon,
The charm more superficial that attends
Her works, as they present to Fancy's choice
Apt illustrations of the moral world,
Caught at a glance, or traced with curious pains.

Through all her transmigrations, till she too
Was purified, had learned to ply her craft
By judgement steadied. Then might we return
And in the rivers and the groves behold
Another face, might hear them from all sides
Calling upon the more instructed mind
To link their images – with subtle skill
Sometimes, and by elaborate research –
With forms and definite appearances
Of human life, presenting them sometimes
To the involuntary sympathy
Of our internal being, satisfied
And soothed with a conception of delight
Where meditation cannot come, which thought
Could never heighten.

Above all, how much
Still nearer to ourselves we overlook
In human nature and that marvellous world
As studied first in my own heart, and then
In life among the passions of mankind
And qualities commixed and modified
By the infinite varieties and shades
Of individual character. Herein
It was for me (this justice bids me say)
No useless preparation to have been
The pupil of a public school, and forced
In hardy independence to stand up
Among conflicting passions and the shock
Of various tempers – to endure and note
What was not understood, though known to be –
Among the mysteries of love and hate,
Honour and shame, looking to right and left,
Unchecked by innocence too delicate
And moral notions too intolerant,
Sympathies too contracted. Hence, when called
To take a station among men, the step
Was easier, the transition more secure,
More profitable also; for the mind

Finally, and above all, O Friend! (I speak
With due regret) how much is overlooked
In human nature and her subtle ways,
As studied first in our own hearts, and then
In life among the passions of mankind,
Varying their composition and their hue,
Where'er we move, under the diverse shapes
That individual character presents
To an attentive eye. For progress meet,
Along this intricate and difficult path,
Whate'er was wanting, something had I gained,
As one of many schoolfellows compelled,
In hardy independence, to stand up
Amid conflicting interests, and the shock
Of various tempers; to endure and note
What was not understood, though known to be;
Among the mysteries of love and hate,
Honour and shame, looking to right and left,
Unchecked by innocence too delicate,
And moral notions too intolerant,
Sympathies too contracted. Hence, when called
To take a station among men, the step
Was easier, the transition more secure,

Learns from such timely exercise to keep
In wholesome separation the two natures:
The one that feels, the other that observes.

Let one word more of personal circumstance –
Not needless, as it seems – be added here.
Since I withdrew unwillingly from France
The story has demanded less regard
To time and place; and where I lived, and how,
Has been no longer scrupulously marked.
Three years, until a permanent abode
Received me with that sister of my heart
Who ought by rights the dearest to have been
Conspicuous through this biographic verse –
Star seldom utterly concealed from view –
I led an undomestic wanderer's life.
In London chiefly was my home, and thence
Excursively, as personal friendships, chance
Or inclination led, or slender means
Gave leave, I roamed about from place to place,
Tarrying in pleasant nooks, wherever found,
Through England or through Wales. A youth – he bore
The name of Calvert; it shall live if words
Of mine can give it life – without respect
To prejudice or custom, having hope
That I had some endowments by which good
Might be promoted, in his last decay
From his own family withdrawing part
Of no redundant patrimony, did
By a bequest sufficient for my needs
Enable me to pause for choice, and walk
At large and unrestrained, nor damped too soon
By mortal cares. Himself no poet, yet
Far less a common spirit of the world,
He deemed that my pursuits and labours lay
Apart from all that leads to wealth – or even
Perhaps to necessary maintenance,
Without some hazard to the finer sense –

More profitable also; for, the mind
Learns from such timely exercise to keep
In wholesome separation the two natures,
The one that feels, the other that observes.

Yet one word more of personal concern –
Since I withdrew unwillingly from France,
I led an undomestic wanderer's life,
In London chiefly harboured, whence I roamed,
Tarrying at will in many a pleasant spot
Of rural England's cultivated vales
Or Cambrian solitudes. A youth – (he bore
The name of Calvert – it shall live, if words
Of mine can give it life,) in firm belief
That by endowments not from me withheld
Good might be furthered – in his last decay
By a bequest sufficient for my needs
Enabled me to pause for choice, and walk
At large and unrestrained, nor damped too soon
By mortal cares. Himself no Poet, yet
Far less a common follower of the world,
He deemed that my pursuits and labours lay
Apart from all that leads to wealth, or even
A necessary maintenance insures,
Without some hazard to the finer sense;

He cleared a passage for me, and the stream
Flowed in the bent of nature.

Having now
Told what best merits mention, further pains
Our present labour seems not to require,
And I have other tasks. Call back to mind
The mood in which this poem was begun,
O friend – the termination of my course
Is nearer now, much nearer, yet even then
In that distraction and intense desire
I said unto the life which I had lived
'Where art thou? Hear I not a voice from thee
Which 'tis reproach to hear?' Anon I rose
As if on wings, and saw beneath me stretched
Vast prospect of the world which I had been
And was; and hence this song, which like a lark
I have protracted, in the unwearied heavens
Singing, and often with more plaintive voice
Attempered to the sorrows of the earth –
Yet centring all in love, and in the end
All gratulant if rightly understood.

Whether to me shall be allotted life,
And with life power to accomplish aught of worth
Sufficient to excuse me in men's sight
For having given this record of myself,
Is all uncertain. But, belovèd friend,
When looking back thou seest, in clearer view
Than any sweetest sight of yesterday,
That summer when on Quantock's grassy hills
Far ranging, and among the sylvan combs,
Thou in delicious words, with happy heart,
Didst speak the vision of that ancient man,
The bright-eyed Mariner, and rueful woes
Didst utter of the Lady Christabel,
And I, associate with such labour, walked

He cleared a passage for me, and the stream
Flowed in the bent of Nature.

Having now
Told what best merits mention, further pains
Our present purpose seems not to require,
And I have other tasks. Recall to mind
The mood in which this labour was begun,
O Friend! The termination of my course
Is nearer now, much nearer; yet even then,
In that distraction and intense desire,
I said unto the life which I had lived,
Where art thou? Hear I not a voice from thee
Which 'tis reproach to hear? Anon I rose
As if on wings, and saw beneath me stretched
Vast prospect of the world which I had been
And was; and hence this Song, which like a lark
I have protracted, in the unwearied heavens
Singing, and often with more plaintive voice
To earth attempered and her deep-drawn sighs,
Yet centring all in love, and in the end
All gratulant, if rightly understood.

Whether to me shall be allotted life,
And, with life, power to accomplish aught of worth,
That will be deemed no insufficient plea
For having given the story of myself,
Is all uncertain: but, beloved Friend!
When, looking back, thou seest, in clearer view
Than any liveliest sight of yesterday,
That summer, under whose indulgent skies,
Upon smooth Quantock's airy ridge we roved
Unchecked, or loitered 'mid her sylvan combs,
Thou in bewitching words, with happy heart,
Didst chaunt the vision of that Ancient Man,
The bright-eyed Mariner, and rueful woes
Didst utter of the Lady Christabel;
And I, associate with such labour, steeped
In soft forgetfulness the livelong hours,

Murmuring of him who (joyous hap!) was found
After the perils of his moonlight ride
Near the loud waterfall, or her who sat
In misery near the miserable thorn –
When thou dost to that summer turn thy thoughts
And hast before thee all which then we were,
To thee, in memory of that happiness,
It will be known – by thee at least, my friend,
Felt – that the history of a poet's mind
Is labour not unworthy of regard:
To thee the work shall justify itself.

The last and later portions of this gift
Which I for thee design have been prepared
In times which have from those wherein we first
Together wantoned in wild poesy
Differed thus far, that they have been, my friend,
Times of much sorrow, of a private grief
Keen and enduring, which the frame of mind
That in this meditative history
Has been described, more deeply makes me feel –
Yet likewise has enabled me to bear
More firmly – and a comfort now, a hope,
One of the dearest which this life can give,
Is mine: that thou art near, and wilt be soon
Restored to us in renovated health,
When (after the first mingling of our tears)
'Mong other consolations we may find
Some pleasure from this offering of my love.

Oh, yet a few short years of useful life,
And all will be complete, thy race be run,
Thy monument of glory will be raised!
Then, though (too weak to tread the ways of truth)
This age fall back to old idolatry,
Though men return to servitude as fast
As the tide ebbs, to ignominy and shame
By nations sink together, we shall still
Find solace in the knowledge which we have,

Murmuring of him who, joyous hap, was found,
After the perils of his moonlight ride,
Near the loud waterfall; or her who sate
In misery near the miserable Thorn;
When thou dost to that summer turn thy thoughts,
And hast before thee all which then we were,
To thee, in memory of that happiness,
It will be known, by thee at least, my Friend!
Felt, that the history of a Poet's mind
Is labour not unworthy of regard:
To thee the work shall justify itself.

The last and later portions of this gift
Have been prepared, not with the buoyant spirits
That were our daily portion when we first
Together wantoned in wild Poesy,
But, under pressure of a private grief,
Keen and enduring, which the mind and heart,
That in this meditative history
Have been laid open, needs must make me feel
More deeply, yet enable me to bear
More firmly; and a comfort now hath risen
From hope that thou art near, and wilt be soon
Restored to us in renovated health;
When, after the first mingling of our tears,
'Mong other consolations, we may draw
Some pleasure from this offering of my love.

Oh! yet a few short years of useful life,
And all will be complete, thy race be run.
Thy monument of glory will be raised;
Then, though (too weak to tread the ways of truth)
This age fall back to old idolatry,
Though men return to servitude as fast
As the tide ebbs, to ignominy and shame
By nations sink together, we shall still
Find solace – knowing what we have learnt to know,

Blest with true happiness if we may be
United helpers forward of a day
Of firmer trust, joint labourers in a work –
Should Providence such grace to us vouchsafe –
Of their redemption, surely yet to come.
Prophets of nature, we to them will speak
A lasting inspiration, sanctified
By reason and by truth. What we have loved
Others will love, and we may teach them how –
Instruct them how the mind of man becomes
A thousand times more beautiful than the earth
On which he dwells, above this frame of things
(Which, mid all revolutions in the hopes
And fears of men, does still remain unchanged)
In beauty exalted, as it is itself
Of substance and of fabric more divine.

Rich in true happiness if allowed to be
Faithful alike in forwarding a day
Of firmer trust, joint labourers in the work
(Should Providence such grace to us vouchsafe)
Of their deliverance, surely yet to come.
Prophets of Nature, we to them will speak
A lasting inspiration, sanctified
By reason, blest by faith: what we have loved,
Others will love, and we will teach them how;
Instruct them how the mind of man becomes
A thousand times more beautiful than the earth
On which he dwells, above this frame of things
(Which, 'mid all revolution in the hopes
And fears of men, doth still remain unchanged)
In beauty exalted, as it is itself
Of quality and fabric more divine.

Notes

NOTES

WAS IT FOR THIS

1–29 The starting-point of *The Prelude* (see Introduction and *1799* I 1n., below). Wordsworth's urgent questions imply a sense of inadequacy, yet reveal at once that childhood has provided him with underlying sources of strength. Revised to form *1799* I 1–26|*1805* I 271–304.

16–19 *Was it for this . . . unrememberable being:* Lines with no counterpart in *1799*, which show Wordsworth distancing himself from the fashion for nostalgic poetry associated with Charlotte Smith, William Lisle Bowles and the early Coleridge.

30–46 First written of the great childhood episodes of *The Prelude*, yet showing, as the boy hangs alone on the cliff-face in the presence of the sublime forces of nature, a complete sureness of touch. Revised to form *1799* I 50–66|*1805* I 333–50.

47–58 Already in this first seemingly unmeditated draft, Wordsworth perceives his theme to be education through the 'eternal things' of nature, which 'sanctify' by their presence the pains and fears of childhood, creating in the process adult security and strength. Preserved almost verbatim as *1799* I 130–41, then heavily revised to form *1805* I 428–41 ('Wisdom and spirit of the universe').

59–75 Lines that present for the first time the central associationist doctrine of *The Prelude*, a way of thinking that comes to seem essentially Wordsworthian, but depends upon Coleridge's reworking of David Hartley (*Observations on Man*, 1749, reissued 1791). Strongly felt, though in themselves unimportant, emotions, coming to be associated with particular landscapes, create for the child a vital imaginative relationship with the natural world. Shortened to form *1799* I 186–98|*1805* I 490–501.

76–97 The woodcock-snaring episode is placed before the bird's-nesting (ll. 30–46, above) in *1799* and later versions of *The Prelude.* Revised to form *1799* I 27–49|*1805* I 309–32.

98–123 Wordsworth's earliest myth of origins, anticipating in important ways both the Infant Babe passage of *1799* (II 267–301) and the pre-existent child of *Intimations*, whose 'birth is but a sleep and a forgetting'. Shortened and revised in *1799* I 375–90|*1805* I 571–85 so as to exclude reference to the Platonic 'eternal spirit' of ll. 104–9.

98–9 *Nor while . . . The mazes of this argument:* Wordsworth at this point in *MS JJ* counts the lines he has written, and makes a fresh start, his sense of purpose marked by the earliest *Prelude* allusions to Milton. By implication Wordsworth too has a 'great argument', his poetry too is 'epic'. Though divesting himself of the Christian panoply of *Paradise Lost*, he too will 'assert eternal providence' (*PL* I 25). Bringing this theme up to date in his account of human consciousness and the education of the mind through nature, Wordsworth makes a further significant allusion. His argument may seem to wander, may seem to have its 'mazes', but he is in control, unlike the fallen angels of *Paradise Lost*, debating theological issues 'in wandering mazes lost' (*PL* II 561).

124–45 Wordsworth's definition of innocent vision – the child's holding of 'unconscious intercourse|With the eternal beauty' – consists of responding to the natural scene with a mind that has no standards of judgment, makes no sophisticated comparisons. Preserved almost verbatim as *1799* I 391–412, then revised to form *1805* I 586–608.

146–50 Lines, not present in later versions, that round off this early *Prelude* draft, giving it the sense of being a completed poem.

THE TWO-PART *PRELUDE* OF 1799

First Part

1–26 *Was it for this . . . thunder-shower:* Like the original *Prelude* draft, *Was It For This*, the two-part version of 1799 begins in unexplained self-reproach. 'This' in ll. 1, 6 and 17 sets up a contrast between Wordsworth's present inactivity (especially his failure to write the philosophical *Recluse*, planned with Coleridge seven months before, in March 1798) and his sense of having been singled out for his vocation as poet by a specially favoured childhood:

> For a time Wordsworth seems to have intended to compose some introductory lines that would explain what it was that 'this' referred to, but to have done so would have spoiled the impact of a rhetorical pattern which had been used in succession by Milton (*Samson Agonistes* 361–3), Pope (1717 *Rape of the Lock* IV 97–102) and Thomson (1746 *Seasons* III 1101–5) . . . Milton's lines are especially important. Manoah, shocked at the condition of his son, 'Eyeless in Gaza at the mill with slaves', reproaches God because it appears no longer possible that Samson can fulfil his appointed task:
>
> For this did the angel twice descend? for this
> Ordained thy nurture holy, as of a plant;
> Select and sacred . . .
>
> Like Samson, with whom Milton of course identifies, Wordsworth has a mission – the writing of the prophetic and redemptive *Recluse* – and he too is failing to fulfil it, despite a childhood in which nurse and Nature had combined to create a 'nurture holy, as of a plant;|Select and sacred'. (*BV* 36–7)

6 *That flowed along:* to intertwine (*WIFT* 6).

7 *Derwent:* The River Derwent runs along a terrace at the foot of the garden of Wordsworth's father's house at Cockermouth.

8 '*sweet birthplace*': A quotation from Coleridge's *Frost at Midnight* of February 1798: 'already had I dreamt|Of my sweet birthplace' (ll. 32–3). Wordsworth, who had written *Tintern Abbey* in July as a companion-piece

to *Frost at Midnight*, seems to have regarded *The Prelude* from the first as the 'Poem to Coleridge' (see Introduction).

14 *earnest:* foretaste, pledge.

16 *Beloved Derwent . . . streams:* Single-line replacement of *WIFT* 16–19.

18 *A naked boy among:* A new detail: 'Beneath thy scars and in' (*WIFT* 21).

19 *Made one long bathing of a summer's day:* A playful allusion to Mulciber's fall from Heaven in *Paradise Lost*: 'from morn|To noon he fell, from noon to dewy eve,|A summer's day' (I 742–4).

21 *coursed:* raced.

22–3 *and dashed the flowers . . . groundsel:* The boy's aggression is for Wordsworth part of a natural and happy childhood.

23 *groundsel:* ragwort (growing two to three feet high on waste ground, with large heads made up of many small yellow daisy-like flowers).

24 *distant Skiddaw's lofty height:* 'all the distant mountains' (*WIFT* 27); standing 3,000 feet above Keswick, Skiddaw is plainly visible nine miles away at Cockermouth.

27–49 Wordsworth has switched the order of his first two childhood episodes, the woodcock-snaring (*WIFT* 76–97) being placed before the bird's-nesting (*WIFT* 30–46).

29 *snapped:* nipped (*WIFT* 77).

34 *springes:* snares; cf. Polonius, 'Ay, springes to catch woodcocks' (*Hamlet* I iii 115) and Thomas Pennant's *Tour of Scotland* (1790) 32 (pointed out, Mary Moorman, *The Early Years* 33): 'Saw on the plain part of these hills numbers of springes for woodcocks, laid between tufts of heath, with avenues of small stones on each side, to direct these foolish birds into the snares, for they will not hop over the pebbles.' Pennant makes clear that the birds were sold at a considerable price, and sent by coach to London.

35 *Gentle powers:* spirits that preside over the child's education; see 68–8n., below.

42 *expectation:* 'hope and fear' (*WIFT* 90).

44 *toils:* labours (also, appropriately, 'trap' or 'snare').

50 *Nor less:* For this *WIFT* 30. Wordsworth's opening question is repeated four times in his original draft, only twice in *1799* and later *Prelude* versions.

55–8 *Though mean . . . raven's nest:* Ravens, largest members of the crow family, are a danger to lambs on Cumbrian hill-farms; Wordsworth's 'inglorious' intention ('view') was to claim a reward paid by the parish for destruction of a nest. To judge from *Wordsworth's Hawkshead* 211–15, he was probably roped, and let down the cliff-face by other boys from the Grammar School.

62 *Shouldering:* Against *WIFT* 42. Both wind and boy 'shoulder' the crag in *1799*.

68–80 *I believe . . . More palpable:* The neo-classical spirit-world that Wordsworth invokes in *1799* Part I comes as a surprise after the single pervading life-force of *Tintern Abbey* and the Platonic world soul of *Was It For This*. In place of a committed pantheist sharing in the life of things, we have polytheism that carries no conviction. But guardian-spirits are common in the eighteenth century, from the sylphs of *The Rape of the Lock* to the Polar Spirit of *The Ancient Mariner*. They enable Wordsworth to express his sense of having been 'Fostered alike by beauty and by fear' (*1805* I 306), without naming too solemnly the power that has singled him out.

76 *With me, though, rarely in my early days:* Last four words pencilled in in *MS V*, lacking in *MS U.* In transcribing *V* Dorothy places commas round 'though rarely' ('With me, though rarely, [in my early days]|They communed'). But the phrasing is awkward, and the implication more so. It is hard to believe that Wordsworth intended to weaken the emphatic claim of l. 80 ('and of their school was I') by stating that gentle powers did indeed commune with him.

81–129 The boat-stealing episode follows *Was It For This* in *MS JJ*, and was probably written within a matter of days.

84 *its usual home 1805:* shows the episode to have taken place on Ullswater, when Wordsworth was travelling between his school at Hawkshead and his grandparents' home at Penrith. For Wordsworth's attempt to work up the experience c. 1788 (in the form of a simile about a shepherd rowing by moonlight), see Carol Landon, 'Sidelights on *The Prelude*', *Bicentenary Studies* 359–62.

89 *Just like a man . . . Though bent on speed:* Wordsworth uses a stilted iambic rhythm to evoke the movement of his boat as it heaves stroke by stroke through the water (recollecting as he does so *PL* XII 1–2, 'As one who . . . bates at noon,|Though bent on speed').

95–6 *one track . . . sparkling light:* Maxwell points to a link with the water-snakes of *The Ancient Mariner*, with their 'tracks of shining white' (l. 266).

100 *that same craggy ridge:* Probably Stybarrow Crag.

109 *instinct:* imbued; if the 'craggy ridge' of l. 100 is Stybarrow, the 'huge cliff' that emerges as the boy rows out from the shore is Black Crag.

124 *blank desertion:* As the avenging mountain-forms invade his mind, the boy is 'deserted' by visual reassurance, mental pictures of day-to-day existence.

130–41 *WIFT* 47–58.

135 *vulgar works of man:* common man-made objects.

143 *stinted:* grudged, partial.

150–85 Sent to Coleridge by Dorothy, 14–21 December 1798, as 'from a description of William's boyish pleasures'.

156–7 *All shod . . . ice:* As Maxwell points out, a reminiscence of Erasmus Darwin's *Botanic Garden* (1791) I iii 570, 'Hang o'er the sliding steel, and hiss along the ice'.

173 *shadow:* reflection (often, at this period, in colour).

182 *her diurnal round:* Cf. Lucy, 'Rolled round in earth's diurnal course|With rocks and stones and trees' (*A Slumber Did My Spirit Seal* 7–8). Both passages are related to Milton, *PL* VII 22, 'Within the visible diurnal sphere', and both written c. November 1798.

183 *train:* succession.

186–98 The central statement from *Was It For This* about the poet's education through nature, originally reading straight on from 'A grandeur in the beatings of the heart' (l. 141 above).

186–9 *Ye powers . . . standing pools:* A case in which Wordsworth's tutelary spirits derive, not from classical or neo-classical literature, but from Shakespeare: Prospero, *Tempest* V i 33, 'Ye elves of hills, brooks, standing lakes and groves'.

194 *Impressed:* stamped, printed; *characters:* marks, letters, signs.

198 *Work:* seethe; see Cowper, *Task* VI 737–8, 'this tempestuous state of human things|Is merely as the workings of a sea'.

198–233 Wordsworth's 'home amusements' section is inserted after Part I has been completed in draft, to make the point that his childhood had its more ordinary, gregarious, side.

210 *With crosses . . . o'er:* noughts and crosses (American tick-tack-toe); Wordsworth has in mind *PL* VIII 83, 'With centric and eccentric scribbled o'er', where man is being mocked for attempting to map the heavens.

215 *loo:* eighteenth-century card game; mentioned in *The Rape of the Lock*, which Wordsworth is imitating in this mock-heroic section, alongside Cowper's *Task* (also dependent on Pope, but distinct in its satirical voice).

225–7 *Meanwhile abroad . . . keen and silent tooth:* Based on Cowper's *Winter Evening* – 'how the frost|Raging abroad, and the rough wind, endear|The silence and the warmth enjoyed within' (*Task* IV 308–10) – but with more obvious reference to Amiens' song in *As You Like It* II vii: 'Blow, blow, thou winter wind . . . thy tooth is not so keen|As man's ingratitude.'

232 *yellings:* Used at this period of noises made by animals (and objects) as well as human beings.

233 *Bothnic main:* the northern Baltic.

236 *milk-white clusters:* hazel-nuts; a reference to *Nutting*, published as a separate poem in *Lyrical Ballads* 1800, but according to Wordsworth first written for *The Prelude.*

258–374 The 'spots of time' sequence, written c. January 1799, is here seen in its original form and original position. In later *Prelude* texts it is elaborated and dispersed, *1799* I 258–79 becoming *1805* V 450–81, and I 288–374 being revised to form *1805* XI 257–388. The link-passage I 279–87 belongs only to *1799.*

258–9 *Ere I . . . Eight summers:* Though Wordsworth claims to have been seven, he had in fact been sent to Hawkshead Grammar School in May 1779 aged nine.

267–70 *I saw . . . bathing:* Records show that Joseph Jackson, schoolmaster of Sawrey at the far end of Esthwaite Water, was drowned while bathing on 18 June 1779. So much, at least, is fact.

279–82 *I might . . . disasters Othello:* I iii 134–5, 'Wherein I spoke of most disastrous chances|Of moving accidents by flood and field'.

287 *archetypes* originals (the permanent forms of nature). Distresses and disasters of the past have stamped on the memory visual images of the countryside where they occurred. These attain within the mind an emotional permanence comparable to that of the natural forms themselves.

290 *fructifying virtue:* the power (Latin *virtus*) to make fruitful, creative.

290–4 *whence, depressed . . . invisibly repaired:* Six months after the writing of *Tintern Abbey* (July 1798) Wordsworth, it appears, is still subject to 'the heavy and the weary weight|Of all this unintelligible world' (*TA* 40–1). The burden now is lightened, however, not by a pantheist seeing 'into the life of things', but by a secular imaginative process, in which the mind – always the agent of its own recovery – is entirely self-nourished, and self-restored.

301–3 *I mounted, and we rode . . . guide:* Lines that catch the five-year-old's sense of pleasure and importance. 'Honest James', fellow horseman in the child's fantasy, was his grandparents' servant at Penrith.

308 *a bottom . . . hung|In irons:* If we assume that the child did stumble on the site of a gibbet, the valley-bottom was Cowdrake Quarry east of Penrith, where Thomas Nicholson had been hanged in 1767 for murdering a local butcher. *The Prelude* is not a record of fact, however; Nicholson's gibbet was still standing (and tenanted) in 1775, and the five-year-old would not have ridden that far. Wordsworth is creating a composite experience, and has chiefly in mind the rotted seventeenth-century gibbet of Thomas Lancaster (who was 'the murderer of his wife') in the meadows at Hawkshead, which we know was an object of terror for him during his schooldays.

312–13 *Only a long green ridge . . . grave:* Wordsworth's language is delicately ambiguous, 'remained' implying that this was the place of execution, whereas 'like a grave' draws attention to the unreliability of the evidence – there are many such long green ridges on the moor. The child knows that a murderer has been hanged in the vicinity; we enter his terrified imagination as he stumbles upon what seems to him the spot.

316 *The beacon . . . summit:* the tall conical stone signal-beacon, built on the hill above Penrith after the Jacobite risings of 1715 and 1719 to give warning of future Scottish invasions. Fires lit on the upper platform were visible twenty miles to the south.

317 *A girl who bore a pitcher on her head:* a cottage-woman fetching water from a stream in the valley – at the time (as Wordsworth says) 'an ordinary sight'.

322 *visionary dreariness:* desolation so extreme as to have a spiritual quality; readers would recollect 'The dismal situation waste and wild' of Milton's hell, where there was 'No light, but rather darkness visible' (*PL* I 60, 63).

324–6 *the naked pool,|The beacon . . . The woman:* 'I have been struck with the important truth', De Quincey (who had read the 1805 *Prelude* in MS) writes in *Suspiria De Profundis*,

> that far more of our deepest thoughts and feelings pass to us through perplexed combinations of concrete objects, pass to us as *involutes* (if I may coin that word) in compound experiences incapable of being disentangled, than ever reach us directly and in their own abstract shapes. (Ward 130)

Note also the pattern of 'involutes' (concrete objects with which the emotions have become involved, or associated, and which thus recall the original feelings) in ll. 341–5, 363–4 below.

329 *a kindred power:* the 'fructifying virtue' of l. 290 above.

331 *The day before the holidays began:* Probably 19 December 1783; the poet was thirteen.

335 *My brothers and myself:* Two of Wordsworth's three brothers were also at Hawkshead Grammar School in 1783: Richard (later a pernickety lawyer), aged fifteen, and John (later the sea-captain), aged just ten. Christopher (later Master of Trinity, Cambridge) joined them in 1785.

335–40 *There was a crag . . . choice uncertain:* Wordsworth is waiting above Hawkshead, and to the north. The horses, sent by his father in Cockermouth, have to go round the central mountains of the Lake District, and may either have come south along the coast, cutting across to Hawkshead via Hardnott and Wrynose Passes, or gone east to Keswick and south via Grasmere and Ambleside.

346 *Those two companions:* Note the touch of humour as Wordsworth draws attention to the non-human 'involutes' (324–6n. above) with which he formed a relationship as he waited. The hawthorn is present in the *Vale of Esthwaite* account (quoted 353–5n.), the 'single sheep' is a narrowing down of the 'poor flocks . . . sad-drooping', and the 'naked wall' replaces 'yon naked rock'.

351 *A dweller in my father's house:* A phrase notable for its biblical ring and for its impersonality. Wordsworth had been born in the house, and spent his childhood there, but the reference hardly makes it sound like home.

352 *orphans then:* The poet's mother had died in March 1778, just before his eighth birthday. His father died on 30 December 1783.

353–5 *The event . . . appeared|A chastisement:* The child feels that he is being punished for looking forward too eagerly to the Christmas holidays – in effect, that he has killed his father. An interesting gloss is put on the child's remorse by a version of the episode written for *The Vale of Esthwaite*, 1786–7, while Wordsworth was still at Hawkshead Grammar School:

> No spot but claims the tender tear,
> By joy or grief to memory dear:
> One evening when the wintry blast
> Through the sharp hawthorn whistling passed
> And the poor flocks, all pinched with cold,
> Sad-drooping sought the mountain-fold,
> Long, long upon yon naked rock
> Alone I bore the bitter shock –
> Long, long my swimming eyes did roam
> For little horse to bear me home,
> To bear me (what avails the tear?)
> To sorrow o'er a father's bier.
> Flow on! In vain thou hast not flowed,
> But eased me of a heavy load;
> For much it gives my heart relief
> To pay the mighty debt of grief.
> With sighs repeated o'er and o'er
> I mourn because I mourned no more! (Oxford I 279–80)

NB The 'bitter shock' of l. 8 is a reference to the weather, not (as some have supposed) the child's bereavement.

358–60 *With trite reflections . . . corrected my desires:* Wordsworth's emphasis on 'trite reflections' ('Put not your trust in the things of this world', and the like) tells us how to read God's 'correction' of the boy's desires. Cowper remarks, *Task* V 875–6, on our practice of 'inventing to ourselves|Gods such as guilt makes welcome'.

367 *indisputable shapes:* As De Selincourt points out, an echo (probably unconscious) of Hamlet's response to the appearance of his dead father on the

battlements at Elsinore: 'Thou comest in such a questionable shape|That I will speak with thee' (I iv 43–4). See *BV* 63–5 (quoted *1805* XI 379–81n.) for discussion of underlying implication, here, and in the deliberate *Hamlet* allusion at *Intimations* 149–50: 'High instincts before which our mortal nature|Did tremble like a guilty thing surprised'. 'Indisputable' is stressed on the second and fourth syllables.

370 *fountain:* stream or well; cf. *Intimations* 153–5, where the 'first affections' and 'shadowy recollections' of childhood,

> be they what they may,
> Are yet the fountain-light of all our day,
> Are yet the master-light of all our seeing . . .

373–4 *unknown to me . . . are brought:* 'Spots of time' shape the adult mind through the powers of association, though it remains unconscious of their workings.

375–90 A cut-down form of *WIFT* 98–123, Wordsworth's earliest discussion of the origins of adult consciousness. It is significant that having (at different stages) inserted the boat-stealing and skating episodes, the 'home amusements' section and the 'spots of time' sequence, he should be returning to the structure of his original draft. Though he is now unwilling to invoke an 'eternal spirit' who is 'the soul|Of our first sympathies' (ll. 108–90), *Was It For This* continues to determine the pattern of his thinking.

375 *sedulous:* anxious; Milton, *PL* IX 27–9, 'Not sedulous by nature to indite| Wars, hitherto the only argument|Heroic deemed'.

376 *collateral:* indirect, sideways, peripheral.

377 *extrinsic passion:* feelings unrelated to the natural scenes that were to have a permanent effect on the poet's mind.

383 *hallowed and pure motions of the sense:* Wordsworth (as Maxwell was first to point out) seems to be 'recalling, and reversing' the implications of *Measure for Measure* I iv 59, 'The wanton stings and motions of the sense'.

385 *intellectual:* spiritual; as in Shelley's Platonist *Hymn to Intellectual Beauty.*

391–412 *WIFT* 124–45.

395 *the eternal beauty:* A Platonist concept, surviving from *Was It For This*, and suggesting the underlying continuity of Wordsworth's thinking. Often it seems in revision that he has decided to be less outspoken, but only the terminology has changed.

396 *organic:* sensuous.

405–6 *linking . . . associated forms:* enjoying the view in and for itself, not by association with earlier experience or with landscape painting.

413 *vulgar:* ordinary, unremarkable.

430–1 *in their substantial . . . brain:* The process of storing up visual images had been described in similarly physical terms at *Pedlar* 32–4: 'on his mind| They lay like substances, and almost seemed|To haunt the bodily sense'.

433 *the impressive agency of fear:* the power of fear to stamp 'impressions' on the memory.

441 *invisible links:* links of association within the mind. As at *WIFT* 59–75, Wordsworth is thinking in terms that go back, via Coleridge, to Hartley's *Observations on Man.* Coleridge regarded Hartley as providing the theologi-

cal basis of Unitarianism, Wordsworth valued him for his account of the workings of the mind.

442 *affections:* emotions.

445–6 *ere the birth . . . snows:* attributing 'flowers' of memory to a period for which in truth the memory is blank; cf. *1850* I 615–16.

447–8 *my friend's so prompt|In sympathy:* The first clear indication that *The Prelude* is being addressed to Coleridge.

449 *With fond and feeble tongue a tedious tale:* A touch of humour that Coleridge would appreciate.

451 *Reproaches from my former years:* Wordsworth's thoughts go back to the mood of self-reproach in which Part I (and *Was It For This*) had opened. Both the happiness and the imaginative power experienced in his 'former years' convict him of the failure to make use of his talent.

453 *honourable toil:* Wordsworth at this stage (February 1799) expected to go straight ahead with *The Recluse*, rather than extending his autobiography.

461 *visionary things:* things seen in the imagination, with the inward eye.

Second Part

1 *Thus far, my friend:* Wordsworth, having completed a version of Part I by the time he and Dorothy left Goslar on 23 February 1799, begins work on Part II c. September, finishing it before the move to Dove Cottage, Grasmere, in mid-December. *MS 18A* preserves an attempt on Part II made in the spring that shows the extent to which Wordsworth depended on Coleridge's approval of his work:

> Friend of my heart and genius, I had reached
> A small green island which I was well pleased
> To pass not lightly by, for though I felt
> Strength unabated, yet I seemed to need
> Thy cheering voice or ere I could pursue
> My voyage, resting else for ever there.

5 *nourishment that came unsought:* Wordsworth's theme in Part I has been the child's unconscious response to the workings of nature upon his imagination. Part II will show how nature in adolescence comes to be 'sought|For her own sake'.

6–7 *From week . . . tumult:* The phase of childhood summed up in *TA* 74–5 as 'The coarser pleasures of my boyish days,|And their glad animal movements'.

16 *a beating mind:* A transferred epithet (it is the heart that beats, not the mind), characteristic of Wordsworth, but deriving in this instance from Shakespeare: Prospero, 'a turn or two I'll walk|To still my beating mind' (*Tempest* IV i 162–3).

18 *And needs:* Read: 'and yet needs'. *monitory voice:* warning, admonishment. Memories of the spontaneous joys of youth show how paltry are the achievements of adulthood.

26 *my corporeal frame:* body; 'this corporeal frame', *TA* 44.

28 *self-presence:* actuality, immediacy (associated with the continuing imaginative 'presence' of the poet's former 'self').

33 *our small market-village:* Hawkshead.

37 *smart assembly-room:* Hawkshead Town Hall, built in 1790, and covered with gravel stucco ('rough-cast') and white-wash. For Wordsworth's consistent dislike of the obtrusiveness of white buildings, see *Guide to the Lakes.*

44 *huckster:* stall-keeper.

50 *collaterally attached:* taken into account for the additional pleasure they could give to the boys' activities.

52 *less grateful else:* otherwise less enjoyable.

55 *plain of Windermere:* level surface of the lake.

56 *bourne:* destination; cf. *Hamlet* III i 79–80, 'That undiscovered country, from whose bourne|No traveller returns'.

58–60 *a sister isle . . . lilies-of-the-valley:* Naming the islands that form the 'archipelago' of Windermere, West notes, '*Grass Holm* is at present shaded with a grove of oaks. And two smaller islets borrow their names from the lilies-of-the-valley which decorate them' (*Guide* 56–7). *umbrageous covert:* shady canopy.

61–3 *a third small island . . . hermit's history: 'Lady Holm*, where in ancient times stood an oratory, is an isle of an oval form, vested with coppice wood' (West, *Guide* 56). *1850* replaces the Gothic details of the 'old stone table', 'mouldered cave' and contemplative hermit (cf. *Tintern Abbey*), with an accurate reference to 'ruins of a shrine|Once to Our Lady dedicate'. It may be that Wordsworth deliberately conflated Lady Holm with St Herbert's Isle on Derwentwater, which does preserve 'A hermit's history'.

78 *delicate viands:* food designed to tempt the palate.

81 *Sabine fare:* Cf. Dryden, *Georgics* II 777, 'frugal Sabines'; Wordsworth may also be thinking of the frugality of Horace on his Sabine farm.

82–6 *little weekly stipend . . . profusely filled:* Wordsworth's pocket-money was sixpence a week in his final year at school, but augmented in January 1787, after the half-yearly holiday, by an extra guinea (worth 42 'weekly stipends').

90 *board:* table, stall.

95–7 *that provoked . . . corporeal appetite:* Food increased the boys' pleasure in landscape; pompous lines that were cut in *1805.*

108–9 *the antique walls|Of a large abbey:* Furness Abbey, built by Cistercian monks in 1127 near Barrow-in-Furness (twenty miles from Hawkshead) was 'dissolved' in 1537 under Henry VIII. Its roof-timbers, stripped of their valuable lead, had long since fallen by Wordsworth's day.

120 *the cross-legged knight:* 'In the middle space, where the first barons of Kendal are interred, lies the procumbent figure of a man in armour, cross-legged' (West, *Guide* 39). The knight is now in the Abbey museum.

121–30 *that single wren . . . such music:*

Like Keats in *Bright Star*, Wordsworth is using the background presence of Shakespeare to enhance a moment of border vision. The famous metaphor of Sonnet 73 – 'Bare ruined choirs, where late the sweet birds sang' – is made actual, just as in *The Ruined Cottage* the broken pitcher of *Ecclesiastes* becomes the 'useless fragment of a wooden bowl'. But though the choirs become the nave of a palpable abbey, the bird remains invisible, intangible, its sourceless song conveying the presence of the sublime. (*BV* 119)

134 *that still spirit of the evening air:* After the direct address to the rocks and streams, it would have been natural to write 'thou, still spirit'. Wordsworth, it seems, wishes to achieve his numinous effect without invoking the spirit-world of Part I.

136 *breathed:* rested the horses – gave them a 'breather'.

139 *the level sand:* Levens Sands, south of Barrow, which would take the riders back to Hawkshead via Greenodd.

140–78 The one section of Part II to be omitted in *1805*; a cut-down version of the Coniston episode is restored in *1850*, as VIII 458–75.

145 *An old hall:* Coniston Hall, with steep Elizabethan 'gavel ends' (gables).

150 *piazza:* colonnade.

153 *chafing-dish:* portable charcoal-stove, used in this case to cook trout or char from the lake.

160 *Himself unseen:* Setting unseen behind the western fells, the sun casts a glow to the east. Wordsworth makes his point by a subdued quotation from *Hamlet*: 'But look the morn, in russet mantle clad|Walks o'er the dew of yon high eastward hill' (I i 166–7).

166–74 Lines drawn appropriately from Wordsworth's schoolboy *Vale of Esthwaite*, which, after their appearance in *1799* (but not in *1805*), are revised to form *Dear Native Regions* (*Poems* 1815).

181 *an inn:* the White Lion, Bowness (now gone).

184 *liveries:* uniformed servants.

185 *the blood-red wine:* A phrase used to sinister effect in the *Ballad of Sir Patrick Spens.*

186 *or ere:* before. *the Hall:* On Belle Isle, completed early 1780s.

208 *The minstrel of our troop:* Identified by Wordsworth as Robert Greenwood, afterwards (like the poet's brother, Christopher) a Fellow of Trinity College, Cambridge. Ann Tyson, Wordsworth's landlady, remembered him simply as 't'lad wi't flute'.

229–30 *To patriotic and domestic love|Analogous:* A very Wordsworthian way of thinking: the moon is valued not for itself (or for its literary associations), but in the deep-down way in which country and family are valued. Compare the patriotic sonnets of 1802–3, heart-felt because they are about the protection of a way of life.

236 *huts:* cottages (built of local slate).

240 *intervenient:* experienced in the midst of other concerns.

251 *that false secondary power:* analytic reason, the tendency to categorize – at the expense of an imaginative perception of wholeness.

255–6 *To thee . . . The unity of all has been revealed:* Coleridge, as a Unitarian, believed in a single God 'who from eternity doth teach|Himself in all, and all things in himself' (*FM* 66–7). The envy in Wordsworth's tones is a reminder that his own faith had no such clear doctrinal basis. Always drawn to the One Life, he seldom commits himself to it (as in *The Pedlar* and *Tintern Abbey*, spring–summer 1798) except when Coleridge is near.

258–9 *to class the cabinet|Of their sensations:* to classify as in a show-case; a rare instance in which Wordsworth's language can be related in detail to a philosophical text. His metaphor of the mind as stocked like a museum collection is drawn from chapter 2 of Locke's *Essay on Human Understanding*: 'The senses at first let in particular ideas, and furnish the yet empty cabinet'.

262 *Hard task to analyse a soul:* Raphael in *Paradise Lost* refers to narrating the war in Heaven as 'Sad task and hard' (V 564). Tacitly Wordsworth is claiming for his own task an importance comparable to Milton's.

269 *The progress of our being:* In his quest for origins, Milton had charted human progress from the Garden of Eden; Wordsworth will trace it from the relationship of mother to infant in the world of everyday experience.

271–2 *when his soul . . . earthly soul:* when his pre-existent soul becomes conscious of its new earthly condition (rather than my timid Norton reading, 'when his soul forms an evident relation with the soul of another human-being'). Though we tend to associate it with Wordsworth's *Intimations* of 1804, the concept of pre-existence is found in Coleridge as early as his sonnet on the birth of Hartley, September 1796: 'and some have said|We lived ere yet this robe of flesh we wore' (ll. 5–6).

275 *Like an awakening breeze:* A draft in *MS RV* had gone still further: 'This passion is the awakening breeze of life' (Parrish 188–9). Behind this life-giving human relationship of mother and child is the 'eternal spirit' of *Was It For This*:

> oh bounteous power,
> In childhood, in rememberable days,
> How often did thy love renew for me
> Those naked feelings which when thou wouldst form
> A living thing thou sendest like a breeze
> Into its infant being. (ll. 109–14)

284 *Tenacious of the forms:* The child learns from the first by storing up 'forms' and associations of the external world; cf. the 'forms of beauty' that are carried away by the adult poet of *Tintern Abbey* 23ff., enabling him later, 'mid the din|Of towns and cities', to 'see into the life of things'.

286 *apprehensive:* suited to learning. *habitude:* relationship – not elsewhere used by Wordsworth, but known to him through Coleridge's section of Southey's *Joan of Arc* (1795), 'holiest habitude|Of constant faith' (II 15–16).

288–90 *there exists . . . sense:* As F. R. Leavis long ago pointed out (*Revaluation*, London, 1936, 160) there is a clear link with *TA* 101–2: 'A motion and a spirit, that impels|All thinking things, all objects of all thought'. In effect the mother's 'belovèd presence' has replaced the divine 'presence' of *TA* 95.

293–4 *The gravitation and the filial bond . . . world:* As in *Was It For This*, Wordsworth is concerned with 'those first-born affinities which fit|Our new existence to existing things' (ll. 120–1), but it is by virtue of his bond with the mother that the child is a part of nature (subject to the gravitational pull of the earth).

302 *the one great mind:* God.

303 *creator and receiver both:* In terms of *Biographia Literaria* chapter 13, the child is capable of the god-like highest powers – at once creative and perceptive – of the primary imagination. Though his major definitions were yet to come, Coleridge (on whom Wordsworth's formulation certainly

depends) had been thinking of the human imagination as imitating God's creativity at least since the Slave Trade lecture of 1795.

304–5 *Working but in alliance . . . beholds:* A retreat from the position in *Tintern Abbey*, where the transcendental 'presence' had dwelt equally in the mind and the blue sky, 'impelling' both. The child is now distinct from the natural world with which he forms an imaginative alliance.

315–16 *this infant sensibility . . . our being:* Portrayed at first as the child at the breast, the infant babe has moved into a symbolic realm, 'powerful' in an array of emotions that he could not possibly have experienced. Wordsworth, however, refuses to think of him as unordinary: his sensibility is the birthright of our being.

320 *chamois:* agile mountain antelope, probably seen by Wordsworth in the Alps.

321 *a trouble came into my mind:* The phase of late adolescence recorded in *Pedlar* 187–9: 'he was o'erpowered|By nature, and his spirit was on fire|With restless thoughts'.

324 *The props of my affections:* Boyish sports which had 'collaterally' supported the growing love of nature.

328 *influxes:* influences.

338–42 *every season . . . else unknown:* Short-lived relationships that each new season offers (with spring flowers, or summer fulness, or falling leaves, or frost) are now, through the power of love, permanently recorded in the mind.

344 *'best society':* It is Adam who, rather surprisingly, comments in Eden, 'For solitude sometimes is best society' (*PL* IX 249).

347 *gentle agitations:* Not dependent on 'By' in the previous line, but the last item in the list that follows 'Hence' in l. 343.

351–71 *For I would walk . . . pursue:* Written originally in February 1798 to describe the Pedlar; adapted for *The Prelude* in autumn 1799 by the simple turning of 'he' to 'I'.

358 *ghostly:* A range of meanings seems to be appropriate, from 'sacred' to 'otherworldly' to 'insubstantial'.

366 *obscure:* Stressed on the first syllable; cf. *PL* II 132, 'with obscure wing'. Wordsworth is Burkean in his association of obscurity with the sublime; see *Sublime and Beautiful* Part II, section iv, 'A clear idea is another name for a little idea'.

377–8 *a superadded soul,|A virtue not its own:* Penetrating to the 'latent qualities| And essences of things' (seeing perhaps into their life), the adolescent Wordsworth is moved by a power that we probably associate with his own creativity (see ll. 411–25 below), but which he feels as an external preternatural force.

379 *the hours of school:* From 6 or 6.30 a.m. in the summer.

380 *our little lake:* Esthwaite Water.

382–3 *a friend . . . loved:* John Fleming, of whom Wordsworth had written in *The Vale of Esthwaite*, 'Friendship and Fleming are the same'.

391–2 *I sat . . . jutting eminence:* Thomson, *Seasons* II 1042, 'Sad on the jutting eminence he sits'.

401 *prospect:* landscape.

411 *plastic:* shaping, creative; another Coleridgean word, cf. *Eolian Harp* 46–8:

> as o'er them sweeps
> Plastic and vast, one intellectual breeze,
> At once the soul of each and God of all.

414–17 *A local spirit ... communed:* The spirit (broadly to be equated with imagination) is 'local' in the sense that it reflects Wordsworth's individuality, refusing to subscribe to 'general tendency' (the norms of human behaviour). Mostly, however, it is willing to take second place to 'external things' (the forms of nature with which the mind interacts).

417 *auxiliar:* enhancing.

424–5 *Hence my obeisance ... transport:* Wordsworth paradoxically gives his 'obeisance' (allegiance) to nature, and experiences 'transport' (rapture – again the sensation of being 'carried away'), because his imagination is able to dominate her, enhance the effect of her workings upon the mind.

426 *still:* always.

428 *analytic industry:* rational thinking.

432 *interminable building:* vast structure (within the mind).

437–41 *or, from excess ... own enjoyments:* Wordsworth is thinking of important lines in the 1798 text of *Frost at Midnight*, not retained in later versions:

> the living spirit in our frame,
> That loves not to behold a lifeless thing,
> Transfuses into all its own delights
> Its own volition ... (ll. 21–4)

446–64 *Pedlar:* 204–22, adapted for *The Prelude* autumn 1799, and incorporating (in the first person) Wordsworth's central pantheist statement of belief from February 1798: 'In all things|He saw one life, and felt that it was joy.' Faith in the One Life is attributed to the past (the poet's 'seventeenth year'), yet by implication has lasted till the present day (see ll. 465ff. below).

463 *grosser prelude of that strain:* sensual enjoyment that prefaces the higher pleasures of response to the One Life.

465 *If this be error:* A sudden concession that reproduces the pattern of *TA* 50ff.: 'If this|Be but a vain belief ...' And cf. Shakespeare, Sonnet 116 ('Let me not to the marriage of true minds|Admit impediments ...'): 'If this be error and upon me proved,|I never writ, nor no man ever loved.'

478–87 *if in these times ... dismay:* Wordsworth is drawing on a letter from Coleridge of September 1799 urging him to incorporate in *The Recluse* an address to

> those, who, in consequence of the complete failure of the French Revolution, have thrown up all hopes of the amelioration of mankind, and are sinking into an almost epicurean selfishness, disguising the same under the soft titles of domestic attachment and contempt for visionary *philosophes*.

479 *waste:* desert.

481–2 *when good men|On every side fall off:* Best known among those who renounced their radical views at this time was James Mackintosh, author of *Vindiciae Gallicae* (1791), a point-by-point reply to Burke's hostile *Reflections on the French Revolution*.

489 *more than Roman confidence:* Maxwell instances the Roman general, Varro, commended after his defeat by Hannibal at Cannae (216 BC) for not despairing of the Republic.

496–7 *Thou, my friend ... other scenes:* Addressing his infant son, Hartley, Coleridge had written in *Frost at Midnight*, 'thou shalt learn far other lore,|And in far other scenes! For I was reared|In the great city' (ll. 50–2). This time there are no inverted commas, but Wordsworth has consciously rounded off the 1799 *Prelude* by quoting in conclusion the poem quoted at the outset ('my "sweet birthplace"', l. 8).

501–5 *The insinuated scoff ... love:* Cf. 'the sneers of selfish men' and 'greetings where no kindness is' (*TA* 130–1).

509–14 *Fare thee well ... mankind:* A signing-off of the poem, but also a parting. While Wordsworth and Dorothy were about to move into Dove Cottage, Grasmere, Coleridge in November 1799, when these lines were written, had decided to go back to his career as a journalist with the *Morning Post* in London.

THE PRELUDES OF 1805 AND 1850

Line numbers in bold type refer to the 1850 text.

Book First

1–54 Commonly referred to as the Glad Preamble (see Wordsworth's backward glance, VII 1–4), ll. 1–54 seem to have been composed on 18–19 November 1799 and inserted in *The Prelude* c. late January 1804. They are the record of a mood of exuberance and optimism as Wordsworth walked from Ullswater to Grasmere to arrange the renting of Dove Cottage, where he and Dorothy would live until 1808. Among literal-minded scholars the poet's metaphor of leaving behind him a city caused confusion that was not resolved until 1970; see John Alban Finch, 'Wordsworth's Two-Handed Engine', *Bicentenary Studies* 1–13.

1–4 *there is blessing ... gives:* Cf. *To My Sister* 5–8, 'There is a blessing in the air,|Which seems a sense of joy to yield ...' and Cowper, *Task* I 155–6, 'we have borne|The ruffling wind, scarce conscious that it blew'.

2,3,5 *it ... it ... its:* A clear case of the poet's executors ignoring his intentions. The printer's copy, *MS E*, reads 'he ... he ... his', making clear his intention to personalize the breeze.

6–7 *a house|Of bondage:* The poet's sense of release is expressed in a quotation from *Exodus* 13.3: 'And Moses said unto the people, Remember this day in which ye came out from Egypt, out of the house of bondage.'

8 *immured:* walled up; Wordsworth's backward reference at VIII 347–53 suggests that his metaphor of the city is a compound of London and the walled city of Goslar, in Saxony, where *1799* Part I was written. For the state of mind represented by the poet's city metaphors, see Lucy Newlyn, 'In City Pent', *RES*, November 1981, 408–28.

9 *at large:* Cowper, *Task* III 18–19, 'I feel myself at large,|Courageous, and refreshed for future toil.'

15 *The earth is all before me:* An allusion to the beautiful last lines of *Paradise Lost*, as Adam and Eve – never before so human – are driven out of Eden:

> Some natural tears they dropped, but wiped them soon;
> The world was all before them, where to choose
> Their place of rest, and Providence their guide.
> They hand in hand, with wandering steps and slow,
> Through Eden took their solitary way.

Wordsworth's poem starts where Milton's leaves off. He too is beginning a new life, but does so joyously and voluntarily.

17–18 *should the guide I choose . . . cloud:* Adam and Eve had been allocated Providence as their guide; Wordsworth is free to choose, and chooses nature – at her least solemn (here, 'a wandering cloud', at ll. 31–2, 'a twig, or any floating thing|Upon the river').

20 *Trances . . . mind:* An important self-borrowing, see 41–7n. below, and Parrish 116–17.

23–4 *That burden . . . weary day:* Reworking of *Tintern Abbey* 39–41: 'the burden of the mystery . . . the heavy and the weary weight|Of all this unintelligible world'.

31–45 Wordsworth's revisions to *1805* I 33–54 are characteristic of many throughout the poem that establish the voice of *1850*: weaker in rhythm, often more formal in diction, tending to smooth away eccentricity, and to sacrifice power, in the name of exactitude.

41–7 *For I, methought . . . creation:* Drawn, together with l. 20 above, from inspired jottings in *MS JJ*, October 1798 (Parrish 116–17). For larger implications, see Introduction; for literary associations of the wind, see M. H. Abrams, 'The Correspondent Breeze' 5–43.

46 *redundant:* overflowing, exuberant.

52 *prowess in an honourable field:* Especially the writing of *The Recluse*; see Introduction.

55–271 Written c. late January 1804 to form a link between the exuberant Preamble and the muted, self-reproachful opening of *1799* ('Was it for this . . .'), incorporated at l. 271.

55 *friend:* Coleridge, to whom all versions of *The Prelude* are addressed.

57 *measured strains:* verse.

60–1 *poetic numbers came|Spontaneously:* A claim nowhere else made by Wordsworth. Though twice offering spontaneity as an ideal in the Preface to *Lyrical Ballads* 1800, he had been careful to stress that poetry was created at a secondary stage – not during the original moment of emotion, but during an imaginative re-experiencing of that moment.

74 *'Twas autumn, and a calm and placid day:* A variant of the opening line of *The Ruined Cottage:* '''Twas summer and the sun was mounted high'.

83 *the very house:* Dove Cottage, in the 'one sweet vale' of Grasmere.

85–7 *some work|Of glory . . . performed:* Wordsworth did, as he intended, make a start on his 'work of glory' soon after arriving at Dove Cottage. *Home at Grasmere*, however, written largely in March 1800, and described in *MS B* (1806) as Book I of *The Recluse*, failed to develop as he had hoped. *The Prelude* and *The Excursion* would be completed, as subordinate parts of the larger scheme, but the philosophical centrepiece that was to carry the poet's redemptive message would never be written.

88 *genial:* pleasant, warm, sympathetic.

90 *that balanced me:* kept me in touch with reality.

88–9 *cloud|Of city smoke:* Wordsworth's adding of detail to his phantom city should be seen not as proof that it existed, but as 'unwillingness to submit the poetic spirit to the chains of fact and real circumstance' (Fenwick Note to *An Evening Walk*).

104 *Eolian visitations:* moments of poetic inspiration; the eolian harp, played on by the wind (and named after Aeolus, Greek god of winds), is a favourite romantic image for inspiration; see Coleridge, *Eolian Harp* (1795), *Dejection: An Ode* (1802); Shelley, *Ode to the West Wind* (1819), etc.

105 *defrauded:* betrayed (by the lack of a creative breeze).

102–3 *shed|Mild influence:* 'the Pleiades ... shedding sweet influence' (*PL* VII 374–5).

112 *sabbath:* day of rest, thus 'peacefulness'.

106 *three days:* An unexplained late correction of *1805* 'two days'; the distance covered, from the foot of Ullswater over the Kirkstone Pass to Grasmere, was approximately 21 miles.

115 *my hermitage:* Appropriate to Wordsworth as the recluse, dedicating himself to 'The holy life of music and of verse'.

121 *self-congratulation:* pleasure in his good fortune; used (as was 'complacency' at the time) without the modern implication of smugness.

124–7 *some determined aim ... interference:* Conscious of following in Milton's footsteps, Wordsworth portrays himself as searching for suitable themes for an epic, modern or from antiquity. There is no reason to believe he actually did so (see Jonathan Wordsworth, 'That Wordsworth Epic', *WC*, winter 1980, 34–5). Not till l. 228 does the poet mention his true ambition, to write a philosophical centrepiece for *The Recluse.*

130 *phantoms of conceit:* images, mental conceptions, that are to be embodied in narrative (given 'a frame of outward life'). *1850* 'airy phantasies' confirms that Wordsworth is thinking of Shakespeare's great lines on poetic creativity, *Midsummer Night's Dream* V i 14–17:

> as imagination bodies forth
> The forms of things unknown, the poet's pen
> Turns them to shapes, and gives to airy nothing
> A local habitation and a name.

132–3 *to such beings temperately ... heart:* Wordsworth had hoped, with due moderation ('temperately'), to confer his own oppressive feelings upon 'beings' created by the imagination.

143–4 *gifts|Of humbler industry:* shorter poems, that would be easier to write, and more immediately rewarding.

151–2 *mother dove|Sits brooding:* 'Dove-like satst brooding' (*PL* I 21); Milton's reference is to the Holy Spirit brooding over Chaos, and making it fruitful.

153–4 *goadings on ... groves:* Cf. the 'tempest' and 'redundant energy' of the Preamble (l. 46 above), and *Castle of Indolence Stanzas* 35–6, 'his own mind did, like a tempest strong,|Come to him thus, and drove the weary man along'.

165–6 *Nor am I naked . . . Forms, images:* More than other poets Wordsworth values the ability to carry 'external things' within the mind; cf. *Tintern Abbey* 24–5, 'These forms of beauty have not been to me|As is a landscape to a blind man's eye'.

169 *manners:* customs, observed ways of life.

178 *Proud spring-tide swellings:* 'tide' is effectively a pun: high tides of springtime are not (in Wordsworth's image) to be confused with a 'sea' of inspiration consistently at the full.

180 *Romantic tale . . . unsung:* Before writing *Paradise Lost* Milton had planned a national epic on King Arthur.

182 *the groves of chivalry:* Wordsworth turns from Milton to Spenser. As De Selincourt notes, the elaborations in *1850* (ll. 170–85) show a 'moral turn of thought' of which the poetry of *1805* had been 'quite innocent'.

185 *hallowing faithful loves:* Spenser in the first stanza of *The Faerie Queene* speaks of 'Fierce wars and faithful loves'.

186–8 *How vanquished Mithridates . . . became|That Odin:* Gibbon, who associates, but does not identify, the two figures, comments significantly, 'This wonderful expedition of Odin . . . might supply the noble groundwork of an epic poem [but] cannot be received as authentic history' (*Decline and Fall of the Roman Empire*, 1776, I 246). Wordsworth would also know of Mithridates (d. 63 BC) in Plutarch's *Lives*, and had doubtless read Southey's *Race of Odin* (1795).

190 *Sertorius:* Roman general (c. 112–72 BC), the subject of one of Plutarch's *Lives* and an ally of Mithridates. Owen, *Annotating Wordsworth* 62–4, notes that Wordsworth's source for the story told in ll. 195–8 is probably George Glas, *History of the Discovery of the Canary Isles* (1764).

199 *like a pestilence:* Wordsworth's astonishing image of the 'soul|Of liberty' as a disease seems to have been suggested by an actual plague brought by the Europeans to the Canaries. According to Glas two-thirds of the 14,000 fighting men succumbed.

205 *that one Frenchman:* 'Dominique de Gourges, a French gentleman who went in 1568 to Florida to avenge the massacre of the French by the Spaniards there' (note to first edition, drawn from Hakluyt's *Navigations*). Wordsworth's language – 'Went single in his ministry' (l. 208), 'Withering the oppressor' (l. 211) – conceals a story of bloodthirsty revenge that would not have made a very heroic poem.

211 *Gustavus:* Gustavus I of Sweden (1496–1560), who raised support among the miners of Dalecarlia and in 1521–3 freed the country from Danish rule.

213 *Wallace:* William Wallace (c. 1272–1305), Scottish general and patriot, captured and executed by Edward I; brought to Wordsworth's mind by the Highland walking tour of August 1803. 'Passed two of Wallace's caves', Dorothy records on the 21st, 'There is scarce a noted glen in Scotland that has not a cave for Wallace or some other hero.'

226–8 *beauteous fabric . . . unsubstantial:* From Prospero's 'Our revels now are ended . . .' *Tempest* IV i 148–63.

228–38 *Then, last wish . . . clearer insight:* Two months after evoking in these lines the 'awful burden' of writing a central section for *The Recluse* (*The Excursion* was planned by March 1804, and *The Prelude* was also to be part of the scheme), Wordsworth was writing desperately to Coleridge to ask for instructions. Coleridge, who was thought to be dying, had promised a 'letter on *The Recluse*'. 'I cannot say', Wordsworth wrote on 29 March, 'what a load it would be to me should I survive you and you die without this memorial left behind.'

233–4 *immortal verse . . . Orphean lyre:* Orpheus was thought of as philosopher as well as poet-musician. Wordsworth is piecing together phrases from Milton: 'airs|Married to immortal verse', *L'Allegro* 136–7, 'Orphean lyre', *PL* III 17.

239–40 *a mockery . . . virtue:* so indecisive as to be capable neither of vice nor of virtue.

248 *Doth lock my functions up:* Pope, *Imitations of Horace* Epistle I i 39–40, 'So slow the unprofitable moments roll,|That lock up all the functions of my soul' (note the use of 'unprofitably' in l. 269; Wordsworth knew Pope extremely well).

262 *interdict:* prohibition; pronounced 'interdite'.

265 *absolute accomplishment:* complete success, fulfilment.

270–1 *Like a false steward . . . renders nothing back:* In the capitalist parable, *Matthew* 25. 14–30, the steward is rebuked for burying, rather than investing, his 'talents' of silver. Making silent use of the pun (the modern word actually derives from the parable), Wordsworth convicts himself of failure to make use of God-given poetic talents. After more than five years he thus neatly provides an antecedent for 'this' in the questioning with which his work on *The Prelude* had originally begun.

271 *Was it for this:* Words with which both the first *Prelude* draft (*Was It For This*, above) and Part I of *1799* had opened. The remainder of Book I in *1805* (and *1850*) is a version of Part I, revised in late January 1804, and without the 'spots of time' sequence (*1799* I 258–374). For the repeated questioning of ll. 271–85, see *1799* I 1n.

275 *holms:* flat ground by the river.

278 *'sweet birthplace':* Drawn from Coleridge, *FM* 33; see *1799* I 8n.

284 *earnest:* foretaste, pledge.

284 *a shattered monument:* Cockermouth Castle.

296 *coursed:* raced.

298 *groundsel:* ragwort; see *1799* I 22–3n.

302 *Indian plains:* American Indian (as in *Complaint of the Forsaken Indian Woman*, 1798).

306 *Fostered . . . fear:* nurtured (in Burkean terms) by the sublime as well as the beautiful; cf. *1799* I 68–80.

308 *belovèd vale:* Esthwaite, site of Hawkshead Grammar School.

306–7 *Ere I had told|Ten birth-days:* The right date (Wordsworth was nine), as against *1805* (eight) and *1799* I 258–8 (seven).

317 *springes:* snares; as at *Hamlet* I iii 115, 'Ay, springes to catch woodcocks'. For an eighteenth-century account of woodcock-snaring on the fells, see *1799* I 34n.

327 *toils:* A double meaning: 'trap' and 'labours'.

326 *cultured:* under cultivation (as opposed to the hillsides, merely grazed by sheep).

339 *lodge:* nest.

342 *the raven's nest:* Ravens are a danger to lambs; the boy's 'inglorious' purpose was to claim the bounty paid by the parish to those who destroyed

their nests. He was probably let down the rockface on a rope (note *1850*'s use of the plural: 'Moved we as plunderers', 'though mean|Our object').

345 *amain:* strongly.

340 *Dust as we are . . . grows:* A line of pious self-abasement first appearing in the base text of *MS D*, c. January 1832 (when the poet was 62).

352 *dark:* mysterious.

363 *nature:* A replacement, in January 1804, for the sub-classical spirit-world of *1799* I 68–81.

360–1 *Straight I unloosed . . . shore:* A replacement for *1805* 376–88, cut in 1832. Ll. 376–82 (introduced in *1805*) are no great loss, but the cutting of ll. 383–8 (going back through *1799* to the early *JJ* drafts) weakens the lead-in to this great episode.

376 *Patterdale:* Ullswater.

388 *Though bent on speed:* 'As one who . . . bates at noon|Though bent on speed' (*PL* XII 1–2).

393–4 *one track . . . sparkling light:* Maxwell points to a Coleridge echo, 'tracks of shining white' (*AM* 266).

406 *a huge cliff:* Probably Black Crag, appearing behind Stybarrow Crag (the 'craggy steep') as the boy rows out from the shore.

407 *instinct:* imbued.

422 *blank desertion:* As the avenging mountain-forms invade his mind, the boy is 'deserted' by visual reassurance, mental pictures of day-to-day existence.

428–89 One of only five passages of *The Prelude* known to Wordsworth's contemporaries before his death in 1850. Printed by Coleridge in *The Friend*, 28 December 1809 (with the title *Growth of Genius from the Influences of Natural Objects on the Imagination in Boyhood and Early Youth*), and by Wordsworth himself in collections from 1815.

428–31 *Wisdom and spirit . . . motion:* In place of the polytheism of *1799* I 130–2, Wordsworth now offers a monotheistic but not specifically Christian conception, close to the immanent life-force of *Tintern Abbey* but with an emphasis on pervading wisdom. The change is largely one of presentation.

435 *vulgar works of man:* common man-made objects.

443 *stinted:* grudged, partial.

460–1 *All shod . . . ice:* As Maxwell points out, a reminiscence of Erasmus Darwin's *Botanic Garden* (1791) I iii 570, 'Hang o'er the sliding steel, and hiss along the ice'.

450 *reflex:* reflection; Wordsworth tried 'shadow' (*1799*), then 'image' (*1805*), before achieving what is surely the most satisfactory reading.

486 *her diurnal round:* Cf. Lucy, 'Rolled round in earth's diurnal course|With rocks and stones and trees' (*A Slumber Did My Spirit Seal* 7–8;) both passages are related to Milton *PL* VII 22, 'Within the visible diurnal sphere', and both are written c. November 1799.

487 *train:* succession.

497 *Impressed:* stamped, printed. *characters:* marks, letters, signs.

501 *Work like a sea:* seethe; see Cowper, *Task* VI 737–8, 'this tempestuous state of human things|Is merely as the workings of a sea'.

511 *milk-white clusters:* hazel-nuts; a reference to *Nutting*, published as a separate poem in *Lyrical Ballads* 1800, but at first written for *The Prelude.*

538 *With crosses . . . o'er:* noughts and crosses (American tick-tack-toe); Wordsworth has in mind a passage in *PL* VIII 83, 'With centric and eccentric

scribbled o'er', where man is being mocked for attempting to map the heavens.

543 *loo:* eighteenth-century card game, mentioned by Pope, whose influence becomes more obvious in the successful *1805* elaboration of the mock-heroic in Wordsworth's home-amusements section.

549 *plebeian cards:* Cf. Pope, *Rape of the Lock* III 54, 'Gained but one trump and one plebeian card'.

562–4 *Meanwhile abroad . . . silent tooth:* Based on Cowper's *Winter Evening* – 'how the frost|Raging abroad, and the rough wind, endear|The silence and the warmth enjoyed within' (*Task* IV 308–10) – but with more pointed allusion to Amiens' song in *As You Like It* II vii:

> Blow, blow, thou winter wind,
> Thou art not so unkind
> As man's ingratitude:
> Thy tooth is not so keen . . .

569 *yellings:* Used of animal noises (and objects) at this period, as well as human beings.

570 *Bothnic Main:* the northern Baltic.

571 *sedulous:* anxious; Milton is 'Not sedulous by nature to indite|Wars, hitherto the only argument|Heroic deemed' (*PL* IX 27–9).

572 *extrinsic passion:* feelings unrelated to the natural scenes that were to have a permanent effect on the poet's mind.

578 *hallowed and pure motions of the sense:* In Maxwell's words, the poet seems to be 'recalling, and reversing' *Measure for Measure* I iv 59, 'The wanton stings and motions of the sense'.

580 *intellectual:* spiritual; as in Shelley's Platonist *Hymn to Intellectual Beauty.*

562–3 *with beauty|Old as creation:* Wordsworth's original phrase, 'With the eternal beauty', persisting from *Was It For This* through *1799* and *1805*, has been modified in case its Platonism should seem unorthodox.

591 *organic:* sensuous.

609 *vulgar:* ordinary, unremarkable.

618–19 *ill-sorted unions . . . fairies:* The union of Titania and Bottom, for instance, in *Midsummer Night's Dream.*

628–9 *in their substantial lineaments . . . brain:* The process of storing up visual images is described in similarly physical terms at *Pedlar* 32–4: 'on his mind|They lay like substances, and almost seemed|To haunt the bodily sense'.

631 *the impressive discipline of fear:* the power of fear to stamp 'impressions' on the memory.

639–40 *invisible links|Allied to the affections:* links of association, valued by Wordsworth for their capacity to conserve and bring to mind past emotions ('affections'); see *1799* I 324–6n. Wordsworth's thinking is a personal redefinition of the associationism of Hartley's *Observations on Man*, which in the mid-1790s had provided the theological basis of Coleridge's Unitarianism.

643–4 *ere the birth . . . snows:* attributing 'flowers' of memory to a period of life for which in truth the memory is blank; see the very late emendation of *1850*, garrulous but explicit.

653 *honourable toil:* Wordsworth, when he wrote these lines in February 1799, expected to go straight ahead with *The Recluse* rather than extending his autobiography.

660 *visionary things:* things seen in the imagination, with the inward eye.

664–71 Wordsworth's concluding paragraph, written late January 1804, states plainly to Coleridge why it is that he prefers to shelve the writing of *The Recluse* in favour of an extended *Prelude*; see Introduction.

Book Second

7 *nourishment that came unsought:* Wordsworth's theme in Book I has been the child's unconscious response to the workings of nature upon his imagination. Book II will show how nature in adolescence comes to be 'sought|For her own sake'.

8–9 *From week . . . tumult:* The phase of childhood summed up in *TA* 74–5 as 'The coarser pleasures of my boyish days,|And their glad animal movements'.

18 *a beating mind:* Prospero, 'a turn or two I'll walk|To still my beating mind' (*Tempest* IV i 162–3).

20 *And needs:* Read: 'and yet needs'. *monitory voice:* warning, admonishment. Memories of the spontaneous joys of youth show how paltry are the achievements of adulthood. *1850* 'Nor needs' shows a change of mind in the poet. Memories of youth are now seen as insufficient in their effect: everyone needs the warning to beware of pride in intellect.

28 *my corporeal frame:* body; 'this corporeal frame' (*TA* 44).

30 *self-presence:* actuality, immediacy (associated with the continuing imaginative 'presence' of the poet's former 'self').

35 *our small market-village:* Hawkshead.

39 *smart assembly-room:* Hawkshead Town Hall, built 1790, and covered with gravel stucco ('rough-cast') and white-wash. For Wordsworth's consistent dislike of the obtrusiveness of white buildings, see *Guide to the Lakes*.

46 *huckster:* stall-keeper.

52 *collaterally attached:* taken into account as the boys plan their otherwise less enjoyable ('grateful', l. 54) pastimes.

57 *plain of Windermere:* level surface of the lake.

58 *bourne:* destination; cf. *Hamlet* III i 79–80, 'That undiscovered country, from whose bourne|No traveller returns'.

60–2 *a sister isle . . . lilies-of-the-valley:* Naming the islands that form the 'archipelago' of Windermere, West notes: '*Grassholme:* is at present shaded with a grove of oaks. And two smaller islets borrow their names from the lilies-of-the-valley which decorate them' (*Guide* 56–7).

unbrageous covert: shady canopy.

63–5 *a third small island . . . hermit's history:* '*Lady-holm*, where in ancient times stood an oratory, is an isle of an oval form, vested with coppice wood' (West, *Guide* 56). Wordsworth clearly knew of the island's association with the Virgin Mary, but in *1799* and *1805* preferred Gothic imprecision: 'old stone table', 'mouldered cave', and a contemplative hermit (as in *Tintern Abbey*, but perhaps borrowed from St Herbert's Isle, Derwentwater). *1850* puts it all straight.

79 *delicate viands:* food designed to tempt the palate.

82 *Sabine fare:* Cf. Dryden, *Georgics* II 777, 'frugal Sabines'; Wordsworth may also be thinking of the frugality of Horace on his Sabine farm.

83 *A little weekly stipend:* Wordsworth's pocket-money was sixpence a week in his final year at school, but augmented in January 1787, after the half-yearly holiday, by an extra guinea (worth 42 'weekly stipends').

91 *board:* table, stall.

101–2 *some famed temple . . . Druids worshipped:* Wordsworth associates the stone circle at Swinside, near Duddon Bridge, with Druids in a footnote to *Evening Walk*; Castlerigg, above Keswick (featured in Keats' *Hyperion*) would also have been in his mind. The circle-builders are no longer believed to have been Druids.

109–10 *the antique walls|Of that large abbey:* Furness Abbey, built by Cistercian monks in 1127 near Barrow-in-Furness (20 miles from Hawkshead) was 'dissolved' in 1537 under Henry VIII. Its roof-timbers, stripped of their valuable lead, had long since fallen by Wordsworth's day.

115–21 *To more than inland peace . . . quietness:* Revision of *1799* II. 112–17 in the name of accuracy (as is so often the case with Wordsworth): on second thoughts, the coast is flat, and too far away. Trees at Furness cannot

> Hear all day long the murmuring sea that beats
> Incessantly upon a craggy shore.

124 *the cross-legged knight:* 'In the middle space, where the first barons of Kendal are interred, lies the procumbent figure of a man in armour, cross-legged' (West, *Guide* 39). The knight is now in the Abbey museum.

125–35 *that single wren . . . such music:*

> Like Keats in *Bright Star*, Wordsworth is using the background presence of Shakespeare to enhance a moment of border vision. The famous metaphor of Sonnet 73 – 'Bare ruined choirs, where late the sweet birds sang' – is made actual, just as in *The Ruined Cottage* the broken pitcher of *Ecclesiastes* becomes the 'useless fragment of a wooden bowl'. But though the choirs become the nave of a palpable abbey, the bird remains invisible, intangible, its sourceless song conveying the presence of the sublime. (*BV* 119)

129–30 *sobbings of the place|And respirations:* A numinous addition to *1799*.

139 *that still spirit of the evening air:* For the relation of Wordsworth's line to the polytheism of *1799* Part I, see *1799* II 134n. above.

141 *breathed:* rested the horses – gave them a 'breather'.

144 *the level sand:* Levens Sands, south of Barrow, which would take the riders back to Hawkshead via Greenodd.

144/5 Omission of the Coniston episode (*1799* II 140–78) is the one major difference between Book II of *1805* and Part II of *1799*.

147 *an inn:* the White Lion, Bowness (now gone).

150 *liveries:* uniformed servants.

151 *the blood-red wine:* A phrase used to sinister effect in the *Ballad of Sir Patrick Spens*.

152 *or ere:* before. *the Hall:* on Belle Isle, completed early 1780s.

174 *The minstrel of our troop:* Identified by Wordsworth as Robert Greenwood,

afterwards (like the poet's brother Christopher) a Fellow of Trinity College, Cambridge. Ann Tyson, Wordsworth's landlady, remembered him simply as 't'lad wi't flute'.

195–6 *To patriotic and domestic love|Analogous:* A very Wordsworthian way of thinking: the moon is valued not for itself (or for its literary associations), but in the deep-down way in which country and family are valued. Compare the patriotic sonnets of 1802–3, heart-felt because they are about the protection of a way of life.

202 *huts:* cottages (built of local slate).

206 *intervenient:* experienced in the midst of other concerns.

219 *succedaneum:* remedy; science, with its reliance on the 'false secondary power' of analytic reason, is merely a support to us in our lack of imaginative vision. We are taught to categorize, instead of perceiving oneness and wholeness.

225–6 *To thee . . . The unity of all has been revealed:* Coleridge, as a Unitarian (at least when these lines were written in 1799), believed in a single God 'who from eternity doth teach|Himself in all, and all things in himself' (*FM* 66–7). Wordsworth's position was never so clear-cut; see *1799* II 256n.

228–9 *to class the cabinet|Of their sensations:* to classify as in a show-case; a rare instance in which Wordsworth's thinking can be related in detail to a philosophical text. His metaphor of the mind as stocked like a museum collection is drawn from chapter 2 of Locke's *Essay on Human Understanding*: 'The senses at first let in particular ideas, and furnish the yet empty cabinet'.

232 *Hard task to analyse a soul:* Raphael in *Paradise Lost* refers to narrating the war in Heaven as 'Sad task and hard' (V 564). Tacitly Wordsworth is claiming for his own task an importance comparable to Milton's.

239 *The progress of our being:* In his quest for origins, Milton had charted human progress from the Garden of Eden; Wordsworth will trace it from the relationship of mother to infant in the world of everyday experience.

241–2 *when his soul . . . earthly soul:* when his pre-existent soul becomes conscious of its new earthly condition (rather than my timid Norton reading, 'when his soul forms an evident relation with the soul of another human being'). Though we tend to associate it with Wordsworth's *Intimations* of 1804, the concept of pre-existence is found in Coleridge as early as his sonnet on the birth of Hartley, September 1796; 'and some have said|We lived ere yet this robe of flesh we wore' (ll. 5–6).

244–57 Cut during the drastic revisions of 1832 and 1838–9.

245 *Like an awakening breeze:* For important earlier phases in Wordsworth's thinking, see *1799* II 275n.

254 *Tenacious of the forms:* The child learns from the first by storing up 'forms' and associations of the external world; cf. the 'forms of beauty' that are carried away by the adult poet of *Tintern Abbey* 23ff., enabling him later, 'mid the din|Of towns and cities', to 'see into the life of things'.

256 *apprehensive:* suited to learning. *habitude:* relationship – not elsewhere used by Wordsworth, but known to him through Coleridge's section of Southey's *Joan of Arc* (1795), 'holiest habitude|Of constant faith' (II 15–16).

258–60 *there exists . . . sense:* As F.R. Leavis long ago pointed out (*Revaluation* 160), there is a clear link with *TA* 101–2: 'A motion and a spirit, that impels|All thinking things, all objects of all thought'. In effect the mother's 'beloved presence' has replaced the divine 'presence' of *TA* 95.

263–4 *The gravitation and the filial bond . . . world:* It is through the bond with his mother that the child becomes a part of nature (subject, in Wordsworth's metaphor, to the gravitational pull of the earth); see *1799* II 293–4n.

245–51 *Is there a flower . . . harm:* Lines added in 1832 that sentimentalize the child's responses, making him (perhaps) a more credible human baby, but weakening the great imaginative claims made by the poetry of *1799* and *1805*. Where before he was 'powerful in all sentiments of grief,|Of exultation, fear, and joy' (*1805* 270–1, cut 1832), now he is a 'Frail creature . . . helpless as frail' (l. 254).

257 *like an agent:* In *1799* and *1805* the child had worked 'as an agent' of God, now he merely resembles one.

273 *creator and receiver both:* In terms of *Biographia Literaria* chapter 13, the child is capable of the god-like highest powers – at once creative and perceptive – of the primary imagination. Though his major definitions were yet to come, Coleridge (on whom Wordsworth's formulation certainly depends) had been thinking of the human imagination as imitating God's creativity at least since the Slave Trade lecture of 1795.

274–5 *Working but in alliance . . . beholds:* A retreat from the position in *Tintern Abbey*, where the transcendental 'presence' had dwelt equally in the mind and the blue sky, 'impelling' both. The child now is distinct from the natural world with which he forms an imaginative alliance.

285 *the infant sensibility . . . our being:* Portrayed at first as the child at the breast, the infant babe has moved into a symbolic realm, 'powerful' in an array of emotions that he could not possibly have experienced. Wordsworth, however, refuses to think of him as unordinary: his sensibility is the birthright of our being.

290 *chamois:* agile mountain antelope, probably seen by Wordsworth in the Alps.

291 *a trouble came into my mind:* The phase of late adolescence recorded in *Pedlar* 187–9: 'he was o'erpowered|By nature, and his spirit was on fire|With restless thoughts'.

294 *The props of my affections:* Boyish sports which had 'collaterally' supported the growing love of nature.

298 *influxes:* influences.

308–12 *every season . . . else unknown:* Short-lived relationships that each new season offers (with spring flowers, or summer fulness, or falling leaves, or frost) are now, through the power of love, permanently recorded in the mind.

314 *'best society':* It is Adam who, rather surprisingly, comments in Eden, 'For solitude sometimes is best society' (*PL* IX 249).

317 *gentle agitations:* Not dependent on 'By' in the previous line, but the final item in a list that follows 'Hence' in l. 313.

321–41 *For I would walk . . . pursue:* Written originally in February 1798 to describe the Pedlar; adapted for *The Prelude* in autumn 1799 by the simple turning of 'he' to 'I'.

328 *ghostly:* A range of meaning seems to be appropriate, from 'sacred' to 'otherworldly' to 'insubstantial'.

336 *obscure:* Stressed on the first syllable; cf. *PL* II 132, 'with obscure wing'.

Wordsworth is Burkean in his association of obscurity and the sublime; see *Sublime and Beautiful* Part II, section iv, 'A clear idea is another name for a little idea'.

347–8 *a superadded soul,|A virtue not its own:* Penetrating to the 'latent qualities| And essences of things' (seeing perhaps into their life), the adolescent Wordsworth is moved by a power that we probably associate with his own creativity (see ll. 381–95 below), but which he feels as an external preternatural force.

349 *the hours of school:* From 6 or 6.30 a.m. in the summer.

350 *our little lake:* Esthwaite Water.

352–3 *a friend . . . loved:* John Fleming, of whom Wordsworth had written in *The Vale of Esthwaite*, 'Friendship and Fleming are the same'.

341–2 *or the vernal thrush . . . the woods:* Rewording by the poet's executors to avoid his revision of 1838–9, in which 'the thrush, high perched,|Piped to the woods his shrill *reveillé*' – sounded a wake-up call.

361–2 *I sat . . . jutting eminence:* Thomson, *Seasons* II 1042, 'Sad on the jutting eminence he sits'.

346–7 *where find|Faith . . . I felt:* The tones of one for whom the 'visionary gleam' has long disappeared. Again an *MS D* revision of 1838–9.

371 *prospect:* landscape.

381 *plastic:* shaping, creative; another Coleridgean word, cf. *Eolian Harp* 46–8:

as o'er them sweeps
Plastic and vast, one intellectual breeze,
At once the soul of each and God of all.

384–7 *A local spirit . . . communed:* The spirit (broadly to be equated with imagination) is 'local' in the sense that it reflects Wordsworth's individuality, refusing to subscribe to 'general tendency' (the norms of human behaviour). Mostly, however, it is willing to take second place to 'external things' (the forms of nature with which the mind interacts).

387 *auxiliar:* enhancing.

394–5 *Hence my obeisance . . . transport:* Wordsworth paradoxically gives his 'obeisance' (allegiance) to nature, and experiences 'transport' (rapture – again the sensation of being 'carried away'), because his imagination is able to dominate her, enhance the effect of her workings upon the mind.

396 *still:* always.

398 *analytic industry:* rational thinking.

402 *interminable building:* vast structure (within the mind).

407–11 *or, from excess . . . own enjoyments:* Wordsworth is thinking of important lines in the 1798 text of *Frost at Midnight*, not retained in later versions:

the living spirit in our frame,
That loves not to behold a lifeless thing,
Transfuses into all its own delights
Its own volition . . . (ll. 21–4)

416–34 *Pedlar:* 204–22, adapted for *The Prelude* autumn 1799, and incorporating (in the first person) Wordsworth's central pantheist statement of belief from February 1798: 'In all things|He saw one life, and felt that it was joy.'

Faith in the One Life is attributed to the past (the poet's 'seventeenth year'), yet by implication has lasted till the present day (see ll. 435ff. below).

413 *the Uncreated:* Wordsworth in *1850* 409–14 not only replaces the great pantheist assertion of *1805* 429–30, but puts a careful theological distance between God, who is uncreated, and his adoring Creation. He wrote the original lines of joy and sharing at the end of the eighteenth century, aged 27; he revised them, with Queen Victoria on the throne, aged almost 70.

433 *grosser prelude of that strain:* sensual enjoyment that prefaces the higher pleasures of response to the One Life.

435 *If this be error:* A sudden concession that reproduces the pattern of *TA* 50ff., 'If this|Be but a vain belief . . .'

448–57 *if in these times . . . dismay:* Wordsworth is drawing on a letter from Coleridge of September 1799 urging him to incorporate in *The Recluse* an address to

> those, who, in consequence of the complete failure of the French Revolution, have thrown up all hopes of the amelioration of mankind, and are sinking into an almost epicurean selfishness, disguising the same under the soft titles of domestic attachment and contempt for visionary *philosophes.*

449 *waste:* desert.

451–2 *when good men|On every side fall off:* Best known among those who renounced their radical ideals at this period was James Mackintosh, author of *Vindiciae Gallicae* (1791), a point-by-point reply to Burke's hostile *Reflections on the French Revolution.*

459 *more than Roman confidence:* Maxwell instances the Roman general, Varro, commended after his defeat by Hannibal at Cannae (216 BC) for not despairing of the Republic.

466–7 *Thou, my friend . . . other scenes:* Addressing his infant son, Hartley, Coleridge had written in *Frost at Midnight*, 'thou shalt learn far other lore,|And in far other scenes! For I was reared|In the great city'.

471–5 *The insinuated scoff . . . love:* Cf. 'the sneers of selfish men' and 'greetings where no kindness is' (*TA* 130–1).

479–84 *Fare thee well . . . mankind:* While Wordsworth and Dorothy were about to move into Dove Cottage, Grasmere, Coleridge in November 1799 (when these lines were written) had decided to go back to his career as a journalist with the *Morning Post* in London.

Book Third

1–167 Probably composed in December 1801, as an extension of the 1799 *Prelude*, to take account of the poet's University education. It is not clear how long at this stage he thought his poem would be. The remainder of Book III belongs to late January 1804.

1 *It was a dreary morning:* Wordsworth arrived in Cambridge on, or soon after, 30 October 1787.

17 *And at the Hoop . . . inn:* As De Selincourt points out (defending the line against Matthew Arnold, who thought it pompous), Wordsworth from the first adopted a playful, somewhat mock-heroic, tone in his account of Cambridge.

16 *spirit:* Sometimes scanned by Wordsworth (and Milton) as a monosyllable; cf. IV 153, 'And swellings of the spirits, was rapt and soothed'.

17 *Some friends I had:* Small as Hawkshead Grammar School was, Wordsworth had nine schoolfriends at Cambridge to support him in his 'strange transformation' (l. 30).

31 *courts:* Cambridge has 'courts', Oxford 'quadrangles'.

36–7 *hair . . . rimy trees:* Visiting her brother in December 1788, Dorothy found the 'smart powdered heads' and academic dress of Cambridge 'odd', 'but exceedingly becoming'. *rimy:* covered with hoar-frost.

42–3 *Smooth housekeeping . . . Liberal:* Taken by Owen to mean 'hospitable both inside and outside the College', but maybe Wordsworth is a more fortunate version of Lamb's Thomas Tame, *Elia* (1823) 8: 'Thomas Tame was very poor. Both he and his wife looked outwardly gentlefolks, when I fear all was not well at all times within.'

44 *The Evangelist . . . was:* St John's College, Cambridge, is dedicated to the Evangelist; St John's, Oxford, to the Baptist.

54 *with a male and female voice:* The hour strikes twice, first with a tenor bell, then with a treble.

55 *pealing organ:* Milton, *Il Penseroso* 161–2, 'let the pealing organ blow|To the full-voiced choir below'.

62–3 *The marble index . . . alone:* Famous lines, added to *The Prelude* in 1838–9, and seemingly distilled from Thomson's little-known elegy on Newton:

> The noiseless tide of time, all bearing down
> To vast eternity's unbounded sea,
> Where the green islands of the happy shine,
> He stemmed alone . . . (ll. 125–8)

Newton's statue is by Roubiliac, 1755.

63 *recusants:* resisters of authority.

65–6 *Examinations . . . balance:* See Daniel's interpretation of the writing on the wall at Belshazzar's feast: 'Thou art weighed in the balances, and art found wanting' (5.27). As Maxwell points out, Wordsworth is punning: 'examination' derives from Latin *examen*, a balance (pair of scales).

75–6 *melancholy thoughts|From . . . family regards:* The poet's family expected him to distinguish himself at Cambridge and gain a Fellowship at St John's, as his uncle, William Cookson, had done before him – and as his younger brother, Christopher, was soon to do at next-door Trinity. Instead, he neglected his academic work, taking a BA without honours in January 1791.

81 *wherefore be cast down:* 'Why art thou cast down, O my soul' (twice repeated in Psalm XLII, 'As the hart panteth after the water-brooks').

83–7 *For (not to speak . . . one far mightier):* A pious replacement of 1838–9 for the bold claim, 'Why should I grieve? I was a chosen son' (originally *Pedlar* 326).

101–7 *What independent . . . night of death:* Again pious elaboration in 1838–9 of a single line (*1805* 108) that had come to seem too bold.

115 *Incumbences:* spiritual broodings.

116 *the upholder:* Punctuation in the manuscripts makes it fairly certain that the 'upholder' is a spiritual principle within the self, equated with 'the tranquil soul'.

121 *That tolerates the indignities of Time:* A memorable line, occurring first in an early revision to *1805* 117–18 that is incorporated in *MS C*:

Which regulates the motion of all life
And tolerates the indignities of time
Till time shall cease.

The underlying and upholding soul is more clearly immortal (in a Christian sense) in *1850*, but from the first there has been the implication that it is beyond, or outside, time. Hence the awe-fulness of the poet's 'incumbencies' (spiritual brooding or overshadowing, *OED*).

121–67 Revised and augmented version of Wordsworth's climax to *The Pedlar* (ll. 330–56), transferred to *The Prelude* in December 1801.

128 *quickening:* life-giving; the material world is presented as drawing nourishment like a plant from an underlying spirit. When transcribing *MS B* in 1805–6, Mary Wordsworth was so conscious of the gardening metaphor that she actually wrote 'quickening soil' for 'quickening soul'.

129 *respired:* breathed; cf. *Kubla Khan* 18, 'As if this earth in fast thick pants were breathing'.

136–7 *in a kindred sense|Of passion:* Wordsworth's 'sense of passion' (mood, experiencing of emotion) is akin to nature's in l. 133.

142–4 *I had a world . . . into my mind:* Though the 'world' exists only within the mind, the fact that it 'lives' for God as well as the poet gives it a certain actuality – enhanced by the use of 'sympathies' in l. 145.

152 *higher up:* further back.

164 *its power:* The 'power' that penetrates exterior forms to find their essences, speaks 'logic' to the soul and 'binds' the senses, can only be imagination.

167 *Did bind my feelings . . . chain:* Wordsworth's senses are not (as one might think) 'bound' in the sense of restricted or controlled, but connected in a 'chain' of beneficial memories and associations. Cf. *Pedlar* 77–81:

the curious links
By which the perishàble hours of life
Are bound together, and the world of thought
Exists and is sustained.

In such a 'chain' the poet's days are 'Bound each to each by natural piety' (*Rainbow* 9).

168 *And here, o friend:* Wordsworth is presumably taking up his story in late January 1804. The new impulse behind composition is his wish to send an extended version of *The Prelude* (in five books, see Introduction) with Coleridge on his voyage to the Mediterranean in search of health.

173–6 *Of genius . . . within me:* That Wordsworth should leave these astonishing claims unmodified in *1850* is a mark of how little, despite concessions to Anglican thinking, he changed in his essential beliefs.

180 *The yoke of earth:* Wordsworth's image of man as harnessed to existence as an ox is harnessed to the plough is used again twice within a matter of weeks: 'years [that] bring the inevitable yoke' (*Intimations* 127), and 'yoke-fellows|To custom' (V 544–5 below).

182 *heroic argument:* Milton describes his 'argument' (theme) in *Paradise Lost* as 'Not less but more heroic' than the battle-poetry of Homer and Virgil (IX 13ff.). In drawing attention to the passage, Wordsworth tacitly places himself in this distinguished tradition. Lines 171–83 offer the new theme of human consciousness, beside which even Milton's Christian epic seems a narrative 'of outward things|Done visibly for other minds'.

188 *Breathings for incommunicable powers:* A strange line that Wordsworth seems to have been perfectly happy with. Are the 'breathings' inept, or inspired (like the breath of I 41)? Are they made by the poet in order to acquire 'incommunicable powers', or in lieu of them?

191 *heartless:* dejected.

191–2 *there's not a man . . . godlike hours:* An assumption on which the entire *Prelude* depends. If moments of transcendence are (however theoretically) within the reach of all, Wordsworth is Everyman, protected from the charge of egotism, and his poem has importance for us all.

201 *Uphold . . . fainting steps:* Seemingly a blend of two passages in *Samson Agonistes*: the opening lines, 'A little onward lend thy guiding hand|To these dark steps', plus l. 666, 'And fainting spirits uphold'.

211–12 *empty noise|And superficial pastimes:* Writing to De Quincey a month or so after composing these lines, Wordsworth is anxious to hear whether Oxford has 'seduced [him] into unworthy pleasures or pursuits' (6 March 1804). 'The manners of the young men' at Cambridge, he recalls, were 'very frantic and dissolute.'

217–28 *Could I behold . . . through the world:* A good example of the unpunctuatable Wordsworth sentence, burdened by parentheses and barely sustained by the triple repetition of 'Could'.

226 *miscellaneous . . . flowers:* undergraduates, pictured improbably as a garland of flowers that Cambridge, their *alma mater*, wears on her brow.

232 *spells seemed on me:* I seemed to be enchanted (to live in a magical world).

235–6 *my heart|Was social:* A corrective to the stereotype of Wordsworth as solitary. To Matthews he wrote on 7 November 1794, 'I begin to wish much to be in town; cataracts and mountains are good occasional society, but they will not do for constant companions'.

240 *divided:* shared.

245 *Unburdened, unalarmed, and unprofaned:* A pattern that Wordsworth probably associates with Milton ('Unshaken, unseduced, unterrified', *PL* VI 89), though it is found also in Spenser and Shakespeare, and imitated by Cowper and others.

248 *Want:* lack.

254 *trivial:* A small but significant change from *1805* 'lazy'.

259 *the second act:* 'opening act' (*1805*) had failed to take into account the early phase when Cambridge turned the poet's mind in on itself.

268 *dark:* unconscious; with undertones perhaps of 'confused' and 'mysterious'.

271 *precincts:* surroundings; often those of a cathedral or place of worship.

274 *Dictators at the plough:* Cincinnatus was ploughing when summoned to become Roman dictator in 458 BC.

274 *the accustomed garb:* Figures in old portraits wore the same academic dress as the poet himself.

276–7 *Beside . . . I laughed with Chaucer:* The Reeve's bawdy tale, concerning two Cambridge undergraduates who 'swyve' a miller's wife and daughter, is set at Trumpington. The fact that Dorothy read the *Miller's Tale* (also very broad in its humour) aloud to the poet on 26 December 1801 suggests that this passage may have been drafted at the same time as 1–167.

283 *I called him brother:* Spenser had been at Pembroke Hall, Cambridge, 1569–76.

284–5 *our blind poet . . . odious truth:* Milton – also a Cambridge man – is seen by Wordsworth in political terms. He is the republican who denounced the Restoration, as Abdiel (associated with Milton himself, and twice referred to in *Paradise Lost* as standing 'single') denounced the fallen angels.

286 *Darkness before . . . behind:* 'In darkness, and with dangers compassed round' (*PL* VII 27).

291–2 *rosy cheeks|Angelical:* Milton, who went to Christ's College, Cambridge in 1625 aged sixteen, was fair as a boy.

295 *My class-fellow:* Edward Birkett from Hawkshead Grammar School was at Milton's old College.

301 *oratory:* shrine.

304 *libations:* offerings of wine, poured out to gods of the classical world. Wordsworth himself is not drinking, but merely 'intoxicated' at the thought of following in Milton's footsteps.

309 *ostrich-like:* Late for chapel (which he was required to attend, see ll. 419–27 below), Wordsworth gathers up his gown, or perhaps the surplice of ll. 316–18, in order to run faster.

310 *opprobrious:* disgraceful.

312 *Cassandra:* daughter of Priam, King of Troy, whose predictions of the destruction of the city were unwelcome and ignored.

319–20 *inferior throng . . . burghers:* townspeople who are grouped low down in the chapel, beneath the organ.

325 *stationed me for:* placed me in a position to receive (note the abasement of *1850*).

339–40 *my life . . . floating island:* Wordsworth's bizarre image derives from a recurring phenomenon on Derwentwater, described in *Guide to the Lakes*: 'there occasionally appears above the surface . . . a considerable tract of spongy ground covered with aquatic plants, which is called the Floating Island' (*Prose Works* II 184).

354 *puissant:* powerful.

371 *Not that I slighted books:* Dorothy comments on 26 June 1791: 'He reads Italian, Spanish, French, Greek and Latin, and English, but never opens a mathematical book.' Unfortunately, maths (such was the dominance of Newton in eighteenth-century Cambridge) was the one subject in which the University held exams, and academic distinction could be achieved.

380 *magisterially:* masterfully; cf. II 387–95.

384 *to science and to arts:* It is not clear what distinction Wordsworth is making. Sometimes he uses science with its modern sense (Natural Science), sometimes (as at l. 427 below) with its earlier, general meaning, 'knowledge'

(Latin *scientia*). 'Arts' is scarcely easier to define at this period. Johnson's *Dictionary* encapsulates the problem: 'Art – A science; as, the liberal *arts*'.

387 *Toil and pains:* industriousness.

388 *bodied forth:* 'as imagination bodies forth|The forms of things unknown' (*Midsummer Night's Dream:* V i 14–15).

392 *congregating temper:* gregariousness, sociability.

401 *The passing day:* the present, as compared to antiquity.

407 *Republican, or pious:* to be seen in terms either of the ideal republic (of Plato or Harrington) or of primitive Christianity.

408 *emblazonry:* embellishment, display of gorgeous colours (in this case, of the imagination).

414 *schools:* academic precincts.

415–16 *to your bells|Give seasonable rest:* Wordsworth's advice to the 'Presidents and Deans' of Cambridge colleges to stop compulsory chapel is never toned down, despite his brother's becoming Master of Trinity.

424–7 *your officious doings . . . Suffers for this:* Fellows of Oxford and Cambridge colleges were not permitted at this period to get married. When they wished to do so, they resigned their Fellowships and went into the Church, carrying with them to their parishes the attitudes towards religion formed at the University.

427 *science:* knowledge, learning; see 384n. above.

431 *Collateral suspicion:* Respect for learning goes with respect for religion.

435 *raised a pile:* Of expectations.

444–6 *though the shades . . . under-coverts:* Extending his metaphor of the ideal university as a 'virgin grove', Wordsworth pictures day-to-day life in terms of cheerful woodlands ('shades') and 'under-coverts' full of songbirds. *indigent of* lacking.

449 *ruminating creatures:* animals that chew the cud (common already as a metaphor for thoughtfulness).

452–4 *the pelican . . . sun himself:* William Bartram, *Travels in North and South Carolina* (1791) 48: 'Behold on yon decayed, defoliated cypress tree, the solitary wood pelican, dejectly perched upon its utmost elevated spire.' Bartram is a source for 'the deep romantic chasm' of *Kubla Khan*, and for tropical imagery in Wordsworth's *Ruth*.

458–9 *the impresses . . . gaudy region:* external influences are of mere gaudiness.

467 *fathered:* traced to a source; cf. the 'unfathered vapour' of VI 527.

468 *curfew-time:* sun-down; leading a frugal life, scholars did not work in the dark by light of expensive candles.

474–7 *that glorious time . . . king:* the Renaissance.

486–7 *'An obolus . . . scholar':* 'I ought to have asked your permission for the scholars and their obolus' (Wordsworth to Coleridge, 29 March 1804). In its original form the story tells of a Byzantine general fallen from power and begging in Constantinople with the words 'Give an obol to Belisarius!'

489 *Bucer, Erasmus, or Melanchthon:* Famous early sixteenth-century scholars, Bucer working in Cambridge and Erasmus in Oxford.

492 *darkly:* confusedly; 'For now we see through a glass, darkly', *I Corinthians* 13.12.

510 *tax:* blame; 'Tax not divine disposal', *Samson Agonistes* 210.

513–14 *passions . . . low and mean:* Enumerated in ll. 533–5 below.

518 *shoal:* crowd.

520 *and not wanting love: 1850* 'yet not wanting' makes the easier reading; however, Wordsworth did not originally see an incongruity in the 'easy minds' possessing love of a kind.

524–41 Cut as early as *MS C*, c. 1819.

540 *the under-soul:* Note the reference back to 'the upholder . . . the tranquil soul' of l. 116, 'Which underneath all passion lives secure'.

542 *this deep vacation:* A quiet joke: term-time at Cambridge was for Wordsworth a 'vacation' from strenuous thought.

546–9 *a shepherd . . . beholds:* Thomson, *Castle of Indolence* (1748) I stanza 30; the shepherd is divorced from reality, not, as one might expect, valued for his imaginative response.

555 *intervenient:* that which 'comes between'; cf. II 206.

556 *visionary:* Cf. the poet's first response to the sights of Cambridge, 'I was the dreamer, they the dream' (l. 28 above).

557 *bolted forth:* driven into the open, like a hunted animal (in this case, forced prematurely into adult life).

563 *to ensue:* Unnecessary words that do not alter the meaning of Wordsworth's sentence, and seem to have no grammatical relation to what has gone before. Yet the lines persist unchanged in *1850*. Could Wordsworth have intended 'to ensure'? A transitive verb would do no harm.

584 *Objects embossed:* standing out in relief. *sedulous:* anxious, diligent (a Miltonic usage, as at I 571).

590–6 *The surfaces . . . to watch:* In evoking 'the surfaces of artificial life' Wordsworth has woven a tapestry ('arras') of allusions to Spenser, *FQ* III xi stanza 28. *state:* formal, pompous.

610 *humourists:* eccentrics, 'humour characters'; applied by Lamb memorably to the clerks of the South-sea House.

618 *hardly:* forcefully.

630–43 Suggested by Cowper, *Task* II 699–750, 'In colleges and halls, in ancient days . . .' but with some reminiscence of Shakespeare's Sonnet 66. Though renouncing personifications in the Preface to *Lyrical Ballads*, Wordsworth used them very effectively for satirical purposes.

634 *And simple pleasure, foraging for death:* Not an easy line. Pleasure either 'forages' on behalf of death, or actually seeks him. Wordsworth could have a situation in mind akin to that of Chaucer's *Pardoner's Tale*, with its revellers who seek death – and of course find him.

637 *bald:* crude, graceless.

644 *notices:* observations.

650 *is still with innocence:* is always, like innocence . . .

652 *cabinet:* display-case; as at II 228.

657 *quickens:* enlivens, animates.

661 *congress:* assemblage, gathering.

669–71 *Thus in submissive idleness . . . away:* As at ll. 542–3 above, Wordsworth plays the idleness of Cambridge off against 'labouring-time' in the outside world.

Book Fourth

1–4 *A pleasant sight . . . Windermere:* Wordsworth was returning to Hawkshead, scene of his schooldays, at the beginning of the Cambridge summer vacation of 1788. He had come by coach to Kendal, then walked ten miles or so, via Crook, to the ridge at Cleabarrow, 500–600 feet above Windermere.

1 *clomb:* climbed; the strong past participle existed both in Cumbrian speech and as a poetic archaism: 'While clomb above the eastern bar|The horned moon' (*AM* 201–2).

11 *that sweet valley:* the Vale of Esthwaite.

14 *Charon:* ferryman of the Greek Underworld, who transported the souls of the dead across the Rivers Styx and Acheron. Doubtless, as De Selincourt commented, an 'inapt allusion', but pleasurable in its incongruity.

17 *my old dame:* Ann Tyson, Wordsworth's landlady at Hawkshead, who died in 1796 aged 83.

20 *good creature:* A term of affection – 'creature' literally meaning 'created one' – not restricted at this period to animals.

40 *froward:* impetuous.

53–4 *my late course . . . enthralment:* life at Cambridge.

66 *habiliments:* clothing.

101–8 *A hundred times . . . yet again:* As at *1799* II 166–74, Wordsworth works into his blank verse adolescent poetry in order to evoke the period at which it was composed. On this occasion it is *The Dog: An Idyllium* of 1786–7:

> If while I gazed, to nature blind,
> In the calm ocean of my mind
> Some new-created image rose
> In full-grown beauty at its birth,
> Then, while my glad hand sprung to thee,
> We were the happiest pair on earth!

The change from 'new-created image' to 'fair enchanting image' (l. 104) is enough to suggest the adult poet's indulgence towards a former self.

114 *passenger:* passer-by. Wordsworth never lost the habit of composing on the roads; see Kilvert's account of his 'crooning out loud some lines of a poem which he was composing' near Ambleside in 1838–9, *1850* XI 377–8n.

130 *consummate:* complete (pronounced 'consùmmit').

140–2 *Gently did my soul . . . her God:* Moses stood unveiled before Jehovah on Mount Sinai, but veiled his shining face when he descended to meet the people (*Exodus* 34.33–4).

150 *I saw but little, and thereat was pleased:* Assuming Wordsworth to be looking at himself on the scales, we expect 'but' for 'and' (he saw little, but what there was was promising). Giving full force to the 'and', we arrive at an odder reading, 'I saw little, and was pleased by that fact'. *1850*, meanwhile, has a reading that makes sense, but surely does not represent the poet's original intention.

157 *Informs, creates, and thaws the deepest sleep:* An echo of Thomson, *Seasons* I 855, 'Adjusts, sustains, and agitates the whole' (Thomson's subject is the inspiring breath of God).

168–80 *meanwhile . . . were there:* Uncomfortably close to self-parody: readers are asked to take seriously that Wordsworth mistook the breathing of the earth ('sobbings of the place|And restrictions', II 129–30 above) for the panting of his dog. *1850* is a considerable improvement.

172 *coppice:* copse, small wood (often of hazels).

184 *prospect:* In this case, the human scene.

199 *To deck some slighted playmate's homely cheek:* A version of *Lycidas* 65, 'To tend the homely slighted shepherd's trade', and intended to be recognized as such.

215 *business:* busy-ness.

237–8 *those fair Seven . . . child:* the Pleiades, otherwise known as the 'Seven Sisters'.

239 *my own belovèd star:* Wordsworth was born under Jupiter, on 7 April 1770.

247–64 *As one who hangs . . . like success:* An epic simile in the tradition of Virgil and Milton, but modelled in fact on Cowper; cf. *Task* III 1–20, quoted IX 5n.

263 *Incumbent:* leaning.

273–4 *gauds|And feast . . . and public revelry:* Milton, *L'Allegro* 127, 'pomp, and feast, and revelry'. *gauds:* pastimes.

283 *grateful:* Not different in meaning from *1805* 'pleasing', but consciously Miltonic.

279 *feeding:* nutritive, spiritually sustaining.

289 *yearnings:* Wordsworth's executors have omitted the adjective 'daily', present in the MSS, so as to reduce a (probably unintended) alexandrine to the standard ten-syllable line.

282 *To nature and to books:* 'Love nature and books', Wordsworth told the undergraduate De Quincey a month or so after writing these lines, 'seek these, and you will be happy. For virtuous friendship, and love, and knowledge of mankind, must inevitably accompany these, all things thus ripening in their due season' (6 March 1804).

291–7 The cutting of *1805* 282–304 down to six-and-a-half lines makes for a smoother lead into the great consecration scene that is to follow, but at a considerable loss.

290 *Contagious air . . . me Hamlet:* II ii 318ff.: 'This most excellent canopy the air, look you, this brave and overhanging firmament . . . it appears no other thing to me but a foul and pestilent congregation of vapours.'

296–8 *The authentic sight of reason . . . faculty of truth:* Not analytic reason, but 'reason in her most exalted mood', showing the influence of Coleridge (and through him, of Kant), and equated at XIII 166–70 with imagination, 'absolute strength|And clearest insight'.

302 *pageant plaything with vile claws:* Wordsworth's imagery in ll. 301–4 unites the mood and diction of *Hamlet* (see 290n. above) with specific reference to a life-sized model of a tiger savaging a white man, captured at Seringapatam in 1799 and probably shown to Wordsworth by Lamb at the East India Company in 1802. See Owen, 'Tipu's Tiger', *NQ* 1970, 379–80, and, better still, the remarkable model itself at the Victoria and Albert Museum.

304 *heartless:* dispiriting.

309 *manners put to school:* the study of human behaviour.

318 *promiscuous rout:* mixed (heterogeneous) company. Wordsworth's model is *PL* I 380, 'the promiscuous crowd stood yet aloof'; as Maxwell points out, 'rout' too is Miltonic in this sense.

319 *tempers:* temperaments.

329 *Two miles I had to walk:* Efforts to place Wordsworth's walk have not been very successful. As elsewhere he is probably conflating memories; Mary Moorman, *The Early Years* 57, points to an interesting statement made by the poet in old age that 'the first voluntary verses' he ever wrote 'were written after walking six miles [from Whitehaven] to attend a dance at Egremont' (private papers).

323–7 *Magnificent|The morning rose . . . the clouds:* Three times in under five lines Wordsworth has altered *1805* by replacing the verb to be. De Selincourt, who regarded the early text in general as more powerful, commented in 1926 'no one can miss the gain in strength and vividness effected by the[se] simple changes'. To judge from his defence of *The Leech Gatherer* to the Hutchinson sisters on 14 June 1802, the younger Wordsworth would have had something to say on the matter: '"A lonely place, a pond", "by which an old man *was*, far from all house or home" – not stood, not sat, but "was" – the figure presented in the most naked simplicity possible.'

335 *grain-tinctured:* An imitation of 'Sky-tinctured grain' (*PL* V 285), though Milton meant blue, and Wordsworth (depending on *OED*, sense 10) means scarlet. *empyrean light:* light from the uppermost heaven, consisting of pure fire; cf. *PL* VI 13–14, 'highest heaven, arrayed in gold|Empyreal'.

338 *Dews, vapours, and the melody of birds:* There is a Miltonic source for this lower Wordworthian style as well as for the poetry of the empyrean: 'fruits and flowers,|Walks, and the melody of birds' (*PL* VIII 527–8).

341–2 *vows|Were then made for me:* As a 'chosen son' (III 82), Wordsworth is 'dedicated' by the higher power (sometimes specifically referred to as nature) that has directed his education. The dedication is to a life of service, by implication as the poet of *The Recluse.*

339 There is no manuscript authority for the punctuation of *1850.*

354 *loose:* undirected.

355 *primitive hours:* times of purer vision.

363–504 Composed in early February 1798 as a separate poem, *The Discharged Soldier*, and incorporated in *The Prelude* in February 1804. *The Discharged Soldier* was first published in its original form (to which reference is made below), by Beth Darlington, *Bicentenary Studies* 433–48.

353–78 Though the episode of the Discharged Soldier is cut by almost a third in *1850*, Wordsworth replaces the brief introduction of *1805* with 14 lines emphasizing the theme of solitude, then inserts eight evoking the Windermere Regatta.

362 *Votary:* one who is bound by vows to a religious life (more loosely, a 'worshipper').

372 *oars with oars contending, sails with sails:* Pleasurable recollection of *Rape of the Lock* I 101–2.

> Where wigs with wigs, with sword-knots, sword-knots strive,
> Beaus banish beaus, and coaches coaches drive.

378 *strenuous idleness:* Horace's famous oxymoron '*strenua nos exercet inertia*' (*Epistles* I xi 28) is quoted by Wordsworth in a letter to Matthews of 17 June 1791: London has whirled him about in 'the vortex of its *strenua inertia*'.

370 *a steep ascent:* Mention in *1850* 370–8 of the poet's returning home after the

Windermere Regatta enables us to identify the 'steep ascent' as Brier's Brow, above the ferry on the Hawkshead side of the lake; see Thompson's *Hawkshead* 139–41.

371–3 *the road's watery surface . . . stream:* Dorothy Wordsworth, 31 January 1798: 'The road to the village of Holford glittered like another stream'. Wordsworth incorporated his sister's note within days (and despite the fact that they were in Somerset, and he was writing about the Lake District).

374 *lapse:* fall, flow; 'And liquid lapse of murmuring streams' (*PL* VIII 263).

400 *step by step led on:* Christ in *Paradise Regained* wanders into the desert, 'Thought following thought, and step by step led on' (I 192).

402 *an uncouth shape:* At *PL* II 666 (note the apocalyptic number), Satan meets Death at the gates of Hell: 'The other shape,|If shape he might be called, that shape had none'. Wordsworth would know Burke's comments on the sublimity of the encounter, and be aware too of illustrations by Fuseli and others.

405–9 *He was . . . day:* A playing down of the obsessional quality of Wordsworth's vision in 1798:

> He was in stature tall,
> A foot above man's common measure tall,
> And lank, and upright. There was in his form
> A meagre stiffness. You might almost think
> That his bones wounded him. His legs were long,
> So long and shapeless that I looked at him
> Forgetful of the body they sustained. (*Discharged Soldier* 41–7)

412 *A milestone:* No milestone survives, but the corner that seems to be described is beyond Far Sawrey, three miles from Hawkshead.

403–4 *To which the trappings . . . back-ground:* Fidgety replacement for the elemental reading of *1805*.

415 *entire. He was: Discharged Soldier:* 55–60 has been omitted at this point, including details of the Soldier's alienation with which Wordsworth had deeply sympathized in 1798:

> His face was turned
> Towards the road, yet not as if he sought
> For any living thing. He appeared
> Forlorn and desolate, a man cut off
> From all his kind, and more than half detached
> From his own nature.

434 *my heart's specious cowardice:* The heart is 'specious' in concealing its true motivation, of fear.

446 *tropic islands:* West Indies. Though his encounter with the Soldier is dated to the long vacation of 1788, the campaigns against the French that Wordsworth has in mind took place in the mid-1790s. By 1796 40,000 British troops had died of yellow fever; others survived in a wasted condition and were reduced to beggary on their return.

463 *And lain:* 'And such the languor of the weary man,|Had lain' (*Discharged Soldier* 119).

468–9 *Discharged Soldier:* 126–32 omitted, including a poignant stress on the Soldier's humanity. As with the Leech Gatherer, and London Beggar of VII 609–23, Wordsworth's concern at this later stage is with the symbolic importance of his solitary figure rather than his pathos.

475 *a strange half-absence:* Cf. *Ruined Cottage* 382–3, 'The careless stillness which a thinking mind|Gives to an idle matter', and the Old Cumberland Beggar's 'fixed and serious look|Of idle computation' (ll. 11–12).

491–2 *But ask . . . required:* An improvement on the wording of 1798, where the poet's reproof is oddly intrusive: 'And told him, feeble as he was, 'twere fit|He asked relief or alms' (*Discharged Soldier* 161–2).

466 *the patient man:* Truer to the Soldier's behaviour than the reading of *Discharged Soldier* and *1805*: 'the poor unhappy man'.

502–4 *Back I cast . . . home:* Not present in *Discharged Soldier.*

469 Inserted in the text of *MS D* (though with a note, 'N.B. Query as to the omission of these three last lines?') is an additional sentence:

> This passed, and He who deigns to mark with care
> By what rules governed, with what end in view
> This Work proceeds, *he* will not wish for more.

Both lines and note persist in *MS E*, and, as Owen points out, there is no warrant for excluding them. 'More' in the final line could of course mean 'greater length'; probably, though, it means 'material of greater importance'. Those who observe that Wordsworth is writing about the growth of the mind will not ask why meeting the Soldier has been significant.

Book Fifth

4 *Thou paramount creature:* A reminiscence of *Hamlet* II ii 315–16, where man is 'the paragon of animals' and yet a 'quintessence of dust'.

7 *I charm away:* Effectively, 'I leave aside' (the image is of magic, as if Wordsworth has Prospero as well as Hamlet in his thoughts).

11–13 *my mind hath looked . . . prime teacher:* Modelled on *FM* 63–8, where God, as the 'great universal Teacher', is to be heard and seen in 'The lovely shapes and sounds intelligible' of the 'eternal language' of nature.

13–16 *intercourse with man . . . participate:* God, as the 'sovereign intellect', has established communication with man through the natural world which is the 'bodily image' of his spiritual presence. As in *Tintern Abbey*, man is not merely aware of the 'soul divine', but 'participates' in it, shares its essence.

17 *As might appear . . . time:* Among Wordsworth's latest revisions; perception of the One Life is now to be seen as a fallible human way of looking at things.

18 *For commerce . . . itself:* as a communication of the human spirit to other human beings.

19 *Things worthy . . . life:* works of art and achievements of the human mind which the poet feels deserve to be permanent.

21 *must perish:* are bound to perish. In the light of ll. 22–3 it seems that it is for man's own good that human achievements (mere 'garments' in l. 23) are impermanent. True immortality will be spiritual.

23–7 *yet man . . . disconsolate:* Wordsworth's meaning seems to be that man, while yet alive (unextinguished), is forced to regret possession of the earthly achievements that he fears to lose, and to live on, abject and disconsolate. The quotation marks draw attention to Shakespeare's Sonnet 64, 13–14, which seem to have influenced both the matter and the cryptic expression of the *Prelude* lines: 'This thought is as a death, which cannot choose|But weep to have that which it fears to lose.'

33 *the living presence:* the presence of life (with an unspoken implication that life is the 'soul divine' of l. 16).

38 *adamantine holds:* impregnable defences.

39–40 *passion . . . soul sublime:* Passion is not merely identified with 'highest reason' (as experienced by the 'soul sublime'), but tacitly equated with imagination, described at XIII 166–70 as 'reason in her most exalted mood'.

41 *The consecrated . . . sage:* works (sacred, because they represent the highest achievements of the human spirit) of the imagination and of the intellect (to be equated, respectively, with poetry and mathematics at ll. 104–9 below).

44–8 *Oh, why . . . frail:* Catching the tones of Milton's lament, 'why was the sight|To such a tender ball as the eye confined' (*Samson Agonistes* 93–4), Wordsworth asks why works of art could not be imprinted on a substance that has the same durability as the human mind that conceived them. It is a question that could be asked only by a poet who feels the mind and human emotion to have the permanence of natural forms.

49 *a friend:* Almost certainly Coleridge (despite the fact that the poem as a whole is addressed to him). There is little to support Smyser's suggestion in 'Wordsworth's Dream of Poetry and Science', *PMLA* 1956, 269–75, that the friend might be Michel Beaupuy, the poet's French mentor in 1792.

53 *on the front of:* immediately following.

55 *kindred hauntings:* similar anxieties; cf. *Brothers* 236, 'hauntings from the infirmity of love'.

56 *Whereupon I told:* Not until the *Prelude* revisions of 1838–9 does Wordsworth claim to have experienced the dream of the arab Quixote himself. De Selincourt, for one, thought the *1805* version of events more probable.

59–60 *famous history . . . Cervantes: Don Quixote.*

67 *Exempt . . . injury* Poetry and geometry have in themselves a perfection (while those who profess them are subject to the 'injuries' of time and chance).

71–139 The great dream-sequence of *The Prelude* has unexpectedly a learned source, in Adrien Baillet's *Vie de Descartes* (1691); see Smyser, cited at 49n. above. Wordsworth has transformed the second of two dreams that Descartes is recorded as having experienced in November 1619. Descartes' dream takes place in a library, and the two 'books' it concerns are literally so: a dictionary and a collection of poetry.

75 *an uncouth shape: 1850* sets up a parallel between the arab Quixote and the Discharged Soldier, also first perceived as 'an uncouth shape' (*1805* IV 402).

79 *A lance he bore:* Quixote at one point famously uses his lance to tilt at windmills (believing them to be giants).

88 *Euclid:* Greek mathematician of the third century BC, whose *Elements* was the basic textbook of geometry used by Wordsworth at Hawkshead Grammar School and (less assiduously) at Cambridge.

97 *ode:* Wordsworth regarded *Tintern Abbey*, because of 'the impassioned music of its versification', as having 'the principal requisites of an ode'.

104–9 *The one . . . hope:* Lines quoted by De Quincey from memory, and brilliantly commented on, *Recollections* 168–9:

> Wordsworth was a profound admirer of the sublimer mathematics; at least of the higher geometry. The secret of this admiration for geometry lay in the antagonism between this world of bodiless abstraction and the world of passion . . . in a great philosophical poem of Wordsworth's, which is still in MS, and will remain in MS until after his death, there is . . . a dream, which reaches the very *ne plus ultra* of sublimity in my opinion, expressly framed to illustrate the eternity, and the independence of all social modes or fashions of existence, conceded to these two 'hemispheres', as it were, that compose the total world of human power – mathematics on the one hand, poetry on the other: 'The one that held acquaintance . . .'

115 *engendered:* created (literally 'bred'); cf. *Brothers* 205–6, 'youth and age|Engendering in the blood of hale four score', where Wordsworth is consciously imitating Shakespeare (*Merchant of Venice* III ii 67–8).

116 *cleave unto:* stick with; cf. the woman's vow in the Marriage Service, 'and forsaking all other, cleave only to him'.

133 *charge:* burden; perhaps 'responsibility'.

137–9 *Whereat I waked . . . side:* As he rounds his dream off with a return to the book and landscape by which it was prompted, Wordsworth shows his awareness of the dream as a literary form, and almost certainly has Chaucer's early vision-poems in mind.

151–2 *the blind and awful lair|Of such a madness:*

> One hasn't in the dream thought of the arab as mad at all, and neither the associations of Don Quixote nor the poet's own identification have led one to think of his mind as a 'blind and awful lair'. The image is violent, shocking, an intrusion of personal terrors into poetry that has seemed to be decorous and assured . . . One is left wondering whether at some level Wordsworth was confronting the possibility that he himself could be mad, crazed by protracted internal thought, deluded in his mission and his aspirations. (*B V* 207–8).

153,156 *Enow:* Archaic plural form of 'enough', used for its poetic quality, but (like 'clomb', IV 1) present in Cumbrian speech.

156–8 *yea, will I say . . . manifest:* Evidence, according to Owen's political reading, that Wordsworth 'foresaw the imminent collapse of Western civilization under French aggression.'

164 *casket:* Immortal verse is 'coffined', subjected to mortality, within the destructible earthly book; cf. the 'shrines so frail' of l. 48.

168 *the best of other thoughts:* the thought of books, nominally Wordsworth's theme in Book V.

171 *travelling back among those days:* returning in his thoughts (and in the narrative of his poem) to childhood.

172 *play an ingrate's part:* be ungrateful; cf. God's unamiable reference to Adam, *PL* III 97–8, 'Ingrate, he had of me|All he could have'.

178 *slender accents:* soft tones; Maxwell draws attention to the 'slender notes' of the redbreast (Cowper, *Task* VI 78), cited by *OED* as the first usage of the word in such a context.

178–9 *some tale|That did bewitch me then:* Cf. Wordsworth's later references to fairy-stories and *The Arabian Nights* (ll. 364–9 and 482–500 below). In 1847 he recalled the happiness of his 'earliest days at school' in terms of being at liberty 'to read whatever books [he] liked' (*Memoirs* I 10). *Don Quixote* is cited, alongside Fielding, *Gil Blas* and Swift.

180 *O friend . . . soul:* Coleridge had addressed Wordsworth in very similar terms in the version of *Dejection: An Ode* printed in the *Morning Post* on 4 October 1802 (Wordsworth's wedding day): 'O lofty poet, full of life and love,|Brother and friend of my devoutest choice . . .'

201 *native prose or numerous verse:* 'in prose or numerous verse' (*PL* V 150); because of the counting of 'feet' involved, verse was often referred to as 'numbers'. *native* natural (not adjusted to metre).

206 *trumpet-tones of harmony:* Homer (representing classical poetry) and the river of Jewish song (the Scriptures) are followed in Wordsworth's thoughts by Milton, whose verse, uniting the two traditions, 'became a trumpet, whence he blew|Soul-animating strains' (*Scorn Not the Sonnet* 13–14).

219–22 *speak of them as powers . . . God:* Wordsworth's own hope was that his poetry might 'become|A power like one of nature's' (XII 311–12).

222 *Or His pure Word . . . revealed:* A reference to Christ's miraculous incarnation as the Word (Logos) become flesh; inserted in revised *MS D*, probably late 1832.

228 *pest:* plague, epidemic; probably modelled on Cowper, *Task* IV 500–1, 'vain the attempt|To advertise in verse a public pest'. Wordsworth turns out to have in mind the late eighteenth-century plague of rationalist educational theories, which might have deprived him and Coleridge of their wandering as children imaginatively through literature.

238 *noosed:* fitted with a halter.

239 *several:* separate.

244–5 *till it hath yielded . . . scythe:* The ox is not turned out to grass until after the first crop of hay has been cut – in terms of the poet's metaphor, till the mower (seen almost as a god) has received the first fruits as an offering. Again Wordsworth is drawing his imagery from Cowper, always present where *The Prelude* adopts a satirical voice: 'of its fruits he sends|Large prelibation' (*Task* V 573–4).

256–7 *Early died . . . mother:* Wordsworth's mother died suddenly in March 1778, when he was nearly eight. He clearly sees no incongruity as the verse moves abruptly from hen to parent.

259–60 *She left us destitute . . . together:* Note the unconscious resentment (and compare the envy of II 261, 'No outcast he, bewildered and depressed'). The family was split up at Ann Wordsworth's death, Dorothy, aged six, being sent to Halifax to be brought up by distant relatives (on the grounds that as a girl she couldn't properly grow up in an all-male household). William was sent to school at Hawkshead a year later, where he and his brothers lived in lodgings.

260–2 *Little suits it . . . others' blame:* Wordsworth thinks it improper to praise his mother by comparison with the relatives who have helped to bring up her orphaned children. Dorothy's first extant letter (to Jane Pollard, July 1787) refers to 'the ill nature of all my relations', and adds:

> Many a time have William, John, Christopher, and myself shed tears together, tears of the bitterest sorrow. We all of us, each day, feel more sensibly the loss we sustained when we were deprived of our parents, and each day do we receive fresh insults.

268 *for times to come: 1805* 'from those to come'; a small revision that wholly changes the meaning.

278 *overweeningly:* presumptuously.

283–4 *from regards . . . promises:* Wordsworth's mother had enjoyed life for what it was, without demanding restlessly whether it had fulfilled its promises, given her her due.

292–3 *the monster birth . . . times:* The 'monster birth', or prodigy, is created by the plague of educational theories, hinted at in ll. 223–45 above. Wordsworth's drift has indeed been scarcely obvious.

294–369 Wordsworth's satirical portrait of the Infant Prodigy created by artificial systems of education was composed in February 1804 to complement *There Was A Boy* (ll. 389–422 below, now first incorporated in *The Prelude*), with its portrayal of education through nature. Broadly the debate could be seen as Locke (*Thoughts on Education*, 1690) and the inculcation of knowledge, versus Rousseau (*Emile*, 1762) and freedom to be a child. But Wordsworth, as De Selincourt points out in a long and useful note, goes beyond Rousseau in his willingness 'to stand aside and leave nature and the child to themselves'. Dorothy Wordsworth's letter to Jane Marshall of 19 March 1797 shows that in the upbringing of Basil Montagu (entrusted to their care in 1796, and now four years old) she and the poet avoided not only system but Rousseau's coercive pointing of the lessons of nature (see l. 334n. below).

298–346 The Infant Prodigy is among the most comprehensively revised passages in *The Prelude.* The final version is 27 lines shorter than *1805*; 35 lines were cut and eight added.

301–3 *Selfishness . . . his name:* Harry Sandford in Thomas Day's morally improving *Sandford and Merton* (1783) has precisely the goody-goody image that Wordsworth is attacking.

304 *Dumb creatures . . . nun:* Wordsworth, who saw Chaucer as the master of the satirical portrait, has in mind the affected tenderness of the Prioress (*General Prologue* 143–50).

306–8 *he is garnished . . . ridiculous:* 'Goodness' is set off to the best advantage: the child's remarks ('notices') are clever, knowing, and his sense of the ridiculous is sharp.

311 *licensed:* unrestrained; cf. Lear's 'all-licensed Fool' (I iv 201).

313 *read lectures:* speak learnedly.

315 *panoply complete:* full armour; cf. Cowper, *Task* II 345, 'armed himself in panoply complete'.

315–18 *fear itself . . . Touches him not:* To be incapable of fear is to be shielded from the major formative influence on Wordsworth's own childhood: 'and I grew up|Fostered alike by beauty and by fear' (I 305–6).

322 *terms of art:* learned terms, jargon.

325–7 *cushion of divine . . . head:* Wordsworth's image is suggested by Cowper's 'plump convivial parson' (*Task* IV 595–8), who 'lays'

> His reverence and his worship both to rest
> On the same cushion of habitual sloth.

The parson's cushion becomes an emblem ('type') of his 'thought profound' because the bible rests on it in front of the pulpit.

328–30 *The ensigns . . . maps:* Flags, orb and sceptre, symbolizing kingship, are replaced by scientific instruments as emblems of the prodigy's intellectual rule.

331 *Ships he can guide . . . sea:* De Selincourt draws attention to Locke's boast in *Some Thoughts Concerning Education* (1690):

> I now live in the house with a child . . . [who] knew the limits of the four parts of the world, could readily point, being asked, to any country upon the globe . . . and could find the longitude and latitude of any place, before he was six years old. (*Educational Writings*, ed. J.L. Axtell, 289)

332 *cunning:* sophistication, complexity.

334 *He knows the policies of foreign lands:* With the prodigy's cult of knowledge compare Basil Montagu's natural curiosity, described by Dorothy Wordsworth on 19 March 1797:

> You ask to be informed of our system respecting Basil. It is a very simple one – so simple that in this age of systems you will hardly be likely to follow it. We teach him nothing at present but what he learns from the evidence of his senses. He has an insatiable curiosity which we are always careful to satisfy to the best of our ability. It is directed to everything he sees: the sky, the fields, the trees, shrubs, corn, the making of tools, carts, &c, &c, &c. He knows his letters, but we have not attempted any further step in the path of book learning. Our grand study has been to make him happy . . .

337–8 *He sifts . . . trust:* Coleridge, whose views on this topic were probably very close to Wordsworth's, had written to Poole on 16 October 1797:

> I have known some who have been *rationally* educated, as it is styled. They were marked by a microscopic acuteness; but when they looked at great things, all became a blank and they saw nothing – and denied (very illogically) that anything could be seen . . . [They] called the want of imagination judgment, and never being moved to rapture, philosophy.

339–40 *The country people . . . experiments:* To the ignorant it seems that the child may be searching for forbidden knowledge. Maxwell points to the magician Glendower's 'deep experiments', *Henry IV Part I* III i 492.

345 *cistern:* water-butt, rain-barrel.

328 *trainer:* gardener (in this case); cf. *Richard II* III iv 63–6.

346–9 *old grandame earth . . . forlorn:* On the face of it, a reversal of *Intimations* 77ff. (also written in February 1804). In the Ode earth, as foster-mother, 'fills her lap with pleasures of her own', tempting the imaginative child to forget his former existence; here, 'grandame earth' (a conflation of *Henry IV Part I* III i 31 and 33) grieves that the unimaginative child rejects her bounty.

350 *Now this is hollow:* Cf. 'Now this is fulsome' from Cowper's account of the 'theatrical clerical coxcomb' (*Task* II 455) on whom later in the year Wordsworth based the 'pretty shepherd' of VII 544–66.

361 *pound:* impound, imprison.

362 *pinfold:* a pound, enclosure for stray animals.

364–7 *Oh, give us . . . St George:* Wordsworth shared Coleridge's view that reading fairy tales 'habituated' the child's mind 'to *the vast*', gave it 'a love of *the great* and *the whole*' (to Poole, 16 October 1797). The wishing-cap of Fortunatus transported him wherever he wished to go; Jack's coat made him invisible while killing giants; Sabra, daughter of the King of Egypt, was rescued by St George from a dragon, and duly married him.

370–422 A sequence put together early in 1799, probably with *The Recluse* rather than *The Prelude* in mind, and forming Wordsworth's first attempt to use *There Was A Boy* as part of a larger discussion of education. In its original form the sequence opened, 'There are who tell us that in recent times|We have been great discoverers'.

371–2 *Who with a broad highway . . . futurity:* The 'workmen' (educationalists) are tacitly compared to Milton's Sin and Death who in *Paradise Lost* build a bridge over Chaos to their new empire on earth (X 282–305). *froward* wayward.

382–3 *would confine . . . engines:* Erasmus Darwin (*Botanic Garden* I i 289–92) had predicted excitedly in 1791 that steam would soon provide power for 'the slow barge', 'the rapid car' and 'the flying-chariot'; despite his *Prelude* reference to 'the very road', however (l. 381), Wordsworth in 1804 is likely to have in mind static engines (pumps, or perhaps machine-looms) that are bolted down. Trevithick's first 'steam-carriage' was tested in 1801.

389–422 Lines published in *Lyrical Ballads* in 1800 as *There Was A Boy*, and regarded by Wordsworth as showing 'one of the earliest processes of nature in the development' of imagination (Preface to *Poems* 1815). In the original draft of *MS JJ*, October 1798, *There Was A Boy* concluded at l. 413, and (despite its impersonal opening line) was offered as the poet's own experience.

390 *Winander:* Windermere.

401 *Responsive to his call:* responsive to my call (*MS JJ*). For the original version read similarly 'my' for 'his' in ll. 405, 408, 410, and 'I' for 'he' in 406.

408 *far into his heart:* De Quincey comments beautifully:

> This very expression, 'far', by which space and its infinities are attributed to the human heart, and to its capacities of reechoing the sublimities of nature, has always struck me as with a flash of sublime revelation. (*Recollections* 161)

410 *unawares:* unconsciously; the word points to a link with the central moment of *The Ancient Mariner* (also a poem about the reciprocal relationship of man and nature): 'A spring of love gushed from my heart,|And I blessed them unaware' (ll. 276–7).

412–13 *that uncertain heaven . . . lake:* 'Had I met these lines running wild in the deserts of Arabia, I should have instantly screamed out "Wordsworth!"' (Coleridge to Wordsworth, 10 December 1798).

414–22 Added to *There Was A Boy* early in 1799, and present in the text as published in *Lyrical Ballads* 1800; see 370–422n. above. As elsewhere in *The Prelude*, Wordsworth blends different facts and events to form an imaginative whole. Though presenting himself as the mimic-hooter of the original poem, he implies in the Fenwick Note (1842) that he had written with William Raincock in mind. Raincock did not however die as a schoolboy at Hawkshead; the person who did so was John Tyson, buried on 27 August 1782 (*Wordsworth's Hawkshead* 56) at the age of twelve (the figure mentioned in *1850*, as against ten in *1805*).

425 *spoken of erewhile:* At IV 14.

433–5 *easily indeed . . . arts and letters:* An unexpected comment. With its young Cambridge headmaster, William Taylor (d. 1786, aged 32), Hawkshead had for a brief period remarkably high academic standards. Wordsworth later claimed to have been a year ahead of his contemporaries in mathematics when he arrived at the university (*Memoirs* I 14). *arts and letters:* literature ('letters') and other branches of study.

450–72 *Well do I call . . . ghastly face:* Written c. January 1799 as the first element in the 'spots of time' sequence, *1799* I 258–74.

450–2 *the very week . . . valley:* Mid-May 1779.

454–6 *that very week . . . not what:* An elaboration belonging to February 1804.

465 *a fish, up-leaping, snapped:* 'a leaping fish disturbed' (*1799*).

444–6 *Drew to the spot . . . deep:* An attempt to dramatize the incident that tends instead to impinge on the child's solitary experience.

470 *the dead man:* Records show that Joseph Jackson, schoolmaster of Sawrey at the far end of Esthwaite Water, was drowned on 18 June 1779. So much, at least, is fact.

472–81 *a spectre shape . . . poesy:* Added in February 1804 with somewhat confusing effects. Wordsworth wishes to tie his 'spot of time' into the discussion of early reading, but in so doing he not only weakens the strong original conclusion ('Rose with his ghastly face', *1799* I 279), but plays down his former emphasis on the sublime. In *1799*, where the Drowned Man is the first element of the 'spots of time' sequence, the episode is classed in an important link-passage (*1799* I 279–87, not found in the later texts) among 'tragic facts|Of rural history, that impressed' the child's mind

> With images to which in following years
> Far other feelings were attached (*1799* I 284–5)

Like the succeeding 'spots', the Esthwaite experience comes, through images implanted in the mind, to have an imaginative value that it did not possess at the time. In *1805* this implication disappears.

484 *abstract:* extract, selection; *The Arabian Nights* made such an impression on Coleridge as a child that his father burned it (to Poole, 9 October 1797).

497 *Religiously:* scrupulously.

524–7 *adventures endless . . . extravagate:* The old warrior (dismantled by time as though he were the castle he once defended) spins stories out of the ideals and ambitions amongst which he wandered as a young man.

533 *elements:* natural forces; cf. *Lear* III ii 16, 'I tax not you, you elements, with unkindness'.

534 *I guess not . . . past:* Wordsworth, who has probably just completed *Intimations*, refuses to speculate on the sources of the child's imaginative power. At l. 561 below, however, he refers to man's 'native continent' of pre-existence.

536 *dubious:* doubtful (because the light is uncertain).

541 *stinted:* diminished, curtailed.

544–5 *yoke-fellows|To custom:* Cf. 'the might of souls . . . while yet|The yoke of earth is new to them' (III 178–80) and years that 'bring the inevitable yoke' (*Intimations* 127).

548 *Forgers of lawless tales:* makers of fairy stories and romance, not subject to the 'law' of probability.

549–50 *the ape|Philosophy:* rationalist philosophers (Locke probably above all), who would suppress imagination in the upbringing of the child.

554–5 *to whom|Earth crouches:* to whom earth itself is obedient.

555 *the elements are potter's clay:* The elements themselves (not the natural forces of l. 533, but earth, air, fire, water, out of which matter is compounded) become malleable in the hands of such writers.

558–67 *It might demand . . . hold of us:* A reference once again to *The Recluse* (cf. *WIFT* 103, 'what might demand a loftier song'), but in an unexpected context. Uncertain as to where material for the philosophical centrepiece of his poem is to come from (see the desperate letter to Coleridge, 29 March 1804), Wordsworth places his emphasis, not on higher truths and imaginative intensity, but on the calmer pleasures of 'growing youth' – 'sober truth, experience, sympathy'. *1850* drops the reference to *The Recluse* (as one would expect), and gives back to childhood its priority.

560–2 *the same isthmus . . . human life:* Wordsworth takes up Pope's famous image of man 'Placed on this isthmus of a middle state' between beast and god (*Essay on Man* II 3) and uses it to convey his sense of life as a journey from the 'native continent' of pre-existence to adult participation. Somewhat incongrously the isthmus (a thin connecting strip of land) in his case consists of the boy's developing response to literature and poetic language.

575–81 *Thirteen years . . . love:* Wordsworth's first extant poem is a celebration of the bicentenary of Hawkshead Grammar School, written at the age of fifteen in 1785. Though openly an imitation of Pope, it is very skilful, and suggests one who has been reading poetry well for some while. *1850* 'twice five years' is not necessarily a boast.

583 *that dear friend:* John Fleming, mentioned at II 352–3.

589 *conning:* memorizing; cf. *Intimations* 102, 'The little actor cons another part'.

594 *in their splendour overwrought:* De Quincey (*Recollections* 166) identifies the verses as by Gray and Goldsmith, both poets whom Wordsworth knew well, though he came to think them 'overwrought'.

598 *inordinate:* As Maxwell points out, 'unordered', rather than the modern sense of 'excessive'.

601–6 *What wonder . . . Kept holiday:* A version of *Pedlar* 315–24, concluding in a touch from *Intimations* 32–3, 'with the heart of May|Doth every beast keep holiday'.

619–24 *Visionary power . . . proper home:*

How much effect are the winds really felt to have in Wordsworth's sentence? Where is it that the enigmatic 'darkness makes abode' – in winds? or in words? What would be the difference if one left the winds out, and read: 'Visionary power|Attends upon . . . the mystery of words'? A great deal falls into place if one realizes that the mighty poet whom Wordsworth has in mind in ll. 618–19 is not Shakespeare, or Milton, or even the Coleridge of the *Eolian Harp*, but his own earlier self. A cluster of verbal echoes refers us back to Alfoxden, and what may well be the earliest lines in *The Prelude*:

> and I would stand
> Beneath some rock, listening to sounds that are
> The ghostly language of the ancient earth
> Or make their dim abode in distant winds.
> Thence did I drink the visionary power. (*1799* II 356–60).

The Wordsworth of Book V is looking back to spring 1798 as the period at which it had seemed possible to perceive directly the transcendental forces of nature . . . In effect he is saying, visionary power is inherent in the language I then used. (*BV* 224–5)

625–6 *circumfused . . . light divine:* In place of the spiritual 'presence' of *Tintern Abbey*, 'interfused' through the natural world, we have the enveloping light of imagination, described by Coleridge in *Dejection: An Ode* as 'This light, this glory, this fair luminous mist,|This beautiful and beauty-making power' (ll. 62–3).

627 *turnings intricate:* As of a winding road.

605 *1805* 630–7 follow this line in the final MS but are omitted by Wordsworth's executors.

Book Sixth

1 *Furness Fells:* Mountainous district of the south-western Lake District, including Coniston and Hawkshead.

5 *the fowler's lure:* lure used by falconers to bring back their hawks; almost certainly an allusion to Marvell's *Horatian Ode*, copied by Wordsworth into *MS W*, used for assembling the five-book *Prelude* of spring 1804; 'where when he first doth lure,|The falconer hath her sure' (ll. 96–7).

6 *Granta's cloisters:* Cambridge (Granta being the old name for the River Cam above Cambridge).

11 *Clothed . . . fern:* By common consent, one of two great lines added to the 1850 *Prelude*; cf. *1850* III 63, 'Voyaging through strange seas of thought alone'. *fern:* bracken.

17 *my own unlovely cell:* There is no reason to think that Wordsworth's room at St John's (now much altered) was anything but rather handsome.

23–5 *read more . . . More promising:* Cut in 1838–9; did the aging Wordsworth think he had been too generous to his undergraduate self?

25 *Two winters:* 1788–9, 1789–90.

26–8 *many books . . . perused:* Wordsworth draws learnedly on Francis Bacon, *Of Studies* (*Essays,* 1597), in making his point that he pursued no settled academic reading: 'Some books are to be tasted, others to be swallowed, and some few to be chewed and digested.'

34–5 *some personal concerns . . . me:* Wordsworth was conscious of family pressure to do well in the University exams and become a Fellow of his College. His uncle, Christopher Cookson, had based a successful career on doing so, becoming tutor to the children of George III; Wordsworth's younger brother, Christopher, was to become a Fellow (and finally Master) of Trinity.

39 *A course of independent study:* For Dorothy's account of her brother's reading in 'Italian, Spanish, French, Greek and Latin, and English' (but never within the set course of mathematics), see III 371n.

42 *This bastard virtue:* Wordsworth fears to offend his relations by planning a course of independent study, so makes a virtue of not doing so.

54 *Unbiassed . . . unawed:* See III 245n.

55 *The poet's soul . . . time:* Wordsworth wrote his first major published poem, *An Evening Walk*, while he was an undergraduate.

58–60 *of which|No few . . . life:* Wordsworth had published *An Evening Walk* (1793), *Descriptive Sketches* (1793) and *Lyrical Ballads* (in three editions, 1798–1802); his unpublished work was still more impressive, including *Salisbury Plain*, *The Borderers*, *The Ruined Cottage*, *Peter Bell*, the two-part *Prelude*, *Home at Grasmere*, many shorter poems (including *The Leech Gatherer* and *Intimations*), and now the sudden *Prelude* extension. Hopes for the future centred on composition of a philosophical section for *The Recluse* (which would never be completed), and a 'dramatic' section (*The Excursion*, planned by March 1804, published in 1814).

61 *this very week:* Wordsworth was 34 on 7 April 1804; Book VI had been started at the end of March, and was complete by 29 April.

50–2 *yet for me . . . Her dew is on the flowers:* A moving statement of faith, created in a revision of early 1832. Wordsworth must be aware as he writes of Coleridge's beautiful terms of praise in *Biographia Literaria.* Chapter 4 had singled him out as carrying the feelings of childhood into adult life, shedding an imaginative light on 'forms, incidents and situations, of which, for the common view, custom had bedimmed all the lustre, had dried up the sparkle and the dew-drops.'

67–9 Owen points to an appropriate borrowing from Milton, *Reason of Church Government* (Yale ed. I 810), 'I might perhaps leave something so written to aftertimes, as they should not willingly let it die.'

81 *our groves:* Gardens belonging to St John's, bordering the Cam, including the site now occupied by the Victorian fourth court.

90 *A single tree:* Connected by the poet's wording with the tree (doubtless in the Lake District) mentioned at *Intimations* 51–2: 'But there's a tree, of many one,|A single field which I have looked upon'.

91–100 *an ash . . . outlandish grace:* Reed points to Wordsworth's dependence on Erasmus Darwin, *The Botanic Garden* (1791), I iv 541–4:

> Round her tall elm with dewy fingers twine
> The gadding tendrils of the adventurous vine;
> From arm to arm in gay festoons suspend
> Her fragrant flowers, her graceful foliage bend . . .

102–4 *The hemisphere . . . tread:* According to the account given in *Biographia*

Literaria chapter 14, it had been agreed during the planning of *Lyrical Ballads* that Coleridge was to contribute poetry of the supernatural, and Wordsworth 'to give the charm of novelty to the things of every day'.

128 *Delusion . . . incident:* Facetious allusion to *Winter's Tale* IV iv 124–5, 'a malady|Most incident to maids'.

129–34 *that overprized . . . simplicity and sense:* the practice of making Latin verses by piecing together phrases from classical authors. Coleridge, in *Biographia Literaria* chapter 1, sees the habit as leading to English 'translations of prose thoughts into poetic language', and recalls a conversation with Wordsworth that probably lies behind these lines.

142 *Indian:* Red Indian, as I 302, and elsewhere in Wordsworth.

124–8 *by what process led . . . without end:* Arrived at in revisions of 1832 and 1838–9. *Those immaterial agents:* the abstract truths of geometry.

150–7 *frequently I drew . . . God:* As in the Quixote Dream (V 49–139), geometry takes its place alongside poetry, both giving entrance to 'the one|Surpassing life' that is beyond space and time.

160–74 *one by shipwreck thrown . . . his feeling:* Drawn from a passage in John Newton's *Authentic Narrative* (1764) copied by Dorothy Wordsworth into *MS 18A* in 1798–9. Newton, slaveship captain turned evangelist, became Vicar of Olney and a friend of Cowper:

> One thing, though strange, is most true. Though destitute of food and clothing, depressed to a degree beyond common wretchedness, I could sometimes collect my mind to mathematical studies. I had bought Barrow's *Euclid* at Plymouth . . . it was always with me, and I used to take it to remote corners of the island by the seaside, and draw my diagrams with a long stick upon the sand. Thus I often beguiled my sorrows, and almost forgot my feeling.

Newton seems to have been an influence both on Wordsworth's *Borderers* and on *The Ancient Mariner.*

189 *tenderness:* susceptibility to impressions (Johnson's *Dictionary*)

192 *melancholy . . . blood:* According to the ancient theory of humours (known to Wordsworth through Ben Jonson among others) melancholy was caused by black bile.

173 *fits of spleen:* gloom, dejection (not here associated with ill-nature).

193–6 *that loved . . . luxurious gloom:* Dorothy Wordsworth, aged 21, writes to Jane Pollard on 30 August 1793: 'the melancholy pleasure of walking in a grove or wood while the yellow leaves are showering around me, is grateful to my mind beyond even the exhilarating charms of the budding trees'. By 1818, Peacock in *Nightmare Abbey* feels that he is fighting a crusade against black bile and poetic affectation.

202 *'Good-natured lounging' Castle of Indolence:* (1748), stanza 15; Wordsworth draws upon Thomson's poem at III 546–9, and had written a witty imitation in 1802.

188–9 Wordsworth's exaggerated self-reproach belongs to 1838–9.

190 *works of art:* man-made beauties, as opposed to natural scenes.

209 *Dovedale:* Derbyshire beauty spot (Lucy Gray is said to have lived 'among the untrodden ways|Beside the springs of Dove').

212–13 *seemed another morn|Risen on mid noon:* Taken word-for-word from Adam's response to the approach of Raphael, *PL* V 310–11.

216–17 *Now . . . Restored to me:* Dorothy is first 'restored' to her brother at Penrith in the summer of 1787, having been living with cousins in Halifax since the death of their mother nine years before.

218 *A gift then first bestowed:* A pun on the name Dorothy; cf. Coleridge to Wordsworth, 23 July 1803, wishing that on their Scottish tour they could make do with a pony, 'and side-saddle for our sister, Gift-of-God'.

220–1 *that monastic castle . . . stream:* Brougham Castle, beside the River Emont near Penrith, is not ordinarily 'monastic' (Peele Castle, for instance, was built by Cistercian monks). Wordsworth perhaps means 'secluded'.

222–6 *A mansion . . . Inspired:* Wordsworth is attracted by Sidney's having written *Arcadia* for his sister, the Countess of Pembroke, but was misled (perhaps by Clarke, *Survey of the Lakes*, 1787) in thinking that Sidney had visited Brougham.

226 *dome:* building (Johnson gives the modern sense as secondary).

233 *Another maid:* Mary Hutchinson, Dorothy's close friend, whom William had known since childhood, and whom he married on 4 October 1802.

242–5 *o'er the Border Beacon . . . golden gleam:* Having revised the Penrith 'spot of time' (*1799* I 296–327) during his recent work towards a *Prelude* in five books, Wordsworth now (April 1804) draws on lines connecting the Beacon and early love which, together with the 'spots of time' sequence, have been laid aside, and will not be encountered by the reader in the final text until XI 320–2:

> Upon the naked pool and dreary crags,
> And on the melancholy beacon, fell
> The spirit of pleasure and youth's golden gleam . . .

248 *I seem to plant thee there:* Coleridge and Wordsworth met eight years later, in September 1795.

249 *Far art thou wandered . . . health:* Coleridge sailed for Malta aboard the Speedwell (note the pun in l. 256) on 9 April 1804, but was thought by the Wordsworths to have left on 22 March.

260 *gales Etesian:* Mediterranean winds (about which Wordsworth probably knew little); given the puns in this passage, Reed may be right to hear in 'Etesian' a 'near anagram' of Coleridge's phonetic spelling of his initials, 'Esteecee'.

255 *several:* separate.

261 An alexandrine, created in Wordsworth's final revisions, probably by mistake.

274–84 *Of rivers, fields . . . long exile:* Wordsworth weaves references to three of Coleridge's most personal poems, *Frost at Midnight* (1798), *Dejection* (the unpublished version, April 1802) and *To the River Otter* (1796) into an evocation of his time as a 'liveried' (uniformed) schoolboy at the 'Blue-coat School', Christ's Hospital, in the City of London. Coleridge's 'long exile' from his Devonshire birthplace, Ottery St Mary, began in September 1782, when he was nine. His father had died the previous year.

286–8 *scarcely had I . . . thither guided:* Wordsworth left Cambridge (settling for a BA without honours) in January 1791; Coleridge matriculated in October.

291–2 *What a stormy course . . . followed:* Coleridge began by winning a University prize; he was the most learned and distinguished undergraduate of his day, and could well have been the most successful. Instead he left Cambridge in December 1794 without a degree. Under the influence of William Frend (tried by the University in 1792 for his 'subversive book' *Peace and Union*, and deprived of his Fellowship), Coleridge had become a Unitarian, and increasingly involved in the Cambridge political scene. He had also got into debt, talked of suicide, and (in December 1793) joined the army as a means of escape. Bought out by his family, he returned to the University, but during the summer vacation of 1794 met Robert Southey with whom he planned a commune (Pantisocracy – the rule of all) in Pennsylvania. His thoughts now on fund-raising, he turned to writing. When at the end of the year he left Cambridge the *Morning Chronicle* was publishing his *Sonnets on Eminent Characters* (heroes of the radical movement). In academic terms Cambridge had been a disaster, but the sonnets were good. Coleridge was launched on his career.

297 *still:* always, ever.

308–11 *toils abstruse . . . words for things:* Wordsworth distinguishes between Coleridge's reading in medieval scholastic philosophy ('the schoolmen') and his excited personal idealism, in which language was used for its own sake, having (in Wordsworth's view) no stable basis. It is not clear whether Wordsworth refers to Platonism as the antecedent of Coleridge's Unitarian pantheism, or sees it in more general terms.

326 *battened on:* grew fat upon.

326–9 *But thou hast trod . . . regrets:* Though Wordsworth is attempting to praise and reassure, he clearly has in the back of his mind *Samson Agonistes* 597–8: 'My race of glory run, and race of shame|And I shall shortly be with them that rest' (*Samson Agonistes* 597–8).

333–4 *now to these . . . leads me:* Having in early March decided to break up the nearly completed five-book *Prelude* and work towards a longer poem, Wordsworth takes as his subject in Book VI the tour of France and the Alps made in the Cambridge long vacation of 1790. He is tracing his own wanderings to be in step with Coleridge, but in doing so he brings to his poem a new political aspect and new scope for exploration of the sublime. Wordsworth has laid aside for future use the Spots of Time (finally XI 257–388) and Climbing of Snowdon (finally XIII 1–65), but cannot have known at this stage in any detail where his poem was leading him.

338–42 *When the third summer . . . distant Alps:* Wordsworth and his Cambridge friend Robert Jones (from mountainous North Wales) set off 'staff in hand, and carrying each his needments tied up in a pocket handkerchief, with about £20 apiece in [their] pockets' (*Memoirs* I 14).

344–5 *Nor entertained . . . dear:* Wordsworth (who should have been studying for his final exams) told no member of the family – not even Dorothy – before setting out.

346 'For nature then . . . To me was all in all' (*TA* 73–6).

347 *mighty forms:* shapes taken by the Alps in his imagination.

353 'Now stand you on the top of happy hours' (Shakespeare, Sonnet 16.)

354 *human nature seeming born again:* 'Few persons', Southey wrote to Caroline Bowles on 13 February 1824,

> but those who have lived in it, can conceive or comprehend what the French Revolution was, nor what a visionary world seemed to open upon those who were

just entering it. Old things seemed passing away, and nothing was dreamt of but the regeneration of the human race.

357 *that great federal day:* 14 July 1790, first anniversary of the fall of the Bastille, was celebrated all over France as the Fête de la Fédération. Helen Maria Williams watched the King in Paris swear an oath of allegiance to the new constitution, and 'caught with enthusiasm the general sympathy':

> It was the triumph of human kind, it was man asserting the noblest privileges of his nature, and it wanted but the common feelings of humanity to become in that moment a citizen of the world. (*Letters Written in France* (1790) 14)

360–1 *Southward thence|We took our way:* Wordsworth kept no journal, but listed the places where he and Jones slept in their three months' journey, of 1,500 miles, through France, Switzerland, northern Italy, southern Germany and the Netherlands; see Donald Hayden, *Wordsworth's Walking Tour of 1790* (Tulsa, 1983).

372 *umbrage:* shade; cf. *Descriptive Sketches* 48, 'road elms rustling thin above my head'.

384–7 *Upon the bosom . . . rocks:* Wordsworth and Jones took a boat again on the Rhine, but the bulk of the tour was on foot *Soane* the River Saône (anglicized as a monosyllable).

396 *great spousals:* The marriage of King and People; see 357n. above. Louis had no intention of keeping his oath. Shortage of money had forced him in May 1789 to summon the Estates General, which no French king had done since 1611. He now found himself forced (he hoped temporarily) to accept the position of constitutional monarch.

399–401 *some vapoured . . . saucy air:* In their joy the 'vapouring' (boastful) delegates resemble the drunken Caliban, Stephano and Trinculo, 'So full of vapour that they smote the air|For breathing in their faces' (*Tempest* IV i 172–3).

403–4 *Guests welcome . . . of old:* Not one of Wordsworth's closer parallels. Three angels visit Abraham in *Genesis* 1.15 to tell him that he is to have a son. Sarah, being 90, laughs; Isaac is duly born.

407, 413 The pleasure Wordsworth takes in the memory, and the infectiousness of his rhythms ('And round and round the board they danced again'), make it hard to believe with Reed that there is an ironic reference to dancing at the murder of General Dillon in 1792, or at the execution of Louis XVI.

409–12 *We bore a name . . . glorious course:* By the 'Glorious Revolution' of 1688 the English had replaced the unpopular Catholic monarch, James II, conferring sovereignty jointly upon Mary Stuart and her Dutch husband, William of Orange. In the process Parliament took steps to limit the sovereign's powers, setting up what to French eyes seemed an enviable constitutional monarchy.

411 *give us hail:* drink to us.

422 *rout:* party.

420–88 Drafted in early summer 1808 as *Tuft of Primroses* 509–69, worked up in *Prelude MSS A* and *B*, and inserted in the text of *C*, c. 1819. Behind these blank-verse accounts lies *Descriptive Sketches* 53–79, written in 1792, two years after Wordsworth's visit to the Chartreuse with Jones on 4–5 August 1790.

422–6 *our eyes had seen . . . blameless inmates:* Wordsworth's claim that he and Jones saw soldiers at the Chartreuse in August 1790 has no basis in fact. It appears in *The Prelude* because: (1) Wordsworth when writing *Descriptive Sketches* in France, in summer 1792, includes a dramatization of the recent expulsion of the monks (carefully describing the section in his synopsis as 'Present state of the Grande Chartreuse'); (2) when drafting the *Tuft of Primroses* (his most forlorn attempt at *The Recluse*) it suited his theme of ruin and loss to play up the drama of the expulsion – 'Alas for what I see! the flash of arms . . .'; (3) it seemed pointless in working up the *Prelude* text to distinguish the events of 1790 and 1792 – more so as the 'military glare' was needed as introduction to nature's rebuke, ll. 431ff.

429 *silence visible:* Cf. Milton's 'darkness visible' (*PL* I 63).

430–5 Nature's rebuke in its original form includes a version of ll. 427–8:

> 'Stay your impious hand . . .
> Oh leave in quiet this embodied dream,
> This substance by which mortal men have clothed –
> Humanly clothed – the ghostliness of things
> In silence visible and perpetual calm.
> Let this one temple last! Be this one spot
> Of earth devoted to eternity!' (*Tuft of Primroses* 537–45)

436 *St Bruno:* Founder of the monastery, and of the Carthusian order, in 1084.

439 *sister streams of Life and Death:* The Guiers Vif and Guiers Mort, rivers below the monastery, referred to in *Descriptive Sketches* 73 as 'the mystic streams of Life and Death'.

440–1 *my heart|Responded:* Wording that first occurs in *MS D*, 1832; in previous versions ll. 441–71 (or their equivalent) are spoken by the voice of nature.

443 *Hail . . . time:* 'Black mists dissolve, break galling chains for ever!' (*MS C*).

464–5 *untransmuted shapes . . . inhabitants:* Mountains surviving unchanged from previous ages, and inhabiting the blue ('cerulean') upper air.

480 *lawns:* open space between woods (Johnson). *Vallombre* 'Name of one of the valleys of the Chartreuse' (note to *Descriptive Sketches*).

483–6 *In different quarters . . . storms:* 'Alluding to crosses seen on the tops of the spiry rocks of the Chartreuse, which have every appearance of being inaccessible' (note to *Descriptive Sketches*). Mountain-top crosses are still to be seen in the area.

487–8 *Yet then . . . insecure:* A striking revision of 1838–9; *MS C* and *D* fair copy read: 'From desperate blasphemers insecure'.

428 *A march . . . of military speed:* Dorothy comments wonderingly to Jane Pollard on 6 October 1790:

> They have frequently performed a journey of thirteen leagues (thirty-nine miles, you know) over the most mountainous parts of Switzerland, without feeling more weariness than if they had been sauntering an hour in the groves of Cambridge.

437 *coverts:* hidden places.

443 *patriarchal dignity of mind:* Dignity such as that of the Old Testament prophets (Owen suggests the dignity of Adam and Eve in Paradise).

509–16 Inserted in 1832. Wordsworth was becoming increasingly conscious of 'evening shadows'.

448 *A green recess:* Shown to Dorothy and Mary by the poet on their Continental tour of 1820, and clearly having special associations for him. To Dorothy the 'shady deep recess' seemed 'the very image of pastoral life, stillness and seclusion' (*Continental Tour*, *Journals*, ed. E. de Selincourt, II 280).

452–61 *That day we first . . . realities:*

> It is not reality that Wordsworth is reconciled to by the glacier, but a symbolic enactment of the potential in which as a poet he needed to believe. Mont Blanc, however beautiful, remains Mont Blanc, a 'soulless image' because it is itself and no more. The mountain represents stasis, the death of imagination, as opposed to stillness, which for Wordsworth contains the possibility of development, change, rebirth . . . The glacier at Chamouni was especially well designed to stir the living thought, release the poet from realities . . . Its 'dumb cataracts' may sound again, once more haunt the listener like a passion; its 'streams of ice' may flow again, frozen though they be; the 'five rivers broad and vast' may be motionless, stopped for ever in their course, but the poet's imagination perceives them still as waves, for ever ready to move on . . . (*BV* 191)

460 *Five rivers broad and vast:* As one might expect, Wordsworth in 1792 had seen the glacier in terms of the picturesque:

> Five streams of ice amid her cots descend,
> And with wild flowers and blooming orchards blend
> (*Descriptive Sketches* 682–3)

473 *such a book:* the 'book' of nature, and of man in his primal state.

483 *The willow wreath:* Symbol normally of the lover's melancholy (as with Viola's 'willow cabin at [the] gate', *Twelfth Night* I v 256), here used to evoke the young poet's sorrows.

489–90 *an under-thirst|Of vigour:* Among many examples of Wordsworth's sense of inner space, cf. 'Hushed, meanwhile,|Was the under-soul' (III 539–40).

495 *clomb:* climbed; see IV 1n.

507 *scruple:* hesitation.

523 *Translated by the feelings:* The peasant's answers are about the road; Wordsworth and Jones are concerned with the inference to be drawn.

524–5 Impressive as the juxtaposition is between Wordsworth's discovery that the Alps have been crossed, in l. 524, and his famous lines upon imagination (ll. 525ff.), this was not the sequence of composition. Rough pencil drafts on the tiny sheets of *MS WW* (beautifuly reproduced, Reed I 356–7) show that Wordsworth originally sought to define his sense of anti-climax in the simile of the Cave of Yordas (finally VIII 711–27).

525–37 In August 1790, imagination (anticipated pleasure at crossing the Alps) had been disappointed. Now, almost fourteen years later, the power asserts itself, taking over the poet's mind as he writes, 'usurping upon' faculties that usually 'rule'; for an extended discussion, see *BV* 174–202, 'Usurpation and Reality: Spring 1804'. Citing Robert A. Brinkley (*WC* 1981, 122–

5), Owen suggests that *1850* may represent 'a real change of mind', in which Wordsworth tries to apply his lines on the grandeur of imagination to the feelings of 1790 rather than to his experience when writing *The Prelude* in 1804.

526 *the eye and progress of my song:* Wordsworth's elegant zeugma is modelled on *Much Ado About Nothing* IV i 229, 'the eye and prospect of my soul'. Rising before the poet's inner eye, the 'unfathered vapour' (a version of Coleridge's 'fair luminous mist' of imagination) halts the progress of the poem.

601 *but with a flash:* Wordsworth's use of the singular (as opposed to *1805* plural, 'flashes that have shown to us'), together with his removal of the 'visitings of awful promise', tends to make his experience seem unique and unsharable. In *1805*, as in *Tintern Abbey*, the poet is one of us – we all 'see into the life of things'.

542 *something evermore about to be:* For Wordsworth the supreme value is not achievement, but aspiration; over the years his poetry gives form to 'an obscure sense|Of possible sublimity' (*Pedlar* Fragment, 1798), the feeling 'that we are greater than we know' (*Duddon* Conclusion, 1820).

543–6 *banners militant . . . reward:* The mind fights beneath 'the banners' (in the name) of 'effort, and expectation, and desire'. It cannot, therefore, win. In Blake's words, 'Energy is eternal delight' (*Marriage of Heaven and Hell*).

547 *access of joy:* Cf. the Pedlar's 'high hour|Of visitation from the living God', glossed similarly as an 'access of mind' (*Pedlar* 107).

559 *rent:* ravine.

561–4 *The torrents . . . voice were in them:* Wordsworth has brought together impressive details from two different parts of *Descriptive Sketches*: 'Torrents shooting from the clear blue sky' (l. 130) and

> Black drizzling crags that, beaten by the din,
> Vibrate as if a voice complained within (ll. 249–50)

565/6 Inserted between these lines c. 1819, and forming part of the *Prelude* text for twenty years, until the revisions to *MS D*, are six magnificent lines:

> And ever as we halted, or crept on,
> Huge fragments of primeval mountain spread
> In powerless ruin, blocks as huge aloft
> Impending, nor permitted yet to fall;
> The sacred death-cross, monument forlorn
> Though frequent, of the perished traveller;

566–72 *The unfettered clouds . . . without end:* It may come as a surprise that Wordsworth at this apocalyptic moment writes with Pope in his thoughts – as well as the expected guides, Milton and Coleridge. Pope defines the Christian tradition from which Wordsworth has subtly departed (and in doing so throws light upon Wordsworth's most bizarre image of unity, 'blossoms upon one tree'):

> All are but parts of one stupendous whole,
> Whose body nature is, and God the soul

That (changed through all, and yet in all the same) . . .
Warms in the sun, refreshes in the breeze,
Glows in the sun, and blossoms in the trees . . .
(*Essay on Man* II 266–72)

Cf. V 560–2n.

568 *workings of one mind:* For the sake of Wordsworth's simile, the 'one mind' does not have to be divine, but in addition to Pope (ll. 566–72n. above), cf. the Unitarian poetry of Coleridge:

There is one mind, one omnipresent mind
Omnific; his most holy name is love. (*1796 Religious Musings* 114–5)

570 *Characters:* letters, handwriting, signs; according to Burnet's *Sacred Theory of the Earth* (1685) the Alps had been formed by the waters of the Flood; cf. Wordsworth's *Pedlar* revisions of spring 1798: 'the day of vengeance when the sea|Rose like a giant from his sleep and smote|The hills' (Butler 166–7). To the imagination, however, the features of the Ravine of Gondo suggest not merely past apocalypse, but the one to come.

572 *Of first, and last, and midst, and without end:* A line that perfectly invokes Wordsworth's independence of his predecessors. Milton in 1667 had correctly applied the same words to God – 'Him first, Him last, Him midst and without end' (*PL* V 165). Coleridge had echoed them in 1795 in a passage written for Southey's *Joan of Arc*, that defines the appropriate use of man's God-given powers:

Him first, Him last, to view
Through meaner powers and secondary things
Effulgent, as through clouds that veil his blaze.

Dealing in the numinous, not the specifically Christian, Wordsworth (fully aware of Milton and Coleridge) leaves out the references to God.

573 *an Alpine house:* Wordsworth and Jones spent the night of 17 August 1790 at the Spittal (inn, lodging-house) of Gondo.

579 *innocent sleep Macbeth:* II ii 33–4, 'innocent sleep,|Sleep that knits up the ravelled sleeve of care'.

587 *Locarno's Lake:* Lake Maggiore.

592 *Abyssinian privacy:* 'Into this part of the globe', the *Encyclopaedia Britannica* (3rd ed. 1797) wrote of Abyssinia, 'the admission of travellers has been supposed extremely difficult, and their return from thence almost impracticable'. Wordsworth may have in mind the Happy Valley of Johnson's *Rasselas*, which had rather too much 'Abyssinian privacy'.

592–5 *I spoke . . . roofed with vines:* See *Descriptive Sketches* 80ff.:

More pleased my foot the hidden margin roves
Of Como, bosomed deep in chestnut-groves . . .
The viewless lingerer, hence, at evening sees
From rock-hewn steps the sail between the trees,
Or marks, mid opening cliffs, fair dark-eyed maids
Tend the small harvest of their garden-glades . . .

622–4 *by report misled . . . from ours:* The hour is sounded, followed by the quarters (in each case a single bell): 1.45 would therefore sound like 4.00 a.m. *report:* sound, message.

631 *bewildered:* lost in the wilds (be-wild-ered).

636 *a dull red image of the moon:* The moon's red image is seen in *Descriptive Sketches* 219–20 by the unfortunate Grison gypsy.

643–4 *insects . . . woods:* 'And insect buzz that stuns the sultry woods' (*Descriptive Sketches* 224).

645 *more by darkness visible . . . than:* When is an oxymoron not an oxymoron? Answer: when you alter the syntax. In Wordsworth's playful allusion to *PL* I 63 (imitated at *1850* 429 above), it is not that the darkness is visible, but that shapes are visible as the result of themselves being dark.

661–72 *Let this alone . . . worship:* Wordsworth had shown a similar anxiety in *Descriptive Sketches* not to be taken for a picturesque traveller: 'I had once given to these sketches the title of picturesque, but the Alps are insulted in applying to them that term' (note to l. 347). The case is more complex than Wordsworth makes it sound; he had learned much from the picturesque tradition (see XI 152–7n.).

667 *a mean pensioner:* one who ungenerously draws pleasure and makes no (imaginative) return.

672–80 *whate'er|I saw . . . circuitous:* Experience of the Alps is seen as flowing into the larger river of the poet's education by bringing out in him the qualities of grandeur and tenderness (the sublime and beautiful again) – the first directly (through response to the mountains); the second by a more subtle process.

684–5 *the nations hailed . . . expectancy:* the new political order for which they had waited so long.

688–9 *the Swiss exulting . . . neighbours:* As the oldest republic in Europe, Switzerland rejoiced that France too should have achieved a measure of political reform (the setting up of a republic was not contemplated by the French themselves in 1790, and didn't take place till September 1792).

691 *the Brabant armies:* armies of the short-lived Belgian republic, suppressed by Leopold II in December 1790.

693 *scarcely of the household . . . life:* hardly grown up.

699 *proper:* own (French *propre*).

Book Seventh

1–56 Written originally as an introduction to Book VIII in early October 1804, when Wordsworth returned to work on *The Prelude* after a break during the summer months. For the somewhat complicated circumstances (and for speculations as to the dating of VII as a whole), see Introduction.

3 *the city's walls:* See I 1–54n. and 8n. The note at this point in the first edition – 'The city of Goslar, in Lower Saxony' – is unhelpful and not written by Wordsworth.

4–13 *I sang . . . last primrose-time:* Giving the impression that the Glad Preamble (*1805* I 1–54) had been his starting-point, Wordsworth distorts the sequence of *Prelude* composition, yet contrives to give a broadly accurate picture. The two parts of the 1799 poem (which in truth preceded the

Preamble) are represented in the 'short-lived transport' and the 'flowing awhile in strength', and the three-year gap in *The Prelude*'s composition, December 1799–January 1804 ('a little space|Before last primrose-time') is correctly marked. *1850*'s late emendation of 'Five years' in line 1 to 'Six changeful years' has the effect of misdating the Preamble, but correctly taking the origins of *The Prelude* back to 1798.

5 *dithyrambic:* fervent, wild.

8 *Scafell:* Locally pronounced 'Scawfle' (note the scansion), and often regarded as the Lake District's highest mountain, though Scafell Pike is slightly taller. *Blencathra:* Chosen for the beauty of its name, and its imposing presence (seen from the road to Keswick and Coleridge).

14–20 *assurances . . . hindrance:* Wordsworth had at first assured himself that he could complete *The Prelude* in five books for Coleridge to take with him to the Mediterranean. Then in March (see Introduction) he had decided to work towards a larger poem and doubtless set himself further targets. In the first six months of the year he had written extraordinarily fast. One 'outward hindrance' during his summer lay-off (July–September) had been the birth of his daughter Dora on 16 August.

30 *their rough lord . . . surly north:* Modelled on Thomson's 'surly Winter', *Seasons* I 11–12: 'And see where surly Winter passes off|Far to the north, and calls his ruffian blasts . . .'

39–41 *A glow-worm . . . Clear-shining:* For the value Wordsworth set on glow-worms, and their 'small circles of green radiance' (*Evening Walk* 278), see especially *Among All Lovely Things My Love Had Been* (April 1802).

50–3 *my favourite grove . . . poet's task:* Wordsworth experiences afresh the 'mild creative breeze' of the Preamble (I 43), but does so now in the setting of Grasmere. He composed frequently in the Ladywood fir-grove near Dove Cottage, and valued it especially for its associations with his brother John; see *When to the Attractions of the Busy World* (1800).

57–9 *Returned . . . gownèd students:* By spending his final long vacation on a tour of the Alps Wordsworth had forfeited any chance of academic success. He returned to Cambridge in October 1790, and took a BA without honours in January 1791.

62 *unfenced regions:* commons; cf. Young, *Night Thoughts* V 740–1: 'Our needful knowledge, like our needful food,|Unhedged, lies open in life's common field . . .'

63–5 *Yet undetermined . . . time:* The true reason why Wordsworth seemed to have a little time was that his family expected him to go into the Church, which he couldn't do until he was 23.

72–4 *at least two years . . . visitant:* Reed conjectures that Wordsworth first visited London at the end of summer 1788 (*Chronology of the Early Years* 81n.).

78 *abroad:* outside, away from home.

80 *affections:* emotions.

85 *Alcairo:* ancient Memphis; De Selincourt points to *PL* I 717–19:

Not Babylon
Nor great Alcairo such magnificence
Equalled in all their glories . . .

Persepolis: Ancient capital of the Persian Empire, sacked by Alexander the Great; cf. Marlowe, 'Is it not passing brave to be a king,|And ride in triumph through Persepolis? (*Tamburlaine* I 717–18).

86 *report by pilgrim friars:* Wordsworth has in mind *Purchas His Pilgrimes* (1625), which in 1797 had provided Coleridge with the opening words of *Kubla Khan.*

94–7 *among our flock . . . traveller:* Philip Braithwaite, who became schoolmaster at Far Sawrey, near Hawkshead, and was visited by Wordsworth in old age (*Wordsworth's Hawkshead* 39–46).

103 *vanity:* fantasy.

110 *equipages:* Perhaps 'carriages with attendant servants' (Norton), but more probably 'retinues', as in life's 'equipage', *Intimations* 105.

114–17 *young Whittington . . . Articulate music:* A dual reference: to the legendary Richard Whittington who as a boy heard the bells of St Mary-le-Bow ring out: 'Turn again Whittington,|Thou worthy citizen,|Lord Mayor of London'; and to Coleridge, who as a boy in Devonshire heard the bells ring 'all the hot fair-day . . .|Most like articulate sounds of things to come' (*FM* 35–8).

119–20 *by simple faith . . . love:* A change of meaning perhaps, but clearer than *1805.*

121–83 A sequence that is very heavily revised in the 1830s. The extent of Wordsworth's cutting is not evident at a glance, as there are considerable insertions too.

123 *Vauxhall and Ranelagh:* London pleasure-gardens, offering balls, masquerades, fireworks etc. Vauxhall, in Lambeth, was larger and more popular; Ranelagh, in Chelsea, charged half a crown admission (five shillings on fireworks-nights) and had a rotunda where Mozart once played.

130 *Whispering Gallery of St Paul's:* Gallery round the inside of the dome, famous for its acoustic effects. A whisper comes full circle.

131 *Giants of Guildhall:* Carved wooden figures of Gog and Magog (1708), destroyed in the London blitz in 1940 (and unimpressively replaced after the war).

132 *Bedlam . . . gates:* Famous London mental hospital, demolished in 1814, whose name (a corruption of Bethlehem) has entered into the language. The figures, representing forms of madness, were carved c. 1680 by Caius Gabriel Cibber, father of Pope's hero in the 1743 *Dunciad*; hence the reference to 'Cibber's brazen brainless brothers' (*Dunciad* I 32).

133–41 Inserted in *MS C* c. 1819.

135 *Monument:* 202-foot stone column erected by Wren at the point where the Fire of London started in 1666.

141 *keen and lively pleasure:* The view that Wordsworth disliked London derives from a series of untypical comments made in 1800, see ll. 700–4n. below. In fact he was delighted as a young man by its colour and bustle, and enjoyed his later visits.

144 *prescriptive:* established.

149–50 *thou monstrous ant-hill . . . world:* Wordsworth's exuberant image is introduced in *MS D* of 1838–9, condensing the original transition of *1805.*

154–243 As Reed suggests, Wordsworth is drawing on the magnificent and mischievous letter that Lamb wrote to him on 30 January 1801 about the pleasures of city life:

I have passed all my days in London, until I have formed as many and intense local attachments as any of you *mountaineers* can have done with dead nature. The lighted shops of the Strand and Fleet Street; the innumerable trades, tradesmen and customers; coaches, wagons, playhouses; all the bustle and wickedness round about Covent Garden; the very women of the town, the watchmen, drunken scenes, rattles – life awake, if you awake, at all hours of the night; the impossibility of being dull in Fleet Street; the crowds, the very dirt and mud, the sun shining upon houses and pavements; the print-shops, the old-book stalls, parsons cheapening books; coffee-houses, steams of soups from kitchens, the pantomimes – London itself a pantomime and a masquerade – all these things work themselves into my mind and feed me without the power of satiating me. The wonder of these sights impels me into night walks about her crowded streets, and I often shed tears in the motley Strand from fulness of joy at so much *life*.

160 *Still:* always.

162 *chariots:* carriages of pleasure, or state (Johnson).

164 *scavenger:* street, or crossing, sweeper, needful when roads were muddy and ladies wore long dresses.

165 *hackney-coaches:* coaches for hire inside London, opposed by Wordsworth to the long-distance coaches (Royal Mails among them) of the next line.

167 *drayman's team:* matched horses pulling a dray (low-sided cart) probably carrying beer barrels.

170 *punctual:* at a certain point (*Latin* punctus).

182 *Boyle:* Robert Boyle (1627–91), chemist, founder-member of the Royal Society.

183 *some Scotch doctor:* James Graham (1745–94) was a confidence trickster who set up a Temple of Health at the Adelphi in London in 1779. Among other remedies customers were offered ethereal medicines, milk and earth baths, and a 'celestial bed' to cure sterility at £50 a night. Wordsworth in his satirical *Imitation of Juvenal* (1796) referred to Graham as 'great high-priest' in 'Health's own temple', but doubted 'If on the couch celestial gold can shed|The coarser blessings of a peasant's bed' (Oxford I 306).

188 *tracts of thin resort:* areas where there were fewer people.

190 *raree-show:* peep-show carried in a box.

198 *thrilled:* pierced (as in 'nostril', where the nose is thrilled).

199 *cries:* Hawkers' proclamations of wares to be sold in the street (Johnson). London cries were famous as the subject of aquatinted costume-studies by Francis Wheatley and others.

200 An octosyllabic line, created during the copying of *MS A* in 1805–6, and persisting (presumably unnoticed) until revisions of 1832 produced the *1850* reading.

202–4 *privileged regions . . . gardens green:* The Inns of Court; Wordsworth seems to have lived with his brother Richard at Staple Inn at the end of 1792, and with the elder Basil Montagu at Gray's Inn early in 1795 (*Chronology* I 138, 163).

209 *Here files of ballads . . . dead walls:* De Selincourt draws attention to Mary Cowden Clarke's recollection in *My Long Life* (2nd ed. 2–3) of ballads for sale, c. 1815, at Cumberland Gate (now Marble Arch): 'The railing adjacent to the gate was at that period (about 1812) permitted to be strung

with rows of printed old-fashioned ballads, such as *Cruel Barbara Allen*, etc.'. *dead:* blank, windowless.

213–14 *That – fronted . . . masquerade:* The advertisement to which Wordsworth points is 'in disguise' – designed to tempt the viewer with its 'most imposing' opening word. *MS X* reveals the secret withheld in later texts: '"Inviting" is the leading word, a bait|Which cannot be resisted' (Reed II 324). 'Imposing' has an elegant double meaning: 'impressive' and 'deceitful'.

216–20 *Behold a face . . . arms:* Samuel Horsey, 'King of the Beggars', is vividly described by Lamb in *A Complaint of the Decay of Beggars in the Metropolis, Elia* 270–1:

> a well-known figure, or part of the figure, of a man, who used to glide his comely upper half over the pavements of London, wheeling along with most ingenious celerity upon a machine of wood . . . He was a grand fragment, as good as an Elgin Marble . . . the man part of a centaur from which the horse-half had been cloven in some dire Lapithan controversy.

226 *field-ward:* Towards the country, still in walking distance (Paddington, for instance, was an outlying village in 1804). *decency* modesty, propriety (implying behaviour suited to one's place in an ordered society).

229 *images:* statuettes, presumably of the Virgin Mary and the Saints.

242 *Lascars:* From the East Indies.

243 *negro ladies . . . gowns:* 'Negro' was not a disparaging term at this period. Wordsworth's sympathy for the sufferings of black people is seen in the sonnets of 1802, *To Toussaint L'Ouverture* and especially *We Had A Fellow Passenger*: 'She was a negro woman driven from France,|Rejected like all others from that race . . .'

248–9 *mimic sights . . . reality:* Representations, such as the panoramas that were a novelty at the end of the eighteenth century (ll. 256–64) or models of famous places (ll. 265–79).

252–3 *subtlest craft . . . purest ends:* imaginative creation.

256–61 *the painter . . . pinnacle:* Thomas Girtin's *Eidometropolis* (on view when Lamb was showing Wordsworth and Dorothy the sights of London in September 1802) was 9 feet high and 216 feet in circumference, and painted from a rooftop near Blackfriars Bridge. It was last heard of in Russia.

257 *circumambient:* surrounding (Latin *circumambeo*, to go round).

258 *pencil:* paintbrush (normal eighteenth-century usage).

260 *commissioned spirits:* The spirit who comes immediately to mind – Satan – had no 'commission' (authority) to place Christ upon a pinnacle.

265 *more mechanic artist:* craftsman.

275–6 *Of Tivoli . . . every tree:* Following Maxwell, the two-line version from *MS C* has been preferred to the three lines of *A* (*Reed* 275–7), which were first left incomplete, then inconclusively revised (Norton at this point is a composite). Wordsworth would have known that Horace, whose Sabine farm was at Tivoli, associated the grotto there with the sibyl Albunea (*Odes* I vii 10–15). The temple, much painted by eighteenth-century British artists at Rome, is dedicated to Vesta.

288 *Half-rural Sadler's Wells:* Sadler's Wells avoided the licence and controls to

which London theatres were subject, by being in 'half-rural' Islington, three miles north.

291 *mauger:* despite (French *malgré*). Regarded by Johnson as archaic, and not elsewhere used by Wordsworth, who perhaps thought it appropriately theatrical: *Twelfth Night* III i 153, 'mauger all thy pride'.

293 *rope-dancers:* A print of Sadler's Wells in 1795 depicts 'TIGHT ROPE DANCING by Mr Richer, whose elegant and admired performances will be relieved and contrasted by the comic dances of Mr Dubois, as Clown of the Rope'; Harry Bearol, *Theatre Notebook* (1951–2) VI 12–14.

294 *posture-masters:* contortionists *harlequins:* clowns, traditionally in particoloured costume. The bluetit of *Kitten and the Falling Leaves* (featuring the infant Dora Wordsworth in autumn 1804) is 'Lithest, gaudiest harlequin,| Prettiest tumbler ever seen (ll. 72–3).

298 *the laws and progress of belief:* An early expression of the Romantic interest in dramatic illusion, leading to Coleridge's famous definition of 'that willing suspension of disbelief for the moment that constitutes poetic faith' (*Biographia Literaria* chapter 14).

306 A quotation from Samson's (and Milton's) lament for his blindness, *Samson Agonistes* 86–9:

> The sun to me is dark
> And silent as the moon
> When she deserts the night,
> Hid in her vacant interlunar cave.

307 *and faith must needs be coy:* Faith has to be 'coy', submissive, if it is to accept such trickery (*1850* neatly removes the awkwardness of *1805*).

310 *here:* At Sadler's Wells.

288 *'forms and pressures of the time':* An appropriate, if inexact, quotation from *Hamlet* III ii 22–4, where the Prince gives his instructions to the Players: 'hold . . . the mirror up to nature', 'show virtue her own feature; scorn, her own image; and the very age and body of the time, his form and pressure'. *pressure:* stamp, impression (and therefore, 'image'), as on a coin.

312 *Thespian times:* the period of Thespis, Greek tragedian of the sixth century BC.

314–26 *some domestic incident . . . marriage bonds:* The 'daring' (presumptuous) brotherhood at Sadler's Wells had on 25 April 1803 put on 'an operatic piece in rhyme' by Charles Dibdin, called *Edward and Susan*, based on a 'domestic incident' in the Lake District. In October 1802, Mary Robinson, daughter of the innkeeper at Buttermere, had married the Hon. Augustus Hope, a Scottish MP and brother to the Earl of Hopetown. Or so it was believed when Coleridge wrote the first of his five articles on the subject for the *Morning Post.* Then it came out that Mary had been deceived, Hope was plain John Hatfield, and the marriage was bigamous. On their walking tour of Scotland, Wordsworth, Coleridge and Dorothy contrived to be present in Carlisle in August when Hatfield was condemned for forgery, then a capital offence (*Journals* I 196). Coleridge (full of righteous indignation, and rather too interested in the wickedness that had been displayed) went to see him in his cell. Hatfield was hanged in September.

De Quincey gives a fascinating and largely credible account of the affair (*Recollections* 66–73).

318 *doubtless treated with irreverence:* The play had been seen in June 1803 by Southey (who slept), Lamb (who laughed), and Mary Lamb, who wrote to the Wordsworths wittily describing the evening's entertainment.

322 *'a bold bad man':* Applied by Spenser to the magician Archimago: 'A bold bad man that dared to call by name|Great Gorgon, Prince of Darkness and dead night' (*FQ* I i stanza 37).

328–9 *When first we saw . . . unheard of:* Wordsworth and Coleridge were waited on by Mary Robinson at the Fish Inn, Buttermere, on 11 November 1799. They could have heard of her by this time had they read Budworth's *Fortnight's Ramble To The Lakes* (1792), where her praises are sung, pp. 202–4.

332 *mien:* manner, looks.

341–5 *For we were nursed . . . stream:* The River Cocker flows from Buttermere to Wordsworth's birthplace, Cockermouth. The poet's sense of himself and Mary as therefore linked in childhood is expressed (tenderly and a little facetiously) through a quotation of *Lycidas* 23, 'For we were nursed upon the self-same hill'. *several* separate.

349 *thy image rose again:* Cf. *TA* 62, 'The picture of the mind revives again', and the rising up of imagination at VI 525–9.

354–5 *Beside the mountain-chapel . . . infant:* Wordsworth could certainly have had local knowledge, but it is odd that his is the only reference to Mary's having had a child by Hatfield. Despite the seeming implication of 'This memorial verse', Mary herself lived on at Buttermere, and on 8 March 1808 (when she was 30) married a local farmer. Perhaps Wordsworth in consigning her to a limbo of the imagination was attempting to distract the curious. De Quincey recalls her as continuing to wait at table, and becoming 'disagreeable' as the result of visitors' attentions.

368–9 *to deal about|Articulate prattle:* make baby-talk.

374 *had been:* would have been.

378 Discarded *MS X* reading (1804): 'A miracle, an infant Hercules'.

387 *treated:* given treats; cf. ''tis a pretty baby-treat' (*Kitten and the Falling Leaves* 41).

397–8 *those who walked . . . fiery furnace:* Shadrak, Meshak and Abednego, 'upon whose bodies', when Nebuchadnezzar had them cast into the furnace, 'the fire had no power, nor was an hair of their head singed' (*Daniel* 3.27).

398–405 *He hath since . . . abasement:*

> The boy amid his fruit and glasses, oaths and indecent speech, has achieved what the child of the Ode cannot achieve, travelling as he does 'daily farther from the east'. Stopped in his perfection, as the Virgin of Michelangelo's Pietà is stopped in hers, he represents the power of imagination over time. (*BV* 301–2)

MS C: shows that Wordsworth replaced this great imaginative poetry with a version of *1850* 370–6 as early as c. 1819.

374 *preferred:* brought forward, raised to heaven.

412 *little more than three short years:* Wordsworth, who was in London early in 1791, harks back to autumn 1787 when he travelled south for the first time, to enter Cambridge. *1850*, 'Four rapid years', alters little.

434 *The sorrow of the passion:* The sadness of his feelings.

406 *By Siddons . . . power:* Sarah Siddons (1755–1831), sister of Charles Kemble, and the greatest actress of her day, was at her peak in the 1790s. Dorothy Wordsworth saw her twice in early December 1797 (see letter to Christopher); Wordsworth nowhere records having seen her, but presumably did.

440 *lustres* chandeliers

459–60 *and makes them|Prate somewhat loudly:* 'Thy very stones prate of my whereabout' (*Macbeth* II i 58). *prate* speak.

470–3 *sportive and alert . . . rustling leaves:* Clearest of the links between Book VII and *Kitten and the Falling Leaves* (c. late October 1804); see Introduction and 294n., 387n. above.

478 *girlish:* innocent, naïve.

490–5 *in itself|Humble . . . sustained:* A version of *Pedlar* 76–81 of February 1798:

> things though low,
> Though low and humble, not to be despised
> By such as have observed the curious links
> With which the perishable hours of life
> Are bound together, and the world of thought
> Exists and is sustained.

The substitution of 'props' (*1805*) for 'links', and 'Rest on each other' (*1805*) for 'Are bound together', removes the original Hartleyan implication of beneficial 'chains' of association at work within the mind; cf. III 167n. above.

505 *obsequious:* obedient.

506 *suburbs of the mind:* 'Dwell I but in the suburbs|Of your good pleasure?'. (*Julius Caesar* II i 285–6).

507–15 *If aught . . . solitude:* By a paradox, 'real grandeur' is to be found (if at all) in moments when the 'gross realities' of the theatre (actors, scenery) that are bodying forth (making 'incarnate') the world of Shakespeare's imagination (see *1850* 484) provoke the mind through their very clumsiness to recognize its own intuitions. *1850* 477–80 admits the possibiity that acting will at times rise 'to ideal grandeur'.

517 *titled higher:* with a higher reputation.

522 *tongue-favoured men:* Cf. Milton's 'Tongue-doughty giant', Harapha (*Samson Agonistes* 1181).

525–6 *One of whose name . . . Familiarly:* William Pitt, Prime Minister 1783–1801, 1804–6.

526–8 *a household term . . . Harry talks of: Henry V* IV iii 51–5:

> Then shall our names,
> Familiar in his mouth as household words –
> Harry the King, Bedford and Exeter,
> Warwick and Talbot, Salisbury and Gloucester –
> Be in their flowing cups freshly remembered.

Dorothy records the emotion she felt in reading the play to Wordsworth in the orchard at Dove Cottage on 8 May 1802.

531–2 *hath yoked . . . his car:* proposes to take a long time. Aurora, Goddess of the Dawn, rises from the sea in her chariot ('car') at daybreak. A further classical reference, to the Hours (Horae), goddesses of the seasons, seems unlikely.

538 *He winds . . . horn:* keeps talking; various heroes from Roland to Astolpho do blow horns, but the chief reference seems to be a facetious one to the gnat of *Lycidas* 28, 'What time the grey-fly winds her sultry horn'.

539 *Words follow words . . . sense:* Wordsworth mimics the elegance, and the balanced phrasing, of Pope, in a line satirizing the orator's reliance on mere form; cf. *1850* IV 372.

512–43 As Maxwell puts it, 'The praise of Burke is perhaps the most striking single example of insertion in later revision [*MS D* 1832] of sympathies alien to the earlier Wordsworth. The answer to the rhetorical question of ll. 540–3 would seem to be "Yes".' In *Reflections on the French Revolution*, published in November 1790, Burke denounced the still peaceful and constitutional French leadership in terms of 'plots, massacres, assassinations'. Two months later, in *Letter to a Member of the National Assembly*, his paranoia took a more extreme form: power in France was 'guided by the prudence of litigious attorneys and jew-brokers . . . by shameless women of the lowest condition' (p. 3). The Assembly was conspiring to subvert the 'principles of domestic trust and fidelity' by propagating the values of Rousseau's *Nouvelle Héloïse* (a book, be it said, of impeccable morality).

514–15 *bewildered men . . . guides:* The group to which (by implication) Wordsworth himself would have belonged. In point of fact, in the early 1790s he had been neither 'confused' nor inclined to listen to Burke. He was a committed republican and admirer of the Revolution. Those dismissed as 'boastful guides' would include Price (*Discourse of the Love of our Country*, 1789), Paine (*Rights of Man*, 1791–2) and Godwin (the first edition of whose *Political Justice* [1793] is committed to the Revolution).

520 *stag-horn branches:* At a certain stage the top branches of an English oak tend to die back, the tree forming a second crown from growth sent out lower down the trunk. Through this new foliage older branches protrude, stag-horn-like, because the wood is so hard that they become seasoned instead of rotting.

527–8 *the vital power . . . Custom:* An aspect of Burke that Wordsworth, with his consistent belief in community, would always have been drawn to.

530 *the allegiance to which men are born:* Allegiance to the monarch, or to a constitution agreed in the past. With Price and Paine, Wordsworth had as a young man refused to accept that future generations could be bound by past decisions. Burke was especially concerned to defend the binding power of the settlement' of 1688 that established British constitutional monarchy (while denying that kingship had actually been conferred).

531 *froward multitude:* wayward, undisciplined. Wordsworth comes near to recalling Burke's notorious reference to the lower classes in *Reflections* as 'the swinish multitude'.

533–4 *the winds . . . chain:* Aeolus, god of winds, kept them chained in a cave. Owen points to Burke's quotation in *Reflections* of *Aeneid* I 140–1 '*Illa se jactat in aula|Aeolus et clauso ventorum carcere regnet*' ('In that hall let Aeolus lord it, and rule in the barred prison of the winds').

538–9 *Wisdom . . . in armour:* Athena, representing wisdom, springs at her birth fully armed from the head of Jove.

540 *Synod:* Parliament.

540–3 *Could a youth . . . uninspired:* Wordsworth's use of the rhetorical question enables him to avoid saying outright that he was himself as a young man inspired by Burke. Haydon's *Diary* quotes him as saying on 23 May 1815: 'You always went from Burke with your mind filled, from Fox with your feelings excited, and from Pitt with wonder . . . at his having had the power to make the worse appear the better reason.'

544–50 Inserted in 1838–9 to replace *1805* 544–6 and offer a positive view of the Church before the satirical portrait that follows.

546–65 Based on Cowper's portrait of the theatrical preacher, *Task* II 430–54, already a model for the Infant Prodigy of Book V (see V 350n.).

550 *lead his voice . . . maze:* Maxwell points to Milton, *L'Allegro* 142, 'The melting voice through mazes running'.

558–65 *he who penned . . . flock:* Wordsworth has his fashionable preacher refer to three popular works of the late eighteenth century: Solomon Gessner's *Death of Abel* (1758, translated by Mary Collyer 1761), Edward Young's *Night Thoughts on Life, Death and Immortality* (1742–5, quoted in *Tintern Abbey*), and James MacPherson's epic 'translations' *Fingal* and *Temora* (1762–3), sited in north-west Scotland ('Morven') and allegedly from the Celtic poet Ossian. Eloquence in Wordsworth's final image is a shepherd's crook entwined with 'flowers' culled from other men's writings.

568 *conventicle:* meeting-place, nonconformist place of worship.

570 *With fondness . . . pedestal:* Read: by fondness . . . (*1850* clarifies the meaning).

576 *candidates for regard:* things, or people, to observe.

588 *in parade:* on show.

591 *the schools:* academic disciplines, faculties at a university.

598–625 Wordsworth's vignette of the workman's love for his child is transferred from Book VIII in the final *Prelude* revisions; for the lines in their earlier form, see *1805* VIII 837–59. Ll. 619–25 were added during the reshuffle.

621 *That huge fermenting mass:* London.

596–7 '*The face . . . mystery*': In contrast to Wordsworth's return to the rural community of Hawkshead in 1788: 'The face of every neighbour whom I met|Was as a volume to me' (IV 58–9).

601–2 *A second-sight procession . . . still mountains:* Wordsworth has in mind the Lake District tradition of 'horsemen-shadows winding to and fro', about which he had first written, *Evening Walk* 183–8.

606 *neither knowing me, nor known:* A biblical usage, cf. *Job* 7.10, 'neither shall his place know him any more', and *Ruined Cottage* 144, 'And their place knew them not'.

607 *far travelled in such mood:* Both 'far-travelled, while experiencing such a mood', and 'far travelled into a mood of this kind'.

615–16 *My mind did . . . waters:* A powerful image of the day: the Industrial Revolution depended on mill-wheels turned 'by the might of waters'.

616–19 *and it seemed . . . universe:* In some ways still more impressive is Wordsworth's original draft in *MS X* (c. November 1804):

and I thought
That even the very best of what we know

Both of ourselves and of the universe,
The whole of what is written to our view,
Is but a label on a blind man's chest. (Reed I 485)

620–2 *on the shape . . . another world:* Comparison with the benign admonishment of the Leech Gatherer ('a man from some far region sent|To give me human strength and strong admonishment', ll. 118–19) points up the London beggar's threatening anonymity:

> There is no comfort this time in the admonishment; the world across the border is suddenly alien . . . Lulled by the second-sight procession that he has created to render tolerable the endless stream of passers-by, conserve his own identity as an artist, Wordsworth is taken completely by surprise. What if his own life and work – *The Prelude* is after all 'the story of the man and who he was' – could be seen by some remote and dispassionate wisdom as 'but a label on a blind man's chest'? (*BV* 306)

628–30 *the solemnity . . . stands still:* The stillness that Wordsworth celebrates in his *Sonnet on Westminster Bridge:* of September 1802.

638–9 *The feeble salutation . . . woman:* A prostitute soliciting; accepted by Lamb the city-dweller as merely part of 'the bustle and wickedness' of Covent Garden (letter to Wordsworth, quoted ll. 154–243n. above).

649–51 *the fair . . . St Bartholomew:* Four-day London street-fair, celebrated in Jonson's play (*Bartholomew Fair*, 1615) and visited by William and Dorothy, with Lamb as guide, in September 1802. The fair, held at Smithfield where Protestant martyrs were burned in the reign of Queen Mary (1553–8), typifies for Wordsworth the anarchy of city life.

652 *finished to our hands:* comes to hand ready-made, requiring no additions of the imagination.

656–8 *she shall lodge . . . platform:* Wordsworth, who throughout Book VII has taken a spectator's (or painter's) view of the colour and bustle of London, now wishes to stand above the fair, offer his readers an aerial panorama.

658–61 *What a hell . . . Monstrous:* Consciously evoking Milton's Hell, where 'nature breeds,|Perverse, all monstrous, all prodigious things' (*PL* II 624–5).

687 *phantasma Julius Caesar:* II i 65, 'Like a phantasma or a hideous dream'.

673 *hurdy-gurdy:* stringed instrument, but played with a rosined wheel rather than a bow.

674 *salt-box:* Self-explanatory; a common musical instrument of the time.

681 *The horse of knowledge . . . pig:* Owen points to a 'mare that tells money' seen by Pepys at Bartholomew Fair on 1 September 1668 and a later 'Arabian pony, who performs the most surprising things with cards'. Toby the Sapient Pig, exhibited in London in 1817, 'could spell, read, cast accounts and play cards', not to mention reading people's thoughts, 'a thing never heard of before in an animal of the swine race'.

685 *wax-work:* Madame Tussaud's horrifying collection, made in Paris during the Reign of Terror, came to London in 1802 and is still on show.

688–9 *all Promethean thoughts . . . dulness:* Prometheus made man out of clay; man when he tries to be similarly inventive produces mere anarchy. 'Dulness' would bring the apocalytic chaos of Pope's *Dunciad* appropriately to mind.

mill: factory.

695–6 *a type not false . . . itself:* As a 'type', or emblem, of the city, Bartholomew Fair is in contrast to the sublime landscape of the Simplon Pass, characterized by 'types and symbols of eternity' (VI 571).

700–4 *The slaves . . . end:* Drawn from a passage drafted for *Michael* in 1800, no doubt in an attempt to rationalize the behaviour of Luke in 'the dissolute city'; rightly cut in Wordsworth's final revisions (1839 or later).

709–12 *him who looks . . . the whole:* Cf. II 220–6, addressed to Coleridge, to whom 'the unity of all hath been revealed'.

745–53 *Think how . . . clouds:* Among Wordsworth's final insertions.

721–9 *to the mind . . . relation:* A revised version of *Pedlar* Fragment, *In Storm and Tempest* 23–31 (early February 1798); Wordsworth had adapted the first 20 lines of the Fragment for *The Prelude* as *1799* II 252–71 (*1805* II 322–41) five years before.

724 *measure:* stature. *prospect:* internal landscape (the mountain has been internalized, first in its stability, then in its changefulness).

738 *meagre lines and colours:* A reflection of Wordsworth's attitude in the last 40 lines, not of Book VII as a whole.

Book Eighth

1–61 A version of Book VIII (consisting of ll. 75–661 and other material discussed in the Introduction) is present in *MS Y* and seems to have been composed in October 1804, before the writing of VII. Ll. 1–61, however, were written after VII was finished. Grasmere Fair is introduced as a parallel to London's Bartholomew Fair (VII 648–94) and a way into the already composed studies of the shepherd's life in VIII. For the original opening of VIII, see VII 1–56.

1–5 *What sounds . . . green field:* Helvellyn (3,118 feet) looks down on Grasmere's tiny annual fair, described by Dorothy Wordsworth in her *Journal* of 2 September 1802.

21 *byre:* cowshed *kine:* cows (the archaic plural, as in Joseph's dream of the seven fat and seven lean kine, *Genesis* 41.2ff.).

20 *traffic:* sale.

22 *chaffering:* bidding, haggling.

24 *bleat the flocks:* A mannerism of eighteenth-century descriptive poetry; cf. Thomson, *Seasons* III 719, 'Vanish the woods'.

32–3 *a speech-maker by rote . . . raree-show:* The peep-show's owner knows by heart the speeches used to heighten each scene in turn.

34 *mountebank:* 'A doctor that mounts a bench in the market and boasts his infallible remedies and cures' (Johnson). Wordsworth may already be drawing on Joseph Cottle's *Malvern Hills* (1798) as he does in the *1850* revisions; see *1850* 48–52n. below.

35 *wain:* wagon.

36–43 *But one is here . . . restlessly:* Wordsworth's charming vignette of the 'sweet lass of the valley' takes its cue from the more open eroticism of Ben Jonson. Farmers in *To Penshurst* (1616) 54–6 send produce

By their ripe daughters, whom they would commend
This way to husbands; and whose baskets bear
An emblem of themselves in plum or pear.

45–55 Added 1838–9, when Wordsworth and Mary (the 'ancient wedded pair' of l. 46) would have been nearly 70.

48–52 'These lines are from a descriptive poem – *Malvern Hills* – by one of Mr. Wordsworth's oldest friends, Mr Joseph Cottle' (note to first edition). Wordsworth had told Cottle the poem was a favourite, and praised the quoted passage as 'super-excellent', in a letter of 27 January 1829. Cottle's lines come from a description of a Whitsun holiday, which Owen suggests may have influenced a number of Wordsworth's detailed observations.

47–8 *the recess . . . Magnificent:* A case of Wordsworth being more Miltonic than Milton. Two echoes are linked from *Paradise Lost* Book II ('this vast recess', l. 254, and 'heaven's whole circumference', l. 353), and a Miltonic construction is used in the placing of the noun between two Latinate adjectives ('Circumambient world|Magnificent'.

55–61 *them the morning light . . . abode:* Wordsworth is reworking a tender passage of Thomson's *Spring*, addressed to 'generous minds', responsive to the presence of God in his creation:

For you the roving spirit of the wind
Blows spring abroad; for you the teeming clouds
Descend in gladsome plenty o'er the world;
And the sun sheds his kindest rays for you,
Ye flower of human race! (*Seasons* I 887–91)

62–74 *With deep devotion . . . playmates:* Not part of the main sequence of *MS Y*, which corresponds broadly to Book VIII, but drafted on spare paper near the beginning of the MS. The backward look at London (l. 63) suggests that the lines were composed, or adapted, to form a transition when, c. late November 1804, Book VIII was fitted with its new opening section (ll. 1–61).

64–119 Cut in 1838–9, after extensive attempts at revision, ll. 64–119 (containing two perfect 'spots of time': the floating island and the shepherd and his dog) are a major loss to the 1850 text. It is not clear where Wordsworth's dissatisfaction lay.

75 *complacency:* contentment (without the modern implication of self-satisfaction).

84 *exhalations:* mists, vapours.

86 *Redounding:* overflowing. *vehement* forceful, active.

93–8 *above my head . . . island:* As in the episodes of the Stolen Boat and the Waiting for the Horses (see *1799* I 84n. and 353–5n.), Wordsworth is recalling a scene first treated in his ambitious schoolboy poem *The Vale of Esthwaite* (1786–7):

And on yon summit brown and bare
That seems such an island in the air
The shepherd's restless dog I mark . . . (Oxford I 270, 13–15)

100–1 *A little pendant area . . . forward:* The inhabitants of Wordsworth's aërial island achieve a stillness and a peace that is the opposite of Claudio's horrifying fantasy of being

> imprisoned in the viewless winds,
> And blown with restless violence round about
> The pendant world. (*Measure for Measure* III i 125–7)

Shakespeare's vision (in this case) is of death as a perpetual restless violence, Wordsworth's (characteristically) is of life stopped in a moment of transcendent calm. (*B V* 289–90)

PL X 313, 'a ridge of pendant rock', may also have contributed to Wordsworth's image.

113 *pervious:* passable (Latin *per*, through, and *via*, way).

117–19 *that deep farewell . . . regions:* Wordsworth brings these Hawkshead reminiscences to an end with an allusion to the Coniston episode, *1799* II 140–78 (dropped from *1805* Book II), which had itself been based on *The Vale of Esthwaite.*

119–43 A paragraph that, as De Selincourt pointed out, is strongly reminiscent in style, construction and phrasing of *Paradise Lost* IV 208–47 (and related passages), while drawing its material from Barrow's *Travels in China* (1804).

121–2 *tract more exquisitely fair|Than:* Cf. Milton's dispraising of other paradises by comparison with Eden: 'Not that fair field|Of Enna' (*PL* IV 268ff.), 'Spot more delicious than those gardens feigned . . .' (IX 439ff.).

122–3 *that paradise . . . or Gehol's famous gardens:* Barrow who had accompanied the ambassador, Lord Macartney, to China, 1792–4, shows that 'Paradise of Ten Thousand Trees' is the Chinese name for Gehol's gardens. On p. 34 of Barrow, Wordsworth would have noticed a comparison between the western part of Gehöl and the grounds of Lowther Castle on Ullswater.

127 *China's stupendous mound:* As Owen points out, Barrow refers to the Great Wall as 'a mound of earth cased on each side with bricks or stone'.

128 *boon nature's lavish help:*

> Flowers worthy of Paradise, which not nice art,
> In beds and curious knots, but nature boon
> Poured forth profuse . . . (*PL* IV 241–3)

130–1 *domes|Of pleasure:* An appropriate allusion to the 'stately pleasure-dome' of *Kubla Khan.*

134–7 *foliage taught to melt . . . pursued:*

> sweet interchange
> Of hill and valley, rivers, woods and plains,
> Now land, now sea, and shores with forest crowned,
> Rocks, dens, and caves (*PL* IX 115–18)

Obsequious: obedient.

152–8 *Man free . . . grace:* After the extravagant claim that the Lake District landscape breathes the 'fragrance' of humanity, Wordsworth offers his social ideal of the independent yeoman-farmer, or 'statesman' (Michael for instance), working his own land in his own time. *native:* natural.

156–8 *still followed . . . grace:* Simplicity, beauty and grace make up man's 'train', attend upon him though unasked, in the paradise of Wordsworth's boyhood.

158/9 *MS Y:* at this point includes the 240-line sequence 'We live by admiration and by love' (*Reed* II 378–88, Norton *Prelude* 500–5), interesting not least because it includes at one point an outright rejection of man in favour of nature:

If upon mankind
He looks, and on the human maladies
Before his eyes, what finds he there to this
Framed answerably? What but sordid men
And trivial occupations and desires
Ignoble and depraved! Therefore he cleaves
Exclusively to nature . . .

'I admire human nature', Keats wrote to Haydon on 22 December 1818, 'but I do not like *men*. I should like to compose things honourable to man – but not fingerable-over by *men*.'

111–20 A case in which *1850* has usefully reduced and tautened the earlier text (*1805* 159–73).

160 *frame:* layout, landscaping.

162 *transport:* joy.

173 *these two principles of joy:* the 'common haunts of the green earth' (l. 166; effectively, nature) and 'ordinary human interests' (l. 167; man, human-heartedness). *principle:* source; as at II 465, 'A never-failing principle of joy'.

181 *Illustrated:* Stressed by Wordsworth on the second and fourth syllables (the word meaning, in origin, 'to throw lustre upon').

183–5 *Not such . . . golden age:* Not literary shepherds, such as those of Greek and Latin pastoral.

129–32 *Not such as Saturn . . . golden age:* Saturn was held to have founded the golden age in Latium (Italy), after being deposed by Jove.

187–90 *As Shakespeare . . . king:* Phoebe in *As You Like It* sighs for the 'false Ganymede' (Rosalind, dressed as a man) after the court of Duke Senior has been exiled to Arden (cf. the elaborations of *1850*). Florizel and Perdita in *The Winter's Tale* are not merely king and queen of the sheep-shearing feast, but heirs to Bohemia and Sicilia.

191–9 *Nor such as Spenser fabled . . . kirk-pillars:* Lines suggested by the *May Eclogue* in Spenser's *Shepheardes Calender.*

193–4 *maids at sunrise . . . maybush:* The custom of going 'a-maying' – cutting and bringing home branches of the maybush (hawthorn) or other blossom on May Morning – is said to have lasted in parts of England until the early nineteenth century.

198 *the maypole dance:* Maypoles were taken down by Act of Parliament in 1644, and though they were replaced when the monarchy was restored in 1660, the custom seems to have been weakened.

198–9 *flowers that decked . . . kirk-pillars:* Spenser, *May Eclogue* 11–13:

home they hasten the posts to dight [decorate]
And all the kirk-pillars ere daylight
With hawthorn buds and sweet eglantine [muskrose]

kirk: church.

202–3 *To drink . . . garlands:* Well-dressing, like the maypole, was a survival of an ancient fertility rite. *1850* 'sainted well' (for *1805* 'favourite') is not inappropriate, however, as the custom became assimilated into Christian tradition.

209 *substantial:* essential, to do with substance.

209/10 *MS Y:* preserves an additional line, 'Set off by nature's weekday help alone'.

211–13 *images of danger . . . forms:* An emphasis on the sublime returns as Wordsworth's thoughts go back to childhood experience. 'Awful powers and forms' cannot (should not) be defined, but 'forms' are doubtless of landscape, and 'powers' are most easily seen in terms of the personified educational forces of *1799* Part I.

221 *my household dame:* Ann Tyson, Wordsworth's landlady at Hawkshead (see IV 17n.).

222–311 The Matron's Tale, composed during Wordsworth's work on *Michael* in autumn 1800, is incorporated in *The Prelude* in *MS Y* (October 1804) and cut before the copying of *MS C* (c. 1819). In *MS Y* the lines are introduced as

A story of a child, a shepherd boy,
Whose perilous adventure pleased me much
To hear while I myself was yet a child.

229–44 *Dove Crag . . . the winds:* Maxwell gives an exhaustive account of the mountain region near Grasmere searched by the shepherd and his son:

Dove Crag Above Ambleside, between the Rydal Valley and Dovedale. Deepdale runs parallel to Dovedale, to the north, with Brotherswater between. Fairfield is to the north-west. Between it and Dove Crag is Hart Crag, not, as on modern maps, Arthur's Seat (Stone Arthur is a lower hill to the south-west, just above Grasmere). St Sunday's Pike (or Crag) is to the north-east, between Deepdale and Grisedale. Seat Sandal (l. 237) is due west of Fairfield, with Grisedale Tarn between. Helvellyn is more than two miles due north, with Striding Edge to the east. Russet Cove (properly 'Ruthwaite', pronounced 'Ruthet') is to the south again, a little further east, on the way back to Grisedale Tarn.

241 *coves:* sheltered recesses in the hills.

245 *devious:* intricate, complicated.

255–7 *he will return . . . mother's side:* Hill-sheep are 'heafed' (from Anglo-Saxon 'heafod', a head) to the area where they are born. They will then return to it instinctively, and (it is always said) do not thrive if moved any distance away from it.

259 An octosyllabic line that persists through *MSS Y*, *A* and *B*, though almost certainly unintended. Wordsworth composed by ear, often dictating his verse. In most cases he probably corrected octosyllabics (a foot too short for the *Prelude*'s iambic pentameter) and alexandrines (a foot too

long) when he noticed them, but maybe there were some that he allowed to stand.

261–2 *that unfenced tract . . . farm belonged:* Farms in mountainous and moorland regions of Britain have typically a few low-lying fields, enclosed and ploughable, together with the right to a very much larger 'sheep-stray' on which their sheep (mostly) remain despite the absence of walls.

284–5 *Thrice did he . . . brink:* Even in so unliterary a poem as the Matron's Tale, Wordsworth is tempted by the convention of thriceness; cf. the death of Dido in *Aeneid* IV 690–2, parodied by Pope in the sylph's attempt to prevent the rape of Belinda's lock: 'thrice they twitched the diamond in her ear,|Thrice she looked back, and thrice the foe drew near' (*Rape of the Lock* III 137–8).

298 *kite:* Large fork-tailed hawk, now so rare in Britain that it has had to be reintroduced.

312–15 *Smooth life had flock . . . shores:* The River Galesus, in Calabria, is celebrated in Horace's *Septimi, Gades* (*Odes* II vi) of which Wordsworth had written a free imitation c. 1791, and in Virgil, *Georgics* IV 126.

316–19 *Smooth life:* The waters of River Clitumnus (also in Calabria) were held to be so pure that they whitened the fleeces of sheep feeding on the banks, making them ready for sacrifice (*Georgics* II 146–8).

321–3 *cool Lucretilis . . . tutelary music:* Horace, *Odes* I xvii 5–14, provides the source of Wordsworth's allusion to Pan, pipe-playing god of pastoral life, in his 'tutelary' role as protector of flocks on the brows of Lucretilis (Monte Genaro, near Horace's farm). *thrilling* piercing, penetrating.

325 *pastoral tract:* region grazed by sheep; Wordsworth has in mind the plain south of the Harz mountains, across which he and Dorothy walked after leaving Goslar on 23 February 1799.

340 *hold:* sheltered or protected spot.

341 *strait where passage is:* narrow place, pass; Wordsworth originally wrote 'pervious strait', a repetition of l. 113 above. The *1805* reading is in effect a translation.

348–9 *the melancholy walls . . . imperial:* As Wordsworth points out in the Fenwick Note to *Written in Germany*, Goslar (where he wrote *Was It For This* and *1799* Part I) 'retains vestiges of ancient splendour' from the time when 'German emperors of the Franconian line' held court there. The first Imperial Diet was held at Goslar in 1009; 789 years later, Wordsworth, protected from the extreme cold by 'a dogskin bonnet', such as German peasants wore, composed daily on the ramparts.

353 *Hercynian:* Harz; Wordsworth and Dorothy left Goslar on 23 February 1799, en route for Göttingen where they visited Coleridge before returning to England. Though they certainly walked through the Harz Forest, there is no record of their movements.

361 *Sagacious:* wise, alert.

365 *A toilsome burden:* Of hay.

368 *enclosures won . . . waste:* 'intakes', mountain-ground that has been cleared and fenced.

371 *office:* job, way of life.

238–51 *When . . . day's march:* Poetic elaboration of *1805* 379–85.

246 *protending:* stretching out.

387 *A freeman:* Cf. the Lake District shepherd of *Home at Grasmere* 441–3, who

is 'a servant' only 'Of the fireside or of the open field,|A freeman, therefore sound and unenslaved'.

390 *native man:* natural man (effectively 'the nature of man').

392–5 *Have felt . . . Presiding:* For the strange status attained by shepherd solitaries in Book VIII see ll. 410–14n. below. *genius:* tutelary spirit ('Henceforth thou art the genius of the shore', *Lycidas* 183).

397 *Seeking the raven's nest:* Cf. the boy Wordsworth as 'plunderer . . . In the high places' (I 333–50).

398–402 *on rainy days . . . Greenland bears:* Based on Thomson, *Seasons* III 725–7:

> Seen through the turbid air, beyond the life
> Objects appear . . . o'er the waste
>   The shepherd stalks gigantic . . .

408 *Above all height:* As Maxwell points out, applied by Milton to God the Father (*PL* III 58).

408–10 *an aërial cross . . . worship:* Wordsworth had alluded to 'crosses seen on the tops of the spiry rocks of the Chartreuse' in a note to *Descriptive Sketches* 71; see *1850* VI 483–6n.

410–14 *Thus was man . . . human nature:*

> The shepherds chosen to show how the poet came to feel 'Love human to the creature in himself' (VIII 77) do nothing of the kind. They are symbolic figures . . . Wordsworth may claim
>
>   thus my heart at first was introduced
> To an unconscious love and reverence
> Of human nature . . .
>
> but there is no reason why we should believe this when it follows the accurate statement, 'Thus was man|*Ennobled outwardly* before mine eyes'. The shepherds take hold of the imagination because they are so removed from the human normality they are supposed to exemplify. (*BV* 282)

417 *creature:* created being.

420–2 *Corin . . . Phyllis:* Stock pastoral names. *coronal:* circle (literally 'garland') of dancers.

423 *for the purposes of kind:* by nature.

432 *the dead letter:* fact, actuality.

432–7 Reed draws attention to Wordsworth's condensing of biblical allusions, 'including ones to *II Corinthians* 3.6, *Ephesians* 1.3, *Leviticus* 26.1, *Deuteronomy* 5.8, and *Isaiah* 44.9–20.'

449 An alexandrine that persists through all revisions – not likely to have been intended in the first instance, but quite possibly noticed by Wordsworth later, and accepted.

471 *the . . . temple's heart:* the soul (synonymous with 'nature's holiest places', X 878).

472–5 *Yet do not deem . . . really so:* The most lame of all Wordsworth's transitions. *1850* is much to be preferred.

476–8 *Nature herself . . . animal activities:* Cf. 'The coarser pleasures of my boyish days,|And their glad animal movements all gone by' (*TA* 74–5) and II 206–8 above, 'nature, intervenient till this time|And secondary, now at length was sought|For her own sake.'

483–5 *three and twenty summers . . . Subordinate to her:* Wordsworth in this account dates his coming to hear 'The still sad music of humanity' (*TA* 92) to 1793, the year of his first visit to Tintern. *1850* 'two-and twenty' dates it to summer 1792 and the learning of political awareness in revolutionary France.

485–6 *awful forms|And viewless agencies:* awe-inspiring natural shapes ('The mountain's outline and its steady form') and invisible influences.

507 *'Mid tossing . . . boats':* From 'I'll never love thee more', by James Graham, Marquis of Montrose (hanged, drawn and quartered, and distributed round the Commonwealth, by Cromwell in 1650), ed. James Watson, *A Choice Collection of . . . Scots Poems:* (3 vols, 1706–11).

521 *A wilfulness of fancy:* The fancy is seen in terms of literary extravagance, largely of the Gothic.

527 *charnelhouse:* Shed where bones were stacked when (in Donne's words) a grave was opened, 'Some second guest to entertain'. The practice of reusing graves persisted well into the nineteenth century.

542 'Through most fantastic windings could I trace' (*MS Y*).

544–59 *when the foxglove . . . ground:* Under the heading of fancy Wordsworth beautifully evokes the sentimental episodes found in his early poetry, and imitated originally from Thomson. The beggar-woman who dies with her infants in *An Evening Walk* had been fancifully introduced by a comparison with a happy family of swans.

556 *lorn:* Correctly a past participle meaning 'lost', but treated in the eighteenth century as a poetic contraction of 'forlorn'.

556–9 *while her little ones . . . ground:* Cf. *Evening Walk* 255–8:

> Oft has she taught them on her lap to play
> Delighted, with the glow-worm's harmless ray
> Tossed light from hand to hand; while on the ground
> Small circles of green radiance gleam around.

567 *Glistered:* gleamed; 'How he glisters|Through my rust', *Winter's Tale* III ii 167–8.

583–5 *Thus sometimes . . . imagination:* As in the 1800 note to *The Thorn* (earliest distinction between fancy and imagination in either Wordsworth or Coleridge) imagination is seen as 'the faculty which produces impressive effects out of simple elements', and is thus allied to superstition.

590–1 *this power . . . passions:* Fancy, which for Coleridge is mechanical ('a mode of memory emancipated from the order of time and space'), is for Wordsworth an expression of emotion, and therefore has a value that Coleridge never conceded.

592 *adulterate:* impure, because lacking the unifying power of imagination (fancy brings together the dissimilar, and enjoys the dissimilarity).

604–5 *a real solid world . . . Of images:* Only Wordsworth could have applied the terms 'real' and 'solid' to images stored up within the mind; cf. *Pedlar* 30–3:

deep feelings had impressed
Great objects on his mind with portraiture
And colour so distinct that on his mind
They lay like substances . . .

605–10 *did not pine . . . knowledge:* For an earlier passage on Coleridge's deprivation as a city child (doubtless his own assessment) see VI 308–11 and n. The joining and disjoining that take place result not from fancy, but from the lack of steadying imaginative knowledge.

616–23 *Meanwhile the man . . . flight:* Wordsworth's reflections at the time of writing (October 1804) seem scarcely more sympathetic, or less self-indulgent, than the fancies of his youth (ll. 610–16).

451 *Nor shall we not be tending:* The clumsy, but deliberate, double negative that Wordsworth and Coleridge inherited from Milton; cf. *PL* II 396, 'Nor could his eye not ken'.

458–75 A version of the Coniston episode, *1799* II 140–74, shortened by omission of the central section (ll. 145–56), but with new introductory lines (*1850* 451–8). The episode had been left out of *The Prelude* when Wordsworth created *1805* Book II in January 1804; it is inserted in Book VIII in 1832, though the text of *1850* is not established until the poet's final revisions.

459 *Thurston-mere:* Lake Coniston.

460–2 *With length of shade . . . cloister:* As Owen points out, the trees beside Coniston are so described both in *The Vale of Esthwaite* and in Wordsworth's *Guide to the Lakes*:

> those aged sycamores which once bordered the bay and promontory, and in such a manner stretched their boughs over the margin of the lake that a boat might have moved under their shade as along a cloister. (*Prose Works* II 307–9)

466 *high eastern hill:* An allusion to *Hamlet* I i 166–7: 'But look the morn, in russet mantle clad,|Walks o'er the dew of yon high eastward hill'.

468–75 *1799:* II 166–74, heavily revised and cast into direct speech. Wordsworth could not insert the lines he had actually written aged sixteen for *The Vale of Esthwaite* (published in 1815 as *Dear Native Regions*) because they were in octosyllabic couplets.

624–31 *There came a time . . . life and joy:* In *1799* II 435–64 perception of the One Life is ascribed to Wordsworth's 'seventeenth year', in *1805* III 121–67 it belongs to his first year at Cambridge; here Wordsworth prefers to leave the chronology vague.

480 *a vital pulse:* A scaling down of *1805*, 'The pulse of being'.

487–8 *though born|Of dust . . . worm:* Lines of 1838–9 that offer not only pious self-abasement, but a major theological change. In *1805* man had been kindred to all forms of creation, because all were permeated by the presence of God; in *1850* he is 'kindred to the worm' (which will presently eat him) because his existence ('born of dust') is similarly corporeal.

647 *the impersonated thought:* Wordsworth's anticipations had embodied ('personated') an unreal concept of what human life would be like. L. 648 provides a gloss.

648 *kind:* human nature.

650–1 *as at large . . . set forth:* In Book III.

666 *essayed:* attempted.

522 *one:* Owen points out that Wordsworth's 'grammar has become vague' as the result of revision, and suggests that 'some such phrase as "I became", parallel to "I was led" (l. 519), must be understood before "one"'.

677 *end:* purpose, divine intention.

680–1 *Erewhile . . . played . . . mantle:* Interesting both for the impression Wordsworth gives of lightheartedness in Book VII's treatment of London (see ll. 689–710n. below), and for another playful allusion to *Lycidas*, where Camus (the River Cam) has a 'mantle hairy . . . enwrought with figures dim' (ll. 104–5). Milton's facetiousness in *Lycidas* licenses Wordsworth's.

683 *inquisition:* enquiry, curiosity.

689–710 *Never shall I . . . thing divine:* The incongruity of Wordsworth's first entry into London coming after a whole book describing his experience there is the result of Book VII having been composed (c. November 1804) after the *MS Y* drafts of VIII in October. Ll. 678–89, looking back to the London book, must have been composed after VII had been completed. They are not present in *MS Y*, and were presumably inserted while Wordsworth was cutting down his drafts to form Book VIII.

694 *itinerant vehicle:* Presumably a stage-coach.

695 *vulgar:* ordinary, undistinguished.

700–2 *great God . . . sway:* Though the experience of entering London is of course a mental one, Wordsworth ascribes to the city a power of its own, the result of its age and history.

711–27 Wordsworth's epic simile of the cave had been originally drafted for Book VI (late March 1804) to evoke the anti-climax of crossing the Alps unawares. *MS WW* shows that it preceded the lines on imagination (VI 525–48).

713 *grotto of Antiparos:* It is not clear how Wordsworth knew of the cavern on the Aegean island of Antiparos. According to the *Encyclopaedia Britannica* (3rd ed. 1797), however, it is 120 yards wide and 60 high, and 'accounted one of the greatest natural curiosities in the world'.

713–14 *den|Of Yordas:* Limestone cave near Ingleton in West Yorkshire, visited by Wordsworth and his brother John in May 1800. Reed points to a 'terrific description' of the cave in an appendix to the sixth edition (1796) of West. The *1850* reference to Yordas as 'that Danish Witch' is perhaps Wordsworth being fanciful.

716–17 *sees, or thinks|He sees:* A direct translation of Virgil, *Aeneid* VI 454 ('*aut videt, aut vidisse putat*') from the poignant account of Aeneas's meeting with Dido in the Underworld. Readers would have recognized the allusion (as they would Milton's, at *PL* I 783–4), and seen its appropriateness as Wordsworth constructs his most elaborate Virgilian simile.

724 *works:* seethes. Applied earlier to the mind (I 419) and to the sea (I 501), 'seethes' has for Wordsworth important associations of creative restlessness.

727 *lifeless as a written book:* For Wordsworth, as for Blake, stasis is death to the imagination; cf. *Marriage of Heaven and Hell* plate 15, where 'living fluids' (imaginative materials, still creative and flexible) are cast into the void, 'and [take] the forms of books and [are] arranged in libraries.'

729 *quickening:* enlivening, coming to life.

734 *magician's airy pageant:* 'like this insubstantial pageant faded' (*Tempest* IV i 155); one of Wordsworth's many references to Prospero.

735 *embodying . . . pressure:* As at *1850* VII 288, a recollection of *Hamlet* III ii 22–4, 'show . . . the very age and body of the time, his form and pressure'. *pressure* imprint.

749 *emporium:* market; for Cowper *Task* III 835–7, London was

> resort and mart of all the earth,
> Chequered with all complexions of mankind
> And spotted with all crimes . . .

749–51 *chronicle at once . . . living residence:* London is valued by Wordsworth for its immense concentration of human emotion. So many lives have been lived there – some of them 'chronicled' (kept fresh in the city's history), most 'buried' – and so many are now being lived. *home|Imperial:* London is at once the centre of a growing empire and 'imperial' in its own dimensions.

755 *craved for power:* For imaginative power, that is.

763 *punctual:* restricted to a point (Latin *punctus*).

612–14 *monuments . . . In earth:* It sounds as if Wordsworth in this late revision is thinking of megalithic stone circles, as he is in the reference inserted at *1850* II 101–2.

771 *popular:* republican, governed by the people (Latin *populus*).

772 *magnanimous:* great of soul (Latin again).

775–6 *their humanizing soul . . . incidents:* English history both lacks the ideals of Greece and Rome and excludes the details of day-to-day existence that might have given it humanity.

620 *their:* Ungrammatical as the result of cutting *1805* 772–3. De Selincourt suggests an emendation to 'its' (which could then refer back to 'history').

786–92 *not seldom . . . nursed:* Because it acts upon Wordsworth's imagination, London is unexpectedly comparable to the natural world. It is 'thronged with impregnations' of the mind, just as the Cumbrian landscape is 'impressed' with associations of 'danger and desire' stored up in boyhood (I 494–501).

802–4 *Neither guilt, nor vice . . . Nor all the misery:* Wordsworth is rewriting his statement of faith in nature, *TA* 129 ff.: 'neither evil tongues,|Rash judgments, nor the sneers of selfish men . . .|Shall e'er prevail against us . . .'

815–16 *seemed brighter . . . counterview:* An example of Wordsworth's painterly sense of *chiaroscuro.*

819–23 *'in the east . . . heavenly fraught': PL* XI 203–7, with slight adaptation; Michael descends to tell Adam and Eve of God's judgement on their trespass. *orient* lit up as by the sunrise. *fraught:* burdened, freighted.

824–7 *Add . . . unity of man:* Lines that read most incongruously after the emphasis on London *dis*-unity at the end of Book VII. It was presumably Wordsworth's sense that London could not be brought under the heading of the unity of man that led him (after completing the drafts of VIII in *MS Y*) to go on and give it a book of its own. Portraying it in VII as an Underworld, he was able to express both the attractiveness of its colour and movement, and the threat he felt in its swallowing up of identity and community.

837–59 Transferred to Book VII in Wordsworth's final revisions, becoming *1850* VII 598–625.

841 *foil:* contrast; a reminder of Wordsworth's true response to London. Tenderness is 'set off by foil'. Man is not unified.

860–70 Drafted in early spring 1804 alongside materials that contributed to Book IV.

680 *'busy hum':* 'Towered cities please us then,|And the busy hum of men . . .' (*L'Allegro* 117–18).

Book Ninth

1–17 No drafts survive, but the bulk of Book IX seems to have been written c. April–May 1804. Ll. 1–17 are added at a later stage, after the composition of Books VIII and VII in October–November, when Wordsworth has a sense of the final shape of his poem. Looking back over the course of his work, he finds in the image of the river (recurrent since the Derwent's flowing along his dreams in the opening lines of *Was It For This*) the means of asserting an organic unity for his poetry. The river 'is an image at once of the poem, and of the mind that is the subject of the poem, and of the poet's mind that is controlling, and failing to control, the narrative' (*BV* 233).

5 *Turns and will measure back his course:* In constructing his epic simile Wordsworth models himself on the beginning of Book III of Cowper's *Task*:

> As one who, long in thickets and in brakes
> Entangled, winds now this way and now that
> His devious course uncertain . . .

8 *motions retrograde:* backward movements.

9–16 Introduced in *MS D* 1832.

10 *precipitate:* expedite, get ahead with.

13–17 *the argument . . . in itself:* As he moves on into his 'argument' (theme) of political involvement, Wordsworth invites a comparison with *Paradise Lost*, warning of material ungenial and forbidding, as Milton (at the beginning of *his* ninth book) warns of the impending Fall:

> No more of talk where God or angel guest
> With man, as with his friend, familiar used
> To sit indulgent . . .
> I now must change
> Those notes to tragic; foul distrust, and breach
> Disloyal on the part of man . . . (*PL* IX 1–7)

31 Wordsworth seems to have spent only four months (January–May) in London during 1791; much of the year was spent in Wales.

36–9 *Led thither . . . Loire:* Cf. Dorothy to Jane Pollard, 7 December 1791:

William is I hope by this time arrived at Orleans, where he means to pass the winter for the purpose of learning the French language, which will qualify him for the office of travelling companion to some young gentleman, if he can get recommended.

36 *scrip and staff:* Obviously there is poetic licence as Wordsworth in this revision of c. 1819 portrays himself and Jones with pilgrim's wallet and staff. His letter to Dorothy of 16 September 1790, however, shows that in the Alps they had bundles 'upon [their] heads, with each an oak stick in [their] hands'.

42–6 *each spot . . . Geneviève:* Once again echoing Milton ('City of old or modern fame', *PL* XI 386), Wordsworth takes his reader to areas of Paris especially associated with the Revolution: the Champs de Mars, where Louis XVI on 14 July 1790 had sworn allegiance to the new Constitution (see VI 357n.); the Faubourg St Antoine, a working-class suburb near to the now dismantled Bastille; Montmartre, revolutionary meeting-place to the north; the church of Ste Geneviève on the Left Bank, where Mirabeau was buried in April 1791 (renamed the Panthéon after Voltaire and Rousseau were brought there for reburial as prophets of the Revolution).

47 *The National Synod and the Jacobins:* Wordsworth told his brother Richard on 19 December 1791 that he had been 'at the National Assembly, introduced by a member'. The Jacobin Club (Society of Friends of the Revolution), whose members dominated the Assembly with their eloquence, held its meetings in a monastery in the Rue St Jacques. At this stage Brissot and the Girondin group were members alongside Robespierre (who would send them to the guillotine in October 1793).

50–1 *The Arcades . . . Orleans:* The courtyard of the Palais Royal was lined on three sides with shopping arcades.

56 *hubbub wild:* Satan as he approaches the realm of Chaos in *Paradise Lost* Book II is met by 'a universal hubbub wild|Of stunning sounds and voices all confused' (ll. 951–2).

63–71 *Where silent zephyrs . . . felt:* The Bastille, royal fortress and prison, symbolic of the tyranny of the Ancien Régime, had been sacked on 14 July 1789, and later dismantled. Now poetic 'zephyrs' (breezes more often to be found sporting with curls) sport with its dust. The sense of incongruity reflected in Wordsworth's language is heightened by memories of himself as the posturing tourist, unconcerned by the grandeur of political events.

68 *incumbences:* moods of thoughtfulness, broodings.

78–80 *the Magdalene . . . tears:* Baroque painting of the penitent St Mary Magdalen, by Charles le Brun (1626–90), displayed (to sounds of religious music, according to Legouis) at the Carmelite convent in the Rue d'Enfer. Now at the Louvre.

81 *my more permanent residence:* Orleans; not always distinguished in the *Prelude* narrative from Annette Vallon's native town of Blois.

97 *the master pamphlets:* English pamphlets that Wordsworth had read before his arrival on the French political scene, presumably including Paine's *Rights of Man* Part I and other replies to Burke's *Reflections on the French Revolution* (November 1790).

103 *organs of the public power:* political groups.

109–11 *the first storm . . . quiet:* It is often forgotten that the Revolution was peaceful for three years between the fall of the Bastille in July 1789 and the events of 10 August 1792 leading to the imprisonment of the King.

116 *Routs:* parties.

118 *Sequestered:* isolated.

125 *patriot:* revolutionary

129 *the city:* Blois now, rather than Orleans; see 81n. above.

131 *seasoned:* In blood.

132–7 *men well-born . . . done:* In spring 1792 the French Army was still staffed by royalist officers, in sympathy with the Austrians against whom (from 20 April) they were supposedly fighting. Austrian troops were waiting on the Rhine, and Marie Antoinette's brother, the Emperor, had declared his intention of restoring Louis to absolute power ('undoing what was done').

136 *Save only one:* The exception was Michel Beaupuy, who converted Wordsworth to the revolutionary cause; see ll. 294ff. below.

147 *temper:* disposition, character.

150 *port:* carriage, bearing.

156–7 *At the hour,|The most important of each day:* Wordsworth's syntax suggests he may be thinking in French: '*A l'heure, la plus importante, du jour*'.

176–7 *Oh, laughter . . . now is:* The historian's 'page' would bring ridicule upon itself by attempting to describe the complexities of the contemporary situation.

179 *Carra, Gorsas:* Journalist deputies of the National Assembly, and members of the Girondin group with whom Beaupuy and Wordsworth were in sympathy. Carra was guillotined on 31 October 1793, Gorsas on the 7th. The story told by Carlyle (*Reminiscences*, Everyman, London, 1972, 532) of Wordsworth's witnessing Gorsas' execution, on an otherwise unrecorded visit to France, is attractive, and beloved of biographers, but in the highest degree unlikely. England and France had been at war for eight months, Wordsworth's French cannot have been perfect, he had no money, and was not by nature a Scarlet Pimpernel. Had either love (a clandestine visit to Annette Vallon) or politics lured him to Paris in October 1793, we should not have to rely for evidence on a conversation alleged to have taken place fifty years later.

184–91 *The men . . . depart:* La Fayette actually called on royalist officers to emigrate so as to clarify the situation. By April 1792 more than half had deserted.

188 *foreign foes:* At this stage Austria and Prussia; England entered the war in February 1793.

202 *polity:* government.

213 *orders and degrees:* social distinctions, either conferred or inherited.

222–6 *It was my fortune . . . blood:* It should be said that Wordsworth, though 'born in a poor district' (l. 218) was born also in a large and handsome house, his father being agent to one of the most powerful landowners in the kingdom.

226–36 *Nor was it least . . . industry:* As in his comments on the Lake District at ll. 222–6, Wordsworth is overstating his claim to have experienced egalitarianism. Cambridge in the late eighteenth century had little resemblance to a republic. The scholars and gentlemen of l. 233 wore different clothes, and led very different lives. Scholars were intent on bettering themselves, first within the University, and then within the Church; by contrast, high-ranking undergraduates had no need to bother with 'talents and successful industry' and, because of the system of ecclesiastical patronage, were frequently in a position to bestow favours on their tutors (Ben Ross Schneider Jr, *Wordsworth's Cambridge Education* 21–4).

233–5 *subservience . . . sovereignty:* A careful removal, in 1832, of the pantheist implications of *1805*, where nature shares in the sovereignty of God.

241 *sanction:* confirm.

254 *A gift . . . soon:* Wordsworth's case was perhaps little different from that of many English people (William Pitt among them) who welcomed the Revolution at its outset because it seemed that the French were catching up – achieving the constitutional rights that had been gained a hundred years earlier by the English 'Glorious Revolution' of 1688.

250–1 *Inflamed by passion . . . injury:* An astonishing attack on the French royalist officers, inserted in *MS C* c. 1819, at a time when Wordsworth was electioneering for the Tories and might well be expected to tone down his contempt. It is an honourable fact that he never ceased to 'hail,|As best, the government of equal rights|And individual worth' (*1850* 241–3).

279–80 *self-devotion . . . confidence:* dedication to the cause, and hopes for earthly well-being (effectively for political justice) felt with the conviction of a Christian martyr.

283 *martial tunes:* Owen points out that the *Marseillaise* was first heard in 1792.

294–5 *Among that band . . . other mould:* Michel Beaupuy, mentioned at l. 136 above, and wholly different in character. *mould:* earth, or clay, from which the human body was traditionally said to have been formed.

298–9 *A meeker man|Than this lived never:* The tones of Chaucer's *General Prologue* appear (cf. ll. 320–1 below, 'Somewhat vain he was|Or seemed so'), suggesting Wordsworth's consciousness of creating a formal portrait of Beaupuy.

303 *sensibly:* perceptibly.

308 *fairy:* magic.

309–13 *By birth he ranked . . . order:* Beaupuy was a nobleman and philosopher, descended on his mother's side from Montaigne. As an aristocratic believer in the Revolution he was by no means alone (see Williams, *Letters Written in France*, passim); among the officers at Blois, however, he was isolated. Aged 36, he befriended the 22-year-old Wordsworth, passing on to him his egalitarian ideals and becoming one of the major influences on his life.

325 *Complacently:* enjoyably, with pleasure.

340–1 *a sounder judgement|Than afterwards:* Probably than in the period 1793–6, after his return to England; cf. Book X.

361/2 *MS Y:* preserves a fine additional line referring to unprincipled wars of conquest: 'The senseless thirst of bloody spoils abroad'.

363 *as it is:* insofar as it is.

368–71 *making social life . . . wise and good:* Social life is to become as pure (through the spreading of knowledge) as personal life is among the wise and good.

383–4 *from the depth|Of shameful imbecility:* Introduced in *MS C* c. 1819, and again showing no slackening of Wordsworth's commitment to the Revolution.

395 *continence:* self-possession.

399–400 *Rotha's stream,|Greta, or Derwent:* Cumbrian rivers: the Rothay flowing into Grasmere, the Greta (beneath Coleridge's house, Greta Hall, Keswick) flowing into Derwentwater, and the Derwent ('fairest of all rivers') flowing from Derwentwater to Wordsworth's birthplace at Cockermouth.

415–24 *Such conversation . . . philosophers:* Wordsworth is drawing appropriately on the *Life of Dion* in North's *Plutarch* (1579), where philosophers play an active part in liberating Sicily from the tyranny of Dionysius the Younger in 357 BC. Dion recruited Eudemus Cyprian and Timonides Leucadian, and together they sailed from the Ionian island of Zante (ancient Zacynthus). Plato had been involved in earlier negotiations.

415 *Attic:* Greek.

430 *accoutred:* equipped, prepared.

431–6 *He perished . . . Lived not to see:* Wordsworth is misinformed as to Beaupuy's later career. As Chief of Staff of the Army of the West he had the task of suppressing the counter-revolution of 'deluded men' in the Vendée, and in October 1793 was badly wounded at Château-Gontier. He survived, however, for three more years, dying at the battle of Elz on the eastern front on 19 October 1796. Though he did not live to see the rise of Napoleon and the creation of a French empire, he took part in the aggressive campaigns of 1794–6 that shocked Wordsworth and other British radicals as a betrayal of the Revolution.

442–3 *High woods and over-arched . . . side:* 'a pillared shade|High overarched, and echoing walks between' (*PL* IX 1106–7).

449 *so met in shades like these:* met as we have done, in shades like these.

454–6 *Angelica . . . as she:* Angelica and Erminia, heroines of Ariosto's *Orlando Furioso* and Tasso's *Gerusalemme Liberata*, evoke the romantic imagination that counterbalances politics in Wordsworth's walks with Beaupuy. In 1789 Wordsworth, who was reading Italian (not part of the syllabus) at Cambridge, had joined in presenting a copy of Tasso to his school library (*Wordsworth's Hawkshead* 144–5).

461–4 *haunt|Of satyrs . . . thrall:* Among possible sources, see especially the stories of Una and Hellenore (*FQ* I vi 13 and III x 43–4).

470–2 *a roofless pile . . . violence abrupt:* It is significant that *Descriptive Sketches*, with its account of the desecration of the Grande Chartreuse (ll. 53–79), is written under the influence of Beaupuy in summer of 1792; see also *1850* VI 420–88.

473 *colloquies:* discussions.

485–93 *that rural castle . . . plain beneath:* De Selincourt's much followed identification of Beauregard as the 'rural castle' and Anne Pisseleu d'Heilly as the particular mistress of Francis I has its problems. Beauregard was built 25 years too late, and in any case is hardly on high enough ground for contact with Francis at Chambord. Anne, meanwhile, first as *fille d'honneur* to the King's mother, then as *maîtresse en titre*, was living at Court, and would have had no cause to signal. Had Wordsworth been concerned with fact he would hardly have let 'name now slipped|From my remembrance' stand for 45 years.

491 *cressets:* flaming torches.

512–16 *a hunger-bitten girl . . . sustenance:*

> It is one of those pieces of writing that would seem inept if they didn't so obviously work. At first the girl is the subject of the central relative clause ('who

crept along'), then with no grammatical transition the heifer turns out to have displaced her . . . No punctuation could contain or imply the poet's meaning, but we become aware through the movement of the syntax that the girl in her poverty and despair has yielded to the dominance of the heifer, which is of course feeding, while she is 'bitten with hunger'. The detail of the cord, not held and controlled, but tied to her as if she were the animal, brings home the cruelty of the situation. (*BV* 252).

517 *heartless:* despairing.

533–4 *whence better days|To all mankind:* Wordsworth assumes, as many did, that the French Revolution (itself modelled on the American) will lead to political reform across the known world.

538 *Captivity by mandate without law:* The *lettre de cachet* (issued by royal or official mandate), with which Vaudracour is threatened at ll. 666–7 below.

541–3 *if not the air . . . Dread nothing:* Wordsworth is being ironic about the likelihood of total change: it is too much to hope that all will breathe the air of liberty, and the human heart have nothing to dread.

551–5 *a tragic tale . . . therein:* Wordsworth's statement that he heard the 'tragic tale' from Beaupuy and others who had played a part in it is corrected in the Fenwick Note to *Vaudracour and Julia* (published as a separate work in 1820), where it is said to be 'faithfully narrated, though with the omission of many pathetic circumstances, from the mouth of a French lady who had been an eye and ear witness of all that was done and said'. To which Wordsworth adds: 'Many long years after I was told that Dupligne [Vaudracour] was then a monk at La Trappe.' Wordsworth, it would seem, heard the story from a woman at Blois (perhaps from others too), and for the sake of continuity transferred it within his poem to Beaupuy. Two other factors have to be taken into account: the similar story of parental tyranny told by Williams in *Letters from France*, and the poet's own recent experience. Early in 1792 Wordsworth had met and fallen in love with Annette Vallon, by whom he had a child, christened in Orleans Cathedral on 15 December as Anne Caroline Wordsworth. Wordsworth and Annette were separated, not by an angry father, but by war (declared in February 1793, two months after the poet's return to London). Annette's two surviving letters, however, leave no doubt that they intended to get married. Williams's story of M and Mme Du Fossé, though it differs in many ways from *Vaudracour and Julia*, resembles it in idiom and atmosphere, and provides the central detail of an aristocratic father willing to imprison his son rather than agree to his marriage with a woman of lower birth. The key to Wordsworth's relationship to Williams's story may be in the fact that in 1793 he was hoping to turn his 'tragic tale' into a novel (*Chronology* I 124). Williams would have been his literary model. *Vaudracour and Julia*, we may assume, has the primary purpose of telling by implication of the poet's relation to Annette. In doing so it broadly follows a story told to him at Blois in 1792, and is written with an eye on the bare heartfelt narrative of *Letters Written in France*.

553–9 *Oh, happy time . . . sequel:* Instead of removing the traces of his story from *The Prelude*, Wordsworth, after publishing *Vaudracour and Julia* separately in *Poems* 1820, permitted his introduction to the lovers' tale to stand. Ll. 557–9, with their incongruous doubling back, and the pointless summary of his untold tale (ll. 559–85), are the product of much reworking in 1832 and 1838–9.

558 *love-knot:* Probably of ribbon.

561 *Young Vaudracour:* Wordsworth takes the name from Lieutenant Vaudracourt in Beaupuy's regiment at Blois.

580 *outside:* surface.

589 *The house . . . shrine:* A recollection perhaps of Criseyde's desolate house, Chaucer, *Troilus and Criseyde* V 551–3:

fayne wolde I kisse
Thy colde dores, dorste I for this route,
And farewel shryne, of which the seynt is oute.

Wordsworth had made a number of translations from Chaucer in 1801.

595 *Overblessed for life:* blest beyond endurance.

615–17 *in a distant town . . . babe was born:* Annette moved from Blois to Orleans to have her child, Mme Du Fossé (in Williams's story), from Rouen to Caen.

631–2 *busy . . . as a swallow|About its nest:* A Dove Cottage touch. 'The swallows come to the sitting-room window as if wishing to build', Dorothy writes in her *Journal*, 16–19 June 1802. 'They swim round and round, and again they come . . . The swallows were very busy under my window this morning.'

638–42 *that darling bard . . . unrelenting east:*

Juliet: Wilt thou be gone? It is not yet near day.
It was the nightingale, and not the lark,
That pierced the fearful hollow of thine ear –
Nightly she sings on yond pomegranate tree –
Believe me, love, it was the nightingale.

Romeo: It was the lark, the herald of the morn;
No nightingale. Look, love, what envious streaks
Do lace the severing clouds in yonder east!
(*Romeo and Juliet* III v 1–8)

650 *A final portion:* A settlement in lieu of his inheritance.

664 *obduracy:* Stressed on the second syllable.

666–7 *The father . . . signet of the state:*

Monsieur Du Fossé received intelligence that his father, irritated almost to madness by the information of his marriage, was making application for a *lettre de cachet* in order to confine his daughter-in-law for the rest of her life, and had also obtained power to have his son seized and imprisoned. (Williams, *Letters Written in France* 130–1)

694 *Self-slaughter:* suicide; 'Or that the Everlasting had not fix'd|His canon 'gainst self-slaughter!' (*Hamlet* I ii 131–2).

715–17 *thought|Unfilial, or unkind . . . breast:* Vaudracour's excessive meekness, paralleled neither in Wordsworth himself nor in Du Fossé, is further evidence of a distinct source.

723 *nice:* fastidious, delicate.

746 *traversed from without:* impinged upon (literally 'crossed') by external pressures.

758–9 *So they fared|Objects of general concern:* 'Everyone sympathized in the fate of this unfortunate young man, and execrated the tyranny of the unrelenting father' (Williams, *Letters Written in France* 168).

785–6 *impressions . . . Friendly to human kindness:* Cf. *Ruined Cottage* 229, 'A power to virtue friendly'.

840 *and be there immured:* remain for the rest of her life within its walls. Williams visits Benedictine and Carmelite convents at Rouen, and learns that the Carmelite nuns 'slept in their coffins, upon straw, and every morning dug a shovel-full of earth for their graves', also that 'they walked to their devotional exercises upon their knees'. At one point she meets nuns who have 'been forced by their parents to take the veil' (Williams, *Letters Written in France* 118–19).

907–8 *Which . . . by some mistake . . . died:* Regarded by De Selincourt as bringing the story to 'a climax of absurdity difficult to parallel in our literature'. Wordsworth's concern, as he said in the Preface to *Lyrical Ballads* 1800, was not with 'action and situation', but with the 'feeling therein developed'. This could lead to a certain perfunctoriness; cf. the removal of Margaret's inconvenient child, at *Ruined Cottage* 345–7, and of Luke to 'a hiding-place beyond the seas' (*Michael* 420–5).

912 *From that time forth he never uttered word:* The last words of Iago, almost verbatim: 'From this time forth I never will speak word' (*Othello* V ii 303).

927 *savage outside:* wild appearance.

929 *intelligence:* communication.

931–5 *Nor could the voice of freedom . . . imbecile mind:* Details which we know from the Fenwick Note did not apply to Dupligne (the Vaudracour of Wordsworth's source), and which seem very probably to come from *Letters Written in France.* For Du Fossé there is a happy ending, but not for one nameless victim of a parental *lettre de cachet*:

> He was confined ten years, and only released when all the prisons were thrown open by order of the National Assembly. But for this unhappy young man their mercy came too late. His reason was gone for ever, and he was led out of his prison, at the age of five-and-twenty, a maniac. (pp. 211–12)

imbecile: is stressed on the second syllable.

Book Tenth

1–8 *It was a beautiful . . . England:* Wordsworth was leaving not only the autumnal beauty of the Loire, but Annette Vallon, who had moved to Orleans in September to have her child. He reached Paris, 'the fierce metropolis', c. 29 October 1792, and was in England by early December. Caroline (whom because of the war he would not meet until 1802, when she was nine) was christened in Orleans Cathedral on the 15th.

4–10 *A day . . . passed on:* Elaboration of 1832 and 1838–9.

5 *tilth:* arable land.

8–9 *From his throne . . . fallen:* Louis XVI was imprisoned after the storming of the Tuileries on 10 August 1792, ending three years' attempt by the leaders of the Revolution to work within the framework of a constitutional monarchy; see ll. 44–8n. below.

9–13 *the congregated host . . . innocuously:* Austrian and Prussian forces, under the bloodthirsty Duke of Brunswick, invaded France on 19 August confident of quickly restoring the monarchy. Written on the 'front' (forehead) of the invasion was the Brunswick Manifesto of 25 July 'giving up the city of Paris to military execution, and exposing it to total destruction' if 'the least outrage' were offered to the French royal family. Longwy and Verdun were taken by the invaders, but on 20 September the cloud 'burst innocuously' as an inexperienced French army won the important battle of Valmy, forcing a retreat to the Rhine.

14–18 *a band . . . victims:* Wordsworth's simile of the coalition armies closing in on the French like trapped animals is shown by the diction ('elate and jocund', 'punctual spot') to be from the first consciously Miltonic. In *1850* it became more obviously so with its reference to *Paradise Lost* XI 391, 'Agra and Lahore of great mogul'.

20 *Rajahs and Omrahs:* Indian princes and nobles; Owen suggests that Wordsworth's image is of a tiger hunt.

23 *to the better cause:* on the part of the French.

24–31 *The state . . . republic:* Despite the example of America, it had not been among the aims of the Revolution that France should become a republic. When she did so, on 22 September 1792, two days after the victory at Valmy, there was little alternative. The revisions of *1850* 34–9 belong to *MS C*, c. 1819, and leave a somewhat confused impression as to Wordsworth's attitudes.

31–4 *Lamentable crimes . . . past:* News of the fall of Verdun to Brunswick's invading army set off four days of mob violence, 2–6 September, in which about half the inmates in the prisons of Paris were executed after summary trials. Though Marat and others were advocating the slaughter of aristocrats, and in other parts of the country there had been purges specifically of priests, four-fifths of those who died in Paris seem to have been ordinary criminals, not royalists. No one ordered the purge, but Danton certainly condoned it.

36 *Ephemeral monsters:* Given the context of senseless violence, Wordsworth may be thinking of the dragon's teeth sown by Cadmus, which sprang up as armed men, but fought each other to death.

42–4 *The prison . . . In bondage:* The Temple was the last home of the royal family, the King and Queen leaving it only to be guillotined (on 21 January 1793 and 16 October), and the Dauphin dying there in 1795.

44–8 *the palace . . . dead and dying:* On 10 August 1792 threats of invasion caused the Paris working-class 'sections' to take control and attack the Tuileries. Four hundred *sans-culottes* were killed by the Swiss Guard, who were then butchered themselves when the King (who had fled to the Assembly) ordered them to lay down their arms. Total numbers killed as the Palace was sacked seem to have been in the region of 1,200. Bodies were burnt in the Place du Carrousel.

62–6 *The fear gone by . . . substantial dread:* The Massacres take on substance – flesh and blood – as Wordsworth in his terror reaches out like Doubting

Thomas to 'feel and touch them'. Links with *The Borderers* (Mortimer to Rivers, IV ii 96–7: 'The proofs, the proofs!|You ought to have seen, to have touched the guilt') suggest the extent to which Wordsworth feels implicated in the violence; see Jonathan Wordsworth, 'Wordsworth's "Dim and Perilous Way"' 205–223.

65 *a little month:* Wordsworth's subdued quotation sets up a parallel between his own response to the Revolution's sudden turn to violence and Hamlet's to his mother's 'o'er hasty marriage' (and collusion in murder): 'A little month . . . a beast that wants discourse of reason|Would have mourned longer' (I ii 147–51).

68 *calendars:* chronicles.

70–74 Reliving his substantial dread of the Massacres, Wordsworth produces five sudden purely apocalyptic lines of interior monologue that are quite unlike anything else he ever wrote . . . The horse is schooled by man against its nature to turn upon the spot (as Danton may induce spontaneous violence to come round), and 'the wind of heaven' that should be freer still, wheels like the horse 'in his own steps'. The poet in his nightmare reverie can turn anything to evidence of cyclical return. Years, tides, days, add their more obvious corroboration, till the argument so commonly and tendentiously used for the Christian afterlife ('all things have second birth') betrays us suddenly into the power of insatiable violence: 'the earthquake is not satisfied at once.' (*BV* 254)

70 *The horse is taught his manage:* schooled to perform particular movements and paces (Wordsworth is probably thinking of the manoeuvre in which a horse turns full circle on its hind legs). I am grateful to Reeve Parker for pointing out to me that the National Convention at this time met at the Manège, previously a riding-school. Owen notes a Shakespearean reference in *As You Like It* I i 11–13: 'His horses are bred better . . . they are taught their manage'.

78–84 Wordsworth in *MS C* (c. 1819) expanded the five great lines of *1805* to thirteen. These were cut to seven in subsequent revisions, but the final text is a mish-mash. As manuscript succeeded manuscript, revision had its own momentum; after 1832 Wordsworth seems never to have turned back to *MS A* or considered reverting to an original reading.

77 '*Sleep no more*': Wordsworth may be thinking not merely of *Macbeth* II ii 35–6 – 'Methought I heard a voice cry "Sleep no more!"|Macbeth doth murder sleep"' – but also of Godwin's powerful and relevant use of the quotation in *Caleb Williams*: 'The ease and lightheartedness of my youth were forever gone. The voice of an irresistible necessity commanded me to "Sleep no more"' (Oxford Novels 138).

83–4 *the Palace Walk|Of Orleans:* the arcades of the Palais Royal, as at IX 51–2.

86–103 *hawkers . . . irresolute friends:* A turning-point of the Revolution, as Louvet accuses Robespierre of aiming at dictatorship – '*Je t'accuse d'avoir évidemment marché au suprême pouvoir*' – and the Girondins (who had indicted Danton in the previous debate for collusion in the September Massacres) fail to press home their advantage. Robespierre is given time to prepare a defence, and survives; power swings away from the moderates as the King is put on trial and executed (21 January 1793); working through the Paris Commune, Robespierre in July 1793 assumes control; in October the Girondin leaders are guillotined.

87–8 *'Denunciation . . . Robespierre':* Pamphlet containing Louvet's speech at the Convention, on sale 30 October 1792.

99 *in the tribune:* on the rostrum.

113–14 *The indecision . . . best:* indecisiveness of the Girondins in the Convention, who 'seemed best' in their intentions; see Mme Jeanne Marie Roland de la Platière (whose death it caused), *Appeal to Impartial Posterity* I 55–6: 'Sometimes for very vexation I could have boxed the ears of these philosophers . . . excellent reasoners all, learned politicians in theory, but totally ignorant of the art of leading men.'

116 *impiety:* lack of scruples, moral standards.

121 *The gift of tongues might fall:* As upon the apostles at Pentecost, *Acts* 2. 2–4.

125 *work of safety:* Glossed by Reed as anticipatory self-protection, but Wordsworth is surely thinking of the defence of republican France (in which, since Valmy, he has total confidence).

134–8 *Yet would I willingly . . . single persons:* Wordsworth's dreams of being the man of the hour were no doubt foolish, but he would have been aware, for instance, of the influence of Tom Paine (in 1792 a member of the National Convention in Paris) on the course of the American Revolution.

137 *still:* always.

139 *Transcendent . . . patrimony:* over and above considerations of region or nationality (Wordsworth is telling himself that even a foreigner might have influence).

141 *objects:* objectives, aims.

144–5 *where evidence divine . . . most sure:* 'Evidence divine' tells man to have faith in the cause that will fulfil his nature.

146–52 *That, with desires heroic . . . safe obedience:* Men are instinctively drawn to the self-reliant and heroic 'spirit' (leader), joining him, and trusting their safety to him, as streams blend themselves in a river.

179–90 Inserted in *MS D* (early 1832) as a continuation to the abstract and not easily intelligible reasonings of *1805* 136–57.

179 *the means:* Probably the leader's human supporters.

183 *A sovereign voice:* conscience.

187 *either sacrifice:* It seems that life as well as death is seen, in the circumstances of betrayal, to be a sacrifice to the 'stern decree' of conscience.

160 *theme:* topic set for composition.

165–6 *to Harmodius . . . Aristogiton:* Athenians who tried to kill the tyrant Hippias and his brother Hipparchus in 514 BC. Harmodius died in the attempt, Aristogiton was captured and executed, but they were widely praised for their good intentions (by Plato, for instance, in the *Symposium*). A Greek drinking song translated by Wordsworth c. 1786 oddly celebrates them as successful in their coup: 'When the tyrant's breast they gored . . . Gave to Athens equal laws' (Oxford I 299).

167 *To Brutus:* The idealist among Caesar's murderers: 'All the conspirators save only he|Did that they did in envy of great Caesar' (*Julius Caesar* V v 69–70).

170 *the godhead which is ours:* Cf. the final words of *The Prelude*, where the mind of man is 'Of substance and of fabric ['of quality and fabric' – 1850] more divine' (than 'the earth|On which he dwells').

171 *charmed:* laid to sleep.

175 *Doth live but by variety of disease:* Not one of Wordsworth's clearer statements. Are the 'diseases' too various to be mortal?

178 *Creed . . . not annulled:* Cut c. 1819; *1850* makes no other substantive change to Wordsworth's moving statement of faith in the Revolution, *1805* 176–88. The 'shameful years' (1794–1804) included the Reign of Terror and the rise of French imperialism.

179 *virtue:* power (Latin *virtus*). *one paramount mind:* the leader whom Wordsworth has posited in ll. 136–75.

180 *those impious crests:* the Jacobins; Wordsworth's metaphor of plumed helmets is taken from *PL* VI 188, 'This greeting on thy impious crest receive'.

183 *immaturity:* It is Wordsworth's consistent view that the people have to be educated to receive power; see *Letter to the Bishop of Llandaff*, c. February 1793.

190 *Compelled . . . absolute want:* Wordsworth's vehemence has the air of self-justification. It cannot have been an easy decision to leave France in autumn 1792, with Annette about to have Caroline. Had the war not intervened he would presumably have scraped together money and returned to get married, but as he left he must have known that the political situation was worsening fast. Englishmen were being arrested in Paris, power was slipping away from the Girondins, the King was on trial for his life – and there can have been little doubt that if he was convicted England would join the war.

222–4 *Dragged by a chain . . . Heaven:* A revision, c. 1819.

191 *else:* otherwise.

194–5 *made a common cause . . . perished:* become more closely associated with the Girondins (imprisoned by Robespierre in July 1793, guillotined in October).

199 *A poet only to myself:* Wordsworth had published almost nothing, but had two major poems, *An Evening Walk* and *Descriptive Sketches*, printed on his return to England (no doubt in the hopes of raising money to get married on).

200–1 *even, belovèd friend . . . unknown:* Wordsworth met Coleridge in September 1795.

202 *a whole year's absence:* November 1791–December 1792; for some reason the period is lengthened in what De Selincourt describes as 'the more decorative version of 1850'.

242 *patriot of the world:* Modelled on Bacon's phrase 'a citizen of the world' (used e.g. by Williams, *Letters Written in France* 14, 'it required but the common feelings of humanity to become in that moment a citizen of the world').

204–10 *a contention . . . English people:* It took 20 years, from the foundation of the Society for the Abolition of the Slave Trade by Clarkson, Wilberforce and others in 1787, for an act to be passed prohibiting the carrying of slaves on British ships (see Wordsworth's sonnet of 1807, 'Clarkson, it was an obstinate hill to climb'). A bill was passed by the Commons in 1792, but thrown out ('baffled', l. 206) by the Lords, as worsening events in France led to a conservative backlash.

218–19 *For me . . . affections:* By contrast, see Cowper's gruesome jocular anti-slave-trade songs of 1788 (e.g. *Sweet Meat has Sour Sauce*) and Coleridge's vehement *Lecture on the Slave Trade* (1795).

248 *levy:* enrolment.

229–30 *the strength of Britain . . . host:* France declared war first (1 February 1793) and England ten days later. Alliances with Prussia and Austria were concluded in July–August. As Wordsworth writes in 1804, the war has still more than nine years to go (ten and a half, if one includes the 'hundred days' and Waterloo, June 1815).

233 *Change and subversion:* Followers of the Revolution are 'subverted' (undermined) by war with the country that embodies their hopes, and will in their own country from this moment be regarded as 'subversive'.

237 *revolution:* Wordsworth's personal 'revolution' (with a small 'r') is caused by England's joining the war against the Revolution (with a capital).

242–4 *with what ungracious eyes . . . regenerated France:* News of the Revolution was in fact welcomed in England. Even Pitt thought at first that the 'convulsions would culminate in general harmony and regular order'. Opinion was turning against France by the time Burke's *Reflections on the Revolution* appeared in November 1790. Corresponding Societies, formed to distribute cheap copies of Paine's *Rights of Man* (March 1791), increased the fears of an English uprising, and from 1793 there was active Government intervention.

248 *foretasted the event:* imagined how it would feel to be at war.

276–9 *As a light . . . tower:* Wordsworth substitutes *1850* 'pliant harebell' and 'tower' for *1805* 'green leaf' and 'tree' in *MS C* (c. 1819).

257 *station:* position, viewpoint

261–3 *When Englishmen . . . shameful flight:* Wordsworth is thinking of British and Hanoverian troops put to flight at Hondschoote and Wattignies, autumn 1793, and perhaps of the disastrous campaign of the grand old Duke of York, summer 1794.

268–9 *bending all|To their great Father:* 'While each to his great father bends' (*Ancient Mariner* 601); compelled to wish for his country's defeat, Wordsworth, amid the 'simple worshippers', is as much an alien as the Mariner himself.

279–80 *in which worst losses . . . best of names:* in which losses (from the point of view of humanity) could seem to be gains.

280–3 *when patriotic love . . . harbinger he is:* Despite the image of John the Baptist giving way to Christ, Wordsworth's point is ironical: patriotic love, rightly so called, gives way to jingoism, a desire for victory in battle regardless of the injustice of the war.

284 *ancient faith:* Presumably in this case democratic ideals, belief in the Revolution, exchanged for the ironically 'higher creed' of loyalty to the Government.

287–9 *in which Experience . . . grey locks:* in which those whose experience should have enabled them to know better join the (bad) cause with youthful enthusiasm.

315 *the red-cross flag:* the white ensign (the red cross of St George, quartered with the union jack on a white background), flown by the British fleet in battle to avoid confusion with the *tricolor*, introduced by the French in 1794. Wordsworth's association is likely to be with pictures of British ships in action; the squadron he watched in July 1793 was under the command of Sir Peter Parker, Admiral of the Blue, and would have flown blue flags.

293–8 *I beheld . . . place of convocation:* Looking back in a note to *Guilt and Sorrow* (1842), Wordsworth wrote:

During the latter part of the summer of 1793, having passed a month in the Isle of Wight, in view of the fleet which was then preparing for sea off Portsmouth at the commencement of the war, I left the place with melancholy forbodings.

298–306 *There I heard . . . pain of heart:* Wordsworth had been more indignant in the fragment *At the Isle of Wight* written at the time:

But hark from yon proud fleet in peal profound
Thunders the sunset-cannon; at the sound
The star of life appears to set in blood (Oxford I 308)

309–12 *Tyrants . . . goaded land waxed mad:* Wordsworth's stay on the Isle of Wight in July 1793 coincided with Robespierre's taking control in Paris. The 'devilish plea' of plotting against the state on behalf of foreign powers was used during the following year to send many hundreds to the guillotine. Robespierre is linked in Wordsworth's language with Milton's Satan, 'the fiend [who] with necessity,|The tyrant's plea, excused his devilish deeds' (*PL* IV 393–4).

313–14 *blasts|From hell . . . heaven Hamlet:* I iv 41, 'Bring with thee airs from heaven, or blasts from hell.'

317 *theirs:* i.e. the faith of those (referring back to l. 315).

317–19 *who throned . . . their god:* The Cathedral of Notre Dame in Paris was reconsecrated on 10 November 1793 as the Temple of Reason. Among those who disapproved, however, was Robespierre. Not content with guillotining Chaumette and other members of the National Convention involved, he himself presided on 8 June 1794 at a Festival of the Supreme Being. As in the final chapter of Rousseau's *Social Contract*, God and an afterlife were presented as the basis of republican 'virtue', the quality in whose name Robespierre chiefly acted, and which above all the Terror was said to protect.

319–21 *the hopes . . . paradise of ages:* Though not regarding the Terror as a purge required in the name of future happiness, Wordsworth himself was capable of thinking that violence had to be accepted as a phase in the revolutionary process; see *Letter to the Bishop of Llandaff* and ll. 749–51 below.

327–8 *The Senate was heart-stricken . . . Uplifted:* Seventy-five right-wing deputies in the National Convention protested after the expulsion of the Girondins on 2 June 1793, but were themselves arrested; there was no further opposition. During Robespierre's year of power, to be 'heart-stricken' was itself a crime. 'A man is guilty against the Republic', Saint-Just told the Convention in January 1794, 'when he takes pity on prisoners. He is guilty because he has no desire for virtue; he is guilty because he is opposed to the Terror.' Such guilt was punishable by death.

329 *Domestic carnage . . . year:* Wordsworth's line makes it sound as if the Terror lasted for years. The first major series of executions was of the Girondin leaders in October 1793; the Great Terror began with the law of 10 June 1794 altering court procedures so that prisoners could be condemned *en masse*; 1,376 people were guillotined in Paris in the 50 days before Robespierre's fall on 27 July.

335–6 *Head after head . . . fall:* Selection for the guillotine was in fact rather capricious. Many were executed with little or no pretext, others (Helen Maria Williams and Tom Paine among them) survived long periods in prison knowing that each day might be their last.

352–4 *The illustrious wife of Roland . . . last words:* Citizeness Jeanne Marie Roland de la Platière (whose *Appeal to Impartial Posterity*, written in prison waiting for execution, reveals more than any book of the period the inside story of the Revolution's struggles for power) went to the guillotine on 8 November 1793. The scene is recorded by her editor, Bosc, in the words of a fellow prisoner:

> she was neatly dressed in white, and her long black hair flowed loosely to her waist . . . She had for the companion to her misfortune a man whose fortitude was not equal to her own, but whom she found means to inspire with gaiety, so cheering and so real that it several times brought a smile upon his face.
>
> At the place of execution she bowed down before the statue of Liberty, and pronounced these memorable words: 'Oh Liberty, how many crimes are committed in thy name!' (*Appeal* II 145–6)

360 *flattered:* filled with unwarranted hope.

362–4 *The Herculean commonwealth . . . cradle:* Hera, jealous wife of Zeus, sent two serpents to kill Heracles, his child by the mortal Alcmene. The 'infant godhead' duly throttled them. The armies of the infant Republic (declared on 22 September 1792) had to cope both with the threat of Austrian and Prussian invaders and with civil war (counter-revolution in the Vendée), but before the death of Robespierre were already turning to the attack.

370 *beat:* Closer probably in Wordsworth's usage to the beat of a heart than the beat of a drum, and often used by him with the force of a transferred epithet; cf. the 'beating mind' of II 18.

378–80 *a sense|Of treachery . . . soul:* Wordsworth in his nightmares is a victim of the Terror, and falsely accused, yet cannot wholly absolve himself from collusion in the violence. His heart has been given to the Revolution for better or for worse.

385 *oppression:* A strong word, but Wordsworth means what he says. Compare his sense of being 'vexed' by his own creativity, and of feeling pleasure as 'a weight'.

388 *creature divine:* Man is at once created by God, and the one created being that is 'instinct with godhead'.

391 *which enables him to be:* which defines his existence as a human being.

392 *sequestered:* alienated. *what a change is here:* Reed points to a silent quotation from *Romeo and Juliet* that has a pleasurable appropriateness. Mercutio is teasing Romeo, who, like Wordsworth, is changing to a 'second love':

> Holy Saint Francis, what a change is here!
> Is Rosaline, that thou didst love so dear
> So soon forsaken? (II iii 65–7)

401 *inflamed:* inspired; the prophets, though dooming their fellows to destruction, are consoled by the powers of the spirit.

408 *consummation:* accomplishment, completion.

411 *rage and dog-day heat:* The rising of the 'dog-stars', Sirius and Procyon, was traditionally the hottest and most feverish time of the year. For Wordsworth 'rage' would have its French connotation of madness – even perhaps (given the dog-stars), of rabies.

413 *in the order of sublimest laws:* Wordsworth glories in the sublimity of the Terror, conscious that Burke has based his 'laws' of the sublime on fear ('terror' with a small 't').

416 *I felt a kind of sympathy with power:* An astonishing statement in its context, but profoundly Wordsworthian. The poet could be said in his writing to replace the Burkean sublime of terror with the sublime of power.

431–2 *'Behold the harvest . . . equality':* The scoffers' taunt has a biblical ring derived partly from the proverb 'As ye sow, so shall ye reap', partly from the mocking of Christ at his crucifixion. *popular:* of the people.

438 *charge:* burden, load, contents; Owen takes Wordsworth's image to be of a bursting cess-pool.

451–5 *That day . . . town of Arras:* Wordsworth and Jones spent the third night (16 July 1790) of their continental tour at Arras, then celebrating the first anniversary of the fall of the Bastille; see VI 352ff.

455–6 *place from which . . . Robespierre:* Robespierre (1758–94) was born at Arras, and represented the town in the National Assembly (variously called at different times) from its first meeting in May 1789. Like so many deputies, he was a lawyer.

457 *the atheist crew:* Words applied by Milton, *Paradise Lost* VI 370, to the fallen angels, who refuse allegiance to God, but do not of course deny his existence. Robespierre detested atheism (in the modern sense of the word), sending to the guillotine most of those who in autumn 1793 had instituted the state religion of Reason; see ll. 317–19n. above.

460–1 *groaned . . . cruel son:* The directions of Robespierre's Committee of Public Safety were carried out in Arras by an ex-priest named (ironically) Le Bon, who was later said by his secretary to have 'killed in a sort of fever'.

462 *As Lear reproached the winds:* The reference to *Lear* III ii 1–24 can be read in two ways: either Wordsworth's quarrel with the image in his mind is as pointless as the mad King's reproaches to the winds, or the town groans under the Terror as Lear complains at the storm. The first, and stronger, reading is pre-empted by the poet's executors, who place dashes at the end of *1850* 503, and after 'winds' in l. 507. Punctuation in the MSS offers no basis for their confidence.

468 *this foul tribe of Moloch:* 'First Moloch, horrid king, besmeared with blood|Of human sacrifice, and parents' tears . . .' (*PL* I 392–3).

469 *regent:* ruler; Robespierre had no elective office or official title, ruling through the Committee of Public Safety and by the support of the Paris sections.

472 *a small village:* Rampside, on the coast north of Barrow-in-Furness and opposite Piel Island, where Wordsworth was staying with cousins in August–September 1794; see *Peele Castle* 1–2: 'I was thy neighbour once, thou rugged pile|Four summer weeks I dwelt in sight of thee . . .'

474–5 *the smooth sands . . . estuary:* Levens Sands, which can still be crossed with a guide when the tide is out, and which formed the main north–south route, cutting across Morecambe Bay; see ll. 515–29 below.

476 *genial:* warm, cheerful.

477–86 *With distant prospect . . . childhood:* Looking east and north Wordsworth sees mountain-tops of the Lake District lit by the sun, and thinks of the hidden valleys below where he has been brought up. To mark the contrast he turns to Milton at his most ornate for the mountainscape, and touches in the 'happy fields' of his childhood in his own less elevated style.

480 *Creatures of one ethereal substance:* beings created from the same heavenly material (clouds and mountains are spiritualized alike by the sun and by the imagination).

481 *consistory:* synod, church council; cf. the 'gloomy consistory', summoned in mid-air by Satan, *PR* I 42.

482 *burning seraphs:* radiant angels; among the angelic 'orders', seraphs are closest to God, living in the realm of pure fire. De Selincourt points to Milton, *At A Solemn Music* 10, 'the bright seraphim in burning row'.

483 *empyrean:* 'the pure empyrean where he sits|High-throned above all height' (*PL* III 57–8).

486 *fulgent:* shining, resplendent; 'At last as from a cloud his fulgent head|And shape star-bright appeared' (*PL* X 449–50).

492 *An honoured teacher of my youth:* William Taylor, brilliant young Cambridge-trained headmaster of Hawkshead Grammar School, died on 12 June 1786, aged 32. His grave may be seen at Cartmell Priory (a church of great beauty) near Ulverston.

499 *A fragment . . . Gray:*

His merits, stranger, seek not to disclose,
Or draw his frailties from their dread abode
(There they alike in trembling hope repose),
The bosom of his father and his God.
(*Elegy* 125–8, with adapted first line)

501 '*My head will soon lie low*': Taylor's moving words were used by Wordsworth, aged sixteen, in his ballad *And Will You Leave Me Thus Alone* (23–4 March 1787):

Heaven told me once – but I was blind –
My head would soon lie low;
A rose within our garden blew
Amid December's snow. (Oxford I 266)

506 *in my own despite:* Cf. *Ruined Cottage* 206–8: 'In my own despite|I thought of that poor woman as of one|Whom I had known and loved.' In each case the reader is surprised by the implied resistance to emotional commitment.

513–14 *when I . . . toilsome songs:* Wordsworth's first extant poem was written at Taylor's suggestion in 1785 to celebrate the bicentenary of Hawkshead Grammar School. Though disparaged by Wordsworth himself (*Memoirs* I 13) as 'a tame imitation of Pope's versification', the poem has considerable power and looks forward to later poetry on the theme of education.

520 *A Romish chapel:* Built, like Piel Castle, by monks from nearby Furness Abbey.

527–8 *shallow stream|Of inland water:* The River Leven, which crosses the Sands, has to be waded; the rest of the two-mile passage is dry-shod. Turner and Cox, among others, have painted the scene that Wordsworth describes; see also Elizabeth Gaskell, *The Sexton's Hero.*

534 *In the familiar language of the day:* going straight to the point.

535 *Robespierre was dead:* News of Robespierre's death (at first very confused) reached London on 16 August 1794; Wordsworth heard it around the 20th.

538 *he and his supporters all were fallen:* Robespierre's fall (dramatized within weeks by Coleridge and Southey) was very sudden. On 27 July 1794 he was outmanoeuvred in the National Convention by Tallien and Barras, and arrested after a painful attempt at suicide. On the 28th he and his 21 closest associates (bar Lebas, who had successfully killed himself) went to the guillotine ('their helper' in l. 549). A further 86 Robespierrists were purged – 71 on the following day – including Samson the executioner.

539–40 *my joy|In vengeance, and eternal justice:* Note the order: Wordsworth makes no bones about a dominant feeling of revenge.

546–8 *They who . . . the Augean stable:* Robespierre, in Wordsworth's unpleasant image, diverts a river of blood to cleanse the Republic, just as Hercules diverts the Rivers Alpheus and Peneus through the stables of King Augeas (choked with 30 years' ox-dung) to accomplish the sixth of his 'labours'.

554 *madding factions:* Cf. 'hissing factionists' (IX 57) and Gray's *Elegy* 73, 'Far from the madding crowd's ignoble strife'.

559–66 *Along that very shore . . . level sand:* Tacitly Wordsworth's exultation and delusive political hopes are compared to the joy of heart with which as a boy he had 'scampered homeward' from Furness Abbey ('St Mary's mouldering fane'), II 135–44. *fane:* temple, church.

566 Repetition of II 144.

XI 1 The decision to divide *1805* Book X into two was taken in 1832. To judge from *MS Z* (April–May 1805), it was a return to Wordsworth's original intention. Why he ever thought having such a weighty book was a good thing is hard to know.

567–72 *From this time . . . past aims:* Authority in France became less efficient as well as 'milder'. The committees through which Robespierre had worked were deprived of their power, and the laws on which he had depended were repealed. With them went the controlled economy which he had devised and enforced. The currency collapsed, starvation was widespread. Lack of effective government led three years later (September 1797) to renewed dictatorship under the Directory, and finally (November 1799) to the rise of Napoleon.

576 *of heartless omen:* discouraging.

589–92 *Such victory . . . noiseless fortitude:* Wordsworth continues to believe not only that the Republic will triumph, but that there will then be a peaceful revolution in Britain.

592–5 *Beholding still . . . same in quality:* Seeing that France resists her attackers as powerfully as before, the poet imagines that her motivation remains as pure.

596 *the two spirits:* the forces of reaction and of truth (Britain and her allies embodying the 'worse' spirit, France the 'better').

598–604 *never dreamt|That transmigration . . . called to:* The 'soul' of France has been replaced. The Republic, created with such high ideals, has suffered a moral fall – is no longer the same being.

604–17 *Youth maintains . . . ordinary practice:* Wordsworth is talking about himself, and the basis of his mistaken judgments in the period after Robespierre's death. The pattern of his thoughts follows his sentence structures: (1) Youth is the period of human life most in touch with nature; (2) nature, in this political phase when 'habit, custom, law' have lost their authority, has unusual scope to influence the judgment; (3) events of the day produced abundant evidence to support warm, or wild, judgments, and to undermine the authority of custom.

617–22 *I could see . . . safety:* Those who, dazed by the Terror, build themselves up a tower of refuge on the basis of seemingly promising news, are (to the Wordsworth of the mid-1790s) as foolish as the builders of Babel (*Genesis* 11.3–9).

625 *conceited:* imagined.

640 *passion over-near ourselves:* material too fraught with emotion to be decorously described.

643 *scorn and condemnation personal:* lampoon, invective; though at times in *The Prelude* an excellent satirist, Wordsworth regards satire as a low form, and personal satire as unacceptable.

645–7 *Our shepherds . . . tool of murder:* Wordsworth's metaphor-mixing indignation against the Pitt Government is oddly reminiscent of *Lycidas* 119–20: 'Blind mouths! that scarce themselves know how to hold|A sheephook'.

647–51 *They who ruled . . .|To imitate:* Despite the example of Robespierre, who lived and died by the guillotine, the British Government longed to imitate repressive French policies. 'These pretended constitutionalists', Coleridge wrote in *The Friend* with this passage in mind, 'recurred to the language of insult, and to measures of persecution. In order to oppose Jacobinism, they imitated it in its worst features: in personal slander, in illegal violence, and even in the thirst for blood' (Rooke II 141).

653–4 *in their weapons . . . reach:* Wordsworth writes as one who has himself been watched by a Home Office informer (at Alfoxden in summer 1797); his image is of rats behind the wainscot.

658 *It hath been told:* In IX 295–543, where Wordsworth, under the influence of Beaupuy, gives his heart to the French people.

660 *polity:* government.

662–5 *I had approached . . . metal which I saw:* According to the fable (which is only partly relevant to Wordsworth's lines) a two-sided shield – one side gold, one silver – is hung at a crossroads. Knights approaching from opposite directions see it differently, and fight to maintain what they see (cf. Joseph Spence, *Moralities* [1753], 99–102).

672–3 *themselves|Felt deeply:* Read: 'though deeply felt'.

677 *sanctuary:* church building where anyone fleeing from civil prosecution could claim protection.

682 *noviciate:* inexperienced, resembling a novice in a religious order; drawn probably from Coleridge, *1796 Religious Musings* 437–8: 'Till then|I discipline my young noviciate thought'.

689–727 Among the few passages of *The Prelude* known in Wordsworth's lifetime; published (with ll. 662–5 above by way of preface) in *The Friend*, 26 October 1809, then in 1815 and Wordsworth's subsequent collections.

690 *auxiliars:* helpers; often used of supporting troops on a battlefield.

694–5 *the meagre, stale, forbidding ways|Of custom:* Wordsworth avoids too close resemblance to *Hamlet* I ii 133–4: 'How weary, stale, flat and unprofitable| Seem to me all the uses of this world!'

697–9 *When reason . . . A prime enchanter:* In a light mockery of his former self, Wordsworth invokes for reason the power of a Prospero.

706 *temper:* temperament.

708 *rapt away:* carried away, enraptured.

709–16 *They who had fed . . . To wield it:* An unexpected self-portrait.

716–19 *they too . . . peaceful selves:* Seemingly a composite portrait of Mary Wordsworth and Wordsworth's brother John, the 'silent poet'.

721 *stuff at hand plastic as they could wish:* ready and malleable material for the imagination to work upon (in its creation of future happiness).

723–7 *Not in Utopia . . . not at all:* 'Paradise and groves|Elysian', Wordsworth had written in the Prospectus to *The Recluse* (1800),

> blessèd islands in the deep,
> Of choice seclusion – wherefore need they be
> A history, or but a dream, when minds
> Once wedded to this outward frame of things
> In love, find these the growth of common day? (ll. 35–40)

There had been no political context in the Prospectus, but in both this poem and *The Prelude* there is the moving emphasis on finding happiness in actuality – in the world that we know and share.

736 *convoked:* called forth, summoned.

739 *still:* always.

XI 160 An alexandrine in the MSS, corrected by the poet's executors, who substituted a dash for the words 'and that'.

749–51 *Not caring . . . futurity:* Wordsworth is impressively clear that some violence and suffering is to be accepted in the early stages of a revolution. In the *Letter to the Bishop of Llandaff* (1793) this is the basis on which he defends the execution of Louis XVI.

751 *happy:* Removed c. 1819, to reduce the line from an alexandrine (presumably unintended) to the regular pentameter.

752–6 *In brief . . . more strong:* In this last phase of Wordsworth's long sentence (beginning at l. 738), he presents himself as the child of nature whose emotions, though they have now found a wider sphere, remain unchanged. Those appropriate to an earlier stage have grown weaker and merged imperceptibly into adult (political) responses.

757–9 *In the main outline . . . France:* For the past hundred lines Wordsworth has been working through a second time the period described in ll. 227–306 above. He has now arrived once more at the outbreak of war (declared by France on 1 February 1793, and Britain on the 11th).

768–9 *What had been a pride|Was now a shame:* Wordsworth, for whom patriotism is an aspect of his early bonding with nature, is thinking of his country's shameful opposition to liberty and the Revolution.

774 *As from the first:* Presumably, as from the early stages of the Revolution.

791–3 *And now, become oppressors . . . conquest:* For eighteen months after their success at Valmy (September 1792) French armies were occupied with defending the borders and suppressing counter-revolution. That they should then turn to the attack made sense in economic terms, though it went against the renunciation of wars of conquest written into the Constitution in May 1790. By the end of 1794 Belgium and Holland had been occupied, Spain and northern Italy invaded. Napoleon meanwhile was rapidly rising through the ranks.

794–6 *and mounted up . . . The scale of liberty:* Liberty, which should be weighing most heavily with the French, is being outweighed by conquest. Wordsworth's image of the balance (scales) is from *Paradise Lost*, where God hangs 'forth his golden scales' in heaven to show Satan his weakness in comparison with Gabriel: 'The fiend looked up · and knew|His mounted scale aloft' (IV 1013–14).

798 *taking to the shame:* accepting, taking for himself, the shame.

800–1 *to prove|Their temper:* test their strength (the metaphor is from 'proving' steel).

803 *Grow into consequence:* become substantial, take on the status of fact.

806–10 *the philosophy . . . ready welcome:* Godwin's *Political Justice* (February 1793) offered a rationalist philosophy in which man's future happiness was to depend on education and the dictates of the mind, freed from emotional ties. The first edition (rewritten in 1796) assumed that Britain would peaceably follow the examples of America and France.

809 *a purer element:* reason.

812–13 *Where passions . . . names:* Having been his disciple in the years 1794–6, Wordsworth exposes the weak point of Godwin's system with brilliant irony. The claims of *Political Justice* had been an act of faith, its dependence on reason emotional.

818–29 *What delight . . . independent intellect:*

> The satire is beautifully controlled – and needs to be, if the writing is to deflect obvious comparisons between Godwinian arrogance and Wordsworthian egotistical solitude. The passage stresses again and again the folly of the individual, the disparity between his assumption of power and powerless actuality. 'Self-knowledge' he clearly does not possess (no one would expect him to, after the ironic 'How glorious'); 'self-rule' is another matter, but confers no right to survey and judge the kingdoms of the world; 'resolute mastery' might be fine in itself, but has no control of nature, time, or place, and cannot change the past; it is true in a way (and a Wordsworthian one) that the basis of social freedom is 'the individual mind', but not when it adopts a posture of superiority, regarding general laws as 'blind constraint' and 'magisterially' assuming that nothing need be taken into account bar such circumstances as happen to penetrate its unwarranted seclusion. (*BV* 267)

833 *a secure intelligence:* a settled mind.

836 *worm-like:* like a caterpillar (commonly called 'worms' at this period, just as butterflies are commonly called 'flies'); Wordsworth draws his image, and the wording of l. 238, from Spenser's delightful mock-heroic *Fate of the Butterfly*.

839 *yet I feel:* to this day I feel.

843–7 *sacrificed . . . false imagination:* To Wordsworth the 'comprehensive mind' (expansive, generous in its imagination) has paradoxically an 'exactness' (precision) that 'scrupulous and microscopic views' cannot achieve; cf. *Not Useless Do I Deem* 58ff.: 'was it meant|That we should pore, and dwindle as we pore,|Forever dimly pore on things minute . . .'

850 *ancient institutions:* Probably Wordsworth means traditional ways of thought, but his attack would be no less relevant to 'institutions' such as the University or the House of Lords.

855–6 *A veil had been|Uplifted:* By the Revolution.

863 *Let loose and goaded:* Wordsworth's mind is released from old ways of thought by the Revolution, but also 'goaded' (a maddening process at l. 312) by the sense of alienation that follows. Hence the reference in the next line to 'what hath . . . been said of patriotic love' (see ll. 253–78 above).

870–1 *A happy man . . . painful things:* Characteristics that Wordsworth had given to his second self, the Pedlar, as early as spring 1798: 'in himself| Happy . . . He could afford to suffer|With those whom he saw suffer' (ll. 279–84).

878 *nature's holiest places:* Cf. ll. 379–80 above, 'the place|The holiest that I knew of – my own soul'.

879 *some dramatic story:* Taking 'dramatic' in rather a literal-minded way, Owen and Reed suggest a reference to Wordsworth's play *The Borderers* (1796–7). Wordsworth, however, is clearly referring to a prospective work – 'Time may come . . .' He is writing in autumn 1804, and on 6 March had told De Quincey of having 'arranged the plan' of *The Excursion* (not a drama, but dramatic in the sense that it is written in dialogue). *The Borderers* lay in the past (Coleridge had known it for more than seven years), and revealed Wordsworth's experience in the Revolution only by implication. *The Excursion*, by contrast, lay in the future, and did indeed tell (in the 'dramatic story' of the Solitary) both of what the poet had learned, and of the errors into which he had been betrayed. See Jonathan Wordsworth, 'That Wordsworth Epic', *WC*, winter 1980, 34–5.

885–6 *a heart . . . turned aside|From nature by external accidents:* Probably the clearest statement as to how Wordsworth came to view his former political self.

889–90 *Dragging all passions . . . to the bar:* As the passions are indicted, called to the bar to explain their right to exist, it is (by implication) Godwinian reason that acts as prosecutor.

892 *titles:* credentials.

898 *in fine:* in the end.

899–900 *Sick, wearied out . . . in despair:* A crisis-point that is of great importance in *The Prelude*, but which Wordsworth does not elsewhere mention. Loss of confidence may well have been associated with reading the impoverished second edition of *Political Justice* at Racedown in March 1796. Godwin on whose thinking Wordsworth had relied for the two past years (and whom he had met personally nine times in London) was in full retreat. On his own admission, five out of the eight books of *Political Justice* 1793 had been rewritten. A work that had looked forward to a chain reaction of beneficent revolutions (America, France, England, and onwards across the known world) now offered the rhetoric of rationalist optimism, divorced from political hope.

XI 306–33 *This was the crisis . . . no admission:* Inserted in its original form in *MS C* c. 1819, but frequently revised as Wordsworth sought to portray his early moral crisis as a 'strong disease' of the soul.

903–4 *Turned towards mathematics . . . evidence:* Wordsworth is turning not to text-book maths (the academic subject he ought to have studied with more vigour at Cambridge), but to the 'independent world|Created out of pure intelligence', discussed in VI 178ff., a 'clear synthesis built up aloft:

Mighty is the charm
Of those abstractions to a mind beset
With images, and haunted by itself . . .

XI 308 *our blessed reason:* Looking back, Wordsworth sees his crisis of confidence as the 'lowest ebb' of the soul, and (confusingly, if one takes into account the original circumstances) thinks of reason as a divine gift wrongly deemed to be inadequate.

XI 309–20 '*The lordly attributes . . . slave of crime*': This speech that Wordsworth puts into the mouth of his former self reads most oddly after *1805* 890–900. Where the early passage shows 'a heart . . . turned aside|From nature by external accidents' (ll. 885–6), *1850* portrays rebellion, 'selfish passion', a questioning of God's purpose in the bestowing of free will.

XI 328–30 *turned to abstract science . . . space and time:* A recollection of Wordsworth's account of the arab's 'stone' in V 103–5, where mathematics is seen in its most exalted form. Representing Euclid's *Elements*, the stone had

held acquaintance with the stars
And wedded man to man by purest bond
Of nature, undisturbed by space or time . . .

905–6 *most precious friend . . . First known to me:* A half-truth: Wordsworth had met Coleridge six months earlier, in September 1795, but did not get to know him until mid-1797 – hence, presumably, the cutting of these lines in *1850*.

908–9 *the belovèd woman . . . days were passed:* Dorothy, with whom Wordsworth had set up house in September 1795 at Racedown in Dorset.

914–15 *a saving intercourse|With my true self:* Cf. *Tintern Abbey* 117ff.: 'in thy voice I catch|The language of my former heart . . .'

920 *office:* role, function, vocation, duty.

921 *And lastly:* Wordsworth's syntax is still dependent on 'Ah then it was' in l. 904.

930–3 *In the catastrophe . . . an Emperor:* Napoleon, who had declared himself Emperor in May 1804, summoned Pius VII to crown him in Paris – then (2 December) took the crown out of his hands and crowned himself. Wordsworth seems to be writing just before the event, 'for so they dream' implying intention on the part of the French. *catastrophe:* dénouement, theatrical climax (not necessarily tragic).

934 *opprobrium:* disgrace.

934–5 *the dog|Returning to his vomit:* Wordsworth's vehement image is from *Proverbs* 26.11, 'As a dog returneth to his vomit, so a fool returneth to his folly' (see also *II Peter* 2.21–2, where the proverb is applied to backsliders who 'have known the way of righteousness'. Having declared themselves a republic in September 1792, the French are returning to monarchy.

935–40 *when the sun . . . opera phantom:* the sun of the Republic, which has touched the clouds with its glory, sets in a grotesque piece of theatre (as Napoleon crowns himself). *gewgaw:* toy, plaything. *machine:* stage-prop.

946–50 *now|Among the basest . . . Timoleon:* Coleridge was in Sicily, part of the kingdom of Naples and regarded as particularly backward, despite a glorious classical past. De Selincourt quotes at length from the *Life of Timoleon* in North's Plutarch, showing Timoleon (d. 337 BC) as a rooter-out of tyrants, establisher of Sicilian democracy, and defender of the island against the Carthaginians.

XI 377–8 *Where Etna . . . Syracuse:* Poetic licence; Mary Moorman, *The Later Years* 504–5, draws attention to Kilvert's account of a meeting between Wordsworth and George Venables when the lines on the mountain's shadow were being composed, c. 1838:

> One evening near Rydal I saw Wordsworth sauntering towards me wearing a shade over his eyes, which were weak, and crooning out loud some lines of a poem which he was composing. I stopped to avoid splashing him and apologised for having intruded upon him. He said, 'I'm glad I met you, for I want to consult you about some lines I am composing in which I want to make the shadow of Etna fall across Syracuse . . . would this be possible?' I replied that . . . the only difficulty was that Etna is exactly north of Syracuse. 'Surely', said Wordsworth, 'it is a little N.E. or N.W.?' And as he was evidently determined to make the shadow fall the way he wanted it, I did not contradict him.
> (Francis Kilvert, *Diary Selections: 1870–79*, ed. William Plomer, 3 vols, London, 1960, I 234)

951 *How are the mighty prostrated:* Strangely inelegant rewording (unchanged in *1850*) of David's lament for Saul and Jonathan: 'The beauty of Israel is slain upon thy high places: how are the mighty fallen' (*II Samuel* 1.119).

953–4 *When the great voice . . . ancient heroes:* The call for liberty?

960 *Strewed with the wreck . . . years:* Cf. Cowper, *Task* II 75–7:

> Alas for Sicily – rude fragments now
> Lie scattered where the shapely column stood;
> Her palaces are dust.

964 *A hope to be deferred:* hope for the distant future.

968–9 *One great society . . . noble dead:* Expanded upon by Wordsworth in *Convention of Cintra* (1809):

> There is a spiritual community binding together the living and the dead, the good, the brave and the wise, of all ages. We would not be [do not wish to be] rejected from this community, and therefore do we hope. (*Prose Works* I 339)

974 *Sirocco:* hot oppressive wind blowing from North Africa.
977 *sanative:* healing, restorative.
981–2 *this last spot . . . Stands single:* Since the breakdown of the Peace of Amiens (1802–3), Britain had been maintaining the war against Napoleon alone.
985 *This heavy time of change for all mankind Lycidas:* 37, 'But oh the heavy change now thou art gone', has been brought into Wordsworth's mind (as De Selincourt points out) by his own use of 'thou art gone' in l. 980.
994 *The gladsome image in my memory:* Wordsworth aged 20 had quite deliberately stored the scenery of the Alps within his memory, reflecting as he did so: 'perhaps scarce a day of my life will pass in which I shall not derive some happiness from these images' (14 September 1790).
996 *at a time, how different:* Wordsworth contrasts the European political scene of 1804 with that of 1790 when 'benevolence and blessedness|Spread like a fragrance everywhere' (VI 368–9).
1002–3 *o flowery vale|Of Enna:*

> that fair field
> Of Enna, where Proserpina gathering flowers
> (Herself a fairer flower) by gloomy Dis
> Was gathered. (*PL* IV 268–71)

1012–13 *Empedocles|Or Archimedes:* Philosopher-poet, supposed to have thrown himself into Etna c. 433 BC, and mathematician (died c. 212 BC) to this day famous for Archimedes' Principle.
1015 *Theocritus:* Greatest of Greek (Sicilian) pastoral poets, died c. 260 BC.
1021–3 *how bees with honey fed . . . muse's nectar:* Story told by Theocritus, *Idyll* VII 78–83. The muse drips nectar on Comates' lips encouraging bees to feed him in the cedar chest where he is imprisoned.
1028 *by this calm fireside:* At Dove Cottage, Grasmere, c. late November 1804.
XI 455 *invaded heavens:* The mountain's height invades the sky.
XI 458 *discipline:* Owen suggests 'instruction'.
XI 460 *sapient:* wise.
1033 *pastoral Arethuse:* Sicilian stream (transformed from a Greek nymph, Arethusa) invoked by Milton, *Lycidas* 85.
1036 *Thou gratulatest:* you greet.
1037 *votary:* devotee.

Book Eleventh (1850 Twelfth)

1 News of the death of his brother John, captain of the *Earl of Abergavenny*, reached Wordsworth on 11 February 1805, and brought work on *The Prelude* to a stop. Ten books were more or less complete. The last three – all of them short – were put together in April and the first half of May, a great deal of old material being used in the process. *MS Z*, fair copy of Books XI and XII, shows that XI began originally at l. 42 below, 'This history, my friend'.
7–8 *Not with these began . . . end:* An affectionate allusion to *Idiot Boy* 445–6: 'And with the owls began my song,|And with the owls must end'.
9–14 *Ye motions of delight . . . silent night:* Found in their original form in a long

sequence at the end of *MS Y* (October 1804), and probably then intended for Book VIII:

> Ye gentle breezes lead me forth again,
> Soft airs and gladdening sunbeams lead me on . . .
>   brooks
> Muttering among the stones, a busy noise
> By day, a quiet one in silent night.

15–22 *And you, ye groves . . . for me:* Drawn (together with XII 47–52 below) from a discarded introductory section to *Nutting*, preserved in *MS 18A* of winter 1798–9. In their original form the lines are addressed, not to 'groves' of everyday experience, but to the polytheist spirits, 'powers of nature', whose 'ministry' oversees the poet's education in *1799* Part I.

23–5 *spring returns|I saw the spring return . . . hope:* Spring 1796; see X 899–90n. Wordsworth's lines are based on *PL* III 41–2: 'Seasons return, but not to me returns|Day, or the sweet approach of even or morn . . .'

XII 31–4 *The morning shines . . . her love:* Wordsworth's tidying-up of *1805* 23–8 is the result of successive revisions, beginning in *MS C* (c. 1819).

29 *complacency:* satisfaction, contentedness.

31 *still:* always.

43 *intellectual:* spiritual.

48–60 *What availed . . . had been:*

> Afloat on the barren seas of Godwinian philosophy, resolutely ignoring signals from the shores of loving relationship (letters, perhaps, from Annette and Dorothy), the poet is a would-be political borderer, crossing the gulf of time to the coasts of futurity. The parenthesis, 'I mean that future times would surely see' . . . mirrors exactly a change to be seen in Godwin himself, as he moved away from a confidence . . . that there would be a speedy and successful revolution in England to a more cautious view [in the 1796 second edition of *Political Justice*] that truth would finally prevail. (*B V* 273)

49 *spells:* the enchantment of Godwinian rationalism.

50–1 *The fragrance . . . shore:* Wordsworth takes his image from *PL* IV 156–65, where Satan's pleasure in the scents of Eden is compared to that of sailors 'Beyond the Cape of Hope' who smell 'odours from the spicy shore|Of Araby the blest'.

69 *purer creatures:* human beings idealized by the imagination.

XII 73–4 *the miserable slave . . . distempered love:* An extraordinarily harsh view of the poets' ideal of man. Owen suggests that the Shakespearean tragic hero is in Wordsworth's mind.

76 *like a monk:* A bigot to the *old* idolatory of Roman Catholicism.

79–81 *as by simple waving of a wand . . . grove:* Another of Wordsworth's many allusions to Prospero's 'Our revels now are ended', *Tempest* IV i 148–58.

82 *syllogistic:* having the appearance of logic, specious.

86–7 *all that reason hath performed . . . refine:* Wordsworth's concession is to reason, not to Godwinian rationalism; note the distinction made at ll. 123–8 below.

108–9 *appanage|Of elements:* dependent elements.

110 *pure forms:* forms exempt from moral judgment, standing outside a moral context (rather than forms that are ideal, 'pure' in the Platonic sense).

116–18 *fell|Beneath . . . Less elevated:* See ll. 148ff. below, 'how feeble have I been'; Wordsworth is referring, somewhat obscurely, to a taste for the picturesque.

123–4 *the grand|And simple reason:* Described at XIII 170 as 'reason in her most exalted mood', and conforming effectively to the Kantian *Vernunft.* In the lines that follow, Wordsworth is scrupulously fair to the lesser, analytic reason (in Kant's terms, *Verstand*, 'understanding'), which has its place but must not be allowed to become an idol. Reason in the sense of Godwinian rationalism (the focus of Wordsworth's attack in Book X) ceases at this point to be a factor in *The Prelude.*

132–3 *a worthy theme|For philosophic verse:* For *The Recluse*, that is, rather than *The Prelude.*

152 *presumption:* presumptuousness; Wordsworth's concern at this point is to show Imagination Impaired (as in the heading of the book) as a prelude to its restoration in the 'spots of time' sequence (ll. 258–389 below). He goes on to accuse himself, with no great conviction, of three distinct forms of presumption that have made him insensitive to the 'soul of nature': (1) the picturesque (ll. 152–7); (2) making aesthetic comparisons (ll. 157–63); (3) the tyranny of the eye (ll. 163–75).

152–7 *even in pleasure . . . my habit:* Wordsworth's disparagement of the picturesque as 'a strong infection of the age' conceals the fact that his developing love of nature at Hawkshead had been influenced by West's *Guide to the Lakes* (third ed. 1784) and Gilpin's *Lakes Tour* (1786), and that he had borrowed from both writers in his poetry. As late as *Tintern Abbey* (July 1798), the 'steep and lofty cliffs' that so memorably 'connect|The landscape with the quiet of the sky' derive from Gilpin's observation of charcoal-burners beside the Wye. Smoke from their fires, he notes (*Wye Tour* 12), 'spreading its thin veil over [the hills], beautifully breaks their lines, and unites them with the sky'.

157–63 *giving way|To a comparison . . . Less sensible:* Though Wordsworth claims to have been more given to aesthetic comparison of natural scenes than to picturesque judgments, no evidence survives of his 'Pampering [him]self with meagre novelties|Of colour and proportion.' It is not easy to believe he ever did so.

163 *sensible:* sensitive, responsive.

167 *creature:* man as created.

170–5 *The state|In which the eye . . . dominion:* Whether or not the dominion of the eye could be said to have impaired Wordsworth's imagination, it is entirely credible that he should think it 'The most despotic of our senses'.

179–80 *summons all the senses . . . themselves:* High-sounding verse; what it could mean is another matter. Under special circumstances some (hardly 'all') senses might perhaps counteract each other. Self-counteraction remains a problem.

183 *power:* imaginative power.

184 *another song:* Again a reference to *The Recluse*; removed from the text c. 1838, the year that Wordsworth conceded to the Boston publisher George Ticknor that the great philosophical poem might never be written.

190 *from hill to hill, from rock to rock:* Wordsworth is quoting from the opening of *To A Daisy* (1802):

> In youth from rock to rock I went,
> From hill to hill, in discontent
> Of pleasure high and turbulent . . .

194 *the inner faculties:* Including, of course, 'that inward eye|Which is the bliss of solitude' (*Daffodils* 15–16, written spring 1804).

199 *a maid:* Mary Hutchinson, who was the same age as Wordsworth ('young as I was then', l. 199), and whom he married on 4 October 1802.

202–3 *critic rules . . . intermeddling subtleties:* 'Critic rules' of the picturesque (as at l. 154 above) and subtleties such as Wordsworth had denounced in *Tables Turned* 26–8:

> Our meddling intellect
> Misshapes the beauteous forms of things,
> We murder to dissect.

205 *genial circumstance:* More than just 'good fortune', 'genial' carrying an implication of warmth, growth-inducing properties, and 'circumstance' meaning in origin 'surroundings'.

213 *nature's inmate:* at one with nature (literally, 'one who dwells with nature'). Tactfully or otherwise, Wordsworth is to be seen applying to his wife lines drafted for his sister. The fragment 'I would not strike a flower' had been addressed to Dorothy, like its companion-piece *Nutting* (c. November 1798):

> For she is nature's inmate, and her heart
> Is everywhere. Even the unnoticed heath
> That o'er the mountain spreads its prodigal bells
> Lives in her love . . .

223–4 *before I was called forth . . . hills:* Before leaving the Lake District for Cambridge, at the age of seventeen.

230–1 *nor . . . survived|The first diviner influence:* Despite *Intimations* 67–8, Wordsworth does not feel that 'Shades of the prison-house' had begun to close upon him personally as the 'growing boy'.

XII 185 *As piety ordained:* A small change from *1805* 'As my soul bade me', but not a small distortion. Wordsworth as Hawkshead had 'worshipped' instinctively – as an act of 'natural piety' – not (as this revision of 1832 implies) through Christian meekness.

240–1 *through the gorgeous Alps|Roaming:* In summer 1790, aged 20; see Book VI.

242 *this degradation:* The impairment of imagination that Wordsworth has attempted to portray in ll. 152–98 above.

244–5 *custom that prepares . . . to least:* Familiarity breeds contempt; the great spiritual aspects of nature come to be undervalued by comparison with superficial attractions.

247 *Or, lastly, aggravated by the times:* By political pressures.

250–6 *I had felt . . . creative soul:* Wordsworth's attempt to impose upon *The*

Prelude a Miltonic structure based on the loss and regaining of paradise (seen first in the five-book version of March 1804) falters because he is unable to say with conviction that his imagination has ever been seriously impaired. Cambridge, though presented as an eddy in the river of his development, does nothing to prevent its onward course. The soul of nature diffuses through London's frightening impersonality 'Composure and ennobling harmony' (VII 740). Political commitment in France betrays the poet into the false hopes and sterile arguments of Godwinian rationalism, but even here we are told at once of recovery and Dorothy's saving presence. There can be no doubt of Wordsworth's wish to show the innocent vision occluded by experience, but he can't bring himself to the belief that it happened. His poem depends far more on the sense of having been, and remained, a 'chosen son'. See *BV* chapter 8, 'Versions of the Fall', especially pp. 274–6.

257–388 Originally consisting of three episodes (*1799* I 258–374), the 'spots of time' sequence provides in all versions of *The Prelude* the rationale for Wordsworth's belief in the capacity of the adult mind to draw strength and inspiration from childhood experience. The individual 'spots' reached the expanded form preserved in *1805* during work on the five-book *Prelude* in early spring 1804. It was at this period that the Drowned Man of Esthwaite (first episode in *1799*, and found at V 450–81 in *1805*) was separated off.

259 *A vivifying virtue:* life-giving power. *1799* 'fructifying virtue' had placed the emphasis on creativity, *1850* 'renovating virtue' (present in Reed's text of the *A/B* Stage) stresses renewal.

270–2 *We have had . . . her will:* Wordsworth's emphasis on the mind as 'lord and master' is the key to his new attitude to the Spots of Time in *1805*. *1799* takes imagination for granted in its quest for continuities in human existence, *1805* exalts it as the triumph of the human mind.

288–9 *a bottom . . . had been hung:* If we assume that the child did indeed stumble on the site of a gibbet, the valley-bottom was Cowdrake Quarry east of Penrith, where Thomas Nicholson had been hanged in 1767. *The Prelude* is not, however, a record of fact. Nicholson's gibbet had not 'mouldered down' in 1775, and a five-year-old would not have ridden that far. Wordsworth is creating a composite experience, and has chiefly in mind a rotted seventeenth-century gibbet in the meadows at Hawkshead, which we know was an object of terror for him during his schooldays.

291–301 *on the turf . . . green sod:* The letters carved in the turf are not present in *1799*, and not likely to have been part of whatever was Wordsworth's original experience; probably he heard of them in the years 1799–1804. Their existence is corroborated by the anonymous *History of Penrith* (1838), which however states that they read 'TPM' (for 'Thomas Parker Murdered'), while Wordsworth regards them as recording 'the murderer's name'.

292 *fell:* fierce; as at l. 318 above, 'I was a fell destroyer', Wordsworth's tones are slightly arch.

294 *monumental:* memorial.

305 *A girl who bore a pitcher on her head:* A cottage-woman fetching water from a stream in the valley – at the time (as Wordsworth says) 'an ordinary sight'.

310 *visionary dreariness:* Wordsworth's readers would recollect 'The dismal situation waste and wild' of Milton's Hell, where there was 'No light, but rather darkness visible' (*PL* I 60–3).

312–14 *the naked pool,|The beacon . . . The woman:* 'I have been struck with the important truth', De Quincey (who had read the 1805 *Prelude* in MS) writes in *Suspiria De Profundis*,

> that far more of our deepest thoughts and feelings pass to us through perplexed combinations of concrete objects, pass to us as *involutes* (if I may coin that word) in compound experiences incapable of being disentangled, than ever reach us directly and in their own abstract shapes. (Ward 130)

Note also the pattern of 'involutes' (concrete objects with which the emotions have become involved, or associated, and which thus recall the original feelings) in ll. 357–9 below.

315–44 *When, in a blessed . . . conclude:* Written in early spring 1804 when Wordsworth was revising the Spots of Time for the five-book *Prelude.* The two 'dear ones' of l. 317 are Mary Hutchinson and Dorothy, and the 'time of early love' was summer 1787 just before he went up to Cambridge. He and Mary would have been seventeen, Dorothy fifteen.

320–5 *Upon the naked pool . . . left behind:* Passion is valued by Wordsworth not so much for its moods as for its intensity and rootedness in the past. Though no one had made such assumptions before, he expects us to accept without question that the pleasures of young love ('youth's golden gleam') can be enhanced by memories of painful early experience.

325–7 *So feeling comes in aid . . . strong:* The creed on which, more than any other, *The Prelude* is built.

332–3 *that thou must give,|Else never canst receive:* Lines that form part of a dialogue with Coleridge, centring upon *Dejection: An Ode* (published in the *Morning Post* as a tribute to Wordsworth on his wedding-day, 4 October 1802): 'Oh Edmund, we receive but what we give,|And in our life alone does nature live'. Coleridge's lines express anxieties that Wordsworth (Edmund) does not feel, but for both poets the capacity to give (outgoing imagination) is associated with ability to perceive and feel intensely.

335–6 *the hiding-places . . . close:* Written probably just before *Intimations* was completed in February 1804. Five years earlier, in *1799* Part II, Wordsworth had spoken confidently of the 'poetic spirit' as 'in some|Through every change of growth or of decay|Preeminent till death' (ll. 306–10).

337–42 *I see by glimpses . . . future restoration:* Lines added after the death of the poet's brother John in February 1805, and conveying the mood in which the last three books of *The Prelude* were put together in April–May.

344–88 In contrast to the previous 'spot', Waiting for the Horses follows the text of *1799* very closely. In the background is an account of the event written for *The Vale of Esthwaite* in 1786–7, as little as two or three years after the death of the poet's father on 30 December 1783; see *1799* I 352n.

345 *The day before the holidays began:* Probably 19 December 1783.

XII 291 *those led palfreys:* A revision of c. 1819, together with 'couched' (for 'was') in l. 300 and 'Sojourners' in l. 307.

349 *My brothers:* Wordsworth's elder brother Richard (a pernickety lawyer, 1768–1816) and John (the sea-captain, 1772–1805).

349–54 *There was a crag . . . choice uncertain:* Wordsworth is waiting above Hawkshead, and a little to the north. The horses, sent by his father in Cockermouth, might be coming over Wrynose Pass and through Little Langdale, or via Keswick and Ambleside.

360 *those companions:* Note the touch of humour as Wordsworth draws attention to the non-human 'involutes' (ll. 312–14n. above) with which he formed a relationship as he waited. The hawthorn is present in the early *Vale of Esthwaite* account (*1799* I 353–5n.), the 'single sheep' is a narrowing down of 'the poor flocks . . . sad-drooping', and the 'naked wall' replaces 'yon naked rock'.

365 *A dweller in my father's house:* Notable both for its biblical ring and its impersonality. Wordsworth had been born in the house, and spent his childhood there, but the reference hardly makes it sound like home.

366 *orphans then:* The poet's mother had died in March 1778, just before his eighth birthday.

367–9 *The event . . . appeared|A chastisement:* The child feels that he is being punished for looking forward too eagerly to the Christmas holidays – that, in effect, he has killed his father.

372–4 *With trite reflections . . . my desires:* Wordsworth's emphasis on 'trite reflections' ('Put not your trust in the things of this world', and the like) tells us how to read God's 'correction' of the child's desires. Cowper remarks, *Task* V 875–6, on our practice of 'inventing to ourselves|Gods such as guilt makes welcome'.

379–81 *the mist . . . indisputable shapes:*

Earlier the mist had obscured the child's view, causing the strained attention that is typical of so many of the border experiences, and that almost invariably prefaces the unexpected. Now, it advances along the roads by which the horses should have come . . . in shapes that indisputably resemble them. But what should one make of the *Hamlet* echo:

> Thou comest in such a questionable shape
> That I would speak to thee. I'll call thee Hamlet,
> King, father, royal Dane. Oh answer me! (I iv 43–5)

It seems an odd chance that this of all passages in Wordsworth's poetry should be linked to the ghost of a murdered father. But in fact there is one other passage, similarly linked, and just as important. Looking backwards to the 'spots of time' in the great ninth stanza of *Intimations*, the poet in 1804 gives thanks not for 'the simple creed|Of childhood'

> But for those blank misgivings of a creature
> Moving about in worlds not realized,
> High instincts before which our mortal nature
> Did tremble like a guilty thing surprised . . .

In this case it seems we have a quotation consciously used, but oddly misapplied: why should the child (as representative of our mortal nature) be connected with the Ghost who at the crowing of the cock, 'started like a guilty thing|Upon a fearful summons' (*Hamlet* I i 148–9)? The answer can only be that at some level the poet associated the 'blank misgivings' and 'high instincts' of childhood with his father's death, and with the guilt that has been taken over from the Ghost.

Infusing the unimportant remembered scene above Hawkshead with emotions occasioned by his father's death, the child gives it lasting power; evoking this power (and consciously deriving it from misplaced guilt), the adult poet visualizes the mist as 'advancing' in shapes that are connected by verbal echo to the ghost of a father who returned to seek revenge. On the level of the poet's intention one assumes that the mist-shapes were unquestionably horses; on another, one indisputably can, and perhaps should, take them to be something far less comfortable. Presumably, writing 100 years before Freud's discussion of the 'uncanny', Wordsworth would have been surprised to think of the forms he had created in the mist, and similarly 'advancing' mountain on Ullswater, in terms of his father; but the man who could write, 'And I grew up|*Fostered* alike by beauty and by fear' (*1805* I 305–6) was not very far from knowing that nature in her 'gentle visitations' had been a replacement for his mother, or that he associated his father with 'severer interventions'. (*BV* 63–4)

381 *indisputable:* Stressed on the second and fourth syllables.

384 *fountain:* stream or well; cf. *Intimations* 151–5, where the 'first affections' and 'shadowy' recollections of childhood,

> be they what they may,
> Are yet the fountain-light of all our day,
> Are yet the master-light of all our seeing . . .

387–8 *unknown to me . . . brought:* Spots of Time shape the adult mind through the powers of association, though it remains unconscious of their workings.

XII 326–35 *and on winter nights . . . hour of . . . ease:* The Spots of Time, which since January 1799 have supported each successive version of *The Prelude* with their theory of the imagination nourished and inspired by early experience, dwindle now to the memories of an old-age pensioner – ways to 'animate an hour of vacant ease'. Though Wordsworth had felt the need to correct his original lines as early as 1832, the text of *1850* is arrived at in a very late revision, 1839 or later. See Jonathan Wordsworth, 'Revision as Making, *The Prelude* and its Peers', *Romantic Revisions*, ed. Robert Brinkley and Keith Hanley, 18–42.

394 *Or otherwise:* or in other ways.

Book Twelfth (1850 Thirteenth)

4–6 *sister horns . . . her bounties:* The two-sidedness of nature – the fact that she contributes equally to emotion and to calm – constitutes her strength, and is the basis of her influence. Attempts (including my own Norton footnote) to give larger meanings to Wordsworth's horn metaphor are no great success. 'Twin peaks' would probably have done as well as 'sister horns', and the 'bounties' of l. 6 require no reference to cornucopias ('horns of plenty').

8–9 *genius . . . peace and excitation:* An interesting Wordsworthian definition, related to the twin influences of beauty and the sublime.

21 *now:* Wordsworth's thoughts have gone back to the period following his

moral crisis of X 888–904. The effect of this backward glance is to identify the crisis of Book XI – never very fully defined or dated (see XI 250–6n.) – with that of X.

24 *a power:* nature; as in ll. 1 and 45.

26 *right reason:* 'reason in her most exalted mood', equated at XIII 170 with 'amplitude of mind' and imagination.

32 *magnanimity:* literally 'greatness of soul'.

XIII 27–8 *trains|To meekness . . . humble faith:* Pious revision of 1838–9.

34–5 *the busy dance|Of things that pass away:* Wordsworth seems to be thinking of 'the quick dance|Of colours, lights, and forms' in London (VII 156ff.).

37–8 *when over fondly set . . . her incumbrances:* Cf. Wordsworth's mockery of the Godwinian former self who, at X 821–3, 'with a resolute mastery' shakes off 'The accidents of nature, time and place|That make up the weak being of the past'.

47–52 *seeing little worthy . . . beauteous world:* Drawn (like XI 15–22) from the unused introduction to *Nutting*, drafted as early as October 1798 in *MS JJ*.

57–9 *I took the intellectual eye . . . little ones:* In the terms of Coleridge's letter to Poole of 16 October 1797 the spiritual ('intellectual') eye perceives 'the great and the whole', whereas those depending on 'the testimony of their senses . . . contemplate nothing but *parts* – and all *parts* are necessarily little'.

64 *The promise of the present time:* political hopes for the future of mankind.

75 *bottomed:* based.

80 *The wealth of nations:* A sideways reference to Adam Smith, *Enquiry into the Nature and Causes of the Wealth of Nations* (1776), is enough to sum up for Wordsworth's reader the impersonality of modern political thinkers ('statists', l. 78). The inverted commas at *1850* 78 are added in 1838–9.

81–2 *having gained . . . of what makes:* The text of *MS Z* is plainer and more to the point: 'having learned|More feelingly to know wherein consists'.

103–5 *that injustice which . . . Ourselves entail:* Since the *Salisbury Plain* poems and *Convict* of 1793–6 Wordsworth had written little poetry of social protest, but his sense of injustice had not diminished.

109 *notices:* observations.

112–277 Old material drafted for Book VIII in *MS Y* (October 1804), and seeming at times anomalous after the full-scale accounts of London in Book VII, and of political involvement in Book X (composed in November–December 1804, after the *Y* materials).

117 *An intermixture of distinct regards:* In effect translated by ll. 118–19. Wordsworth requires that 'regards' (sights, experiences) of a more personal kind should be mingled with affairs of the outer world; cf. the 'individual sights|Of courage, and integrity, and truth' (VIII 839–40).

120 *that great city:* A reference to VIII 824–7 where 'the unity of man' is 'affectingly set forth' among 'the multitudes|Of that great city'. The link of course had more point before the *MS Y* drafts used to form the central section of Book XII were separated from the materials of Book VIII (see 112–277n.).

128 *untoward:* intractable, obstinate, unfavourable; used by Wordsworth in *The*

Leech Gatherer to describe his thoughts of poets being brought 'to despondency and madness'.

136 *In my esteem, next to such dear delight:* Interlined in *MS Z*; a reminder that Wordsworth's revision tends at all periods to elaboration.

139–40 *and teach . . . fields and groves:* References in ll. 143–4 to the cottage-bench and well confirm that Wordsworth has in mind the Pedlar who tells the story of Margaret in *The Ruined Cottage*: 'Together did we make the hollow grove|Ring with our transports' (*Pedlar* 323–4).

141–2 *where if we meet a face . . . friend:* To be placed alongside IV 58–9, 'The face of every neighbour whom I met|Was as a volume to me', and contrasted with the London experience of VII 597–8, 'the face of everyone|That passes by me is a mystery.'

149–50 *one bare steep . . . feet had trod:* The road to the village of Isel over Watch Hill, which can be seen from the house at Cockermouth where Wordsworth passed the first years of his life (De Selincourt).

158 *bedlamites:* madmen ('Bedlam' being a corruption of London's Bethlehem Hospital for the Insane).

174 *estate:* condition, place in society.

185–204 Like the Matron's Tale (VIII 222–311) surplus material drafted for *Michael* in *MS J* (autumn 1800), and incorporated into *Prelude MS Y* four years later.

187–8 *A gift . . . Of vulgar nature:* a gift merely of nature.

189 *Retirement MS J:* 'Refinement' looks a better reading, and was perhaps lost through hasty copying in *MS Y*.

194–7 *True is it . . . and poverty:* A passage that had been impressively simple in *MS J*:

> These deem that bonds of natural amity
> Do seldom lay strong hold upon the hearts
> Of men in low estate, true inference
> When want and the excess of poverty

204 *that inference:* The inference of ll. 185–93 that feeling goes along with cultivation. On 14 January 1801 Wordsworth had told Charles James Fox that *The Brothers* and *Michael* 'were written with a view to show that men who do not wear fine clothes can feel deeply.'

215–19 *flattering thus . . . universal heart:* Cf. Wordsworth's vehement letter to John Wilson of 7 June 1802:

> People in our rank in life are perpetually falling into one sad mistake . . . that of supposing that human nature and the persons they associate with are one and the same thing. Whom do we generally associate with? Gentlemen, persons of fortune, professional men, ladies, persons who can afford to buy, or easily procure, books of half a guinea price . . .

231–59 A passage that contains striking echoes of Wordsworth's poetic manifesto of 1800, the Prospectus to *The Recluse.* The number of echoes increases in revision. L. 251 (echoing Prospectus 16–18) is present in *MS Y*; ll. 239–40 and 243 make their appearances in *MS Z*, the first recalling Prospectus

28–9, the second ('Nor uninformed by books, good books though few') being close to parody in its recollection of Prospectus 11–12: 'fit audience let me find, though few!|"Fit audience find, though few", thus prayed the bard'.

238–9 *through unadulterated ears|Pour rapture:* For 'ears' Wordsworth originally wrote 'hearts' (*MS Y*). It is hard to know which reading is the more incongruous. *unadulterated:* uncorrupted.

245 *Sorrow that is not sorrow:* Cf. Wordsworth's wish in *Intimations* 186–7 to find strength 'In the soothing thoughts that spring|Out of human suffering'.

254–5 *Who to the letter ... soul:* who judge the inward soul by outward appearances.

260 *mould:* composition (the 'earth' from which man was made at Creation).

261 *Who are their own upholders:* Cf. the 'visitings|Of the upholder, of the tranquil soul' (III 115–16).

263–4 *Expressing ... native passion dictates:* The ideal of the perfect natural expression of emotion that lies behind the Preface to *Lyrical Ballads* 1800.

264–74 *Others too ... among them:* Wordsworth has in mind his brother John, the 'silent poet' (drowned at sea four months after these lines were drafted in *MS Y* – and two months before they were incorporated into Book XII).

272 *Words are but under-agents ... souls:* The prefix 'under' works in different ways, suggesting the unimportance of words as such to those who speak 'the language of the heavens', but implying too that the 'silent poet' is peculiarly in touch with the sources of Wordsworthian power; cf. the 'under-soul' of III 539–40 and 'under-presence' of XIII 71–3. As 'under-agents' in the soul, 'words' are non- or pre-verbal communication.

274 *They do not breathe among them:* In their highest moments 'silent poets' do not live ('breathe') in the world of 'words' (articulate language).

280 *the inner frame:* Effectively, the soul.

286–9 *I felt ... passion makes it:* Beauty is in the eye of the beholder.

301 *poets, even as prophets:* As 'Prophets of nature' Wordsworth and Coleridge will, in the final lines of the poem, 'speak|A lasting inspiration', instructing their age in the paramount beauty of the mind.

303 *his peculiar dower:* his personal talent, endowment.

308 *influx:* inspiration.

309–12 *work of mine ... nature's:* Wordsworth's most concise and powerful statement of his ambition as a poet.

312–14 *To such mood ... raised:* Wordsworth's claim is to have been exalted during his experience on Salisbury Plain in summer 1793 into a mood in which he was uniquely inspired, 'enabled to perceive|Something unseen before' (ll. 304–5). He crossed the Plain on foot, with little or no food, his thoughts on the war with France – 'more like a man|Flying from something that he dreads, than one|Who sought the thing he loved' (*TA* 71–3). *Sarum:* Latin name of Salisbury.

315 *downs:* chalk-hills, unploughed at this date, and used only for grazing sheep..

320–36 *I had a reverie ... the dead:* Wordsworth is drawing heavily (at times verbatim) on his anti-war poem *Salisbury Plain*, perhaps begun on the spot (see ll. 358–9 below), and certainly completed by April 1794:

Much of the wonders of that boundless heath
He spoke, and of a swain who far astray
Reached unawares a height and saw beneath
Gigantic beings ranged in dread array.
Such beings, thwarting oft the traveller's way,
With shield and stone-axe stride across the wold . . .

And oft a night-fire mounting to the clouds
Reveals the desert, and with dismal red
Clothes the black bodies of encircling crowds.
It is the sacrificial altar fed
With living men! How deep it groans – the dead
Thrilled in their yawning tombs their helms uprear;
The sword that slept beneath the warrior's head
Thunders in fiery air; red arms appear
Uplifted through the gloom and shake the rattling spear. (ll. 172–89)

323 *wold:* open countryside.

330 *desert:* desolate, unpopulated area (not in this case sandy)

332–3 *how deep the groans . . . gigantic wicker:* According to Aylett Sammes, *Britannia Antiqua Illustrata* (1676), the Druids performed human sacrifices by burning their victims in a huge basketwork statue of a man. Taking his cue from Erasmus Darwin (who depended on Sammes) Wordsworth writes at a later stage in *Salisbury Plain*:

Though from huge wickers paled with circling fire
No longer horrid shrieks and dying cries
To ears of demon-gods in peals aspire . . .

Blake's imagination too was caught by

that holy fiend
The wicker man of Scandinavia, in which cruelly consumed
The captives reared to heaven howl in flames among the stars . . .
(*Jerusalem* II, plate 47)

333 *thrills:* pierces.

335–6 *the pomp|Is for both worlds . . . dead:* the spectacle ('pomp') is shared by the 'living' (those burning the captives in the 'wicker') and the already dead wakening in their burial-mounds ('monumental hillocks').

339 *the downy plain:* Salisbury Plain is a plateau composed of chalk downs.

342–3 *figuring o'er|The untilled ground:* making a design on the unploughed turf.

343 *divine:* deduce.

344 *infant:* early.

347–53 *I was gently charmed . . . sound:* The transition from Wordsworth's creative reverie of ll. 320–36 to the mere 'antiquarian's dream' of ll. 338–53 reproduces exactly the pattern of *Salisbury Plain*, the stanzas quoted above being followed by a vision of Druid astronomers:

Long-bearded forms with wands uplifted show
To vast assemblies, while each breath of night
Is hushed, the living fires that bright and slow
Rounding the etherial plain in order go.
Then as they trace with awe their various files
All figured on the mystic plain below,
Still prelude of sweet sounds the moon beguiles
And charmed for many a league the hoary desert smiles. (ll. 191–8)

356–65 *Nor is it, friend, unknown . . . reflected:* Wordsworth's meaning is somewhat obscured by the use of 'it' in l. 356 to refer to the experience that has just been described. Pleased by reading Wordsworth's poem in 1795–6 (in its later form, *Adventures on Salisbury Plain*), Coleridge has himself given pleasure by pointing to its transformation of 'present things'. According to chapter 4 of *Biographia Literaria* (dictated in 1815, ten years after the *Prelude* lines) it was *Salisbury Plain* that alerted Coleridge to Wordsworth's

> original gift of spreading the tone, the atmosphere, and with it the depth and height of the ideal world round forms, incidents and situations, of which, for the common view, custom had bedimmed all the lustre, had dried up the sparkle and the dew drops.

358–9 *some imperfect verse . . . composed:* Wordsworth, who was given to composing as he walked, may well have begun *Salisbury Plain* on the spot in late July–early August 1793, but much of the poem was probably written in North Wales in the weeks that followed. Sense of the poetry's imperfection led to his withholding publication (except of the section revised for *Lyrical Ballads* as *The Female Vagrant*) until *Guilt and Sorrow:* of 1842.

367–8 *the mind . . . Witness and judge:* As 'witness' the mind offers the evidence of memory, as 'judge' it has therefore the right to pronounce upon its own past.

XIII 362 *We were as strangers:* Wordsworth met Coleridge briefly at Bristol in September 1795, and sent him a copy of *Adventures on Salisbury Plain* early in 1796.

XIII 363–5 *verse, however rude . . . light from far:* De Selincourt points out that Wordsworth is 'confusing and combining the impression made on Coleridge by [*Salisbury Plain*] with that made by *Descriptive Sketches* some time earlier.' See *Biographia Literaria* chapter 4:

> During the last year of my residence at Cambridge I became acquainted with Mr Wordsworth's . . . *Descriptive Sketches*, and seldom, if ever, was the emergence of an original poetic genius above the literary horizon more evidently announced.

370 *about this period:* To be specific would not have helped. Wordsworth in Book X had brought his story down to 1796 (at least), and in Book XIII he was about to use as his climax the ascent of Snowdon which had taken place in 1791. Though it needs a forward movement, *The Prelude* does not depend on chronological sequence.

370–9 *sight|Of a new world . . . sees:* Though Wordsworth does not say so directly, the 'new world' of imaginative giving and receiving is the pantheist world of *Tintern Abbey.* As its basis it has the divine principle ('That whence our dignity originates') that is present at once in 'the round ocean and the living air . . . and in the mind of man' (*TA* 99–100), and that constitutes the 'pure spirit and best power|Both of the object seen and eye that sees'.

Book Thirteenth (1850 Fourteenth)

1–65 The great Snowdon episode that forms the imaginative climax of *The Prelude* was written in February–early March 1804 to open the last book of the five-book *Prelude.* It describes an event that took place in summer 1791. When Wordsworth abandoned the five-book scheme, c. 10 March 1804, he could have inserted the Climbing of Snowdon in its chronological position between the French visits of 1790 and '92 (Books VI and IX). Instead he set it aside to be the climax of the new longer poem. As such it is assigned to no date or period. It is an event of the mind, and takes place 'on one of these excursions'.

2 *a youthful friend:* Robert Jones, Cambridge friend and fellow 'mountaineer' (VI 340), with whom Wordsworth stayed on a number of occasions in North Wales after undertaking the Continental tour of 1790.

XIV 3 *Cambria:* Wales.

3 *Bethgelert's huts:* the cottages of Beddgelert, featured in watercolours of the period, notably by John Varley.

11 *glaring:* Cf. *Ruined Cottage:* 2–3, 'the uplands feebly glared|Through a pale steam'.

15 *pilot:* guide.

17 *chat:* Not elsewhere used by Wordsworth, who is expressing mild contempt. Pope, *Rape of the Lock* II 17–18, rhymes the word with 'singing, laughing, ogling, and all that'.

25 *barking turbulent:* A touch of mock-heroic humour: Wordsworth pairs Anglo-Saxon noun with Latin Miltonic adjective, and enters into the dog's 'own great joy'.

39–40 *instantly a light . . . Fell like a flash:* Related to the 'pleasant instantaneous light' that 'startles the musing man' in *Night-Piece* 7–8, but far more dramatic.

45–6 *their dusky backs upheaved . . . ocean:* As he portrays the mist that is an emblem of human creativity, Wordsworth's mind turns to Milton's account of Creation, *PL* VII 285–7:

> the mountains huge appear
> Emergent, and their broad backs upheave
> Into the clouds . . .

51 *Usurped upon:* For the metaphor of usurpation, so important to Wordsworth at this period, see *BV* 174–202, 'Usurpation and Reality: Spring 1804'.

54–9 *And from the shore . . . voice:* The numinous blue chasm at the centre of the Snowdon mistscape had made its appearance in Wordsworth's poetry within a year of his night-time climbing of Snowdon in summer 1791. Not in a Welsh scene, however, but in a description of the Alps:

> A mighty waste of mist the valley fills,
> A solemn sea, whose vales and mountains round
> Stand motionless, to awful silence bound.
> A gulf of gloomy blue, that opens wide
> And bottomless, divides the midway tide . . .
> Loud through that midway gulf ascending sound
> Unnumbered streams with hollow roar profound.
> (*1793 Descriptive Sketches* 495–505)

Many of the details that the Snowdon lines share with *Descriptive Sketches* derive from a mist-scene quoted from Beattie's *Minstrel* (1771) by James Clark, *Survey of the Lakes* (1787) 73, but the blue chasm seems to be Wordsworths's personal observation, or personal invention.

57–9 *A deep and gloomy breathing-place . . . voice:* Wordsworth's 'breathing-place' chasm is akin to the fountain of *Kubla Khan* ('As if this earth in fast thick pants were breathing'), but more personal in its implications. Clark (see previous note) had emphasized that as one climbs through mist 'every sound is much more distinctly heard than at any other time'; Wordsworth has the streams and torrents blend into a single voice, which (even before the allegorization of ll. 66–73) it is not difficult to associate with a welling up of the unconscious.

63 *the homeless voice:* Numinous by virtue of having no apparent source – 'Not to be tracked and fathered' (III 467).

65 *The soul, the imagination of the whole:* As Wordsworth mounts towards the conclusion of his poem, the revelation offered on Snowdon is of the identity of soul and imagination.

XIV 61–2 *Heard over earth and sea . . . heavens:* Nebulous, safe, apologetic lines, designed (in 1838–9) to replace the too daring implications of *1805*. No other passage of *The Prelude* suffered as greatly in revision as did the Climbing of Snowdon, because no other passage shows so powerfully the grandeur and independence of Wordsworth's early thinking.

66–73 *A meditation . . . Or vast in its own being:* Wordsworth's 'meditation' on the Climbing of Snowdon is written fourteen months after the episode itself (ll. 10–65) in May 1805. It expresses the poet's most advanced thinking on imagination, and should not be taken as literally corresponding to a train of thought on the mountain in 1791:

> Though Wordsworth is now explaining things that before had been unstated, the poetry has lost none of its fluidity. The opposition between soul and imagination is beautifully taken up in 'The sense of God, or whatsoe'er is dim|Or vast in its own being'. In the spacial quality of 'under-presence', 'dim' and 'vast', one responds again to the power of the 'deep and gloomy breathing-place'. But this is not all. The meditation is said to rise within the poet, well up of its own accord from those same interior depths from which had 'Mounted the roar of waters, torrents, streams/Innumerable'. The meditation too is a sense of God, or the godlike in man, produced by the soul/imagination. (*B V* 323).

72–3 *The sense of God . . . own being:* One of the great moments in Wordsworth's poetry, as he brings his poem to a climax that leaves open the nature of his spiritual experience. An equal grandeur is claimed for the mind if what it perceives is its own internal vastness, rather than the presence of God. Coleridge could not have accepted such a formulation (though he would have known it was true to Wordsworth), but in terms of *Biographia Literaria* chapter 13 Wordsworth's lines evoke the primary imagination in its highest mood. Through an act that is at once perceptive and creative, the human mind is shown to possess godlike powers.

XIV 63–77 *When into air . . . mortal privilege:* A rewriting of Wordsworth's *1805* 'meditation' (ll. 66–73) that leaves none of the great claims standing, and not a single line untouched. Again, 1838–9.

XIV 64–5 *given to spirits . . . chance human wanderers:* In *1805* there had been no implication of sharing the vision with Jones and the shepherd; the poet had been no aimless 'wanderer', but a 'chosen son'.

XIV 70–4 *There I beheld . . . continuous stream:* The great and wholly accessible poetry of *1805* 68–73 has been replaced by lines of remarkable obscurity. It is far from clear how a mist-covered landscape could typify the 'acts' and 'possessions' of an intellect, let alone 'what it has and craves' (ll. 67–8), but the remainder of the passage presents still greater difficulties. Where in *1805* the mighty mind had been imaged in the mistscape with the 'blue chasm' at its centre, now the mind (with a hint from Milton's Holy Spirit brooding over Chaos, *PL* I 21–2) broods above the abyss, detached from it and listening externally to its voices. Is it perhaps the moon that Wordsworth now thinks of as typifying the mind?

XIV 74–7 *a mind sustained . . . mortal privilege:* Owen notes: 'Sense obscure . . . But it seems likely that "of transcendent power" and "of more than mortal privilege" are parallel phrases referring to "recognitions".' 'More than mortal privilege' he then glosses as 'the privilege of immortality'. His reading can hardly be ruled out, but it may be simpler to see the mind as sustained by recognitions of power in sense, to which the specially privileged soul may give ideal form.

75 *Exhibited by putting forth:* demonstrated by analogy.

79 *So moulds them, and endues, abstracts, combines:* Transforming the mountain-slopes with a sea of mist, nature performs a function akin to the secondary (less important) powers of the human imagination, as defined in *Biographia Literaria* chapter 13: 'It dissolves, diffuses, dissipates in order to recreate . . . at all events it struggles to idealize and to unify'. Coleridge is not on record as having made his distinction between the primary and secondary imaginations by 1805, but the closeness of his wording in this instance suggests that he may have done so in conversation. There can be no doubt that Wordsworth's thinking depends upon him; see Jonathan Wordsworth, 'The Infinite I AM', *Coleridge's Imagination*, ed. Gravil, Newlyn and Roe, 22–52.

81–4 *Does make one object . . . but feel:* Working on the five-book *Prelude* in February–early March 1804, Wordsworth drafted six further examples of interaction between the mind and nature to follow the Climbing of Snowdon. First of these was the exquisite study of a horse singled out by the 'abrupt and unhabitual influence' of moonlight:

One evening, walking in the public way,
A peasant of the valley where I dwelt
Being my chance companion, he stopped short
And pointed to an object full in view
At a small distance. 'Twas a horse, that stood
Alone upon a little breast of ground
With a clear silver moonlight sky behind.
With one leg from the ground the creature stood,
Insensible and still; breath, motion, gone,
Hairs, colour, all but shape and substance gone,
Mane, ears, and tail, as lifeless as the trunk
That had no stir of breath. We paused awhile
In pleasure of the sight, and left him there,
With all his functions silently sealed up,
Like an amphibious work of nature's hand,
A borderer dwelling betwixt life and death,
A living statue or a statued life.

Beautiful as they are, the lines were never published by Wordsworth.

84–119 *The power . . . external universe:* Possession of 'the glorious faculty' of imagination defines the Wordsworthian elect ('higher minds'), controlling their relation not only to the natural world but to every aspect of existence.

93 *native:* natural.

94–6 *for themselves create . . . instinct:* Emphasis once again on the imagination as both creative and perceptive.

98–9 *They build . . . From least suggestions:* In Wordsworth's earliest recorded definition (Note to *The Thorn*, 1800), imagination had been 'the faculty that produces impressive effects out of simple elements'.

101 *calls:* stimuli, excitements.

103–5 *By sensible impressions . . . invisible world:* As in Blake, the senses are a barrier to perception of the divine: 'If the doors of perception were cleansed everything would appear to man as it is, infinite' (*Marriage of Heaven and Hell*, plate 14).

XIV 114 *That flesh can know:* As opposed to the bliss known to heavenly beings; a revision probably dating from late 1832.

108–11 *consciousness|Of whom they are . . . impressions:* For the truly imaginative, all experience is a confirmation of identity.

113 *Whether discursive or intuitive:* The Kantian distinction between 'discursive' understanding and 'intuitive' reason. Describing reason as the 'being' of the soul, Raphael (*PL* V 487) makes the discursive/intuitive distinction for Adam, commenting: 'discourse|Is oftest yours [human], the latter most is ours [angelic]|Differing but in degree, in kind the same.' Milton's lines are quoted by Coleridge in *Biographia Literaria* chapter 10, and in chapter 13 are picked up in his reference to the secondary imagination as identical to the godlike primary 'in the *kind* of its agency . . . differing only in degree'. To judge from *Prelude* XIII Coleridge must have pointed Milton's lines out to Wordsworth before his departure for Malta in spring 1804, and passed on to him the equation of intuitive reason with the primary imagination.

XIV 126–7 *that peace . . . understanding:* 'The peace of God which passeth all understanding' (*Philippians* 4.7). Ll. 127–9, with their reassuring Christian view-point, belong to 1838–9.

127 *And yet . . . undiminished powers:* Wordsworth's line belongs to the same month (February 1804) as *Intimations* iv–xi and *1805* XI 335–6 ('The hiding-places of my power|Seem open, I approach, and then they close'), but adopts a surprisingly confident tone.

128 *whatever falls:* From Fortune's revolving wheel (see l. 129).

131–2 *never . . . Did tamper with myself:* Made clear in *1850* 150–1.

136 *with jealousy:* watchfully, scrupulously.

141 *a universe of death:* Drawn from Milton's Hell, *PL* II 622–4: 'A universe of death . . . Where all life dies, death lives, and nature breeds|Perverse all monstrous, all prodigious, things'. Significantly Wordsworth had evoked the same passage in his account of the perversion of nature in London's Bartholomew Fair (VII 687ff.).

143–4 *To fear and love . . . ends:* Cf. the statement of Wordsworth's theme at I 305–6: 'Fair seed-time had my soul, and I grew up|Fostered alike by beauty and by fear.' Fear ends in love, because painful (sublime) experiences are formative, leading to love of nature.

XIV 179–87 *There linger . . . Almighty's Throne:* Though the *1850* replacement of *1805* 159–65 is not arrived at until 1838–9, Wordsworth redefines the 'higher love' of *1805* in specifically Christian terms as early as c. 1819 (see Introduction).

163 *a diffusive sentiment:* Cf. II 420ff. (written originally for *The Pedlar*, spring 1798): 'I felt the sentiment of being, spread|O'er all that moves and all that seemeth still . . .'

166 *intellectual:* spiritual.

167–70 *imagination . . . exalted mood:* An extreme statement of the powers of the primary imagination, but one that is in line with the poetry and thinking of Wordsworth and Coleridge. This higher imagination is godlike and thus equivalent to 'absolute [spiritual] strength'; 'clearest insight' speaks for itself; 'amplitude of mind' implies magnanimity (literally 'greatness of soul'), the outgoing, expansive power of imagination; intuitive reason ('reason in her most exalted mood') has been the theme of Book XIII and is later equated with the primary imagination in *Biographia Literaria.*

172–84 *we have traced . . . infinity and God:* Modelling his imagery to some extent on the sacred river Alph of *Kubla Khan*, Wordsworth now offers the river that has been recurrent in *The Prelude* from the opening lines of *Was It For This* and *1799*, as symbolic of the organic structure of his poem.

183 *The feeling of life endless:* Though *Intimations* alludes in February 1804 to 'the faith that looks through death', Wordsworth seems to have had no confidence in an afterlife when his brother John was drowned in February 1805. A letter to Beaumont of 12 March (six weeks before this section of *The Prelude* was written) shows him arguing himself into an acceptance of 'the supposition of *another* and a *better* world'.

XIV 205 *human Being:* human existence.

188 *Dividually:* separately. In practice it would be hard to define outgoing 'spiritual love' (such as that shown in the Ancient Mariner's blessing of the watersnakes) as distinct from the primary imagination.

193 *this ability:* the capacity for spiritual love.

208 *female softness:* Valued highly by Wordsworth in men; cf. the shepherd's attention to his infant son, *Michael* 162–8.

209 *little loves and delicate desires:* A reflection of Dorothy's tenderness in *The Sparrow's Nest*, 'And humble cares and delicate fears' (l. 18), which is strengthened in *1850*. In the background (as Reed points out) are the 'soft and delicate desires' of Claudio, *Much Ado About Nothing* I i 303.

211–14 *Child of my parents . . . imbibed:* Apart from his tribute to Dorothy's tenderness in *The Sparrow's Nest*, Wordsworth has in mind *To A Butterfly*: 'she, God love her, feared to brush|The dust from off its wings' (ll. 17–18).

222–3 *the very going-out of youth . . . reached:* Book XII had ended with the crossing of Salisbury Plain in summer 1793, and Book XIII opened with the ascent of Snowdon two years earlier. It is not in Wordsworth's interests to be precise about chronology. The 'later seasons' of Dorothy's influence (l. 215) include the Racedown period, 1795–7.

225–6 *that beauty . . . terror in it:* Milton's sense of the terror that exists in love (effectively of the presence of the sublime within the beautiful) is expressed by Satan, new-landed in Eden and confronted by the beauty of Eve: 'She fair, divinely fair, fit love for gods,|Not terrible, though terror be in love|And beauty' (*PL* IX 489–91).

228 *reckless of:* unconcerned by.

236–44 *At a time . . . refined humanity:* The period associated in *Tintern Abbey* with coming to hear 'The still sad music of humanity', and marked by composition of *The Ruined Cottage* in early summer 1797.

XIV 266–75 *Thereafter came . . . the dewy grass:* In an early form, Wordsworth's tribute to his wife is inserted into *The Prelude* c. 1819. The vagueness of 'Thereafter' is strategic. After their 'blessed time of early love' (*1805* XI 317) in 1787, Mary had been displaced in Wordsworth's thoughts by Annette (and Caroline). The war, however, had kept him and Annette apart from autumn 1792 for almost ten years. Before the end of this period – perhaps when Mary came to visit Dorothy at Racedown, November 1796–June 1797 – she and Wordsworth had (privately) come together again. They were married in October 1802.

XIV 268–9 *no more a phantom to adorn|A moment:* A reference to the touching Lucy poem written for Mary in spring 1804:

> She was a phantom of delight
> When first she gleamed upon my sight,
> A lovely apparition sent
> To be a moment's ornament . . . (ll. 1–4)

249 *Placed on this earth to love:* Cf. the poignant final lines of Coleridge's *Pains of Sleep* (1803) 'To be beloved is all I need,|And whom I love I love indeed.'

253–7 *the life|Of all things. . . Interposition:* Through Coleridge's loving companionship Wordsworth came at Alfoxden to accept a Unitarian belief (merely 'interposed', not argued or preached) in the One Life.

XIV 282–7 *Thus fear relaxed . . . eternity:* A revision of *1805* 253–5 made in 1839 or later. For no obvious reason Coleridge (d. 1834) is credited with having rescued Wordsworth from fear and self-hauntings. At Alfoxden? Or is Coleridge being transported in the poet's fancy back to the period of the Racedown crisis of confidence, spring 1796?

257 *closelier gathering:* more personal, more immediate in their concerns.

264–5 *a reason . . . pathetic truth:* reason at her most personal – as opposed to 'reason in her most exalted mood' (l. 170 and n. above), which is imagination.

268 *Where man is sphered . . . God animates:* Man's proper place ('sphere') is earth, but earth is animated by God.

271 *consummation:* perfecting.

273–8 *We have reached . . . should endure:* Wordsworth thinks of himself as having brought his story up to the period of *Lyrical Ballads*, when (in March 1798) *The Recluse* was first projected.

274 *which was our object from the first:* Not strictly true; see Introduction.

280 *Of books how much:* Addressing Coleridge, with his massive reading, Wordsworth is conscious of not having stressed the role of literature in his education, though he had attempted to do so in Book V.

282–8 *nature's secondary grace . . . moral world:* The habit of drawing moral truths from nature ('Consider the lilies of the field . . . They toil not, neither do they spin . . .') was foreign to Wordsworth though he could indulge in it on occasion. In *The Primrose on the Rock* (1831) the flowers are 'faithful to the stems', the stems 'faithful to the root', and 'God upholds them all'.

291–4 *In turn might fancy . . . judgement steadied:* As in Book VIII, Wordsworth sets a value on fancy that Coleridge could not have accepted; see VIII 590–1n.

294–306 *Then might we return . . . never heighten:* Strangely opaque lines (cut with no loss in *1850*), perhaps about anthropomorphic readings of nature.

308 *that marvellous world:* the world of human consciousness and emotion.

316 *a public school:* Founded in 1584, Hawkshead Grammar School was (as Eton, Winchester, Westminster had originally been) public in the sense of being a Grammar School, open to all.

329–31 *keep|In wholesome separation . . . observes:* It is interesting that Wordsworth, who placed so much emphasis on emotion, should value reserve and the ability to keep one's feelings to oneself.

334 *Since I withdrew unwillingly from France:* In November 1792, leaving behind Annette and the newborn Caroline.

338–43 *Three years . . . wanderer's life:* December 1792–September 1795.

349–67 *A youth . . . bent of nature:* Raisley Calvert, younger brother of Wordsworth's schoolfellow William (who lent the poet and Dorothy their first, temporary, home together at Windy Brow, Keswick in spring 1794), died of tuberculosis in 1795 aged 22, leaving Wordsworth £900 to free him from taking a job and enable him to write.

356 *no redundant patrimony:* a limited family fortune.

360 *mortal:* earthly, mundane.

368–9 *further pains . . . seems not to require:* Wordsworth has it in common with Milton that many of his weakest lines occur in moments of transition.

372 *the termination of my course:* death.

373–7 *even then . . . I said . . . reproach to hear:* A reference back to the self-reproach – 'Was it for this' – in which composition of *The Prelude* had begun in

October 1798; see the openings of *Was It For This* and *1799*, and *1805* 271ff. Reed points also to *Genesis* 3.8–13, as Adam and Eve hear the reproachful voice of God, walking in the garden.

377–80 *Anon I rose . . . I had been|And was:* Based on the 'prospect wide|And various' shown to Eve in her dream, *PL* V 86–9.

383 *Attempered:* suited; cf. the 'rural ditties' of *Lycidas* 32–3, 'Tempered to the oaten flute'.

385 *gratulant:* capable of giving pleasure.

387–90 *aught of worth|Sufficient . . . uncertain:* On 6 March 1804, at the moment of embarking on the full-length *Prelude*, Wordsworth had told De Quincey: 'This poem will not be published these many years, and never during my lifetime till I have finished a larger and more important work [*The Recluse*] to which it is tributary.' In sight of completing the 'tributary' poem, Wordsworth comments to Beaumont on 1 May 1805: '[It is] a thing unprecedented in literary history that a man should write so much about himself.'

393–8 *That summer . . . Lady Christabel:* summer 1798, on the Quantock Hills above Alfoxden. *The Ancient Mariner* was in fact completed in March, and *Christabel* Part I in April.

394 *sylvan combs:* wooded hollows; pronounced 'cooms' (to rhyme with 'tombs').

399–403 *I, associate . . . miserable thorn:* Looking back on the partnership that produced *Lyrical Ballads*, Wordsworth pokes fun at himself for his 'murmuring' of *The Idiot Boy* aloud during composition, and for the lugubrious refrain of *The Thorn*: 'Oh misery, oh misery,|Oh woe is me, oh misery!'

416–17 *a private grief|Keen and enduring:* Another reference to the death of John Wordsworth, captain of the *Earl of Abergavenny*, drowned off the Dorset coast on 5 February 1805.

421–7 *a hope . . . offering of my love:* As Wordsworth brings his poem to a close in early May 1805 Coleridge has been abroad for over a year. When he did finally return, the 'offering of . . . love' was read to him at Coleorton in January 1807. Coleridge responded in his last major poem, *To William Wordsworth*:

> o great bard,
> Ere yet that last strain dying awed the air,
> With stedfast eye I viewed thee in the choir
> Of ever-enduring men. (ll. 47–50)

429 *thy race be run:* Wordsworth is talking to himself. It is perhaps the thought of having to go on and write *The Recluse* in Coleridge's absence that brings the dispirited Samson to his mind: 'My race of glory run, and race of shame,|And I shall shortly be with them that rest' (ll. 597–8).

432 *old idolatry:* Wordsworth models the conclusion of *1805* on that of *1799*, where (in spite of his dismay at rising French imperialism) he had lamented the weakness of those in England who betrayed the ideals of the Revolution:

> if in these times of fear,
> This melancholy waste of hopes o'erthrown,

If, mid indifference and apathy
And wicked exultation, when good men
On every side fall off, we know not how,
To selfishness . . . (*1799* II 478–83)

436 *the knowledge which we have:* Wordsworth's emphasis on knowledge is surprising, but consistent. In announcing the scheme for *The Recluse* to Tobin on 6 March 1798 he refers to lines already written, as conveying 'most of the knowledge of which [he is] possessed'. *Home at Grasmere* (written for *The Recluse* in 1800) looks forward to a millennium of human happiness that 'love|And knowledge will . . . hereafter give|To all the vales of earth and all mankind' (ll. 254–6).

442 *Prophets of nature:* The conclusion to *1799* is buoying Wordsworth up, enabling him to feel confident in a shared prophetic role. Coleridge, in the earlier lines, had been 'in many things' the poet's brother, but 'chiefly' in his 'deep devotion' to nature (II 508–9).

XIV 446 *faith:* a telling replacement for 'truth' (*1805*), made in 1832.

449 *revolutions:* changes (as of Fortune's wheel – though of course including Revolution with a capital 'r').

452 *Of substance and of fabric more divine:* Not merely a resonant conclusion. The mind shares with the rest of nature the animating presence of God, but is more 'divine' in that it alone possesses the God-given power of imagination that enables it to perceive the presence that it shares.

AFTERWORD: THE POET AS REVISOR

It is not chance that Wordsworth's revisions of *The Prelude* were mainly for the worse. Given his methods of working – the creative process that he describes for us in the Preface to *Lyrical Ballads* – we should expect it to be so. Twice in the Preface Wordsworth tells us that 'poetry is the spontaneous overflow of powerful feelings', and twice he modifies his statement. First we are told that the poet must be a person 'of more than usual organic sensibility [who has] also thought long and deeply', next that poetry 'takes its origin from emotion recollected in tranquillity'. It is the words that follow that are chiefly important:

> the emotion is contemplated till by a species of reaction the tranquillity gradually disappears, and an emotion, similar to that which was before the subject of contemplation, is gradually produced, and does itself actually exist in the mind.

'In this mood', Wordsworth concludes, 'successful composition generally begins, and in a mood similar to this it is carried on.' These are not theoretical statements, the poet has observed his own mental process and tells us precisely what he sees.

Revision, if it is to be enhancing, has to be similarly imaginative. It must be accompanied by a re-experiencing of the mood in which composition originally took place – a mood that was itself a reliving of earlier experience. Revisions carried out over many years, as they were in key passages of *The Prelude*, are not likely to meet this requirement. Re-entering the original mood becomes progressively more difficult. And it becomes more and more probable that revisions will be carried out for reasons that are at odds with the poet's original intentions, interests, inspiration.

One might assume that what goes for Wordsworth would go for all Romantic poets. Coleridge, though, is on the whole a good reviser. Twenty years after writing *The Eolian Harp* he adds lines perfectly in keeping with his early pantheist self: 'Oh! the one Life, within us and abroad . . .' Though the original 1798 text of *Frost at Midnight* is a wonderful poem, Coleridge improves upon it successively in 1817 and 1828. To *Christabel* (written 1798–1800, published 1816) he adds in 1828 lines of immense importance, bringing out a wounded human side to the demonic Geraldine:

Yet Geraldine nor speaks nor stirs;
Ah! what a stricken look was hers!
Deep from within she seems half-way
To lift some weight with sick assay,
And eyes the maid and seeks delay . . .

Wordsworth, by contrast, is a bad reviser at the height of his powers. The point is made by revisions to the two-part *Prelude* incorporated in *1805*. In February 1804 (when he wrote some of his greatest poetry, including two-thirds of the *Intimations Ode*, *Daffodils* and the Climbing of Snowdon) Wordsworth replaced his beautiful account of the setting of Furness Abbey –

In more than inland peace
Left by the winds that overpass the vale,
In that sequestered ruin trees and towers,
Both silent and both motionless alike,
Hear all day long the murmuring sea that beats
Incessantly upon a craggy shore.

– with the lame prosaic rhythms and sadly diminished claims of *1805* II 115–21:

To more than inland peace
Left by the sea-wind passing overhead
(Though wind of roughest temper) trees and towers
May in that valley oftentimes be seen,
Both silent and both motionless alike;
Such is the shelter that is there, and such
The safeguard for repose and quietness.

'By the imagination', Wordsworth told Crabb Robinson in 1816, 'the mere fact is . . . connected with that infinity without which there is not poetry.' Yet fact it was that prompted his revision of the Furness lines. One cannot hear the sea at the site of the Abbey. The beautiful fantasy that one might do so is removed by the poet in a mood utterly at odds with his original creativity.

As the revisions of *The Prelude* go on – small ones at different times, huge ones c. 1819, in 1832, and 1838–9 – the chance that they will be for the better diminishes. In many ways Wordsworth remains an independent thinker: what other poet in 1850 supported the ideals of the French Revolution, or hailed 'As best, the government of equal rights|And individual worth'? And at all stages he remains capable of producing sudden new impassioned poetry – the account of Newton,

with his prism and silent face,
The marble index of a mind for ever
Voyaging through strange seas of thought alone.

But increasingly the drive behind *Prelude* revision becomes the leaving of a gift for posterity. Instead of re-entering imaginatively the early experiences that have been his inspiration, Wordsworth is tidying them up. The changing of three small words right at the end of his poem says it all. As prophets of nature, he and Coleridge had seemed in *1805* to be 'sanctified|By reason and by truth'. In *1850* they are 'sanctified|By reason, blest by faith'.